CW00544058

JIVIA

CIMA

Subject P3

Risk Management

Study Text

Published by: Kaplan Publishing UK

Unit 2 The Business Centre, Molly Millars Lane, Wokingham, Berkshire RG41 2QZ

Acknowledgements

We are grateful to the CIMA for permission to reproduce past examination questions. The answers to CIMA Exams have been prepared by Kaplan Publishing, except in the case of the CIMA November 2010 and subsequent CIMA Exam answers where the official CIMA answers have been reproduced. Questions from past live assessments have been included by kind permission of CIMA,

Notice

Kaplan Publishing's learning materials are designed to help students succeed in their examinations. In certain circumstances, CIMA can make post-exam adjustment to a student's mark or grade to reflect adverse circumstances which may have disadvantaged a student's ability to take an exam or demonstrate their normal level of attainment (see CIMA's Special Consideration policy). However, it should be noted that students will not be eligible for special consideration by CIMA if preparation for or performance in a CIMA exam is affected by any failure by their tuition provider to prepare them properly for the exam for any reason including, but not limited to, staff shortages, building work or a lack of facilities etc.

Similarly, CIMA will not accept applications for special consideration on any of the following grounds:

- failure by a tuition provider to cover the whole syllabus
- failure by the student to cover the whole syllabus, for instance as a result of joining a course part way through
- failure by the student to prepare adequately for the exam, or to use the correct pre-seen material
- errors in the Kaplan Official Study Text, including sample (practice) questions or any other Kaplan content or
- errors in any other study materials (from any other tuition provider or publisher).

British Library Cataloguing in Publication Data

A catalogue record for this book is available from the British Library.

ISBN: 978-1-78740-983-5

Printed and bound in Great Britain

Contents

Page

Introduction

How to use the Materials

These official CIMA learning materials have been carefully designed to make your learning experience as easy as possible and to give you the best chances of success in your objective tests.

The product range contains a number of features to help you in the study process. They include:

- a detailed explanation of all syllabus areas

- extensive 'practical' materials

- generous question practice, together with full solutions.

This Study Text has been designed with the needs of home study and distance learning candidates in mind. Such students require very full coverage of the syllabus topics, and also the facility to undertake extensive question practice. However, the Study Text is also ideal for fully taught courses.

The main body of the text is divided into a number of chapters, each of which is organised on the following pattern:

- **Detailed learning outcomes.** These describe the knowledge expected after your studies of the chapter are complete. You should assimilate these before beginning detailed work on the chapter, so that you can appreciate where your studies are leading.

- **Step-by-step topic coverage.** This is the heart of each chapter, containing detailed explanatory text supported where appropriate by worked examples and exercises. You should work carefully through this section, ensuring that you understand the material being explained and can tackle the examples and exercises successfully. Remember that in many cases knowledge is cumulative: if you fail to digest earlier material thoroughly, you may struggle to understand later chapters.

- **Activities.** Some chapters are illustrated by more practical elements, such as comments and questions designed to stimulate discussion.

- **Question practice.** The text contains three styles of question:

    - Exam-style objective test questions (OTQs).

    - 'Integration' questions – these test your ability to understand topics within a wider context. This is particularly important with calculations where OTQs may focus on just one element but an integration question tackles the full calculation, just as you would be expected to do in the workplace.

-     'Case' style questions – these test your ability to analyse and discuss issues in greater depth, particularly focusing on scenarios that are less clear cut than in the objective tests, and thus provide excellent practice for developing the skills needed for success in the Management Level Case Study Examination.

- **Solutions.** Avoid the temptation merely to 'audit' the solutions provided. It is an illusion to think that this provides the same benefits as you would gain from a serious attempt of your own. However, if you are struggling to get started on a question you should read the introductory guidance provided at the beginning of the solution, where provided, and then make your own attempt before referring back to the full solution.

If you work conscientiously through this Official CIMA Study Text according to the guidelines above you will be giving yourself an excellent chance of success in your objective tests. Good luck with your studies!

Quality and accuracy are of the utmost importance to us so if you spot an error in any of our products, please send an email to mykaplanreporting@kaplan.com with full details, or follow the link to the feedback form in MyKaplan.

Our Quality Co-ordinator will work with our technical team to verify the error and take action to ensure it is corrected in future editions.

Icon explanations

 Definition – These sections explain important areas of knowledge which must be understood and reproduced in an assessment environment.

 Key point – Identifies topics which are key to success and are often examined.

 Supplementary reading – These sections will help to provide a deeper understanding of core areas. The supplementary reading is **NOT** optional reading. It is vital to provide you with the breadth of knowledge you will need to address the wide range of topics within your syllabus that could feature in an assessment question. **Reference to this text is vital when self-studying.**

 Test your understanding – Following key points and definitions are exercises which give the opportunity to assess the understanding of these core areas.

 Illustration – To help develop an understanding of particular topics. The illustrative examples are useful in preparing for the Test your understanding exercises.

Study technique

Passing exams is partly a matter of intellectual ability, but however accomplished you are in that respect you can improve your chances significantly by the use of appropriate study and revision techniques. In this section we briefly outline some tips for effective study during the earlier stages of your approach to the objective tests. We also mention some techniques that you will find useful at the revision stage.

Planning

To begin with, formal planning is essential to get the best return from the time you spend studying. Estimate how much time in total you are going to need for each subject you are studying. Remember that you need to allow time for revision as well as for initial study of the material.

With your study material before you, decide which chapters you are going to study in each week, and which weeks you will devote to revision and final question practice.

Prepare a written schedule summarising the above and stick to it!

It is essential to know your syllabus. As your studies progress you will become more familiar with how long it takes to cover topics in sufficient depth. Your timetable may need to be adapted to allocate enough time for the whole syllabus.

Students are advised to refer to the examination blueprints (see page P.13 for further information) and the CIMA website, www.cimaglobal.com, to ensure they are up-to-date.

The amount of space allocated to a topic in the Study Text is not a very good guide as to how long it will take you. The syllabus weighting is the better guide as to how long you should spend on a syllabus topic.

Tips for effective studying

(1) Aim to find a quiet and undisturbed location for your study, and plan as far as possible to use the same period of time each day. Getting into a routine helps to avoid wasting time. Make sure that you have all the materials you need before you begin so as to minimise interruptions.

(2) Store all your materials in one place, so that you do not waste time searching for items every time you want to begin studying. If you have to pack everything away after each study period, keep your study materials in a box, or even a suitcase, which will not be disturbed until the next time.

(3) Limit distractions. To make the most effective use of your study periods you should be able to apply total concentration, so turn off all entertainment equipment, set your phones to message mode, and put up your 'do not disturb' sign.

(4) Your timetable will tell you which topic to study. However, before diving in and becoming engrossed in the finer points, make sure you have an overall picture of all the areas that need to be covered by the end of that session. After an hour, allow yourself a short break and move away from your Study Text. With experience, you will learn to assess the pace you need to work at. Each study session should focus on component learning outcomes – the basis for all questions.

(5) Work carefully through a chapter, making notes as you go. When you have covered a suitable amount of material, vary the pattern by attempting a practice question. When you have finished your attempt, make notes of any mistakes you made, or any areas that you failed to cover or covered more briefly. Be aware that all component learning outcomes will be tested in each examination.

(6) Make notes as you study, and discover the techniques that work best for you. Your notes may be in the form of lists, bullet points, diagrams, summaries, 'mind maps', or the written word, but remember that you will need to refer back to them at a later date, so they must be intelligible. If you are on a taught course, make sure you highlight any issues you would like to follow up with your lecturer.

(7) Organise your notes. Make sure that all your notes, calculations etc. can be effectively filed and easily retrieved later.

Progression

There are two elements of progression that we can measure: how quickly students move through individual topics within a subject; and how quickly they move from one course to the next. We know that there is an optimum for both, but it can vary from subject to subject and from student to student. However, using data and our experience of student performance over many years, we can make some generalisations.

A fixed period of study set out at the start of a course with key milestones is important. This can be within a subject, for example 'I will finish this topic by 30 June', or for overall achievement, such as 'I want to be qualified by the end of next year'.

Your qualification is cumulative, as earlier papers provide a foundation for your subsequent studies, so do not allow there to be too big a gap between one subject and another. For example, P3 *Risk management* builds on your knowledge of risks and controls from P2 *Advanced management accounting* as well as your understanding of the digital environment from the E pillar papers.

We know that exams encourage techniques that lead to some degree of short term retention, the result being that you will simply forget much of what you have already learned unless it is refreshed (look up Ebbinghaus Forgetting Curve for more details on this). This makes it more difficult as you move from one subject to another: not only will you have to learn the new subject, you will also have to relearn all the underpinning knowledge as well. This is very inefficient and slows down your overall progression which makes it more likely you may not succeed at all.

Also, it is important to realise that the Strategic Case Study (SCS) tests knowledge of all subjects within the Strategic level. Please note that candidates will need to return to this material when studying SCS as it forms a significant part of the SCS syllabus content.

In addition, delaying your studies slows your path to qualification which can have negative impacts on your career, postponing the opportunity to apply for higher level positions and therefore higher pay.

You can use the following diagram showing the whole structure of your qualification to help you keep track of your progress. Make sure you seek appropriate advice if you are unsure about your progression through the qualification.

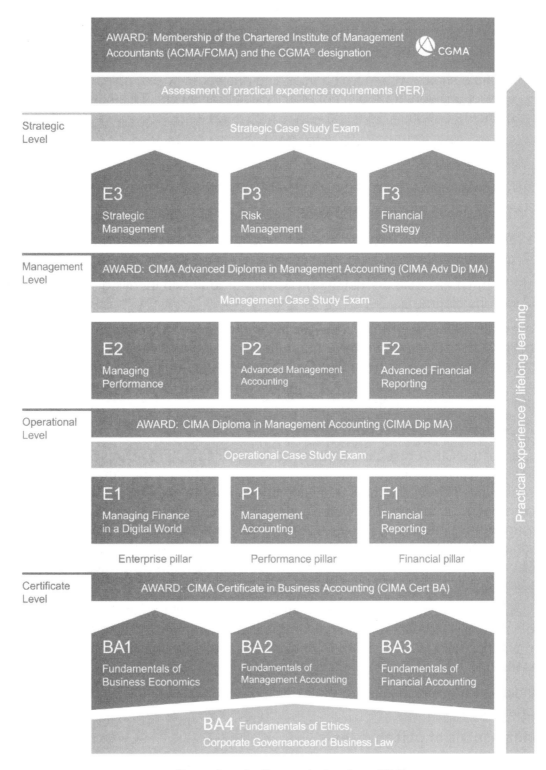

Reproduced with permission from CIMA

Objective test

Objective test questions require you to choose or provide a response to a question whose correct answer is predetermined.

The most common types of objective test question you will see are:

- Multiple choice, where you have to choose the correct answer(s) from a list of possible answers. This could either be numbers or text.

- Multiple choice with more choices and answers, for example, choosing two correct answers from a list of eight possible answers. This could either be numbers or text.

- Single numeric entry, where you give your numeric answer, for example, profit is $10,000.

- Multiple entry, where you give several numeric answers.

- True/false questions, where you state whether a statement is true or false.

- Matching pairs of text, for example, matching a technical term with the correct definition.

- Other types could be matching text with graphs and labelling graphs/diagrams.

In every chapter of this Study Text we have introduced these types of questions, but obviously we have had to label answers A, B, C etc. rather than using click boxes. For convenience, we have retained quite a few questions where an initial scenario leads to a number of sub-questions. There will be no questions of this type in the objective tests.

Guidance re CIMA on-screen calculator

As part of the CIMA objective test software, candidates are now provided with a calculator. This calculator is on-screen and is available for the duration of the assessment. The calculator is available in each of the objective tests and is accessed by clicking the calculator button in the top left hand corner of the screen at any time during the assessment. Candidates are permitted to utilise personal calculators as long as they are an approved CIMA model. Authorised CIMA models are listed here: https://www.cimaglobal.com/Studying/study-and-resources/.

All candidates must complete a 15-minute exam tutorial before the assessment begins and will have the opportunity to familiarise themselves with the calculator and practise using it. The exam tutorial is also available online via the CIMA website.

Candidates may practise using the calculator by accessing the online exam tutorial.

Fundamentals of objective tests

The objective tests are 90-minute assessments comprising 60 compulsory questions, with one or more parts. There will be no choice and all questions should be attempted. All elements of a question must be answered correctly for the question to be marked correctly. All questions are equally weighted.

CIMA syllabus 2019 – Structure of subjects and learning outcomes

Details regarding the content of the new CIMA syllabus can be located within the CIMA 2019 professional syllabus document.

Each subject within the syllabus is divided into a number of broad syllabus topics. The topics contain one or more lead learning outcomes, related component learning outcomes and indicative knowledge content.

A learning outcome has two main purposes:

(a) To define the skill or ability that a well prepared candidate should be able to exhibit in the examination.

(b) To demonstrate the approach likely to be taken in examination questions.

The learning outcomes are part of a hierarchy of learning objectives. The verbs used at the beginning of each learning outcome relate to a specific learning objective, e.g.

Calculate the break-even point, profit target, margin of safety and profit/volume ratio for a single product or service.

The verb '**calculate**' indicates a level three learning objective. The following tables list the verbs that appear in the syllabus learning outcomes and examination questions.

The examination blueprints and representative task statements

CIMA have also published examination blueprints giving learners clear expectations regarding what is expected of them.

The blueprint is structured as follows:

- Exam content sections (reflecting the syllabus document)
- Lead and component outcomes (reflecting the syllabus document)
- Representative task statements.

A representative task statement is a plain English description of what a CIMA finance professional should know and be able to do.

The content and skill level determine the language and verbs used in the representative task.

CIMA will test up to the level of the task statement in the objective tests (an objective test question on a particular topic could be set at a lower level than the task statement in the blueprint).

The format of the objective test blueprints follows that of the published syllabus for the 2019 CIMA Professional Qualification.

Weightings for content sections are also included in the individual subject blueprints.

CIMA VERB HIERARCHY

CIMA place great importance on the definition of verbs in structuring objective tests. It is therefore crucial that you understand the verbs in order to appreciate the depth and breadth of a topic and the level of skill required. The objective tests will focus on levels one, two and three of the CIMA hierarchy of verbs. However, they will also test levels four and five, especially at the management and strategic levels.

Skill level	Verbs used	Definition
Level 5 **Evaluation** How you are expected to use your learning to evaluate, make decisions or recommendations	Advise	Counsel, inform or notify
	Assess	Evaluate or estimate the nature, ability or quality of
	Evaluate	Appraise or assess the value of
	Recommend	Propose a course of action
	Review	Assess and evaluate in order, to change if necessary
Level 4 **Analysis** How you are expected to analyse the detail of what you have learned	Align	Arrange in an orderly way
	Analyse	Examine in detail the structure of
	Communicate	Share or exchange information
	Compare and contrast	Show the similarities and/or differences between
	Develop	Grow and expand a concept
	Discuss	Examine in detail by argument
	Examine	Inspect thoroughly
	Interpret	Translate into intelligible or familiar terms
	Monitor	Observe and check the progress of
	Prioritise	Place in order of priority or sequence for action
	Produce	Create or bring into existence
Level 3 **Application** How you are expected to apply your knowledge	Apply	Put to practical use
	Calculate	Ascertain or reckon mathematically
	Conduct	Organise and carry out
	Demonstrate	Prove with certainty or exhibit by practical means
	Prepare	Make or get ready for use
	Reconcile	Make or prove consistent/compatible

Skill level	Verbs used	Definition
Level 2 Comprehension What you are expected to understand	Describe	Communicate the key features of
	Distinguish	Highlight the differences between
	Explain	Make clear or intelligible/state the meaning or purpose of
	Identify	Recognise, establish or select after consideration
	Illustrate	Use an example to describe or explain something
Level 1 Knowledge What you are expected to know	List	Make a list of
	State	Express, fully or clearly, the details/facts of
	Define	Give the exact meaning of
	Outline	Give a summary of

Information concerning formulae and tables will be provided via the CIMA website, www.cimaglobal.com.

SYLLABUS GRIDS

P3: Risk Management

Analyse, evaluate and manage strategic, operational and cyber risks

Content weighting

Content area		Weighting
A	Enterprise risk	25%
B	Strategic risk	25%
C	Internal controls	25%
D	Cyber risk	25%
		100%

P3A: Enterprise risk

Not all intended strategies are implemented due to various factors. These factors constitute the operating enterprise-wide risks of the organisation. This section covers how to identify, evaluate and manage these risks.

Lead outcome	Component outcome	Study text chapter
1. Analyse sources and types of risk.	Analyse:	
	a. Sources of risks	1
	b. Types of risks	1
2. Evaluate risk.	a. Evaluate the impact of risk	2
	b. Assess the likelihood of risks	2
	c. Analyse the interaction of different risks	2 and 4
3. Discuss ways of managing risks.	Discuss:	
	a. Roles and responsibilities	5 and 6
	b. Risk tolerance, appetite and capacity	2
	c. Risk management frameworks	2
	d. Risk analytics	1, 2 and 4

P3B: Strategic risk

A fundamental risk of the organisation is that its strategy is the wrong one and that even if implemented perfectly, it will achieve the wrong outcome for the organisation. In addition, some risks are of such high significance that they can affect the very existence of the organisation. This section covers where these risks emanate from, evaluates them and explains how oversight of such risks is critical to the governance of the organisation.

Lead outcome	Component outcome	Study text chapters
1. Analyse risks associated with formulating strategy.	a. Analyse relevance of the assumptions on which strategy is based.	3
	b. Discuss potential sources and types of disruptions to strategy.	3
2. Evaluate the sources and impact of reputational risks.	Evaluate:	
	a. Sources of reputational risk	4
	b. Impact of reputational risk on strategy	4
3. Explain governance risks.	Explain:	
	a. The role of board and its committees in managing strategic risk	5
	b. Failure of governance and its impact on strategy	5

P3C: Internal controls

Control systems are an integral part of managing risks. Various control frameworks have been developed to assist in this process. In addition, the internal audit function performs a vital role in helping to implement and monitor implementation and adherence to the control frameworks. This section covers how internal control systems can be used effectively in the risk management process.

Lead outcome	Component outcome	Study text chapters
1. Analyse internal control systems.	a. Discuss roles and responsibilities for internal controls.	6 and 7
	b. Discuss the purpose of internal control.	6
	c. Analyse the features of internal control systems.	6
2. Recommend internal controls for risk management.	a. Discuss the Committee of Sponsoring Organisations of the Treadway Commission (COSO) internal control and risk management framework.	2 and 6
	b. Assess control weakness.	6
	c. Assess compliance failures.	6
	d. Recommend internal controls for risk management.	6
3. Discuss various issues relating to internal audit in organisations.	Discuss:	
	a. Forms of internal audit	7
	b. Internal audit process	7
	c. Effective internal audit	7
	d. The internal audit report	7

P3D: Cyber risk

In a digital world one of the major threats is cyber risk. How are data and operating systems protected from unauthorised access and manipulation? How are breaches identified, analysed, remedied and reported? These are some of the questions covered in this section.

Lead outcome	Component outcome	Study text chapters
1. Analyse cyber threats.	Analyse:	
	a. Nature and impact of cyber risks	8
	b. Types of cyber risks	8
	c. Risk of security vulnerabilities.	8
2. Review cyber security processes.	Review:	
	a. Cyber security objectives	8 and 9
	b. Security controls	9
	c. Centralisation in cyber security	9
3. Discuss cyber security tools and techniques.	Discuss:	
	a. Forensic analysis	10
	b. Malware analysis	10
	c. Penetration testing	10
	d. Software security	10
4. Evaluate cyber risk reporting.	a. Evaluate cyber risk reporting frameworks	10

Risk

Chapter learning objectives

Lead	Component
A1. Analyse sources and types of risk	(a) Analyse sources of risk (b) Analyse types of risk
A3. Discuss ways of managing risks	(d) Discuss risk analytics

 1   What is risk?

There are many different ways of defining risk including the following:

- Risk is a condition in which there exists a quantifiable dispersion in the possible outcomes from any activity. (CIMA official terminology)

- Risk can be defined as the combination of the probability of an event and its consequences (ISO Guide 73)

- Risk in business is the chance that future events or results may not be as expected.

Risk is often thought of as purely bad (pure or **'downside'** risk), but risk can also be good i.e. the results may be better than expected (speculative or **'upside'** risk) as well as worse.

In order to assess and measure the risks that an organisation faces, a business must be able to identify the principal sources of risk. Risks facing an organisation are those that affect the achievement of its overall objectives (which should be reflected in its strategic aims). Risk should be managed and there should be strategies for dealing with risk.

Risk and uncertainty

The term 'risk' is often associated with the chance of something 'bad' will happen, **and that a future outcome will be adverse. This type of risk is called 'downside' risk** or **pure risk**, which is a risk involving the possibility of loss, with no chance of gain.

Examples of pure risk are the risk of disruption to business from a severe power cut, or the risk of losses from theft or fraud, the risk of damage to assets from a fire or accident, and risks to the health and safety of employees at work.

Not all risks are pure risks or downside risks. In many cases, risk is two-way, and actual outcomes might be either better or worse than expected. **Two-way risk** is sometimes called **speculative risk**. In many business decisions, there is an element of speculative risk – and management are aware that actual results could be better or worse than forecast.

For example, a new product launch might be more or less successful than planned, and the savings from an investment in labour-saving equipment might be higher or lower than anticipated.

Risk is inherent in a situation whenever an outcome is not inevitable. **Uncertainty**, by contrast, arises from ignorance and a lack of information. By definition, the future cannot be predicted under conditions of uncertainty because there is insufficient information about what the future outcomes might be or their probabilities of occurrence.

In business, uncertainty might be an element to be considered in decision-making. For example, there might be uncertainty about how consumers will respond to a new product or a new technology, or how shareholders will react to a cut in the annual dividend. Uncertainty is reduced by obtaining as much information as possible before making any decision.

 Why incur risk?

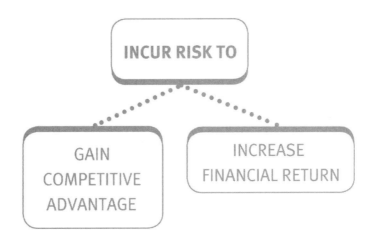

It is generally the case that firms must be willing to take higher risks if they want to achieve higher returns:

- To generate higher returns a business may have to take more risks in order to be competitive.

- Conversely, not accepting risk tends to make a business less dynamic, and implies a 'follow the leader' strategy.

- Incurring risk also implies that the returns from different activities will be higher – 'benefit' being the return for accepting risk.

- Benefits can be financial – decreased costs, or intangible – better quality information.

- In both cases, these will lead to the business being able to gain competitive advantage.

For some risks, the level of risk is rewarded with a market rate of return e.g. quoted equity – where a shareholder invests in a company with the expectation of a certain level of dividend and capital growth. However, for other risks there may not be a market rate of return e.g. technology risk – where a company invests in new software in the hope that it will make their invoice processing more efficient. The important distinction here is that the market compensates for the former type of risk, but might not for the latter.

 Benefits of taking risks

		Activity risk	
		Low	High
Ability to gain competitive advantage	Low	2 Routine	4 Avoid
	High	1 Identify and develop	3 Examine carefully

Focusing on low-risk activities can easily result in a low ability to obtain competitive advantage – although where there is low risk there is also only a limited amount of competitive advantage to be obtained. For example, a mobile telephone operator may produce its phones in a wide range of colours. There is little or no risk of the technology failing, but the move may provide limited competitive advantage where customers are attracted to a particular colour of phone.

Some low-risk activities, however, will provide higher competitive advantage – when these can be identified. If these can be identified, then the activity should be undertaken because of the higher reward. For example, the mobile phone operator may find a way of easily altering mobile phones to make the processor faster. Given that mobile phone users like their phone to respond quickly, there is significant potential to obtain competitive advantage. However, these opportunities are few and far between.

High-risk activities can similarly generate low or high competitive advantage. Activities with low competitive advantage will generally be avoided. There remains the risk that the activity will not work, and that the small amount of competitive advantage that would be generated is not worth that risk.

Other high-risk activities may generate significant amounts of competitive advantage. These activities may be worth investigating because of the high returns that can be generated. For example, a new type of mobile phone providing, say, more accurate facial recognition features to enable quicker access, recognising a partially obscured face may provide significant competitive advantage for the company; the risk of investing in the phone is worthwhile in terms of the benefit that could be achieved.

The point is, therefore, that if a business does not take some risk, it will normally be limited to activities providing little or no competitive advantage, which will limit its ability to grow and provide returns to its shareholders.

2 CIMA's risk management cycle

Risk management should be a proactive process that is an integral part of strategic management.

This perspective is summarised in **CIMA's risk management cycle**, illustrated below:

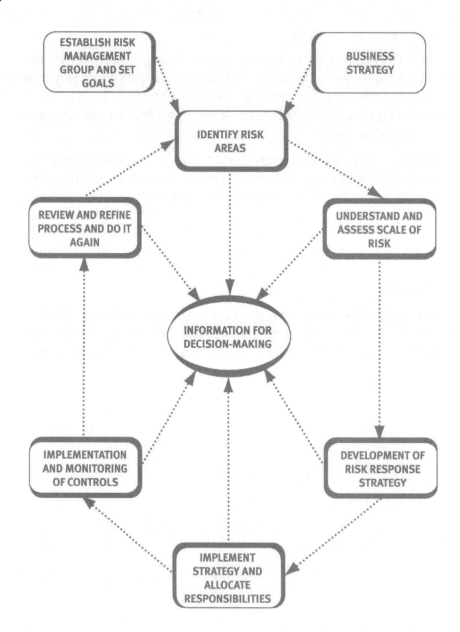

Source: Chartered Institute of Management Accountants (2002), Risk Management: A Guide to Good Practice, CIMA.

The risk management cycle is a very important tool for your exam.

Test your understanding 1

CIMA's Risk Management Cycle identifies various activities that should be undertaken during risk management.

Which of the following options shows the steps in the correct order?

A   Identify risk areas; Develop risk response strategy; Allocate responsibilities; Establish risk management group.

B   Establish risk management group; Identify risk areas; Allocate responsibilities; Develop risk response strategy.

C   Allocate responsibilities; Identify risk areas; Develop risk response strategy; Establish risk management group.

D   Establish risk management group; Identify risk areas; Develop risk response strategy; Allocate responsibilities.

3   Types and sources of risk for business organisations

Identifying and categorising risks

- Many organisations categorise risks into different types of risk. The use of risk categories can help with the process of risk identification and assessment.

- There is no single system of risk categories. The risk categories used by companies and other organisations differ according to circumstances. Some of the more commonly-used risk categories are described below. It is important to note that risks can fit into more than one risk category, the descriptions that follow are a guide and not designed to be definitive rules.

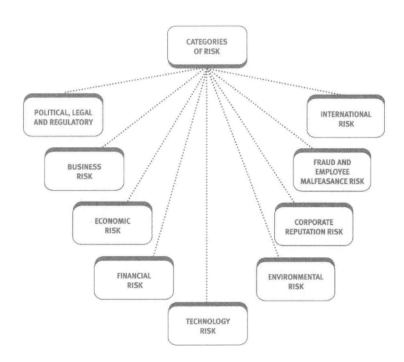

Political, legal and regulatory

These are the risks that businesses face because of the regulatory regime that they operate in. Some businesses may be subject to very strict regulations, for example companies that could cause pollution, but even companies that do not appear to be in a highly regulated industry have some regulatory risk. For example, all companies are subject to the risk of employment legislation changing or customers taking legal action.

This risk can be broken up into different types:

Political risk   Risk due to political instability. Generally considered to be external to the business.

Legal/litigation risk   Risk that legal action will be brought against the business.

Regulatory risk   Risk of changes in regulation affecting the business.

Compliance risk   Risk of non-compliance with the law resulting in fines/penalties, etc.

More on political, legal and regulatory risks

Political risk depends to a large extent on the political stability and the political institutions in the country or countries in which an organisation operates. A change of government can sometimes result in dramatic changes for businesses. In an extreme case, for example, an incoming government might nationalise all foreign businesses operating in the country. Even in countries with a stable political system, political change can be significant. For example, an incoming new government might be elected on a platform of higher (or lower) taxation.

Legal risk or litigation risk arises from the possibility of legal action being taken against an organisation. For many organisations, this risk can be high. For example, hospitals and hospital workers might be exposed to risks of legal action for negligence. Tobacco companies have been exposed to legal action for compensation from cancer victims. Companies manufacturing or providing food and drink are also aware of litigation risk from customers claiming that a product has damaged their health.

Regulatory risk arises from the possibility that regulations will affect the way an organisation has to operate. Regulations might apply to businesses generally (for example, competition laws and anti-monopoly regulations) or to specific industries.

Compliance risk is the risk of losses, possibly fines, resulting from non-compliance with laws or regulations. Measures to ensure compliance with rules and regulations should be an integral part of an organisation's internal control system.

Business risk

Business risk is the risk businesses face owing to the nature of their operations and products. Some businesses for instance are reliant on a single product or small range of products, or they could be reliant on a small key group of staff. The risks can be considered in different categories:

Strategic risk	Risk that business strategies (for example, but not limited to acquisitions/product launches) will fail.
Product risk	Risk of failure of new product launches/loss of interest in existing products.
Commodity price risk	Risk of a rise in commodity prices (e.g. oil).
Product reputation risk	Risk of change in product's reputation or image.
Operational risk	Risk that business operations may be inefficient or business processes may fail.
Contractual inadequacy risk	Risk that the terms of a contract do not fully cover a business against all potential outcomes.
Fraud and employee malfeasance	Considered separately later.

More on business risks

Business risks for a company are risks arising from the nature of its business and operations. Some businesses are inherently more risky than others.

- **Strategic risks** are risks arising from the possible consequences of strategic decisions taken by the organisation that impact the long term future of the organisation. For example, one company might pursue a strategy of growth by acquisitions, whilst another might seek slower, organic growth. Growth by acquisition is likely to be much more high-risk than organic growth, although the potential returns might also be much higher. Strategic risks are not limited to acquisitions and growth, but anything that should be identified and assessed at senior management and board of director level. Strategic risks can appear as sources of likely disruption to a whole industry, and that makes them very powerful. There is more detail on strategic risk in later chapters.

- **Product risk** is the risk that customers will not buy new products (or services) provided by the organisation, or that the sales demand for current products and services will decline unexpectedly. A new product launched on to the market might fail to achieve the expected volume of sales, or the take-up could be much slower than expected. For example, the demand for 'third generation' (3G) mobile communications services was much slower to build up than expected by the mobile telephone service providers, due partly to the slower-than-expected development of suitable mobile phone handsets.

- **Commodity price risk.** Businesses might be exposed to risks from unexpected increases (or falls) in the price of a key commodity. Businesses providing commodities, such as oil companies and commodity farmers, are directly affected by price changes. Equally, companies that rely on the use of commodities could be exposed to risks from price changes. For example, airlines are exposed to the risk of increases in fuel prices, particularly when market demand for flights is weak (so increases in ticket prices for flights are not possible).

- **Product reputation risk**. Some companies rely heavily on brand image and product reputation, and an adverse event could put their reputation (and so future sales) at risk. Risk to a product's reputation could arise from adverse public attitudes to a product or from adverse publicity: this has been evident in Europe with widespread hostility to genetically-modified (GM) foods. There could also be a risk from changes in customer perceptions about the quality of a product. For example, if a car manufacturer announces that it is recalling all new models of a car to rectify a design defect, the reputation of the product and future sales could be affected.

- **Operational risk** refers to potential losses that might arise in business operations. It has been defined broadly as 'the risk of losses resulting from inadequate or failed internal processes, people and systems, or external events' (Basel Committee on Banking Supervision). Operational risks include risks of fraud or employee malfeasance, which are explained in more detail later. Organisations implement internal control systems to manage operational risks.

- **Contractual inadequacy risk** may arise where a business has negotiated contracts and other business transactions without adequate consideration of what may happen if things don't go according to plan. For example, a building company may have a fixed completion date for the construction of a house. If it is not completed on time, they may have to pay compensation to the house purchaser. Similarly, there is also a risk that the purchaser will not have the funds when payment is due. This risk may be mitigated by having terms in the contract setting out what rights the company will have in such circumstances. Clearly, if the building company does not consider either or both of these possibilities when agreeing to build the house, then there is an unidentified and unquantified risk of loss.

Test your understanding 2

Which of the following would normally be classified as an operational risk?

Select ALL that apply

A   The risk that a new product will fail

B   The risk of competitors cutting costs by manufacturing overseas

C   The loss of an experienced supervisor

D   Raw materials being wasted during the production process due to untrained staff

Test your understanding 3

Which of the following would normally be classified as a strategic risk?

A   Human error

B   Information technology failure

C   Fraud

D   Stricter health and safety legislation

Test your understanding 4

Company Q assembles circuit boards for mobile telephones and relies on suppliers to manufacture one of their key components. This component contains a highly toxic, expensive chemical which is currently in scarce supply across the world.

Company Q has one main supplier of the component. This supplier is based in a developing country with low labour costs. The supplier has developed a great deal of expertise in handling the toxic chemical and keeping waste to a minimum. However, there have been allegations that rivers local to the supplier have been polluted with toxic waste from the chemical. There are also rumours that the supplier does not provide adequate safety equipment for staff working with the chemical. The supplier has informed Company Q that price rises may occur since safe storage of the chemical is becoming more expensive.

> **Which of the following represent strategic risks to Company Q?**
>
> Select ALL that apply.
>
> A   Risk that the supplier's employees are injured through unsafe handling of toxic chemicals.
>
> B   Risk that pollution from local rivers is proved to be the result of the supplier's processes and waste.
>
> C   Risk that the supplier is unable to source adequate quantities of chemical.
>
> D   Risk that the supplier's storage facilities become more expensive.
>
> E   Risk that the developing country in which the supplier is based introduces a minimum wage.

Economic risk

This is the risk that changes in the economy might affect the business. These changes could be inflation, unemployment rates, international trade relations or fiscal policy decisions by government. Again, this risk is considered to be external to the business.

The 'credit crunch'

In 2008 there was global banking crisis which then led to what has since been called a 'credit crunch' and, for some countries, recession. This section looks at the causes of the banking crisis and its knock-on effects.

Contributory factor 1: US sub-prime mortgage lending

In 2001 the US faced recession, due partly to the events of 9/11 and the Dot com bubble bursting, so the US government was keen to stimulate growth. As part of this, in 2003, the Federal Reserve responded by cutting interest rates to 1% – their lowest level for a long time.

Low interest rates encouraged people to buy a house backed by a mortgage, resulting in house prices rising due to the increased demand for housing. As house prices began to rise, mortgage companies relaxed their lending criteria and tried to capitalise on the booming property market. This boom in credit was also fuelled by US government pressure on lenders to grant mortgages to people who, under normal banking criteria, presented a very high risk of default. These were the so called 'sub-prime mortgages', with many borrowers taking out adjustable rate mortgages that were affordable for the first two years.

This 'sub-prime market' expanded very quickly and by 2005, one in five mortgages in the US were sub-prime. Banks felt protected because house prices were continuing to rise so if a borrower defaulted the bank would recover its loan.

In 2006 inflationary pressures in the US caused interest rates to rise to 4%. Normally 4% interest rates are not particularly high but, because many had taken out large mortgages, this increase made the mortgage payments unaffordable. Also many homeowners were coming to the end of their 'introductory offers' and faced much higher payments. This led to an increase in mortgage defaults.

As mortgage defaults increased the boom in house prices came to an end and house prices started falling. In some areas the problem was even worse as there had been a boom in the building of new homes, which occurred right up until 2007. It meant that demand fell as supply was increasing – causing prices to collapse. Banks were no longer able to recover their loans when borrowers defaulted. In many cases they only ended up with a fraction of the house value.

Contributory factor 2: 'Collateralised debt obligations' or CDOs

Normally if a borrower defaults it is the lending bank or building society that suffers the loss. As a result they are very diligent in verifying the credit worthiness of potential borrowers and whether they have the income and security to repay loans. However, in the US, mortgage lenders were able to sell on mortgage debt, in the form of CDOs, to other banks and financial institutions. This was a kind of insurance for the mortgage companies. It meant that other banks and financial institutions shared the risk of these sub-prime mortgages.

Using the income from their mortgage book as security, banks sold CDO bonds with a three-tier structure:

(1) Tier 1 was "senior" or "investment grade" and supposed to be very low risk but with a low return.

(2) Tier 2 was the "mezzanine tranche" and had medium risk and medium return

(3) Tier 3 was the "equity tranche" and had highest risk and return.

As money was received on mortgages, it was used to pay the Tier 1 bond holders their interest first, then Tier 2 and finally Tier 3, so if borrowers defaulted, then Tier 3 holders would suffer first and so on, like a waterfall effect.

Unfortunately losses were so great that Tier 3 and Tier 2 and in some cases Tier 1 investors were affected. At the very least, the value of Tier 1 bonds fell due to the perceived risks.

Contributory factor 3: Debt rating organisations

The CDO bonds were credit-rated for risk, just like any other bond issues. Maybe because these sub-prime mortgage debts were bought by 'responsible' banks like Morgan Stanley and Lehman Brothers, or maybe because they didn't fully understand the CDO structures, risk agencies gave risky Tier 1 debt bundles AAA safety ratings. Normally AAA would denote extremely low risk investments.

This encouraged many banks and financial institutions to buy them, not realising how risky their financial position was. The trillions of dollars of sub-prime mortgages issued in the US had thus become distributed across the global markets, ending up as CDOs on the balance sheets of many banks around the world.

Many commentators have seen this factor as an example of regulatory failure within the financial system.

Contributory factor 4: Banks' financial structure

Unlike most other commercial enterprises, banks are very highly geared with typically less than 10% of their asset value covered by equity. A drastic loss of asset value can soon wipe out a bank's equity account and it was this risk which led some banks to start selling their asset-backed securities on to the market.

However, the sellers in this restricted market could not find buyers; as a result, the values at which these "toxic assets" could be sold fell and many banks around the world found themselves in a position with negative equity.

Contributory factor 5: Credit default swaps

As an alternative (or in addition) to using CDOs, the mortgage lenders could buy insurance on sub-prime debt through credit default swaps or CDSs.

For example, AIG wrote $440 billion and Lehman Brothers more than $700 billion-worth of CDSs. These were the first institutions to suffer when the level of defaults started to increase.

Warren Buffett called them "financial weapons of mass destruction".

Contributory factor 6: Risk-takers

There is a school of thought that the risk-takers were taking risks they didn't understand. Some risks can be easily understood, however, others are far more complicated.

Implication 1: the collapse of major financial institutions

Some very large financial institutions went bust and others got into serious trouble and needed to be rescued. For example,

- In September 2008 Lehman Brothers went bust. This was the biggest bankruptcy in corporate history. It was 10 times the size of Enron and the tipping point into the global crash, provoking panic in an already battered financial system, freezing short-term lending, and marking the start of the liquidity crisis.

- Also in September 2008 the US government put together a bailout package for AIG. The initial loan was for $85bn but the total value of this package has been estimated at between 150 and 182 billion dollars.

- In the UK the Bank of England lent Northern Rock £27 billion after its collapse in 2007.

Implication 2: the credit crunch

Banks usually rely on lending to each other to conduct everyday business. But, after the first wave of credit losses, banks could no longer raise sufficient finance.

For example, in the UK, Northern Rock was particularly exposed to money markets. It had relied on borrowing money on the money markets to fund its daily business. In 2007, it simply couldn't raise enough money on the financial markets and eventually had to be nationalised by the UK government.

In addition to bad debts, the other problem was one of confidence. Because many banks had lost money and had a deterioration in their balance sheets, they couldn't afford to lend to other banks. Even banks that had stayed free of the problem began to doubt the credit worthiness of other banks and, as a result, became reluctant to lend on the interbank market.

The knock on effect was that banks became reluctant to lend to anyone, causing a shortage of liquidity in money markets. This made it difficult for firms to borrow to finance expansion plans as well as hitting the housing market.

Many companies use short-term finance rather than long-term. For example, rather than borrowing for, say, 10 years a company might take out a two year loan, with a view to taking out another two year loan to replace the first, and so on. The main reason for using this system of "revolving credit" is that it should be cheaper – shorter-term interest rates are generally lower than longer-term. The credit crunch meant that these firms could not refinance their loans causing major problems.

Implication 3: government intervention

Many governments felt compelled to intervene, not just to prop up major institutions (e.g. Northern Rock and AIG mentioned above) but also to inject funds into the money markets to stimulate liquidity.

Efforts to save major institutions involved a mixture of loans, guarantees and the purchase of equity.

Usually, central banks try to raise the amount of lending and activity in the economy indirectly, by cutting interest rates. Lower interest rates encourage people to spend, not save. But when interest rates can go no lower, a central bank's only option is to pump money into the economy directly. That is quantitative easing (QE). The way the central bank does this is by buying assets – usually financial assets such as government and corporate bonds – using money it has simply created out of thin air. The institutions selling those assets (either commercial banks or other financial businesses such as insurance companies) will then have "new" money in their accounts, which then boosts the money supply.

In February 2010 the Bank of England announced that the UK quantitative easing programme, that had cost £200bn, was to be put on hold.

The end result was that many governments found themselves with huge levels of debt with the corresponding need to repay high levels of interest as well as repay the debt.

Implication 4: recession and "austerity measures"

The events described above resulted in a recession in many countries. Despite the falling tax revenues that accompany this, some governments would normally try to increase government spending as one measure to boost aggregate demand to stimulate the economy.

However, the high levels of national debt have resulted in governments doing the opposite and making major cuts in public spending.

Implication 5: problems refinancing government debt

In 2010/2011 some countries tried to refinance national debt by issuing bonds:

* A problem facing the Spanish government at the end of 2010/2011 was the need to raise new borrowing as other government debt reached maturity. Spain successfully sold new bonds totalling nearly €3 billion on 12/1/11 in what was seen as a major test of Europe's chances of containing the debt crisis gripping parts of the region. This was in addition to the Spanish government cutting spending by tens of billions of euros, including cuts in public sector salaries, public investment and social spending, along with tax hikes and a pension freeze.

* The problem of refinancing is more severe for countries whose national debt has a short average redemption period (Greece is about 4 yrs) but much less of a problem where the debt is long dated (e.g. the UK where the average maturity is about 14 yrs).

For others they needed help from other countries and the International Monetary Fund (IMF).

* Greece received a €110 billion rescue package in May 2010.

* At the end of 2010 Ireland received a bailout from the EU, the UK and the IMF. The total cost is still being debated but could be as high as €85 billion.

Financial risk

Financial risk is a major risk that affects businesses and this risk is studied in much more depth in F3, an awareness of financial risk is sufficient for P3.

Financial risk is the risk of a change in a financial condition such as an exchange rate, interest rate, credit rating of a customer, or price of a good.

The main types of financial risk are

Credit risk   Risk of non-payment by customers.

Political risk   Risk arising from actions taken by a government that affect financial aspects of the business.

Currency risk   Risk of fluctuations in the exchange rate.

Interest rate risk Risk that interest rates change.

Gearing risk   Risk in the way a business is financed (debt vs. equity) (sometimes this is considered part of interest rate risk).

More on financial risks

Financial risks relate to the possibility of changes in financial conditions and circumstances. There are several types of financial risk.

- **Credit risk.** Credit risk is the possibility of losses due to non-payment by debtors. The exposure of a company to credit risks depends on factors such as:
  - the total volume of credit sales
  - the organisation's credit policy
  - credit terms offered (credit limits for individual customers and the time allowed to pay)
  - the credit risk 'quality' of customers: some types of customer are a greater credit risk than others
  - credit vetting and assessment procedures
  - debt collection procedures.

- **Currency risk.** Currency risk, or foreign exchange risk, arises from the possibility of movements in foreign exchange rates, and the value of one currency in relation to another.

- **Interest rate risk.** Interest rate risk is the risk of unexpected gains or losses arising as a consequence of a rise or fall in interest rates. Exposures to interest rate risk arise from:
  - borrowing
  - investing (to earn interest) or depositing cash.

- **Gearing risk.** Gearing risk for non-bank companies is the risk arising from exposures to high financial gearing and large amounts of borrowing.

Technology risk

Technology risk is the risk that technology changes will occur that either present new opportunities to businesses, or on the down-side make their existing processes obsolete or inefficient.

More on technology risk

Technology risk arises from the possibility that technological change will occur. Like many other categories of risk, technology risk is a two-way risk, and technological change creates both threats and opportunities for organisations.

There are risks in failing to respond to new technology, but there can also be risks in adopting new technology. An example of over-investing in new technology was the so-called 'dot.com boom' in the late 1990s and early 2000s. For a time, there was speculation that Internet-based companies would take over the markets of established 'bricks and mortar' companies.

To varying degrees, established companies invested in Internet technology, partly as a protective measure and partly in order to speculate on the growth of Internet commerce. (Whereas most established companies survived the collapse of the 'dot.com bubble' in 2001 – 2002, many 'dot.com' companies suffered financial collapse.)

Cyber risk   Cyber risk is a focus area for organisations now. It is the risk of financial loss, disruption, or damage to an organisation caused by issues with the information technology systems they use.

Cyber risk and how to deal with it is covered in detail in chapters 8, 9 and 10.

Environmental risk

Environmental risk is the risk that arises from changes in the environment such as climate change or natural disasters. Some businesses may perceive this risk to be low, but for others, for example insurance companies, it can be more significant. Insurance companies have to take environmental risks into account when deciding policy premiums, and unusual environmental circumstances can severely alter the results of insurance businesses.

More on environmental risk

Environmental risk arises from changes to the environment:

*   over which an organisation has no direct control, such as global warming

*   for which the organisation might be responsible, such as oil spillages and other pollution.

To ensure their long-term survival, some companies should consider the sustainability of their businesses. When raw materials are consumed, consideration should be given to ensuring future supplies of the raw material. For example, companies that consume wood and paper should perhaps show concern for tree planting programmes, and deep-sea fishing businesses should consider the preservation of fishing stocks.

The Japanese tsunami

The Japanese tsunami of 2011 illustrates very well the fact that some risks can be understood and others are far more complicated.

The Japanese have some of the best flood defence systems in the world, being on the edge of a plate system and regularly experiencing tremors. However, even the best defence system is built with a risk factor included – using probabilities and modelling by water engineers. Whilst it is not possible to prevent a tsunami, in some particularly tsunami-prone countries some measures have been taken to reduce the damage caused on shore. Japan has implemented an extensive programme of building tsunami walls of up to 4.5 m (13.5 ft) high in front of populated coastal areas. Other localities have built floodgates and channels to redirect the water from incoming tsunami. However, their effectiveness has been questioned, as tsunami are often higher than the barriers. For instance, the Okushiri, Hokkaidō tsunami which struck Okushiri Island of Hokkaidō within two to five minutes of the earthquake on July 12, 1993 created waves as much as 30 m (100 ft) tall – as high as a 10-story building. The port town of Aonae was completely surrounded by a tsunami wall, but the waves washed right over the wall and destroyed all the wood-framed structures in the area. The wall may have succeeded in slowing down and moderating the height of the tsunami, but it did not prevent major destruction and loss of life.

On 11 March, 2011 a 10-meter tsunami slammed into the Japanese city of Sendai killing hundreds and sweeping away everything in its wake. The wall of water was triggered by the country's biggest ever earthquake. Cars, lorries and boats bobbed like toys as a wave of debris spread over huge swathes of north-eastern Japan.

An after effect of the tsunami was the malfunctioning of a nuclear plant in Fukushima, north of Tokyo, where the reactor's cooling system overheated. Other nuclear power plants and oil refineries had been shut down following the 8.9 magnitude quake. Engineers opted to cover the plant in concrete, the technique used at Chernobyl 25 years ago, however this failed and experts have since tried to plug the leak using an absorbent polymer. An exclusion zone of 30 kilometres has been advised by the Japanese government, which will be long-term. It is thought the crack in reactor number two is one source of leaks that have caused radiation levels in the sea to rise to more than 4000 times the legal limit. Food products and water supplies have been affected. Scientists in Europe are convinced this scenario could happen closer to home. They have been working on an early warning system for countries surrounding the Mediterranean Sea. The region along the Turkish coast in the Eastern Mediterranean is considered the most vulnerable.

In these scenarios, engineers have tried to learn from the past and estimate what might happen in the future. However, with the best will in the world it is sometimes impossible to ascertain all the implications of a single event, such as a tsunami.

Fraud risk

Fraud risk (a type of operational business risk) is the vulnerability of an organisation to fraud. Some businesses are more vulnerable than others to fraud and as a result have to have stronger controls over fraud. Fraud risk is a risk that is considered controllable by most businesses.

> **More on fraud risk**
>
> Fraud risk is the vulnerability of an organisation to fraud. The size of fraud risk for any organisation is a factor of:
>
> - the probability of fraud occurring, and
>
> - the size of the losses if fraud does occur.
>
> For example, a bank will be subject to much higher fraud risk than a property investment company due to the desirability of money and the potential value that theft could achieve; it is unlikely that someone will steal a building from an investment company.
>
> Fraud risk should be managed, by:
>
> - fraud prevention: ensuring that the opportunities to commit fraud are minimised
>
> - fraud detection and deterrence: detection measures are designed to identify fraud after it has occurred. If employees fear that the risk of detection is high, they will be deterred from trying to commit fraud.
>
> The management of fraud risk should be an element of an organisation's internal control system.

Corporate reputation risk

Reputation risk is for many organisations a down-side risk as the better the reputation of the business the more risk there is of losing that reputation. A good reputation can be very quickly eroded if companies suffer adverse media comments or are perceived to be untrustworthy.

This could arise from:

- environmental performance

- social performance

- health & safety performance.

More on corporate reputation risk

Many large organisations are aware of the potential damage to their business from events affecting their 'reputation' in the opinion of the general public or more specific groups (such as existing customers or suppliers).

Some organisations succeed in being perceived as 'environmental-friendly', and use public relations and advertising to promote this image.

For many organisations, however, reputation risk is a down-side risk. The risk can be particularly significant for companies that sell products or services to consumer markets. There have been cases where a company's reputation has been significantly affected by:

- employing child labour in under-developed countries or operating 'sweat shops' in which employees work long hours in poor conditions for low pay

- causing environmental damage and pollution

- public suspicions about the damage to health from using the company's products

- investing heavily in countries with an unpopular or tyrannical government

- involvement in business 'scandals' such as mis-selling products

- management announcements about the quality of the product a company produces.

Managing reputation risk can be complicated by the fact that many of these factors lie outside the control of the organisation. For example, many companies outsource production to third parties who operate in countries where labour costs are cheaper. Such arrangements can work well, although major multinational corporations have had their reputations tarnished by being associated with third parties who used dubious employment or environmental policies in order to keep costs down.

Reputational risk is covered in detail in Chapter 4.

Test your understanding 5

During their work on Worldcom and Enron, Arthur Anderson (chartered accountants and registered auditors) failed to identify serious irregularities in these companies. This led to their demise.

This was mainly due to which ONE of the following?

A   Business risk

B   Political risk

C   Environmental risk

D   Reputation risk

Employee malfeasance risk

Malfeasance means doing wrong or committing an offence. Organisations might be exposed to risks of actions by employees that result in an offence or crime (other than fraud). This, like fraud risk, is a type of operational business risk.

More on employee malfeasance

Examples of employee malfeasance are:

* deliberately making false representations about a product or service in order to win a customer order, exposing the organisation to the risk of compensation claims for mis-selling

* committing a criminal offence by failing to comply with statutory requirements, such as taking proper measures for the safety and protection of employees or customers.

Risks from illegal activities by employees should be controlled by suitable internal controls, to ensure that employees comply with established policies and procedures.

Risks in international operations

International businesses are subject to all the risks above but also have to consider extra risk factors, which could be due to the following:

Culture   A UK business may fail in a venture overseas because it does not adapt to the overseas culture. Good knowledge of local culture can, however, give companies an advantage.

Litigation   There is a greater litigation risk in overseas operations as the parent company management may not understand the legislation well and are therefore more at risk of breaching it.

Credit   There is often a greater difficulty in controlling credit risk on overseas sales. Chasing debts is more difficult and expensive.

Items in transit There is a greater risk of losses or damage in transit if companies are transporting goods great distances

Financial risks These include foreign exchange risks, and interest rate risk and are considered in more detail in F3.

More on risks in international operations

Companies that engage in international operations could face substantial risks in addition to country risk.

- There could be significant **cultural differences** between the various countries in which the company operates. There could be a risk that products, services and business practices that are acceptable in one country will be unacceptable in another. Failure to understand a national or local culture could mean that a company will fail to succeed in establishing its business.

- A lack of understanding of local legislation could expose an organisation to **litigation risk**. When legal action is initiated in a different country, a company has to appoint lawyers to represent them and rely on their advice on the appropriate and necessary steps to take.

- When a company exports goods to other countries, there is a **risk that the goods will be held up or lost in transit**, and the loss might not always be covered by insurance. For example, goods might be held up in customs due to inadequate import documentation.

- When a customer in another country buys goods on credit, the exporter is exposed to credit risk. However, the **credit risk is often greater**, because in the event of non-payment by the customer, legal action might be more difficult to arrange (and more expensive) and the prospects of obtaining payment might be much lower.

Test your understanding 6

A company has performed a SWOT analysis and has identified two main threats:

- new legislation covering one of their products; and

- the bank asking for their loan to be repaid immediately since the company failed to pay their most recent instalment after the interest rate rose.

Which categories of risk are they best described by?

Select ALL that apply

A   Financial risk

B   Political risk

C   Reputation risk

D   Economic risk

Test your understanding 7

Risk identification and management are the responsibility of:

Select ALL that apply

A   The Board

B   The risk manager

C   The audit committee

D   Non-executive directors

Test your understanding 8

Miney plc ("Miney") is a global company – incorporated in the USA – that extracts valuable minerals from the earth.

Mining is a risky business with a death toll averaging 100 deaths per annum in the USA alone. Miney has recently had a coal mine collapse killing two men and trapping four others for three days. The accident made the national news each day and Miney became a household name. Miney is financed purely by equity and has a large cash balance and no debt. It has come to the attention of the Board that the future price of coal is forecast to fall, as renewable energy sources becomes more reliable.

Which THREE of the following risks would you identify as most critical for Miney to assess?

A   Financial risk

B   Project risk

C   Reputation risk

D   Production risk

E   Health and safety risk

F   Commodity price risk

Test your understanding 9

AW company is expanding geographically and has just appointed Miss X as divisional manager of their new branch in Country B. AW has never operated in Country B before but has a history of successful divisional expansion in other countries.

Which of the following could help Miss X minimise the risks facing AW Company relating to cultural and legal differences between Country B and AW's current working practices.

Select ALL that apply.

A Recruitment of local staff.

B Employing a local firm of solicitors to advise Miss X on local legislation and working practices.

C Replication of previous divisional expansion plans.

D A marketing campaign to introduce Country B to AW Company.

E Secondment of staff from within AW who are experienced in setting up new divisions.

Test your understanding 10

Historically, X has done business with several non-democratic or repressive governments.

In the light of this, which TWO of the following risks should the directors of X be most concerned with?

A Technology risk.

B Corporate reputation risk.

C Economic risk.

D Fraud risk

E Business risk

F Financial risk.

Test your understanding 11

You are a management accountant working on proposals to build a dam in a developing country in order to generate hydro-electric power and enable many homes to have electricity for the first time. The dam is being financed by international aid, the total amount of which is currently uncertain.

You have been made aware of a pressure group which disagrees with the proposals since construction of the dam will damage the local eco system. The pressure group have vowed to disrupt the project directly through protests.

You are also aware of negative media coverage of the dam which accuses your company of making excessive profits from the project. In addition, the bank financing the initial stages of the project has contacted the directors to ask that its involvement in the project not be publicised as it believes it will damage its reputation.

Your company's directors have asked you to present a briefing on the project at their next board meeting.

Which of the following should you include as risks to the project's progression in your briefing to the board?

Select ALL that apply.

A   Risk the international aid is not received or inadequate to fund the project.

B   Risk of negative media coverage for the company.

C   Threats from the pressure group to disrupt the project directly.

D   Risks that the local eco system will be damaged.

E   Threat that the bank will pull out due to risks to their reputation.

Test your understanding 12 – ZXC (Case Study)

Scenario

The ZXC company manufactures aircraft. The company is based in Europe and currently produces a range of four different aircraft. ZXC's aircraft are reliable with low maintenance costs, giving ZXC a good reputation, both to airlines who purchase from ZXC and to airlines' customers who fly in the aircraft.

Trigger

ZXC is currently developing the 'next generation' of passenger aircraft, with the selling name of the ZXLiner. New developments in ZXLiner include the following:

•   Two decks along the entire aircraft (not just part as in the Boeing 747 series) enabling faster loading and unloading of passengers from both decks at the same time. However, this will mean that airport gates must be improved to facilitate dual loading at considerable expense.

- 20% decrease in fuel requirements and falls in noise and pollution levels.

- Use of new alloys to decrease maintenance costs, increase safety and specifically the use of Zitnim (a new lightweight conducting alloy) rather than standard wiring to enable the 'fly-by-wire' features of the aircraft. Zitnim only has one supplier worldwide.

Many component suppliers are based in Europe although ZXC does obtain about 25% of the sub-contracted components from companies in the USA. ZXC also maintains a significant R&D department working on the ZXLiner and other new products such as alternative environmentally friendly fuel for aircraft.

Although the ZXLiner is yet to fly or be granted airworthiness certificates, ZXC does have orders for 25 aircraft from the HTS company. However, on current testing schedules the ZXLiner will be delivered late. ZXC currently has about €4 billion of loans from various banks and last year made a loss of €2.3 billion.

Task

Write a report to the directors of ZXC identifying the sources of risk that could affect ZXC, and evaluating the impact of the risk on the company.

(30 minutes)

Test your understanding 13 – Smart meters (Case study)

Scenario

E is an electricity company that has a large number of customers. All customers' homes have electricity meters with mechanical dials that turn to record the consumption of electricity. Most homes have their meters indoors. Customers have to provide E with regular readings from their meters in order to ensure that they are billed properly for their electricity consumption. Customers can log into their accounts online to input their readings or they can telephone E's call centre to give an operator a reading.

E has a policy that customers must allow an inspector to read their electricity meters at least once per year. This inspection has two purposes. The first is to ensure that the customer has not been consistently understating the figures in order to underpay for their electricity and the second is to ensure that the meter has not been tampered with in order to reduce the readings according to the dials. The meters are designed so that they are difficult to dismantle without causing obvious damage and they also have a seal that is made out of soft metal that will be broken if the meter is ever opened.

E's inspectors generally visit all the homes within a particular area in the course of an evening. As most customers are at home then it is an efficient way to conduct the annual checks. If a customer is not at home the inspector leaves a card to request an opportunity to inspect the meter. If the customer does not respond to the card within seven days E will send up to four weekly reminders. Almost all customers comply with these requests but a very small minority do not respond and E can apply to the courts for the right to force entry when that happens.

Trigger

E is considering the replacement of its electricity meters with new "smart meters" which will be located in customers' homes. These will record consumption electronically rather than mechanically. The information will be stored on the meter. The same wires that carry electricity can be used to transmit data to and from the meters and E's IT system will send coded messages to meters to request readings as and when required. It is envisaged that these electronic readings will normally be once every three months, but there is very little to prevent E from reading some meters far more often.

Each meter will be fitted with a chip that will transmit a warning if it is tampered with either physically or electronically. The memory on the meters is not affected by power cuts and the meters can restart themselves without losing any data if a power cut occurs.

Task

Write a report to the Board of E which:

(a) Discusses the potential benefits for E that may come about from the introduction of smart meters; and

(b) Evaluates FOUR risks that might arise from the introduction of smart meters and suggests how each risk might be dealt with.

(45 minutes)

4 Chapter summary

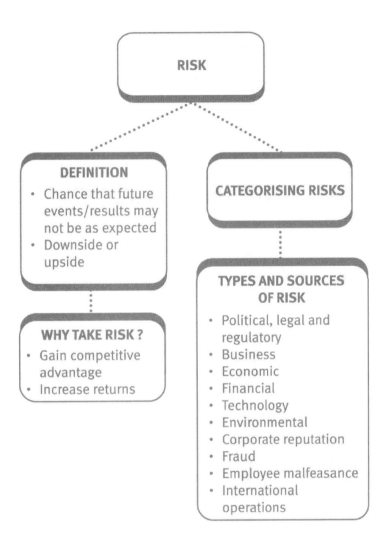

Test your understanding answers

Test your understanding 1

The correct answer is D – Per CIMA's risk management cycle, a risk management group should be formed, risks identified, understand their scale, develop a strategy, implement and allocate responsibility, control and review.

Test your understanding 2

The correct answers are C and D – A and B are strategic level risks.

Test your understanding 3

The correct answer is D – A, B and C are operational risks.

Test your understanding 4

A, B and C

- Option A: If publicised, poor treatment of employees at Company Q's main supplier could greatly increase reputation risk to Company Q. This may influence Q's performance over a long period of time since it may lose support from customers, shareholders and employees. The fact that Q Company may not be able to meet it strategic objectives as a result makes this a strategic risk.

- Option B: See explanation above, Company Q will be associated with the pollution and held responsible for it.

- Option C: Would almost certainly compromise Company Q's ability to meet its' strategic objectives.

- Option D: Would not affect Company Q's performance over a long period of time. It may lead to a reduction in profit margins but only if the supplier successfully negotiates a price increase.

- Option E: See explanation for Option D above.

Test your understanding 5

The correct answer is D – Arthur Anderson consequently lost their reputation as being the number one accountancy firm in the world and consequently many of their customers.

Test your understanding 6

The correct answers are A and B – New legislation is covered within political risk. The repayment of the loan is covered within financial risk.

Test your understanding 7

The correct answers are A, B, C and D – All staff in an organisation are responsible for risk.

Test your understanding 8

C, E and F

A   Financial risk – low risk due to lack of debt finance

B   Project risk – large one off projects are not a major aspect of the company's business model

C   Reputation risk – high due to accident

D   Production risk – despite the accidents, there is not a high risk of production shortages

E   Health and safety risk – high due to accident and potential for injury in the industry

F   Commodity price risk – high due to threat from renewable sources

Test your understanding 9

A and B only

- Options A and B will help Miss X understand local practices.

- Option C – Previous divisional expansion plans are likely to be culturally appropriate to other countries and not Country B.

- Option D – a marketing campaign may cause more cultural issues.

- Option E – see explanation for option 3 above.

Test your understanding 10

B and D

- X should be concerned with their reputation but also the risk of fraud and corruption when dealing with non-democratic governments is greater (option D).

Test your understanding 11

A, C and E

- Options A, C and E will disrupt or halt the project directly.

- Option B is a risk to the company and not the project.

- Option D is not a risk to the project's progression although it may end up causing reputation risk for the company.

Test your understanding 12 – ZXC (Case Study)

To: The directors of ZXC

From: A.N. Accountant

Date: Today

Subject: Sources and evaluation of risk at ZXC

This report covers the identification of risk at ZXC and evaluates each risk in turn. Recommendations for risk reduction are not given at this time.

Product/market risk

This is the risk that customers will not buy new products (or services) provided by the organisation, or that the sales demand for current products and services will decline unexpectedly.

For ZXC, there is the risk that demand for the new aircraft will be less than expected, either due to customers purchasing the rival airplane or because airports will not be adapted to take the new ZXLiner.

Commodity price risk

Businesses might be exposed to risks from unexpected increases (or falls) in the price of a key commodity.

Part of the control systems of the ZXLiner rely on the availability of the new lightweight conducting alloy Zitnim. As there is only one supplier of this alloy, then there is the danger of the monopolist increasing the price or even denying supply. Increase in price would increase the overall cost of the (already expensive) ZXLiner, while denial of supply would further delay delivery of the aircraft.

Product reputation risk

Some companies rely heavily on brand image and product reputation, and an adverse event could put its reputation (and so future sales) at risk.

While the reputation of ZXC appears good at present, reputation will suffer if the ZXLiner is delayed significantly or it does not perform well in test flights (which have still to be arranged). Airline customers, and also their customers (travellers) are unlikely to feel comfortable flying in an aircraft that is inherently unstable.

Currency risk

Currency risk, or foreign exchange risk, arises from the possibility of movements in foreign exchange rates, and the value of one currency in relation to another.

ZXC is currently based in Europe although it obtains a significant number of parts from the USA. If the €/$ exchange rate became worse, then the cost of imported goods for ZXC (and all other companies) would increase. At present, the relatively weak US$ is in ZXC's favour and so this risk is currently negligible.

Interest rate risk

Interest rate risk is the risk of unexpected gains or losses arising as a consequence of a rise or fall in interest rates. Exposures to interest rate risk arise from borrowing and investing.

As ZXC do have significant bank loans, the company is very exposed to this risk.

Gearing risk

Gearing risk for non-bank companies is the risk arising from exposures to high financial gearing and large amounts of borrowing.

Again, ZXC has significant bank loans. This increases the amount of interest that must be repaid each year.

Political risk

Political risk depends to a large extent on the political stability in the countries in which an organisation operates, the political institutions within that country and the government's attitude towards protectionism.

As ZXC operates in a politically stable country this risk is negligible.

Legal risk or litigation risk

The risk arises from the possibility of legal action being taken against an organisation.

At present this risk does not appear to be a threat for ZXC. However, if the ZXLiner is delayed any further there is a risk for breach of contract for late delivery to the HTS company.

Regulatory risk

This is the possibility that regulations will affect the way an organisation has to operate.

In terms of aircraft, regulation generally affects noise and pollution levels. As the ZXLiner is designed to have lower noise and pollution levels than existing aircraft then this risk does not appear to be a threat to ZXC.

Technology risk

Technology risk arises from the possibility that technological change will occur or that new technology will not work.

Given that ZXC is effectively producing a new product (the ZXLiner) that has not actually been tested yet, there is some technology risk. At worse, the ZXLiner may not fly at all or not obtain the necessary flying certificates.

Economic risk

This risk refers to the risks facing organisations from changes in economic conditions, such as economic growth or recession, government spending policy and taxation policy, unemployment levels and international trading conditions.

Demand for air travel is forecast to increase for the foreseeable future – this will lead to a demand for aircraft which ZXC will benefit from. The risk of product failure is more significant than economic risk.

Environmental risk

This risk arises both from changes to the environment over which an organisation has no direct control, such as global warming, and from those for which the organisation might be responsible, such as oil spillages and other pollution.

ZXC is subject to this risk – and there is significant debate concerning the impact of air travel on global warming. At the extreme, there is a threat that air travel could be banned, or made very expensive by international taxation agreements, although this appears unlikely at present.

Conclusion

ZXC will suffer from many risks which will impact on the company. The likelihood and impact of each varies, by risk and over time. ZXC should implement reduction strategies where possible.

Test your understanding 13 – Smart meters (Case study)

To: The Board of E

From: A.N. Accountant

Date: Today

Subject: Smart meters and risk

Introduction

This report discusses the benefits of introducing Smart Meters at E, and then evaluates four risks arising from this action. Recommendations are then made to reduce the risks identified.

(a) **The introduction of Smart Meters**

Smart meters will offer the potential to dramatically reduce operating expenses. E will not require meter inspectors to visit customers' homes. There will be far fewer transactions involving call centre staff and so numbers can be reduced there too.

The new meters may reduce customer fraud and so enhance revenues. The fact that they are electronic and not mechanical will make it far harder to tamper with readings.

E will be able to gather a great deal of information about individual customers. At present, E can tell how much electricity is being drawn from the grid, but it cannot identify the specific customers who are using it. The new meters will make it possible to identify customers whose demand changes in response to, say, a major sporting event. That may make it easier for E to predict demand in advance of such events and so plan more easily.

E may also be able to gather valuable marketing information. For example, some customers will have larger increases in consumption when the weather is cold. E could target such customers with offers of alternative pricing plans or discounts on home insulation.

(b) **Risks**

Customer fraud

If customers learn how to interfere with the meters then E may lose significant amounts of revenue. The new meters may be more difficult to manipulate, but history suggests that electronic safeguards can be defeated. For example, mobile phones can be unlocked and dvds can be pirated despite safeguards.

E could compare patterns of energy consumption within neighbourhoods and could identify customers whose readings seem low. Those customers' meters could be inspected for any modification. E should publicise any criminal prosecutions as a deterrent to other customers.

Installation

The installation of these new meters will be a significant undertaking. E will have to arrange access to every customer's home in order to fit the new meters. The logistics of this will be complicated because of customers' work patterns and availability because of work and so on. The old system will have to operate in parallel with the new while this work is being undertaken and so staff will be stretched.

E may offer discounts or rebates to customers who offer access at convenient times. The discounts should be self-financing if they are funded out of the cost savings of managing a customer's account once the smart meter has been installed.

IT issues

It will be difficult for E to fully test this system before installation. There will be large numbers of smart meters in the system and they will be communicating over long distances. There could be unforeseen problems with data being corrupted or lost. If that happens then the original meters will have been removed and there will be no effective way to put the system back.

It would be ideal if E could select a system that has already been used successfully by another electricity company. It would be preferable to apply a proven system even if there are more up to date versions of the technology that might offer enhancements.

Financial cost

There will have to be a significant investment in this new system and the anticipated benefits may not be realised. The shareholders and other stakeholders may be concerned that E is taking a reckless risk by making a substantial investment in a new technology. An adverse outcome could mean lower profits or higher prices for consumers.

E could possibly transfer some of the risk by paying a third party to design and implement the new system. The contract could specify penalties for any shortcomings in the operation of the new system.

Conclusions

E would appear to benefit from the introduction of Smart Meters. However, several risks may arise with their introduction. These risks can be reduced, in part, by the measures suggested in this report.

Risk management

Chapter learning objectives

Lead	Component	
A2. Evaluate risk exposure	(a)	Evaluate the impact of risk
	(b)	Assess the likelihood of risks.
	(c)	Analyse the interaction of different risks
A3. Discuss ways of managing risk.	(b)	Discuss risk tolerance, appetite and capacity
	(c)	Discuss risk management frameworks
	(d)	Discuss risk analytics
C2. Recommend internal controls for risk management	(a)	Discuss the COSO risk management framework

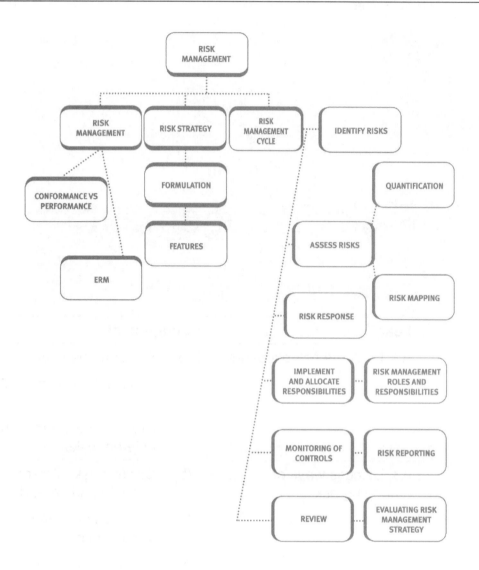

 1   Risk management

Risk management is defined as:

'the process of understanding and managing the risks that the organisation is inevitably subject to in attempting to achieve its corporate objectives'

CIMA Official Terminology

- The traditional view of risk management has been one of protecting the organisation from loss through conformance procedures and hedging techniques – this is about avoiding the **downside** risk.

- The new approach to risk management is about taking advantage of the opportunities to increase overall returns within a business – benefiting from the **upside** risk.

- The following diagram shows how risk management can reconcile the two perspectives of conformance and performance (as discussed previously in chapter 1).

Source: IFAC (1999) Enhancing Shareholder Wealth By Better Managing Risk

Enterprise Risk Management (ERM)

Enterprise risk management is the term given to the alignment of risk management with business strategy and the embedding of a risk management culture into business operations.

It has been defined as:

'A process, effected by an entity's board of directors, management and other personnel, applied in strategy setting and across the enterprise, designed to identify potential events that may affect the entity, and manage risk to be within its risk appetite, to provide reasonable assurance regarding the achievement of entity objectives.'

Committee of Sponsoring Organisations of the Treadway Commission (COSO) (2003)

Risk management has transformed from a 'department focused' approach to a holistic, co-ordinated and integrated process which manages risk throughout the organisation.

The key principles of ERM include:

- consideration of risk management in the context of business strategy
- risk management is everyone's responsibility, with the tone set from the top
- the creation of a risk aware culture
- a comprehensive and holistic approach to risk management
- consideration of a broad range of risks (strategic, financial, operational and compliance)
- a focused risk management strategy, led by the board (embedding risk within an organisation's culture).

The COSO ERM Framework is represented as a three dimensional matrix in the form of a cube which reflects the relationships between objectives, components and different organisational levels.

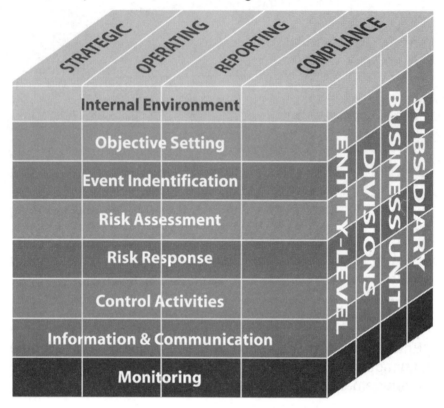

- The four objectives (strategic, operations, reporting and compliance) reflect the responsibility of different executives across the entity and address different needs.

- The four organisational levels (subsidiary, business unit, division and entity) emphasise the importance of managing risks across the enterprise as a whole.

- The eight components must function effectively for risk management to be successful.

The eight components are closely aligned to the risk management process addressed previously, and also reflect elements from the COSO view of an effective internal control system:

- **Internal environment:** This is the tone of the organisation, including the risk management philosophy and risk appetite (see later in this chapter).

- **Objective setting:** Objectives should be aligned with the organisation's mission and need to be consistent with the organisation's defined risk appetite.

- **Event identification:** These are internal and external events (both positive and negative) which impact upon the achievement of an entity's objectives and must be identified.

- **Risk assessment:** Risks are analysed to consider their likelihood and impact as a basis for determining how they should be managed.

- **Risk response:** Management selects risk response(s) to avoid, accept, reduce or share risk. The intention is to develop a set of actions to align risks with the entity's risk tolerances and risk appetite.

- **Control activities:** Policies and procedures help ensure the risk responses are effectively carried out.

- **Information and communication:** The relevant information is identified, captured and communicated in a form and timeframe that enables people to carry out their responsibilities.

- **Monitoring:** The entire ERM process is monitored and modifications made as necessary.

 Risk management and shareholder value

Ernst and Young (2001) have developed a model of shareholder value in which:

Shareholder value = Static NPV of existing business model + Value of future growth options

which more simply put is: 'the sum of the value of what a company does now and the value of what they could possibly do in the future'.

Good risk management allows businesses to exploit opportunities for future growth while protecting the value already created. By aligning risk management activity to what the shareholders consider vital to the success of the business, the shareholders are assured that what they value is protected. Ernst and Young identify four stages:

(a) Establish what shareholders value about the company – through talking with the investment community and linking value creation processes to key performance indicators.

(b) Identify the risks around the key shareholder value drivers – the investment community can identify those factors that will influence their valuation of the company. All other risks will also be considered, including those not identified by investors.

(c) Determine the preferred treatment for the risks – the investment community can give their views on what actions they would like management to take in relation to the risks. The risk/reward trade-off can be quantified by estimating the change in a company's market valuation if a particular risk treatment is implemented.

(d) Communicate risk treatments to shareholders – shareholders need to be well informed, as a shared vision is important in relation to the inter-related concepts of risk management and shareholder value.

> ## Test your understanding 1
>
> IFAC highlighted two aspects of risk management which link risk aversion and risk seeking activities. They are:
>
> A   Compliance and strategy
>
> B   Conformance and performance
>
> C   Compliance and conformance
>
> D   Performance and strategy

> ## Test your understanding 2
>
> In 2003 the Committee of Sponsoring Organisations (COSO) outlined six key principles of Enterprise Risk Management (ERM).
>
> **Identify which of the following is/are included.**
>
> Select ALL that apply
>
> A   Consideration of risk management in the context of business strategy
>
> B   The creation of a risk aware culture
>
> C   Consideration of a narrow range of risks, mainly financial
>
> D   Risk management is the responsibility of the Risk Committee
>
> E   A comprehensive and holistic approach to risk management

ERM – Integrating strategy with performance 2017

In 2017 COSO produced an update to the ERM framework. The update uses a new diagram – the double helix (shown below) – and the key principle is that ERM should be ingrained into everything the organisation does including setting the mission, vision and core values of the entity.

Risk is inherent in everything an entity does and it is therefore a risk that a strategy chosen by an entity may not be in line with the stated mission, vision and core values.

ENTERPRISE RISK MANAGEMENT

MISSION, VISION, & CORE VALUES — STRATEGY DEVELOPMENT — BUSINESS OBJECTIVE FORMULATION — IMPLEMENTATION & PERFORMANCE — ENHANCED VALUE

 Governance & Culture

 Strategy & Objective-Setting

 Performance

 Review & Revision

 Information, Communication, & Reporting

The double helix is broken down into five components:

1   Governance and culture

This relates to the internal environment and emphases the importance of the tone of the organisation. It also includes ethical behaviour and understanding the risk appetite of the entity.

2   Strategy and objective setting

This component is possibly the main focus to the update; it emphases the importance of making sure ERM and objective setting is aligned to risk appetite in the strategic planning stage – to make sure that the strategy can be implemented successfully. This component therefore helps to minimise the risk of the wrong strategy being chosen.

3   Performance

This combines the components from the original cube of event identification, risk assessment and risk response. It involves maintaining a focus on identifying internal and external events (both positive and negative) which could impact upon the achievement of an entity's objectives, assessing the likelihood and impact of these events to prioritise their importance, and then developing a response to accept, reduce, avoid or share the risk.

4   Review and revision

Policies and procedures to help ensure the risk responses are effectively carried out, through the selection of key metrics. This ensures that the entire ERM process is monitored and modifications made as necessary.

5   Information, communication and reporting

As always, it is vitally important that the relevant information is identified, captured and communicated in a form and timeframe that enables people to carry out their responsibilities. And that this information is reported to the right people and levels, be that directors or shareholders.

The cube or the helix

It is important to note that COSO has not withdrawn the cube (which is why it remains part of the P3 syllabus). The cube also provides a useful background to the development of the 2017 update.

COSO want to encourage organisations to identify the framework that works best for their situation, giving the company the best chance to improve their performance and of achieving their strategy and objectives.

Benefits of ERM

Benefits of effective ERM include:

- enhanced decision-making by integrating risks
- reduced performance fluctuations and fewer interruptions to operations
- the resultant improvement in investor confidence, and hence shareholder value
- focus of management attention on the most significant risks
- a common language of risk management which is understood throughout the organisation enabling performance improvement
- increased ability to benefit from upside risk and reduced susceptibility to downside risk
- reduced cost of finance through effective management of risk.
- improved utilisation of resources
- increased opportunities for the organisation

> **Test your understanding 3**
>
> Q Co is a new organisation, but management are keen to maximise their chances of achieving their objectives by using ERM. They have recently met to discuss the controls they will use to mitigate the risks they considered to be the most significant.
>
> **Which one of the ERM Integrating strategy with performance 2017 components does this best describe:**
>
> A   Information, communication and reporting
>
> B   Review and revision
>
> C   Governance and culture
>
> D   Performance
>
> E   Strategy and objective setting

2   Risk management strategy

Formulation of a risk strategy

- For many businesses the specific formulation of a risk strategy has been a recent development.
- In the past, a formal strategy for managing risks would not be developed, but rather it would be left to individual managers to make assessments of the risks the business faced and exercise judgement on what was a reasonable level of risk.
- This has now changed: failure to properly identify and control risks has been identified as a major cause of business failure (take Barings Bank as an example).

A framework for board consideration of risk is shown below:

Formulating a risk management strategy

A risk management strategy needs to be developed to ensure that the risk exposures of the organisation are consistent with its risk appetite. At the very least, the risk management capability within the organisation should be sufficient to:

- review its internal control system and its adequacy at least annually,
- ensure that controls are properly implemented, and
- monitor the implementation and effectiveness of controls.

However, the investment by the organisation in risk strategy should be largely determined by the performance requirements of its business objectives and strategy:

- **Risk appetite** can be defined as the amount of risk an organisation is willing to accept in pursuit of value. This may be explicit in strategies, policies and procedures, or it may be implicit. It is determined by:
    - **risk capacity** – the amount of risk that the organisation can bear, and
    - **risk attitude** – the overall approach to risk, in terms of the board being risk averse or risk seeking.
- The way that the organisation documents and determines the specific parts of its risk strategy should link to the business strategy and objectives
- Overall risk management strategy is concerned with trying to achieve the required business objectives with the lowest possible chance of failure. The tougher the business objectives, however, the more risks will have to be taken to achieve them.
- **Residual risk** is the risk a business faces after its controls have been considered (see later in this chapter for more details).

More on risk appetite

To bring risk management into line with strategic management, an organisation should define the amount of risk it is prepared to take in the pursuit of its objectives. This willingness to accept risk can be stated in a mixture of quantitative and qualitative terms. For example:

- The board of directors might state how much capital they would be prepared to invest in the pursuit of a business objective and the size of the loss they would be willing to face in the event that results turn out badly.

- Risk can also be stated qualitatively, for example in relation to the organisation's reputation.

In practice, in a large organisation, there will be different levels of risk appetite for different operations or different profit centres/investment centres within the business.

Risk appetite factors

The factors, or business strategies, which could affect the risk appetite of the board of a company include:

Nature of product being manufactured	A high risk of product failure in certain products (e.g. aircraft) must be avoided due to the serious consequences of such an event. This will, out of necessity, limit the risk appetite of the board with regard to these specific products. For other products the risk of failure will be less (e.g. a fizzy drink having small changes from the normal ingredients – customers may not even notice the difference). Additionally if a business is taking significant risks with part of its product range it may be limited in the risk it can take with other products.
The need to increase sales	The strategic need to move into a new market will result in the business accepting a higher degree of risk than trying to increase sales or market share in an existing market. At that stage the business will appear to have a higher risk appetite.
The background of the board	Some board members may accept increased risk personally and this may be reflected in the way they manage the company.
Amount of change in the market	Operating in a market place with significant change (e.g. mobile telephones) will mean that the board have to accept a higher degree of risk. For example, new models of phone have to be available quickly.
Reputation of the company	If the company has a good reputation then the board will accept less risk – as they will not want to lose that good reputation.

Test your understanding 4

The amount of risk an organisation is willing to accept in the pursuit of value is known as their:

A   Risk map

B   Risk appetite

C   Risk culture

D   Risk thermostat

Features of a risk management strategy

In a CIMA and IFAC (International Federation of Accountants) joint report in 2004 – Enterprise Governance – the following key features of a risk management strategy were identified:

- Statement of the organisation's attitude to risk – the balance between risk and the need to achieve objectives.

- The risk appetite of the organisation.

- The objectives of the risk management strategy.

- Culture of the organisation in relation to risk (and the behaviour the organisation expects from individuals with regard to risk-taking).

- Responsibilities of managers for the application of risk management strategy.

- Reference should be made to the risk management systems the company uses (i.e. its internal control systems).

- Performance criteria should be defined so that the effectiveness of risk management can be evaluated.

An alternative risk management process

The Institute of Risk Management (IRM) developed a risk management process containing three elements:

(1)   **Risk assessment** is composed of the analysis and evaluation of risk through the process of identification, description and estimation.

       The purpose of risk assessment is to undertake risk evaluation. Risk evaluation is used to make decisions about the significance of risks to the organisation and whether each specific risk should be accepted or treated.

(2)   **Risk reporting** is concerned with regular reports to the board and to stakeholders setting out the organisation's policies in relation to risk and enabling the effective monitoring of those policies.

> (3) **Risk treatment** (risk response) is the process of selecting and implementing measures to modify the risk.
>
> Residual risk reporting will therefore follow risk treatment.

3 Identifying, measuring and assessing risks

Chapter 1 examined the different types of risks faced by an organisation. It is key, however, that businesses can identify the risks they face and evaluate the effect of these risks on the business. Some risks will be relatively easily borne by businesses, but others will be more difficult and more serious in their implications.

Risk identification

- The risk identification process will often be controlled by a **risk committee** or risk management specialists (see later in this chapter).

- The risks identified in the process should be recorded in a **risk register**, which is simply a list of the risks that have been identified, and the measures (if any) that have been taken to control each of them.

- There are a variety of methods that can be used by businesses to identify the risks that they face.

The risk register

The risk register is a very important and practical risk management tool that should be used by all companies. It takes several days, if not weeks, to produce, and needs to be reviewed and updated regularly – often annually (in conjunction with corporate governance guidelines).

The risk register is often laid out in the form of a tabular document with various headings:

(1)   The **risk title** – stating what the risk might be.

(2)   The **likelihood** of the risk – possibly measured numerically if a scale has been set e.g. 1 is unlikely, 5 is highly likely.

(3)   The **impact** of the risk should it arise. Again this might be graded from, say, 1 (low impact) to 5 (high impact).

(4)   The **risk owner's** name will be given – usually a manager or director.

(5)   The **date** the risk was identified will be detailed.

(6)   The date the risk was last considered will be given.

(7)   **Mitigation actions** should be listed i.e. what the company has done so far to reduce the risk. This might include training, insurance, further controls added to the system, etc.

(8)   An **overall risk rating** might be given e.g. 1/10, so that management can immediately see which risks are the ones they should be concentrating on.

(9)   **Further actions** to be taken in the future will be listed (if any).

(10) The **'action lead'** name will be detailed i.e. who is responsible for making sure that these future actions are implemented.

(11) A **due date** will state when the date by which action has to be implemented.

(12) A risk level target might be given i.e. a score lower than that given in step 8 above. This might mean that by implementing a control, the risk rating is expected to lower from, say, 8 to, say 2 (the target risk level).

For example, using the steps detailed above, one row of a tabulated risk register might show:

(1)   Loss of personal data i.e. unsecure use of mobile devices could result in personal identifiable information being lost, stolen or unauthorised access gained.

(2)   Likelihood = 3

(3)   Impact = 5

(4)   Risk owner = Mike Smith (IT manager)

(5)   1.1.X2

(6)   2.2.X4

(7) Staff receive training every 2 years which highlights the risks. All laptops are encrypted. Regular audits are undertaken. Any incidents are reported to the Audit Committee.

(8) Overall risk rating = 7

(9) Encryption technology to be implemented which meets industry standard.

(10) Mike Smith

(11) 31.7.X4

(12) Risk level target = 3

Test your understanding 5

Risk registers would normally detail which of the following:

Select ALL that apply

A   Risk level before controls are implemented

B   Risk level after controls are implemented

C   Responsibility for managing risks

D   The total cost of a control being implemented

More on risk identification

Some of the common methods of risk identification include:

PEST/SWOT analysis	PEST (Political, Economic, Social, Technological) and SWOT (Strengths, Weaknesses, Opportunities, Threats) are very well known and familiar business analysis tools. These models can be used to assess risks by providing a framework to identify and think about the risks in the organisation.
External advisors	Companies may employ external risk consultants who will advise on key risks and processes that can be used to limit and control those risks. Consultants have access to other businesses and as a result may have pools of knowledge not available internally.
Interviews/questionnaires	The company may conduct interviews or send questionnaires to key business managers asking them to indicate principal risks.

Internal audit	One of the functions of internal audit should be to provide recommendations on controlling risk. As part of their work therefore, internal audit assess where the organisation faces risk.
Brainstorming	The business may decide to use more informal brainstorming meetings to assess the risks it faces. These meetings have the advantage of accessing many different viewpoints.

Any of these methods identify risks but at the end of the process it is important that the organisation determines which its principal risks are. It is these principal risks that will determine the controls that need to be put in place and the systems that will have to be introduced to control and manage the risks.

 ## Quantification of risk exposures

Quantification of risk is important in understanding the extent and significance of risk exposure. This can be done by measuring the impact of the risk factor (such as exchange rates) on the total value of the company, or on individual item such as cash flow or costs.

- Risks that are identified should be measured and assessed. The extent to which this can be done depends on the information available to the risk manager.

- In some companies, particularly in the banking and insurance industries, many risks can be measured statistically, on the basis of historical information.

- In many other situations, the measurement and assessment of risk depends on management judgement.

Some quantitative techniques include:

- expected values and standard deviation
- volatility
- value at risk (VaR)
- regression analysis
- simulation analysis

Expected values and standard deviation

- Some risks can be measured using expected values.

    Expected value = Σ prob X

    where prob = probability, X = outcome

Expected value of risk

When statistical estimates are available for the probabilities of different outcomes and the value of each outcome, risk can be measured as an expected value of loss or gain.

Expected value of loss = p × L

Where:

p is the probability that the outcome will occur

L is the loss in the event that the outcome does occur.

Example

The finance director of a company has to prepare an assessment of credit risk for a report to the board. The company has annual credit sales of $12 million, and customers are given 60 days (two months) credit. Experience shows that:

- irrecoverable debts written off amount to 1.5% of total annual credit sales

- 10% of irrecoverable debts written off are subsequently recovered by legal action.

Required:

(a)   What is the credit risk exposure of the company?

(b)   What is the expected loss each year due to credit risk?

Solution

(a)   The total exposure to credit risk can be expressed either as the total annual credit sales ($12 million) or the exposure to unpaid debts at any point in time ($12 million × 2/12 = $2 million).

(b)   For a full year the expected value of loss is = $12 million × 1.5% × 90% = $162,000

The standard deviation is a measure of the dispersion of the possible values of a given factor, such as cash flow, from the expected value or mean. Thus the standard deviation provides a measure of volatility – the greater the standard deviation, the greater the risk involved.

Volatility

- Another way of assessing risk might be looking at potential volatility. For example, a company might calculate an expected value based on a range of probabilities but also assess the potential variation from that expected outcome (range or standard deviation).

Test your understanding 6 – Volatility (Integration)

The following are the forecast purchases of raw materials in a future month:

£200,000   30% probability

£250,000   50% probability

£300,000   20% probability

Calculate the upside and downside volatility from expected purchases.

Value at risk

Value at Risk (VaR) allows investors to assess the scale of the likely loss in their portfolio at a defined level of probability. It is becoming the most widely used measure of financial risk and is also enshrined in both financial and accounting regulations.

VaR is based on the assumption that investors care mainly about the probability of a large loss. The VaR of a portfolio is the maximum loss on a portfolio occurring within a given period of time with a given probability (usually small).

- Calculating VaR involves using three components: a time period, a confidence level and a loss amount or percentage loss.

- Statistical methods are used to calculate a standard deviation for the possible variations in the value of the total portfolio of assets over a specific period of time.

- Making an assumption that possible variations in total market value of the portfolio are normally distributed, it is then possible to predict at a given level of probability the maximum loss that the bank might suffer on its portfolio in the time period.

- A bank can try to control the risk in its asset portfolio by setting target maximum limits for value at risk over different time periods (one day, one week, one month, three months, and so on).

- VaR may be calculated as standard deviation × Z-score (the Z-score can be found from the normal distribution tables).

Normal distribution

Normal distributions can be found when we measure things such as:

- Exam results

- Staff performance gradings

- The heights of a group of people etc

A normal distribution has the following characteristics:

The mean is shown in the centre of the diagram and the curve is symmetrical about the mean. This means that 50% of the values will be below the mean and 50% of the values will be above the mean.

Note: The mean, median and mode will all be the same for a normal distribution.

How far the values spread out from the mean is the standard deviation. This can be seen in the following diagram:

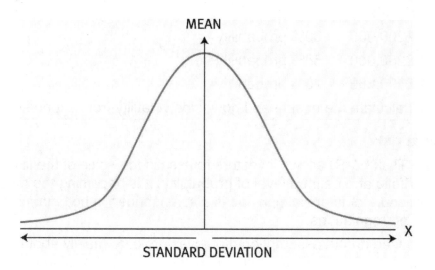

The total area under the curve is equal to 1.

If we can think of a standard normal distribution curve with three standard deviations as follows:

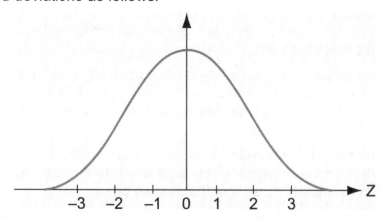

In general 68% of values are within one deviation (between -1 and 1), 95% of values are within two standard deviations (between -2 and 2) and 99.7% of values are within three standard deviations (between -3 and 3).

From this we can see that if we look at a set of data which fits a normal distribution the majority of values will occur closer to the mean, with fewer and fewer occurring the further from the mean we move.

A standard normal distribution has:

a mean of 0

a standard deviation of 1.

This special distribution is denoted by z and can be calculated as:

$$z = \frac{x - \mu}{\sigma}$$

Where:

z is the score

x is the value being considered

μ is the mean

σ is the standard deviation

This calculation is used to convert any value to standard normal distribution.

Looking up the normal distribution tables

Once we have calculated our 'z score' we can look this up on the normal distribution table to find the area under the curve, which equates to the percentage chance (probability) of that value occurring.

So if we calculated a z score of 1.00. From the table the value is 0.3413.

This means that (0.3413 ÷ 1.0) or 34.13% is the area shown from 0 -1 on the diagram

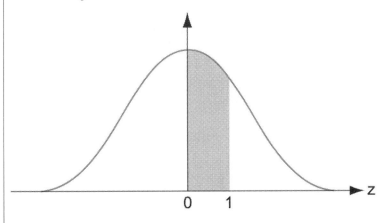

From this we can deduce that 34.13% would be the area shown from 0 -1 on the diagram. So we can say that 68.26% of values will fall within one standard deviation (-1 to 1).

VaR calculation

For VaR, there are two types of calculation to consider:

(1) The confidence level that the result will be above a particular figure – this is referred to as a one tail test.

(2) The confidence level that a figure will be within a particular range – this is referred to as a two tail test.

In both cases we are working backwards from the percentage to find the value of x.

One tail test

If you are asked to calculate the 95% VaR, this is a one tail test. As we are looking at risk, it is usually about being 95% certain that the outcome will be above a particular value.

50% of the distribution is on one side of the mean, within the tables we are looking for as close to 0.4500.

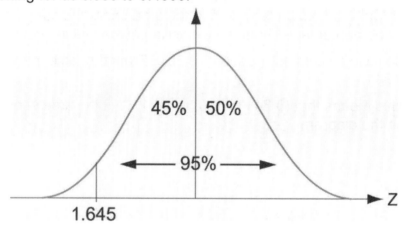

Two tail test

If you are asked about being 95% certain the result is within a range, the area would look like this:

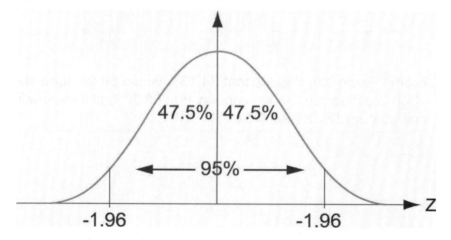

We would be looking for 0.4750 in the tables, 47.5% above and below the mean.

One tail test

Z is a bank. The management accountant of Z has estimated that the value of its asset portfolio at year end will be $1,500 million, with a standard deviation of $300 million.

Calculate the value at risk of the portfolio, at a 97.5% confidence level. (Express your answer in $, rounded to the nearest million.)

Solution

The Z value for a one-tail 97.5% confidence level is 1.96 (from the Normal Distribution tables).

VaR = standard deviation × Z value, so the

VaR = USD 300 million × 1.96 = USD 588 million

This means there is a 2.5% chance that the value of the portfolio will be (1,500 – 588) $912 million or below.

Two tail test

AL plc, a UK based company are expecting to receive $10 million from a US customer. The value in pounds is dependent on the exchange rate between the dollar and pound.

The mean exchange rate is $1.25/£ and the daily volatility of the pound/dollar exchange rate is 0.25%.

What is the range of values that AL plc will be 95% confident of receiving in 1 day?

Solution

The mean value of the $10 million is £8 million ($10 million ÷ $1.25/£) The daily standard deviation is (0.25% × £8 million =) £20,000

As we are looking at a range, this is a two tail test, to be 95% confident this will be within 47.5% of the mean on either side.

First find 0.4750 in the normal tables, this is a z value of 1.96. VaR = Z × Std deviation = 1.96 × 20,000 = £39,200

This means that AL plc is 95% confident that the value will be within £39,200 of the mean.

Therefore AL plc is 95% confident the sterling amount will be between £7,960,800 & £8,039,200.

Given the 1-day VaR, we can easily calculate the VaR for longer holding periods as:

n day Var = 1 day Var × √n

The VaR increases with the holding period. Thus, the longer the holding period, the greater the VaR.

Example of VaR

Suppose a UK company expects to receive $14 million from a US customer. The value in pounds to the UK company will depend on the exchange rate between the dollar and pounds resulting in gains or losses as the exchange rate changes. Assume that the exchange rate today is $1.75/£ and that the daily volatility of the pound/dollar exchange rate is 0.5%.

Calculate the

(a)   1-day 95% VaR

(b)   1-day 99% VaR.

The value of the $14 million today is £8 million ($14 million ÷ $1.75/£) with a daily standard deviation of £40,000 (0.5% × £8 million).

(a)   The standard normal value (Z) associated with the one-tail 95% confidence level is 1.645 (see Normal Distribution tables). Hence, the 1-day 95% VaR is 1.645 × £40,000 = £65,800. This means that we are 95% confident that the maximum daily loss will not exceed £65,800. Alternatively, we could also say that there is a 5% (1 out of 20) chance that the loss would exceed £65,800.

(b)   The standard normal value (Z) associated with the one-tail 99% confidence level is 2.33 (see Normal Distribution tables). Hence, the 1-day 99% VaR is 2.33 × £40,000 = £93,200. Thus, there is a 1% (1 out of 100) chance that the loss would exceed £93,200.

If we wanted to calculate the VaR for longer period, say 5 days, at the 95% level the calculation would be:

5 day 95% VaR = 1 day 95% VaR × $\sqrt{5}$ = £65,800 × 2.236 = £147,133

There is a 5% chance that the company's foreign exchange loss would exceed £147,133 over the next 5 days.

Similarly, the 30-day 99% VaR would be:

1 day 99% VaR × $\sqrt{30}$ = £93,200 × 5.477 = £510,477

This illustrates the longer the holding period, the greater the VaR.

More on value at risk (VaR)

The Basel committee established international standards for banking laws and regulations aimed at protecting the international financial system from the results of the collapse of major banks. Basel II established rigorous risk and capital management requirements to ensure each bank holds reserves sufficient to guard against its risk exposure, given its lending and investment practices. Regulators require banks to measure their market risk using a risk measurement model which is used to calculate the Value at Risk (VaR).

However, the global financial crisis has identified substantial problems with banks governance procedures in terms of understanding operational risk and applying risk measurement models like VaR. This has been emphasised by the number of banks that have failed or required government support – Northern Rock and Bradford and Bingley in the UK; Bear Sterns and Washington Mutual in the US amongst others.

Test your understanding 7

A company expects to receive $10 million from a US customer. The value in £ will depend on the exchange rate changing. Assume that the exchange rate today is $1.6667 / £ and that the daily volatility of the £/$ exchange rate is 0.5%.

Required:

What is the 10 day 95% VaR?

Test your understanding 8 – Value at risk (Integration)

A bank has estimated that the expected value of its portfolio in two weeks' time will be $50 million, with a standard deviation of $4.85 million.

Required:

Calculate and comment upon the value at risk of the portfolio, assuming a 95% confidence level.

Regression analysis

This can be used to measure a company's exposure to several risk factors at the same time. This is done by regressing changes in the company's cash flows against the risk factors (changes in interest rates, exchange rates, prices of key commodities such as oil). The regression coefficients will indicate the sensitivities of the company's cash flow to these risk factors.

The drawback with this technique is that the analysis is based on historical factors which may no longer be predictors of the company in the future.

Simulation analysis

This is used to evaluate the sensitivity of the value of the company, or its cash flows, to a variety of risk factors. These risk factors will be given various simulated values based on probability distributions, and the procedure is repeated a number of times to obtain the range of results that can be achieved.

The mean and standard deviation are then calculated from these results to give an expected value and measure of the risk.

This technique can be complex and time-consuming to carry out, and is limited by the assumptions of the probability distributions.

Other methods of measuring or assessing the severity of an identified risk include:

- scenario planning – forecasting various outcomes of an event;

- decision trees – use of probabilities to estimate an outcome;

- sensitivity analysis – asking 'what-if?' questions to test the robustness of a plan. Altering one variable at a time identifies the impact of that variable.

Drawbacks of the quantification of risk

Once a risk has been quantified, there is a problem – whether anyone really knows what it means. Unless you are a trainee or qualified accountant (or similar) this is unlikely, hence risks are often left unquantified.

Risk or assurance mapping

A common qualitative way of assessing the significance of risk is to produce a **'risk map'** or sometimes called an **'assurance map'**.

- The Board, the Risk Committee, the Audit Committee and senior management from various departments will all be involved in the preparation of the map.

- The map identifies whether a risk will have a significant impact on the organisation and links that into the likelihood of the risk occurring.

- The approach can provide a framework for prioritising risks in the business.

- Risks with a significant impact and a high likelihood of occurrence need more urgent attention than risks with a low impact and low likelihood of occurrence.

- A well-structured risk map will highlight where there are gaps in assurances over significant risk areas.

- Also, duplicated or potentially burdensome assurance processes may be identified.

- Risks can be plotted on a diagram, as shown below.

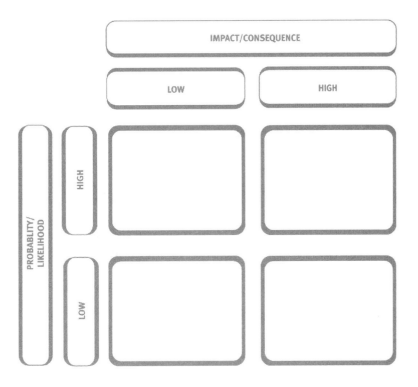

 More on risk mapping

The potential loss from an adverse outcome is a function of:

- the probability or likelihood that the adverse outcome will occur, and

- the impact of the outcome if it does occur.

When an initial review is carried out to identify and assess risks, the assessment of both probabilities and impact might be based on judgement and experience rather than on a detailed statistical and numerical analysis.

- In an initial analysis, it might be sufficient to categorise the probability of an adverse outcome as 'high', 'medium' or 'low', or even more simply as 'high' or 'low'.

- Similarly, it might be sufficient for the purpose of an initial analysis to assess the consequences or impact of an adverse outcome as 'severe' or 'not severe'.

Each risk can then be plotted on a risk map. A risk map is simply a 2 × 2 table or chart, showing the probabilities for each risk and their potential impact.

Example

The following simple risk map might be prepared for a firm of auditors

		Impact/consequences	
		Low	**High**
	High	New audit regulations for the profession	Loss of non-audit work from existing clients
Probability/likelihood	**Low**	Increases in salaries above the general rate of inflation	Loss of audit clients within the next two years.

Using a risk map

A risk map immediately indicates which risks should be given the highest priority.

- High-probability, high-impact risks should be given the highest priority for management, whether by monitoring or by taking steps to mitigate the risk.

- Low-probability, low-impact risks can probably be accepted by the organisation as within the limits of acceptability.

- High-probability, low-impact risks and low-probability, high-impact risks might be analysed further with a view to deciding the most appropriate strategy for their management.

For each high-probability, high-impact risk, further analysis should be carried out, with a view to:

- estimating the probability of an adverse (or favourable) outcome more accurately, and

- assessing the impact on the organisation of an adverse outcome. This is an area in which the management accountant should be able to contribute by providing suitable and relevant financial information.

An alternative layout for a risk map (other than the cruciform style shown above) would be a tabular format. The table might have the following columns:

(1) The risk name e.g. fraud.

(2) The likelihood of that risk arising e.g. medium.

(3) The impact of the risk if it does arise e.g. high.

(4) Controls already in place.

(5) The risk owner i.e. the name of a manger or director who watches out for this risk arising.

(6) Whether assurance is sufficient. This might be given a score out of, say, 10, or a yes/no type response.

(7) Controls to be implemented in the future.

Test your understanding 9 – Restaurant (Integration)

Suggest a risk that could be included in each quadrant for a restaurant.

Test your understanding 10

The loss of lower-level staff would best fit which category of a risk map?

A   Low likelihood; low consequence

B   High likelihood; low consequence

C   Low likelihood; high consequence

D   High likelihood; high consequence

Test your understanding 11

The axes of a risk map include:

Select ALL that may apply

A   Likelihood

B   Volatility

C   Consequences

D   Certainty

Test your understanding 12

HH Ltd is a private rehabilitation centre which provides services for people recovering from debilitating injuries. These services include a supported re-introduction to living at home through independent living units where clients can 'practice' living alone but with medical support on hand should they need it.

The managers of HH are aware they operate in a high risk industry. Clients are often prescribed strong medications which must be administered correctly by HH staff and there are two ongoing legal disputes over injuries that have occurred to clients in HH's independent living units. Some of HH's managers believe these risks are simply part of their business model and unavoidable, whereas others are of the opinion that a formal risk management policy should be devised.

The directors have suggested the managers get together to carry out a risk mapping exercise.

> **Which of the following are benefits from a risk mapping exercise?**
>
> Select ALL that apply.
>
> A   Managers will reach a consensus on which are the key risks facing HH and will be able to target the most significant.
>
> B   Managers can use the existence of the risk map to prove they have not been negligent in the legal disputes concerning injured clients.
>
> C   The risk of medication being wrongly administered can be assessed and a policy devised to reduce it going forward.
>
> D   The risk of injury to clients accessing the independent living units can be assessed and prioritised and a policy devised to reduce it going forwards.
>
> E   The existence of a risk map may prevent managers wasting time dealing with trivial risks.

4   Risk response strategy

So far we have considered the types of risk a company could be exposed to and the way it may choose to assess, measure and bear those risks. The next area is to look at the formulation of a strategy to respond to those risks, the general methods that can be used to treat risks and the implementation of such a strategy.

The management of risks involves trying to ensure that:

* Exposure to severe risks is minimised.

* Unnecessary risks are avoided.

* Appropriate measures of control are taken.

* The balance between risk and return is appropriate.

The estimate of the potential loss for each risk should be compared with the acceptable risk limit for the company. If the risk is greater than the acceptable limit, the next stage is to consider how the risk should be managed or controlled, to bring it down in size.

 Risk treatment (management) methods

Assuming that the business does want to manage its risks a number of methods can be used. These methods will limit the risks, and the overall risk management strategy may define how the risks will be managed and the way these methods will interact.

Avoid risk

- A company may decide that some activities are so risky that they should be avoided.

- This will always work but is impossible to apply to all risks in commercial organisations as risks have to be taken to make profits.

Transfer risk

- In some circumstances, risk can be transferred wholly or in part to a third party.

- A common example of this is insurance. It does reduce/eliminate risks but premiums have to be paid.

Pool risks

- Risks from many different transactions can be pooled together: each individual transaction/item has its potential upside and its downside. The risks tend to cancel each other out, and are lower for the pool as a whole than for each item individually.

- For example, it is common in large group structures for financial risk to be managed centrally.

Diversification

- Diversification is a similar concept to pooling but usually relates to different industries or countries.

- The idea is that the risk in one area can be reduced by investing in another area where the risks are different or ideally opposite.

- A correlation coefficient with a value close to –1 is essential if risk is to be nullified.

 Managing risk by diversification

The syllabus refers specifically to the principle of diversifying risk, but states that numerical questions will not be set. It will therefore be useful to look in more detail at the effect of diversification on risk.

- Risk can be reduced by diversifying into operations in different areas, such as into Industry X and Industry Y, or into Country P and Country Q.

- Poor performance in one area will be offset by good performance in another area, so diversification will reduce total risk.

- Diversification is based on the idea of 'spreading the risk'; the total risk should be reduced as the portfolio of diversified businesses gets larger.

- Diversification works best where returns from different businesses are negatively correlated (i.e. move in different ways). It will, however, still work as long as the correlation is less than +1.0.

- Example of poor diversification – swimming costumes and ice cream – both reliant on sunny weather for sales.

- Spreading risk relates to portfolio management, as an investor or company spreads product and market risks.

- The most common form of diversification attempts to spread risk according to the **portfolio** of companies held within a group – based on links within the supply chain

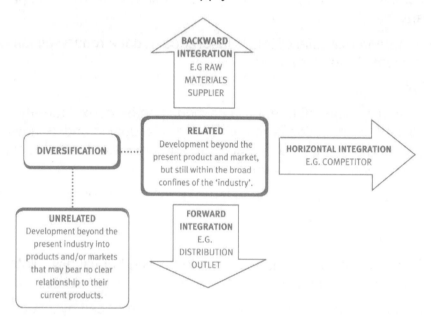

Spreading risk by portfolio management

Within an organisation, risk can be spread by expanding the portfolio of companies held. The portfolio can be expanded by integration – linking with other companies in the supply chain, or diversification into other areas.

This is development beyond the present product and market, but still within the broad confines of the 'industry'.

- **Backward integration** refers to development concerned with the inputs into the organisation, e.g. raw materials, machinery and labour.

- **Forward integration** refers to development into activities that are concerned with the organisation's outputs such as distribution, transport, servicing and repairs.

- **Horizontal integration** refers to development into activities that compete with, or directly complement, an organisation's present activities. An example of this is a travel agent selling other related products such as travel insurance and currency exchange services.

Unrelated diversification

This is development beyond the present industry into products and/or markets that may bear no clear relationship to their present portfolio. Where appropriate an organisation may want to enter into a completely different market to spread its risk.

Problems with diversification:

- If diversification reduces risk, why are there relatively few conglomerate industrial and commercial groups with a broad spread of business in their portfolio?

- Many businesses compete by specialising, and they compete successfully in those areas where they excel.

- Therefore, it is difficult for companies to excel in a wide range of diversified businesses. There is a possible risk that by diversifying too much, an organisation might become much more difficult to manage. Risks could therefore increase with diversification, due to loss of efficiency and problems of management.

- Many organisations diversify their operations, both in order to grow and to reduce risks, but they do so into related areas, such as similar industries (e.g. banking and insurance, film and television production, and so on) or the same industry but in different parts of the world.

- Relatively little advantage accrues to the shareholders from diversification. There is nothing to prevent investors from diversifying for themselves by holding a portfolio of stocks and shares from different industries and in different parts of the world.

Test your understanding 13

Risk reduction can be achieved using which of the following theories?

A   Management theory

B   Systems theory

C   Portfolio theory

D   Contingency theory

Test your understanding 14 – Diversification (Integration)

Evaluate whether it is always a good business strategy for a listed company to diversify to reduce risk

Risk reduction

- Even if a company cannot totally eliminate its risks, it may reduce them to a more acceptable level by a form of internal control.

- The internal control would reduce either the likelihood of an adverse outcome occurring or the size of a potential loss.

- The costs of the control measures should justify the benefits from the reduced risk.

- More will be seen on internal controls in chapter 6.

Hedging risks

- Hedging is considered in detail in F3.

- The concept of hedging is reducing risks by entering into transactions with opposite risk profiles to deliberately reduce the overall risks in a business operation or transaction.

Risk sharing

- A company could reduce risk in a new business operation by sharing the risk with another party.

- This can be a motivation for entering into a joint venture.

 Risk management using TARA

An alternative way of remembering risk management methods is via the mnemonic '**TARA**':

Transference. In some circumstances, risk can be transferred wholly or in part to a third party, so that if an adverse event occurs, the third party suffers all or most of the loss. A common example of risk transfer is insurance. Businesses arrange a wide range of insurance policies for protection against possible losses. This strategy is also sometimes referred to as **sharing.**

Avoidance. An organisation might choose to avoid a risk altogether. However, since risks are unavoidable in business ventures, they can be avoided only by not investing (or withdrawing from the business area completely). The same applies to not-for-profit organisations: risk is unavoidable in the activities they undertake.

Reduction/mitigation. A third strategy is to reduce the risk, either by limiting exposure in a particular area or attempting to decrease the adverse effects should that risk actually crystallise.

Acceptance. The final strategy is to simply accept that the risk may occur and decide to deal with the consequences in that particularly situation. The strategy is appropriate normally where the adverse effect is minimal. For example, there is nearly always a risk of rain; unless the business activity cannot take place when it rains then the risk of rain occurring is not normally insured against.

Risk mapping and risk responses

Risk maps can provide a useful framework to determine an appropriate risk response:

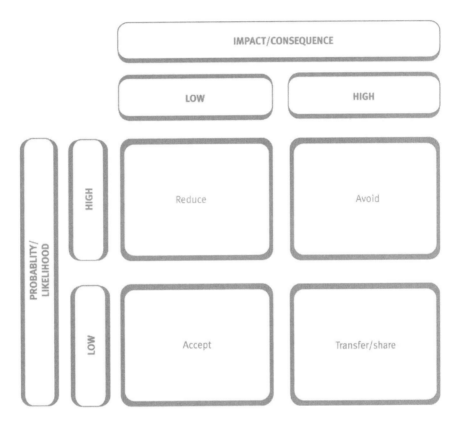

Test your understanding 15

The death of, or serious injury to, a member of staff at work would best fit which category on a risk map?

A   Low likelihood; low consequence

B   High likelihood; low consequence

C   Low likelihood; high consequence

D   High likelihood; high consequence

Test your understanding 16

A risk identified as having a low frequency and a high severity should be managed by:

A   Avoiding

B   Accepting

C   Transferring

D   Reducing

Test your understanding 17

P Company is a large international fast food retailer with plans to expand on a global scale. JZ is a manager who has relocated to Country X to begin an aggressive standardised expansion plan.

Five restaurants have opened so far in the cities of Country X but the response from the local population has been poor. Initial sales targets have not been met and the Board of P Company believes that further expansion into Country P is at risk and it is possible the plan will be abandoned.

JZ believes that the restaurants have not been immediately successful because the population of Country X, although affluent and well educated, are not used to the concept of 'fast food'. Restaurants in Country X are typically expensive and serve fresh food to order.

Which of the following are appropriate risk management responses for JZ to discuss with The Board?

Select ALL that apply.

A   P Company should embark on a marketing campaign within Country X.

B   The menus of restaurants in Country X should be modified to reflect local tastes with more fresh food included.

C   P Company should stop expansion plans in Country P and choose a more appropriate location.

D   P Company should replace JZ as the manager of expansion in Country X.

E   P Company should abandon their standardised plan in Country X and instead tailor their branding and products to be in line with successful local restaurants.

5 The risk cube

Another way of considering risk and its management is to use the risk cube.

Risk equals the volume of the cube

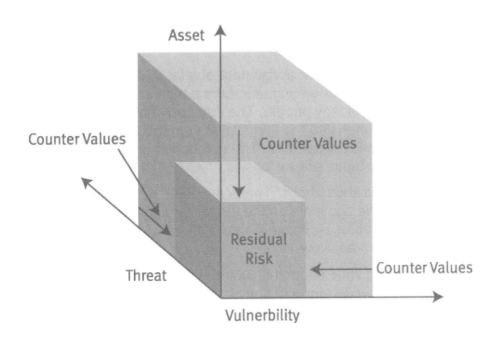

Risk is seen as some combination of a **threat**, exploiting some **vulnerability**, that could cause harm to an **asset**.

Residual risk is the combined function of:

- a threat less the effect of threat-reducing safeguards;
- a vulnerability less the effect of vulnerability-reducing safeguards; and
- an asset less the effect of asset value-reducing safeguards.

Managing the risk can be undertaken by reducing the threat, reducing the vulnerability and/or reducing the asset value.

For example, imagine a company sells machine parts on credit to industrial customers.

The threat might be that the customer doesn't pay for their machine parts.

The vulnerability might be that the selling company has a low cash balance and therefore needs the funds to pay its own suppliers.

The asset is the receivable due.

The threat-reducing safeguards might include performing a credit check on all customers.

The vulnerability-reducing safeguards might include holding a minimum cash balance at all times to ensure sufficient cash is available to pay suppliers.

The asset-reducing safeguards might include setting a limit on each receivable balance, so that once it is reached no further goods would be supplied to a customer until payment was made.

Test your understanding 18 – Twinkletoes (Case study)

Scenario

You are the management accountant of a large private company, Twinkletoes. Twinkletoes manufactures a high volume of reasonably priced shoes for elderly people. The company has a trade receivables ledger that is material to the financial statements containing four different categories of account. The categories of account, and the risks associated with them, are as follows:

(i)   small retail shoe shops. These accounts represent nearly two thirds of the accounts on the ledger by number, and one third of the receivables by value. Some of these customers pay promptly, others are very slow;

(ii)   large retail shoe shops (including a number of overseas accounts) that sell a wide range of shoes. Some of these accounts are large and overdue;

(iii) chains of discount shoe shops that buy their inventory centrally. These accounts are mostly well-established 'high street' chains. Again, some of these accounts are large and overdue; and

(iv)   mail order companies who sell the company's shoes. There have been a number of large new accounts in this category, although there is no history of irrecoverable debts in this category.

Receivables listed under (ii) to (iv) are roughly evenly split by both value and number. All receivables are dealt with by the same managers and staff and the same internal controls are applied to each category of receivables. You do not consider that using the same managers and staff, and the same controls, is necessarily the best method of managing the receivables ledger.

Trigger

Twinkletoes has suffered an increasing level of irrecoverable debts and slow payers in recent years, mostly as a result of small shoe shops becoming insolvent. The company has also lost several overseas accounts because of a requirement for them to pay in advance. Management wishes to expand the overseas market and has decided that overseas customers will in future be allowed credit terms.

Task

Management has asked you to classify the risks associated with the receivables ledger in order to manage trade receivables as a whole more efficiently. You have been asked to classify accounts as high, medium or low risk.

Write an email to the finance director:

(a) Classifying the risks relating to the four categories of trade receivables as high, medium or low and explain your classification (**Note**: More than one risk classification may be appropriate within each account category.)

(b) Describing the internal controls that you would recommend to Twinkletoes to manage the risks associated with the receivables ledger under the headings: all customers, slow paying customers, larger accounts, and overseas customers.

(30 minutes)

6 ISO 31000

ISO 31000 is a group of standards designed to provide guidance on risk management. It comes from the International Organisation for Standardisation.

International Organisation for Standardisation

The International Organisation for Standardisation is an independent non-government group. It develops voluntary international standards which help facilitate international trade by providing confidence that an overseas organisation is working to an appropriate level.

The standards are related to a wide range of areas from quality, safety, reliability to cyber security (more later) and risk management.

As this chapter has highlighted there are many different ways an organisation can choose to manage risk, from accepting that the risk exists to reducing or avoiding it altogether.

The standard is designed to be open, it is not developed for any particular industry, subject matter field or any organisation with a particular management system in place. It provides best practice structure and guidance for any organisation concerned with risk management.

It follows a lot of the processes outlined in this chapter:

- Risk assessment (including identification and evaluation)
- Risk treatment
- Monitoring and review
- Recording and reporting

In the risk treatment the standard suggests seven ways an organisation mays choose to deal with risk:

- Avoiding the risk

- Accepting the risk

- Removing the risk source

- Changing the probability

- Changing the outcome

- Sharing the risk

- Retaining the risk

 ISO 31000: options for risk treatment

In choosing the right risk treatment an organisation must review the potential upside from taking a course of action against costs and effort involved and the potential downside of implementation. The options are not necessarily mutually exclusive and may not be appropriate in all situations.

The suggestions follow the TARA approach, but with slightly more detail.

Transfer

- Sharing the risk (for example through contracts, buying insurance);

Avoid

- Avoiding the risk by deciding not to start or continue with the activity that gives rise to the risk.

Reduce

- Changing the probability

- Changing the outcome

- Removing the risk source – this is probably what all organisations would like to do, but in reality it is very difficult to achieve and rather than a removal of the risk source, a reduction in the impact or likelihood of the risk source is more likely.

Accept

- Accepting or increasing the risk in order to pursue an opportunity

- Retaining the risk by informed decision

ISO 31000 versus COSO ERM

This chapter covers both ISO31000 and COSO ERM as standards and frameworks to help guide risk management. Some risk management practitioners have strong views as to which of these is the best one to follow.

Ultimately both approaches are helpful to an organisation, they give guidance and structure on a key area.

There isn't a definitive right or wrong way to deal with risks and most organisations would benefit from using either or both of the approaches to help manage their risk.

7   Risk reporting

Risk reports now form part of UK annual reports. It is an important disclosure requirement. (Examples of these are available on larger companies' websites. Candidates are encouraged to read some.)

Managers of a business, and external stakeholders, will require information regarding the risks facing the business. A risk reporting system would include:

- A systematic review of the risk forecast (at least annually).

- A review of the risk strategy and responses to significant risks.

- A monitoring and feedback loop on action taken and assessments of significant risks.

- A system indicating material change to business circumstances, to provide an 'early warning'.

- The incorporation of audit work as part of the monitoring an information gathering process.

Marks and Spencer plc – Risk report extract

Marks and Spencer are a UK retail company, within Marks and Spencer's annual report for 2020 there is a risk management section. This has been duplicated in part below.

It states their approach to risk management and key areas of focus:

Risk management

Effective risk management is an essential tool for our business to support the delivery of our transformation and to respond effectively to the challenges facing our company, the retail sector and the communities we serve.

Approach to risk management

Our approach to risk management is simple and practical. The Audit Committee, under delegated authority from the Board, is accountable for overseeing the effectiveness of our risk management process, including identification of the principal and emerging risks facing M&S. The Group Risk Policy was formally reviewed and revised during the year to ensure it remains fully aligned with business needs and our corporate governance responsibilities. An overview of the key features of the Policy and the principal risks and uncertainties are set out on the following pages.

The risk management process mirrors the M&S operating model with each business and functional area being responsible for the ongoing identification, assessment and management of their existing and emerging risks. The output of these assessments are ultimately aggregated to compile an overall Group-level view of risk. This process includes:

- Risks being consistently identified, measured and reported against set criteria which considers both the likelihood of occurrence and potential impact to the Group.

- Each business and functional area maintaining detailed risk registers and mitigation plans which are approved by their respective leadership teams and discussed with the executive directors.

- Direct reporting of risk and mitigating activities by each of our business and functional leadership teams to the Audit Committee on an annual basis.

- A formal half-yearly review of all risk registers by the Group Risk team.

- Development of an overarching summary of risks, combining both top-down and bottom-up perspectives, to provide a consolidated view of Group-level risks.

- A full review of the principal risks and uncertainties at least twice a year by the Audit Committee.

- Swift action to reassess risk across the business in response to significant changes or events, such as the Covid-19 pandemic.

The overall assessment considers the impact of changes in the external environment, our strategy and transformation programme, core operations and our engagement with external parties. It also includes proactive consideration of emerging risks where the full extent and implications may not be fully understood but need to be tracked.

The output from the above process is subject to periodic review and challenge with the executive directors. Subsequently, the principal risks are submitted to the Audit Committee ahead of final review and approval by the Board.

The directors' assessment of the long-term viability of M&S is also reviewed annually, mindful of the principal risks faced. The approach for assessing long-term viability can be found later in the report.

Principal risks and uncertainties

During the course of the year, the business has continued to develop and adhere to our risk management disciplines and managed risks in line with good practice, including adoption of the requirement to formally consider potential emerging risks.

Our established processes had operated to allow consideration of the principal risks and uncertainties to be completed in accordance with the methodology outlined on the previous page, and in line with our year-end timetable prior to the outbreak of Covid-19 in the UK. The impact of the pandemic on the UK has, however, triggered the need to consider both the specific consequences of the virus and its impact on the underlying principal risks being managed by the business.

The disclosure below has therefore been structured to provide an overview of the actions taken in response to the virus, the most significant risks associated with the pandemic and details of how it has impacted the broader set of principal risks and uncertainties.

Covid-19

The impact of Covid-19 on the business is explained in various parts of the Strategic Report. Consequently, the narrative included in the business updates should be read in conjunction with the disclosure below to provide an understanding of the risks and, in some instances, opportunities, facing M&S.

Our response

From the initial reports of the outbreak in China, the crisis management and business continuity protocols for the business were effectively invoked and have, since January, provided a framework to support our response. The following key actions have been undertaken to manage the impact of the pandemic on our business:

(Three of the many key actions are detailed below.)

- Reacted immediately to government guidance by closing clothing outlets, Clothing & Home store sections, cafés and M&S Bank services.

- Introduced distancing and hygiene measures in stores and depots to keep customers and colleagues safe

- At a leadership level, streamlined structures were implemented to accelerate decision-making by a group of the executive and managing directors of our family of businesses

Changes to our risk profile

The table below summarises the key potential risk implications of the pandemic and how these link to the core principal risks that remain in place.

(Three of the many key potential risk implications are detailed below.)

Risk category	Risk description	Relevant principal risk
Protecting customers and colleagues	An inability to maintain and, where needed, adapt operational protocols to safeguard customers, colleagues and other partners involved in running our business during extended lockdown or a period of transitional social distancing would impact the continued operation of stores and breach our responsibilities to all key stakeholders.	Legal and regulatory compliance
Clothing & Home inventory management	A failure to effectively manage the implications of the lockdown period on all aspects of the Clothing & Home supply chain and inventory management would adversely impact customer experience, trading performance, liquidity, operational efficiency and third-party relationships for an extended period.	Trading performance (clothing & Home)
Liquidity	Significantly reduced trading over an extended and currently undetermined timeframe, combined with an inability to effectively manage expenditure against revised targets, would impact the business's ability to operate within committed credit facilities.	Liquidity and funding

In addition to the risks noted above, many of the principal risks prior to the pandemic remain the same in substance but have been amplified by the current events – for example, our ability to effectively respond to Brexit, the transformational improvements needed to the supply chain, maintaining controls over food safety, the potential risk of disruption to critical third-party relationships or readiness to execute the launch of M&S products with Ocado Retail. Where this is the case, the effect has been noted in the relevant section below.

Emerging risks

It is also important to note that, in many respects, the impact of Covid-19 has the characteristics of an emerging risk as well as changing the principal risk profile today, as future events, and their impact on our business and the global community we work within, cannot be determined with any certainty. We will therefore continue to monitor and respond to further changes as needed in the months ahead. As a consequence, the nature and magnitude of the ongoing events will continue to change the risk profile in currently unknown way.

(Two of the many principle risks and mitigating actions are detailed below.)

Trading performance recovery

A failure of our Food and/or Clothing & Home business to effectively and rapidly respond to the pressures of an increasingly competitive and changing retail environment, including the impact of Covid-19, would adversely impact customer experience, operational efficiency and business performance.

M&S competes with a diverse range of retailers – in both Food and Clothing & Home – in an increasingly challenged sector faced with continued cost and pricing pressures, shifts in consumer behaviours and broader macroeconomic uncertainties. Delivering the right product ranges that appeal to our customers, clear and simple pricing architecture and availability are critical to the growth of our business.

In addition, Covid-19 has had, and continues to have, a significant negative impact on our trading performance in line with UK retail more widely. Managing the growth in surplus stock resulting from the lockdown is an area of business focus.

Delays in implementing the targeted transformational improvements, or the business recovery plans in response to Covid-19, across the business could negatively impact business performance.

Mitigating activities

- Continued to strengthen capabilities of our senior leadership teams in both Food and Clothing & Home through targeted recruitment.

- Established operating model consisting of a family of accountable businesses who share M&S brand values, colleagues and support functions, technology and customer data.

- Managing directors for each of these businesses who have full accountability for their performance including for marketing, supply chain, finance and technology.

- Individual Business Boards to enable executive oversight and effective governance of each business.

- Continued delivery against business-specific transformation plans incorporating discipline around cost, prices, availability, value, ranges, broadening customer appeal and promotions across both businesses.

- Development, ongoing update and monitoring of business specific planning for the business restore as future stages of the lockdown are communicated. This includes development of a clear strategy to manage the wide-ranging implications of the lockdown period on all aspects of the Clothing & Home supply chain and inventory management.

- Planned improvements to online trading by delivering both the Ocado online launch in Food and our online ambitions for Clothing & Home.

Information security

Failure to adequately prevent or respond to a data breach or cyber-attack could adversely impact our reputation, result in significant fines, business disruption, loss of stakeholder confidence, and/or loss of information for our customers, employees or business.

The increasing sophistication and frequency of cyber-attacks in the retail industry, coupled with the Data Protection Act (DPA), highlight the escalating information security risk facing all businesses. Our reliance on a number of third parties hosting critical services and holding M&S and customer data also means the information security risk profile is changeable.

This risk also increases as we develop our digital capabilities. For example our dependency on the availability of, and access to, insightful data across our business and/or with the increasing shift online.

In addition, the risk of a data breach or misuse is impacted by Covid-19 as there is the potential for:

- An increase in targeted phishing campaigns.

- New risks linked to working from home and the usage of personal devices.

- Increased reliance on third parties supporting critical support services.

Mitigating activities

- Dedicated Information Security function, comprising a multi-disciplinary operation of information security specialists and support services and capabilities, with a 24/7 Security Operation Centre.

- Continued focus on improving controls, policies, and procedures in line with our environment and threat landscape, including heightened areas of risk due to Covid-19.

- Maintained focus on scanning our threat environment.

- Established third-party assurance programme.

- Focused security assurance, overall operational rigor and security hygiene around significant change activities.

- Network of Data Protection Compliance Managers in priority business areas to oversee and address compliance.

- Mandatory information security and data protection training for colleagues, including responsibilities for the use of personal data.

- Corporate Security team with a focus on improving the physical security environment.

(The risk report continues for several pages covering many other risks.)

Test your understanding 19

A recent SWOT analysis carried out within Y Company showed that the organisation is now subject to more diverse threats than previously documented. This is mainly due to deregulation of Y Company's industry and consequently many new entrants. These new entrants, often from other countries, are able to undercut Y Company on price and so gain market share.

The directors believe they have appropriate measures in place to identify and manage the new risks that Y Company faces but are concerned that Y Company's stakeholders should be able to access information relating to company's most up to date risks. Y Company's risk profile has evolved since the prior year.

The company wishes to convey, via an annual risk report, that risk remains a key consideration in all strategic decision making.

Which of the following should be included in Company Y's risk reporting system?

Select ALL that apply.

A   A detailed review of Y Company's risk strategy and responses to risks it faces.

B   A monitoring and feedback loop on action taken and assessments of significant risks such as those resulting from new entrants.

C   A system indicating material change to Y Company's industry circumstances, to provide an 'early warning'.

D   The incorporation of audit work as part of the monitoring and information gathering process.

E   A systematic review of the risk forecast (at least quarterly).

8 Gross and net risk

Risk reports should show:

* the **gross risk** = an assessment of risk **before** the application of any controls, transfer or management responses, and

* the **net risk** (or **residual risk**) = an assessment of risk, taking into account the controls, transfer and management responses i.e **after** any controls have been implemented to facilitate a review of the effectiveness of risk responses.

An example of gross and net risk assessments, utilising the risk map (impact/likelihood matrix) is shown below:

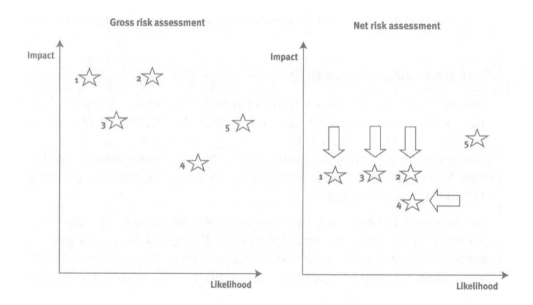

If the residual risk is considered to be too great then the company will need to:

- not expose itself to the risk situation; or
- put in place better controls over the risk.

The amount of residual risk a company can bear is ultimately a management decision.

- It is possible to measure that residual risk, possibly as a proportion of profit/capital/turnover, in order to help management make that judgement.

Ability to bear risk

One approach to assessing the ability to bear a risk is to consider its financial consequences in relation to:

- the organisation's profits
- return on capital employed
- the organisation's expenditure budget (not-for-profit organisations).

For example, suppose that the financial consequences of a particular risk have been estimated as a potential loss of $200,000. For an organisation making annual profits of, say, $200 million, this might seem relatively insignificant. On the other hand, for an organisation with annual profits of just $250,000, say, the risk would be much more significant.

An organisation might establish policy guidelines as to the maximum acceptable residual risk for any individual risk, or set risk limits to the maximum acceptable loss on particular operations.

Gross and net risk example

Using the earlier example of the risk register we can show gross and net (or residual risk):

(1) Loss of personal data i.e. unsecure use of mobile devices could result in personal identifiable information being lost, stolen or unauthorised access gained.

(2) Likelihood = 3

(3) Impact = 5

(4) Risk owner = Mike Smith (IT manager)

(5) 1.1.X2

(6) 2.2.X4

(7) Staff receive training every 2 years which highlights the risks. All laptops are encrypted. Regular audits are undertaken. Any incidents are reported to the Audit Committee.

(8) Overall risk rating = 7 **(Gross risk)**

(9) Encryption technology is implemented which meets industry standard.

(10) Mike Smith

(11) 31.7.X4

(12) Risk level = 3 **(Net or residual risk)**

By implementing the encryption technology the risk has reduced from a score of 7 to a score of 3. This means that there is still some risk but far less than there was. Management will have to consider whether a level 3 risk is acceptable or whether further controls need to be implemented to achieve a lower score, and at what cost.

Test your understanding 20

TGDW are assessing a new contract to provide maintenance services for a prestigious office complex. Should the complex be unable to function for more than 5 hours due an error or omission by TGDW, they will face a fine of sufficient magnitude to cause the company severe financial difficulty. The directors assessed the gross risk as high impact and due to the complexity of the systems maintained there is high probability of an error occurring. The client is unwilling to reduce the penalty or to change the criteria and TGDW's internal controls are already at a high level.

Using TARA what action should TGDW take?

A   Transfer

B   Avoid

C   Reduce

D   Accept

9   Evaluating risk management strategy

Once the company has established its risk strategy and decided in what areas it will reduce its risks and the methods it will use to achieve the desired reductions, the strategy should be evaluated.

The purpose of the evaluation is two-fold, as shown below:

Has the strategy been successful?

Within the risk management strategy, targets should be included to enable the company to assess whether the risk strategy objectives have been achieved. For example, a company might set a target for risk of faulty products at a set number or percentage level and then formulate a risk strategy to achieve that level. In order to assess this, a control mechanism will need to be set up. The basic control idea is that the company compares the actual results with a required target and assesses whether the target has been achieved. If not, the reasons must be investigated and action taken, including possibly a re-assessment of the risk strategy

Do benefits outweigh costs?

- The costs and benefits of risk measures such as internal controls can be evaluated, and a cost-benefit comparison carried out.

- The benefits from risk controls should preferably be measured and quantified, although some benefits (such as protecting the company's reputation) might have to be assessed qualitatively.

- The evaluation process should be based on the principle that the costs of a control measure should not exceed the benefits that it provides.

  - For example, a company could be very concerned about theft of petty cash and therefore introduce controls limiting the cash held to £25 and also requiring daily reconciliations of the cash balance by the financial controller, with observation by a member of the internal audit department.

  - This control would probably reduce theft, but would be very expensive for the company to operate and as a result the costs would exceed the benefits. The controls set up must be proportionate to the potential losses that could occur if the risk results in losses

Cost-benefit example

A manufacturing company is concerned about the rate of rejected items from a particular process. The current rejection rate is 5% of items input, and it has been estimated that each rejected item results in a loss to the company of $10.Each day 600 items go through the process.

It is estimated that by introducing inspections to the process, the rejection rate could be reduced fairly quickly to 3%. However, inspections would result in an increase of costs of $70 per day.

Required:

How should this control through inspection be evaluated?

Solution

The example is a simple one, but it is useful for suggesting an approach to risk management and control evaluation.

What is the objective of the control?

Answer: To reduce losses from rejected items from the process, initially from 5% to 3% of input.

What is the expected benefit?

Answer: A reduction in rejects by 2% of input, from 5% to 3%. The reduction in rejects each day is (2% × 600) 12. Since each reject costs $10, the total daily saving is $120.

What is the expected cost of the control?

Answer: $70 per day. Therefore the control appears to be worthwhile in achieving the objective.

Is the control effective?

Answer: This should be established by monitoring actual results. For example, if the control costs $70 each day, but succeeds in reducing the rejection rate from 5% to just 4% (a reduction of 1%), the benefits would be only $60 each day and the control would not be cost-effective (unless the savings are more than $10 per unit).

Interaction between risks

Risk identification is very important, because risks are often interrelated. This means that if one risk is more likely or will have a more significant impact for an organisation, then it may be more likely to be exposed to other risks or more susceptible to other risks.

This is a theme throughout P3, but it is highlighted to here to make sure that it is something that is in your thought processes as you go through the rest of the material.

Here are some examples:

Compliance risk ⟶ Reputation risk

Environmental risk ⟶ Reputation risk

Fraud risk ⟶ Reputation risk

Compliance risk ⟶ Litigation risk

Interaction between risks

A café in a busy seaside resort would have compliance risk, it will be assessed on its food hygiene and if it did not meet the standards that have been set it may receive fines and it would be published on government websites and also on review websites that the food hygiene is poor.

This leads to other risks:

- Financial risk in that it will have to pay any fines it receives by a particular date.

- Reputation risk because customers are likely to check these things and avoid cafés that do not perform well on this criteria and also warn friends, family and colleagues.

- Litigation risk because someone may become ill after eating at the café due to the poor food hygiene and may take legal action against the café.

Test your understanding 21

WZL Plc a waste disposal company, have been found to have knowingly breached environmental legislation about the disposal of hazardous waste. This is an example of a compliance risk and they stand to receive a substantial fine as a result. The issue occurred because an employee, despite training and internal policies, ignored the information that the customer provided about the waste and how hazardous it was.

Which of the following risks are likely to increase as a result of this breach?

Select ALL that apply

A   Financial risk

B   Reputational risk

C   Commodity price risk

D   Economic risk

E   Currency risk

F   Fraud risk

Another consideration in the interaction between risks is the combining of risks. Sometimes for the end result to occur, multiple risks have to combine. Some of the techniques in this chapter, such as expected values, can help to quantify that combination.

Risks combining

A company could be considering the risk of somebody breaking into a warehouse to steal some of the inventory. The company has controls in place already, with an alarm system fitted, and security guards patrolling the warehouse.

They have identified the following:

- The risk of an intruder getting past the alarm is 30%

- The risk of an intruder getting past the guards is 25%

This means the overall risk of the intruder getting in is:

$$0.3 \times 0.25 = 0.075 \text{ or } 7.5\%$$

Designing safeguards

An organisation could be considering appropriate safeguards and have estimated the following:

- There is a one in ten chance that a thief could get past CCTV

- a one in ten chance of getting past an alarm system, and

- a one in ten chance of beating the door locks.

The odds of a successful burglary would be $0.1 \times 0.1 \times 0.1 = 0.001$ or one in a thousand.

The key point is than none of the controls are particularly effective by themselves. That is a useful point in designing safeguards because a security device that was 99.999% effective might cost far more than three **independent** safeguards that are each only 90% secure.

The odds have to be independent.

As each control or safeguard is commonly used, a skilled individual who is capable of deceiving the CCTV might also be able to bypass the alarm and the door lock.

In the real world, tiny risks cannot always be accepted. There have been major industrial accidents that occurred because of "almost impossible" combinations of events. Therefore each organisation would need to make the assessment based on their situation.

One of the treatments of risk discussed in this chapter is diversification and the idea of creating a portfolio of products or services to help manage risks. This is another example of how risks interact. In this case we are considering the upside and downside risk that we first discussed in chapter 1.

Planning would need to be carried out by the organisation to achieve this portfolio effect. The planning could involve assessing the market in terms of the choices available to customers but also in terms of the likely behaviour of the customers, as well as the likely costs and return on the investment.

The aim of this planning would be to make sure the products or businesses that are added to the portfolio will have different risks. This mean that the products within the portfolio could offset one another – one product does well while another struggles, for example selling warm clothes and light clothes should mean that the business would have a good chance of making sales regardless of the weather or time of year.

In an ideal world all of the products in the organisation's portfolio would do well, but if demand is affected by different factors then they might tend to even out overall.

10 Risk management roles and responsibilities

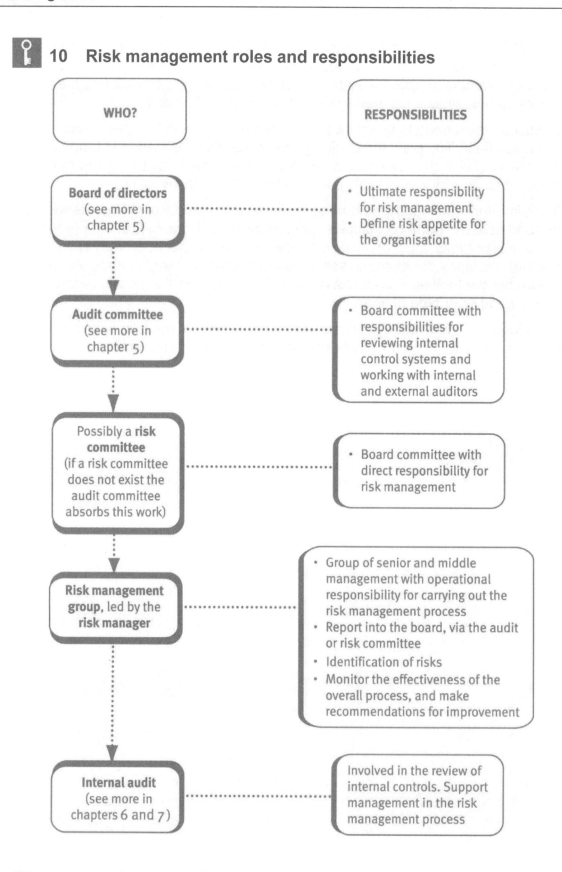

If the company being considered is divisional there may be a **risk officer** for each division who will help to identify and manage tactical and operational level risks.

All **employees** have a role and responsibility for risk too. You should be **aware** of possible risks (through policies issued and training given) and you should be **audible** if you believe a risk needs to be managed (by reporting it to your manager or by whistleblowing).

Roles of the risk committee

In broad terms, the risk (management) committee within an organisation has the following main aims:

- Raising risk awareness and ensuring appropriate risk management within the organisation.

- Establishing policies for risk management.

- Ensuring that adequate and efficient processes are in place to identify, report and monitor risks.

- Updating the company's risk profile, reporting to the board and making recommendations on the risk appetite of the company.

Supporting these objectives of the risk (management) committee, there are many secondary objectives. These objectives may also be contained in the terms of reference of the risk (management) committee.

- Advising the board on the risk profile and appetite of the company and as part of this process overseeing the risk assurance process within the company.

- Acting on behalf of the board, to ensure that appropriate mechanisms are in place with respect to risk identification, risk assessment, risk assurance and overall risk management.

- Continual review of the company's risk management policy including making recommendations for amendment of that policy to the board.

- Ensuring that there is appropriate communication of risks, policies and controls within the company to employees at all management levels.

- Ensuring that there are adequate training arrangements in place so management at all levels are aware of their responsibilities for risk management.

- Where necessary, obtaining appropriate external advice to ensure that risk management processes are up to date and appropriate to the circumstances of the company.

- Ensuring that best practices in risk management are used by the company, including obtaining and implementing external advice where necessary.

Roles of the risk committee

Typical activities carried out by a risk manager include:

- Provision of overall leadership for risk management team.

- Identification and evaluation of the risks affecting an organisation arising from that organisation's business, operations and policies.

- Implementation of risk mitigation strategies including appropriate internal controls to manage identified risks.

- Seeking opportunities to improve risk management methodologies and practices within the organisation.

- Monitoring the status of risk mitigation strategies and internal audits, and ensuring that all recommendations are acted upon.

- Developing, implementing and managing risk management programmes and initiatives including establishment of risk management awareness programmes within the organisation.

- Maintaining good working relationships with the board and the risk management committee.

- Ensuring compliance with any laws and regulations affecting the business.

- Implementing a set of risk indicators and reports, including losses, incidents, key risk exposures and early warning indicators.

- Liaising with insurance companies, particularly with regards to claims, conditions and cover available.

- Depending on specific laws of the jurisdiction in which the organisation is based, working with the external auditors to provide assurance and assistance in their work in appraising risks and controls within the organisation.

- Again, depending on the jurisdiction, producing reports on risk management, including any statutory reports (e.g. Sarbanes-Oxley (SOX) reports in the US).

Northern Rock

A failure of risk management

Perhaps the most interesting example of risk and control was the case of Northern Rock. In September 2007 Northern Rock plc was a top five UK mortgage lender, on the FTSE 100 index with over £100 billion in assets. Northern Rock raised over 70% of the money it used in its growing mortgage lending business from banks and other financial institutions. Following the global credit crunch that resulted from the crisis in the US sub-prime (high risk) mortgage sector, banks stopped lending to each other and Northern Rock could not raise sufficient cash to cover its liabilities.

A bank run (the first on a UK bank for 150 years) on Northern Rock by its customers led to the government providing 'lender of last resort' funding and guarantees for the bank's depositors totalling about £20 billion. The result was a 90% fall in the bank's share price, a deteriorating credit rating and a loss of reputation. The CEO resigned and several directors also left the board.

Northern Rock had a formal approach to risk management, including liquidity, credit, operational and market risk, fully described in its Securities and Exchange Commission filings. Northern Rock's assets were sound so there was no significant credit risk. Market risk was also well managed in terms of interest rate and foreign exchange exposure. However, despite formal procedures and a demonstrated compliance with regulations, there was an assumption by managers that access to funds would continue unimpeded. The US sub-prime crisis led to liquidity risk materialising, causing the Northern Rock problems. The consequence was also the loss of reputation that followed press reports which blamed the bank's management for not having a contingency plan to cover the possibility of disruption to its funding – an operational risk. It is likely that the board of Northern Rock failed in monitoring both liquidity risk and the effectiveness of the existing controls.

The lesson of Northern Rock is that we need to move beyond the tick-box approach to compliance and that good governance requires a more insightful approach to risk management and internal control.

 An example of how risk could be dealt with in a retail chain

A retail group has 480 stores and sales of £1.5 billion. Risk management is part of the internal audit function. The internal auditor/risk manager has said that the motivation for risk management is to 'establish best practice in corporate governance' but also commented that the business recently had 'problems with its fundamental controls' when 'senior management were looking at refinancing so took their eye off the ball'.

The risk management process commenced with a brainstorming session by the internal audit team. They considered 'risk drivers' to identify what could go wrong and what controls could be put in place to address these risks. The team then held interviews with all managers to determine the effectiveness of these controls using a scale from 1 to 5. The threat of a control gap was identified and recommendations were made. This list looked like a risk register, although the group did not call it that. The internal auditor/risk manager did not see value in a risk register, but rather saw risk management as a high level concern.

The group's Risk Management Committee (RMC) meets every 2 months, comprising all business (executive) directors. The list given by the internal audit team to RMC showed the monetary value of a 'fundamental control breakdown', from which was deducted the monetary value arising from controls implemented, to give a 'residual risk' (i.e. the risk after controls) and this was assigned a probability. These values were admittedly subjective. The RMC considered the risk maps, which showed the percentage probability of a threat arising and the residual monetary risk after taking account of controls. The whole process had been centrally driven, with a concern for 'high level' risks. The big risks identified through this process were: supply chain, suppliers, people management, rebates, cost base, key processes, property management, market share, product offering and pricing, brand management, strategic management, integration and change, systems and business continuity.

The group's most recent development is a Key Control Improvement Plan (KCIP) that provides recommendations to address the risks. It summarises each risk (the example of supply chain failure was given) and the 'mitigating factors' (i.e. controls) and what still needs to be done.

The Audit Committee (AC) of the Board is made up of four non-executive directors, the external auditors, the finance director and the internal auditor/risk manager and is responsible for monitoring progress in relation to the risk maps. The risk maps also drive the audit plan which is agreed by the AC, the business directors and the RMC.

The most significant issues are dealt with, for example, purchase ordering and goods received, new stores, margins. Results are provided to the RMC and AC where the value of the report is greater than £250,000. Internal audit now has more exposure to decision-makers, as the risk management role had given them a high profile.

Going forward, the internal auditor/risk manager wants to implement a Risk Intelligence Report to provide early warning of risks. This will involve looking at key performance indicators to identify what the business should be concerned with. The manager also wants to introduce a Risk Management Marketing Plan to help communicate risk and to pass on the responsibility to other managers – with senior managers making presentations to RMC. The internal auditor/risk manager expects it to take another 2 years to establish risk management in the organisation. More 'bottom up' controls need to be introduced and risk management needs to be embedded at the cultural level.

An example of how risk could be dealt with in an engineering consultancy

This organisation is privately owned with 3,500 employees. A review of its financial performance had revealed that the estimated cost of project over-runs, non-productive time and contractual penalties incurred was about 2% of annual turnover. This represented an opportunity loss of about £3 million per annum against reported profits of about £5 million.

However, the main driver behind risk management was to address the rapidly increasing cost of professional indemnity insurance. Premiums had increased to several million pounds and its excess had increased from £5,000 to £500,000 per annum over the last few years. The organisation had appointed a risk manager, adopted an offshore 'captive' insurer and implemented a management development programme to improve the skills of all its managers. This had included a substantial content on risk awareness.

One of the ways in which it was helping its managers to understand risk was to undertake risk assessments as part of every project bid and to reflect each risk in pricing. During contract negotiations, each risk could be discussed between the lead consultant and the client. The value of the risk could be discussed – in terms of the control devices that could be put in place by the client to reduce the risk and hence reduce that component of the project price that reflected the risk.

It was anticipated that this collaboration between consultant and client would reduce risk and lead to a more profitable outcome for both parties.

Test your understanding 22 – L tinned foods (Case study)

Scenario

L manufactures a range of very high quality tinned foods. The company was established eight years ago and it has grown steadily by selling to independent grocers in prosperous areas. Most consumers associate tinned food with poor quality and are unwilling to pay high prices. However, the consumers who buy L's products are willing to pay a premium for higher quality.

L's only large customer is H, a major supermarket chain that has a reputation for selling high-quality produce. L began sales to H just under a year ago, with H purchasing small quantities of L's most popular product in order to assess demand. After a successful period of test marketing, H started to place larger orders with L. Now H accounts for 20% of L's sales by volume.

Trigger

L has traditionally had a functional organisational structure. There is a director in charge of each of sales, production, finance and human resources. Each director has a team of senior managers who support their function. The hierarchy for organising and supervising staff is generally based on this functional structure. The only exception arose on the appointment of EJ, who is the Account Manager in charge of L's dealings with H. H insisted on the appointment of a designated account manager as a condition of placing regular, large orders with the company. EJ is the designated point of contact on all matters between L and H.

EJ's job description states that she is responsible for all decisions, including pricing, relating to L's relationship with H and that she is expected to base all such decisions on the promotion of L's commercial interests.

There have been a number of complaints from L's managers since EJ's appointment. These include several occasions when staff have received contradictory instructions. For example, EJ has ordered the production department to give priority to H's requests for large deliveries, even though that has led to regular orders to other customers being delayed. EJ has also told the staff in the credit control department not to press H for payment even though the company had several overdue invoices.

L's Sales Director believes that the company could sell even greater quantities to H and that other large supermarket chains will start placing orders in the near future once H has demonstrated that there is a demand for high quality tinned food. She has warned L's Chief Executive that additional account managers will have to be employed in the event that L starts to supply further supermarket chains.

Task

Write a report to the Board of L which:

(a)   Evaluates the potential risks that might arise from L's appointment of an account manager to deal with H's business; and

(b)   Recommends, stating reasons, the changes that L's board should introduce in order to minimise the threats arising from having an autonomous account manager.

(40 minutes)

Test your understanding 23 – Dental practice (Case study)

Scenario

D is a dental practice that was established eight years ago. The practice was founded by six dentists, each of whom has an equal share.

Trigger

The six dentists have decided that they should undertake a formal evaluation of the risks affecting their business. To that end, they have engaged a consultant to act as a facilitator.

The facilitator began with a brainstorming session. The dentists were provided with a flipchart and they were asked to list as many risks as they could think of. Then the risks were transferred to a risk map based on the TARA framework. A simplified version of the risk map is shown below:

		Impact/consequences	
		Low	**High**
Probability/likelihood	**High**	<u>Reduce</u> Negligence claims arising from failed dental implants	<u>Avoid</u> Cross infection
	Low	<u>Accept</u> Spiral staircase	<u>Transfer/share</u> Unknown allergies

All six dentists agreed that each of these risks is worth classifying, but there was considerable debate as to where each should appear on the risk map. The facilitator has used the opinion of the dentist who identified the risk as a starting point and has asked for some discussion as to how best to classify each.

Dental implants

Dental implants are false teeth that are rooted in the patient's jaw using titanium screws. Fitting an implant is a very time-consuming and expensive procedure that costs the patient in excess of GBP 2,000. The patient's bone structure usually accepts the implant and fuses with it to form a very strong bond. In 3-5% of cases the implant causes an adverse reaction and has to be removed. The practice warns patients of this possibility and does not offer any refund in this event because the failure is beyond the dentist's control. Some patients who suffer an adverse reaction do seek compensation despite these warnings, alleging negligence on the part of the dentist.

Cross infection

Cross infection can occur when patients pass infections on to the dental staff (and vice versa) or when dental instruments transmit infections between patients. Apart from the need to work in close proximity to the patient, dental procedures always involve contact with the patient's saliva and can sometimes involve contact with blood if a tooth is extracted or the patient's gums bleed.

Spiral staircase

The dental surgery is located one floor up from street level. Patients enter via a narrow hallway and climb to the reception using a narrow spiral staircase. The building cannot be remodelled to accept a lift or a more suitable staircase.

Unknown allergies

The dentists are often required to prescribe antibiotics and other drugs in order to treat gum infections. These can cause severe allergic reactions that are impossible to foresee unless the patient has been prescribed that drug in the past and has notified the practice of this allergy.

Task

(a) Discuss the benefits that the dental practice may obtain from the risk mapping exercise described above.

(b) Critically evaluate the placing of each of the identified risks in the risk map, stating with reasons whether or not you agree with the placement.

(30 minutes)

Test your understanding 24 – B bank (Case study)

Scenario

The B Bank is a large international bank. It employs 6,000 staff in 250 branches and has approximately 500,000 borrowers and over 1,500,000 savers. The bank, which was founded in 1856, has an excellent reputation for good customer service. The bank's share price has increased, on average, by 12% in each of the last 10 years.

Trigger

There has been much adverse media coverage in many countries, including B Bank's home country, about the alleged excessive bonuses received by the directors of banks. A meeting of central bank governors from many nations failed to reach agreement on how to limit the size of directors' bonuses. The governor of the central bank in B Bank's home country is particularly concerned about this issue, and consequently put forward the following proposal:

"Directors of banks will be asked to pay a fee to the bank for the privilege of being a director. This fee will be set by the remuneration committee of each bank. Directors will be paid a bonus based solely on appropriate profit and growth indicators. The more the bank succeeds, the higher will be the bonus. This proposal directly links performance of the bank to directors' pay. I see this as a more realistic option than simply limiting salaries or bonuses by statute as proposed at the recent central bank governors' conference."

B Bank board and strategy

The constitution of the board of B Bank is in accordance with the internationally agreed code of corporate governance.

Overall board strategy has been to set targets based on previous (profitable) experience, with increased emphasis on those areas where higher potential profits can be made such as mortgage lending (this is discussed below). The bank's executive information systems are able to compute relative product profitability, which supports this strategy. This strategy generated substantial profits in recent years. The last major strategy review took place four years ago. Non-executive directors do not normally query the decisions of the executive directors.

In recent years, the profile of the major shareholders of the bank has moved. Traditionally the major shareholders were pension funds and other longer term investors but now these are overshadowed by hedge funds seeking to improve their short-term financial returns.

One of the major sources of revenue for the bank is interest obtained on lending money against securities such as houses (termed a "mortgage" in many countries) with repayments being due over periods varying between 15 and 25 years. Partly as a result of intense competition in the mortgage market, the values of the mortgages advanced by B Bank regularly exceed the value of the properties. For example, B Bank has made advances of up to 125% of a property's value. Internal reports to the board estimate that property prices will reverse recent trends and will rise by 7% per annum for at least the next 10 years, with general and wage inflation at 2%. B Bank intends to continue to obtain finance to support new mortgages with loans from the short-term money-markets.

Task

Write a report to the Board:

(a) Evaluating the proposal made by the governor of the central bank; and

(b) Evaluating the risk management strategy in B Bank (except for consideration of directors' remuneration). Your evaluation should include recommendations for changes that will lower the bank's exposure to risk.

(45 minutes)

Test your understanding 25 – W consumer (Case study)

Scenario

W is a leading manufacturer of consumer electronics devices. The company has a significant share of the markets for mobile phone and personal music players ("mp3 players").W's main areas of expertise are in design and marketing. The company has a reputation for developing innovative products that set the trend for the market as a whole. New product launches attract a great deal of press interest and consequently W spends very little on advertising. Most of its promotional budget is spent on maintaining contact with leading technology journalists and editors.

<u>Manufacturing and supply</u>

W does not have a significant manufacturing capacity. New products are designed at the company's research laboratory, which has a small factory unit that can manufacture prototypes in sufficient quantity to produce demonstration models for test and publicity purposes. When a product's design has been finalised W pays a number of independent factories to manufacture parts and to assemble products, although W retains control of the manufacturing process.

W purchases parts from a large number of suppliers but some parts are highly specialised and can only be produced by a small number of companies. Other parts are standard components that can be ordered from a large number of sources. W chooses suppliers on the basis of price and reliability.

All assembly work is undertaken by independent companies. Assembly work is not particularly skilled, but it is time consuming and so labour can cost almost as much as parts.

- W has a large procurement department that organises the manufacturing process. A typical cycle for the manufacture of a batch of products is as follows:

- W's procurement department orders the necessary parts from parts suppliers and schedules assembly work in the electronics factories.

- The parts are ordered by W but are delivered to the factories where the assembly will take place.

- The finished goods are delivered directly to the customer.

This is a complicated process because each of W's products has at least 100 components and these can be purchased from several different countries.

Supplier communications

W insists on communicating with its suppliers via electronic data interchange (EDI) for placing orders and also for accounting processes such as invoicing and making payment. This is necessary because of the degree of coordination required for some transactions. For example, W may have to order parts from one supplier that are then delivered to another supplier to carry out some assembly work. Both suppliers have to be given clear and realistic deadlines so that the resulting assemblies are delivered on time to enable W to meet its own deadlines.

Trigger

W recently launched a new range of mp3 players. The launch of the first batches of players attracted a great deal of adverse publicity:

The supplier which produces the unique memory chips used in the mp3 player was unable to meet the delivery deadlines and that delayed the launch. The supplier owns the patent for the design of these memory chips.

Supplies of the memory chip are now available. The assembly factories have been asked to increase their rates of production to shorten the timescale now that the memory chips have become available.

Task

Write a report to W's finance director:

(a) Evaluating THREE operational risks associated with the manufacture of W's products including an explanation of how each of these risks could be managed; and

(b) Evaluating the risks associated with the use of EDI for managing W's ordering and accounting processes.

(45 minutes)

Test your understanding 26 – SPM (Case study)

Scenario

SPM is a manufacturer and distributor of printed stationery products that are sold in a wide variety of retail stores around the country. There are two divisions: Manufacturing and Distribution. A very large inventory is held in the distribution warehouse to cope with orders from retailers who expect delivery within 48 hours of placing an order.

SPM's management accountant for the Manufacturing division charges the Distribution division for all goods transferred at the standard cost of manufacture, which is agreed by each division during the annual budget cycle. The Manufacturing division makes a 10% profit on the cost of production but absorbs all production variances. The goods transferred to Distribution are therefore at a known cost and physically checked by both the Manufacturing and the Distribution division staff at the time of transfer.

Trigger

The customer order process for SPM's Distribution division is as follows:

- SPM's customer service centre receives orders by telephone, post, fax, email and through a new on-line Internet ordering facility (a similar system to that used by Amazon). The customer service centre checks the creditworthiness of customers and bundles up orders several times each day to go to the despatch department.

- All orders received by the despatch department are input to SPM's computer system which checks stock availability and produces an invoice for the goods.

- Internet orders have been credit checked automatically and stock has been reserved as part of the order entry process carried out by the customer. Internet orders automatically result in an invoice being printed without additional input.

- The despatch department uses a copy of the invoice to select goods from the warehouse, which are then assembled in the loading dock for delivery using SPM's own fleet of delivery vehicles.

- When SPM's drivers deliver the goods to the customer, the customer signs for the receipt and the signed copy of the invoice is returned to the despatch office and then to the accounts department.

- SPM's management accountant for the Distribution division produces monthly management reports based on the selling price of the goods less the standard cost of manufacture. The standard cost of manufacture is deducted from the inventory control total which is increased by the value of inventory transferred from the manufacturing division. The control total for inventory is compared with the monthly inventory valuation report and while there are differences, these are mainly the result of write-offs of damaged or obsolete stock, which are recorded on journal entry forms by the despatch department and sent to the accounts department.

Due to the size of inventory held, a physical stocktake is only taken once per annum by Distribution staff, at the end of the financial year. This has always revealed some stock losses, although these have been at an acceptable level. Both internal and external auditors are present during the stocktake and check selected items of stock with the despatch department staff. Due to the range of products held in the warehouse, the auditors rely on the despatch department staff to identify many of the products held.

Task

(a) Evaluate any weaknesses in the risk management approach taken by SPM's Distribution division and how this might affect reported profitability. **(30 minutes)**

(b) Recommend internal control improvements that would reduce the likelihood of risk. **(15 minutes)**

 Test your understanding 27 – ABC (Case study)

Scenario

The operations division of ABC, a listed company, has responsibility to maintain and support the sophisticated computer systems used for call centres and customer database management. These are relied on by the organisation's retail customers as many of their sales are dependent on access to these systems, which are accessed over the Internet.

Although there is no risk management department, ABC has a large number of staff in the operations division devoted to disaster recovery. Contingency plans are in operation and data are backed up regularly and stored off-site. However, pressures for short-term profits and cash flow have meant that there has been a continuing under-investment in capital equipment.

Trigger

A review of disaster recovery found that although data were backed up there was a real risk that a severe catastrophe such as fire or flood would have wiped out computer hardware and although data back-up was off-site, there was no proven hardware facility the company could use. While managers have relied on consequential loss insurance, they appear to have overlooked the need to carry out actions themselves to avoid or mitigate any possible loss.

Task

Write a report to the Board:

(a) Advising on the main business issue for ABC and the most significant risks that ABC faces; **(10 minutes)**

(b) Advising them on their responsibilities for risk management and recommending a risk management system for ABC that would more effectively manage the risks of losing business continuity. **(30 minutes)**

(c) Evaluating the likely benefits for ABC of an effective risk management system for business continuity. **(5 minutes)**

11   The exams

The models and frameworks detailed in this chapter are a starting point for the exam, however, candidates need to be able to use their common sense in order to relate this material to exam questions in both the P3 objective test and the strategic case study exam.

12   Chapter summary

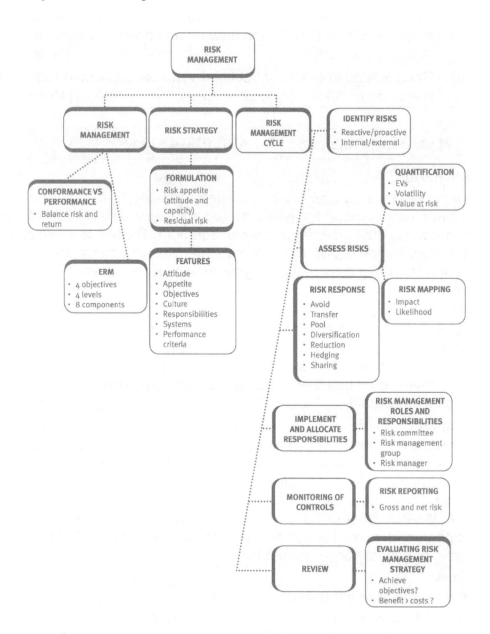

Test your understanding answers

Test your understanding 1

The correct answer is B – By definition.

Test your understanding 2

A, B and E

COSO considers a WIDE range of risks, and is the responsibility of EVERYONE.

Test your understanding 3

D

The management are working on their risk response, which is included in the performance component.

Test your understanding 4

The correct answer is B – A risk map assesses an organisation's risks on the basis of likelihood and consequence.

Risk culture is the set of shared attitudes, values and practices that characterise how an entity considers risk in its day-to-day activities.

Risk thermostat is the notion that everyone has a propensity to take risks. This varies by person and is influenced by potential rewards and any previous 'accidents'.

Test your understanding 5

The correct answers are A, B and C – The total cost of a control is not normally detailed on the risk register.

Test your understanding 6 – Volatility (Integration)

The expected value of purchases is:

	£
£200,000 × 0.3	60,000
£250,000 × 0.5	125,000
£300,000 × 0.2	60,000
	245,000

The volatility therefore is:

Downside (£300,000 – £245,000)	£55,000
Upside (£245,000 – £200,000)	£45,000

The volatility is the possible amount away from the expected value.

Test your understanding 7

The value of $10 million today is £6 million ($10 m/$1.6667) with a standard deviation of £30,000 (0.5% × £6 million).

The one-tail 95% confidence level is 1.645.

Hence a five day 95% VaR is 1.645 × £30,000 × √10 = £156,058

Test your understanding 8 – Value at risk (Integration)

At the 95% confidence level the value at risk = 1.645 × 4.85 = $8 million (1.645 is the normal distribution value for a one-tailed 5% probability level – this can be taken from the normal distribution tables).

As the information is for the 2 week period, and not a daily mean or standard deviation, there is no need to use the n day VaR adjustment.

There is thus a 5% probability that the portfolio value will fall to $42 million or below.

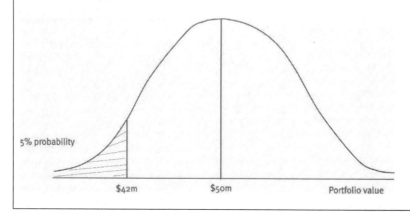

Test your understanding 9 – Restaurant (Integration)

For a restaurant:

		Impact/consequences	
		Low	**High**
	High	A staff member is taken ill and cannot work	Head chef resigns
Probability/likelihood	**Low**	Accept Spiral staircase	Ingredient prices Several customers suffer from food poisoning

Each suggestion could arguably be in a different quadrant, depending on the restaurant. These are just suggestions.

Test your understanding 10

The correct answer is B – Low-level staff frequently change jobs in order to progress. The severity is low as they are unlikely to be well-trained/highly skilled and could be replaced fairly quickly and easily.

Test your understanding 11

The correct answers are A and C – The axes are likelihood/probability and impact/severity/consequences.

Test your understanding 12

C, D and E

- Option A – managers may not agree on the key risks facing HH. The risk map will force them to discuss risks but not to reach a consensus.

- Option B – the legal disputes are ongoing and a new risk map is unlikely to help with historical cases.

- Options C, D and E are benefits.

Test your understanding 13

The correct answer is C – Portfolio theory seeks to diversify the company's activities which can reduce risk (by not putting all your eggs in one basket).

Test your understanding 14 – Diversification (Integration)

Arguments for and against diversification:

For

- Reduces risks and enables company to give more predictable return to investors.

- Attracts investors who want low risk investments.

Against

- Management may not understand all the businesses that the company operates in – increases the risk.

- It is not necessary to diversify for investors – they can diversify themselves by investing in a number of different companies.

- New business areas can attract risks – for instance going into a new country may increase the risk of not understanding a company culture.

Test your understanding 15

The correct answer is C – The likelihood of this event would hopefully be low as several controls preventing this should be in place. Staff would refuse to work otherwise. The consequence of such an event would be high as it would likely lead to an investigation, legal proceedings, compensation and reputational risk.

Test your understanding 16

The correct answer is C – Low frequency/high severity risks are often transferred, by using insurance for example.

Test your understanding 17

A and B only

- Option A: Is appropriate since the population of Country X are not familiar with fast food.

- Option B: Often organisations need to adapt their standardised products because of cultural differences.

- Option C: Significant investment is likely to have already occurred in Country X and simply pulling out before embarking on other risk response plans is unlikely to be appropriate at this point. In addition, the entire strategy of P Company is based around geographical expansion. It will be more difficult in some countries to establish the brand.

- Option D: The poor performance of restaurants in Country P is unlikely to be JZ's fault rather it is due to rolling out standardised products in culturally diverse locations. In fact, since JZ has now built up some experience in Country X, she should be retained to continue expansion.

- Option E: The global brand of P Company is based on uniformity and although small tweaks to this make sense to enable the restaurants to 'fit' with the local culture, the brand needs to be consistent with values applied globally.

Test your understanding 18 – Twinkletoes (Case study)

To: The Finance Director

From: The Management Accountant

Date: Today

Subject: Risk management at Twinkletoes

Dear Finance Director,

Please find attached my classification of risks for receivables and a recommendation for internal controls.

(a) **Classification of risks for receivables**

(i) **Small retail shoe shops**

Despite the fact that individual accounts in this category have small balances, the category as a whole is significant to Twinkletoes because of the total amounts owed (one-third of total receivables), the rising level of irrecoverable debts and the adverse effect of slow payers on cash flow. It is likely that most of these accounts individually are low risk because customers pay promptly and the amounts are small. Accounts that are significantly overdue may be classified as medium risk, but probably only if they are substantial accounts, because all entities must expect to experience a small number of small irrecoverable debts. If, however, a large number of accounts are significantly overdue, they may be classified as high risk.

(ii) **Large retail shoe shops**

Some of these accounts are large and overdue and may therefore be classified as medium or high risk. However, as the total value of such accounts is around 22% of total receivables and the total value of the overdue accounts may be small in relation to total receivables, the classification should probably only be medium risk. The classification for accounts that are not overdue may be low risk

Overseas accounts. Whilst these might at first appear to be at risk because the accounts are being lost, they represent a small proportion of accounts by both number and value (customers currently pay in advance). This means that they may be viewed as low risk.

(iii) **Chains of shoe shops**

As with the large shoe shops, large and overdue accounts might be classified as medium or high risk. However, 'high street' chains of well-established shops are less likely to become insolvent than less well-established entities and therefore represent a lower risk. This means that the classification may be low risk, even for accounts that are large and overdue.

(iv) **Mail order companies**

New accounts generally represent an increased risk of irrecoverable debts and a large number of new accounts increases this risk. However, there is no history of irrecoverable debts in this category at all so the new accounts may therefore be classified as medium risk. Existing accounts within this category may be classified as low risk because there is no history of irrecoverable debts.

(b) **Internal controls**

(i) **All customers**

I would recommend that:

- credit checks be performed when new customers seek credit, and that cash in advance or on delivery is required where large orders are placed by new customers;

- credit limits be set for all customers based on the length of the relationship with the customer, the volume of sales and their payment history;

- payment terms be set (say, 30 days for local customers, 45 days for overseas customers);

- insurance be taken out against the risk of irrecoverable debts.

These controls will help ensure that accounts do not become overdue, damaging the company's cash flow and increasing the risk of irrecoverable debts.

(ii) Slow paying customers

I would recommend that:

- dedicated staff are assigned to chase slow payers regularly for outstanding amounts and to ensure that a `stop' is put on accounts that are significantly overdue;

- legal action is taken against those customers owing large amounts for long periods for which there are no good reasons.

(iii) Larger accounts – large shops, chains of shops and mail order companies

I would recommend that:

- dedicated staff are assigned to manage the relationship with larger customers, particularly the mail order companies.

(iv) **Overseas customers**

I would recommend that:

- overseas customers be allowed a credit period of say, 45 days in order to permit the required bank transfers to take place;

- overseas customers be required to pay in the currency used by Twinkletoes (except perhaps for large orders which may be backed by government guarantees) or in a stable currency which does not fluctuate significantly against the currency used by Twinkletoes.

If you have any queries, please do not hesitate to ask.

Best wishes

Management Accountant

Test your understanding 19

B, C and D

- Option A – responses to significant risks only.

- Option E – such a review should be carried out at least annually.

Test your understanding 20

B – avoid

It would appear that the gross risk cannot be reduced since the client will not renegotiate the level of the penalty. The impact then remains high and as TGDW's internal controls are already at a high level it is unlikely that the likelihood can be reduced.

As the likelihood is high then it is unlikely that TGDW will able to get insurance against this event occurring so transference is not possible.

Acceptance is unthinkable in this case and there appears to be no further scope for reduction.

Therefore unless TGDW are an exceptionally risk seeking organisation they will need to avoid this risk.

Test your understanding 21

A, B and F

- Option A – as they will receive a significant fine, this will increase the financial pressure on the company.

- Option B – as disposal of waste is their core work, companies may be reluctant to use them having breached regulations.

- Option F – the issue occurred through employee malfeasance, and suggests a lack of controls are in place which could mean that fraud is more likely.

- Option C, D and E – There are no commodities or foreign currencies involved and economic risk links to how changes in the economy will affect the business.

Test your understanding 22 – L tinned foods (Case study)

To: The Board of L

From: A.N. Accountant

Date: Today

Subject: Risks and recommendations regarding account managers

Introduction

This report evaluates the potential risks that might arise from L's appointment of an account manager to deal with H's business. It then goes on to recommend the changes that L's board should introduce in order to minimise the threats arising from having an autonomous account manager.

(a) **The risks of appointing an account manager**

L has effectively introduced a matrix management structure with respect to its dealings with H. This has the potential for a number of upside risks. In particular, it means that H's interests will be kept under constant review by a designated manager. Thus, there is less risk that H's business will be lost because of an oversight or a breakdown in communications. If any of the decision makers at H require anything then they know to contact EJ and she will then be responsible for dealing with their request.

There are a number of downside risks arising from this arrangement. The most obvious of these is that there may be a conflict between EJ's role as an account manager and the roles of the other functional managers within L. H is an important customer, but it accounts for only 20% of sales by volume and so it could be argued that the smaller customers are, collectively, far more important than H. Presumably, H is capable of negotiating significant trade discounts and so the additional volume of business is unlikely to be particularly profitable.

EJ's role may be important, but there is a danger that it will lead to dysfunctional behaviour on her part. She will be motivated to retain H's business because that is the whole point of her employment. H will be aware of that and may start to pressure her into granting further discounts, extensions of credit and other concessions.

EJ has already disrupted transactions involving existing customers with whom L has an established relationship. The most immediate threat is that those customers may cease trade with L. It is also possible that such behaviour will lead to conflict between EJ and the functional managers, which will waste time. The functional managers may also become demotivated if their efforts are thwarted by EJ.

Junior staff will also be confused by contradictory instructions. If they are unsure whether to obey EJ or their usual functional managers then they may delay acting in order to seek clarification. Once they start to question instructions from their superiors then the overall control environment may be undermined.

(b) **Recommendations for change to reduce the threat of autonomous account managers**

Firstly, there has to be clear communication between the account manager and the functional managers. It should be made clear that any conflict should be discussed and, if possible, resolved by compromise. If, for example, H wishes to place a large and urgent order then it may be possible to ask the production manager to increase output so that all potential sales can be made without disappointing existing customers. That will reduce the threat of disagreement between the account manager and the functional managers.

It should be made clear that any conflict that cannot be resolved by compromise should be dealt with in a manner that is in L's overall best interests. It should be made clear that any dysfunctional behaviour will be regarded as a disciplinary matter. That will reduce the threat that the account manager will be tempted to act in H's best interests rather than L's.

Subordinate staff should be free to state that any instruction contradicts policy or a previous request. It should then be the functional or account manager's responsibility to seek a compromise so that subordinate staff have an agreed instruction. That will avoid the stress and confusion that will arise for junior staff if they are caught between competing managers.

Ideally, the account manager should have been appointed from within L and it should be made clear that the appointee's continued employment is not conditional on retaining H as a customer. An internal appointee will, hopefully, have a more immediate loyalty to L than to H. The assurance of continuing employment will reduce the extent to which H might pressure the account manager.

There should be a clear policy for resolving conflicts between managers. It may be that the appropriate functional manager should make the final decision, on the basis that the business from H is worth only 20% of the company's sales by volume, and those may be subject to a substantial discount because H is the company's largest customer. That should lead to a consistent response to any conflicts between managers.

Conclusion

There are several risks arising from the appointment of an account manager, however, these risks can be reduced by improving communication, having a clear policy for conflict resolution and implementing disciplinary action if necessary.

Test your understanding 23 – Dental practice (Case study)

(a)   The risk-mapping exercise is not an objective process and so the resulting diagram is not an objective or "correct" representation of the risks faced by the practice. The dentists should not risk relying too heavily on the map itself to determine their overall risk-management strategies.

The main benefit to be had from this exercise is that the dentists will have the opportunity to discuss the risks facing the practice.

This communication will mean that each of the dentists is made aware of the threats that have been identified by each of the others. That should mean that each of them will have a more comprehensive understanding of the risks faced by the practice as a whole.

The discussion will also ensure that there is an opportunity to address colleagues' understanding of identified risks. It may be that some dentists are devoting too much time and effort to managing trivial risks. Conversely, potentially serious risks could be misunderstood and overlooked. The discussion will enable the dentists to reach some agreement as to the most appropriate response to each risk. A consensus opinion is more likely to be balanced and logical than any individual view.

The fact that the risks have been identified and discussed can be recorded for future reference. In the event that the practice is ever accused of negligence then the fact that a risk was discussed and a response put in place may enable the dentists to argue that they acted with reasonable skill and care. That, of course, implies that an appropriate response has been put in place for any identified risks.

Dental implants

It is logical to state that the probability of occurrence is high if this is a relatively common procedure. Presumably the failures are caused by random factors that are out of the dentist's control, such as the patient's overall health or dental hygiene and so the laws of probability will mean that failures will occur from time to time.

It is natural for a patient who has spent a significant amount of money on a procedure to be aggrieved if that procedure fails and so the practice may be accused of malpractice. Patients may discount the risk of failure when agreeing to the implant because the probability seems reasonably remote when looking ahead and making plans.

The impact of a claim will be low because it is a known risk that the patient has agreed to accept. It will be both difficult and expensive for a patient to pursue any formal claim for a refund or a repeat procedure.

Cross infection

It is important to be clear about whether the likelihood is expressed in terms of gross risk or net. Every dental procedure puts the dental staff in close proximity to the patient and will involve contact with body fluids. The gross risks are, therefore, high. The net risks of cross infection can, however, be minimised through good hygiene, such as the dentist and the nurse wearing disposable gloves that are changed between patients and also face masks to reduce the risk of transmitting respiratory infections.

Spiral staircase

The staircase could prevent disabled or infirm patients from obtaining access to the practice. It may be that a potential patient will choose to make this a matter of principle and complain that the practice has not made adequate provision for the disabled. Legally, the practice is not under any obligation to do more than make reasonable provision for access and there is no practical solution that could be offered.

It is unlikely that the impact will be significant. The practice is already well established, so it has already attracted a viable number of patients who can cope with this access problem. Any complaints can be addressed by a polite comment to the effect that the practice is located in a building that cannot accommodate a lift or a conventional staircase.

Given that there is no viable response to this risk, it really has to be accepted in almost any case. Dealing with it would require an extreme and potentially disproportionate response, such as moving to new premises.

Allergies

The probability that a patient will suffer an allergic reaction is low. Pharmaceutical products are tested to ensure that they do not generally cause reactions. Patients will, hopefully, be aware of most allergies that they suffer from and the dental practice can record those in patient files.

The impact of an allergic reaction is probably not high for the practice, despite the fact that it could be a serious matter for the patient. Provided the dentist has prescribed the antibiotic in good faith there is very little risk that the practice will be in trouble for prescribing a relevant drug to treat an infection. The dentist should always check that the patient's medical history is up to date in order to ensure that there is no reason to avoid any particular medication. Provided that has been done, any reaction will be viewed as an unfortunate accident rather than medical negligence.

The impact of causing an infection will be high. This is a preventable problem and so there is a risk that any failure will constitute medical malpractice. In the event that a patient complains to the health authorities or the dentists' professional body there could be a significant penalty. There could also be a serious threat of adverse publicity, with patients choosing to use another dental practice.

Test your understanding 24 – B bank (Case study)

To: The Board of B Bank

From: A.N. Accountant

Date: Today

Subject: Directors bonuses and risk management

Introduction

This report covers an evaluation of the governor's suggestion and an evaluation of B banks risk management strategy.

(a) **Evaluate the proposal made by the governor**

The governor of the central bank in B Bank's country has suggested that directors of banks pay a fee, and that the bonuses will be based on profit and growth indicators.

Director's viewpoint

From the view point of the banks directors this will not be a welcome solution. The amount of the fee will be questioned – will it be the same for all directors? What will the fee be used for? Will it be returned when a director retires? It is likely that there will be much unrest and argument before this proposal is accepted.

The remuneration committee is to set the fee. Presumably the committee should be an independent one consisting of non-executive directors (NEDs). The NEDs should not be included under the heading of 'directors' and need not pay a fee.

The target of 'appropriate profit and growth indicators' is very vague. What is appropriate to one person e.g. a director may not be appropriate to an investor.

However, the idea of linking profits and bonuses is a better idea than simply paying out large bonuses with little justification (even when a bank has made a loss).

The linking of bonuses with profit may, however, encourage the directors to take excessive risks in order to boost their bonuses.

Staff viewpoint

The staff of B Bank may not be happy with this proposal since there is no mention of them receiving a bonus. They may fear that all profits are paid out to the directors when they feel that they have worked hard.

The directors may not accept this proposal either if they consider the fact that many external factors out of their control can affect the bank's profits. They may work extremely hard and still make a loss in extreme circumstances due to, say, a fall in the demand for mortgages.

Central bank's viewpoint

Finally, the proposal may go against any future decision by the governors of the central banks in other nations.

However, on the plus side, at least the governor in B Bank's home country is trying to alleviate the adverse media coverage by doing something rather than delaying the issue.

(b) Evaluation of the risk management strategy

In the past a formal strategy for managing risks would not be made but rather it would be left to individual managers to make assessments of the risks the business faced and exercise judgement on what was a reasonable level of risk.

This has now changed: failure to properly identify and control risks has been identified as a major cause of business failure e.g. Barings Bank.

Risk management strategy

CIMA identified the following key features of a risk management strategy:

- A statement of the organisation's attitude to risk – the balance between risk and the need to meet objectives

- The risk appetite of the organisation

- The objectives of the risk management strategy

- The culture of the organisation in relation to risk

- The responsibility of managers for the application of risk management strategy

- Reference should be made to the risk management systems the company uses. i.e. its internal control systems

- Performance criteria should be defined so that the effectiveness of risk management can be evaluated

B Bank meets only a few of these criteria.

B Bank's risk management strategy

A statement of B Bank's attitude to risk and risk appetite is not mentioned in the scenario. However it can probably be assumed that they are risk takers as they are able to achieve an increase in share price of 12% per annum, and attract hedge funds as investors. From the view point of the investors, B Bank's risk management strategy is good.

The culture of B Banks managers will probably be one of risk seeking in order to provide the high returns mentioned. (A risk averse manager would feel very uncomfortable in these surroundings.) The staff at B Bank may or may not like the risk management strategy. If it provides them with high salaries then they are probably happy. However, these high salaries may only be short-term if an incorrect decision is made in the future and the bank hits hard times or goes bust. Then the staff may have been happier with lower salaries and job security.

Since a risk management strategy is not formally mentioned it is difficult to say whether managers have been allocated responsibility for the application of risk management. For the bank to have traded successfully for over 150 years, some risk management must take place, however, this should be formalised.

The risk management systems will include the bank's executive information system (EIS). It is able to compute product profitability which supports the targets set on previous profitable experience. On the plus side, having an EIS is an advantage for B Bank; however, it is not being used to its full potential. (See recommendations below.)

Also, B Bank has non-executive directors (NEDs) but they are a poor internal control since they do not question the decisions of the executive directors.

Performance criteria to assess the effectiveness of the risk management strategy are not mentioned in the scenario, other than the targets set on previous experience. It seems that while B Bank is successful, the targets will just roll forward without any reference to what is happening in the external environment of B Bank.

Evaluation of the risk management strategy in B Bank is two-fold:

Has the strategy achieved its objectives? This is hard to say since no formal strategy has been set.

Do the benefits outweigh the costs? Most certainly yes. Since the setting of the strategy cost nothing (no strategy was set) and large returns have been achieved, then the benefits have far outweighed the costs.

Conclusions and recommendations

Overall, the current risk management strategy in B Bank is not good enough. In order to lower the bank's exposure to risk the following recommendations are made:

A major strategy review needs to be performed as soon as possible since the last one was four years ago and much has changed since then. The management appear to be adopting an incremental approach to planning ahead (using previous profitable experiences as the basis for their targets). The past is not always a good indicator of the future and this could be a very dangerous philosophy. B Banks directors need to formally identify the banks attitude to risk, set up a risk committee, and communicate their risk attitude and appetite to its management and investors. They also need to perform an environmental analysis in order to prepare themselves for events that may affect them in the future. E.g. a further fall in house prices.

More effective NEDs need to be appointed who will query the decisions of the executive directors. They may also be able to provide further experience and insight into the banking industry and its environment that the executive directors don't have, or don't have the time to consider.

The property price trend into the future needs to be corroborated with external information, not just internal reports. B Bank should obtain independent, external advice on this in case their internal department is wrong in its prediction.

Currently B Bank is obtaining finance to support new mortgages with loans from the short-term money-markets. This is a very dangerous practice should the source of finance dry up. The principle of 'matching' should be adopted whereby long-term assets (mortgages) are matched with long-term loans (liabilities). This will secure the finance required for the duration of the mortgage and avoid 'renewal risk'.

B Bank may wish to seek new investors. The current investors – hedge funds, may be driving B Bank down a risky road in order to provide them with short-term financial returns. B Bank was founded in 1856 and presumably has the objective of continuing in business into the future. Taking high risks to provide high returns may prevent this objective from being met.

Conclusion

There appear to be more negative viewpoints than positive viewpoints regarding the governor's proposal and B Bank's risk management strategy could be significantly improved.

Test your understanding 25 – W consumer (Case study)

To: The finance Director

From: A.N. Accountant

Date: Today

Subject: Evaluation of operational risk and the use of EDI at W

Introduction

This report covers the evaluation of operational risks at W and suggests management techniques to reduce those risks. It then goes on to consider the risks in using EDI.

(a) **Operational risks**

W is dependent upon a small number of third parties for the manufacture of critical components. If a supplier defaults on a delivery then W may run out of product to sell. The likelihood of this is impossible to predict, but it is a risk that is not under W's direct control. The best safeguard against such problems would be to have more than one potential supplier for any given item. W should make sure that it owns the patents for any components or processes that it relies on, or that it has a licence in place just in case it needs to move to an alternative supplier. Penalty clauses will not mitigate losses in the event of any disruption, but they may concentrate the attention of its suppliers.

W has no direct control over the quality of its products, which may lead to customer dissatisfaction. Parts are sourced from many different suppliers and so it will be difficult for W to ensure that every component is manufactured to the required tolerances. Manufacturing staff at the component and assembly factories will not feel that they are part of W and they may resent the fact that they do not enjoy the security of working for a large organisation. The owners and managers of the factories may not feel that there is a huge incentive to do much more than meet the minimum standards for quality and delivery because they may be replaced at the conclusion of their contract. W can control that risk by introducing quality checks on both components and finished goods. W could request samples on a random basis and check these thoroughly. W could also have a policy of rewarding reliable suppliers by retaining them and giving them as much work as possible so that they have an incentive to exceed expectations.

The global nature of W's manufacturing process creates logistical problems for manufacturing. Manufacturing may be disrupted by delays in delivery, which could be outside the control of W and its suppliers. For example, electronic components are frequently transported by air freight, which can be affected by weather or industrial action. Goods crossing international borders can be delayed by customs inspections. One way round this would be to localise sources as much as possible, with suppliers for minor parts such as screws and plastic cases chosen for proximity to the assembly factories even if they are not necessarily the cheapest. W might use a specialist logistics company to manage the transport of parts and assemblies so that there is clarity as to who is responsible for any logistical problems. W might also have a policy of keeping safety stocks of all but the most expensive parts and assemblies to cover any disruption.

(b) **EDI**

EDI is potentially more efficient than more traditional methods of communication. W has a very complicated manufacturing process and EDI makes it possible to break the task of ordering and paying for a batch of completed mp3 players much simpler. In theory, this system will reduce W's staffing costs considerably. The system will place orders and will keep track of inventory as it is received. The bookkeeping will be done automatically because invoices will be received, recorded and passed for payment electronically.

The problem with W is that it does not really have a long-term relationship with all of its suppliers. It is possible that many of the suppliers it uses will be replaced in the medium or even the short term if a cheaper source becomes available. For example, a shift in currencies could make an alternative source of labour for fabrication tasks cheaper than the present supplier.

Potential suppliers might not be prepared to install the necessary technology and that could restrict W's sources.

Another problem is that W might find it difficult to manage the processing of invoices and payments. A supplier could invoice W for parts or fabrication work on sub-assemblies that are delivered to another third party. W will have no way of verifying that the goods being invoiced were, in fact, delivered in good order and so the system will not be able to make payment. Suppliers could be reluctant to accept orders unless they are likely to be paid for promptly and efficiently.

On a related matter, the lack of human interaction could complicate the manufacturing process. Suppliers of even small parts could delay the completion of finished products if their IT systems accept electronic orders without any consideration of whether the requested delivery dates are feasible. A manager in the sales office could review incoming orders and ensure that the necessary capacity is available.

Conclusions

There are several risks identified in this report and risk management recommendations made. Although EDI would help W, there are many issues which need to be resolved first before EDI could be implemented.

Test your understanding 26 – SPM (Case study)

(a) Risk management is the process by which organisations systematically identify and treat upside and downside risks across the portfolio of all activities with the goal of achieving organisational objectives. Risk management increases the probability of success, reduces both the probability of failure and the uncertainty of achieving the organisation's objectives. The goal of risk management is to manage, rather than eliminate risk. This is most effectively done through embedding a risk culture into the organisation.

For SPM's Distribution division, there is a risk of stock losses through theft, largely due to the lack of separation of duties. This lack of separation occurs because the Distribution Division:

- enters all orders to the computer;

- selects all stock from the warehouse;

- despatches all goods to customers;

- receives the signed paperwork evidencing delivery;

- writes off stock losses due to damage and obsolescence;

- carries out and to a large extent controls the annual physical stocktake.

This lack of separation of duties could result in stock losses or theft that is not identified or not recorded and any stock losses or theft may be disguised during the stocktake due to the expertise of the Distribution division which the auditors appear to rely on.

These stock losses or theft may not be accurately recorded and the reported profits of SPM may overstate profits if physical inventory does not match that shown in the accounting records. Stock of stationery is easy to dispose of and losses can easily happen due to error or carelessness, for instance through water damage, dropping and so on. The possibility of theft of stock which can readily be sold in retail stores is also high and the consequences of not identifying stock losses or theft might be severe over a period of time. There is a risk that inventory records may substantially overstate the physical stock. There is a serious limitation of accounting here as it relies on computer records and a stocktake process that may be severely impaired and hence there may be hidden losses not reflected in SPM's reported financial statements.

Fraud is dishonestly obtaining an advantage, avoiding an obligation or causing a loss to another party. Those committing fraud may be managers, employees or third parties, including customers and suppliers. There are three conditions for fraud to occur: dishonesty, opportunity and motive. If stock theft is occurring, the weakness in systems due to the lack of separation of duties provides an opportunity. Personnel policies and supervision may influence dishonesty and employment or social conditions among the workforce may influence motive.

As for all other risks, a risk management strategy needs to be developed for fraud. This strategy should include fraud prevention; the identification and detection of fraud and responses to fraud.

Existing risk treatment does not appear to be adequate due to the lack of separation of duties, the possibility of fraud and the reliance of internal and external auditors on the Distribution division's staff.

(b)   The main recommendation is for the separation of duties in SPM's distribution division. The customer service centre should process all customer orders, even though this may mean transferring staff from the despatch department. It may be more effective to use a document imaging system to reduce paperwork by converting orders into electronic files that are capable of being read by computer programs and transferred to the despatch department. Further separation can be carried out by sending signed paperwork evidencing delivery to the accounts department and for all write offs of stock losses due to damage or obsolescence to be carried out by the accounts department. Finally, the reliance on Distribution staff for stocktaking needs to be reduced and accountants and internal auditors need to play a more prominent role in physical counting and reconciling to computer records.

The second recommendation is for greater emphasis on controls to prevent dishonesty. These include pre-employment checks, scrutiny of staff by effective supervision, severe discipline for offenders and strong moral leadership. Motive can be influenced by providing good employment conditions, a sympathetic complaints procedure, but dismissing staff instantaneously where it is warranted.

Test your understanding 27 – ABC (Case study)

To: The Board

From: A.N. Accountant

Date: Today

Subject: Risk management

Introduction

This report covers:

(a) The main business issue for ABC and the most significant risks that ABC faces;

(b) The Board's responsibilities for risk management and recommending a risk management system for ABC that would more effectively manage the risks of losing business continuity;

(c) An evaluation of the likely benefits for ABC of an effective risk management system for business continuity.

Risks

(a) A review of disaster recovery had identified a lack of hardware back-up as costs had been continually deferred from year to year to maintain current profits. This has an effect on business continuity for both ABC and its retail customers. Insurance is only one type of risk treatment and ABC has overlooked the need to address business continuity more proactively and comprehensively.

The pressure on short-term profits and cash flow is important to recognise but the short-term view may lead to medium- and long-term problems if under-investment continues. This needs to be the focus of a risk management exercise to properly assess, evaluate, report and treat the business continuity risk.

Although a severe catastrophe may have a small likelihood of occurrence, the impact will be severe and insurance cover is unlikely to be adequate as ABC will not have taken adequate steps to mitigate the loss. Customer awareness of the risk is likely to result in customers moving their business elsewhere. Public disclosure or a severe catastrophe will have a major impact on the reputation of ABC and on ABC's share price.

(b) **Board responsibilities**

The board is responsible for maintaining a sound system of internal control to safeguard shareholders' investment and the company's assets. When reviewing management reports on internal control, the board should consider the significant risks and assess how they have been identified, evaluated and managed; assess the effectiveness of internal controls in managing the significant risks, have regard to any significant weaknesses in internal control; consider whether necessary actions are being taken promptly to remedy any weaknesses and consider whether the findings indicate a need for more exhaustive monitoring of the system of internal control.

Risk management is the process by which organisations systematically identify and treat upside and downside risks with the goal of achieving organisational objectives. The goal of risk management is to manage, rather than eliminate risk. Initially, there needs to be a commitment from the board and top management in relation to risk management generally and business continuity in particular, even if this means a short-term detrimental impact on profitability. The board of ABC, through the audit committee, needs to be more involved in the risk management process. Individual responsibilities for risk management need to be assigned and sufficient resources need to be allocated to fund effective risk management for business continuity.

ABC needs to identify its appetite for risk, and a risk management policy needs to be formulated and agreed by the board. The risk management process needs to identify and define risk, which needs to be assessed in terms of both likelihood and impact. For ABC, the risks have been clearly defined: a loss of business continuity caused by a major catastrophe and the consequent loss of reputation this would involve.

The likelihood of fire, flood, terrorist or criminal activity and so on needs to be assessed, particularly in terms of the risk avoidance processes that are already in place. For example, ABC needs to evaluate whether there has been flooding in the area before, whether water pipes run near the computer facility, whether fire prevention measures are in place, whether firewalls are in place and have been tested so as to reduce the likelihood of attack via the Internet. An assessment of probability of these and other catastrophes should be made. Although these may be low probability events, the impact on the business of any such catastrophe will be severe

Risk evaluation determines the significance of risks to the organisation and whether each specific risk should be accepted or treated. It should be emphasised that these risks cannot be accepted but do need to be treated. Risk treatment (or risk response) is the process of selecting and implementing measures to reduce or limit the risk. The existing contingency plans need to be examined in detail. While data appear to be backed up regularly and stored off-site, there seems to be inadequate back-up for hardware. Risk treatment will involve deciding the most cost-effective method by which to manage the risk. A preferred solution given the reliance of ABC's customers on the system is to have a remote site equipped with a second system that data can be restored onto. While this is the most expensive option there may be business benefits in having two sites. A second solution may be to outsource the back-up facility so that ABC contracts with a third party to have a system available if one is needed. A third option is to negotiate with suppliers as to the availability of other sites and the replacement of equipment on a short notice basis. Finally, insurance coverage needs to be reviewed and the mitigation decided in consultation with ABC's insurers. The present method of risk management that relies only on off-site data back-up is inadequate to assure business continuity.

As business continuity is so important, the board and audit committee need to be involved in the decision-making process about risk treatment. There needs to be regular risk management reporting to assess the control systems in place to reduce risk; the processes used to identify and respond to risks; the methods used to manage significant risks and the monitoring and review system itself. Reporting should take place to business units, senior management, internal audit, the board and the audit committee.

(c) **The benefits of effective risk management**

For ABC, the benefits include the maintenance of profitability in the medium- and longer-term and the avoidance of sudden losses if business continuity is impeded. The major benefit for ABC in such a case is the avoidance of profit warnings and major exceptional items. Additional benefits may include more cost-effective insurance cover and reduced premium cost. If the recommendations are adopted, despite the increased costs that will almost necessarily be incurred, the board of ABC will have greater degree of assurance that business continuity will be safeguarded in the event of a catastrophe, will continue to satisfy its customers and will maintain its reputation with customers, the public and investors.

Conclusions

The main risk for ABC is the lack of a disaster recovery plan as this has an effect on business continuity.

The board is responsible for maintaining a sound system of internal control to safeguard shareholders' investment and the company's assets.

The benefits of effective risk management outweigh the costs.

Strategy risk

Chapter learning objectives

Lead	Component	
B1. Analyse risks associated with formulating strategy	(a)	Analyse relevance of the assumptions on which strategy is based.
	(b)	Discuss potential sources and types of disruptions to strategy.

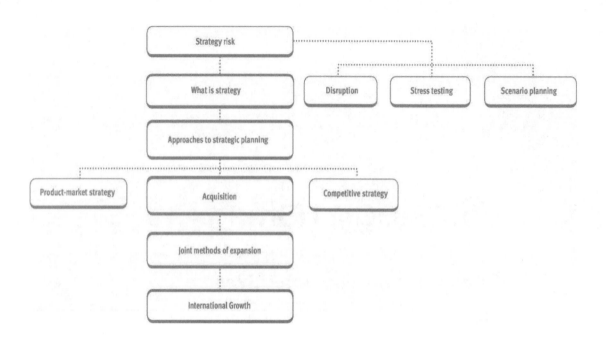

 ## 1   Introduction

In this chapter we look at the risks involved with strategy formulation and assumptions on which the strategy is based. The process of strategy formulation is a core topic in E3 and is developed further there, in P3 we are focussed on the risks. However, before we look at the risks involved, we will first look at what we mean by the word 'strategy'.

2   What is strategy?

Strategy can be defined in a number of different ways, including:

'A course of action, including the specification of resources required, to achieve a specific objective.'

CIMA official terminology

'Strategy is the direction and scope of an organisation over the long term: which achieves advantage for the organisation through its configuration of resources within a changing environment, to meet the needs of markets and to fulfil stakeholder expectations.'

Johnson, Scholes and Whittington (Exploring corporate strategy)

The core of a company's strategy is about choosing:

*   **where** to compete and

*   **how** to compete.

It is a means to achieve **sustainable competitive advantage**.

In terms of risk management, the test of a good strategy is whether it enables an organisation to use its resources and competencies advantageously in the context of an ever changing environment.

Strategic (or corporate) planning involves formulating, evaluating and selecting strategies to enable the preparation of a long-term plan of action and to attain objectives.

Levels of strategy

Strategy can be broken down into three different levels

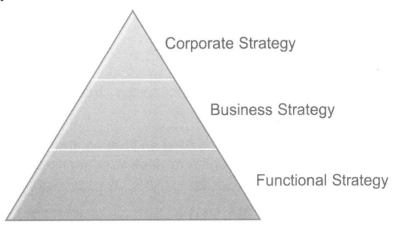

Corporate (or strategic) level

This is the highest level of strategy within the organisation and examines the strategies **for the organisation as a whole**. In particular it focuses on which businesses and markets the organisation should operate within.

Corporate strategy is therefore often concerned with issues such as:

* acquisitions, disposals and diversification

* entering new industries

* leaving existing industries.

Business (or management) level

Having selected a market, the organisation must develop a plan to be successful in that market. Business strategy therefore looks at **how the organisation can compete successfully in the individual markets** that it chooses to operate within.

Business strategy is concerned with issues such as:

* achieve advantage over competitors

* meet the needs of key customers

* avoid competitive disadvantage.

Corporate strategy affects the organisation as a whole, but business strategy will focus upon **strategic business units (SBUs).** An SBU is a unit within an organisation for which there is an external market for products distinct from other units.

Functional (or operational) level

This level of strategy is concerned with how the component parts of the organisation in terms of resources, people and processes are pulled together to form a strategic architecture which will effectively deliver the overall strategic direction. It looks at the **day to day management strategies of the organisation**.

Operational strategy is concerned with:

- human resource strategy
- marketing strategy
- information systems and technology strategy
- operations strategy.

These could be unique to the SBU and benefit from being individually focused or the corporate unit may seek to centralise them and so benefit from synergy

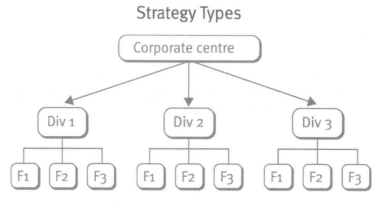

Strategy Types

✓ One corporate strategy

✓ Three business strategies

✓ A choice for functional strategies

Remember that all three levels should be linked. A risk for the corporate or business level strategy is that it will only succeed if it is supported by appropriate operational strategies.

For instance, a hotel chain may pursue a high level strategy of 'excellence in customer care', but achieving the goal will be at risk if staff do not clean the rooms to an appropriate standard or cook the meals in line with hygiene requirements, etc. Therefore the day to day activities **must** be focused on achieving the corporate level strategy.

It is worth mentioning that formulating the strategy is the easy part. Aligning and implementing the strategy can be the difficult part. Football clubs around the world will all have strategies in place to win their league. Only one team per league will actually do so!

Levels of planning

Gap is an international clothing retailer. Classification of different levels of planning could be as follows.

Strategic

- Should another range of shops be established to target a different segment of the market? (Gap opened Banana Republic, a more up-market chain to do just that.)

- Should the company raise more share capital to enable the expansion?

Business

- Which geographical markets should the new range of shops open in?

- How often should inventories be changed to ensure the business keeps up with changing fashions?

- What prices should be charged in the new stores relative to rivals?

Operational

- How will suitable premises be found and fitted out for the new range of shops?

- Which staff should be hired for the new stores?

- Which IT systems need to be installed in the stores?

Gap's strategic decision to create the Banana Republic chain had to be supported by new business and operational level strategies. For example, a risk Gap faced was that poor business strategies for Banana Republic (such as pricing goods too high relative to rivals) would have led to the failure of the new stores. Likewise, poor operational strategies (such as poor training for employees in the new stores) would risk damaging Banana Republic's brand and ruin Gap's overall strategic level strategy.

Whichever approach is chosen, remember that most different types of organisation will need a strategy. This will include companies (large and small), unincorporated businesses, multinational organisations and not-for-profit organisations such as charities, schools and hospitals, etc.

Anywhere that is likely to have a management accountant is likely to need a strategy. Remember that the exam itself will be based on any of these types of organisation. Be prepared for a wide range of scenarios!

The strategic planning process

Having an appropriate strategy is seen as vital to the future success of most organisations. So how does an organisation create a strategy?

There are a number of different models that can be adopted. There is no single 'best' approach – it simply depends on which one each organisation feels is the most appropriate for their needs.

The rational model

The rational model is a logical, step-by-step approach. It requires the organisation to analyse its existing circumstances, generate possible strategies, select the best one(s) and then implement them.

The rational model follows a series of set stages as shown in the diagram below:

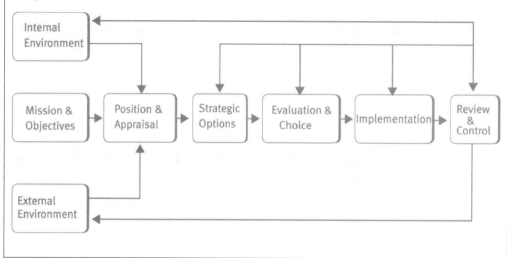

Johnson, Scholes and Whittington took the stages from the rational model and grouped them into three main stages:

- Strategic analysis

- Strategic choice

- Strategic implementation

Our main focus in P3, is strategic choice, and in particular the associated risks involved with the choices that an organisation has.

The following diagram illustrates some of the key considerations in this stage.

> **Strategic choice**
> - Strategies are required to 'close the gap'
> - Competitive strategy – for each business unit
> - Directions for growth – which markets/products should be invested in
> - Whether expansion should be achieved by organic growth, acquisition or some form of joint arrangement.

The JSW approach

A full-price airline in considering setting up a 'no-frills', low-fare subsidiary. The strategic planning process, according to JSW, would include the following elements:

Strategic analysis: Competitor action, oil price forecasts, passenger volume forecasts, availability of cheap landing rights, public concern for environmental damage, effect on the main brand.

Strategic choices: Which routes to launch? Set up a subsidiary from scratch or buy an existing low-cost airline? Which planes to use? Which on-board services to offer?

Strategic implementation: Setup of new subsidiary. Staff recruitment and training. Acquisition of aircraft and obtaining of landing slots.

Test your understanding 1

Which THREE of the following are stages in the rational model of strategic development?

A   Implementation

B   Strategic analysis

C   Mission and objectives

D   Review and control

E   Strategic planning

F   Operational strategy

Benefits of deliberate long-term planning

Benefits of adopting a long-term planning approach (such as the rational model discussed above) include:

- **Forces managers to look ahead** – formal planning methodologies require managers to identify changes in the organisation's circumstances and look at ways to deal with them. This will help to ensure that the organisation stays relevant in its market and survives in the long term.

- **Identifies key risks** – by undertaking detailed analysis, management can identify key external and internal risks and create plans to mitigate them.

- **Improved control** – the organisation is forced to identify a mission and objectives. This will be communicated to management, meaning that they know what targets they are working towards/being assessed against. This will also improve goal congruence.

- **Encourages creativity** – management will have to generate ideas for the organisation, meaning that it can benefit from their experience and ability to innovate.

2.1 Risks of formal planning

The risks of formal, long-term planning include:

- **Setting corporate objectives** – it may be difficult for the organisation to create an overall mission and objectives. This is often due to the contradictory needs of key stakeholders. For example, maximising profit for shareholders may require restructuring the organisation which causes employee redundancy.

- **Short-term pressures** – The pressures on management are often for short-term results. It can therefore be difficult to motivate managers by setting long-term strategies when short-term problems can consume their entire working day.

- **Difficulties in forecasting accurately** – it may be hard to identify long-term trends in the market – particularly as industries are becoming increasingly reliant on the rapidly changing world of technology. This may make it difficult to create a strategy that is effective for the organisation over several years.

- **Bounded rationality** – the internal and external analysis undertaken as part of long-term strategic planning is often incomplete. Any strategies developed by the organisation based on this incomplete analysis may be ineffective.

- **Rigidity** – Once a long-term plan is created, managers often believe it should be followed at all costs – even if it is clearly no longer in the best interests of the organisation. This can also lead to the long-term strategy stifling initiative as managers refuse to act 'outside the plan'.

- **Cost** – the strategic planning process can be costly, involving the use of specialists, sometimes a specialist department, and taking up management time.

- **Management distrust** – the strategic planning process involves the use of management accounting techniques, including forecasting, modelling, cost analysis and operational research. This may be unfamiliar to some managers, leading to resistance. It is worth noting that many academics mistrust these models – not just managers!

Alternatives ways to develop strategies

Strategies are not always formally planned. In reality, strategies may evolve in response to unexpected events that impact on the organisation. Mintzberg referred to these as emergent strategies.

Logical Incrementalism (initially developed by Lindblom) suggests that current strategy tends to be a small-scale extension of past policy, rather than radical change. He does not believe that the rational model of decision-making is sensible and suggests that, in the real world, it is rarely used.

This is because:

- Strategy is not usually decided by autonomous strategic planning teams that have time to impartially sift all the information and possible options before deciding on the optimal solution.

- Instead, managers have to sift through the options themselves. Due to time and knowledge constraints (also known as bounded rationality), they usually only choose between relatively few options.

- This typically leads to strategy being small scale extensions of past policy – in other words, managers try to make small changes to what they know has worked well in the past.

This approach to strategy has a number of advantages over the traditional rational model. In particular it is often more acceptable to stakeholders as consultation, compromise and accommodation are built into the process. In addition, it is less of a cultural shift for the organisation to adopt an incremental approach to strategy as the organisation will not be trying to implement major shifts in its activities.

However, incrementalism may mean that the organisation has no overall long-term plan, causing it to suffer from strategic drift, eventually leading to it being unable to meet the needs of its customers. In addition, it could mean that the organisation fails to make major changes if needed.

The emergent model

Pfizer, a multinational pharmaceutical company, developed a drug known as Sildenafil in an attempt to deal with high blood pressure in patients.

The drug was ultimately unsuccessful, but patients in the test groups reported an interesting side-effect. Pfizer sold the drug as Viagra and started a new multi-billion dollar market.

2.2 Problems with a lack of formal planning

There are a number of practical risks involved with not undertaking a formal planning approach.

- **Failure to identify threats** – the business is not being forced to look ahead. This means that it may fail to identify key threats, and so will not have contingency plans in place to deal with them, should they arise.

- **Strategic drift** – the organisation does not have an overall plan for the future, meaning that it may be difficult for it to effectively compete in its market in the long term.

- **Difficulty in raising finance** – investors typically like to know what plans the organisation has for the future. If the company does not have a formal plan, it may be difficult to convince shareholders and banks (amongst others) that the company is a worthwhile investment.

- **Management skill** – freewheeling opportunists require managers that are highly skilled at understanding and reacting to the changing market. Less able or experienced managers will find this a difficult approach to use.

Test your understanding 2

NerdyWordys is a data analytics company specialising in review management software. They offer a service to help organisation make sense of all the reviews and commentary about their products on social media using linguistics and artificial intelligence (AI). It is small company with only 2 directors, one specialising in AI and another in linguistics.

When they set up the company two years ago, they did produce a very formal long term plan, considering the external environment, their skills and where they saw the business going. They intend to review this again in two years' time.

What are the risks to NerdyWordys of this type of planning?

Select ALL that apply.

A   An initial failure to match their strengths to opportunities

B   Strategic drift

C   Difficulties accurately forecasting demand

D   Failure to identify key risks to the strategy when they started

E   Failure to react to a dynamic environment

2.3 Which approach to strategy should we adopt?

We have identified different approaches to developing a strategy. While we have already mentioned that there is no 'correct' approach, it is important that you understand the risks associated with each approach and align them to the risk appetite of each firm in order to choose the approach that is most appropriate.

More formal planning approaches, such as the rational model (and to a degree the emergent model) tend to suit organisations which:

- exist in relatively stable industries, meaning there is sufficient time to undertake detailed strategic analysis

- have relatively inexperienced managers, as the formal planning approach helps to ensure they are familiar with the organisation, as well as providing a series of guidelines they can follow to help them develop a strategy.

More informal approaches tend to suit organisations which:

- are in dynamic, fast changing industries where there is little time to undertake formal strategic analysis

- have experienced, innovative managers who are able to quickly identify and react to changes in the organisation and its environment

- do not need to raise significant external finance (external investors typically prefer a formal planning approach).

Test your understanding 3

EJS Plc is a digital image printing company. They operate solely through their website and allow organisations and individuals to set up an account and upload digital images directly from various mobile devices to be printed in a variety of ways (on mugs, t-shirts, phone cases and even on photo paper).

They have a very informal approach to planning and believe that flexibility in developing product ideas is the key to their success so far in the industry.

What are the THREE biggest risks to EJS from this approach to strategic planning?

A   Failure to capitalise on their popularity and offer an app for easier access

B   Difficulty forecasting

C   A rigid approach to sales channels

D   Difficulty establishing corporate sales

E   Failure to react to a dynamic environment

F   A rigid approach stifling creative product ideas

Test your understanding 4

Boris has decided to set up an independent coffee shop in a country with a strong economy. He has analysed the industry and made the choice to offer premium coffee with a friendly, personal service in a city centre location.

He's identified a basement property with minimal windows and only accessible by steep steps on a busy street, with a local train station at the top of the street that is used by thousands of commuters every day. At the bottom of the street there is a bus stop where several bus services drop off most people who are arriving in the city centre. It is also near to several large employers such as universities and local council offices. The street that he has chosen has also has two major coffee chains based on street level at the top and the bottom of the street.

What are the biggest risks to Boris' strategy?

Select ALL that apply

A   Premium coffee will be unattractive to people in a city

B   The footfall in the area chosen will be insufficient for the shop to make a profit

C   The basement location may mean that passers-by do not see the shop

D   Customers dislike a friendly personal service in this industry

E   The property chosen will make it difficult for Boris to differentiate his coffee shop from the other city centre shops

F   The major chains have better locations and busy commuters will choose the most convenient shop to get their coffee from.

Test your understanding 5 – HAA – (Case Style)

You are Ali, a management accountant working for HAA plc – a computer games company that operates in country F. You have just found the following note from your manager on your desk:

NOTE

Hi Ali,

As I'm sure you're aware, HAA is planning to expand abroad, into the European market. To support this, we have undertaken a detailed review of our existing operations and the European market. This has been used to produce a three-year budget and operational plan for our proposed European operations.

The European electronics market has always been seen as a difficult market for new entrants. This is due to the fast-moving, innovative nature of the companies currently operating there. HAA has a high spend on research and development and our directors feel that the company is well placed to compete with European games manufacturers.

I'm meeting with the directors in fifteen minutes so I need you to make some brief notes for me evaluating our current approach to strategic planning. Can you explain the risks of the current approach?

Thanks

Required:

Draft a response to your manager, as requested.

(15 minutes)

Strategic planning for not-for-profit organisations (NFPs)

Strategic planning

Many of the organisations in exam questions will be profit-seeking businesses. However, some may involve charities, councils, schools, hospitals and other organisations where profit is not the main objective. With such an 'NFP' a discussion of objectives is likely to be problematic for the following reasons:

- It is more likely to have multiple objectives. A large teaching hospital may want to give the best quality care and treat as many patients as possible and train new doctors and research new techniques. Conflict is inevitable.

  This is not just an issue for NFPs, profit-seeking organisations also have multiple stakeholders with conflicting demands.

- It will be more difficult to measure objectives. How can one measure whether a school is educating pupils well? Performance in exams? Percentage going on to university? Percentage getting jobs? Percentage staying out of prison once they leave?

- There may be a more equal balance of power between stakeholders. In a company, the shareholders hold ultimate power. If they do not use it, the directors generally get their way. In a school, the balance of power may be more even (or even undefined) between parents, governors, the headmaster and the local education authority.

- The people receiving the service are not necessarily those paying for it. The Government and local NHS trusts determine a hospital's funding, not the patients. Consequently there may be pressure to perform well in national league tables at the expense of other objectives.

In spite of these problems, NFPs are still likely to need strategies. In the UK, for example, many public sector organisations have to produce strategic plans for between one and five years ahead as this is a Government requirement.

One of the reasons for this is that the public sector is required to hit certain targets and key performance indicators (KPIs), which are set by central government. In a company these targets and KPIs are used to ensure that the business is competitive. For a public sector organisation, they are used by the government to exert control over the activities of the organisation and to ensure that the government's funding is being used appropriately.

The 3Es

Public sector organisations and charities often have difficulty in using traditional private-sector-based approaches to objective setting since they do not make a profit by which their success or failure can be measured. One way to address this problem is to use the following approach.

The 'three **E**s approach' of the Audit Commission:

- **Economy** looks solely at the level of inputs, e.g. did the hospital spend more or less on drugs this year? Or on nurses' wages?

- **Efficiency** looks at the link between outputs and inputs (the internal processes approach). This approach looks at how well inputs have been used to achieve outputs – it is a measure of efficiency. For example, what was the average cost per patient treated? What was the average spend per bed over the period? What was the bed occupancy rate that this achieved?

- **Effectiveness** looks at the outputs (the goal approach). This looks at the ultimate objectives of the organisation, i.e. at output measures. For example, for an NHS hospital, have the waiting lists been reduced? Have mortality rates gone down? How many patients have been treated?

The best picture of the success of an organisation is obtained by using all of the above approaches and by examining both financial and non-financial issues. Think about effectiveness meaning 'doing the right things' and efficiency 'about doing things right'.

The 3Es

Consider O – a large teaching hospital based in a major city which is funded by the Central Government. O may want to analyse its value for money using the 3Es in the following ways:

Economy:

O is given an annual budget by the Central Government. Economy is likely to look at whether this budget has been met. Has O spent more overall than expected? Has more or less been spent on drugs or wages than predicted? These would help O measure if it has been economical with the use of its funds.

Efficiency:

How well have O's inputs been used to generate its desired outputs? This looks at O's internal processes and could include measures such as the average cost per patient, average spend per hospital bed, or the spend per student in the period.

Effectiveness:

This looks solely at the outputs of O's operations. For example, has O had a higher or lower mortality rate than expected? What percentage of students have qualified or passed exams? How long is the patient waiting list at O?

2.4 The risks associated with the 3Es

The 3Es do have some risks associated with their use:

- The wrong choice of measures – just because you can measure something doesn't mean you should.

- The measures can give contradictory results, and that may mean you prioritise one or two of the measures over the others.

- Internal confusion over which measures to prioritise, leading to demotivated workers and all measures being missed.

- Economy and efficiency can be in conflict with effectiveness, given that spending more can improve effectiveness or spending less (and improving economy/efficiency) can reduce the effectiveness.

- Economy and efficiency are often viewed as easier to measure than effectiveness and so can be the focus of performance measures or audits.

The wrong Es

A local authority claims handling unit was being measured on the time taken to process a claim – efficiency. What you measure affects the way people behave and so, to make sure their efficiency rating was high, the team discovered it was quickest to pay every claim that came in without investigating if the claim was legitimate.

Test your understanding 6

H College is a government funded provider of education to several thousand students in country G. It aims to ensure that at least 75% of all exams sat by its students are passed.

In the last year, it achieved a pass rate of 75% on its exams (the same as the previous year). The head of the college claimed that this was in spite of the government limiting H College's budget rise to 3%, which meant that H College was unable to provide the level of service it had in previous years. Inflation in the economy of country G is 2%.

The government's official auditor has discovered that the cost per student has risen by 5% in H College over the last year, due to internal problems in operations.

H College is expected to offer value for money (VFM).

Which aspect of VFM has H College managed to achieve over the last year?

A   Efficiency

B   Economy

C   Effectiveness

D   Ethical behaviour

3   Approaches to strategic planning

While each aspect of strategic planning is important, firms may prioritise the perspectives in different ways:

- A traditional approach – stakeholders

- A 'market-led' or 'positioning' approach

- A 'resource-based' or 'competence-led' approach

Different priorities

A traditional approach – stakeholders

The traditional approach starts by looking at stakeholders and their objectives (e.g. increase EPS by 5% per annum). The emphasis is then on formulating plans to achieve these objectives.

This approach can be particularly useful for not-for-profit organisations where a discussion of mission and objectives is often key.

A 'market-led' or 'positioning' approach

The more modern 'positioning' approach starts with an analysis of markets and competitors' actions before objectives are set and strategies developed.

The essence of strategic planning is then to ensure that the firm has a good 'fit' with its environment. If markets are expected to change, then the firm needs to change too. The idea is to be able to predict changes sufficiently far in advance to control change rather than always having to react to it.

A 'resource-based' or 'competence-led' approach

Many firms who have found anticipating the environment to be difficult have switched to a competence or resource-based approach, where the emphasis of strategy is to look at what the firm is good at – its core competences.

Ideally these correlate to the areas that the firm has to be good at in order to succeed in its chosen markets (its critical success factors – these are also difficult for competitors to copy.

3.1 The key risks for each of the differing priorities

- **A traditional approach – stakeholders**

  Objectives are very important but this approach can be risky if objectives are set in isolation from market considerations and are thus unrealistic.

- **A 'market-led' or 'positioning' approach**

  The main risk with the positioning approach lies in predicting the future. Some markets are so volatile that it is impossible to estimate further ahead than the immediate short term.

- **A 'resource-based' or 'competence-led' approach**

  The risk is that the company become obsessed by the things that they can do and lose sight of what is happening in the market and what the customers want – leading to products becoming overly complicated and containing features the customer does not want or understand.

Test your understanding 7

J Ltd is a company which offers home television repairs to customers. It has an excellent reputation for customer service and good quality workmanship. J feels that this has given it a competitive advantage in the market.

J is considering launching a car maintenance and repair service. It feels that its excellent reputation is likely to make such a move successful.

Which of the following are the key risks that J will face given the approach to strategic planning they are adopting?

Select ALL that apply

A   Issues predicting where the market will change

B   Unrealistic objectives

C   Losing touch with what the market demands

D   Stifling creativity through a rigid approach

Test your understanding 8 – GYU – (Case Style)

You have just received an email from your manager.

To: A

From: A. B Jones

Date: 17/05/XX

Subject: GYU

Hi A,

You may not have heard of GYU – they are a new client of ours. GYU is a large company which manufactures mobile phone handsets. This is an extremely competitive market and GYU has recently been struggling to keep up with other companies in its sector. This is due to the fast-paced nature of the market. New handsets with increasingly complex features are constantly being launched by competitors and the directors of GYU are concerned that the range of handsets manufactured by the company are beginning to look dated.

This has caused a sharp fall in GYU's cash balances and in response, for the first time in its history, GYU has had to cut its dividend. The fall, which was around 10%, was met with an angry response by shareholders and GYU's share price has fallen significantly since the announcement.

While GYU's position appears weak, it is still seen as a market leader in the production of mobile handset software. While the reviews of its handsets are no longer entirely favourable, most customers agree that the software on the mobile phones is significantly superior to that produced by any of GYU's competitors.

I'm about to have a meeting with GYU's directors for the first time and I think they will ask me to advise them about the three different approaches to strategy that GYU could use and in particular the risks that are associated with each one.

I'd like you to email me back in the next fifteen minutes and tell me your thoughts on these matters.

Required:

Reply to the manager as requested.

(15 minutes)

4 Strategic analysis and choice

Once the position has been identified, the organisation will be aware of its environment and the current strategic capability of the organisation. The questions then becomes "What should we do now to enable us to have the best chance of achieving our objectives?" In other words, which strategy should we follow?

There are many ways to achieve the end result! There is no one strategy that should be deployed in any given circumstance, rather a range of possible strategies that could be used singly or jointly.

4.1 Key decisions to make

As part of strategic choice there are three key levels of strategy to consider:

(1) **Where to compete?**

Which markets/products/SBUs should be part of our portfolio?

(2) **How to compete?**

For each SBU, what should be the basis of our competitive advantage?

(3) **Which investment vehicle to use?**

Suppose an attractive new market has been identified. Should the organisation enter the market via organic growth, acquisition or some form of joint expansion method, such as franchising?

5 Competitive strategy

Porter's generic strategies suggests that competitive advantage arises from the selection of a generic strategy which best fits the organisation's environment and then organising value-adding activities to support the chosen strategy.

		Competitive stance	
Strategic scope	*Broad scope. Targets whole market.*	Cost leadership	Differentiation
	Narrow scope. Targets one segment	Focus	

Cost leadership – being the lowest-cost producer.

Differentiation – creating a customer perception that the product is superior to that of competitors so that a premium can be charged, i.e. that it is different and that customers are willing to pay more for this difference.

Focus – utilising either of the above in a narrow profile of market segments, sometimes called niching.

Porter argues that organisations need to address two key questions:

• Should the strategy be one of differentiation or cost leadership?

• Should the scope be wide or narrow?

He argues that organisations can run the risk of trying to satisfy all three and end up being 'stuck in the middle'. This seems to suggest that Porter was advocating that organisations need to make a basic competitive decision early on in the strategic determination process.

5.1 Cost leadership strategy

This approach is based upon a business organising itself to be the lowest-cost producer.

Note that this does not mean producing an inferior product – cost leadership means that the organisation's product is comparable to those of its rivals, but is made more efficiently.

Cost leadership

Potential benefits are:

- business can earn higher profits by charging the same price as competitors or even moving to undercut where demand is elastic

- let's company build defence against price wars

- allows price penetration entry strategy into new markets

- enhances barriers to entry

- develops new market segments.

Care needs to be taken when deciding on a pricing strategy as a cost leader. Cutting prices to below those of rivals can trigger a damaging price war, as well as potentially suggesting to customers that the product is inferior to those produced by more expensive competitors. Cost leaders may therefore choose to sell their products at a comparable price to those charged by rivals, but earn more profit which can be reinvested (such as in advertising, expansion or research and development) to gain competitive advantage.

Value chain analysis is central to identifying where cost savings can be made at various stages in the value chain. Attainment depends upon arranging value chain activities so as to:

- reduce costs by copying rather than originating designs, using cheaper materials and other cheaper resources, producing products with 'no frills', reducing labour costs and increasing labour productivity.

- achieve economies of scale by high-volume sales allowing fixed costs to be spread over a wider production base.

- use high-volume purchasing to obtain discounts for bulk purchase.

- locate in areas where cost advantage exists or government aid is possible.

- obtained learning and experience curve benefits.

Risks:

- There is no fall back if the leadership position is lost, for example strengthening of the currency may make imports of substitute goods cheaper.

- The organisation must continually adapt to ensure unit prices are kept low and consumer needs are met.

5.2 Differentiation strategy

This strategy is based upon the idea of persuading customers that a product is superior to that offered by the competition. Differentiation can be based on product features or creating/altering consumer perception (i.e. through superior brand development to rivals). Differentiation can also be based upon **process as well as product**. It is usually used to justify a higher price.

 Differentiation

Benefits:

- Products command a premium price so higher margins.

- Demand becomes less price elastic and so avoids costly competitor price wars.

- Life cycle extends as branding becomes possible – hence strengthening the barriers to entry.

Value chain analysis can identify the points at which these can be achieved by:

- creating products which are superior to competitors by virtue of design, technology, performance, etc. Marketing spend becomes important

- offering superior after-sales service by superior distribution, perhaps in prime locations

- creating brand strength

- augmenting the product, i.e. adding to it.

- packaging the product

- ensuring an innovative culture exists within the company.

Risks:

- there is a need to continually innovate to defend the position

- smaller volumes

- associated costs, such as marketing, are higher

- performance in a recession may be poor.

5.3 Focus strategy

This strategy is aimed at a segment of the market rather than the whole market. A particular group of consumers are identified with similar needs, possibly based upon age, sex, lifestyle, income or geography and then the company will either differentiate or cost focus in that area.

Focus

Benefits:

- smaller segment and so smaller investment in marketing operations
- allows specialisation
- less competition
- entry is cheaper and easier.

Requires:

- reliable segment identification
- consumer/customer needs to be reliably identified – research becomes even more crucial
- segment to be sufficiently large to enable a return to be earned in the long run
- competition analysis – given the small market, the competition, if any, needs to be fully understood
- direct focus of product to consumer needs.

Risks:

- if successful it may attract other cost leaders/ differentiators due to potential low barriers to entry
- low volumes may be sold.

Niching

Niching can be done via specialisation by:

- location
- type of end user
- product or product line
- quality
- price
- size of customer
- product feature.

If done properly it can avoid confrontation and competition yet still be profitable.

The key risks to consider for the market niche:

- the niche must be large enough in terms of potential buyers
- the niche must have growth potential and predictability
- the niche must be of negligible interest to major competitors
- the firm must have strategic capability to enable effective service of the niche.

Cost leadership

Casio Electronics Co. Ltd – Casio has sold over 1 billion pocket calculators. It follows an industry-wide cost leadership approach. Its calculators are certainly not inferior products, being able to perform over two hundred basic scientific functions. How does it do it? Consider its value chain:

- Operations – mass manufactured in China, which has cheaper labour and economies of scale.
- Operations – 'buttons', display and instructions manuals are multi– lingual – reducing the need to make calculators specific to one target country.
- Procurement – mass purchase/production of components.
- Outbound logistics – packaging is robust, yet allows a considerable number of calculators to be shipped at any time.

Differentiation

British Airways (BA) is a multinational passenger airline. It has adopted a differentiation approach by offering passengers a higher-quality experience than many of its rivals. This allows it to charge a premium for its flights compared to many other airlines. Again – examination of its value chain may help to explain how it achieves this:

- Procurement – prime landing slots are obtained at major airports around the world.
- Procurement – high-quality food and drink is sourced from suppliers.
- Operations – well-maintained, clean and comfortable aircraft are sourced.
- Operations – high numbers of attendants on each flight.
- Marketing – advertising based on quality of service provided.
- Human resources – training in customer care and the recruitment of high-quality staff.

> **Focus**
>
> Ferrari is an example of a company that focuses on a niche market in the automobile industry. It produces extremely high quality cars which command a high premium price. However, this means that Ferrari only has a very small percentage of the global car market, as the majority of consumers are unable to afford its high sales prices.
>
> This is a risk of the focus approach. The niche targeted may be small and fail to justify the company's attention. In addition the niche may shrink or disappear altogether over time as consumer tastes and fashions change.

5.4 Risks of Porter's generic strategies

In spite of its popularity, there are a number of problems with Porter's generic strategies model, including:

- Porter argues that any business that attempts to adopt more than one of the generic strategies will become 'stuck in the middle'. He suggested that this is because a business will be unable to successfully implement more than one at the same time, leading to strategic drift. In reality this may be too simplistic.

  A number of companies do not fit into one of the classic generic strategies and adopt a 'hybrid' approach. Successful UK supermarket chain Sainsbury's uses a slogan 'Live well for less', suggesting to its potential customers that its products are both lower price than rivals and good quality – both differentiation and cost leadership.

- Cost leadership in itself may not give competitive advantage.

  Failure to pass on cost savings to customers through lower prices may mean that the business fails to gain an edge over rivals. Passing on the cost savings may trigger a price war with rivals, meaning that the company fails to benefit from the strategy.

- Differentiation may not always lead to a business being able to command a high price for its goods. It may be used to generate increased sales volume – which Porter argued was typically the purpose of a cost leadership approach.

Test your understanding 9

Company W makes motor vehicles. Several years ago, W restructured its value chain to significantly reduce production costs and improve quality. This was in response to similar activities by its W's major rivals.

Because of this, W has been able to maintain its prices at only a slightly higher level than those of its competitors, while continuing to produce a wide range of cars that are tailored to a variety of market segments.

W has recently decided to undertake a significant investment in advertising, as it feels that its brand is one of the most recognised in the market. W wishes to further increase the desirability of its brand, which it feels could allow it to raise its prices slightly in the coming year, while still maintaining its overall sales volume.

Applying porter's generic strategy model, what are the most likely risks of W's current approach?

Select ALL that apply

A   As the lowest cost producer they could lose their advantage if one of their competitors makes significant cost savings.

B   The market is not big enough to generate growth opportunities.

C   Brand perception helps generate sales.

D   Low volumes will be sold as the segmentation leads to a narrow market.

E   Marketing costs are higher to protect the firms image

F   They may suffer in a recession

Test your understanding 10

Y is a small business that sells furniture in country H. It is considering its future corporate strategy.

The furniture market is dominated by large manufacturers, who have large factories as well as close relationships with key suppliers of raw materials. Y is currently the twentieth largest manufacturer of furniture in country H.

Y's market analysis has identified that there are a moderate number of self-employed individuals in country H who work from home and who desire standard office furniture that is also fashionable. However, there are several companies who have built up established brand names in this sector of the market.

Y currently makes furniture for small to medium sized businesses (such as desks and office chairs). Products in this segment of the market are fairly generic as businesses typically choose a furniture supplier based on price. There are a large number of other suppliers of this style of furniture in country H – including several of the larger manufacturers.

Y is concerned that it lacks the appropriate skills to make other types of furniture.

Considering Y's strategy, which of the following are the most likely risks that Y will face?

A   A small niche with limited growth

B   Lack of differentiation

C   Inability to compete on costs due to economies of scale

D   Poor marketing effort to publicise the unique nature of their products

E   Too many competitors targeting the same niche as them

 Test your understanding 11 – AVA – (Case style)

You work as a senior manager for AVA, an airline company that offers regular passenger flights from several countries in country L to destinations all over the world.

AVA is a long-established company which has historically offered a low-cost service with few passenger comforts or luxuries. Customers have to book seats online, with no chance for interaction with an AVA staff member. Seats (which are renowned by customers for their lack of leg room) cannot be pre-booked and AVA has a poor record for delays and cancellations.

In spite of this, AVA has managed to achieve reasonable profits by being able to offer its flights at extremely low prices. In recent years, however, the company's profits have fallen as the economy of country L has started to recover from a long recession. This has led the company to start looking at ways of improving profitability.

Your manager, the finance director (FD) of AVA sends you the below email:

To: Senior manager

From: Johan O'Leary, FD

Date: 16/09/XX

Subject: AVA Strategic direction

I'll get straight to the point, the directors feel that the company is missing out on the lucrative first class service market – currently dominated by several major international airlines which are significantly larger than AVA. While first class travellers require more services and better facilities, these types of customers pay a significantly higher ticket price.

The company would therefore convert the front section of several of its aircraft into 'first class' with fewer seats and more leg room. Passengers could book these seats through a separate system which would enable them to speak to an adviser if they had any problems. AVA would also offer free food and drink on the flight to first class passengers. This service would not be available to standard class customers.

The airplanes that AVA upgraded would all be based on one of its major routes, to maximise potential appeal.

The directors are concerned that we may be susceptible to certain risks. They would like to examine our existing and first class strategies using Porter's generic strategies, in particular focussing on the risks of these strategies for AVA.

Please have the report on my desk in thirty minutes, so I have time to consider it before speaking to the other directors.

Thanks

FD

Required:

Draft the report as requested in the FD's email.

(30 minutes)

6   Product-market strategy

6.1 Ansoff's matrix

The product/market growth framework

Ansoff's matrix provides a commonly used model for analysing the possible strategic directions that an organisation can follow. It is therefore useful in areas of strategic choice:

		Products	
		Existing	*New*
Markets	Existing	Market penetration	Product development
	New	Market development	Diversification

Ansoff

Market penetration

The main aim is to increase market share using existing products within existing markets.

Approach

First attempt to stimulate **usage by existing customers:**

- new uses of advertising
- promotions, sponsorships
- quantity discounts.

Then attempt to attract **non-users** and **competitor customers** via:

- pricing
- promotion and advertising
- process redesign, e.g. Internet/e-commerce

Key notes:

Considered when:

- overall market is growing
- market not saturated
- competitors leaving or weak
- strong brand presence by your company with established reputation
- strong marketing capabilities exist within your company.

Market development

Aims to increase sales by taking the present product to new markets (or new segments). Entering new markets or segments may require the development of new competencies which serve the particular needs of customers in those segments, e.g. cultural awareness/linguistic skills.

Movement into overseas markets is often quoted as a good example as the organisation will need to build new competencies when entering international markets.

Approach

- Add **geographical** areas – regional and national
- add **demographic** areas – age and sex
- new **distribution** channels.

Key notes

- **Slight** product modifications may be needed
- advertising in different media and in different ways
- research – primary research at this point given significance of the investment
- company is structured to produce one product and high switching costs exist for transfer to other product types
- strong marketing ability is needed, usually coupled with established brand backing, e.g. CocaCola

Product development

Focuses on the development of new products for existing markets.

Offers the advantage of dealing with known customer/consumer bases.

Approach:

- develop product features of a significant nature
- create different quality versions.

Key notes:

Company needs to be innovative and strong in the area of R&D and have an established, reliable marketing database.

Constant innovation allows for the developing sophistication of consumers and customers and ensures that any product-related competitive advantage is maintained.

Diversification

New products to new markets.

Key notes:

Appropriate when existing markets are saturated or when products are reaching the end of their life cycle. It can spread risk by broadening the portfolio and lead to 'synergy-based benefits', allegedly.

This approach goes through periods of being in and out of favour, and debate continues about whether this is a good strategic option. Critics argue that it is madness to take resources away from known markets and products only to allocate them to businesses that the company essentially knows nothing about. This risk has to be compensated for by higher rewards, which may or may not exist.

Brand stretching ability is often seen as being the critical success factor for successful diversification – this is a possible discussion point. The new business and its strategy may well have 'teething problems' with its implementation and this may damage brand reputation.

Reasons suggested:

- Objectives can no longer be met in known markets – possibly due to a change in the external environment.

- Company has excess cash and powerful shareholders;

- Possible to 'brand stretch' and benefit from past advertising and promotion in other SBUs.

- Diversification promises greater returns and can spread risk by removing the dependency on one product.

- Greater use of distribution systems and corporate resources such as research and development, market research, finance and HR leading to synergies.

Ansoff

- Kellogg's have repositioned their products through various advertising campaigns (**market penetration**). For example, the 'have you forgotten how good they taste?' campaign was to remind adults, who buy cereals for their children, of the virtues of their product.

- Kwik Fit, a motor repair company, took the opportunity to cross sell insurance to customers on their database who had visited their outlets to have equipment fitted (**product development – 'piggybacking'**).

- Kaplan now sell their ACCA courses in Eastern Europe and Asia, amongst other countries, rather than just their traditional UK markets (**market development**).

- Virgin, a multinational conglomerate, has expanded into a wide range of different activities, including airlines, trains, cosmetics, wedding wear and so on (**diversification**).

6.2 Risks

Market penetration

Market penetration is the lowest risk option in Ansoff's matrix, but given the risk reward trade off, it is also likely to yield the lowest return. The key risk therefore is that it does not generate the returns the organisation requires.

For example, a company could increase their advertising spend significantly, but they may well have already reached all of their target market already and so fail to increase sales.

Product development

Product development increases risk for an organisation – R&D costs can be significant in product design and development. If the resultant product is not appropriate for their core market or if a competitor gets to the market quicker or with a better product, then the new product may fail, leading to significant losses.

Market development

New markets can be very varied. The company could be selling to a new segment (for example age range or sex), or it could be selling in a new country. However an organisation chooses to develop its market it must do thorough research into whether their entry into the market is viable. Failure, as well as significant cost of entry and exit, could also lead to reputational damage too.

Market development failures

- Monsoon clothing entered the male clothing market for a time, having previously focussed on the female market. For a variety of reasons, most prominently a lack of awareness of them selling clothes to the male market, the development didn't work.

- Marks and Spencer have on numerous occasions attempted to enter mainland Europe, but have failed to get their strategy right. So far the development has not worked, sometimes leading to a downturn in fortunes in their core UK market as a result of their efforts.

Diversification

The riskiest option in Ansoff's matrix. There are different types of diversification, related (for example vertical integration) or unrelated. Both have their risks.

- **Related** is less risky, either buying a supplier or customer. For example a chain of pubs buying a brewery (or vice versa). There is knowledge and similarities to the current operations, but it can increase your reliance on the market you serve and reduce choice. If for example you bought a supplier and then had issues it would not be as easy to switch supplier given you now owned a competitor.

- **Unrelated** is the most risky approach, this is entering a market with no common thread to the current operations. The key risks with this are a lack of knowledge and skills, the cost of entry, the time it would take to develop share in that market. Sometimes this leads companies to acquire an existing company to enter into that market.

7 Acquisition

Businesses may choose to grow in one of several main ways, including acquisitions, mergers or organic growth.

 Acquisition refers to a corporate action in which a company buys most, if not all, of the target company's ownership stakes in order to assume control of the target firm.

 Mergers are business combinations that result from the creation of a new reporting entity formed from the combining parties.

Note that, for our purposes there is little or no strategic difference in risks between an acquisition and a merger.

 Organic growth is growth through internally generated projects, such as increased output, customer base expansion, or new product development.

Acquisition may be more expensive than organic growth because the owners of the acquired company will need to be paid for the risks they have already taken. On the other hand, if the company goes for organic growth it must take the risks itself so there is a trade-off between cost and risk.

A company can gain synergy by bringing together complementary resources in their own business and that being acquired. Synergy is defined as **'the advantage to a firm gained by having existing resources which are compatible with new products or markets that the company is developing'.**

For example, sales synergy may be obtained through the use of common marketing facilities such as distribution channels. Investment synergy may result from the joint use of plant and machinery or raw materials.

An acquisition must add value in a way the shareholder cannot replicate in order to avoid the risks associated with diversified companies (see Ansoff).

Acquisition v organic growth

Benefits of acquisitions over organic growth

Acquisition has some significant benefits over internal growth.

- High-speed access to resources – this is particularly true of brands; an acquisition can provide a powerful brand name that could take years to establish through internal growth.

- Avoids barriers to entry – acquisition may be the only way to enter a market where the competitive structure will not admit a new member or the barriers to entry are too high.

- Less reaction from competitors – there is less likelihood of retaliation from existing companies because an acquisition does not alter the overall capacity of the competitive arena.

- It can block a competitor – if Kingfisher's bid for Asda had been successful it would have denied Walmart its easy access to the UK.

- It can help restructure the operating environment – some mergers of car companies were used to reduce overcapacity.

- Relative price/earnings ratio – if the P/E ratio is significantly higher in the new industry than the present one, acquisition may not be possible because it would cause a dilution in earnings per share to the existing shareholders. But if the present company has a high P/E ratio it can boost earnings per share by issuing its own equity in settlement of the purchase price.

- Asset valuation – if the acquiring company believes the potential acquisition's assets are undervalued, it might undertake an asset-stripping operation.

7.1 Risks associated with growth by acquisition

There are some considerable risks associated with this method of growth

- Acquisition may be more costly than internal growth because the owners of the acquired company will have to be paid for the risk already taken. On the other hand, if the company decides on internal growth, it will have to bear the costs of the risk itself.

- There is bound to be a cultural mismatch between the organisations – a lack of 'fit' can be significant in knowledge-based companies, where the value of the business resides in individuals.

- Differences in managers' salaries – another example of cultural mismatch that illustrates how managers are valued in different countries.

- Disposal of assets – companies may be forced to dispose of assets they had before the acquisition. The alliance between British Airways and American Airlines was called off because the pair would have had to free up around 224 take-off and landing slots to other operators.

- Lack of knowledge – despite due diligence, there is the risk of not knowing all there is to know about the business it seeks to buy.

- Reduction in return on capital employed – quite often an acquisition adds to sales and profit volume without adding to value creation

7.2 The key control for an acquisition

Due diligence

Due diligence is an investigation of a business prior to signing a contract. It relates to the process through which a company will evaluate a target and their assets prior to acquisition. Due diligence should provide information that allows for more informed decision making regarding the acquisition. There is always risk involved in any acquisition, but the work done here is designed to help reduce the uncertainty and control the risks that the acquirer will face as they go through the acquisition and afterwards as the company looks to make a success of the combined entity.

Although due diligence usually goes beyond simply looking at financial information, it is likely that this will be the main part of the investigation. Due diligence is a control to reduce the likelihood of overpaying for a target company

This process is particularly important if a private company is the target. As such, they would not have been subject to the same scrutiny as a listed company. Due diligence would be the first opportunity for the acquirer to obtain some of the information on the target as it would not be available from public sources.

Possible areas of focus for due diligence:

- Financial statements

- Strategic Fit

- Employee/Management Issues

- Property

- Competition commission

- Intellectual Property

- Contract review

- Pending litigation

- Tax

- Insurance

If both parties are aware of the due diligence activities that are likely to be carried out, the process is more likely to run smoothly and effectively.

Due diligence considerations in more detail

Financial statements

Review of the historic financial statements, considering:

- financial metrics
- reasonableness of the financial forecasts
- verification of the assets owned and their value
- analytical review of annual, quarterly, monthly financial statements, potentially going back several years

This may reveal important information and background knowledge about the financial performance (past and future) which may impact the price a company is willing to pay. External auditors may be used to verify the financial information represents a true and fair view.

Strategic Fit

Due diligence is not only assessing the target company's potential future performance per the financial forecasts, it is also designed to understand how the target will fit strategically within the combined entity. Considerations would be:

- potential enhancements after the acquisition
- cost savings and other synergies
- time and cost of integration.

Employee/Management Issues

Acquisition is a time of change and potential unease amongst staff. The due diligence team will also want to look at whether there are any underlying issues that may cause disruption in the future. Acquiring information on the target company's organisational structure, labour disputes, employee benefits (profit sharing, pension plans and so on) would be useful to gauge any potential issues but also compare with our own arrangements.

For example, if talent management at the acquiring company is very important it will be important to consider whether aligning the two entity's policies in the future may cause turbulence not just to the target's employees, but to the acquirer too.

Property

A review of any premises the target owns or leases should be undertaken to consider if they are in line with the acquirer's plans would be essential. It is unlikely that all the target companies' locations would be kept after acquisition, so the best locations should be identified and any locations no longer required should be reviewed in terms of break clauses or saleability.

Competition commission

If the acquisition or merger is related to companies competing in the same industry, thought must be given to the combined market share that would materialise. Significant market share could prove problematic giving rise to regulatory issues with any Competition Commission in affected countries.

Intellectual Property

An acquisition or merger is rarely carried out just because of financial assets. One of the main reasons in the modern age is the intellectual property of the target and this may also require valuation. This is likely to include, but not limited to:

- website operations

- mobile apps

- data analytics processes.

The due diligence team may want to look at whether the target has taken appropriate steps to protect its intellectual property (including confidentiality agreements with current and former employees regarding any data analytics processes).

Contract review

The due diligence process is likely to review the material contracts the target holds in order to fully understand its commitments. These may involve supplier or customer contracts. The acquirer may want to ensure these contacts will be carried forward under new ownership. Although laborious, a contract review is critical. Without it, the acquirer may not be aware of costs, such as terminating a contract early, which can pose significant financial and operational obligations that require consideration.

Pending litigation

The acquirer needs to know whether there are any ongoing claims, closed claims or pending litigation. Acquiring a huge legal case would not be ideal as part of any deal.

Tax

In any acquisition the buyer would need to consider the tax situation of the target company, reviewing any tax returns and getting an understanding of any tax balances or correspondence with the tax authorities of the relevant countries. As with the litigation, the buyer does not want to end up acquiring a large tax liability.

Insurance

It will be important to check what insurance policies the target has in place. If the policies do not appear appropriate in terms of the level of cover or excesses, then break clauses and costs to improve the cover would need to be ascertained.

8   Joint methods of expansion

8.1   Joint development methods

These include:

- joint venture
- strategic alliances
- franchising
- licenses
- outsourcing

In any joint arrangement key considerations are:

- sharing of costs
- sharing of benefits
- sharing of risks
- ownership of resources
- control/decision making

Joint development methods

Joint venture

A separate business entity whose shares are owned by two or more business entities. Assets are formally integrated and jointly owned.

A very useful approach for:

- sharing cost
- sharing risk
- sharing expertise.

In the UK, an example of a joint venture is Virgin Trains – a company whose share capital is 51% owned by the Virgin Group and 49% owned by Stagecoach. The joint venture allowed the two companies to work together to take advantage of the privatisation of the nationalised British Rail.

Strategic alliance

A strategic alliance can be defined as a cooperative business activity, formed by two or more separate organisations for strategic purposes, that allocates ownership, operational responsibilities, financial risks, and rewards to each member, while preserving their separate identity/autonomy.

Alliances can allow participants to achieve critical mass, benefit from other participants' skills and can allow skill transfer between participants.

The technical difference between a strategic alliance and a joint venture is whether or not a new, independent business entity is formed.

A strategic alliance is often a preliminary step to a joint venture or an acquisition. A strategic alliance can take many forms, from a loose informal agreement to a formal joint venture.

Alliances include partnerships, joint ventures and contracting out services to outside suppliers.

Seven characteristics of a well-structured alliance have been identified.

- **Strategic synergy** – more strength when combined than they have independently.

- **Positioning opportunity** – at least one of the companies should be able to gain a leadership position (i.e. to sell a new product or service; to secure access to raw materials or technology).

- **Limited resource availability** – a potentially good partner will have strengths such as access to scarce resources that complement weaknesses of the other partner. One of the partners could not do this alone.

- **Less risk** – forming the alliance reduces the risk of the venture.

- **Co-operative spirit** – both companies must want to do this and be willing to co-operate fully.

- **Clarity of purpose** – results, milestones, methods and resource commitments must be clearly understood.

- **Win-win** – the structure, risks, operations and rewards must be fairly apportioned among members.

Some organisations try to retain some of the innovation and flexibility that is characteristic of small companies by forming strategic alliances (closer working relationships) with other organisations. They also play an important role in global strategies, where the organisation lacks a key success factor for some markets.

An example of a strategic alliance is that pursued by Starbucks in 2012, in an attempt to break into the Indian coffee shop market. It formed an alliance with Tata Global Beverages – a large Indian drinks company – with both parties investing $80m in order to open a number of Starbucks stores across India. Starbucks had significant experience of running coffee shops, while Tata had strong local knowledge of the growing Indian drinks market.

Franchising

The purchase of the right to exploit a business brand in return for a capital sum and a share of profits or turnover.

- The franchisee pays the franchisor an initial capital sum and thereafter the franchisee pays the franchisor a share of profits or royalties.

- The franchisor provides marketing, research and development, advice and support.

- The franchisor normally provides the goods for resale.

- The franchisor imposes strict rules and control to protect its brand and reputation.

- The franchisee buys into a successful formula, so risk is much lower.

- The franchisor gains capital as the number of franchisees grows.

- The franchisor's head office can stay small as there is considerable delegation/decentralisation to the franchisees.

A classic example of franchising is McDonalds. Within the UK, for example, around half of all McDonalds restaurants are franchises.

Licensing

The right to exploit an invention or resource in return for a share of proceeds. Licensing differs from a franchise because there will be little central support.

In the UK, many beers such as Heineken and Fosters were 'brewed under licence' in the UK for many years, with the original companies that developed the beers simply taking a share of the proceeds from the local brewers.

Outsourcing

Outsourcing means contracting out aspects of the work of the organisation, previously done in-house, to specialist providers. Almost any activity can be outsourced – examples include information technology or payroll.

Mobile telecommunications company O2 has recently announced plans to outsource its customer contact centres in the UK.

The public sector may also undertake outsourcing. For example, in 2013 Barnet Council in London announced plans to outsourced much of its corporate procurement, IT and HR services to Capita – a private sector company.

8.2   Key risks of joint development methods

Regardless of the choice of collaboration an organisation uses, the key risks of partnering with a third party are:

- **Strategic fit** – the partner chosen needs to have a similar strategy because by association the two (or more) collaborating firms will affect each other's reputation.

Innocent and McDonalds

Innocent collaborated with McDonalds for a time, Innocent effectively used them as a distribution channel for their smoothies.

The smoothies became a healthy option in McDonalds Happy Meals. The logic being that McDonalds wanted to portray themselves as offering healthier alternatives (they have since gone on to offer a lot more healthy options), Innocent saw it as an excellent way to increase the opportunities for people to choose one of their smoothies. It seemed the perfect opportunity.

The collaboration was given a reasonable time, but ultimately did not last. The smoothies were not a popular choice, McDonalds customers stuck with their core options of milkshakes and fizzy drinks, and Innocent in particular received a lot of criticism for collaborating with a firm that many stakeholders felt went against a lot of the core values that Innocent stood for.

- **Cost sharing** – the two companies will have to come to an agreement over how costs are split or who bears particular costs. This can be difficult and can lead to disagreements

- **Knowledge sharing** – by partnering with a firm, there is a risk that an organisation may have to reveal some of its trade secrets, depending on how close the collaboration is. Careful consideration must be given to who a company collaborates with and what skills and knowledge they share in the collaboration.

- **Profit sharing** – the ultimate aim for most collaborations is to increase the collaborating organisations' ability to make money, therefore a key discussion point must be how the profits are split and it must be deemed proportionate to the risks each party is taking on in the collaboration.

- **Loss of control** – partnering with other organisations requires trust that the partner will perform its work to the same standard as normal. Any issues with quality of product or service will have a knock on effect to the reputation of the other organisation.

Amazon

Internet retailer Amazon operate what many people refer to as a network organisation, where a network of companies collaborate to provide the customer with the goods they desire.

For example, one company manufactures the product, a retailer may offer it for sale through the amazon website, payment is made via a credit or debit card provider and then delivery is made by a logistics/courier firm.

If anyone of these collaborating organisations do not carry out their role in the collaboration to the appropriate standard it can tarnish the reputation of Amazon. This is one of the reasons Amazon ask for feedback – there will be strict targets for customer satisfaction levels imposed on those organisations allowed to use the Amazon platform.

- **Loss of development opportunities** – collaboration is often used to enter into a new geographic market or offer a service/product the company did not previously provide. If an alternative approach had been used then an organisation could have developed these skills themselves rather than effectively outsourcing them.

Test your understanding 12

H Ltd wishes to rapidly expand its popular chain of retail stores, but does not have the capital needed to do so. It has decided to consider joint development methods in order to aid its growth, but H Ltd's owner T is uncertain about which method to use.

T is unwilling to allow any other individual or organisation to have significant influence over H's strategic operations as she is used to having the final say over all major decisions within the company.

T wishes to avoid any damage to H's brand name. As such, she wants staff to continue to be trained centrally, as well as all fixtures, fittings and inventory to be purchased from authorised suppliers only.

Which of the following methods of joint development would be most appropriate for H Ltd?

A   Licensing

B   Franchising

C   Joint venture

D   Strategic alliance

> ### Test your understanding 13 – (integration question)
>
> Which of licensing, joint venture, strategic alliance and franchising might be the most suitable for the following circumstances?
>
> (1) A company has invented a uniquely good ice cream and wants to set up an international chain of strongly branded outlets.
>
> (2) Oil companies are under political pressure to develop alternative, renewable energy sources.
>
> (3) A beer manufacturer wants to move from their existing domestic market into international sales.

9 International growth

When deciding whether to expand abroad, a business has several possible strategies that it can adopt:

- **Exporting strategy** – the firm sells products made in its home country to buyers abroad. This often starts with the receipt of a chance order or perhaps poor sales at home force the business to export or collapse.

- **Overseas manufacture** – the firm may either manufacture its products in a foreign country and then either import them back to its home country or sell them abroad. Either way, the firm is involved in direct foreign investment because it is purchasing capital assets in another country. For example, Nissan Motors is a Japanese company, but operates plants to build its motor vehicles across the world, including North-East England.

- **Multinational** – these firms co-ordinate their value-adding activities across national boundaries. For example, a multinational car manufacturer will have engine plants in one country, car body plants in another and electrics in a third. Production capacity is often duplicated around the world. Not all overseas manufacturers could be classed as multinationals, but Nissan Motors, manufactures in over 20 countries so could be classed as both a multinational and an overseas manufacturer.

- **Transnational** – these are 'nation-less' firms that have no 'home' country. Employees and facilities are treated identically, regardless of where they are in the world. The company may be listed on several national stock exchanges. This is often considered to be (currently) largely theoretical.

When deciding between which approaches to take if expanding abroad, consideration should be given to the risks of international growth:

- **Political risk** – the risk that government policy may make it difficult to operate successfully in the new country.

- **Foreign exchange risk** – the risk that earnings could be reduced by currency fluctuations.

- **Need for capital investment** – this will be lower if an exporting strategy is used.

- **Risks to customer relationships** – given the distance between the manufacturer and its foreign consumers, this can be hard to maintain in an exporting strategy.

- **Increased risks in the supply chain** – manufacturing at a distance from your target market will increase the cost of getting the units to them.

- **Ethical risks** – if operating in countries with less developed labour laws, should the company take advantage of this to keep costs low?

- **Cultural risks** – managing operations in foreign countries can be difficult due to differences in language and customs. This can also make advertising and operational control difficult.

Test your understanding 14

YH operates a large number of food production facilities, based in country N. In particular, YH's operations focus on the growing and harvesting of soft fruit. YH then sorts and grades the fruit, before shipping it to retailers, such as large supermarkets.

YH has struggled to find the amount of farmland it needs in order to expand its production in its home country. In recent years, therefore, YH has been buying farmland and facilities in several new countries around the world. This has allowed it to expand its sales into a number of new geographical markets and grow its business.

This business model has been so successful that a significant majority of YH's fruit is now grown abroad, with some of it even being brought back into country N to meet demand from YH's customers.

Which of the following options is the best match to the international growth strategy being adopted by YH?

A   Transnational

B   Exporting

C   Multinational

D   Overseas manufacture

---

10 Disruption

In the modern business world, a key strategic risk to consider is disruption, or, to use its full name, disruptive innovation.

10.1 What is disruptive innovation?

A disruptive innovation is new development, commonly involving advancement in technology, that changes (disrupts) an existing market or potentially creates a new market, that leads to the replacement of an existing market and can often lead to well-known firms or products having a significant drop in sales.

Amazon

One of the biggest disruptors is online retailer, Amazon. The simplicity, range of products and the competitive pricing has made them very hard to ignore for consumers around the world.

They have contributed towards many leading companies struggling or failing. In the UK, the online retailer has been partly responsible for the failure of Woolworths, the struggles at music retailer HMV, and the department stores Debenhams and House of Fraser.

Focussing on the department stores, the unique selling point of the department store was the range of goods that were available under one roof, but now people have that range of goods – and more – available to them on one internet site or mobile phone application. Now, with the introduction of the virtual assistant in an ever increasing number of homes, consumers do not even need to open an app or go online – they can buy from Amazon by just saying a few words. This has been one of the key consideration for Amazon – finding ways to make the purchase easier for the consumer.

Amazon are now moving outside of retail and attempting to disrupt markets such as healthcare, logistics and even home security.

10.2 The role of technology in disruption

Technological advancements play a huge part in disruptive innovation – where a company or an individual identifies how technology can be used to make life easier. Sometimes the disruption is an unintended consequence of the technological advancement, sometimes the intended disruption doesn't materialise.

Disruption is not always the end

Disruption itself is nothing new, it has been happening for many years, it is just that the frequency of disruption is increasing, making it more of a concern for organisations.

When the television set first started appearing in people's homes in the late 1920s, and then again when home video was first introduced in the late 1970s and early 1980s, through VHS and Betamax videos, commentators were predicting the end of cinemas.

Cinemas still exist, because they have a unique selling point that cannot be replicated in the home, even with the continued improvement of the home experience. Cinemas have improved their offerings (including more comfortable seating, better sound, bigger screens) to remain relevant and competitive.

10.3 Considerations for successful disruption

Another concern regarding disruption, strategy and technology is choosing the right platform to take to market. The platform must be one that enables the disruptor to maximise the returns from their disruption. Some of the factors that influence the success of the disruptors are:

- **Simplicity** – the ease of ordering on Amazon is one of their reasons for success as a disruptor.

- **Resources** – using less of a scarce resource or generally being more environmentally friendly. For example LED light bulbs use significantly less power than incandescent light bulbs and last longer.

- **Cost** – a key consideration for most purchasers whether they are individual consumers or businesses and the reason that many battles are won. VHS became the industry standard in home video ahead of Betamax because it was cheaper – even though it was a technically inferior product.

- **Accessibility** – the ability to use a device or application makes it a more appealing alternative. For example, WhatsApp as a group messaging service, is available on all smart phones, while iMessage is only available on iOS (Apple) devices. Another example is Blu-ray becoming the industry standard for high quality images on DVD over Toshiba's HD DVD. One of the factors was that millions of people had the facility to play Blu-ray DVDs through their PlayStation while very few HD DVD players had been sold.

- **Quality** – doing something significantly better than it is currently done can also be a source of disruption.

Being out-disrupted

In the 1990s Sony were investing in production of a MiniDisc that was going to disrupt the CD market. The MiniDisc would be smaller than the CD, provide better quality audio and wouldn't skip if they were knocked (so would be more popular for use while exercising).

The MiniDisc provided all these things, but just as it was breaking into the market the MiniDisc was disrupted by digital music. MP3 & MP4 players such as Apple's iPod entered the market offering all benefits of the MiniDisc but also used less resources and increased accessibility by not needing a disc to play music. Instead all music was stored in files on the device giving access to hundreds or thousands of songs depending on the internal storage on the device.

MP3 and MP4 players have now been disrupted by increased connectivity and improved data access. Rather than have a certain number of songs stored on a device and pay for an individual song or album, consumers can pay a monthly fee to a music provider and stream (the simultaneous delivery and use of the media as opposed to downloading a media file, then playing it later) music through mobile telephone networks or using WiFi, giving them access to limitless songs at the touch of a screen.

Electronic maps

Another example of disruption is the market for maps. Previously companies who produced maps would regularly (at least annually) update and reprint all maps. Walkers, hikers, taxi drivers, haulage drivers, a huge variety of people and workers would require up to date information about routes and locations.

Technological advancements mean that most people now have an electronic device either specifically for this (Satellite navigation systems) or a device that provides a similar service (most smart phones). These electronic maps are live, so are updated constantly, and those used on the roads even include traffic updates.

At present map companies have not gone out of business. There is still a demand for paper maps as electronic data coverage is not comprehensive enough in most countries. Most map companies have changed their mode of operation to produce paper maps on demand, therefore reducing overhead costs and having a more flexible business model, but also using their brand name in the industry to launch applications for smart devices and making money from these applications.

Accept change and challenge the current

Disruption requires someone or some people to think differently, Apple has already appeared in this text book as an example of a company that has done things differently. Steve Jobs once said "You can't just ask customer what they want and then try to give that to them. By the time you get it built, they'll want something new."

Another example of someone who challenges current concepts is Elon Musk such as:

- how we pay for things – PayPal

- how we interact with computers – setting up a company called Neuralink that is working on developing a brain-computer interface

- transportation:

- electric cars – Tesla

- SpaceX – working on reducing the cost of transportation in space

- The Boring Company – working on an underground hyperlink between New York City, Philadelphia, Baltimore and Washington DC, with the aim of reducing the transport from New York to Washington DC to less than 30 minutes.

Elon Musk is prepared to try something new and do things differently. He probably accepts that not all of the companies he has set up will be successful, but he knows that one of the ways to be successful is to do things differently.

Test your understanding 15

Ebaps Ltd is an online sandwich delivery company, based on the outskirts of a major city. The company was set up in an attempt to disrupt the lucrative lunchtime sandwich market of the city centre and surrounding out of town business parks.

A customer goes onto the website before 10:30 in the morning and design their sandwich from the wide variety of choices including different types of bread, spreads, meats, cheeses and other additions like olives and sundried tomatoes. They enter their delivery postcode and select a timeslot for delivery to their office or potentially their home if they live within the postcode areas that Ebaps deliver to (this area includes all the lucrative city centre locations and surrounding area). The delivery is carried out by the company's own delivery drivers who are specifically employed on a part time basis by Ebaps.

As the range is breads and fillings are so extensive Ebaps have chosen to charge a premium for the product and service they are offering and each additional sandwich filling increases the costs. The premium is also required as they do not yet have economies of scale, and the choice of fillings they want to offer means their ingredients are quite expensive and have a short useful life before they go off.

After a promising start, the company started to have issues with production (incorrect fillings in the sandwiches) and delivery (delivery drivers being unable to find the offices). Sometimes, by the time the sandwiches were delivered, the customer had been hungry, unable to wait for their delivery slot and visited one of the many cafes, sandwich shops, supermarkets or takeaways in the city centre. When the sandwich arrived late or with a slight issue over the contents, the customer rejected it and refused to pay.

After redesigning their menu to streamline the choice, initiating an online payment process and reducing the delivery radius, the company ceased trading after 2 years.

What are reasons that the disruption failed?

Select ALL that apply.

A   The range of choice made ordering and meeting the order too complex.

B   The failure to develop a smartphone application for ease of ordering

C   High cost in comparison to the established competitors

D   Poor quality ingredients and choice

E   The traditional market was much more accessible

F   The target market was too small to make the business viable

Other types of disruption

In late 2019 and early 2020 a new strain of the coronavirus emerged known as Covid 19. At the time of writing this text book the longer terms implications of Covid 19 are being assessed, but it is safe to say that it has had significant impact businesses on a global scale.

It has already caused significant disruption in the professional exams and training industry. In response to the disruption CIMA launched remote testing allowing students to sit objective tests and case study exams from home.

Kaplan Financial followed government advice and when the UK Government advised to work from home if possible, all training that had previously taken place in a Kaplan training location went online. This was not an easy task and various departments had to work together to overcome many issues.

To illustrate this, there was a significant effort communicating with all students – to let them know not to go into a Kaplan training location – and getting all the textbooks – that were in Kaplan training locations ready for courses that were about to start – back to the Kaplan Publishing Warehouse in Wokingham and then sent out individually to each student at their correct home address.

The examples above are some short term challenges, but the pandemic has continued to influence the strategic discussions of the leadership team within Kaplan.

11 Scenario planning

Competence slip and organisational failure have been linked to the notion that management have failed to grasp the way that society is moving and have not conceptualised a possible future marketplace. It has been suggested that managers need a picture or scenario of where the world may be in a few years' time.

For example, how would an accountancy training college meet its objectives under the following circumstances?

(1) a merger between three accountancy bodies

(2) wide demand for computer-based training

(3) changes to immigration laws leading to a reduction in the number of overseas students.

11.1 The steps involved in scenario planning

Scenario planning involves the following steps:

(1) Identify high-impact, high-uncertainty factors in the environment.

Relevant factors and driving forces could be identified using a strategic analysis framework such as a PEST analysis. Once identified, factors need to be ranked according to importance and uncertainty.

For example, in the oil industry there may be a need to form a view of the business environment up to twenty-five years ahead and issues such as crude oil availability, price and economic conditions are critical.

(2) For each factor, identify different possible futures.

For example, oil companies would consider possible political uncertainty in oil-producing countries and the attitudes of future governments to climate change, pollution and energy policy.

Precision is not possible but developing a view of the future against which to evaluate and evolve strategies is important.

At 3M, for example, the general manager of each business unit is required annually to describe what his or her industry will look like in fifteen years.

(3) Cluster together different factors to identify various consistent future scenarios.

For example, two key factors may have been identified as:

(a) the threat of new entrants

(b) new legislation that may reduce the potential for profit.

Clearly, if new legislation is passed that reduces industry profit potential, then the likelihood of new entrants will fall.

This process usually results in between seven and nine mini-scenarios.

(4) 'Writing the scenario' – for the most important scenarios (usually limited to three), build a detailed analysis to identify and assess future implications.

As part of this, planners typically develop a set of optimistic, pessimistic and most likely assumptions about the impact of key variables on the company's future strategy.

The result of this detailed scenario construction should include:

-    financial implications – anticipated net profits, cash flow and net working capital for each of three versions of the future

-    strategic implications – possible opportunities and risks

-    the probability of occurrence, usually based on past experience.

(5)   For each scenario, identify and assess possible courses of action for the firm.

For example, Shell was the only major oil company to have prepared for the shock of the 1970s oil crisis through scenario planning and was able to respond faster than its competitors.

Some strategies make sense whatever the outcome, usually because they capitalise on or develop key strengths of the firm. For example, the firm concerned may have a global brand name and could seek to strengthen it by increasing its advertising spend in the short term.

However, in many cases, new resources and competences may be required for existing strategies to succeed. Alternatively, entirely new strategies may be required.

(6)   Monitor reality to see which scenario is unfolding.

(7)   Revise ("redeploy") scenarios and strategic options as appropriate.

Construction of scenarios

These need to be well thought out if they are to be effective. Hence the following should be considered: .

- use a team for a range of opinions and expertise

- identify time-frame, markets, products and budget

- stakeholder analysis – who will be the most influential in the future?

- trend analysis and uncertainty identification

- building of initial scenarios

- consider organisational learning implications

- identify research needs and develop quantitative models.

As mentioned above, Shell makes use of scenario planning extensively in order to predict future changes in the energy industry so that it can attempt to prepare for them.

 How useful is scenario planning?

The downside

- Costly and inaccurate – uses up substantial resources and time

- tendency for cultural distortion and for people to get carried away

- the risk of the self-fulfilling prophecy, i.e. thinking about the scenario may be the cause of it

- many scenarios considered will not actually occur.

The upside

- Focuses management attention on the future and possibilities
- encourages creative thinking
- can be used to justify a decision
- encourages communication via the participation process
- can identify the sources of uncertainty
- encourages companies to consider fundamental changes in the external environment.

Test your understanding 16

Which THREE of the following are disadvantages of scenario planning?

A   Bounded rationality

B   Reduced communication within the organisation

C   High cost

D   Risk of self-fulfilling prophecy

E   Wastes management time

F   Discourages creative thinking

Test your understanding 17 – UHJ (Case style)

UHJ is a multinational company, based in Europe, which manufactures aircraft components. This is a fast–moving, dynamic market with a large number of innovative competitors attempting to take UHJ's market share.

UHJ recently expanded into the North American market and set up a new division with two factories on the west coast. Since this expansion, however, the North American market has been hit by a significant economic downturn. This downturn has continued for the last year and analysts are uncertain of how far and when it will recover.

This has led to a large reduction in orders for aircraft components and has meant that the North American division of UHJ is now barely breaking even. Its future profitability for the next few years depends on a large order from a North American airline, VTH. VTH will announce a decision on this order next month.

UHJ has recently been approached with an offer by one of its rivals to buy the factories for what UHJ considers to be a fair price. UHJ wishes to avoid closing the factories as it feels that the closure costs and redundancy payouts that would be required would be extremely high.

Your manager has recently attended a seminar on scenario planning, but is concerned that she did not fully understand what is involved.

She has asked you to prepare for her some briefing notes, explaining what scenario planning is and how it would benefit UHJ.

Required:

Prepare the briefing notes as requested by your manager.

(10 minutes)

Test your understanding 18 – NSF – (Case style)

The National Sports Foundation (NSF) for Country Z is a public body which operates within the central government department for Sport and Culture. NSF's role is to support and develop a sporting environment across all communities in Country Z and to increase the number of people participating in sport.

NSF is mainly funded by the Government of Country Z. Up until 2010, it employed several hundred staff and also relied upon thousands of volunteers throughout Country Z to run the various sporting clubs and associations, such as amateur football clubs and children's out-of-school sports activities. Following cuts in Government funding in 2010, NSF's level of staffing was considerably reduced. This resulted in NSF relying more on private sector partnerships and volunteers.

Until three years ago, the economic, social and technological environment in Country Z had been relatively stable, with NSF receiving guaranteed funding from the Government and the numbers of sports participants and volunteers being reasonably predictable. Therefore, the Board of NSF has not considered frequent and regular environmental analysis to be necessary.

NSF's Board has been taken by surprise by the changes that have occurred in the environment in the last three years. In addition to Government funding cuts, local administrative government bodies have been forced to sell off local community sports grounds and facilities to raise finance. Furthermore, the level of financial and operational support provided by private sector organisations has also declined due to similar economic challenges. Increasingly stricter regulations and rules have resulted in fewer volunteers throughout the country.

The rapid growth in technology-based entertainment products has been blamed for the reduction in the number of young people participating in sports. In addition, NSF has failed to consider the changing demographics and ageing population of Country Z and the impact that this will have on sports participation in future years.

The Chair of the Board of NSF has recently attended several conferences where the value of undertaking thorough 'environmental analysis' has been discussed. The Chair now realises that there is a serious gap in NSF's knowledge about the environment in which it operates and considers that if NSF is to continue successfully in the future then it must improve its foresight to actively plan for the future.

The Chair has therefore contacted you and asked you to produce some briefing notes to help apply this knowledge to NSF. The email is shown below:

To: A. Waterman

From: C. H. Airman

Date: 15/08/XX

Subject: Scenario planning for NSF

Hi A,

Hope you are well. As you know I have recently attended a number of conferences on foresight and scenario planning and I want to try and decide how they could be applied to NSF. I know this is a topic you have studied recently and I would like you to outline a few things for me.

I need you to analyse each of the key stages that would be included in a scenario planning process which could be used by NSF.

I'm going into a meeting with the other board members about this in about thirty minutes, so please email back by then.

Kind regards

C.H.

Required:

Draft the email requested by the Chair.

(30 minutes)

11.2 Game theoretic approaches to strategic planning

A key aspect of strategic planning is anticipating the actions of competitors and acting accordingly. Game theory has been used to great effect in this matter. The results are derived using mathematical modelling, although the mathematics are not necessary for this subject.

Game theoretic approaches to strategic planning

Game theory

In many markets it is important to anticipate the actions of competitors as there is a high interdependency between firms – i.e. the results of my choice depend to some extent on your choices as well.

Game theory is concerned with the interrelationships between the competitive moves of a set of competitors and, as such, can be a useful tool to analyse and understand different scenarios.

Game theory has two key principles:

(1) Strategists can take a rational, informed view of what competitors are likely to do and formulate a suitable response.

(2) If a strategy exists that allows a competitor to dominate us, then our priority is to eliminate that strategy.

Despite the simplicity of these principles, game theory has become very complex.

Many of the bidders for third-generation mobile phone licences in the early 2000s, and the governments auctioning those licences, used game theory principles. In the UK this resulted in over a hundred rounds of bidding and revenue raised of £22 billion.

Example

The most famous example of game theory is the "Prisoner's dilemma" game. This can be applied to companies as follows:

Suppose there are two companies, A and B, who between them dominate a market. Both are considering whether to increase their marketing spend from its current low level.

- If just one firm decides to increase its spend, then it will see its returns increase.

- However, if both increase the spend then both end up with lower returns than at present.

These could be shown by the following pay-off table (figures = net profit).

		Competitor A	
		High spend	Low spend
Competitor B	High spend	A = 5 B = 5	A = 3 B = 10
	Low Spend	A = 10 B = 3	A = 7 B = 7

Viewed individually the dominant strategy for both firms is to invest heavily. Taking A's perspective:

- If B does not increase spending, then the best plan of action for A would have been to invest heavily.

- If B does increase spending, then the best plan of action for A would have been to invest heavily.

However, the end result ("equilibrium") is likely to be that both firms increase spending and thus end up worse off than if they had both kept their marketing spend at its current low level. Some degree of collusion to keep the spend low would benefit both parties.

Note: The original version of the prisoners' dilemma.

Suppose two accomplices perpetrate a crime together and are later arrested by the police.

Unfortunately the police have insufficient evidence for a conviction, and, having separated both suspects, visit each of them to offer the chance of betraying their accomplice. Suppose the possible outcomes are as follows:

- If one testifies (defects from the other) for the prosecution against the other and the other remains silent (cooperates with the other), the betrayer goes free and the silent accomplice receives the full 10-year sentence.

- If both remain silent, both prisoners are sentenced to only six months in jail for a minor charge.

- If each betrays the other, each receives a five-year sentence.

Each prisoner must choose to betray the other or to remain silent. Each one is assured that the other would not know about the betrayal before the end of the investigation.

How should the prisoners act?

The unique equilibrium for this game is that rational choice leads the two players to both play defect, even though each player's individual reward would be greater if they both played cooperatively.

Application

A common application of this is to price wars. Price wars between two evenly matched competitors usually results in lower profits for all concerned and no change in market share. No one wins, except the customer.

12 Stress testing

12.1 What is stress testing?

A stress test in the business world is a way of analysing a business to consider how well it could cope in difficult conditions. When a business is doing well it can be difficult to identify how it would fare if there was a sudden downturn in the economic environment.

Bank of England

The Bank of England conducts annual stress tests on each of the major UK based banks.

The stress tests were brought in as a result of the financial crisis in 2008-2009, and the tests are designed to simulate scenarios that are similar or worse than what happened in the financial crisis.

Some of the scenarios used in 2018 were:

- Property prices falling by 33%

- Interest rates rising to 4%

- UK GDP falling by almost 5%

The results are published and if a bank fails the stress test – as well as the reputation damage it would cause – it may be required to reduce dividend payments to shareholders to improve its capital position.

12.2 How to stress test

In terms of a business conducting its own stress test, Robert Simons, a Harvard business professor, suggested there are 7 questions that organisations should try to answer to check if their business is robust enough. The questions break down into 4 keys areas:

Prioritisation

- Who is your primary customer?

- How do your core values prioritise shareholders, employees, and customers?

Measurement

- What critical performance variables are you tracking?

- What strategic boundaries have you set?

Productivity

- How are you generating creative tension?

- How committed are your employees to helping each other?

Flexibility

- What strategic uncertainties keep you awake at night?

Stress testing – 4 key areas

Prioritisation

Simons' view is that people who work for the organisation cannot be customers, and to refer to any internal people/departments as a customer means the organisation will lose focus on the true purpose.

Once your primary customer is established the majority of resources should be used to make sure the company is delivering for their needs.

In a similar way, the core values of a business must be clearly defined and statements that list multiple desirable actions don't work. There is no right stakeholder to prioritise, but a company must decide if it's the shareholder, the customer or the employees that come first, and make sure their behaviours are then consistent with this.

Measurement

There are various well known saying around this: "If it matters, measure it", "what gets measured gets done".

The key is not to have too many measures on any scorecard but to identify the key factors that drive performance and focus on those.

The boundaries refer to keeping focus on the parameters that are important and not to drift away from these, by telling employees where to focus or where not to. Where to focus is often viewed as the safer option, while where not to focus allows more creativity.

Productivity

The reference to creative tension is unusual, but the idea is that disagreement challenges the norms and can produce different ideas and outcomes. Diverse opinions and ideas lead to new ways to do things. Often idea generation is often associated with a positive outlook, but it can actually be the opposite. A positive outlook may be lead to people insisting that everything will eventually work out, but a pessimistic view that things are not working, can often lead to a positive change.

Commitment to each other, links back to the theory of why organisations exist – that working effectively together helps us achieve our goals more easily than working alone. If employees feel that they are being treated fairly and trust each other they will achieve greater results.

Flexibility

Finally, as with any control system, flexibility is important – being able to change approach in the ever changing world in which businesses operate: customer preferences change, technology is moving at an incredible pace, at some point your business model will become outdated.

Any organisation must be willing to adapt to the new requirements placed on it. To achieve this everyone must be focussed on what it happening in the external environment and feedback anything unusual so that action can be taken.

Stress testing

Who is your primary customer?

M&S have always tried to appeal to a range of age groups, but M&S are struggling to keep pace with all the different clothing options available. Shoppers are now confused by their range of brands and don't know which brands are aimed at them. Critics of M&S suggest this is one of their biggest problems and that to turnaround their recent decline they need to clearly define who they are selling to.

How do your core values prioritise shareholders, employees, and customers?

Shareholders

Many companies state in their mission that their purpose is to maximise shareholder wealth through the industry they operate in. Companies such as Kerr-McGee Corporation (an energy company in America bought by Anadarko another American energy company) and financial services company Citigroup are both examples of companies who make reference to only one stakeholder in their mission with a clear prioritisation of shareholders.

Employees

Virgin founder, Richard Branson, believes that the employee should be a company's number one priority. He says that if the employee is happy and proud of the brand they work for, then that will show in the work that they do, so the customer will get excellent service. They will therefore also be happy and more likely to return and that leads to shareholder satisfaction too.

Customers

Google's mission statement since it started in 1998 has been "to organise the world's information and make it universally accessible and useful." Serving the end users has been at the heart of what Google does from the day it was founded and is one of the core reasons for its success.

What critical performance variables are you tracking?

After the rise of various performance management tools, such as the balanced scorecard, emphasised the importance of collecting a range a data to assess performance, companies have gone metric crazy. Now the advice is to focus on a few key metrics. DHL are an example of where the board became frustrated by the amount of time spent reviewing operational data without any real benefit coming from it. They analysed what stakeholders were really interested in and streamlined the review process.

What strategic boundaries have you set?

Apple are well known for setting strategic boundaries. In 1998 Steve Jobs reduced the product portfolio by over 70% so the company could focus on doing a few things very well. The results were incredible, from a company struggling and making losses in 1997, Jobs turned Apple into the biggest global brand. He famously said, "Focus means saying no to the hundred other good ideas."

How are you generating creative tension?

The matrix structure is an example of how a company can develop creative tension, having dual management means extra pressure on an employee to deliver. Many people find that pressure can help them perform and if managed well it can help companies succeed. Many companies have used the matrix structure successfully – for example P&G and Kraft.

How committed are your employees to helping each other?

While Henry Ford gets all the credit in business strategy textbooks and articles, he had a team working with him. Clarence Avery was the lead developer, Peter Martin the head of assembly and Charles Sorensen was the assistant to Peter Martin. All these people combined to help create the assembly line that the model T car so famously came from.

What strategic uncertainties keep you awake at night?

When Alan Mulally became the CEO at Ford in 2006, Ford were heading towards a $17 billion loss. He implemented a colour coding system for weekly meetings with his executives. As normal, green meant good, yellow meant new issues, red meant problems. Mulally couldn't understand why all the charts were green at the first meeting as a company heading for a $17 billion loss could not all be green. One unit head put up a red chart and highlighted an issue he was having in Canada. Mulally applauded the unit head's honesty and then discovered other areas were having the same issues. Through collaboration they were able to find a solution, and that changed the culture at Ford to one where people shared issues to find solutions.

12.3 Stress testing for nonfinancial companies

This section started with an example about the Bank of England, linked into the financial crash of 2008. As the example suggests it is now common place for companies in the financial sector like banks and mortgage lenders to use stress testing. It is less prevalent in companies outside financial sector.

These nonfinancial companies are not immune from risks and therefore could also benefit from stress testing too. One of the biggest current risks to organisations is related to cyber security (discussed in more detail later), but the risks of cyber-attacks are not limited to banks, or financial services organisations; any company with an online presence can be affected.

The failure of a company, whoever they may be, can have a knock on effect to society (through job losses) and other companies (lost customers or loss of a key part of the supply chain). The process would be the same, regardless of whether it was a financial or nonfinancial organisation.

The need for stress testing

Stress testing can play a strategic role. The results of a stress test can indicate why strategy may not be successfully realised or implemented, it can identify areas of inefficiency and it can make a business more 'agile' and adaptable to changes in its business environment.

Stress testing allows risks to be quantified. Many businesses might be able to state that sales will fall if the economy were to move into a recession, but a company who has stressed tested its budgets for such an event would be able to say not only by how much sales would fall, but also to explain the impact on profits and cash as well as the company's plans to minimise the impact and adjust its strategies.

Stress tests may be imposed on the business by lenders. If, say, a company is borrowing money in order to finance a new project and the loan will last 10 years, a lender may want to know how the company will cope with a rise in interest rates or if the project returns are only half of what the company are expecting.

There may also be infrequent expenditure that is not accounted for in the budget. For example, if an employee leaves and has to be replaced there will be costs involved in recruitment, training and lost productivity. These are often not planned for in the budget but should be stress tested. In simple terms, the organisation can then set cash aside for these instances of infrequent and sometimes unexpected elements of expenditure. This is preferable to having all 'available' cash tied up in investments leading to a short-term shortage of cash available to meet the extra burden placed on the organisation.

Stress testing is not just testing for the survival of the organisation. It may be that an organisation expects sales to increase by 40% this year and has therefore put in place an employee recruitment programme throughout the year. If sales fail to increase by 40% the company may not go out of business, but it will need to consider what to do with any staff recruited or how to delay or cancel any outstanding recruitment. Warning signs need to be identified and plans put in place for when these warning signs are triggered.

If, for example, sales fail to increase at all in the first quarter, then it is unlikely that annual sales will rise by 40%. So the company could place all second quarter recruitment on hold and look for ways to redeploy any staff already recruited (which might in itself create growth elsewhere in the business).

Considering these events prior to the budget launch will allow the company to more quickly and effectively react to the stresses placed on the budget. This proactivity is much better than being reactive to changes in the organisation's environment. In choosing to outline the ways in which stresses might affect the company's position, more informed decisions can be made about where it is the company's focus should lie.

Sources of business stress

There are many sources of stress that may be placed on an organisation (both internally and externally) such as:

- technology which makes the product obsolete or uncompetitive

- changes in customer or consumer tastes

- the economy changes from a boom to a recession (or vice versa)

- rivals creating a better product or finding ways to stand out better to customers

- a cybersecurity attack

- a workforce strike

- failure of or faults in production systems.

This list is not comprehensive and every organisation will face many more risks than these. But the list should illustrate that the stresses can come from both internal and external events.

Organisations should be constantly assessing these stresses and then testing their budgets to evaluate their ability to cope with any or all of them at any point in time. Stress testing will also identify correlations between events – how, for example, changes in the strength of the economy might also impact on the relative strength of a country's currencies. The impact of both events happening concurrently might then be stress tested.

Stress testing goes beyond simple 'what-if' analysis which often focuses on changing one or two variables in the budget. Stress testing evaluates the impact of entire scenarios on an organisation. For example, a company that exports to foreign markets might assess how a change in currency movements could impact on its business. The currency fluctuations may impact on the company sales price, but it may also impact on the entire domestic economy so that unemployment rates change, consumer spending levels change or inflation rates change. These changes could impact on a number of variables in the budget system such as sales volume, wage rates, import costs etc.

Stress testing and software

Stress tests are usually computer-generated simulation models that test hypothetical scenarios. Major organisations will have developed their own software and systems which tailor the tests to their situations. But smaller organisations should also be stress testing their budgets even if it is using bespoke and simple software such as Excel.

The scenarios that are planned for and tested for should be plausible. Stress testing can be a complicated, time-consuming and expensive exercise. It is therefore important that risks and events are evaluated for plausibility before the stress testing process is initiated. The resources available for the testing must also be considered – so that smaller organisations might only test 5 or 6 events whereas larger organisations might test up to 20 events.

Tesco: Covid-19 response

Tesco and other supermarkets in the UK were widely praised for their response to the Covid-19 pandemic in 2020.

Tesco CEO, Dave Lewis, attributed their ability to deal with the restrictions imposed on working in the UK during the pandemic to a "doomsday exercise" the company carried out in 2016.

The management exercise was based on the idea that the head office in Welwyn Garden City where around 6,000 employees are based, would have to shut down completely. At the time it was considered "ridiculous" and "extreme", but as it turns out the exercise showed incredible foresight.

During the period where the UK government advised that people should work from home where possible and only leave their house for very limited reasons there were fewer than 30 people (less than 1% of the workforce) working at the Tesco head office, the CEO being one of them.

As a result of the management exercise carried out in 2016, the organisation already had all of the equipment in place for remote working and some of the teams had been using video calling applications to "gather staff together" remotely for two years or more.

In mid-February, before restrictions were introduced in the UK, Tesco had already started to implement their plans to maintain their food supply in preparation for what they anticipated to happen. Some of the changes introduced included:

- one-way systems in stores
- physically distanced queueing
- protective equipment for in store workers
- Tesco almost doubled capacity for delivery and click and collect in a 6-week period

The way shoppers behaved changed significantly too, Lewis commented that "transactions were down 48% but basket size (the amount bought in a transaction) had more than doubled" as shoppers were looking to reduce the number of times they went to a supermarket in line with government guidance.

Tesco were well placed to adapt to the changes caused by the pandemic because they had incorporated into their planning extreme events, which many thought were unlikely to happen, showing the benefit of stress testing.

Test your understanding 19

Lerlaid is a local fruit and vegetable delivery business specialising in supplying the hospitality sector and has built up a very loyal customer base of cafes, pubs and restaurants in the surrounding area. The managing director is very proud of the quality of produce that Lerlaid supplies and believes this is key to their success so far.

The managing director is concerned by the increasing incidents of extreme situations impacting the world and trading conditions, from ecological factors like climate change and extreme weather through to cyber attacks and sharp economic changes. As such, she would like to carry out a stress test on the business model that Lerlaid use.

She is happy with the prioritisation of customer satisfaction through quality produce, she knows how hard her employees work, and while they don't always agree with each other, robust exchanges often lead to improved performance.

Which of the four key areas of stress testing still need to be covered?

Select ALL that apply.

A   Flexibility

B   Productivity

C   Confidentiality

D   Advocacy

E   Measurement

F   Prioritisation

13 Summary

By the end of this chapter, you should be able to discuss:

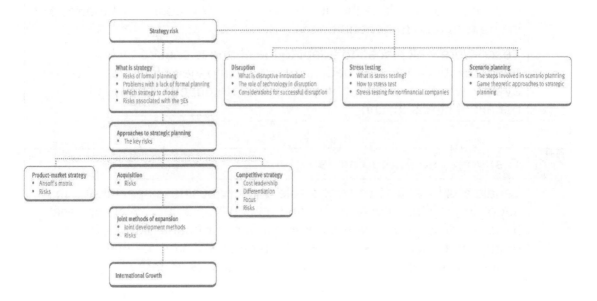

Test your understanding answers

Test your understanding 1

The correct answers are A, C and D.

Test your understanding 2

The correct answers are C and E

It will be very difficult to forecast demand in a dynamic environment such as this and particularly so when a company is just starting out.

They are planning on continuing with the same plan for 4 years, this is a long time, particularly in a rapidly changing environment and the strategy may fail to take advantage of technological advancements.

A, B and D are both risks of the less formal approach to planning,

Test your understanding 3

The correct answers are A, C and D

A and C, despite their informal approach to planning, they are being rigid in only selling though their website. Competitors are likely to offer an app for mobile devices offering a more user friendly interface than having to open the web page each time customers want to print an image.

D, because of the lack of planning they may find it hard to meet large orders, and upset some corporate customers. Also they may not be able to get finance from a bank to expand into larger corporate sales opportunities.

B they don't try to forecast with this approach.

E is a risk of a formal planning approach

F they have a very flexible approach to products

Test your understanding 4

The correct answers are C, E and F

The basement location sounds inappropriate for a premium coffee shop, it will be hard to see, and some people will be unable to access it. The major chains are closer to the commuters and busy commuters will generally choose convenience and not walk far for a coffee.

A is incorrect as there are high numbers of both independent and chain coffee stores in most cities like the one described.

B is incorrect as the area appears to have excellent footfall, it is just the specific location (basement) that limits the footfall.

D is incorrect as customers rarely complain about friendly, efficient service.

Test your understanding 5 – HAA – (Case Style)

Meeting notes

Current approach to strategy

HAA is currently using the rational model to develop its strategies. This involves taking a logical, step-by-step approach. HAA has clearly done this by undertaking such detailed planning, including strategic analysis of the market and the production of detailed operating plans.

The key advantage of such an approach to HAA is the level of understanding it will give them in the new market. They are currently not used to operating in the European market, so the initial strategic analysis they have performed will be invaluable. It will give them a picture of their own capabilities as well as the European market they will be entering.

Risks

However, the new European market is fast-moving and the rational approach has a tendency to be rigid and slow to react to changes in the external environment. This means that HAA could go in with a sound strategy but because it is following a three year plan, the strategy could become outdated very quickly.

In particular the European market is more high-tech and the level of innovation by competitors means that HAA will have to be prepared to quickly change its approach to deal with unexpected developments in the market. As the company has produced a detailed operational plan, this may stifle their ability to innovate at the same rate as their competitors.

In addition, given the lack of experience that HAA has in the European market, any detailed forecasts it produces may prove to be unreliable. This may cause it to make inaccurate decisions based on flawed market predictions. If these forecast are not revisited and flexed based on the information they gain as they develop into the new market, the company could become uncompetitive in this new market place very quickly.

Test your understanding 6

The correct answer is C

Effectiveness looks at the outputs of the organisation. As H has achieved its goal of a 75% pass rate, it has been effective.

Economy looks at the level of inputs – in this case, inputs have risen by 3% in the year (above inflation), but the efficiency with which H has used these inputs has fallen significantly. These factors would indicate a lack of efficiency and economy.

Test your understanding 7

The correct answer is C

J has identified a key resource or capability – its strong reputation. It is now looking for new ways to capitalise on this. The risk with this approach is losing touch with what the market wants.

Test your understanding 8 – GYU – (Case Style)

There are three main approaches to strategic planning that GYU could take.

Traditional

This would involve GYU examining its key stakeholders and developing objectives that will meet their needs. The two key stakeholders in the scenario are GYU's customers and shareholders. The shareholders are clearly upset with the reduction in their dividend and will expect GYU to reverse this in coming years. The customers will be looking for handsets with more features and that are less 'dated'.

Risks

Unfortunately, while these are important objectives, they may be difficult for GYU to accomplish in the short term. Given the poor level of its finances, it may struggle to either increase dividends or invest enough in research and development to update its product line.

Market-led

This will involve the examination of GYU's competitors and market. Doing so should help GYU to ensure that it is competitive in what is a very fast-paced market.

Risks

While this appears to have been a weakness of GYU's to date (given the fact that it seems to have fallen so far behind many of its competitors), it may be inherently difficult to achieve in the mobile phone handset market. As the market is changing so rapidly, it may be difficult for GYU to accurately predict future trends and create appropriate strategies.

Resource-based

This involves GYU focusing its business strategies on areas that it is good at. For GYU, its key area of skill is in the production of mobile handset software. It is acknowledged to be the market leader in this area and it appears to be very important to customers. Any future strategies should therefore be based around leveraging this area of skill.

For example, if it feels unable to produce handsets that are competitive, GYU could consider focusing on producing software which could then be licensed on other manufacturer's handsets. If this is a big enough market, this could help GYU to turn its business around.

Risks

The issue with this approach is that the company starts to lose connection with the customers and how they operate the software. They may begin to create applications that appeal to the software developers but that the customer doesn't understand how to use or doesn't want the features that have been developed.

Conclusion

Based on the information provided, the resource–based approach seems most likely to be best for GYU, as long as they maintain a focus on how the consumer feels about our software.

Test your understanding 9

The correct answers are E and F.

W is currently trying to gain competitive advantage by using its brand name to differentiate it from its rivals. Marketing costs can be higher with this approach and differentiators are often susceptible to tough economic conditions.

A is a risk of being a cost leader

B and D are risks of focussing

C is a benefit of differentiation.

Test your understanding 10

The correct answer is A, C and E

Its size prevents it from achieving the economies of scale of its larger rivals, so it cannot compete on cost leadership.

Y's current customers seem to mainly be interested in price, so a differentiation strategy and any marketing based on that approach would not be worthwhile.

Finally, there seems to only be one niche market that Y has identified – that of home workers. However this is a relatively small part of the market and it appears to be well served by the several existing companies.

Overall, this is a very difficult market for Y as it will find it difficult to find a way to outcompete its rivals.

Test your understanding 11 – (Case Study)

Report

To: J. O'Leary, FD

From: Senior manager

Date: 16/09/XX

Title: Risks of AVA first class offering

Introduction

Porter argued that organisations could adopt one of three main strategies in order to gain competitive advantage – focus, differentiation and cost leadership. This report will use Porter's model to analyse AVA's strategies, particularly the first class one.

Current strategy in AVA

AVA has previously adopted a classic cost leadership approach. It has removed a number of 'extras' from the service it provides to customers – such as excess leg room, direct customer service and seat reservations.

AVA has done this in order to keep its costs low. These savings can then be passed onto the customer in the form of low ticket prices, driving up demand and enabling AVA to outcompete its rivals.

Cost leadership requires the price elasticity of the market to be high – in other words if AVA offers a low price for its product it needs to be able to generate a high volume of sales. This will allow it to cover its high fixed costs in spite of the relatively low contribution made by each ticket sale.

The risk with this approach is that as the economy in country L has returned to growth, it is likely that customers will have more disposable income and therefore be willing to spend more money on flights with additional features – such as increased leg room. AVA has started to see the effect of this as its passenger numbers start to fall.

First class strategy in AVA

AVA's proposed approach is to offer a section of 'first class' seats to customers at the front of each airplane which provide more leg room and free food and drink, as well as better customer service.

This seems to be an attempt to move into a differentiation approach, where AVA will be starting to charge a premium for some of its flights due to additional features that wealthier clients may value. For this to work, AVA must be able to offer a real alternative to the existing first class airline services – either through the actual services offered to its customers or through its brand name and image. The move into first class flights would help to improve AVA's profitability as first class tickets command higher margins than AVA's standard tickets.

Expansion into the first class market would provide a limited amount of diversification for AVA. Its low cost approach would seem to be struggling as customers are able to afford better quality flights and this problem is likely to continue as the economy grows.

Risks of the proposal

There are a number of practical problems with the proposals.

Firstly, AVA may be struggling to attract more affluent customers as the new first class model is inconsistent with its brand image. AVA has a poor reputation in the market for comfort and reliability – things that are likely to strongly appeal to first class customers. This may confuse both markets, alienating the declining core market, worried that they are not getting the cheapest deal available as they may be concerned they are partially funding the first class passengers. It would also be unlikely a first class passenger would choose to pay a high price for any AVA offering based on the current brand and reputation of the firm.

In addition, the first class market is already dominated by several major airlines that have experience of catering to the needs of this market segment. Unless AVA is able to find some way of offering extra services or features that these rivals don't offer, it is unlikely that it will ever outperform them in the market.

Staffing considerations are an issue for AVA too, staff may feel that their position is under threat as they joined to offer a particular service for AVA. They may worry that this will mean that new staff will be recruited to serve the customers who buy the new first class service, meaning less standard staff are needed, and may start looking for alternative employment.

The company may also experience cultural problems – staff who are required to serve both types of customers on a flight may find it difficult to differentiate their behaviour and offer an excellent service to some customers but not others, leading to complaints from first class customer who are not getting the premium treatment they expect.

Offering the service on its more popular routes will also reduce the availability of seats for the core market, these popular routes may be suffering less reduction than some other flights and they may reduce the sales to the core market further.

Conclusion

Overall by proceeding with its first class strategy, AVA risks becoming 'stuck in the middle' and failing to compete effectively within the market. It may therefore wish to consider an alternative plan which is more in keeping with its current strategy.

Test your understanding 12

The correct answer is B

T has two major requirements – consistency with the existing H stores and the need to retain control of H and its operations.

Licensing another organisation to trade as H would not allow T to maintain control over the day to day operations of the new stores.

Strategic alliances and joint ventures, by their nature, would require T to form partnerships with third party organisations who would work together (or set up a jointly owned company) to operate the new H stores. Again, this would lead to H losing control and being forced to compromise with the other organisation(s) she had entered an alliance with.

Franchising would allow H to control many of the day to day operations of the new stores and would also enable her to still make the key strategic decisions for the organisation. The franchisee would have to work within the preset guidelines in the franchise agreement, which may include central training of staff and supplier selection.

Test your understanding 13 – (integration question)

(1)　A franchise arrangement would work well here. There is more than just manufacturing involved – there is the whole retail offering, and entering into franchise agreements would be a quick, effective way of expanding.

(2)　Unless the oil companies felt that, because of their size, there was no need for joint research, development, marketing and lobbying, a strategic alliance of some sort could be useful. Research costs and findings could be shared. Together they could bring powerful pressure to bear on governments to, for example, allow more generous time scales for implementation of the new technology. Alternatively, the new energy technology could be developed within a joint venture organisation.

(3)　Almost certainly, this company would expand by licensing local brewing companies to make and distribute its product.

Test your understanding 14

The correct answer is D

YH is currently manufacturing (or growing) the bulk of its products overseas to meet demand, with some of this produce even finding its way back to country N. This would suggest an overseas manufacture strategy.

YH does grow some of its fruit in its home country, but given that this constitutes a minority of its goods, it cannot be convincingly matched to an exporting strategy.

As YH does not obviously coordinate value adding activities between its overseas facilities (they are all similar growing and processing facilities in each country) it is not a multinational. The fact that it still has a home country in which it is based would indicate that it is not a transnational.

Test your understanding 15

The correct answers are A, C and E

Key considerations in disruption are simplicity, cost and accessibility. The range of options made choosing a sandwich more complicated for the customer and increased the likelihood of mistakes in making the sandwiches. The high volume of existing competition with simple fillings and lower selling prices made the traditional market more accessible ad appealing.

The lack of smartphone application is not an issue as most of the target market would have access to a computer in their work.

While quality is a key factor in successful disruption the quality and choice of ingredients were not the issue, but mistakes in production meant customers were put off using the service again.

The lunchtime sandwich market is large and very already very competitive so it wasn't the size of the market.

Test your understanding 16

The correct answers are A, C and D

Test your understanding 17 – UHJ (Case Study)

Briefing Notes

To: Manager

From: UHJ Senior Manager

Date: Today

Title: Scenario planning

UHJ is faced with a dynamic and rapidly changing environment in the North American market. Scenario planning is the detailed and credible analysis of how the business environment might develop in the future, based on various environmental influences and drivers for change. The target for this analysis should be areas where the organisation considers there to be a high degree of uncertainty or opportunity.

Scenario planning would therefore enable UHJ to calculate and examine various possible strategic outcomes.

For example, UHJ would be able to examine the possible impact of the economic downturn lasting for several years, or alternatively beginning to reverse immediately. It could also compare combinations of events, such as:

- the sale of the division, followed by an economic recovery, but the loss of the VTH order

- the retention of the division, followed by a continuation of the economic downturn, along with the acquisition of the VTH order

and so on.

This approach will have two key benefits:

(1)   It will help the directors of UHJ to see 'worst case' scenarios. Should the North American economy suffer a prolonged downturn and the division lose the VTH order, there could be a significant impact on the division, along with the rest of the company. This may help the directors to decide how much of a risk maintaining the North American division is and whether it would be best to sell immediately.

(2)   Scenario planning will also help the directors to anticipate potential problems with, or opportunities from, the North American division. For example, if UHJ wants to sell the division and the VTH order is lost, the price it achieves from the sale may well be much lower than is currently on offer. Alternatively, the market may recover in the near future and the sale of the division now may compromise UHJ's future growth prospects.

Test your understanding 18 – NSF – (Case style)

To: C.H. Airman

From: A. Waterman

Date: 15/08/XX

Subject: Scenario planning for NSF

Dear C.H.

Thank you for your email.

Scenario planning, as a tool, will provide NSF with a better understanding of what could happen in the environment in which it operates and help to minimise surprises.

The stages could be as follows:

(1) Define the scope of the scenario

NSF will need to decide what knowledge is most important to it. Consideration of its most important market segments and customers and the time frame it wishes to consider (i.e. how far into the future) should be paramount. It will need to decide whether the scenario is to be focussed on a specific issue e.g. the impact of the technology on the participation of children or a more blue sky approach where it asks a question such as; 'what is the future of community participation in sport in Country Z?'

(2) Identify and map the major stakeholders

A consideration of who the main stakeholders are in the sporting environment should be undertaken and how they are likely to drive change over the period under consideration. For NSF this would most probably include the Government of Country Z (as the main funder), its volunteers and its customers. All of these stakeholders would need to be evaluated in terms of their impact and power to influence the future activities of NSF.

(3) Identify the basic trends and uncertainties affecting the business

In assessing the trends and factors that would be identified in an environmental analysis and considering how they may change in the future, NSF would most probably want to focus upon the technological advances and the increasing use of the internet by children and young adults and its effect upon sport participation. Since it is very dependent upon the Government for its revenue it would also consider the trends in the economy which would affect its income. Also the changing demographics would be a major consideration for NSF.

(4)   Identify the key trends and uncertainties

Of the basic trends that have been identified NSF would need to decide which are the key uncertainties. These trends and uncertainties will be the 'drivers for change' which will require contingency planning activities and will shape the future of the industry. In the case of NSF this would certainly include the declining Government funding and societal and demographic changes. These will be the main drivers forcing change in NSF.

(5)   Construct initial scenario themes, or skeleton outlines

Possible future scenarios should then be created by forming the key trends and uncertainties into coherent themes. Usually two alternative scenarios are produced but more can be identified if necessary. NSF might develop one scenario where the economy continues to be depressed and funding continues to decline with sport becoming less important to society. This would be the 'negative' scenario. The alternative 'positive' scenario might feature a booming economy with many members of society both volunteering and actively participating in sport activities.

(6)   Check for plausibility and internal consistency

Effective scenarios are both internally consistent and plausible. This means that different directions that the trends have taken in the scenario could logically happen together and the events described could happen within the timescale chosen.

(7)   Develop learning scenarios

The next stage would be to 'flesh out' the scenarios so that they become full descriptions of the sector and conditions that are expected to prevail in the future timeframe. This is often done by writing a detailed piece of narrative. The managers of NSF would need to consider the detailed aspects of each scenario in terms of impact upon NSF's staff, possible plans for re-training, more detailed financial analysis and an overall view of the sporting environment in Country Z.

Note: There is no one perfect method of producing scenario plans and the following answer is one of a number of ways in which scenarios can be developed. Candidates will be rewarded for appropriate stages which are applied to the NSF.

I hope this helps you for your meeting – if you need any more information, please let me know.

Kind regards

A.

Test your understanding 19

The correct answer is E

The strategic uncertainties that keep the managing director awake at night are the increasing frequency of extreme events. This would fit into flexibility.

Prioritisation has been dealt with by the clear primary customer and focus on quality produce.

Productivity has been considered through the willingness of staff to discuss difficult issues and seek an appropriate resolution.

Confidentiality and advocacy are not part of the four key areas that Robert Simons identified.

That leaves measurement as not having been covered.

Reputational risks

Chapter learning objectives

Lead	Component
A2. Risk exposure	(c) Analyse the interaction of different risks
A3. Discuss ways of managing risk	(d) Discuss risk analytics.
B2. Evaluate the sources and impact of reputational risks	(a) Evaluate sources of reputational risk (b) Evaluate impact of reputational risk on strategy.

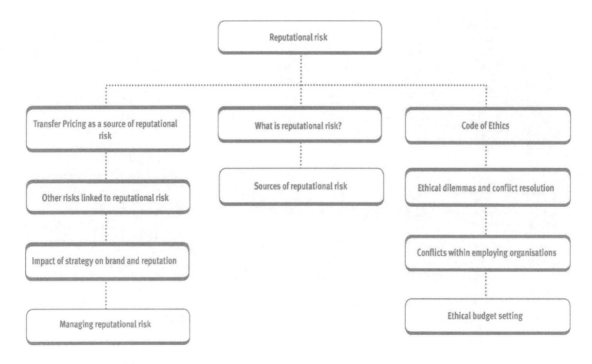

1 Reputational risk

1.1 Introduction

In this chapter we look at risks involved with the reputation of an organisation and what an organisation can do to mitigate them. Before we look at the risks involved, we will first look at what we mean by reputation.

Reputation is defined as the beliefs or opinions that are generally held about someone or something.

1.2 What is reputational risk?

Reputational risk is therefore the likelihood of losses occurring due to a deterioration in the belief or opinion held about someone or something.

Reputation is an area that organisations are increasing their focus upon, partially because there have been some high profile instances of reputational damage in recent times, and partially because of the rise in social media giving more customers a voice.

Reputational damage can be caused by many factors such as dishonesty, incompetence, activities that do unnecessary harm to the environment or unethical behaviour. It can be caused by an individual or by the behaviour of a company as a whole.

Johnson & Johnson: good and bad reputation

In 1982, Johnson & Johnson were widely praised for their handling of a series of deaths that were caused by poisoned Tylenol (a product they make).

The CEO made the decision to recall all Tylenol products. The decision raised some eyebrows amongst analysts as it reduced their market share from over 30% to under 10% and the view was they would never recover.

However, it transpired that the company were subject to a sabotage and were seen as one of the victims. As a result of their prompt actions, and the ensuing investigations, their reputation was enhanced and they regained a market share of over 30%.

In 2010, the company was in the news again, once again related to Tylenol. Customers started to complain of a musty, mildew smell from the product in 2008 and there were complaints of stomach pains. The company decided not to report the concerns. In 2009 it started to recall certain batches of Tylenol. As the number of recalled batches started to increase, anxiety grew amongst customer about what was wrong and whether they were impacted. At a similar time a rival started to give away bottles of their own version of the medicine and Johnson & Johnson lost significant market share as a result of their slow response.

Their response was widely derided and held up as a perfect example of how to damage the reputation of a company.

CIMA survey

CIMA conducted a global survey in 2013 of over 1,500 finance leaders. It found that companies are beginning to put a higher priority on reputation and in some cases are putting reputation before profit. The survey identified three main factors behind this: an increase in the need for transparency, the increased use of social media (more on social media in chapter 8) and incidents happening at a competitor or other leading organisation that led to reputational damage.

2 Sources of reputational risk

2.1 What could cause reputational risk?

The sources of reputational risk are many and very diverse. It could manifest itself in anything from accounting deficiencies, poor customer service, lack of IT security or failure to meet expected standards of quality. All of these could lead to media coverage resulting in negative perceptions of the brand and company. These negative perceptions can then lead to investors and customers going elsewhere.

Tesco's accounting issues

In 2014 Britain's biggest supermarket chain revealed it had overstated its profits by around £250 million. In August that year it told the market half year profits would be £1.1 billion, but 4 weeks later it announced the overstatement. The issue related to discrepancies between when profits from deals with suppliers were accounted for and when costs were paid.

This lead to over £214 million in fines and compensation claims, but also reputational damage. Investors no longer trusted the company and started to sell their shares - the share price fell by over 50% in a year.

2.2 Social and environmental considerations

The PESTEL framework can often help identify the sources of reputational risk. From that framework, two key areas to consider are social and environmental. Some factors are very obvious, for example it would be detrimental to a firm's reputation to encourage an unhealthy lifestyle, endorse violence, be involved with forced labour, or knowingly damage areas of outstanding natural beauty or of significant historical interest. However most social and environmental considerations are more complex than these examples.

Environmental considerations and reputational risks

Environmental legislation may have been identified as being particularly important to a chemicals producer. A company in this sector is likely to get significant bad press if they are not compliant with legislation.

It should therefore set up a series of targets to measure compliance. For example:

- level of fines

- number of environmental prosecutions

- number of environmental enforcement actions

- number of 'notifiable' incidents (local legislation will define what is 'notifiable' and what is not)

- percentage of employees working within an ISO 14001 compliant Environmental Management System

- the firm's rating in independent benchmarking such as the 'Business in the Environment' Index.

Facebook

One of the biggest social media companies Facebook are facing reputational issues from a variety of sources. There is public concern about issues from the spread of fake news on its platform to the misuse of data in the Cambridge Analytica scandal.

This has led to user numbers declining in its most valuable markets, the US, Canada and Europe. While overall Facebook is still growing, losing user numbers in these key markets is a concern.

Facebook aim to give people the opportunity to express their views. However the line between opinion and fact can sometimes be hard to identify. There is also a risk of data misuse: selling the data on its users provides Facebook with a business opportunity for Facebook, but it can only do so if it complies with the legislation about data use (see chapter 8). Non-compliance could lead to significant reputational damage as well as fines.

2.3 Business ethics

- Ethics is a set of moral principles that guide behaviour, based on what is 'felt' to be right.

- Comprises principles and standards that govern business behaviour.

- Actions can be judged to be right or wrong, ethical or unethical by individuals inside or outside the organisation.

For example, is it ethical to:

- experiment on animals?

- drill for oil?

- build roads through the countryside?

- allow smoking in public areas?

- pay senior executives large increases in salary?

- train students to pass exams?

Different individuals will have different views on each of these issues.

Illustration – Nestle and Ethics

Nestlé was criticised in the past for taking advantage of the poor and uneducated populations in developing countries in order to increase their own profits.

The company gave gifts and incentives to local health officials, as encouragement for promoting their baby milk formula and therefore discouraging breast feeding. Nestlé employees were heard telling midwives that 'all western women use formula to feed their babies, so that they grow up big and strong'.

Nestlé didn't educate mothers about sterilising bottles and therefore mothers mixed the formula with dirty water at the cost of many babies' health. The free samples provided to mothers in hospitals and clinics soon dried up, but not before the mothers and babies had become reliant on them because the mothers had stopped producing their own milk. The mothers then had to pay almost western prices for the baby milk formula, a price that most families could not afford.

Apart from any moral duty to be ethical, the prime purpose of a business is to maximise shareholder wealth and the chance of this happening is increased by the adoption of ethical behaviour.

Test your understanding 1 (integration)

Required:

How can the adoption of ethical behaviour by an organisation help to assist to maximise shareholder wealth?

2.4 Corporate social responsibility

 Corporate social responsibility (CSR) refers to the idea that a company should be sensitive to the needs of all stakeholders in its business operations and not just shareholders. As such, ethics is just one dimension of corporate social responsibility.

CSR and risk management

By aligning the company's core values with the values of society, the company can improve its reputation and ensure it has a long term future.

Benefits of a CSR strategy

- Differentiation – the firm's CSR strategy can act as a method of differentiation.
- High calibre staff will be attracted and retained due to the firm's CSR policies.
- Brand strengthening – due to the firm's honest approach.
- Lower costs – can be achieved in a number of ways, e.g. due to the use of less packaging or energy.

- The identification of new market opportunities and of changing social expectations.

- A resultant overall increase in profitability.

- NPVs will also increase due to increased sales, lower costs, an extended project life and a lower level of risk.

Test your understanding 2 (integration)
Required: Many commentators believe that CSR is a morally correct pursuit, but there are powerful arguments against it. Identify and discuss these arguments.

CSR and metrics

It is really important for the organisation to have some clear goals in mind with regards to its CSR strategy.

Remember, **things that get measured get done** more often than things that are not measured. Therefore, the company should measure the result of any CSR programme using appropriate metrics.

Illustration – Tesco and performance metrics
In the Tesco illustration earlier, one of the issues that led to the overstatement in profit was the push to achieve and improve profit performance as a key performance metric. As the half year profits release approached, heads of division were reported to be putting pressure on buyers to "find an extra £30 million". This would have flowed down through the organisation, creating a pressure to achieve the profit target in any way. The CEO that came in after the scandal recognised the culture needed to change and that integrity needed to be central to the way the business behaved.

Illustration – The influence of metrics on the banking crisis
The collapse of Lehman brothers, a sprawling global bank, in September 2005, almost brought down the world's financial system. The then governor of the bank of England, Mervyn King, criticised City banks who rewarded staff with huge sums for taking risks and concluded that the credit crisis was caused, in part, by bankers betting on high-risk complex financial products. A culture of risk taking had developed due to the huge potential bonuses and rewards offered to bankers.

3 Code of ethics

As Chartered Management Accountants, students throughout the world have a duty to observe the highest standards of conduct and integrity, and to uphold the good standing and reputation of the profession. They must also refrain from any conduct which might discredit the profession. Members and registered students must have regard to these guidelines irrespective of their field of activity, of their contract of employment or of any other professional memberships they may hold.

The Institute promotes the highest ethical and business standards, and encourages its members to be good and responsible professionals. Good ethical behaviour may be above that required by the law. In a highly competitive, complex business world, it is essential that CIMA members sustain their integrity and remember the trust and confidence which is placed on them by whoever relies on their objectivity and professionalism. Members must avoid actions or situations which are inconsistent with their professional obligations. They should also be guided not merely by the terms but by the spirit of this Code.

CIMA members should conduct themselves with courtesy and consideration towards all with whom they have professional dealings and should not behave in a manner which could be considered offensive or discriminatory.

CIMA has adopted a code of ethics based on the IFAC (International Federation of Accountants) code of ethics which was developed with input from CIMA and the global accountancy profession. The CIMA Code of Ethics is freely available on CIMA's website – https://www.cimaglobal.com/Professionalism/Ethics/CIMA-code-of-ethics-for-professional-accountants/.

If a member cannot resolve an ethical issue by following this code or by consulting the ethics support information on CIMA's website, he or she should seek legal advice as to both legal rights and any obligations (s)he may have.

The code of ethics is in three parts:

- Part A establishes the fundamental principles of professional ethics and provides a conceptual framework for applying those principles.

- Parts B and C illustrate how the conceptual framework is to be applied in specific situations:

    – Part B applies to professional accountants in business.

    – Part C applies to professional accountants in public practice.

3.1 Fundamental principles

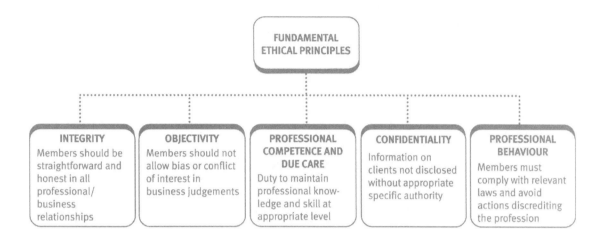

 ### More on fundamental ethical principles

Integrity

Integrity implies fair dealing and truthfulness.

Members are also required not to be associated with any form of communication or report where the information is considered to be:

- materially false or to contain misleading statements

- provided recklessly

- incomplete such that the report or communication becomes misleading by this omission.

Objectivity

Accountants need to ensure that their business/professional judgement is not compromised because of bias or conflict of interest.

However, there are many situations where objectivity can be compromised, so a full list cannot be provided. Accountants are warned to always ensure that their objectivity is intact in any business/professional relationship.

Professional competence and due care

There are two main considerations under this heading:

(1) Accountants are required to have the necessary professional knowledge and skill to carry out work for clients.

(2) Accountants must follow applicable technical and professional standards when providing professional services.

Appropriate levels of professional competence must first be attained and then maintained. Maintenance implies keeping up to date with business and professional developments, and in many institutes completion of an annual return confirming that continuing professional development (CPD) requirements have been met.

Where provision of a professional service has inherent limitations (e.g. reliance on client information) then the client must be made aware of this.

Confidentiality

The principle of confidentiality implies two key considerations for accountants:

(1)   Information obtained in a business relationship is not disclosed outside the firm unless there is a proper and specific authority or unless there is a professional right or duty to disclose.

(2)   Confidential information acquired during the provision of professional services is not used to personal advantage.

The need to maintain confidentiality is normally extended to cover the accountant's social environment, information about prospective clients and employers and also where business relationships have terminated. Basically there must always be a reason for disclosure before confidential information is provided to a third party.

The main reasons for disclosure are when it is:

(1)   permitted by law and authorised by the client

(2)   required by law, e.g. during legal proceedings or disclosing information regarding infringements of law

(3)   there is professional duty or right to disclose (when not barred by law), e.g. provision of information to the professional institute or compliance with ethical requirements.

Professional behaviour

Accountants must comply with all relevant laws and regulations.

There is also a test whereby actions suggested by a third party which would bring discredit to the profession should be avoided.

An accountant is required to treat all people contacted in a professional capacity with courtesy and consideration. Similarly, any marketing activities should not bring the profession into disrepute.

Test your understanding 3

The fundamental ethical principles include:

Select ALL that apply

A   Communication

B   Objectivity

C   Professional competence and due care

D   Integrity

Test your understanding 4

Fair dealing and truthfulness is implied within the ethical principle of:

A   Confidentiality

B   Objectivity

C   Professional competence and due care

D   Integrity

Test your understanding 5

Compliance with all relevant laws and regulations is implied within the ethical principle of:

A   Professional behaviour

B   Objectivity

C   Professional competence and due care

D   Integrity

Test your understanding 6

Zahra is a CIMA Member in Practice, and advises a range of individual clients and organisations.

A client has called Zahra, asking for her annual accounts to be finalised as a matter of urgency. Apparently, one of Zahra's staff promised that the accounts would be completed a week earlier. Zahra asks her staff member, a part-qualified accountant, to tell her the situation relating to the client's accounts. The staff member says that the accounts need another four or five hours' work. As it is Friday, the staff member offers to complete the accounts at home, over the weekend, and to deliver them to the client on the way to work on Monday morning.

For Zahra to allow this would be in breach of which ONE of the following fundamental ethical principle (according to CIMA's Code of Ethics)?

A   Integrity

B   Objectivity

C   Professional competence and due care

D   Confidentiality

E   Professional behaviour

Test your understanding 7

L is a CIMA Member in Practice, and advises a range of individuals and organisations. An owner manager of one of L's clients has contacted her to ask if she can urgently contact the bank on the client's behalf in order to give a credit reference. Without an injection of funds from the bank, the client's business will be unable to continue trading. The client, a personal friend of L's has asked for this to be done as a 'favour'. Both L and the client are aware that the business' cash flow problems are severe and a positive reference would be misleading.

For L to give the bank a positive credit rating would be in breach of which fundamental ethical principles?

Select ALL that apply.

A   Integrity.

B   Objectivity.

C   Professional Competence and Due Care.

D   Confidentiality.

E   Professional Behaviour.

3.2 Conceptual framework approach

- The circumstances in which management accountants operate may give rise to specific threats to compliance with the fundamental principles.

- It is impossible to define every situation that creates such threats and specify the appropriate mitigating action.

- A conceptual framework that requires a management accountant to identify, evaluate and address threats to compliance with the fundamental principles, rather than merely comply with a set of specific rules which may be arbitrary, is, therefore, in the public interest.

Ethical threats

- The self-interest threat

  May occur due to personal financial interest in a situation creating conflict.

- The self-review threat

  May occur when previous judgement needs to be re-evaluated by the member responsible for that judgement.

- The advocacy threat

  May occur when a member promotes a position or opinion to the point that subsequent objectivity may be compromised.

- The familiarity or trust threat

  May occur when, because of a close or personal relationship, a member becomes too sympathetic to the interests of others.

- The intimidation threat

  May occur when a member may be deterred from acting objectively by threats, whether real or perceived.

- The adverse interest threat

  May occur when a member does not act with integrity because their interests are opposed to the employer.

Test your understanding 8

Ali is a CIMA member, working as Financial Controller of a listed public company.

Ali's wife owns a large number of shares in the company, and Ali knows that the share price depends, to some extent, on the reported profits. Ali is responsible for producing the published accounts of the company.

This represents which type of ethical threat (according to CIMA's Code of Ethics)?

A   self interest

B   self review

C   advocacy

D   intimidation

E   familiarity

3.3 Ethical issues as sources of risk

- As stated above, CIMA's code of ethics has a 'threats and safeguards' approach to resolving ethical issues.

- If identified threats are other than clearly insignificant, a management accountant should apply safeguards to eliminate the threats or reduce them to an acceptable level such that compliance with the fundamental principles is not compromised.

- Note that the ethical threat does not necessarily have to relate to personal ethics but could focus on a business decision and its possible implications.

Ethical safeguards

Safeguards

Safeguards are actions or other measures that may eliminate threats or reduce them to an acceptable level.

There are two basic types of safeguards:

- Safeguards created by the profession, legislation or regulation
    - Educational, training and experience requirements for entry into the profession.
    - CPD requirements.
    - Corporate governance regulations.
    - Professional or regulatory monitoring and disciplinary procedures.
    - External review by a legally empowered third party of the reports, returns, communications or information produced by a professional accountant
- Safeguards in the work environment
    - Firm-wide safeguards
    - Engagement-specific safeguards

Test your understanding 9

One of B Company's products, a computer printer, has been found to be at risk of setting alight if left plugged in for long periods of time. The directors of B Company are meeting to decide whether to begin a universal recall of the product or do nothing and just settle any claims for compensation as they arise.

B company's risk assessment concluded that due to safety mechanisms built in to the printer, serious injuries as a result of the fault are very unlikely and that the likelihood of fire in the first place is less than 1 in 100,000.

Which of the following are likely risks to B Company if they decide not to recall the product?

Select ALL that apply.

A   Risk that the company's sales of other products suffer if knowledge of the fault becomes public

B   Risk that the cost of compensation claims outweigh the cost of the recall

C   Risk that serious injury occurs and a recall is necessary anyway

D   Risk that the company's decision not to recall the product becomes public and the company is seen as unethical.

Test your understanding 10

D is an importer and processor of a product called R33, which is a material used in many household products. It is mined in some of the world's poorest countries where large communities rely on it for their incomes. These incomes support education, sanitation and health facilities in these countries.

Recently, independent research discovered that R33 was very harmful to human health, particularly in its raw mined form. Some of the respiratory diseases it caused remained inactive in the body for decades. Doctors had suspected this to be the case but it had never been confirmed before.

The board of D have met to discuss a report commissioned on whether the health risk to workers could be managed with extra internal controls over safety measures. The report concluded that, unless expensive redesign of facilities took place and breathing apparatus was issued to all employees, this was unlikely. The report also pointed out that the workers in the poorest nations were more afraid of losing their jobs than the health implications of working with R33.

The board recognise they have an ethical dilemma associated with how they manage the risks associated with the mining of R33.

Which of the following statements are correct with respect to the ethical dilemma associated with risk management in this case?

Select ALL that apply.

A   The board of D has a duty towards its employees to safeguard their health and so must act on the report, regardless of whether this leads to job losses.

B   D has a duty to the local communities supported by its mines which are under threat because of the report findings.

C   If the workers in the poorest developing countries are willing to take the risks to their health, D has a duty to keep providing work.

D   Legally, D must provide the safety equipment and redesign the facilities regardless of cost.

E   D can choose to ignore the report and continue with its existing risk management strategies.

CIMA's Financial Management magazine has a section on ethical dilemmas each month.

4   Ethical dilemmas and conflict resolution

4.1   What is an ethical dilemma ?

- A dilemma will only occur if there are two or more interests at stake, even if it is only an ethical duty to oneself.

- An ethical dilemma exists when one or more principles of the code are threatened.

- You may have discovered something unethical, illegal or fraudulent going on where you work, or perhaps you feel that you have been asked to do something that compromises your professional integrity.

- Conflicts of interest and confidentiality issues are also ethical problems.

- In general, ethical issues should be dealt with by taking actions (called safeguards) to reduce them to a level where they are no longer significant or of any consequence.

4.2 Ethical conflict resolution

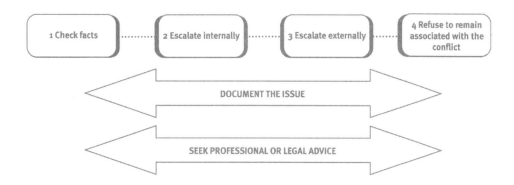

CIMA recommends the following process for addressing situations of ethical conflict:

- Gather all facts and relevant information.

- Ascertain the ethical issues involved and identify the fundamental principles related to the matter in question.

- Escalate concern internally, i.e. to direct management.

- Escalate issue further to your manager's boss, the Board or a non-executive director (following any internal grievance or whistleblowing procedure).

- Seek advice from CIMA.

- Report externally to auditors or relevant trade/regulatory body.

- Remove yourself from the situation.

Throughout the process, document the steps you take to resolve the issue. For example, raise your concern in writing and keep copies of relevant correspondence. This will allow you to demonstrate how you dealt with the problem should you ever need to do so.

 Ethics and CIMA

Going downhill fast

Danielle Cohen shares the true story of a CIMA member who contacted the institute's ethics helpline for advice. His problem stemmed from allowing what seemed, on the face of it, a minor issue to snowball into a job-threatening situation.

Andrew was the management accountant of a small firm that was part of a plc. His boss, Chris, was the firm's CEO. Several months before Chris had approached him with a query about the month-end figures that Andrew has produced, saying that they must be wrong. At the time there was a certain amount of confusion, because their firm had just taken over another small company, so Andrew adjusted them as instructed.

Next month Chris questioned the numbers again, and Andrew duly changed them once more. This happened at several more month-ends until he began to suspect that Chris's reasons for changing the numbers might not be valid – and that the business was simply not performing. He raised the issue with his boss, who assured him that he would sort everything out. Relieved that Chris recognized that the matter needed to be dealt with, Andrew dropped it.

At the end of the firm's financial year, Chris announced that he had, as promised, found a solution to the problem of the ongoing adjustments. Unfortunately, this was very different from what Andrew was expecting. Chris proposed that he own up to the discrepancies, admit that they were the result of a simple error and then resign to prevent any further questions from being asked. In return for carrying the can, Andrew would receive a glowing reference – on the understanding, of course, that he kept quiet about the whole affair.

Shocked and unsure about what to do, Andrew contacted CIMA's ethics helpline. He had gone from accepting a small month-end adjustment to his figures to finding himself about to lose a job. Our guidance to Andrew was that he should consider taking the problem to more senior people in the group, since raising it with Chris wasn't an option. Andrew had some concerns about the possible repercussions of doing this, particularly because Chris was well respected in the group, and he was worried that his version of events would not be believed. The lack of an internal grievance or whistle blowing procedure made it hard for him to predict how his case would be handled.

Given all these factors, Andrew questioned whether quitting was an acceptable solution. A good reference had been promised, but was this pledge worth anything coming from Chris? And how would he explain to any future employer why he had left? And what would happen if a colleague were to complain to CIMA about his lack of competence? If this were to happen, he could potentially lose his membership. Even worse, lying to accept responsibility would be another breach of CIMA's code of ethics. If discovered, this would also have consequences for his membership.

After further discussion, Andrew identified a potential ally (a financial controller) at group level. He arranged a meeting through a trusted colleague in order to minimize the chances of discovery by Chris.

We suggested that Andrew should speak to the Institute's legal advice line for expert guidance on his legal obligations and employment rights, and also to the whistle-blowing advice line for free, confidential, independent advice on raising his concerns.

Andrew spoke to the financial controller and Chris was eventually forced to resign. But Andrew's ongoing compliance with his boss's wishes was enough to have tarnished his reputation. A few months later he resigned of his own accord.

Andrew's case is a reminder of how crucial it is to use your professional judgment, heed the warning signs and establish the facts at the first sign of an ethical dilemma. Armed with these and CIMA's code of ethics, you can decide whether or not you need to act and, if so, what that action should be.

So how exactly do you know when an ethical dilemma is an ethical dilemma? As Oscar Wilde observed: 'Morality, like art, means drawing a line someplace.' When the amount of money is not material, the report is only for internal purposes or when no one else seems to think there's an issue, how can you be sure where that line is?

Taking time to consider the situation from all angles will help you to know for sure. In the code of ethics, the line is where a threat to our fundamental principles is anything more than trivial. Although the changes that Andrew made to the numbers in that first month might not have been material, the pattern that they established was. If he had stood up to Chris the first time he was asked to adjust the figures, the situation might never have developed.

Danielle Cohen is CIMA's ethics manager. This article appeared in Financial Management, November 2007.

Test your understanding 11

The procedure for ethical conflict solution is:

A   To check the facts; escalate internally; escalate externally; dissociate with the conflict

B   To check the facts; escalate externally; escalate internally; dissociate with the conflict

C   To check the facts; dissociate with the conflict; escalate internally; escalate externally

D   Escalate internally; escalate externally; check the facts; dissociate with the conflict

Test your understanding 12

JJ is the management accountant at D Co, a small family company run by a board of three directors who are husband, wife and son. There are no other managers within the organisation.

The son also owns another company with his wife and JJ is aware that he has been selling D Co's products to this company at prices below cost. This has caused the profit margin in D Co to fall considerably. The son has now asked JJ to alter the figures in the management accounts before signing them off as he would prefer to explain the transactions to his parents at a later date.

JJ is certain that the other directors know nothing about the sales and realises that disclosure of the situation will have long term implications for the future of D Co including JJ's job.

Which of the following courses of action appear reasonable for JJ at this stage?

Select ALL that apply.

A   Alter the figures since a professional accountant in business should support the objectives established by their employer.

B   Report the correct figures directly to the board of directors.

C   Obtain advice on the best course of action from other managers within D Co.

D   Seek legal advice.

E   Follow the formal dispute resolution process within D Co.

F   Ask the son to speak to his parents immediately since changing the figures is not possible.

4.3   Case study – Nike

Nike is one of the famous franchises in the world that sells sportswear for all ages. But it is mostly famous for athlete shoes and apparel and it is also one of the major manufacturers of sport equipment. The slogan for Nike is "Just Do It". Nike was founded in January 1962 in Oregon, United States by Philip Knight and Bill Bowerman. Nike has around 700 retail outlets spread all over the world, and approximately 45 offices outside the United States employing 30,000 people all over the world. The company had a revenue excess of $16 billion in 2007. Nike's factories are mostly located in Asian countries like Pakistan, India, Malaysia, China, Indonesia, Philippines, Taiwan, Vietnam and Thailand.

The primary stakeholders of the company will be the shareholders, business partners, the employees, and the customers/ consumers. What the shareholders and the investors want from the company is that it achieves its profits, the employees of the expect work satisfaction, pay, and good supervision and the customers are concerned with quality, safety and availability of services when they require them. When any primary stakeholder group is not satisfied the organisation's progress becomes questionable.

The secondary stakeholders of the company would be the community. Most companies like Nike exist under a charter or licenses and operate within the limits of safety laws, environmental protection and other laws and regulations. The socially responsible organisations like Nike should consider the effect of their actions upon all stakeholders. What all of these stakeholders want from the company is that the company is ethically and socially responsible and when this secondary stakeholder group becomes dis-satisfied, the reputation of the company gets tarnished (for example, the debate about sweatshops tarnished the reputation of Nike).

Issues faced by Nike:

- Child labour and the sweat shop problem;

- Workers given a very low wage, and overtime in countries like Vietnam, China and Indonesia under a subcontract;

- Poor or squalid working conditions and forced labour in the factories that manufacture their products;

- Environmental damage done to society by air and water pollution, noise, and change in the climate due to pollution. (Stockdale & Crosby, 2004)

There are different kinds of guiding principles that can prevent Nike type scandals, and this is what the company did:

PR campaign

Nike decided to use a PR campaign to repair its social image after the sweatshop debate. The PR campaign covered the following actions:

Employment Practices

The management of Nike looked at its employment practices; it made sure that the company was following appropriate policies on recruitment, training, health, safety and welfare. Management also oversaw environmental practices – to make sure that the company followed responsible procedures regarding waste disposal and avoidance, and energy inputs.

Training Plan

They conducted and designed a training program for the employees. Management remembered that training and development programs are not universal solutions to every need of the company – effective job design, selection, placement and other activities of the HR department are also very important.

Assessing Performance

They set targets and identified a range of performance measure standards. For performance to be rated accurately, management must assess every relevant performance dimension.

Ethical Responsibility

The management of Nike understood that ethical responsibility was needed within the company – because it is the obligation of an organisation's management to make decisions and take actions that will grow the welfare and interest of society and the organisation. This would include activities and commitments related to human rights, governance and ethics, development, working conditions of the employees, community involvement, customer satisfaction, relations with the company's suppliers and customers and respect for diverse cultures and different people.

4.4   Case study – BP

BP plc is one of the largest oil and alternative energy companies in the world. It has set targets with regard to reducing its CO_2 emissions and the development of alternative sources of energy such as solar power. However, in recent years BP's environmental image has been tarnished. Whether BP has acted unethically is considered to be ambiguous by some.

British Petroleum plc developed their image considerably. They altered the meaning of BP to mean 'Beyond Petroleum' and aimed to 'reduce … greenhouse gas emissions by 10%' (Bulkin, 2010) between 1990 and 2010 – which they did successfully. This signalled their intent to either aid the environment with their business practices or simply to cultivate a 'greener' image to ensure the ever more environmentally aware public would favour their products, and to capture the developing market for alternative energy. BP's ethical stand point appears to consider the broader responsibilities contributing to their businesses' decisions and policies. However it is necessary to established whether ethical decisions and Corporate Social Responsibility (CSR) are based upon intentions, goals, outcomes; or, a mixture of each.

BP have adopted a 'progressive approach to environmental protection'; setting targets and producing reports on their environmental development progress. The 'Ethical Conduct Policy' considers factors such as adhering to Human Rights regulations; ensuring that all operations are fair and legal, and dismissing those who act unlawfully (as they did in 2006); and zero tolerance of bribery or gifts as facilitation payments. These factors are demonstrated by management in decisions, policies and actions. Moreover, pledging its name to the United Nations Global Compact (UNGC) and partnering the Red Cross's appeal for financial support all demonstrate BP's commitment to being a ethically astute corporate citizen. Therefore, can it be argued that BP is an ethical company? Or are these actions simply the mask of an organisation whose only responsibility is to its shareholders and top management?

Many of BP's actions have, contrastingly, been regarded as extremely unethical e.g. the Alaskan oil spills, Texas City refinery fire, treatment of Colombian farmers and the explosion in the Gulf of Mexico. Decisions were made which ultimately lead to destructive consequences for many stakeholder groups. The complex ethical dilemmas facing BP are thus: how to weight emphasis on different stakeholders, to what extent are immediate mistakes and unethical practices allowable in pursuit of a better, more sustainable future; and, to what extent is it ethical to publicise the firm's ethics and CSR for the predominant purposes of profit maximisation.

It could be argued that BP should: adopt riskier strategies that result in higher returns; cut safety costs; and exploit small minorities. The results could provide a benefit for a great number of people over time. Adopting this view, FDI host nations, customers and shareholders would benefit most, leading to greater levels of investment and higher revenues. Thus, more investment could then be made by BP to develop alternative energy sources and create a more sustainable future. So exploitation of, and accidents regarding, small numbers of employees, the environment, and local communities can all be seen as blips, even calculated casualties, in the pursuit of a better world.

However, environmental destruction and human deaths would widely be considered unethical. This contradicts the human rights of the employees. Therefore short-term operational decisions, such as ensuring that safety standards are appropriate for employees should be implemented; rather than pursuing additional profits and hiding behind a mask of public relations. Viewed from this perspective, 'calculated casualties' don't provide the greatest amount of good; it simply highlights an unethical and ruthless pursuit of profits. BP's employees could be seen to act unethically as the immediate results of some decisions induce suffering and detrimental effects to the environment, employees and local communities. The firm's "green-washing" of its CSR to gain public approval of its practises and generate profits, could be considered unethical.

An alternative view of BP's ethical behaviour suggests that those who are in charge of safety should ensure that their job has been completed thoroughly. BP should not view the employees or environment as factors of production used to maximise profits for shareholders; suggesting that any reduction of safety is acting unethically and irresponsibly. Some say that BP's CSR and sustainability image are a marketing gimmick.

Thus, it can be seen that one view provides a moral standpoint for BP; looking to the future as it attempt to pioneer alternative energy sources; aiming to please the greatest number of people. However, another view demonstrates that BP acts selfishly to maximise profits quickly. Another view suggests that BP's decision makers employ unethical practices. They don't just fail to consider all stakeholders, but consciously exploit many in order to increase efficiency and cut costs, often at the expense of safety.

However, traditional ethical theories should not be viewed as complete 'rules', but as contributing to a wider ethical understanding for decision making. BP's business actions are complex and have implications for all stakeholders. Senior management will often squeeze deadlines which force decision makers to 'cut corners'. Hence, an variety of ethical perspectives are needed to conclude on whether the actions that lead to the Texas City Fire, the Gulf of Mexico explosion and other events, were a result of conscious unethical decision making or unexpected and unfortunate casualties of good business practice in the pursuit of future global improvements. However, it could conversely be argued, that BP is simply a collection of human beings who have limited insight into the full consequences of their actions and thus, are justified in pursuing their own self-interests, regardless of other human's demands. Therefore, interpretation of BP's CSR and ethical policy is ambiguously subjective and open to conflicting perspectives.

5   Conflicts within employing organisation

- It is important to consider exercising ethical principles in conducting and reporting on internal reviews.

- There may be times, however, when a professional accountant's responsibilities to an employing organisation and their professional obligations to comply with the fundamental principles are in conflict.

- Ordinarily, a professional accountant in business should support the legitimate and ethical objectives established by the employer and the rules and procedures drawn up in support of those objectives.

- Nevertheless, where compliance with the fundamental principles is threatened, a professional accountant in business must consider a response to the circumstances.

5.1 Pressures that may be faced

A professional accountant may be put under pressure by managers, directors or other individuals to:

- act contrary to law or regulation

- act contrary to technical or professional standards

- facilitate unethical or illegal earnings management strategies

- lie to, or otherwise intentionally mislead (including misleading by remaining silent) others, in particular:

  - the auditors of the employing organisation

  - regulators

- Issue, or otherwise be associated with, a financial or non-financial report that materially misrepresents the facts, including statements in connection with, for example:

  - the financial statements

  - tax compliance

  - legal compliance

  - reports required by securities regulators.

5.2 Safeguards to be applied

The significance of threats arising from such pressures, such as intimidation threats, should be evaluated. If they are other than clearly insignificant, safeguards should be considered and applied as necessary to eliminate them or reduce them to an acceptable level. Such safeguards may include:

- obtaining advice where appropriate from within the employing organisation, an independent professional advisor or a relevant professional body.

- the existence of a formal dispute resolution process within the employing organisation.

- seeking legal advice.

6   Ethical budget setting

Conflicting objectives

Imagine you are a manager and you help upper management establish the master budget (the planning phase). Furthermore, you are evaluated based on achieving budgeted profit on a quarterly basis (the control phase). You will receive a $10,000 quarterly bonus, in addition to your basic salary, if you meet or exceed budgeted profit. There is an inherent conflict between the planning and control phases of this process. You are helping the company plan, but you also want to be sure budgeted profit is as low as possible so you can get the $10,000 bonus.

Establishing a sales and profit budget that is considerably lower than what is likely to happen causes problems for the entire organisation. Production may be short of materials and labour, causing inefficiencies in the production process. Selling and administrative support may be lacking due to underestimating sales. Customers will not be satisfied if they must wait for the product. The dilemma you face as a manager in this situation is whether to do what is best for you (set a low profit estimate to earn the bonus) or do what is best for the company (estimate accurately so the budget reflects true sales and production needs).

Organisations must recognize this conflict and have processes in place to ensure both the interests of individual employees and the interests of the organisation as a whole are served. For example, employees can be rewarded not just for meeting goals but also for providing accurate estimates. Perhaps a long-term share option incentive system would provide motivation to do what is best for the organisation. Whatever incentive system is implemented, organisations must promote honest employee input and be aware of fraudulent reporting to achieve financial targets.

Undue pressure

Imagine another ethical scenario – your manager is pressurising you to meet the budget. This could involve you and your staff working overtime that you don't want (and are not contracted) to do, through to 'window dressing' of the actual results by delaying or pulling forward costs and revenues in to the required time period to meet the budget.

You know that your manager will not be happy if you don't meet the budget. What should you do?

There are two main courses of action available to you:

You could do as you are told. This would keep your manager happy and probably make your life easier. It may enable you and your manager to earn a reward or bonus. However, if you lose the trust of your staff or effectively mislead higher management by lying about the state of the budget then this is not good for you or the company. It is likely to become apparent in the near future and it is an unethical course of action.

You could work as hard as you can to meet the budget but if it doesn't work out, then take the wrath of your manager. This is probably the most ethical course of action, but it may make your job harder in the future. Your manager might be angry with you and make your future working life difficult. However, there are other courses of action open to you. You could face your manager and state that he or she is being unreasonable, and unethical in their request. If this falls on deaf ears and your position becomes untenable, then you could escalate your concerns to a higher level of management, human resources or perhaps the audit committee. They should take your issue seriously and investigate the manager's actions. Your manager, if found to have exerted undue pressure on you, should be reprimanded and probably investigated further since their actions may not have been a 'one-off' incident. Their 'moral compass' may be questionable and at this point high level management should ask whether they want such a manager working for their company. However, in some cases, high level management may also agree with the manager 'pushing' to meet targets. At this point you should question whether you want to work for such an organisation. CIMA's code of ethics suggests that resignation may be your final option.

Test your understanding 13

CIMA's code of ethics identifies six categories of common threat.

Which of the following are part of the six threats?

Select ALL that apply

A   Self interest

B   Self review

C   Familiarity

D   Confidentiality

E   Advocacy

Test your understanding 14

When you form a close relationship with others so that your professional judgement becomes compromised this is considered to be the threat of:

A   Self review

B   Self interest

C   Familiarity

D   Advocacy

> ### Test your understanding 15
>
> **Safeguards against ethical threats might include:**
>
> Select ALL that apply
>
> A   Intimidation
>
> B   Disciplinary actions
>
> C   Disclosure of confidential information
>
> D   Training
>
> E   Internal control systems
>
> F   Inducements

7   Impact of strategy on brand and reputation

7.1   The difference between brand and reputation

To understand how your strategy impacts brand and reputation, it's first important to make sure that the difference between these two words is clear. They are often used as if they are the same thing and they are not.

- **Brand** – is something that the organisation can control to a certain extent. It's about what the organisation does and how it approaches its products, services and interactions.

- **Reputation** – is what people think about an organisation, and crucially what they communicate about an organisation. This is much harder to control – doing the things that the brand sets out is a good way to go about building a reputation, but it doesn't guarantee it.

> ### Illustration – your brand versus your reputation
>
> If we view ourselves as an organisation then our brand is what we say we are going to do and our reputation is whether we keep to our word.
>
> Imagine you borrow some money from a friend. You may promise to pay them back next week, when you have been paid. This sounds good, and is the right thing to say to reassure someone that they will get their money back.
>
> If you then don't pay the money back when you have been paid as you said you would, the chance of that friend lending you money again is reduced – by not keeping to your promise you have broken their trust.
>
> In the same way, a customer that is disappointed by an organisation is likely less to come back.

7.2 How strategy helps

So where does the strategy come in? In the previous chapter we discussed what strategy is:

'A course of action, including the specification of resources required, to achieve a specific objective.'

An organisation needs to develop appropriate strategies, to make sure it understands its environment and what it can do internally and makes the right choice about where and how to compete. Having the right strategy also links to conveying the right brand image to achieve success in the market place the organisation has chosen.

It also involves developing strategies to ensure the organisation has the right resources available and the right people in place, with the time they need to do the job well, to deliver on their brand and their strategic promise and to achieve a good reputation.

It's important that the board recognises that managing the brand and reputation is difficult – it is much more than a public relations exercise or a marketing message. Without delivering on the promise, they are just words, which eventually people stop believing.

Like most risks, it requires the whole organisation to work together, which is why the strategy chosen and the message the board conveys to the rest of the organisation is so important.

 Illustration – Consistency

The organisation as a whole must work together to deliver the strategy and brand – this gives the reputation the best chance of aligning to the brand.

If different functions across an organisation interpret the message the board sends out in different ways, they will act in a different ways and this can lead to confusion internally and as a result the external perception of the company is unlikely to be as the board originally set out.

7.3 Strategic alignment

Strategic alignment starts at the very top of an organisation and is about the board making sure that the strategic goals, the company culture and business processes align for the reason the organisation exists, achievement of the mission.

If the board gets this right, then the organisation has the best chance of enabling the reputation to match the brand they promise.

Illustration – Southwest Airlines versus Northwest Airlines

Southwest Airlines is a low cost airline based in America, which was established in 1967, and set out a very clear vision:

"To become the world's most loved, most flown and most profitable airline."

By acting out their mission or purpose:

"Connecting people to what's important in their lives through friendly, reliable and low-cost air travel."

To achieve this, they recognised the importance of aligning the people that work for their organisation and as part of that they had this motto to help instil the correct culture:

"If employees are happy, satisfied, dedicated, and energetic, they'll take real good care of the customers. When the customers are happy, they come back. And that makes the shareholders happy".

They recognised the link between their stakeholders (from shareholders, to employees, to customer and beyond), a consistent message coming from the top of the organisation that sets out the brand promise, and also the culture within the organisation to fulfil that promise and allow them to develop a reputation that aligns with it.

According to a US Department of Transportation Origin and Destination survey in for the 12 months to the end of June 2018, Southwest Airlines carried the most passengers in the US. Their website also states they have achieved 46 consecutive years of profitability.

By contrast Northwest Airlines, who were founded in 1926 but no longer exist, had a brand promise of:

"Safety. Reliability. Comfort. Fairness. Courtesy. Honesty"

Sounds like a great brand promise, but it needs to be aligned throughout the organisation.

The connection was never made and, as an example of the issues that Northwest airlines had with their staff, in 1998 they were in dispute with their pilots and shutdown the airline for more than two weeks as they couldn't agree a deal with their union. The pilots were unhappy, other staff were affected by the shutdown and the connection between the strategic aims, the culture and brand promise was never aligned. Their promise was broken on many occasions leading to them filing for bankruptcy in 2005 and eventually merging with Delta Air Lines.

> ### Illustration – Toyota
>
> Toyota are often cited for adopting new techniques, from TQM to JIT production and Lean manufacturing. It is unsurprising to find that Toyota were very quick to understand the need for their strategy, culture and brand to align to give them the reputation they needed to continue their success.
>
> The company have always followed guiding principles such as being true to your duties and creating a good atmosphere at work, but in 2001 they adopted the Toyota Way. This linked performance with respect for people, giving employees the opportunities to develop and perform and stating specifically that "a relationship of mutual trust and mutual responsibility between labour and management" is essential; they now give stable employment and improving work conditions the highest priority.
>
> This feeds through to the way their staff behave and fulfil the brand promises they make.
>
> When the Toyota Way was founded in 2001, the company was for a long time the third largest automotive manufacturer in the world, behind General Motors and Ford, but in 2006 they became the largest and have held that title every year since (apart from 2011 when an earthquake and tsunami disrupted production).

8 Transfer Pricing as a source of reputational risk

In an organisation with profit centres and investment centres, there will almost certainly be some inter-connection between different centres. Some profit centres will supply goods and services to others.

When inter-divisional (inter-company) trading takes place between profit centres, the centre providing the goods or services to the other will want to earn income from the transfer. Unless it receives income from the transfer, it will make a loss on the transaction.

For example, if Division A provides items to Division B that cost $10 each to make, Division A must earn at least $10 from the transfer, otherwise it will make a loss. If decision making is delegated to profit centre management, the manager of Division A would refuse to supply Division B unless it is allowed to earn income of at least $10 for each unit.

Inter-divisional transfers must therefore be priced. The price of the transfer is the **transfer price.**

- The transfer is treated as an internal sale and an internal purchase within the organisation. It provides sales income to the supplying division and is a purchase cost for the receiving division.

- The sales income of one division is offset by the purchase cost of the other division. The transfer therefore affects the profits of the two divisions individually, but has no effect on the profit of the organisation as a whole.

Setting a transfer price: Inter-divisional trading policy

The transfer price for inter-divisional transactions is significant because:

- it determines how the total profit is shared between the two divisions, and

- in some circumstances, it could affect decisions by the divisional managers about whether they are willing to sell to or buy from the other division.

Both divisions must benefit from the transaction if inter-divisional sales are to take place.

- A selling division will not agree to sell items to another division unless it is profitable for the selling division to do so.

- Similarly, a buying division will not wish to purchase items from another division unless it is profitable for the division.

Transfer prices have to be established and agreed. They could be decided either centrally or locally.

- They could be imposed by head office.

- Alternatively, they could be decided by commercial negotiation between the profit centre managers.

- If decentralisation is to delegate the power of decision making to profit centre managers, they should have the authority to agree transfer prices by discussion or negotiation between themselves.

Inter-divisional trading should take place within a broad company policy, that:

- for a 'selling division', given the choice between making a sale to an external customer or supplying goods or services to another division within the group, **the preference should be to sell internally**

- for a 'buying division', given the choice between purchasing from an external supplier or from another division within the company, the **preference should be to purchase internally.**

However, a division should be allowed to sell externally rather than transfer internally, or buy externally rather than internally, if it has a good commercial reason. Good commercial reasons would include an external customer offering a higher price, or an external supplier offering a lower price.

Objectives Of Transfer Pricing

(1) Goal Congruence

Within a divisionalised company, divisional managers will have responsibility for, and will be judged on, their division's performance. They will act independently, autonomously and selfishly in the best interests of their own division. They neither know nor care what is happening in other divisions.

It is the task of the management accounting system in general, and the transfer pricing policy in particular, to ensure that what is good for an individual division is good for the company as a whole.

(2) Performance Measurement

The transfer pricing system should result in a report of divisional profits that is a reasonable measure of the managerial performance.

(3) Maintaining Divisional Autonomy

One of the purposes of decentralisation is to allow managers to exercise greater autonomy. There is little point in granting additional autonomy and then imposing transfer prices that will affect the profitability of the division.

(4) Minimising the global tax liability

When a divisionalised company operates entirely within one tax regime the transfer pricing policy will have a minimal impact on the corporate tax bill. However multinational companies can, and do, use their transfer pricing policies to move profits around the world and thereby minimise their global tax liabilities.

(5) Recording the movement of goods and services

In practice, an extremely important function of the transfer pricing system is simply to assist in recording the movement of goods and services.

(6) A fair allocation of profits between divisions

Most of the advantages claimed for divisionalisation are behavioural. Insofar as transfer pricing has a material effect on divisional profit it is essential that managers perceive the allocation of corporate profit as being fair if the motivational benefits are to be retained.

Needless to say, a number of these objectives can conflict with each other, and prove difficult to achieve in practice. It is highly unlikely that any one method would meet all the firm's requirements in all circumstances the best that can be hoped for is a reasonable compromise.

8.1   International Transfer Pricing

Transfers within an international group will often be cross-border, between divisions in different countries. With international transfers and international transfer pricing, the issues already described in this chapter still apply. In addition, other factors need to be considered.

8.2   Different tax rates

A multinational company will seek to minimise the group's total tax liability. One way of doing this might be to use transfer pricing to:

* reduce the profitability of its subsidiaries in high-tax countries, and

* increase the profitability of its subsidiaries in low-tax countries.

Changes in the transfer price can redistribute the pre-tax profit between subsidiaries, but the total pre-tax profit will be the same. However, if more pre-tax profit is earned in low-tax countries and less profit is earned in high-tax countries, the total tax bill will be reduced.

Taxation and Transfer Pricing

International and intra-group trading is a very important part of business today. One-third of the UK's exports to Europe are intra-group transactions. Foreign-owned assets in Europe and the USA have increased considerably. In one decade, foreign-owned assets in the USA tripled, but the tax paid changed very little, as more than half the companies involved reported no taxable income.

International intra-group transfer pricing has its own special considerations, and so a multinational organisation will have matters other than behavioural ones to consider when it sets its transfer prices. There is a natural inclination to set transfer prices in order to minimise tax payments.

Taxation

If a group has subsidiaries that operate in different countries with different tax rates, the overall group corporation tax bill could be reduced by manipulating the transfer prices between the subsidiaries.

For example, if the taxation rate on profits in Country X is 25 per cent and in Country Y it is 60 per cent, the group could adjust the transfer price to increase the profit of the subsidiary in Country X and reduce the profit of the subsidiary in Country Y.

Thus, if the subsidiary in Country X provides goods or services to the subsidiary in Country Y, the use of a very high transfer price would maximise the profits in the lower-tax country, and minimise the profits in the higher-tax country.

There is also a temptation to set up marketing subsidiaries in countries with low corporation tax rates and transfer products to them at a relatively low transfer price. When the products are sold to the final customer, a low rate of tax will be paid on the difference between the two prices.

According to a survey by Ernst and Young, more than 80 per cent of multinational companies viewed transfer pricing as a major international tax issue, and more than half of those companies saw it as the major issue. The taxation authorities in most countries monitor transfer prices in an attempt to control the situation and in order to collect the full amount of taxation due. Double taxation agreements between countries mean that companies pay tax on specific transactions in one country only. However, if the company sets an unrealistic transfer price in order to minimise tax, and the tax authority spots this, the company will pay taxation in both countries, that is, double taxation. This additional payment can amount to millions of pounds and, as a result, is quite an effective deterrent. On the other hand, the gains of avoiding taxation may be even greater.

There have been many cases of transfer price fixing for one reason or another over the years. One of the most notorious of UK transfer pricing cases was that of Hoffman La Roche, as it was then called. Hoffman La Roche had developed the drugs Librium and Valium. The products were imported into the UK at prices of $437 and $979 per kilo, respectively. The UK tax authority accepted the prices; however, the Monopolies Commission sprang into life and questioned the prices on the grounds that the same chemical ingredients, which were unbranded, could be obtained from an Italian company for $9 and $28 per kilo. Hoffman La Roche argued on two grounds: (1) that the price was not set on cost but on what the market would bear, and (2) they had incurred the research and development costs and so had to recover those in the price. However, this was not accepted and they were fined $1.85 m in 1960.

In the UK, Nissan was caught for unpaid tax of $237m for falsely inflated invoices that were used to reduce profits. The freight charges were inflated by 40–60 per cent by a Norwegian company. The next year Nissan was required to pay $106 m in unpaid tax in the USA because the authorities felt that part of their USA marketing profits were being transferred to Japan as transfer prices on imports of cars and trucks were too high. Interestingly, the Japanese tax authorities took a different view and returned the double tax, which is a very rare occurrence.

Most countries now accept the Organisation for Economic Co-operation and Development's (OECD) guidelines. These guidelines were produced with the aim of standardising national approaches to transfer pricing as part of the OECD's charter to encourage the freedom of world trade. They provide guidance on the application of 'arm's length' principles. They state that where necessary transfer prices should be adjusted using an 'arm's length' price, that is, a price that would have been arrived at by two unrelated companies acting independently. There are three methods the tax authorities can use to determine an arm's length price.

The first is the comparable price method. This is the most widely used and involves setting the arm's length price by using the prices of similar products, that is, the market price or an approximation to one. The method is known as using comparable uncontrolled prices (CUPS) and is the preferred method wherever possible. This may seem a straightforward basis but, as most international trade is carried out between related companies, meaningful comparisons are hard to find. For example, at one time in the UK, it was possible to use independent car distributorships to find a CUP but now that car manufacturers have developed their own dependent distributor networks, finding arm's length comparability is much more difficult.

Where a CUP cannot be found, or is inappropriate, one of two gross margin methods should be used. These involve a review of gross margins in comparable transactions between uncontrolled organisations. The resale price method is used for the transfer of goods to distributors and marketing operations where goods are sold on with little further processing. The price paid for a final product by an independent party is used and from this a suitable mark-up (to allow for the seller's expenses and profit) is deducted. The second gross margin method is the cost-plus method. Here an arm's length gross margin is established and applied to the seller's manufacturing cost.

These methods are of little help when attempting to establish an arm's length price for intangible property such as a patent right or trade name. Also, much of the data needed may not be in the public domain and so setting fair transfer prices is not easy. In the past, this did not matter so much but today it is often up to the taxpayer to 'prove' the price.

For example, the US section 482 regulations on transfer pricing cover 300 pages and the onus is on the taxpayer to support the transfer price with 'timely' documentation. If this is not done, a non-deductible penalty of up to 40 per cent of the arm's length price may be levied. In the past in the UK, it was up to the tax authorities to detect cases of inappropriate transfer pricing. This left the UK vulnerable to a certain amount of tax leakage. But now under the self-assessment regulations, the onus has switched to the taxpayer to provide correct information. Failure to demonstrate a reasonable attempt at an arm's length price in the tax return will give rise to a penalty of 100 per cent of any tax adjustment. Other European countries are also tightening their regulations in response to the USA and OECD's moves.

> To safeguard the position, the taxpayer may enter into an Advanced Pricing Agreement (APA) with the relevant two tax authorities involved. This is a new approach and is done in advance to avoid any dispute and the costly penalty of double taxation and penalty fees. According to the Ernst and Young survey referred to earlier, more than 60 per cent of companies intend to do, or are doing this.

8.3 Government action on transfer prices

Governments are aware of the effect of transfer pricing on profits, and in many countries, multinationals are required to justify the transfer prices that they charge. Multinationals could be required to apply 'arm's length' prices to transfer prices: in other words, they might be required under tax law to use market-based transfer prices, to remove the opportunities for tax avoidance.

It is also possible, on the other hand, that some countries wishing to attract business might have tax laws that are very favourable to business. A country with the status of a 'tax haven' might offer:

* a low rate of tax on profits
* a low withholding tax on dividends paid to foreign holding companies
* tax treaties with other countries
* no exchange controls
* a stable economy
* good communications with the rest of the world
* a well-developed legal framework, within which company rights are protected.

Multinationals might set up subsidiary companies in tax havens, trade through these companies, and hope to reduce their total tax liabilities.

8.4 Transfer pricing to manage cash flow

Some governments might place legal restrictions on dividend payments by companies to foreign parent companies.

In this situation, it would be tempting for a multinational to sell goods or services to a subsidiary in the country concerned from other divisions in other countries, and charge very high transfer prices as a means of getting cash out of the country.

This tactic is not possible, however, when the country's tax laws require that transfer prices should be set on an arm's length basis.

Transfer pricing at Starbucks

Starbucks – the international coffee chain, has been in the UK news over the past few years due to its Board declaring it profitable in the UK, yet reporting losses in its financial statements, and paying very little or no UK corporation tax.

Over a three year period Starbucks has reported no profit and paid no UK tax on UK sales of £1.2 billion. (By comparison, McDonalds had a tax bill of £80 million on £3.6 billion of UK sales.)

This apparent contradiction arises from perfectly legal tax avoidance – a tactic used by many multi-nationals the world over.

Starbucks achieves this, in part, through transfer pricing. Starbucks buys coffee beans for the UK through a Switzerland based subsidiary. Before the beans reach the UK they are roasted at the subsidiary in Amsterdam.

The tax authorities in the Netherlands and Switzerland require Starbucks to allocate some profits from its UK sales to its Dutch roasting and Swiss trading units.

The Dutch roasting plant declares a small operating profit, while in Switzerland the Swiss trading unit is not required to publish accounts. Corporate profits are taxed at 24% in the UK, 25% in the Netherlands, but as low as only 5% in Switzerland. In this way it minimises its UK tax bill.

Starbucks was subject to a UK customs enquiry in 2009 and 2010 due to its transfer pricing practices, but it was resolved without further action or penalties. HMRC declined to comment.

9 Other risks linked to reputational risk

9.1 Fraud

Fraud can be defined as:

'Dishonestly obtaining an advantage, avoiding an obligation or causing a loss to another party'.

Prerequisites for fraud

There are three prerequisites for fraud to occur

- **Dishonesty** on the part of the perpetrator.
- **Opportunity** for fraud to occur.
- **Motive** for fraud.

In more detail:

- an ability to **rationalise** the fraudulent action and hence act with **dishonesty** – virtually anyone can justify almost any dishonest or illegal action that they undertake. The idea is that many people obey the law because they believe in it and/or they are afraid of being shamed or rejected by people they care about if they are caught. However, some people may be able to rationalise fraudulent actions as:

  - necessary – especially when done for the business

  - harmless – because the victim is large enough to absorb the impact

  - justified – because 'the victim deserved it' or 'because I was mistreated.'

- a perceived **opportunity** to commit fraud – this can cover a vast range of circumstances, from the board of directors (whose position almost always gives some opportunity to publish fraudulent statements) to members of staff or the general public who think that the system might be weak.

- a **motive,** incentive or pressure to commit fraud – this can range from the members of the board wishing to maximise the value of their performance-related remuneration packages to greed on the part of a dishonest employee or third party.

All three factors generally exist within all organisations and at all levels.

There is more detail on fraud in Chapter 6.

9.2   Link to reputational risk

If a fraud becomes public knowledge it can affect a company's reputation. The control systems within the company will be considered weak, which will worry investors. The share price may fall (dependent on the size of the fraud and the investors' opinion of it). Future investors will be wary and it could prevent the company from raising future finance.

(In the past companies have adopted two different attitudes to the disclosure of fraud – admit to it, or hide it. Hiding fraud is unethical. Also, often the press find out and the consequences are worse than they would have been if the company had come clean in the first place.)

9.3   Bribery

Bribery occurs when someone in a position of trust receives a benefit as a reward for voluntarily acting in breach of that trust. The benefit can take many forms including, but not limited to cash, luxurious gifts or favours to the individual.

9.4 Link to reputational risk

If an organisation is found to have been involved in bribery, then as with fraud it can lead to negative connotations.

A writer for the Harvard Business School, George Serafeim, stated that 'bribery's most significant impact is its negative effect on employee morale', highlighting that reputational risk can lead to issues other than just reduced sales, and declining share price. In the same way that a good reputation can attract employees, reputational damage can lead to loss of skilled workers.

10 Managing reputational risk

Warren Buffett, a famous American businessman, once said "It takes 20 years to build a reputation and five minutes to ruin it. If you think about that, you'll do things differently".

A good reputation therefore has many benefits from attracting higher calibre employees to attracting loyal customers. This can then lead to higher sales, both from these satisfied customers, and from new customers attracted as a result of referrals. Such a positive image can then lead to easier access to finance and a share price that outperforms the market. Finally, a good reputation can help build relationships with legislators and regulators which could mean being meaningfully involved in discussions around changes in regulations.

There are many ways to manage reputational risk, here are some examples:

- governance
- employee relations
- environmental awareness
- external relations
- risk professionals
- a policy framework
- risk sensing tools

More on managing reputational risk

In more detail:

Governance

There is more detail on governance in chapter 5 and in the ERM section of chapter 2. It is important for the board of directors to be aware and open minded about the possible reputational damage that the company could cause through its actions. In particular they must be alert to new risks that are not currently included in the risk register or risk management processes of the company.

A culture of doing the right thing, again linking to one of the ERM principles – the control environment – will help set the appropriate tone.

Employee relations

In line with the ERM framework, every single person within the organisation has a responsibility to manage risk, including reputation risk. Using bribery as an example, it doesn't have to be a senior figure accepting or making the bribe, it could be someone working at an operational level, but the bribe could still lead to concerns over the culture within the organisation.

Regular communication with the workforce, including training and education on the potential for reputational risk, should be provided – reminding them about the ways to deal with any concerns.

External relations

Transparency with stakeholders should be as great as is possible without giving away information that provides a competitive advantage. There must be clear and transparent communication with stakeholders about what the organisation is doing and why it is doing it.

Environmental awareness

This relates to being aware of not only the impact that the company and its supply chain is having on the environment, but also changes in beliefs about how society should interact with the environment. For example, diesel engines were previously perceived to be more environmentally friendly than petrol, and there is now a much increased awareness of the damage that single use plastic is having on the environment.

Monitoring

Monitoring can mean internal monitoring of certain metrics or controls to ensure that policies and procedures are being undertaken as they should. It can also be applied to monitoring of external sources, for example social media, to gain an awareness of what is being said about the company, the competitors and potentially the industries the company is involved in.

Risk professionals

A company could employ or hire the services of an expert in risk and risk management. These individuals could review known risks and mitigation strategies, but also consider emerging risks relating to strategy and the changing environmental and social factors.

Policy framework

Setting up a framework relating to risks, and in particular highlighting reputational risk, can help employees with identification of potential issues, and will also enable clear and consistent assessment and management of risks.

Risk sensing tools

As the rise of social media is part of the reason for an increased focus on reputational risk, organisations are investing significantly in tools to analyse text and linguistics used in social media posts and reviews to understand what is being said about their firm. They are aiming to do this in real time, so they effectively have a live feed of public opinion, giving them time to act quickly and avoid surprises.

10.1 How to respond in a crisis

Prevention is an excellent approach, but the reality is, as with every risk, complete prevention is unrealistic, so it is also sensible for an organisation to have a crisis response plan for an event that may damage their reputation. Options a company could use:

- setting up a crisis response team
- scenario planning

Reputation crisis response

Crisis response team

Having a team of people who are responsible for coordinating a companywide response will help make sure the message is consistent with the overall strategy, brand and culture of the firm.

Having a crisis response team should include a clear escalation policy for the whole company. This should include who should be informed and when and what any individual should say should a new reporter phone or ask any questions outside the companies premises.

Scenario planning

As reputational risk is becoming more and more of a strategic issue, it makes sense to use strategic tools to assist with risk management and responses.

A risk committee, or potentially the crisis response team, could model various reputational issues, for example a backlash from customers on social media and plan a coordinated and considered response to such events, rather than having a reactive response that could lead to further issues.

Test your understanding 16 – Private hospital (Case study)

Scenario

A private hospital has a canteen that provides staff and visitors with subsidised meals and refreshments. The canteen's selling prices are supposed to cover running costs, so that there is no net cost to the hospital. Over the past eighteen months the canteen has been reporting losses that have been increasing steadily despite monthly sales remaining constant. The cost of purchases has grown substantially for no apparent reason. The purchasing of supplies and the choice of suppliers is the sole responsibility of the Canteen Manager. The current Canteen Manager has been in post for almost two years.

Trigger

The hospital's Chief Executive asked the Head of Internal Audit to investigate why the canteen was making losses and a thorough investigation was conducted under the supervision of F, an experienced auditor and qualified accountant. The internal audit team discovered that the losses started shortly after the Canteen Manager changed suppliers. F compared the invoiced prices charged by the new supplier with those charged by the former supplier and discovered that the new supplier was significantly more expensive.

F interviewed the Canteen Manager, who claimed the change in suppliers was because the new supplier was more reliable and provided higher quality products. F was suspicious and contacted a number of alternative suppliers. None of the potential suppliers whom F contacted would have charged as much as the canteen was paying for basic commodities such as rice and potatoes. Furthermore, the canteen's invoices showed that it was paying far more than the normal market price for branded goods, such as crisps and chocolate bars.

F was in the Canteen Manager's office one lunch time, saw a laptop computer open at an email to the supplier and investigated further. The Canteen Manager had been using a personal email account to email the owner of the supplier on a daily basis. The emails revealed that:

- the owner had been inflating the selling prices of all goods sold to the hospital by 20%;

- the Canteen Manager passed these inflated invoices for payment; and

- the owner then paid half of the 20% that had been overcharged to the Canteen Manager in cash.

F confiscated the laptop, which was the Canteen Manager's personal property, and submitted it, along with a full report, to the Head of Internal Audit.

Two weeks later, F was asked to meet with the hospital's Chief Executive. The hospital's directors had discussed the report carefully and had interviewed the Canteen Manager and decided that they did not wish to refer the matter to the police. The Canteen Manager had been accompanied by a lawyer, who stated that the Canteen Manager denied all charges of fraud and pointed out that there was very little evidence to support F's accusations. F could have easily falsified the emails on the laptop and the owner of the food supplier had supplied the lawyer with a statement that no payments had been made to the Canteen Manager. The Chief Executive had agreed that the hospital would return the Canteen Manager's laptop and would make him a substantial payment in return for his agreement to resign quietly. The Chief Executive had also promised that the Canteen Manager would receive a positive reference. F was asked to destroy any remaining notes and documents relating to this investigation and to remain silent, not discussing the case with anyone either within the hospital or any third parties.

Task

(a) Critically evaluate the decision by the Chief Executive to pay the Canteen Manager to resign quietly.

(b) Advise F on the ethical issues arising from destroying the notes taken and maintaining silence on this investigation.

(30 minutes)

Test your understanding 17 – M mobile telephones (Case study)

Scenario

M is the leading retailer of mobile telephones in its home country. The company has almost 100 branches, with at least one branch in every major town and city. Some branches are located within walking distance of one another.

M has a highly aggressive management team. It views sales growth as the key to the company's continuing success. It believes that increasing their share of the retail market will enable M to negotiate large discounts from manufacturers and network providers. It also creates economies of scale in the advertising and promotion of the company and its services.

Two years ago the directors abandoned traditional budgeting and target setting. They decided that budgets did not necessarily give branch staff a sufficient incentive to maximise sales because they tended to work towards achieving but not surpassing sales targets. They introduced a new management control system with the following features:

- Shop sales are recorded using electronic point of sales (EPOS) cash registers that are linked to head office. Every sale indicates the branch and the member of staff responsible for the sale. These transactions are recorded in real time during the course of the day.

- A terminal in every shop lists a running total of that shop's sales for the day, analysed between each member of sales staff. The terminal also indicates the shop's ranking for the day relative to all of M's other shops.

- Every shop manager must be at work at least an hour before the shop opens. During that hour the manager receives a telephone call from the regional sales manager to discuss the previous day's sales and the likely sales during the day ahead.

- Each shop manager is permitted considerable freedom to introduce special offers and promotions, subject to achieving an acceptable margin on each sale made.

- At the end of every week the manager and staff of the ten shops with the highest sales are given a substantial bonus. The manager and staff at the ten shops with the poorest sales are given one week's notice to improve or they face being moved to other shops or even dismissal.

- Sales have grown rapidly since this system was introduced, although the rate of growth has been declining recently.

The Director of Human Resources has investigated staff absenteeism and turnover and has discovered that many of M's branch managers and sales staff have been with the company for several years. They seem to thrive in the competitive environment and the company pays staff with good sales records a substantial salary compared with other retailers. M also suffers a high staff turnover every year and some members of staff are frequently absent for health reasons, with their doctors certifying them as ill due to stress-related conditions.

Trigger

M's Chief Accountant is concerned that the company's management accounting systems are unethical and she has provided the board with a copy of CIMA's Code of Professional Ethics.

Task

Write a letter to the Board advising on the ethical implications of their approach to personnel management.

(20 minutes)

Test your understanding 18 – Grove council (Case study)

Scenario

Grove Council is the local government authority responsible for the running of public services in a district of approximately 200 square miles and with a population of over 300,000. The Grove district comprises a mixture of towns, villages and rural areas.

The Council employs approximately 13,000 staff in a wide variety of occupations. The Council is responsible for the maintenance of the entire public infrastructure in its area of responsibility, including the roads and sewerage systems. The Council also manages education and cares for vulnerable residents such as the elderly and infirm. The Council has a divisional structure, with divisions taking responsibility for specific matters such as education, roads and so on throughout the Grove district.

Employment law requires that every employer, including Grove Council, must maintain a register of all workplace injuries sustained by employees. There is no precise definition of a reportable injury, but Council guidelines indicate that anything that requires a dressing, such as a bandage or sticking plaster, must be reported as minor injuries. Injuries are classified as "serious" if they require the victim to be absent from work for more than three days and "severe" if they require admission to hospital or involve a fatality.

Trigger

The latest injury statistics show that there were 150 injuries during the last year, of which 20 were serious injuries and 3 were severe. The Council's Director of Operations (DO) is satisfied with these figures because the number of injuries is no worse than in previous years. The DO holds the view that such figures are to be expected given the diverse range of jobs, many of which are risky, throughout the Council. The Chief Executive of the Council does not share these views: but believes that the Council should try to prevent all injuries by eliminating accidents in the workplace.

The Chief Executive asked Grove Council's internal audit department to review the systems for reporting injuries. As part of their response a CIMA qualified member of internal audit was sent to investigate the repair depot that maintains the Council's fleet of vehicles. The depot employs a team of over 40 mechanics and is equipped with a full range of welding and lifting equipment.

The depot's injury register had only two entries for the year prior to the internal audit visit. Both injuries were severe and each involved an injury that required an ambulance to be called and an employee to be admitted to hospital.

On enquiry, several of the mechanics explained that the small number of reports is due to the depot manager refusing to record injuries unless they are either serious or severe. Several of the depot mechanics are trained in first aid and no records are kept of any injuries that they treat. All of the mechanics refused to put these allegations in writing for the internal auditor.

The internal auditor asked the Head of Internal Audit to send an urgent report to the Chief Executive, but the Head of Internal Audit refused to do so on the grounds that there was insufficient evidence of manipulation. The Head of Internal Audit threatened to suspend the internal auditor if these allegations were repeated to anyone else either inside or outside of the Council. The internal auditor is dissatisfied with the Head of Internal Audit's response and is considering whether to take the matter further.

Task

As the internal auditor prepare briefing notes, which may be used in a meeting with the Audit Committee, covering:

(a)   An analysis of the ethical dilemma faced by the internal auditor.

(b)   The recommended course of action that the internal auditor should take if Head of Internal Audit cannot be persuaded to draw the allegations of under-reporting of injuries to the attention of the senior management of Grove Council.

(30 minutes)

Test your understanding 19 – SPQ (Integration)

As a CIMA member, you have recently been appointed as the Head of Internal Audit for SPQ, a multinational listed company that carries out a large volume of Internet sales to customers who place their orders using their home or work computers. You report to the Chief Executive although you work closely with the Finance Director. You have direct access to the Chair of the audit committee whenever you consider it necessary.

One of your internal audit teams has been conducting a review of IT security for a system which has been in operation for 18 months and which is integral to Internet sales. The audit was included in the internal audit plan following a request by the Chief Accountant. Sample testing by the internal audit team has revealed several transactions over the last three months which have raised concerns about possible hacking or fraudulent access to the customer/order database. Each of these transactions has disappeared from the database after deliveries have been made but without sales being recorded or funds collected from the customer. Each of the identified transactions was for a different customer and there seems to be no relationship between any of the transactions.

You have received the draft report from the internal audit manager responsible for this audit which suggests serious weaknesses in the design of the system. You have discussed this informally with senior managers who have told you that such a report will be politically very unpopular with the Chief Executive as he was significantly involved in the design and approval of the new system and insisted it be implemented earlier than the IT department considered was advisable. No post-implementation review of the system has taken place.

You have been informally advised by several senior managers to lessen the criticism and work with the IT department to correct any deficiencies within the system and to produce a report to the Audit Committee that is less critical and merely identifies the need for some improvement. They suggest that these actions would avoid criticism of the Chief Executive by the Board of SPQ.

Required:

Explain the ethical principles that you should apply as the Head of Internal Audit for SPQ when reporting the results of this internal review and how any ethical conflicts should be resolved.

(20 minutes)

Test your understanding 20 – Erasmus (Integration)

You are the newly-appointed financial controller of Erasmus, a fully owned subsidiary of the Think Group. The following matters have come to your attention:

(1) Your assistant, a newly-qualified Management Accountant, is heavily in debt to a junior member of the finance staff, who has a considerable amount of personal wealth in spite of her fairly junior position in the company.

(2) The CEO of the company was in the habit of making accounting adjustments to the financial statements prepared by the finance director in order to 'smooth out variances' if actual performance was not going to plan.

(3) A member of your department, another Management Accountant, recently made significant errors in completing the sales tax returns to the tax authorities, which resulted in a fine and interest charges for an underpayment of the sales tax liability.

Required:

Discuss how you would deal with each of these three problems in order to bring about an improvement in the ethical standards in the systems of management. Indicate any problems you might expect to arise when you attempt to bring about change.

(15 minutes)

Test your understanding 21 – Five ethical situations (Integration)

In all of the ethical situations below, the people involved are qualified members of CIMA.

- A applies for a job and enhances her CV by indicating she obtained first time passes in all her examinations, although she actually failed three exams at the first attempt.

- B is the management accountant in C Ltd. B is paid a bonus based on the profits of C Ltd. During accounts preparation B notices an error in the inventory calculation which has the effect of overstating profits. B decides to take no action as this would decrease the bonus payable.

- D is responsible for the purchase of computer equipment in E Ltd. Quotes from three suppliers have been received for installation of new hardware; one supplier, F Co, has promised a 10% discount, payable to D, if their quote is accepted.

- G is preparing the management accounts in H Ltd. Part of the information presented to her indicates that H Ltd entered into an illegal agreement with I Ltd to fix price increases in the goods H and I supply. H and I together supply 90% of the total market. The price setting enabled H and I to obtain higher than expected profits for their sales.

- J is preparing the management accounts for K Ltd. L, the senior management accountant, has instructed J to omit the negative overhead variance from the accounts on the grounds that they show an 'unacceptable loss' with the inclusion of the variance.

Required:

(a) Explain how professional codes of ethics address possible conflicts of interest facing accountants. **(15 minutes)**

(b) For each of the situations above:

(i) Identify and explain the ethical threat to the accountant.

(ii) Discuss the ethical safeguards available to overcome that threat. **(30 minutes)**

11 Chapter summary

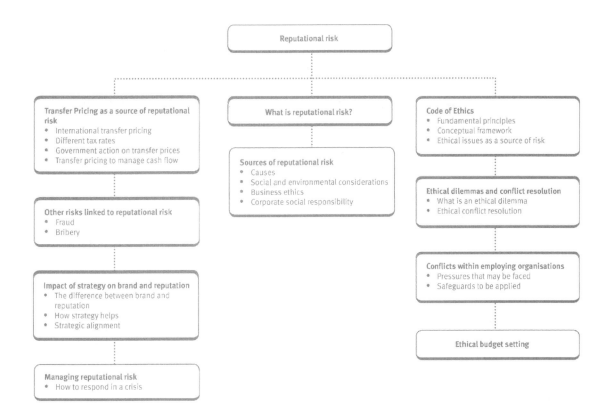

Test your understanding answers

Test your understanding 1

- Ethical behaviour is likely to be favoured by:
    - customers: resulting in higher sales volumes and/or prices
    - employees: resulting in the attraction/retention of the best employees and increased employee productivity.
    - business collaborators: resulting in increased opportunities for profitable projects.
- Ethical behaviour reduces risk and gives access to cheaper funds which in turn increase project NPVs.
- Unethical behaviour will, at some point be discovered resulting in a damage to reputation and potential legal charges.

Test your understanding 2

- The purpose of a business is to make profits. Profit is a good thing in its own right as it supports stable employment, innovation, allows higher taxes to be paid and makes economies richer. Companies have no need to feel guilty about making profits and buying off some of that guilt by embarking on good works.
- The prime stakeholders are the shareholders and directors should always attempt to maximise shareholder wealth. If directors embark on a CSR programme, have shareholders given permission? It is, after all, shareholders' money that is being used.
- CSR allows directors to feel generous and righteous – but with someone else's money. Better, perhaps, that directors and shareholders make private donations out of their remuneration and dividends.
- What is the democratic basis which companies use to choose between CSR projects? Simply choosing a project because the chief executive likes it does not mean the money is being well spent – the project could be already well-funded.

Test your understanding 3

The correct answers are B, C and D

The fundamental principles are integrity, objectivity, professional competence and due care, professional behaviour and CONFIDENTIALITY (not communication).

Test your understanding 4

The correct answer is D

By definition.

Test your understanding 5

The correct answer is A

By definition.

Test your understanding 6

C

Allowing a part-qualified colleague to complete the work at home exposes the firm to a high risk that the work will be rushed and not up to the quality expected.

Test your understanding 7

A, B and E

- Option A – Integrity implies fair dealing and truthfulness. L would not be telling the truth if she provided the reference.

- Option B – L's objectivity is likely to be threatened anyway given she is a personal friend of the client.

- Option C – There is nothing to suggest L is compromising her duty to maintain her skills.

- Option D – The client is clearly giving L permission to contact the bank.

- Option E – Giving a misleading reference would discredit the accountancy profession if knowledge of it became public.

Test your understanding 8

A

Ali can benefit directly from any manipulation or questionable judgements that Ali makes concerning the accounts.

Test your understanding 9

A and D

- Option A – Potential customers may see B's products as less safe as a result of the issue.

- Option B – Unlikely given B Company's risk assessment.

- Option C – As option 2 above.

- Option D – A recall is more ethical since, if successful, it will prevent injury completely.

Test your understanding 10

A and B

- Option A: The board has a fiduciary responsibility to its employees. It could be argued this responsibility is more important than ever when employees are vulnerable – for example in very poor countries.

- Option B: If it is no longer safe to mine R33, the communities are indeed under threat since the mining is their main source of funds.

- Option C: The board of D has a duty to set a suitable 'tone from the top' and a high level commitment to internal controls and risk management. They must conduct regular risk assessments and would be unable to ignore the findings of the report.

- Option D: The poorest nations are unlikely to have detailed employment laws with regards to safety.

- Option E: See Option C above.

Test your understanding 11

The correct answer is A

The correct order of events is to firstly check the facts. Then once you are sure of the facts to escalate internally. If the issue cannot be resolved internally then you should escalate it externally e.g. call CIMA. Finally if the ethical issue continues you should dissociate with the conflict i.e. possibly resign

Test your understanding 12

B, D and F

- Option A: This is not appropriate since the employer's objectives are fraudulent.

- Option B: This is a reasonable course of action although it will cause upset.

- Option C: There are no other managers in D Co.

- Option D: This is a reasonable, although expensive course of action.

- Option E: D Co is a small, family-run business, which is unlikely to have a formal dispute resolution process.

- Option F: This is the most immediately practical although may not get results since the son may refuse to comply.

Test your understanding 13

The correct answers are A, B, C and E

The six ethical threats are self-interest, self review, advocacy, intimidation, familiarity and adverse interest.

Test your understanding 14

The correct answer is C

By definition.

Test your understanding 15

The correct answers are B, D and E

Training, disciplinary actions and internal control systems should help to safeguard against ethical threats.

Intimidation, inducements and disclosure of confidential information may cause ethical issues.

Test your understanding 16 – Private hospital (Case study)

(a) It would be unacceptable for the Chief Executive to make this arrangement in order to protect the reputations of the hospital's senior management. If the public becomes aware of the fraud then the fact that the senior management team had not detected it sooner could lead to criticism of the hospital's governance arrangements.

The Chief Executive may have been acting in the best interests of the hospital. Under the circumstances, it would have been necessary to have suspended the manager from duty on full pay until the allegations could be properly investigated. It would almost certainly have been impossible for this investigation to reach a satisfactory conclusion and so the suspension would have been prolonged and expensive. Paying the manager to leave made it possible to restrict the cost of the settlement to the agreed sum.

The hospital would also have been unable to appoint a replacement Canteen Manager while the investigation was still in progress. The payment will leave the post vacant and so a new appointment can be made to this important role. Staff may be demotivated if they discover that the control system had broken down in this way and that a major fraud had been committed. Paying the manager to leave quietly will enable the directors to maintain the impression that the control environment is functioning.

The payment will, of course, come from funds that had been intended to treat patients. Even if the payment is justified as the least expensive resolution of this problem, it is undesirable for hospital resources to be spent in this way.

(b) Qualified accountants are generally subject to ethical codes that are almost identical to CIMA's Code of Ethics for Professional Accountants. That code applies within the company and to contact with third parties. Thus, F is subject to a formal duty to respect the confidence of the hospital and not divulge this arrangement to anybody else, either within the hospital or outside of it.

This duty of confidence does not necessarily apply in every case. F has a wider duty to the stakeholders involved and so society in general. F could breach this duty of confidence if doing so was in the public interest. F should consider that possibility, although it seems unlikely to be the case given the facts. The amounts stolen from the hospital are unlikely to be sufficiently large as to warrant breach of confidence. On the other hand, the fact that the manager will receive a positive reference could mean that he will be able to repeat the fraud, which could create some justification for F to report the matter to, say, the police.

F is obliged to act with integrity. It could be argued that F has already discharged his responsibility by reporting the suspected fraud to the head of internal audit, who has clearly reported the matter to senior management. It appears that the management team has reached a decision that is in the hospital's best interests and so there is no real need for F to take any further action.

Test your understanding 17 – M mobile telephones (Case study)

Address

Date

Dear Board of Directors,

Re: Ethical principles

CIMA's Code of Professional Ethics states that a professional accountant is required to comply with five fundamental principles.

Integrity

A person should be straightforward and honest in all professional and business relationships.

Objectivity

A person should not allow bias, conflict of interest or undue influence of others to override professional or business judgements.

Professional competence and due care

A person has a continuing duty to maintain professional knowledge and skill at the level required to ensure that an employer or customer receives a competent professional service.

Confidentiality

A person should respect the confidentiality of information acquired as a result of professional relationships and should not disclose any such information to third parties without proper authority.

Professional behaviour

A person should comply with relevant laws and regulations and should avoid any action that discredits the company.

Not all of M's directors will be professional accountants but the code of ethics will still be appropriate to a professional company such as M and its directors. The Director of Human Resources is concerned that M has a high staff turnover, linked to the high absence rate due to 'stress related conditions' at M. The highly competitive environment at M is being blamed for this.

Sales have grown rapidly although the rate is now slowing. It is possible that in the past sales staff have been adopting an aggressive sales technique which only works once with customers, since they are not pleased with their purchase and don't return to make another. This is a short-sighted sales technique, where sales growth will be high at first, but then fewer repeat purchases are made and sales staff struggle to meet their objectives in the future.

Staff will become very worried about the implications of failing to meet the sales objectives if they think that they have only a week to correct their actions, or face being moved to another shop or dismissed. Moving to another shop may be inconvenient for their home life, and dismissal would be worrying in that they may not be able to find another job quickly, becoming unable to provide for any family they may have.

If moving to another store is seen as a threat by staff then this is unethical, since professional staff and companies should not use threats to incentivise their staff.

The employer has a responsibility to treat information about their employees in confidence. If the staff's results are being published, anyone can identify under-performers, which breaches confidentiality.

The environment at M may suit certain individuals who thrive on competition, but for others it will be very stressful if they are not natural sales people and they have dependents that rely on their salary. From a director's point of view, working a member of staff so hard that they become ill is unethical.

Sales staff may be driven to 'hard-sell' products to customers, and may even tell un-truths to secure a sale. This goes against the principle of integrity stated in the code of ethics. M's reputation will become tarnished if it becomes public knowledge that their employees mislead customers into buying a product that is not suitable for them.

Similarly rewarding a member of staff for high sales that may not have been made ethically will reflect badly on the management of M.

New staff members are unlikely to meet the sales growth objective straight away. They will be unfamiliar with some of the products and could misadvise a customer. They should be allowed a period of settling in. The new staff are possibly the major part of the high staff turnover at M.

The high absenteeism and staff turnover is not good for M as it is very costly to pay someone to be off work or to frequently recruit new members of staff.

New staff will learn sales techniques from the more established staff members, which may not always be ethical sales methods. The element of competition may lead them to lack objectivity in their sales dealings. Older sales staff should not have undue influence over the new staff, and the new staff should be encouraged to have their own ethical principles.

I hope this clarifies any queries you had. Should you require any further information, please do not hesitate to ask.

Yours sincerely,

A.N. Accountant

Test your understanding 18 – Grove council (Case study)

Briefing notes

To: Audit Committee

From: Internal auditor

Date: Today

Subject: Ethics

(a)   The internal auditor has reason to believe that records are being falsified that could threaten the health and safety of staff at the depot. If members of staff stop reporting minor cuts and bruises then the Council will not be aware of risks that could result in a more serious accident, such as a safety issue with a particular machine. That could lead to avoidable accidents occurring because the need for repairs or modifications was not apparent. Remaining silent about these allegations could be viewed as a breach of the requirement to apply professional competence and due care.

Bypassing the Head of Internal Audit by reporting directly to the Chief Executive or another senior officer would breach the duty to demonstrate professional behaviour. But the internal auditor is subordinate to the head of department who has ruled that the matter is to be taken no further. Any report that cannot be substantiated could lead to a waste of time and effort and could undermine the credibility of internal audit.

Any report to a third party would breach the internal auditor's duty of confidence. As an employee, there is a duty not to divulge any information to a third party. As a CIMA member, the internal auditor is also bound by CIMA's Code of Ethics for Professional Accountants, which makes that duty even more significant.

(b)   The internal auditor should consider whether there is any reason to believe that inaction is likely to lead to a serious risk to life or health. If the records that are being suppressed relate to trivial cuts and bruises and are unlikely to leave staff exposed to more serious risks then there is no need to do anything further.

It would be possible to approach the depot manager and seek an explanation as to whether these allegations are true. If the manager makes a genuine commitment to report honestly then the problem will be resolved.

If a review of the facts suggests that the depot's reporting practices are significantly increasing the risk of severe injuries then the auditor should take matters further. The depot had two out of only three severe injuries for the Council as a whole. Failing to act on such information could be viewed as criminal negligence.

Any report should be made in the first instance to an appropriate senior Council officer, possibly addressed to the Chief Executive in the first instance. There is only a need to report to a third party, such as the Health and Safety Executive, if the risk is high enough to justify the breach of confidence and the internal report is ignored.

If the Head of Internal Audit is bypassed then the auditor may feel it necessary to resign.

Test your understanding 19 – SPQ (Integration)

The fundamental principles that relate to the work of accountants as internal auditors are integrity (acting honestly and avoiding misleading statements); objectivity (impartiality and freedom from conflicts of interest); professional competence and due care; confidentiality; professional behaviour and the avoidance of conduct that might bring discredit to CIMA; and technical competence (the presentation of information fully, honestly and professionally).

Most of these principles apply in the present case. If the evidence justifies it, integrity and objectivity require that it be brought to the audit committee's attention. However, professional and technical competence requires that the Head of Internal Audit be confident in the audit findings before doing so.

CIMA's Ethical Guidelines describe the process for resolving ethical conflicts. Accountants working in organisations may encounter situations which give rise to conflicts of interest, ranging from fraud and illegal activities to relatively minor situations. An ethical conflict is not the same as an honest difference of opinion.

CIMA members should be constantly conscious of, and be alert to factors which give rise to conflicts of interest. In the present case, the ethical conflict is the real or perceived pressure placed on the Head of Internal Audit not to embarrass the Chief Executive. There is also the question of divided loyalty to the Chief Executive, to the audit committee, and to the Head of Internal Audit's professional responsibilities as a CIMA member.

Although it has not been suggested to the Head of Internal Audit that the matter not be reported, there is a suggestion that the report be softened and that work carry on behind the scenes to improve the system.

However, it is important that a draft report be produced and submitted for comment before it is sent to the audit committee. This presents the opportunity for other views to be aired. One course of action may be to discuss the matter with the Finance Director to determine his/her view and with the Chief Executive to determine that person's reactions to the draft audit report.

When faced with ethical conflicts, members should:

- Follow the organisation's grievance procedure.

- Discuss the matter with the member's superior and successive levels of management, always with the member's superior's knowledge (unless that person is involved).

Discussion with an objective adviser or the professional body may be useful to clarify the issues involved and alternative courses of action that are available, without breaching any duty of confidentiality. Throughout, the member should maintain a detailed record of the problem and the steps taken to resolve it.

If an ethical conflict still exists after fully exhausting all levels of internal review, the member may have no recourse on significant matters other than to resign and report the matter to the organisation. Except when seeking advice from CIMA or when legally required to do so, communication of information regarding the problem to persons outside the employing organisation is not considered appropriate.

Test your understanding 20 – Erasmus (Integration)

(1) **Indebtedness of the assistant to the junior staff member**

This situation might call into question the independence and objectivity of the assistant in carrying out her work within the finance function. It could also threaten my own position, if it were generally known that a member of my staff is receiving financial assistance from a junior colleague.

The position of the assistant is difficult, because she is presumably unable to repay the debt immediately, and she might be unaware of the fact that she has put the internal audit section into an embarrassing position.

I should discuss the position with her, and explain the problem that it has caused. She should be reminded of CIMA's ethical guidelines about the need to maintain objectivity and independence. I should find out how quickly she plans to repay the debt. If this will not happen quickly, I should ask whether she might be able to obtain a loan to repay the debt. (The company might possibly be willing to provide a loan for such a purpose.)

If the assistant is unable to agree to my suggestion, I should have to consider recommending that she should be moved to another position where her independence and objectivity would not be compromised.

(2) **CEO's accounting adjustments**

It is my responsibility to provide the CEO with financial information that is competently and accurately prepared. The CEO presumably shares the financial information with board colleagues and the board of the parent company. I need to consider whether any adjustments made by the CEO to financial statements that I prepare will bring my integrity into question.

I should resist attempts by the CEO to amend financial results to make them seem better than they actually are. It would be particularly worrying if figures have been altered in order to improve the financial rewards for the CEO. On the other hand, some prudent adjustments to the figures might be justifiable.

I should discuss the situation with the finance director and the CEO, and establish whether the CEO intends to continue altering financial statements in the future, and the reasons for doing so. If the situation cannot be resolved, I should have to consider my position within the company. I should not remain in a position where I know that my integrity is being compromised.

(3) **Errors in the sales tax returns**

CIMA members have an ethical duty to carry out their work with professional competence. Technical competence means that the staff in my department should understand the necessary rules in relation to the tax work they do. Ignorance is no excuse for mistakes, and a repetition of the errors – and the fine – must be avoided.

I need to ensure that the staff who carry out specialist tasks are competent to carry them out. Training should be provided if required. Suitable instructions and guidance should also be available for reference.

Test your understanding 21 – Five ethical situations (Integration)

(a) There are a number of possible threats to fundamental ethical principles which lead to conflicts of interest affecting accountants in their work. Professional codes of ethics aim to enable the accountant to understand how to resolve these conflicts of interest.

Conflicts of interest and their resolution are explained in the conceptual framework to the code of ethics. A framework is needed because it is impossible to define every situation where threats to fundamental principles may occur or the mitigating action required. Different assignments may also create different threats and mitigating actions – again it is not possible to detail all the assignments an accountant undertakes. The framework helps to identify threats – using the fundamental ethical principles as guidance. This approach is preferable to following a set of rules which may not be applicable in a particular case.

Once a material threat has been identified, mitigating activities will be performed to ensure that compliance with fundamental principles is not compromised.

Where conflicts arise in the application of fundamental principles, the code of ethics provides guidance on how to resolve the conflict.

The conceptual framework:

– provides an initial set of assumptions, values and definitions which are agreed upon and shared by all those subject to the framework.

– is stated in relatively general terms so it is easy to understand and communicate.

– recognises that ethical issues may have no 'correct' answer.

– provides the generalised guidelines and principles to apply to any situation.

(b) **Situation 1**

Ethical threat – dishonesty

Accountants need to be honest in stating their level of expertise – and not mislead employers by implying they have more expertise than they actually possess. In this situation, A is implying she was better at studying for her exams than her actual exam success rate. This may make the potential employer view A more favourably, or enable A to meet a recruitment criteria of 'first time passes only' for success in obtaining the job.

Ethical safeguards

It is difficult to stop provision of incorrect information in this instance.

However, A should be following the fundamental ethical principle of integrity in applying for the job. Alternatively, the potential employer could ask all applicants to confirm that information provided is accurate as a condition of employment. Any errors or omissions found later could act as initial grounds for disciplinary action.

Situation 2

Ethical threat – overstatement of profits and salary

B's bonus is determined by the same accounts that B is working on. The threat is that B will overstate profits in some way to ensure that the bonus payable is as high as possible. Again, accountants should act with integrity and honestly, although these ideals conflict in this case with B's remuneration.

Ethical safeguards

The main safeguard will be to ensure that someone other than B determines the amount of B's bonus (and checks the accounts produced) – or that the bonus is not linked to the accounts that B is preparing. This removes the conflict of interest.

Situation 3

Ethical threat – receipt of bribes/gifts

D stands to gain 10% of a contract price by accepting the quote from F rather than another company. This means D's objectivity may be breached leading to a preference for the quote from F. There is also an issue of confidentiality because presumably D will want to keep the payment 'secret' from E Ltd so the employer does not know of the inducement.

Ethical safeguard

From D's point-of-view, the obvious ethical safeguard is not to accept the bribe. This removes the objectivity issue leaving D free to choose the best system rather than the one with the most financial advantage. Alternatively, D can inform the senior management and/or board of E Ltd, provide the relevant information on the three quotes, and let the board make the final decision. Should the board choose F then again D should not accept the bribe.

Situation 4

Ethical threat – price fixing

In most situations, G would keep the affairs of the client confidential, and would be acting with integrity in taking this action. However, there is a conflict as H and I appear to have been acting illegally; increasing their profits at the expense of their customers. G can either choose to keep quiet about the situation or disclose the information to relevant third parties, effectively 'blowing the whistle' on H and I.

Ethical safeguards

G could report to the ethics committee or audit committee in H, should the company have either of these committees. As long as some appropriate action was taken, then this relieves G from external reporting obligations. External disclosure should only be made after taking into account various issues such as the gravity of the matter, the number of people affected and the likelihood of repetition. As many people are affected and repetition seems likely then external disclosure is likely to be appropriate.

Situation 5

Ethical threat – incorrect financial information

Accountants need to be able to prepare information honestly and with objectivity. However, in this situation, J is being pressured into producing information which will be incorrect, simply to show K Ltd in a better light. The instruction provides a conflict with J's integrity because she wants to follow the instructions of L but may not be able to do so because this would be dishonest.

Ethical safeguards

J needs to consult with other people apart from L in an attempt to determine the correct course of action. J can consult with any committee charged with governance (e.g. the audit committee or ethics committee) or if necessary take advice from her professional body. If after these discussions, the situation cannot be resolved, J may have to consider resignation.

Corporate governance

Chapter learning objectives

Lead	Component	
A3. Ways of managing risk	(a)	Roles and responsibilities.
B3. Explain governance risks	(a)	Explain the role of board and its committees in managing strategic risk.
	(b)	Explain failure of governance and its impact on strategy.

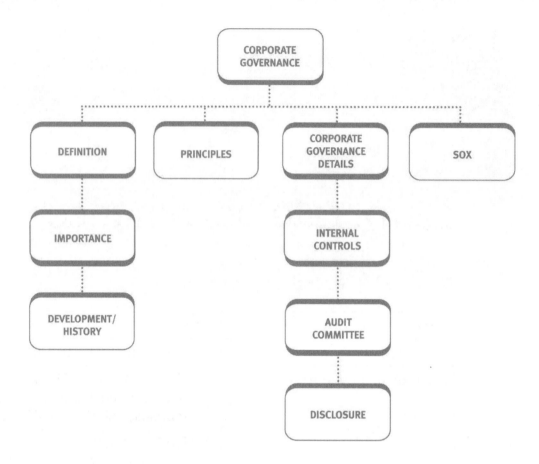

 1   What is corporate governance?

Corporate governance has been defined in many different ways, but generally it can be described as:

'the system by which companies are directed and controlled in the interest of shareholders and other stakeholders'.

There are different codes and practices around the world but they tend to cover similar areas:

*   The role of the board of directors.

*   The reliability of financial reports and the relationship between the company and its auditors.

*   The interest of the company's shareholders in the company.

Importance of corporate governance

*   In most developed countries, listed companies are required to operate systems of corporate governance laid down either by statute or by professional organisations (such as the Securities and Exchange Commission (SEC) in the US or the Financial Conduct Authority (FCA) and Prudential Regulation Authority in the UK).

*   The requirements are often given the support of the stock exchanges, in that they are built into listing rules

- The development of corporate governance codes is closely associated with the UK, hence the UK is a useful model to discuss best practice.

- The UK Corporate Governance Code follows a principles-based approach (see next section), and is endorsed by the London Stock Exchange. The US system has been much more legislative with the introduction of the Sarbanes-Oxley Act of 2002 (to be discussed later in this chapter).

- It should be appreciated that corporate governance has links to risks and internal controls. Whilst good corporate governance cannot stop company failure or prevent companies failing to achieve their objectives, it is a major help, and well-run companies tend to achieve their objectives in a less risky way. As a result it is part of risk reduction.

Development of corporate governance

- Governance regulations have developed largely as a result of a series of corporate failures in the 1980s and early 1990s.

- The corporate governance themes that began to emerge from these collapses were:

  - poorly-run companies, especially companies with a board of directors dominated by a single chair/chief executive figure, and companies with 'greedy' or 'fat cat' directors (demonstrating the agency problem of a company failing to operate in the best interests of its shareholders)

  - poor financial reporting, raising questions about auditing and internal control systems, and

  - an apparent lack of interest by the major investment institutions in the performance of the companies in which they invested.

- The UK Corporate Governance Code was developed further in accordance with the 2008–09 global financial crisis.

Company collapses

Several issues or problems appear to emerge when there is a corporate governance 'scandal' and a company has collapsed.

- The company has not been well-run by its board of directors.

- In many cases, there has been an individual who has dominated the board and exerted excessive influence on decision-making by the board. In many cases, this individual held the positions of both chair of the board and chief executive officer.

- A board of directors might have lacked sufficient breadth of knowledge and experience to appreciate the problems the company was in and the risks it faced.

- Companies were being run in the interests of the executive directors, who received high remuneration packages and generous bonuses, but the rewards were not being given for the achievement of objectives that were in the best interests of the shareholders. The interests of the directors were not properly aligned with those of the shareholders.

- Financial reporting was unreliable and the published accounts did not seem to give any indication of the true financial position of the company. In some cases there was a suspicion that the auditors were not sufficiently independent of the company and so not fulfilling their responsibilities adequately. Alternatively, the auditors were accused of doing their job badly or of being misled by the company's directors and management. (In 2002 audit firm Arthur Andersen collapsed from the consequences of its involvement in the Enron scandal.)

- Whenever a company collapsed unexpectedly, there have been suspicions that the internal control system was ineffective. There usually appears to have been inadequate risk management generally.

- Questions have also been asked about major institutional shareholders, and whether they could have done more to identify problems in companies and persuade or force the directors to make improvements.

Maxwell Communications Corporation

Robert Maxwell was born in to extreme poverty in Czechoslovakia in 1923. By the time of his death (accident or murder was never established) in 1991 he was a media mogul, having built a publishing empire that spanned the world. In the weeks that followed his death however, news emerged of the state of his company's finances.

After the Second World War he set up Pergamon Press publishing scientific journals. It became very profitable and he turned his attention to politics, later becoming a Member of Parliament for the Labour Party. His relationship with the Party was an uneasy one since anyone who criticised him was confronted in the courts. This was when signs emerged of his dishonesty.

In 1969, Maxwell agreed a takeover bid for Pergamon by Leasco (an American financial and data processing group). The profits of Pergamon were questioned by Leasco and eventually talks fell apart as a Department of Trade and Industry (DTI) enquiry ensued. Inspectors found that the profits depended on transactions with Maxwell family private companies. The DTI concluded that Maxwell 'is not a person... who can be relied upon to exercise proper stewardship of a publicly quoted company'.

In 1980 Maxwell took over the troubled British Printing Corporation renaming it Maxwell Communications Corporation. In 1984 he bought Mirror Group Newspapers (MGN) and Macmillan publishers, which put his company further into debt. In 1991 he floated MGN as a public company desperate to raise cash that would save the Group from bankruptcy (with debts over £2 billion). After Maxwell's death it transpired that he had taken money from the pension funds to keep the companies afloat and boost the share price.

Enron

In December 2001, US energy trader Enron collapsed. Enron was the largest bankruptcy in US history. Even though the United States was believed by many to be the most regulated financial market in the world, it was evident from Enron's collapse that investors were not properly informed about the significance of off-balance sheet transactions. US accounting rules may have contributed to this, in that they are concerned with the strict legal ownership of investment vehicles rather than with their control. By contrast, International Accounting Standards follow the principle of 'substance over form'. There were some indications that Enron may have actively lobbied against changing the treatment in US financial reporting of special purpose entities used in off-balance sheet financing. Overall, there was a clear need for greater transparency and trust in reporting.

The failure of Enron also highlighted the over-dependence of an auditor on one particular client, the employment of staff by Enron who had previously worked for the auditors, the process of audit appointments and re-appointments, the rotation of audit partners and how auditors are monitored and regulated.

As a consequence of the failure of Enron and WorldCom, the United States has introduced Sarbanes-Oxley legislation to address many of the criticisms of reporting and auditing practice. In their comments on the failure of Enron, the Association of Certified Chartered Accountants recommended the need for global financial markets to have a global set of principles-based financial reporting standards and a global code of corporate governance, arguing that legalistic, rules-based standards encourage creative, loophole-based practice.

Former chief executive Kenneth Lay died in 2006 before he could stand trial. Enron's former chief financial officer Andrew Fastow was sentenced in late 2006 to six years in prison for stealing from Enron and devising schemes to deceive investors about the energy company's true financial condition. Lawyers have to date won settlements totalling $US 7.3 billion from banks including JPMorgan Chase, Bank of America, Citigroup, etc.

Barings Bank

Barings Bank was Britain's oldest merchant bank, having existed for 200 years before it collapsed as a result of uncontrolled derivatives trading by Nick Leeson in the bank's Singapore office.

The collapse of Barings Bank in 1995 was caused by Nick Leeson, a 26-year-old dealer who lost £800 million in unauthorised dealings in derivatives trading from his base in Singapore. Leeson suppressed information on account '88888' which he used for trading between 1992 and 1995, which management was unaware of. The losses wiped out the Bank's capital.

As only a small amount of money (a margin) is needed to establish a derivatives position, it is possible to face financial obligations beyond an organisation's ability to pay. Therefore, strict controls are needed. There are many risk management and control lessons to be learned from the failure of Barings.

Barings had placed Nick Leeson in charge of both the dealing desk and the back office. The back office records, confirms and settles trades made by the front office and provides the necessary checks to prevent unauthorised trading and minimise the potential for fraud and embezzlement. In this dual position, Leeson was able to relay false information back to London.

An internal audit report in August 1994 concluded that Leeson's dual responsibility for both the front and back office was an excessive concentration of powers and warned of the risk that Leeson could override controls. The internal auditors' responsibility was to make sure the directors were aware of the risk they were facing by not implementing the separation of duties. However, directors did not implement these recommendations. Their response was that there was insufficient work for a full-time treasury and risk manager. There was also a lack of supervision of Leeson by Barings' managers, either in Singapore or London.

Senior managers of Barings had a superficial knowledge of derivatives, did not understand the risks of the business, did not articulate the bank's risk appetite or implement strategies and control procedures appropriate to those risks.

When the Singapore exchange made margin demands on Barings, large amounts of cash had to be paid out but still no steps were taken by the London head office to investigate the matter. Eventually, the amounts required were so great that Barings were forced to call in receivers. The trading positions taken out by Leeson were unhedged and the cost of closing out the open contracts was US$1.4 billion.

The information in this case study comes from the Report of the Board of Banking Supervision (BoBS) Inquiry into the Circumstances of the Collapse of Barings.

Worldcom

WorldCom filed for bankruptcy protection in June 2002. It was the biggest corporate fraud in history, largely a result of treating operating expenses as capital expenditure.

WorldCom (now renamed MCI) admitted in March 2004 that the total amount by which it had misled investors over the previous 10 years was almost US$75 billion (£42 billion) and reduced its stated pre-tax profits for 2001 and 2002 by that amount.

WorldCom stock began falling in late 1999 as businesses slashed spending on telecom services and equipment. A series of debt downgrades had raised borrowing costs for the company, struggling with about US$32 billion in debt. WorldCom used accounting tricks to conceal a deteriorating financial condition and to inflate profits.

Former WorldCom chief executive Bernie Ebbers resigned in April 2002 amid questions about US$366 million in personal loans from the company and a federal probe of its accounting practices. Ebbers was subsequently charged with conspiracy to commit securities fraud, and filing misleading data with the Securities and Exchange Commission (SEC). Scott Sullivan, former chief financial officer, pleaded guilty to three criminal charges.

The SEC said WorldCom had committed 'accounting improprieties of unprecedented magnitude' – proof, it said, of the need for reform in the regulation of corporate accounting.

Parmalat

In December 2003, Italian dairy-foods group Parmalat, with 36,000 employees in 30 countries, went into bankruptcy protection with US$ 8–10 billion of vanished assets. The company was 51% owned by the Tanzi family.

Parmalat defaulted on a US$185 million bond payment that prompted auditors and banks to scrutinise company accounts. Thirty-eight per cent of Parmalat's assets were supposedly held in a bank account in the Cayman Islands but no such account ever existed. Letters received from the bank by auditors were forgeries.

Parmalat has been one of the largest financial frauds in history. The company falsified its accounts over a 15-year period. This was not identified by two firms of auditors, Grant Thornton and Deloitte Touche Tohmatsu. At least 20 people have been involved in the fraud, including members of the Tanzi family, the chief financial officer, board members and the company's lawyers. Calisto Tanzi the founder and chief executive was arrested on suspicion of fraud, embezzlement, false accounting and misleading investors.

Tanzi admitted that he knew the accounts were falsified to hide losses and the falsified balance sheet was used to enable Parmalat to continue borrowing. He also confessed to misappropriating US$620 million, although prosecutors believe it could be as much as US$1 billion.

Equitable Life

During the 1960s to 1980s the 242-year-old Equitable Life had sold thousands of policies with guaranteed returns, some as high as 12%. The company ran into problems in 2000 when it closed to new business after years of excessive returns to special policy holders had left the company with no money to absorb a deterioration in the value of its stock market investments. It had a 'black hole' in its finances estimated at £4.4 billion because it had been paying out more to policy holders than it held in reserves. Equitable lost a case in the House of Lords in 2000 that led to a further deterioration in its financial position of £1.5 billion.

A report by Lord Penrose published early in 2004 said that the former management was primarily culpable for Equitable's near collapse, aided by the failure of regulators to identify the mutual insurer's financial position. The autocratic former Chief Executive and chief actuary Roy Ranson was blamed for keeping regulators and the board of Equitable in the dark about the precarious state of Equitable's financial position throughout the 1990s. The Penrose report also said that there had been weaknesses in the way that insurance companies were supervised throughout that period. The 'light touch' approach to regulation had not been changed to meet the requirements of an increasingly sophisticated and risky investment industry.

The Penrose report said that management had been dominated by 'unaccountable' actuaries, a board of non-executives who had no idea what was going on at the company they were charged with overseeing and, a regulator that failed to act as any kind of protector for policy holders.

Lord Penrose said, "The board at no stage got fully to grips with the financial situation faced by the Society. Information was too fragmented [and], their collective skills were inadequate for the task".

Test your understanding 1

The lack of knowledge and supervision by management, and the excessive concentration of power placed on one employee enabling the overriding of controls was prevalent at:

A   Enron

B   Maxwell Communications Corporation

C   Barings Bank

D   Worldcom

Test your understanding 2

Money secretly taken from the pension fund to keep the company afloat and boost the share price was the cause for concern at:

A   Enron

B   Maxwell Communications Corporation

C   Barings Bank

D   Worldcom

- The most recent update in 2018, the focus areas were Directors' Remuneration to reduce the likelihood of excessive pay and bonuses, and running the organisation with a long term view.

Volkswagen

In September 2015, Volkswagen Group, the German multinational automotive manufacturing company, were issued with a notice of violation of the Clean Air Act by the United States Environmental Protection Agency. The Agency found that Volkswagen had deliberately programmed certain diesel engines vehicles to automatically activate their emission controls to meet US standards during laboratory testing but emit more than 40 times more nitrogen oxide emissions in real world driving conditions.

This is an example of managers prioritising short term profitability and receiving their bonuses over the interests of shareholders. For a decision of this nature to have been taken, the tone from the top of the group appears to be inappropriate. Since the scandal, various investor advisory groups have criticised the responses to the issue. For a period of time one of the criticisms was that the senior managers of the Volkswagen group had not been held accountable for intentionally cheating on the test, although charges have been brought now.

> The group have failed to publish reports into the issue despite promising it would make certain documents public. This shows a lack of transparency towards shareholders and other stakeholders.
>
> After the scandal, a management board was set up to lead integrity and legal affairs but high profile members of this board then left raising concerns that the internal investigations and culture of the organisation were at fault and there was little desire to make meaningful change.
>
> One of the changes the company did make was to change the remuneration policy for the directors, reducing the bonuses available, but this was also criticised by advisory groups as the reduction in bonuses was accompanied by what was described as "drastic and unexplained increases in base salary".

2 Principles of good corporate governance

The Listing Rules of the London Stock Exchange require each listed company to state in its annual report:

- How it has applied the principles of the UK Corporate Governance Code.
- Whether or not it has complied with the provisions of the Code throughout the accounting period.

Although there are some legal requirements relating to corporate governance, the main approach is that listed companies are required to 'comply or explain' with the provisions of the Code. This is referred to as a principles-based approach.

The Code is constantly evolving and in the most recent update the principles of the UK Corporate Governance Code relate to the following areas:

- Board Leadership and Company Purpose
- Division of Responsibilities
- Composition, Succession and Evaluation
- Audit, Risk and Internal Control
- Remuneration.

Board leadership and company purpose

The focus on this principle appears to have increased. The provisions here were predominantly included in the principle previously called 'Relations with shareholders'.

Every company should be headed by an effective and entrepreneurial board which is collectively responsible for the long-term success of the company, creating wealth for shareholders and benefitting the community. This board should be responsible for setting the purpose, values and strategy of the company and making sure the culture is aligned with them. The members of the board should lead by example with regard to the culture of their organisation and behave with integrity.

It is the board responsibility to make sure appropriate resources are available to help the company meet its objectives and review performance, this includes creating and monitoring controls to review and manage the risks it faces.

The board as a whole has responsibility for ensuring that a satisfactory dialogue with shareholders and stakeholders takes place. The board should engage with them and encourage participation from them. One of these stakeholder groups is the employees and to help this stakeholder group the company should develop policies and procedures consistent with the values of the company. There should also be a facility for employees to raise any issues.

Board leadership and company purpose

The board should consider the strategy upon which the company intends to generate wealth over the long term and report on both opportunities and risks to the continued success of the business.

The board should pay particular attention to the workforce and assess if the culture is appropriate for the policies and procedures that are aligned to the company's purpose, values and strategy. If there are any issues, corrective action should be taken and explained within the annual report.

The chair should ensure that the views of shareholders are communicated to the board as a whole. The chair should discuss governance and strategy with major shareholders. The senior independent director should attend sufficient meetings with a range of major shareholders to listen to their views in order to help develop a balanced understanding of the issues and concerns of major shareholders.

The chairs of the audit, remuneration and nomination committees should also engage with the shareholders with regard to their areas of responsibility.

The interests of key stakeholders should be considered and details of discussion around these interests should be described in the annual report. In particular, there is guidance for engaging with the workforce either through:

- a director appointed from the workforce

- a formal workforce advisory panel

- a designated non-executive director

If one of these options is not implemented the alternative arrangements and their efficacy should be explained.

A formal whistleblowing policy should be in place for the workforce to raise concerns in confidence and – if desired – anonymously. Any concerns should be reviewed and followed up on by the board.

The board should seek to identify any conflicts of interest and ensure there do not compromise the company's ability to achieve its objectives.

Directors should record any concerns they have about the operations of the board in the board minutes and if a NED resigns they should provide a written statement about any concerns they had to the chair, which should be circulated to the board.

If more than 20 percent of shareholders vote against a board recommendation for a resolution, then an explanation should be given regarding what actions the board will take to understand the shareholders concerns. The views received and actions taken should be published within 6 months of the shareholders meeting.

Division of responsibilities

There should be a clear division of responsibilities and no single individual should have unfettered powers of decision (See Maxwell illustration earlier.). The chair is responsible for leadership of the board and ensuring its effectiveness. Non-executive directors should constructively challenge and help develop proposals on strategy.

- There should be a clear division of responsibilities between running the board (the role of the chair) and the executive responsibility for the running of the company's business (the role of the CEO).

- The roles of chair of the board and CEO should not be held by the same individual.

This was not the case at Marks and Spencer plc in 2008 when they appointed Stuart Rose as CEO and Chair. The company stated that it was a temporary role for 3 years until they identified a new CEO from within the company. Major shareholders – Legal and General, didn't agree with this and a heated debate ensued, not least because the dual role went against the then called UK 'Combined Code' of corporate governance. Other investors, Schroders, said that M&S were setting an 'appalling example' to other UK companies.

The Board eventually agreed to Stuart Rose being put up for re-election every year, and they appointed a new 'heavy weight' NED as senior independent director to 'keep an eye on him'.

Many smaller investors were very happy with the arrangement.

Stuart Rose remained CEO and Chair at M&S for over two years until Marc Bolland (formerly of Morrisons) took over as CEO and Robert Swannell took over as Chair (also chair of HMV).

The Chair and CEO in more detail

Chair

The chair should be independent on appointment. The following are situations that could appear to impair independence:

- was an employee within the last 5 years

- represents a significant shareholder

- has close family ties with Co.

- holds cross-directorships or has significant links with directors through in other companies or bodies

- receives other pay or benefits in addition to a directors' fee

- had material business relationship with the Co. within the last 3 years

- has served on the board for more than 9 years.

The chair should not remain the chair beyond 9 years from the date of their first appointment to the board. This can be extended for a limited period if it helps the succession planning and development of a diverse board. An explanation should always be provided if this is the case.

The specific responsibilities of the chair, inter alia, are to:

- provide leadership to the board, supplying vision and imagination, working closely with the CEO

- take a leading role in determining the composition and structure of the board which will involve regular assessment of the
  - size of the board
  - balance between executive directors and NEDs
  - interaction, harmony and effectiveness of the directors

- set the board's agenda and plan board meetings

- chair all board meetings, directing debate toward consensus

- ensure the board receives appropriate, accurate, timely and clear information

- facilitate effective contribution from NEDs

- hold meetings with the NEDs, without the executive directors present

- chair the AGM and other shareholders' meetings, using these to provide effective dialogue with shareholders

- discuss governance and major strategy with the major shareholders

- ensure that the views of shareholders are communicated to the board as a whole

CEO

The specific responsibilities of the CEO, inter alia, are to:

- develop and implement policies to execute the strategy established by the board

- assume full accountability to the board for all aspects of company operations, controls and performance

- manage financial and physical resources

- build and maintain an effective management team

- put adequate operational, financial, planning, risk and internal control systems in place

- closely monitor operations and financial results in accordance with plans and budgets

- act as an interface between board and employees

- assist in selection and evaluation of board members

- represent the company to major suppliers, customers, professional associations, etc.

Test your understanding 3

One person has carried out the roles of CEO and chair since BB Co was floated on the stock exchange 20 years ago. Recently, analysts have begun to criticise this policy explaining that since the CEO acts as her own boss because she has no chair to report to, unchecked risk taking may result and although this can produce strong short-term results it can also ending up harming a company.

The board of BB Co however believes that a single Chair/CEO may provide advantages in both leadership and oversight in light of his or her superior knowledge of the organisation.

Best practice dictates that the roles should be separated.

Which of the following could be improved by splitting the roles of CEO and Chair?

Select ALL that apply.

A   Accountability.

B   Transparency.

C   Compliance.

D   Speed of decision making.

E   Unity of leadership.

Non-Executive Directors (NEDs)

Non-executive directors should scrutinise the performance of management in meeting agreed goals and objectives and monitor the reporting of performance. They should satisfy themselves on the integrity of financial information and that financial controls and systems of risk management are robust and defensible. They are responsible for determining appropriate levels of remuneration of executive directors and have a prime role in appointing and, where necessary, removing executive directors, and in succession planning.

The Code states as a principle that the board should include a balance of NEDs and executives. This is to reduce an unfavourable balance of power towards executives.

The board should consist of half independent NEDs excluding the chair.

One NED should be the senior independent director who is directly available to shareholders if they have concerns which cannot or should not be dealt with through the appropriate channels of chair, CEO or finance director.

These functions are, to some extent, carried out as part of their positions on key committees – remuneration committee, nominations committee and audit committee – as well as discussions as part of the main Board.

Further details on NEDs

Roles

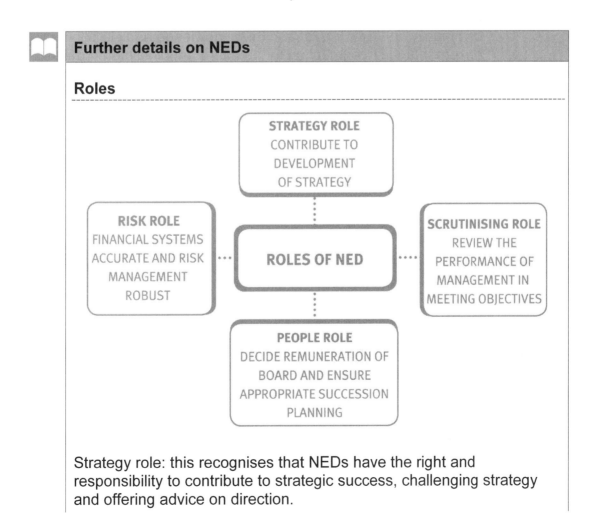

Strategy role: this recognises that NEDs have the right and responsibility to contribute to strategic success, challenging strategy and offering advice on direction.

Scrutinising role: NEDs are required to hold executive colleagues to account for decisions taken and results obtained. They should meet without the chair present at least annually (or more if necessary) to review the chair's performance.

Risk role: NEDs ensure the company has an adequate system of internal controls and systems of risk management in place.

People role: NEDs oversee a range of responsibilities with regard to the appointment and remuneration of executives and will be involved in contractual and disciplinary issues.

Effectiveness

To be effective, a NED needs to:

- build a recognition by executives of their contribution in order to promote openness and trust

- be well-informed about the company and the external environment in which it operates

- have a strong command of issues relevant to the business

- insist on a comprehensive, formal and tailored induction, continually develop and refresh their knowledge and skills to ensure that their contribution to the board remains informed and relevant

- ensure that information is provided sufficiently in advance of meetings to enable thorough consideration of the issues facing the board

- insist that information is sufficient, accurate, clear and timely

- uphold the highest ethical standards of integrity and probity

- question intelligently, debate constructively, challenge rigorously and decide dispassionately

- promote the highest standards of corporate governance and seek compliance with the provisions of the Combined Code wherever possible.

Independence

The primary fiduciary duty that NEDs owe is to the company's shareholders. They must not allow themselves to be captured or unduly influenced by the vested interests of other members of the company such as executive directors, trade unions or middle management.

There are also concerns over the recruitment of NED's and the challenge that this may bring to independence.

Recruiting those with previous industry involvement can result in a higher technical knowledge, a network of contacts and an awareness of what the strategic issues are within the industry. While these might be of some benefit to a NED's contribution, they can make the NED less independent as prior industry involvement might also reduce the NED's ability to be objective and uncontaminated by previously held views.

Accordingly, it is sometimes easier to demonstrate independence when NEDs are appointed from outside the industry.

In practice, many companies employ a mix of NEDs, and it is often this blend of talents and areas of expertise that is what makes a non-executive board effective.

Reasons for NED independence

- To provide a detached and objective view of board decisions.

- To provide expertise and communicate effectively.

- To provide shareholders with an independent voice on the board.

- To provide confidence in corporate governance.

- To reduce accusations of self-interest in the behaviour of executives.

Threats to independence

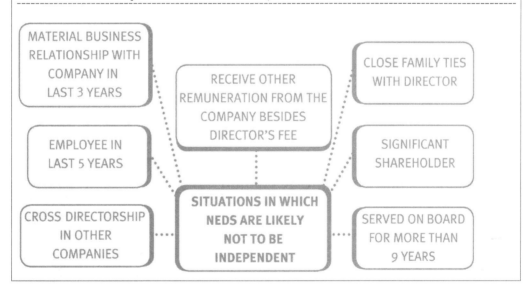

Test your understanding 4

A Company is a large retailer which operates supermarkets all over Country E. It has a board of 11 directors, 5 of whom are non-executive (NED). None of the directors have any experience of the grocery market in Country E and over half are newly appointed (within the last year).

Country E's industry is fast moving and dynamic. The executive directors are finding it time consuming to explain strategic decisions to the NED's and when they do, a perceived lack of understanding on the NED's part often leads them to disagree with the executive directors and delay things further.

The CEO has suggested that the executive directors meet without the NED's in order to make strategic decisions on a timely basis. These decisions could then be explained to the NED's at a later date.

Which of the following may be consequences of the NED's only finding out about strategic decisions after they are made?

Select ALL that apply.

A   Management's performance in meeting objectives will not be assessed by the NED's.

B   NED's will be unable to ensure risk management processes and systems are robust.

C   Decisions will be more relevant to the business since they will be made by the most knowledgeable staff.

D   Strategic decisions may not be made in the best interests of stakeholders.

E   The NED's will be able to concentrate on other aspects of their role and improve their knowledge about A Company since time will be saved.

Composition, succession and evaluation

There should be a formal procedure for the appointment of new directors to the board and an appropriate succession plan for the board and senior management, not just the CEO. Appointments and succession plans should be based on ability to do the roles and with that context, enable diversity (social, ethnic, gender).

The board and its committees should have the appropriate balance of skills, experience, independence and knowledge. All directors should be able to allocate sufficient time to the company to discharge their responsibilities effectively.

All directors should be subject to an annual evaluation regarding whether they are contributing appropriately. There should also be an annual review of the board's composition and how effective the members of the board are at working together to achieve company objectives and diversity. All directors should be submitted for re-election at regular intervals, subject to continued satisfactory performance.

Nomination Committees

The need for nomination committee is identified in many codes of best practice.

In terms of best practice, a majority of the members of the nomination committee should be independent non-executive directors.

The chair can be on the committee, but should not chair the committee when it is deciding on the appointment of a new chair.

As an example, the UK Corporate Governance Code requires that **there should be a formal, rigorous and transparent procedure for the appointments of new directors to the board.**

The main responsibilities and duties of the nominations committee are to:

- Review regularly the structure, size and composition of the board and make recommendations to the board.

- Consider the balance between executives and NEDs on the board of directors.

- Ensure appropriate management of diversity to board composition.

- Provide an appropriate balance of power to reduce domination in executive selection by the CEO/chair.

- Regularly evaluate the balance of skills, knowledge and experience of the board.

- Give full consideration to succession planning for directors.

- Prepare a description of the role and capabilities required for any particular board appointment including that of the chair.

- Identify and nominate for the approval by the board candidates to fill board vacancies as and when they arise.

- Make recommendations to the board concerning the standing for reappointment of directors.

- Be seen to operate independently for the benefit of shareholders.

There should be a formal and thorough review of the board performance, including, chair, committees and individual directors on an annual basis. Consideration should be given to involving an external party in this review on occasion, for FTSE 350 companies this should be every three years.

The chair is responsible for acting on the results of the review, including celebrating the strengths and improving the weaknesses identified. Directors should take appropriate individual action to develop any areas of weakness that have been identified within their responsibility.

The annual report and the nomination committee

The work that the nomination committee does should be included in the annual report, details could include:

- The process it uses for succession planning and how any appointments were made during the period, including a reference to how this incorporates diversity.

- How any board evaluation has been carried out, the results of this evaluation and action taken.

- Any policy on diversity, how it links to objectives and how the implementation of the policy is progressing.

- The gender split of the board, the first level of management below the board and their direct reports, plus the company secretary.

The need for succession planning

A lot of companies have a succession plan for the role of chief executive officer that is not always the case with the rest of the board. According to a 2018 survey by Robert Half Management Resources, almost half of more than 1,100 chief financial officers surveyed do not have a succession candidate in line.

It is estimated that it can take longer than six months to search for an appropriate candidate to fill the CFO, this then leads to a gap in the strategic leadership of an organisation, where productivity could decline and decisions made without appropriate consideration.

Also, if good quality finance professionals, do not have appropriate career progression opportunity at their current employer they may look elsewhere for the opportunity to become a CFO.

The work that the nominations committee does is therefore vital for the strategic benefit of a business, but also for the retention and progression of their workforce.

Audit, risk and internal control

The board should create policies and procedures to make sure that internal and external audit are independent and effective, and that financial statements are produced with integrity.

The board should present a balanced and understandable assessment of the company's position and prospects.

The board is responsible for determining the nature and extent of the significant risks it is willing to take in achieving its strategic objectives. The board should maintain sound risk management and internal control systems. The board should establish formal and transparent arrangements for considering how they should apply the corporate reporting and risk management and internal control principles and for maintaining an appropriate relationship with the company's auditor.

 Audit committee

The board should establish an audit committee of at least three, or in the case of smaller companies two, independent non-executive directors. The company chair should not be a member of the committee. The board should satisfy itself that at least one member of the audit committee has recent and relevant financial experience. The committee should, overall, be competent in the sector the company operates in.

The audit committee's role is:

- to monitor the integrity of the financial statements of the company and any formal announcements relating to the company's financial performance, reviewing significant financial reporting judgements contained in them;

- to, if asked by the board, provide appropriate guidance about if the annual report is fair, balanced and clear enough for the shareholders to assess the company's performance and strategy;

- to review the company's internal financial controls and, unless expressly addressed by a separate board risk committee composed of independent directors, or by the board itself, to review the company's internal control and risk management systems;

- to monitor and review the effectiveness of the company's internal audit function and if there is not one, to consider if there is a need for one on an annual basis and make the appropriate recommendation to the board;

- to make recommendations to the board, for it to put to the shareholders for their approval in general meeting, in relation to the appointment, re-appointment and removal of the external auditor and to approve the remuneration and terms of engagement of the external auditor;

- to review and monitor the external auditor's independence and objectivity and the effectiveness of the audit process, taking into consideration relevant UK professional and regulatory requirements;

- to develop and implement policy on the engagement of the external auditor to supply non-audit services, taking into account relevant ethical guidance regarding the provision of non-audit services by the external audit firm, and to report to the board, identifying any matters in respect of which it considers that action or improvement is needed and making recommendations as to the steps to be taken.

The terms of reference of the audit committee, including its role and the authority delegated to it by the board, should be made available.

A separate section of the annual report should describe the work of the committee in discharging those responsibilities.

The audit committee should review arrangements by which staff of the company may, in confidence, raise concerns about possible improprieties in matters of financial reporting or other matters. The audit committee's objective should be to ensure that arrangements are in place for the proportionate and independent investigation of such matters and for appropriate follow-up action.

The audit committee should monitor and review the effectiveness of the internal audit activities. Where there is no internal audit function, the audit committee should consider annually whether there is a need for an internal audit function and make a recommendation to the board, and the reasons for the absence of such a function should be explained in the relevant section of the annual report.

The audit committee should have primary responsibility for making a recommendation on the appointment, re-appointment and removal of the external auditor. If the board does not accept the audit committee's recommendation, it should include in the annual report, and in any papers recommending appointment or re-appointment, a statement from the audit committee explaining the recommendation and should set out reasons why the board has taken a different position.

The annual report should explain to shareholders how, if the auditor provides non-audit services, auditor objectivity and independence is safeguarded

Risk management and internal control

The board are responsible for carrying out a thorough review of both emerging risks and key risks that have been identified as either likely or that have a significant impact on the competitive strategy, reputation or future performance of the company or both. The board should incorporate in the annual report a description of the key risks, the processes in place to identify emerging risks and how these risks are being dealt with.

The board should, at least annually, conduct a review of the effectiveness of the company's risk management and internal control systems and should report to shareholders that they have done so. The review should cover all material controls, including financial, operational and compliance controls.

The board should also state whether they consider it appropriate to use the going concern basis of accounting in preparing the financial statements and make it clear if there are any uncertainties over the company's ability to continue to operate like that into the future and meet the obligations as they fall due, including any assumptions in reaching that conclusion.

Remuneration

Levels of remuneration should be appropriate to the strategy and lead to long term sustainable success.

No director should be able to decide their own remuneration.

There should be a clear process to the policy for establishing the remuneration of directors and senior management.

Directors should exercise discretion and consider wider business issues, the performance of the company and how the individual has performed when authorising remuneration levels.

Remuneration Committees

The board should establish a remuneration committee of at least three, or in the case of smaller companies two, independent non-executive directors. In addition the company chair may also be a member, but not chair, of the committee if he or she was considered independent on appointment as chair. Before becoming chair of the remuneration committee the individual should have been a member of a remuneration committee for at least 12 months.

The remuneration committee should have delegated responsibility for setting remuneration for all executive directors and the chair, including pension rights and any compensation payments. The committee should also recommend and monitor the level and structure of remuneration for senior management. The definition of 'senior management' for this purpose should be determined by the board but should normally include the first layer of management below board level.

The remuneration committee should consider overall company remuneration policy, the approach to rewards and incentives and the impact on culture when setting director remuneration.

Remuneration should align with creating long term shareholder value, and so should promote long term shareholdings by directors. The remuneration committee develop a policy for post employment shareholding.

Pension contributions rates for executive directors should be in line with the rest of the workforce. Basic salary should be the only basis for pension contributions and the pension contributions should be considered in any decisions about increasing in basic salary

Levels of remuneration for non-executive directors should reflect the time commitment and responsibilities of the role. Remuneration for non-executive directors should be in line with the Articles of Association. Remuneration for non-executive directors should not include share options or other performance-related elements.

Remuneration schemes should include the option to use judgement in share awards and prevent formulaic outcomes. Particularly, there must be the option to withhold share awards in situations where it would be inappropriate to award shares.

Notice or contract periods should be set at one year or less. If it is necessary to offer longer notice or contract periods to new directors recruited from outside, such periods should reduce to one year or less after the initial period. The remuneration committee should carefully consider what compensation commitments (including pension contributions and all other elements) their directors' terms of appointment would entail in the event of early termination. The aim should be to avoid rewarding poor performance. They should take a robust line on reducing compensation to reflect departing directors' obligations to mitigate loss.

The remuneration committee should make available its terms of reference, explaining its role and the authority delegated to it by the board. Where remuneration consultants are appointed, a statement should be made in the annual report including whether they have any other connection with the company.

Director remuneration policy and procedures

The remuneration committee should address the below considerations when setting up the policy and procedures.

- **clarity** – the remuneration should be transparent and help shareholders and employees engage effectively.

- **simplicity** – the remuneration structure should be easy to understand.

- **risk** – remuneration policy should consider the risks such as reputational damage for excessive pay, or behavioural implications for performance related pay are identified and mitigated.

- **predictability** – the range of rewards should be made clear to individuals, plus any potential for judgement changes.

- **proportionality** – the policy should not reward poor performance and the link between award, strategy and long term company performance should be clear.

- **alignment to culture** – consideration of the company purpose, values and principles should be incorporated to encourage appropriate behaviours.

Remuneration committee and the annual report

The work of the remuneration committee is vital to the company and therefore it should be detailed in the annual report. These are some of the things that could be included:

- the strategic reasoning behind directors' remuneration policies, structures and KPIs.

- an explanation about why the remuneration is reasonable, using both internal and external information, such as ratios and pay gaps.

- an explanation of how the remuneration relates to the policy and practices for director remuneration.

- whether the policy was applied as intended, and if not why not, and how it will have been changed.

- what communication there has been with shareholders and employees about remuneration and the impact this has had on policy.

- what communication there has been with employees about director's remuneration and how consistent this is with the overall pay structure.

- whether any judgement has been used regarding remuneration and why.

Test your understanding 5

PK is a large listed company. The remuneration committee consists of four Directors with the Finance Director chairing the committee. The other three members are NED's although only two of these have been assessed as independent by the nominations committee. The remuneration committee has responsibility for both executive and non-executive pay policy with these policies being put forward by approval at the AGM by shareholders.

What actions should PK take to comply with best practice corporate governance?

Select ALL that apply.

A   The Finance Director should resign from PK

B   The remuneration committee should not have responsibility for NED remuneration

C   The non-independent NED should resign from the remuneration committee

D   The Finance director should resign from the remuneration committee

E   All NEDs on the remuneration committee should be replaced

Remuneration policy – The Sage Group plc

The following is an extract of the Remuneration Report (2011) of The Sage Group plc:

'Remuneration Policy

The Remuneration Committee, in setting the remuneration policy, recognises the need to be competitive in an international market. The Committee's policy is to set remuneration levels which ensure that the executive directors are fairly and responsibly rewarded in return for high levels of performance. Remuneration policy is designed to support key business strategies and to create a strong, performance orientated environment. At the same time, the policy must attract, motivate and retain talent... The Remuneration Committee considers that a successful remuneration policy must ensure that a significant part of the remuneration package is linked to the achievement of stretching corporate performance targets... generating a strong alignment of interest with shareholders... Around 75% of each executive's total compensation value is delivered through performance-related incentives, and is therefore 'at risk' if stretching performance targets are not reached.

Performance Share Plan (PSP)

The Committee established the PSP as the Group's main long-term equity incentive to drive financial and market performance... The individual limit on award levels under the Plan is 300% of salary. PSP awards will normally have a maximum value of 210% of salary. This represents a 'core' award to the value of 140% of salary, which, if maximum EPS (earnings per share) growth is attained, and TSR (total shareholder return) performance is ranked upper quartile against the comparator group, could rise to 210% of salary...

A sliding scale based on EPS is used. 25% of the award vests at the end of the period if the increase in EPS exceeds RPI (retail prices index) by 9% over the period; 100% of the award vests at that time only if RPI is exceeded in that period by 27%.

Awards are also subject to a TSR 'multiplier' whereby the level of vesting based on EPS achievement is adjusted according to TSR performance over the same three year period compared with a group of international software and computer services companies.' (These include Adobe Systems, Cap Gemini, Microsoft, Oracle, SAP amongst others.)

The Report goes on to detail audited information including outstanding awards granted to each director under the PSP. For example, the Chief executive Officer's details were:

	Awarded 1 Oct 2010 number	Awarded during the year number	Vested during the year number	Lapsed during the year number	Awarded 30 Sept 2011 number	Vesting date
G S Berruyer	361,647	–	(95,167)	(266,480)	–	3 March 2011
	745,649	–	–	–	745,649	3 March 2012
	507,280	–	–	–	507,280	4 March 2013
	–	737,795	–	–	737,795	10 March 2014
Total	1,614,576	737,795	(95,167)	(266,480)	1,990,724	

- 'The market price of a share on 10 March 2011, the date of the awards made in the year ended 30 September 2011 was 272.1p.

- The market price of a share on 3 March 2011, the date the above awards vested in the year ended 30 September 2011 was 280.8p. The market price of a share on 3 March 2008, the date on which these awards were granted was 202.25p.'

As you will be able to calculate from the illustration, the awards are well-worth receiving if company performance meets the targets set. The targets are reasonably straightforward, there being only two – EPS and TSR; however, the calculation of the award does become reasonably complicated.

The time period for tie-in is 3 years which is in line with the UK stock exchange listing rules/the UK Corporate Governance Code, whereby directors should get a reasonable time to prove themselves but not so long that the company cannot refresh the Board should it wish to.

3 Directors' remuneration

Remuneration is defined as payment or compensation received for services or employment and includes basic salary, bonuses and any other economic benefits.

Behavioural impact

Whatever remuneration package is determined, it is essential to ensure that the directors' objective is to do a good job for the stakeholders of the company.

The remuneration package should be motivational, not too small or too easily earned. The remuneration committee should design a package that attracts, retains and motivates the director. This should take into account the market rate i.e. comparable companies remuneration packages.

Components of the directors' remuneration package

- Basic salary – covering the job itself, the skills required, the directors' performance, their contribution to company strategy and market rates;

- Performance-related pay – remuneration dependent on the achievement of some performance measure. This could be short-term e.g. a bonus paid to the director at the end of the accounting year for achieving a certain level of profit or earnings per share, or long-term e.g. executive stock options. Stock/share options are contracts that allow the director to buy shares at a fixed price. If the share price rises above the exercise price the director can sell the shares at a profit. This encourages the director to manage the company in such a way that the share price increases, therefore share options are believed to align the directors' goals with those of the shareholders. Problems arise when the directors' actions are solely focussed on the share price to the exclusion of other stakeholder objectives. Also, if the share price rises too much the director could be tempted to sell their shares and retire, which defeats the objective of trying to tie the director in to the company for the long-term.

- Pension contributions – the remuneration committee should consider the pension consequences of increases in basic salary;

- Benefits in kind – are various non-wage compensations e.g. a company car, or health insurance.

Share (stock) options

Bonuses to directors based on the current year's profit can lead to short termism, in that the directors will maximise the current year's profit by not investing in new products and not developing existing ones (these costs would reduce the current year's profit). Not investing in new products and not developing existing ones will adversely affect future profits and may threaten the long-term existence of the business.

It is argued that share options are an effective way of paying directors and of avoiding short-termism, as the value of a share should be a reflection of the long-term profitability of the company.

Until recently, there has been no charge in the company's profit and loss account for share options, so the shareholders are not aware of the value of the options granted to the directors. However, share options can be very valuable to directors. Excluding the cost of share options from the financial statements understates directors' remuneration.

The grant date is the date when the employee and employer enter into an agreement that will entitle the employee to receive an option on a future date, provided certain conditions are met.

The service date is the date or dates on which the employee performs the services necessary to become unconditionally entitled to the option.

The vesting date is the date when the employee, having satisfied all the conditions becomes unconditionally entitled to the option.

The exercise date is when the option is taken up.

Normally, the option is granted at the market price of the shares at the grant date (e.g. 250p a share). If, at the exercise date of, say, 30 June 2010, the value of the shares is 290p, the director will buy the shares from the company for £2,500,000 and immediately sell them in the market for £2,900,000, making a gain of £400,000. If the value of the shares is less than 250p on 30 June 2010, the director will not purchase the shares (as he/she would make a loss), so the director's gain on the option will be zero.

Interestingly, most directors of UK listed companies buy and sell the shares at the exercise date (30 June 2010 in this case). Only a small minority of directors buy the shares at the option price and continue to hold them.

Share options as a measure of long-term profitability

The 'theory' of share options is that the share price on 30 June 2010 will be based on the company's long term profitability, so if the company is doing well, the share price will be higher and the director's profit on buying the shares (and subsequently selling them) will be higher. So the director's gain on selling the shares will reflect the director's success in increasing the long-term profits and hence the share price of the company.

To a certain extent, this 'theory' is correct in that the share price tends to increase if the company's profitability increases. However, share price movements also depend on other factors, such as the general price movement of other shares and investors' views about the future profitability and growth in the particular type of trade the company is in. For instance, in late 1999 and early 2000 there was an enormous increase in the value of telecom and dot.com shares, yet many of these companies had never made a profit. Thus, the increase in the share price did not depend on the profitability of the companies, and it could be argued that the prices of these shares increased because this was a fashionable sector of the market in which to invest. At the same time as the increase in value of telecom and dot.com shares there was a substantial fall in the value of other shares, including well-known retailers. Sometimes, share prices were falling, despite the fact that the companies' profits were increasing. So, it can be seen that the increase in the share price of a company may be more related to market conditions than its long-term profitability. Thus, awarding options on shares may not be a very effective way of paying directors, as the change in the share price may have little to do with profitability of the company and the directors' contribution to increasing those profits.

Regarded as a way of boosting productivity and employee retention, share options have become less popular since the economy turned bearish. Fuelled in the late 90s by dot com promises of untold future wealth, option-holding employees had little or no prospect of realising any value. When the economy suffered, staff became more interested in staying in progressive, well-paid jobs with quantifiable packages, so there has been less reason to implement schemes. (Some employers had been accused of using share options for employees as a way to pay salaries of less than the market rate.)

Microsoft is an example of a company that has ended its own option scheme. It decided to grant shares instead (not options on shares), explaining this practice is recorded on balance sheets, giving analysts a better view of the company's financial state and workers a tangible incentive.

To compound matters, the International Accounting Standards Board requires that firms put the cost of share-based awards through their financial statements.

Executive Share Options (ESOPs)

Executive share options (ESOPs) have been blamed for almost every business scandal that has made the headlines since the new millennium.

An ESOP is part of a manager's remuneration package. The features generally involve the following:

- Each eligible manager is granted an allocation of options as part of his or her annual remuneration. The number of options will generally be decided by the remuneration committee, comprising non-executive directors.

- The options themselves will normally have a striking price that is equal to, or slightly higher than, the share price at the date the options are granted.

- There is usually a vesting period of a few years that must pass before the options can be exercised. If the manager resigns or leaves the company during that period then the options will lapse.

- The options can normally be exercised on a specific date at the end of the vesting period.

(The vesting period and the fact that the options must be exercised on a very specific date make them more difficult to value than the more typical traded options that can be bought and sold by third parties.)

There are two main reasons why shareholders might be keen to reward their directors with options.

- If the directors hold large numbers of options then they will have a financial incentive to maximise the share price. Provided the share price exceeds the exercise price at the relevant date the directors can exercise their options and buy shares for less than their market value. They will then either retain those shares as an investment (acquired at a bargain price, so providing an attractive return) or resell them at a guaranteed capital gain. If the share price does not rise during the vesting period then the directors will receive little or no value and so they will have a direct financial stake in delivering an increased share price.

- An investment opportunity that would be attractive to the shareholders because the potential returns are high might be unacceptable to the directors because they will be exposed to the risks of it going wrong and the loss of their jobs. For example, a new product that fails might have a very limited impact on shareholders' total investment portfolios but could end the careers of the directors who were responsible for recommending that it should proceed.

Thus, if the shareholders really wish to align the directors' interests with their own they need to find some way to encourage the directors to accept the risks that they would choose to accept for themselves and ESOPs provide the answer.

If the directors hold large numbers of options then they will have an economic interest in accepting risky investment opportunities that they might otherwise be inclined to reject. If the investment succeeds and the share price rises then their options will be worth far more at the exercise date and they will not be exposed to any specific loss (at least on their options) if the investment fails and the share price plummets.

Thus, ESOPs give the shareholders the reassurance that the directors will wish to work hard to increase the share price and also accept realistic risks provided the potential return is high enough. They will also encourage the directors to take a long-term view and to remain with the company rather than move elsewhere and lose their options.

Directors should only be permitted to hold share options of any kind if they are honest and upright individuals. Clearly, many company directors are both but there will always be a few dishonest individuals in every walk of life. For example, in the past directors have purchased call options with their own money and then manipulated the share price by distorting the financial statements so that the options could be exercised at a massive profit. It was felt that company directors had too much of an incentive to cheat and manipulate when they held options and so it became illegal for them to own them.

In the late 1980s company directors were being accused of taking excessive salaries and bonuses and steps were taken to reduce the amounts being paid. In the USA a law was passed to restrict remuneration to $1m per annum. Shareholders were nervous that such a limit would give directors very little incentive to work hard and so ESOPs were used as a way round the restriction. It is extremely difficult to value the options granted under ESOPs and this meant that they were not accounted for in the total disclosed in the financial statements.

Major scandals such as Worldcom in the 1990s and the Credit Crunch in the late 2000s have been blamed on the pressures created by the possibility of directors earning huge amounts from any manipulation of the share price, timed to coincide with the exercise date of ESOP options.

Test your understanding 6

Which of the following executive remuneration package elements will best align the interests of executive directors and shareholders?

A   Cash bonus paid to director if company achieves profit growth targets

B   Cash bonus paid if director achieves a range individual performance related targets

C   Share option bonus scheme that is paid if company achieves profit growth targets

D   Private Health insurance for director and immediate family

Test your understanding 7

Which of the following are principles of the UK Corporate Governance Code:

Select ALL that apply

A   The role of chair and CEO should be separate

B   Non-executive directors should be appointed

C   The Board should meet once per month

D   The Board is responsible for determining the nature and extent of the significant risks the company will face

 4   Corporate governance and internal controls

The **board** is responsible for:

- maintaining a sound system of internal control,
- reviewing the effectiveness of internal controls, and
- reporting to shareholders that this review has been carried out.

It is the responsibility of **management** to:

- identify and evaluate the risks faced by the company, for consideration by the board
- design, operate and monitor a suitable system of internal control.

FRC's Risk Guidance

In 1999 a report was published called the Turnbull Report. This was, at the time, the most specific report regarding the requirements for internal control. (See Internal Control: Guidance for Directors on the Combined Code 1999 and revised 2005). It has been superseded by the FRC's Guidance on Risk Management, Internal Control and Related Financial and Business Reporting in September 2014.

The Turnbull Report required that internal controls should be established using a **risk-based approach.** Specifically a company should:

- Establish business objectives.
- Identify the associated key risks.
- Decide upon the controls to address the risks.
- Set up a system to implement the required controls, including regular feedback.

In establishing this structure, the Turnbull Report summarised the way that businesses should be controlled (and also how this subject links the topics of risk and control).

In addition, the Turnbull Report addressed the responsibilities of directors and management in relation to risk and control, as discussed above.

Turnbull suggested and the most recent FRC guidance still does suggest that directors should review internal controls under the five headings that COSO identified:

- Control environment.

- Risk assessment.

- Control activities.

- Information and communication.

- Monitoring.

The Turnbull Report went on to suggest that internal audit makes a significant and valuable contribution to a company.

Test your understanding 8

The Turnbull Report required that:

A   Internal controls should be established using a risk-based approach

B   The CEO and chair are separate roles

C   An audit committee is set up

D   Director's remuneration is fully disclosed

Test your understanding 9

The principles of good corporate governance in the UK Corporate Governance Code include:

Select ALL that apply

A   Division of responsibilities

B   Composition and succession

C   Audit, risk and internal control

D   Remuneration

E   Board leadership and company values

More on reviewing the effectiveness of internal controls

Management is accountable to the board for monitoring the system of internal control. The board has a responsibility for reviewing its effectiveness.

To review the effectiveness of the internal control system, the board should not rely on the existence of suitable embedded internal control processes. It should also receive regular reports on risks and controls, in addition to carrying out an annual assessment.

When reviewing reports on internal control, the board should:

- consider the significant risks and how they have been identified, evaluated and managed

- assess the effectiveness of the internal controls for managing each significant risk

- consider whether any controls are weak and action is necessary to strengthen them

- consider whether the causes of the failing or weakness indicate poor decision-taking

'The board should summarise the process it has applied in reviewing the effectiveness of the system of risk management and internal control. The board should explain what actions have been or are being taken to remedy any significant failings or weaknesses. Where this information has been disclosed elsewhere in the annual report and accounts, for example in the audit committee report, a cross-reference to where that information can be found would suffice. In reporting on these actions, the board would not be expected to disclose information which, in its opinion, would be prejudicial to its interests.' (FRC Guidance on Risk Management, Internal Control and Related Financial and Business Reporting).

The annual assessment of the system of internal control should consider:

- the changes since the assessment carried out in the previous year

- the scope and quality of management's ongoing monitoring of risks and of the system of internal control

- the extent and frequency of the communication of the results of this monitoring to the board

- the extent and frequency of internal control weaknesses and failing that have been identified during the year

- the effectiveness of the company's public reporting processes.

More on board's statement on internal control

The annual report should provide sufficient meaningful and high-level information to enable the shareholders to understand the main features of the company's risk management processes and system of internal control.

At the very least, the board should disclose:

- that there is an ongoing process for identifying, evaluating and managing the significant risks faced by the company

- that this process has been in place throughout the year

- that the process is regularly reviewed by the board.

The statement should include an acknowledgement by the board that it is responsible for the company's system of internal control and for reviewing its effectiveness.

The board should also summarise the process by which it reviewed the effectiveness of the control systems, whether that review was conducted directly or through, say, an audit committee.

 ## 5   Corporate governance and the audit committee

Audit committees were first required under the Cadbury Code (and are now required by the UK Corporate Governance Code) in response to criticisms of the relationship between the directors and the auditors.

It was felt that the auditors were not sufficiently independent of the board of directors and that, as a result, the auditors were not providing their monitoring and reporting role as they should be.

Particular criticisms of the relationship were about:

- Remuneration of the auditors – decided by the directors.

- Appointment of the auditors – at the discretion of the directors in practice.

- Reports of the auditors – received by the directors.

- The directors had the power to give other lucrative work to auditors.

To address these concerns, audit committees were to be established.

- Audit committees are made up of non-executive directors (at least one of which should have recent relevant financial experience) and have formal terms of reference.

- There should be as many meetings as the audit committee's role and responsibilities require. It is recommended the audit committee should meet at least three times per year, and also at least once a year have a meeting with the auditors without the presence of any executive directors.

Responsibilities of an audit committee

The responsibilities of the audit committee would typically include:

- Review of the financial statements, and any interim reports produced.

- Review of the company's system of internal financial controls.

- Discussion with the auditors about any significant matters that arose on the audit.

- Review of the internal audit programme and significant findings of the internal auditors.

- Recommendations on the appointment and removal of the auditors.

- The setting of the audit fee in discussion with the auditors.

- Review of the audit report and any management letter provided by the external auditors.

- Review all the company's internal control and risk management systems (unless this is delegated to a separate risk committee).

- Ensure that a system is in place for whistleblowing.

Audit committee and financial reporting

The key roles of the audit committee are 'oversight', 'assessment' and 'review' of other functions and systems in the company.

The audit committee should review the significant financial reporting issues and judgements in connection with the preparation of the company's financial statements. Management is responsible for preparing the financial statements and the auditors are responsible for preparing the audit plan and carrying out the audit.

The audit committee needs to satisfy itself that the financial statements prepared by management and approved by the auditors are acceptable.

It should consider:

- the significant accounting policies that have been used, and whether these are appropriate

- any significant estimates or judgements that have been made, and whether these are reasonable

- the method used to account for any significant or unusual transactions, where alternative accounting treatments are possible

- the clarity and completeness of the disclosures in the financial statements.

The committee should listen to the views of the auditors on these matters. If it is not satisfied with any aspect of the proposed financial reporting, it should inform the board.

Audit committee and internal control

In relation to internal controls, the audit committee should:

- review the company's internal **financial** controls

- review **all** the company's internal control and risk management systems, unless the task is taken on by a separate risk committee or the full board

- give its approval to the statements in the annual report relating to internal control and risk management

- receive reports from management about the effectiveness of the control systems it operates

- receive reports on the conclusions of any tests carried out on the controls by the internal or external auditors.

Audit committee and internal audit

The audit committee should monitor and review the effectiveness of the company's internal audit function. If the company does not have an internal audit function:

- the committee should consider annually whether there is a need for an internal audit function and make a recommendation to the board, and

- the reasons for the absence of an internal audit function should be explained in the relevant section of the annual report.

Where a company does have an internal audit function, the audit committee has an important role in preserving the independence of the internal audit function from pressure or interference.

The audit committee should:

- approve the appointment or termination of appointment of the head of internal audit

- ensure that the internal auditor has direct access to the board chair and is accountable to the audit committee

- review and assess the annual internal audit work plan

- receive a report periodically about the work of the internal auditor

- review and monitor the response of management to the findings of the internal auditor

- monitor and assess the role and effectiveness of the internal audit function within the company's overall risk management system.

Audit committee and external auditors

The audit committee is responsible for oversight of the company's relations with its external auditors. The audit committee should:

- have the primary responsibility for making a recommendation to the board on the appointment, re-appointment or removal of the external auditors

- 'oversee' the selection process when new auditors are being considered

- approve (though not necessarily negotiate) the terms of engagement of the external auditors and the remuneration for their audit services

- have annual procedures for ensuring the independence and objectivity of the external auditors

- review the scope of the audit with the auditor, and satisfy itself that this is sufficient

- make sure that appropriate plans are in place for the audit at the start of each annual audit

- carry out a post-completion audit review.

Test your understanding 10

P Company follows a principles based code of corporate governance and has both an audit committee and a risk committee.

Which of the following roles would be carried out by the audit committee?

Select ALL that apply

A   Review of the financial statements, and any interim reports produced.

B   Review of the company's system of internal financial controls.

C   Discussion with the auditors about any significant matters that arose on the audit.

D   Recommendations on the appointment and removal of the auditors.

E   Act on any recommendations put forward by the auditors in the management letter.

F   Review all the company's internal control and risk management systems.

Test your understanding 11

Within the UK Corporate Governance Code it states that the chair should arrange for several stakeholder groups to attend the AGM. These include:

Select ALL that apply

A   The audit, remuneration and nomination committees

B   The directors

C   The Chief Executive Officer

D   The chair of the audit, remuneration and nomination committees

E   All non-executive directors

Test your understanding 12

Responsibilities of an audit committee include:

Select ALL that apply

A   Review of the financial statements and any interim reports produced

B   Review of the company's system of internal financial controls

C   The detection of fraud

D   Ensuring a system is in place for whistleblowing

Lehman Brothers

Lehman Brothers was founded in 1850 and by 2008 it was the fourth largest investment bank in America, behind only Goldman Sachs, Morgan Stanley and Merrill Lynch. It employed over 25,000 people globally, but on September 15th 2008 it filed for bankruptcy and started what many people called the credit crunch or global financial crisis.

There are usually many reasons why something goes wrong, and in this case, many reasons why a business fails, but one area that was certainly a large factor in the failure on Lehman Brothers was Corporate Governance, or poor corporate governance to be precise.

It wasn't that they didn't have a board of directors, it was more the makeup of that board. There were 10 people on the board at Lehman went it filed for bankruptcy. And for an investment bank, it was very lacking in financial expertise at board level; there are different reports about exactly how many had financial experience, but they generally range between zero and two.

A diverse range of skills is often considered a good thing, but included on the board at Lehman, and reportedly on the audit committee, and the finance and risk committee, was a theatrical producer. One former

CEO on the board may provide useful insights, but Lehman Brothers didn't just have one former CEO – they had at least five – but not very much experience in other key business areas.

There were some undoubtedly talented people on the Lehman Brothers board, but they were often carrying out too many roles to be effective for Lehman. One member of Lehman board, whose roles included Chair of the nominations committee, member of the remuneration committee and also part of the risk committee, was also reportedly serving on at least three other boards at the same time.

Finally, the Chair and CEO of the board was the same person, and based on some of the descriptions of his character, and the fact that according to some reports he asked the firm's chief risk officer to leave the boardroom during key discussions, it does not sound like the dual role was appropriate.

6 International developments

Sarbanes-Oxley Act

The US financial world was rocked by a number of very serious financial scandals around 2000/2001, the most well known of which were Enron and Worldcom. The problems of Enron and Worldcom brought into question US accounting practices (for example, by exploiting loopholes in US accounting, Enron did not show its problems in its statement of financial position) and also the corporate governance exercised by directors. In order to restore confidence in the results of US companies the Sarbanes-Oxley Act was introduced.

- The SOX legislation is extremely detailed and carries the full force of the law behind it.

- The Act also includes requirements for the Securities and Exchange Commission (SEC) to issue certain rules on corporate governance.

- It is relevant to US companies, directors of subsidiaries of US listed businesses and auditors who are working on US listed businesses.

Differences to the UK Code

Overall the two main differences between SOX and the UK Code are:

(i) **Enforcement**

   The UK Code is a series of voluntary codes (a **'principles-based** approach') whereas SOX takes a robust legislative approach which sets out clear personal responsibility for some company directors with a series of criminal offences that are punishable by fines (both company and its officers) or lengthy jail sentences (a **'rules-based** approach').

(ii) **Documentation**

   SOX creates a much more rigorous demand for evidencing internal controls and having them audited.

Key points of SOX

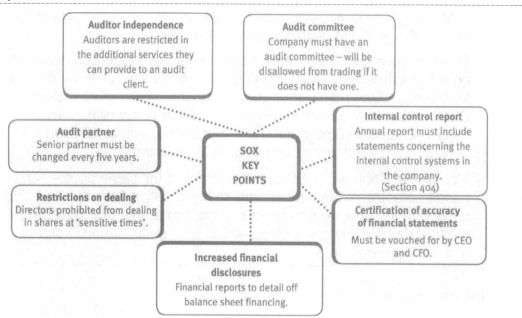

Auditor independence
Auditors are restricted in the additional services they can provide to an audit client.

Audit committee
Company must have an audit committee – will be disallowed from trading if it does not have one.

Audit partner
Senior partner must be changed every five years.

SOX KEY POINTS

Internal control report
Annual report must include statements concerning the internal control systems in the company.
(Section 404)

Restrictions on dealing
Directors prohibited from dealing in shares at 'sensitive times'.

Certification of accuracy of financial statements
Must be vouched for by CEO and CFO.

Increased financial disclosures
Financial reports to detail off balance sheet financing.

UK Code vs. SOX

Most countries in the world now have Governance codes, and this chapter has looked at the UK Code and SOX, as they provide good examples of a Principles (UK Code) and a Rules (SOX) based approach.

Certification of accuracy the financial statements

A rules based approach gives personal responsibility for the accuracy of the firm's financial statements to its principal executive officer (CEO) and the chief financial officer (Finance Director), who must provide a signed certificate to the Securities and Exchange Commission (SEC) vouching for the accuracy of the statements signed by the two officers above. It is a criminal offence to file defective financial statements.

The CEO and CFO must also hand back any bonuses for previous years if the financial statements need to be amended due to defective financial statements.

This is a far more specific requirement than in a principles based code which would only provide for a statement about the responsibility of the board for preparing financial statements and a going concern statement.

Increased financial disclosures

Whilst a principles based code would focus more on directors and their accountability to shareholders, a rules based code would be likely to include a number of provisions for greater, or more rapid, disclosure of financial information:

- In its financial reports the company must disclose details about its off balance sheet transactions and their material effects.

- Material changes should be disclosed on a rapid and current basis i.e. new off balance sheet transactions, loss of a major customer or a one-off writing down charge.

Internal control report

Companies need to include a report on 'internal control over financial reporting' in their annual report. This must:

- Include a statement of management's responsibility for adequate control systems.

- Identify the framework to evaluate internal control.

- Provide an assessment of the effectiveness of internal control and any material weakness.

Again this follows the principles based approach quite closely regarding the board's responsibilities and the role of the audit committee in reporting on the effectiveness of financial controls

Audit committee

In the same way as the UK Code, SOX requires companies to comply with certain audit committee requirements. However, the US stock exchanges are prohibited from listing any firm that does not comply.

As per the Combined Code the committee should:

- Be independent (in the UK NEDs).

- Have responsibility for appointing and compensating auditors.

- Oversee the auditors.

- Establish whistleblower procedures regarding questionable accounting or audit matters.

Unlike the UK Code, however, the rules based SOX goes much further in restricting auditors and non-audit work. A number of specific non-audit activities are explicitly prohibited.

Whilst the principles based example of the UK Code discourages auditors carrying out non-audit work, an explanation of how companies safeguard auditor independence in the annual report is usually sufficient if additional work is carried out.

The rules based approach of SOX also requires a compulsory rotation of the lead audit partner working on a corporate client.

Test your understanding 13

In the US, the accuracy of the financial statements is vouched for by:
Select ALL that apply

A   The board of directors

B   The audit committee only

C   The chief financial officer

D   The chair only

E   The chief executive officer

Test your understanding 14

The most heavily regulated corporate governance provisions are in:

A   The UK

B   The US

C   Canada

D   South Africa

The risk of no corporate governance

Imagine a poor country with no corporate governance at all. Should we trade with businesses within that country? Do we have a responsibility to encourage corporate governance?

In answer to the first question – should we trade with that country, the answer could be 'yes' or 'no'. Firstly – yes, the country is poor, prices might be low, the population might need employment. Our company could benefit from lower prices and benefit from good public relations by providing much needed jobs.

However, without corporate governance, businesses may not operate to the standards expected of our own country which could bring reputation risk. We might not be able to trust them.

So maybe the answer should be 'no'. The overseas company may be badly run by its management, with total disregard for the 'rules' we operate within our own country. The benefits to us now may be outweighed by any future costs in terms of lost reputation should an adverse event occur.

In answer to the second question – should we encourage corporate governance, then the answer should probably be 'yes'. Our richer countries' success may be founded on operating within the guidelines of corporate governance – well-run companies following the 'rules'. The poorer country companies might learn from this and see that more profit can be made through trade with other countries that comply with corporate governance.

This will not happen overnight and is not costless. However, by asking those poorer companies to make small changes over time (such as having non-executive directors or not dealing using bribes) we would encourage trade with them, which in itself would bring monetary advantage which could be reinvested to improve their company in the future.

Test your understanding 15

Country N is a poor developing nation with no corporate governance structures in place. Several large international organisations have recently publicised decisions not to trade with Country N because its government and business structures are seen as corrupt and its treatment of workers is poor.

Company Q, one of the world's largest manufacturers has however decided to maintain its relationship with Country N, from where it sources many of its components at competitive prices. Company Q has issued a media statement detailing how it intends to encourage the government and companies within Country N to adopt corporate governance 'best practice'.

Which of the following are reasons why Company Q might encourage Country N to adopt corporate governance principles rather than simply cease trading with them?

Select ALL that apply.

A   If Country N follows best practice corporate governance this will attract trading partners and potentially increase the wealth of the nation.

B   Company Q will be able to continue to source it's components from Country N without disruptions to supply whilst carrying out plans to encourage corporate governance best practice.

C   Company Q is likely to satisfy stakeholders who are concerned about CSR through encouraging better working conditions in Country N.

D   Company Q may be seen as ethical and progressive if it encourages better governance standards in Country N.

E   If suppliers in Country N improve the way they are controlled, there are less likely to be problems with the components Company Q purchases.

The Harvard Law School in the US produced a report in 2013 considering the Board's responsibility towards managing its stakeholders interests. It is reproduced, in part, below:

Companies today are being called upon by their stakeholders to not only boost their profits, but also to help address some of their country's most challenging problems, including those concerning economic development and the environment. Corporate stakeholders (which typically include shareholders, employees, customers, suppliers, the general public, governments and regulators) are demanding that companies recognise their responsibilities in addressing those problems. As a result, companies are increasingly working with stakeholders to understand their views and concerns on various environmental, social, corporate governance and economic issues and to incorporate and address those views and concerns in the company's strategic decision-making processes.

The Corporate Social Responsibility (CSR) report can be a key component of a company's stakeholder engagement strategy.

Why should the Board be responsible for managing stakeholders' interests?

Corporate Value. Stakeholder engagement includes the formal and informal ways a company stays connected to its stakeholders (the individuals or parties that have an actual or potential interest in or impact on the company, its operations and financial results). Stakeholders often have the ability to influence the success (or failure) of a company at various levels. A primary objective of corporate stakeholder engagement is to build relationships with stakeholders to better understand their perspectives and concerns on key issues (including CSR issues) and to integrate those perspectives and concerns (when and where feasible and prudent) into the company's corporate strategy.

Companies tend to recognise certain value associated with stakeholder engagement, including:

- enabling informed board and management decision making;

- avoiding or reducing business risks due to better business intelligence;

- developing and expanding business opportunities, brand value and reputation; and

- bringing diverse perspectives together to facilitate innovation;

all of which help drive long-term sustainability and shareholder value.

Rise in Shareholder Activism. Shareholder activism on CSR issues continues to rise, necessitating further engagement between companies and their shareholders and other stakeholders. Related stakeholder concerns can be proactively discussed and addressed, companies may be able to avert a potentially costly and prolonged proxy fight, and relationships between companies and their stakeholders may be nurtured.

Rise in Sustainable and Responsible Investing. Stakeholder engagement and understanding and addressing stakeholders' CSR concerns have become especially important as shareholders and potential investors are increasingly evaluating CSR issues when analysing investment decisions. Under sustainable and responsible investing ("SRI") principles, investors apply various CSR criteria in their investment analysis. It has been reported that SRI grew by more than 22% to $3.74 trillion in managed assets during the period from 2010–2012. For instance in 2011, the California Public Employees' Retirement System ("CalPERS"), as part of its "total fund" approach to investment, adopted three core themes for integrating CSR issues into its investment decisions: (1) corporate governance (including issues such as shareowner rights and executive compensation), (2) climate change (including issues related to water stress, carbon emissions, energy efficiency, clean technology and renewable energy) and (3) human capital (including issues of health and safety, responsible contracting and diversity).

Why CSR and the CSR Report?

CSR is defined many ways but generally refers to how a company addresses and manages its environmental, social, corporate governance and economic impacts and how such impacts may affect the company's stakeholders. CSR provides companies an opportunity to strengthen their business (through cost savings, risk mitigation and value enhancement) while contributing to society. CSR should focus on the important areas of interaction between the company and its key stakeholders and address value creation actions as part of the company's strategy.

A 2013 global consumer survey reported that CSR remains a powerful differentiator, influencing both consumer behaviour and corporate reputation. Nearly all consumers in that survey noted that when companies engage in CSR they have a more positive image of the company, would be more likely to trust that company and would be more loyal to that company. Consumer respondents added that it is acceptable if a company is not perfect, provided that the company is honest and transparent about its CSR efforts.

The CSR report, therefore, provides a company with an opportunity to communicate its CSR efforts to the company's stakeholders and to discuss (within the confines of a single document) certain company successes and challenges on a wide array of CSR issues, including corporate governance, climate change, employee and supplier diversity initiatives, and community investments and partnerships. The CSR report is also a medium for transparency (which often improves a company's reputation with certain stakeholders, particularly shareholders, employees, suppliers and communities within which the company operates) and may be used as an effective outreach tool as part of an ongoing shareholder relations campaign. In addition, the CSR report provides existing and potential investors with CSR information to assist in analysing investment decisions.

The CSR Report

Corporate CSR reports address issues most important to each of the company's key stakeholders, for example:

Shareholders – addressing the company's business model and corporate governance, including disclosing the role of the board in risk management, in sustainability reporting and in evaluating CSR performance.

Employees – addressing diversity, health and safety, training and mentoring, employee relations, and wages and benefits.

Customers – addressing customer service and privacy.

Suppliers – addressing labour standards and whether suppliers are required to implement their own CSR programs.

Communities – addressing corporate philanthropy and charitable contributions, community investment and partnerships, volunteerism and the environmental impact of operations.

Governments and Regulators – addressing lobbying, public policy and the effects of and compliance with environmental regulations.

Other Considerations

With respect to CSR, the CSR report and stakeholder engagement, a company and/or its board of directors may also want to consider the following:

CEO Responsibility and Board Oversight. The chief executive officer should ultimately be responsible for establishing effective communications with the company's stakeholders with CSR oversight by the board or board committee (or committees). Such oversight may include (1) review of CSR trends and impacts on the company's operations, financial results and stakeholders and (2) periodic updates from the chief executive officer/ management concerning the company's positions on and actions taken relating to relevant CSR issues and how such positions and actions have affected or may affect stakeholders.

Focus on Impact. Because management time and resources are limited, companies should focus on those CSR issues that may have the greatest impact on them and their operations and finances.

Stock Exchange Reporting Initiatives. Although the CSR report is not currently mandated by any federal law or regulation, there is a reported global effort by certain groups, including investors, to mobilize stock exchanges to adopt a listing requirement regarding sustainability (CSR) reporting. Regulators in the United Kingdom, for example, are requiring companies listed on the main market of the London Stock Exchange to publish full details of their greenhouse gas emissions for reporting years ending on or after September 30, 2013. While there currently is no mandatory sustainability (CSR) reporting requirement for companies listed on the New York Stock Exchange or NASDAQ, both exchanges have joined the United Nations' Sustainable Stock Exchanges initiative, which aims to explore how exchanges can work together with investors, regulators and listed companies to enhance corporate transparency on CSR issues and encourage responsible long-term approaches to investment.

Identify Corporate Team. Companies should identify the corporate team that will be responsible for their CSR report and include, at a minimum, employees from their investor/public/community relations, legal, compliance, regulatory and human resources departments.

Other Components of Stakeholder Engagement. The CSR report is only one component of an effective stakeholder engagement strategy. Other components of such strategy may include supplemental reports (e.g., Carbon Disclosure Project reports), regulatory filings, the annual meeting of shareholders and direct dialogue with stakeholders (e.g., community town hall and employee as well as supplier meetings).

Test your understanding 16
Generally share options should not be awarded to non-executive directors. However, if they are awarded the non-executive director may sell them:
A   Whenever he or she wants to
B   When they leave the non-executive Board
C   At nil profit
D   At least one year after leaving the non-executive board

7   Governance and strategy

The implications of governance for strategy
The results of the increasing focus on governance issues are as follows:
• Increasing power of governance bodies.
• Increasing shareholder power, ensuring that companies are run with shareholders' interests prioritised.
• Greater pressure on boards to formulate strategy and be seen to control the businesses concerned.
• Greater scrutiny of quoted businesses, resulting in more short-termism.
• Greater emphasis on risk assessments, so directors may feel pressured to undertake lower-risk (and hence lower-return) projects.
• Greater scrutiny of mergers and acquisitions in particular.

How does corporate governance impact organisational strategy?

Corporate governance is very important to help maximise the effectiveness of an organisation's strategy. This is for a number of reasons.

- Corporate governance works to ensure that no individual can dominate the board of directors (by ensuring the CEO and Chair roles are separated as well as the presence of independent non-executive directors). This helps to ensure that no-one is powerful enough to force through inappropriate or ineffective strategy. The non-executive directors should be able to impartially assess whether a proposed strategy is in the best interests of the organisation.

- Corporate governance should help to improve the diversity of the board of directors. This allows the board to identify a wide range of possible strategies, as well as analyse them from a variety of different viewpoints.

- Adequate internal audit and control systems should ensure that the board has accurate information about the current operations of the company. This will enable them to develop more effective strategies for the organisation. In addition, strong internal control increases the chance that the organisation will be able to implement its strategies successfully.

- Having good corporate governance is attractive to investors. This will make it easier for the organisation to raise the funding necessary to invest in the new strategies that they have identified.

It is therefore extremely important that companies consider corporate governance principles if they wish to develop and implement successful strategies.

HMV

HMV was the place to go for music in the 1980s, and in the 1990s the company expanded its range to take advantage of technological advancements and was the place to go for videos, DVDs, computer games and other things as well as music. Such was its power and dominance, it was charging nearly £20 for a CD and the House of Commons investigated its huge profits in the 1990s.

The music retailer, should therefore have been perfectly placed to continue the technological progression and become the place to download digital music, and then set up a streaming service.

The Managing Director at the time, Steve Knott, described digital music as "just a fad". Instead of the board assessing the risks and opportunities around them, developing an appropriate digital strategy that would enable them to compete with the likes of Amazon or iTunes, HMV failed to adapt their strategy to the market conditions and continued to do more of the same. They acquired Waterstones, a book retailer that was also struggling with online and digital rivals. This failed to change their fortunes and was eventually sold to pay off debts in 2011.

HMV still did not embrace digital music, and eventually entered administration for the first time in 2013. They were taken out of administration by Hilco. Under their new ownership they finally launched a music download service, almost 10 years after iTunes had launched and around 6 years after Amazon offered such a service.

By this time the trend for consuming music was changing from digital downloads to streaming services such as Spotify, who launched in 2008. HMV entered administration again in December 2018.

Test your understanding 17

According to the UK Corporate Governance Code, committees should include non-executive directors.

Which of the following committees does the code stipulate should include non-executive directors?

Select ALL that apply

A   The risk committee

B   The nominations committee

C   The audit committee

D   The remuneration committee

Test your understanding 18 – H electronics (Integration)

H is a company that manufactures basic electronic components such as capacitors and printed circuit boards for the IT industry. The company has recently appointed K as a non-executive director. K was the founder and chief executive of a quoted executive recruitment consultancy and employment agency. She has stood down from that role and has accepted the position on H's board in order to seek fresh challenges.

H's board meets twice every year for a formal discussion of company strategy. These meetings tend to look back at H's performance for the previous half-year. This discussion mainly focuses on a report based on the monthly management accounts for the previous half year and then briefly considers the future impact of these. Monthly management accounts are presented to the board at their monthly board meetings.

K has attended two of the meetings relating to strategy. At the conclusion of the second meeting she expressed two concerns about the half-yearly board meetings. Firstly the meetings focus on feedback rather than feed forward. K argued that the board should be constantly forward looking and aiming to identify new opportunities. K believes that historical summaries of past performance distract from the need to plan for the future. Secondly, K believes that the half-yearly meetings focus on details associated with the existing business model rather than strategic direction. She believes that it would be a more productive use of the board's time at these meetings to work towards identifying strategic opportunities that might be pursued over the next three to five years. When she was chief executive of her employment agency the board met at least once per year and frequently more often to think about new strategies that might be pursued.

H's Production Director has complained that K has really misunderstood the board's responsibility for the management of H. The Production Director believes that her first argument is invalid because the distinction between feedback and feed forward control is more about day to day tactical management rather than strategic management. The Production Director believes that feed forward is more about fine tuning rather than strategic management. The Production Director also believes that K's comments about strategic direction demonstrate a very limited understanding of manufacturing electronics. H must respond and react to the requirements of the IT industry. H cannot really innovate. The life cycle of the company's products is such that changes to H's strategic direction happen infrequently. The Production Director has suggested that K should restrict her comments to the information prepared for consideration by the full board, especially as she has come from the service sector and has no real understanding of manufacturing.

Required:

(a) Evaluate the respective arguments put forward by K and by the Production Director concerning the need for H's full board to be forward looking rather than focussing on past performance.

(b) Evaluate K's argument that H's board should review the company's strategic direction at its half-yearly meetings.

(c) Evaluate the Production Director's argument that K should not comment on the manner in which H is run because of her background and lack of experience in a manufacturing company.

(45 minutes)

Test your understanding 19 – C consultancy (Case study)

Scenario

C is a partnership that offers a range of consultancy services involving structural engineering. The firm specialises in examining plans prepared by architects to ensure that the buildings being planned are structurally sound. This requires careful consideration of the design and the materials being used to ensure that the resulting building will be stable and can withstand the effects of the wind and other forces of nature. C specialises in major contracts and the firm often advises on complex designs that use innovative building techniques.

C has a reputation for having a competitive culture. The firm offers salaries that are much higher than the industry average. There is an "up or out" culture which means that qualified staff must demonstrate the potential to be promoted to the next level of seniority within a relatively short period or they will be encouraged to leave.

C has 45 partners, all of whom are qualified structural engineers, and approximately 400 professional staff. C's professional staff comprises engineers at different stages in their careers, ranging from team leaders to junior trainees. The team leaders are all experienced engineers who are eligible for promotion to partnership in the event that a vacancy arises. Selection for partnership depends on the ability to consistently complete assignments to a high standard and within budget.

Trainee engineers are appointed on a three year contract, during which time they are expected to pass their professional exams. C takes on approximately 50 trainees every year. Those trainees who demonstrate the necessary qualities to succeed in C are offered the opportunity to stay with the firm at the conclusion of their training contracts. Those who do not receive such an offer must leave.

Each partner is responsible for a portfolio of assignments, and each portfolio is accounted for as a profit centre. Partners are expected to be aware of the opportunities to bid for assignments and to win new business despite competition from other engineering firms. C has a reputation for bidding aggressively and accepting tight deadlines. Each partner is responsible for a portfolio of assignments, each of which will involve a team leader and several assistants. Professional staff time is charged to assignments on an absorption costing basis and the firm's time recording system calculates a notional profit for each assignment based on the cost of time charged against the fee generated.

At the end of every financial year each partner receives an equal share of the firm's annual profit, but it is a matter of pride for each partner to generate more profit for the firm than he or she receives from the annual profit share.

All partners enjoy equal seniority and major strategic decisions are decided by a simple majority vote of the partnership. The firm is managed on a day to day basis by a management committee which comprises three partners. Every partner is expected to take a turn as a member of the management committee at some stage in his or her career. One person joins the committee every year to take over from the committee member whose term of office has expired. The third year of service on the management committee is spent as the firm's managing partner. There is no additional reward for serving on the management committee, but during that year the committee members are not expected to be responsible for a full complement of assignments and the managing partner is not expected to be responsible for any assignments.

Task

As an external consultant, write a letter to the audit committee evaluating the strengths and weaknesses of C's governance arrangements with respect to the partnership and its management committee.

(20 minutes)

Test your understanding 20 – P chemicals (Case study)

Scenario

P is a major quoted company that manufactures industrial chemicals. The company's Board comprises a Chief Executive and five other executive directors, a non-executive chair and four non-executive directors.

Trigger

Two of the non-executive directors have served on P's board for five years. The company has a policy of asking non-executive directors to stand down after six years and so the Chair has established a Nominations Committee to start the process of selecting replacements.

Three replacements have been suggested to the Nominations Committee. The nominees are:

- S, who is on the main board of C Pensions, an investment institution which owns 5% of P's equity. S has worked for C Pensions for 20 years and has always worked in the management of the company's investments, initially as an analyst and more recently as director in charge of investments. Before working for C Pensions, S was an investment analyst with an insurance company for 15 years.

- T, who is a CIMA member, is about to retire from full-time work. T has had a varied career, completing the CIMA qualification while working as a trainee accountant with a food manufacturer, then as a management accountant with an engineering company and finally as a senior accountant with a commercial bank. T was promoted to the bank's board and has been Finance Director for eight years.

- U, who is a former politician. After a brief career as a journalist, U became a member of parliament at the age of 35. After spending 20 years as a politician, including several years as a government minister, U has recently retired from politics at the age of 55. U already holds two other non-executive directorships in companies that do not compete with and are not in any way connected to P.

The Chair of P is keen to recruit more non-executive directors as a matter of priority because the Remuneration Committee faces a difficult task. The executive directors are presently remunerated with a combination of a salary and executive stock options. P's shareholders have expressed concern about the pressures created by these stock options and have asked that they be replaced by individual bonuses that reflect the personal contribution made by each of the executive directors.

The Chair and the non-executive directors are discussing the level of bonus that should be awarded for the current year. This has been complicated because P made a loss for the first time. The Chief Executive has stated that it would not be appropriate to accept a bonus from a loss-making company, but the other executive directors claim that the loss was attributable to economic and industrial conditions and that their leadership minimised the loss. All of the executive directors other than the Chief Executive have asked for substantial bonuses to reflect their leadership in difficult times.

Task

Prepare a briefing note to the Chair, in your capacity as a non-executive director, which:

(a) Evaluates the suitability of each of the three nominees.

(30 minutes)

(b) Discusses the problems associated with determining a suitable level of bonus for each of P's executive directors. **(20 minutes)**

Test your understanding 21 – JKL (Case study)

Scenario

JKL is a profitable but small FTSE 500 company in a technology-related service industry with annual sales of £150 million. Its gearing is 50% of total assets, secured by a mortgage over its main site. The industry is highly competitive but there are major barriers to entry for new competitors and the long-term future of JKL is considered by industry analysts to be sound.

The Board comprises a non-executive chair, a chief executive who has a large shareholding, an executive finance director, operations director and marketing director and a non-executive director with wide knowledge of the industry and who retired from the company 3 years ago. The board only has one committee, an audit committee. The audit committee consists of the chair, non-executive director and finance director.

There is no internal audit function in JKL but the external auditors are relied on to report on any weaknesses in control and their letter of engagement authorises them to carry out work over and above the financial audit in relation to internal control. The external auditors have always given a 'clean' audit report to the company and have reported that internal controls within JKL are sound. There is no formal risk management process in place in JKL although board meetings routinely consider risk during their deliberations.

Trigger

The chair and chief executive both believe that compliance with corporate governance reforms will not benefit JKL and is likely to be too costly. This is disclosed in JKL's Annual Report.

Task

Write a report to the Chair

(a)   evaluating the key reforms and best practice in:

  –   corporate governance

  –   risk management that have taken place over the last few years and which affect JKL;   **(30 minutes)**

and

(b)   with reasons, which (if any), of those reforms should be adopted by the company.   **(15 minutes)**

Test your understanding 22 – HFD (Case study)

Scenario

HFD is a registered charity with 100 employees and 250 volunteers providing in-home care for elderly persons who are unable to fully take care of themselves. The company structure has no shareholders in a practical sense although a small number of issued shares are held by the sponsors who established the charity many years previously. HFD is governed by a seven-member Board of Directors. The Chief Executive Officer (CEO) chairs the board which comprises the chief financial officer (CFO) and five independent, unpaid non-executive directors who were appointed by the CEO based on past business relationships. You are one of the independent members of HFD's board.

The CEO/Chair sets the board agendas, distributes board papers in advance of meetings and briefs board members in relation to each agenda item. At each of its quarterly meetings the Board reviews the financial reports of the charity in some detail and the CFO answers questions. Other issues that regularly appear as agenda items include new government funding initiatives for the client group, and the results of proposals that have been submitted to funding agencies, of which about 25% are successful. There is rarely any discussion of operational matters relating to the charity as the CEO believes these are outside the directors' experience and the executive management team is more than capable of managing the delivery of the in-home care services.

The Board has no separate audit committee but relies on the annual management letter from the external auditors to provide assurance that financial controls are operating effectively. The external auditors were appointed by the CEO many years previously.

Trigger

HFD's Board believes that its corporate governance could be improved by following the principles applicable to listed companies.

Task

Prepare briefing notes for a meeting with the Board:

(a) Recommending how HFD's Board should be restructured to comply with the principles of good corporate governance.

(30 minutes)

(b) Explaining the aspects of CIMA's ethical principles and the conceptual framework underlying those principles which you would consider relevant to continuing in your role as an independent member of HFD's Board. **(20 minutes)**

Test your understanding 23

Which of the following is NOT a strategic aim of corporate governance?

A   To reduce costs within the organisation

B   To increase the organisation's transparency to stakeholders

C   To improve investor confidence in the organisation

D   To ensure that the organisation abides by relevant laws and acts ethically

Test your understanding 24 – ADF – (Case Study)

You are the Finance Director of ADF – a large national firm that retails clothes direct to the public through a chain of 250 high-street stores in country F. You have just received the following email from the Managing Director (MD), Carlos Smith:

To: Anne Accountant

From: Carlos Smith

Date: 1/5/20XX

Subject: Review of corporate governance arrangements

Hi Anne,

As you may be aware, we are currently reviewing our corporate governance arrangements within the company after some of our investors expressed concerns. I felt that you would be the right person to ask about this as I'm aware you've studied this topic.

You're probably aware that ADF's executive directors are all employees who have worked their way up through the company. Half of the board is made up of non–executive directors.

If you remember, the Chair of the board is a retired director of a major electrical retailer. All of the other non–executive directors are personal friends of his and were appointed on his recommendation.

As you know, only one member of the board is female. All the directors are from country F and between the ages of 45 and 55.

The company does have a small internal audit department but this is understaffed. The Head of Internal Audit has stated several times that the work undertaken on ADF's stores is minimal and that a number of stores have never been visited by internal audit.

As we discussed at the Board meeting last week, the company is concerned that its current market is saturated and is looking to expand abroad into neighbouring countries, though the Chair has expressed concern over this as he feels it is too risky.

I'd be grateful if you could identify any weaknesses in our corporate governance. Please could you explain how each weakness will affect the company strategically? I'm meeting a few other Board members to discuss this in 20 minutes, so I be grateful if you could give this some urgent attention.

Thanks

Carlos

Required:

Draft a reply to Carlos, as requested.

(20 minutes)

8 Chapter summary

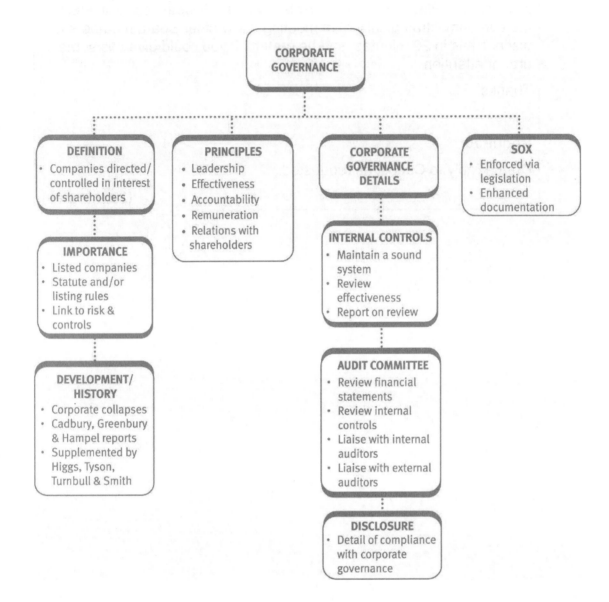

Test your understanding answers

Test your understanding 1

The correct answer is C – Nick Leeson had responsibility of both the back and front office dealings of Barings Bank, dealing with issues that none of his managers understood.

Test your understanding 2

The correct answer is B.

Test your understanding 3

A, B and C

- Option A: Yes because the CEO has a named person (The Chair) in addition to the NED's to whom he or she must account for the company's performance and his or her own behaviour.

- Option B: Yes – It is clear that the CEO is directly involved in the management of the company and the chair can adopt a more supervisory position.

- Option C: Yes – It is considered best practice because it provides a reassurance to the shareholders and ensures compliance with relevant codes.

- Option D: No – It could be argued that decision making is quicker with just one leader who does not need to seek the approval of the chair.

- Option E: No – There is a danger that the leadership becomes fragmented, especially if the two most senior members of staff do not agree and cannot provide a united front. This can lead to a lack of goal congruence in an organisation.

Test your understanding 4

D and E

- Option A – The NEDs will still be able to assess management's performance in meeting objectives; it is the objectives themselves they will not be involved in setting.

- Option B – provided the NEDs are informed on a timely basis about strategic decisions they will be able to carry out their risk role.

- Option C – it appears that the EDs are no more knowledgeable than the NEDs in this scenario.

- Option D – The role of the NED is to scrutinise decisions made by EDs and act on behalf of shareholders and other stakeholders. Without this involvement there is a risk decisions are made in the best interests of the executive directors. This is a key reason why NEDs should be involved in strategic decision making.

- Option E – It cannot be disputed that time will be saved and the NEDs could use it to carry out other duties. This does not make the proposal correct.

Test your understanding 5

B, C and D

The remuneration committee should consist of independent NEDs and should not consider NED remuneration. This should be decided by the board as a whole and/or shareholders depending on the specific requirements in the company Articles of Association.

A – there is no need for the FD to resign from the company but they shouldn't be on the remuneration committee.

E – there is no need to replace all NEDs

Test your understanding 6

C

Whilst the best trigger for the awarding of a bonus would be the director achieving a range of individual performance targets, share options would best align remuneration to shareholder interests as both parties would want the company share price to rise to maximise their individual financial return.

Test your understanding 7

The correct answers are A, B and D – The Board should meet regularly, not necessarily monthly.

Test your understanding 8

The correct answer is A – By definition.

Test your understanding 9

The correct answers are A, C and D – Composition and succession should also include evaluation. Values should instead read as purpose.

Test your understanding 10

A, B, C and D

- Option E the audit committee would review the management letter and actions taken by the board but not take action themselves.

- Option F would be carried out by the risk committee.

Test your understanding 11

The correct answers are B, C and D – Only the chairs of each of these committees are suggested to attend.

Test your understanding 12

The correct answers are A, B and D – The detection of fraud is management's responsibility. The audit committee could advise on any fraud found.

Test your understanding 13

The correct answers are C and E – In the US, the accuracy of the financial statements is vouched for by the chief financial officer and the chief executive officer.

Test your understanding 14

The correct answer is B – The US has a 'rules-based' corporate governance provision. This has been prompted by the higher number and higher value of corporate scandals occurring there.

Test your understanding 15

B, C, D and E

- Option A – is a reason why good governance may benefit Country N. It is not specific to Company Q.

- Option B, C, D and E all relate to Company Q.

Test your understanding 16

The correct answer is D.

Of the options provided this would be the best way to maintain independence of the non-executive director.

Test your understanding 17

The correct answer is B, C and D –

A risk committee can be staffed entirely by executive directors as the make-up is not discussed in the code. The other committees are covered by the corporate governance code and should include non-executive directors. In the case of the audit committee and the remuneration committee, they should staffed entirely by NEDs.

Test your understanding 18 – H electronics (Integration)

(a) K's basic argument is that the board ought to be forward looking, with a view to setting a strategic direction for H. That is a far more constructive approach to running the company than focussing on past performance. Part of her concern may be due to the fact that the half-yearly reports are really just an amalgamation of the monthly management accounts that have already been considered by the executive directors during their monthly meetings

The Production Director's response is logical because the present arrangements appear to focus on looking at H's present position and reflecting on the effectiveness of its strategies. That is not as pointless nor is it as backward looking as K suggests. H's management team is aware that the board will be looking at performance on a half-yearly basis and so there will always be an incentive to perform well in terms of working towards the company's strategic objectives. Presumably the main board has agreed that six months is a suitable interval over which to review progress, although it is also clearly only a brief period in terms of the company's product life cycle.

The Production Director could be correct in the sense that feed forward control is largely about determining corrective action on the basis of predicted results. Strategic management should be largely about setting targets and developing tactics to achieve those results. Feed forward control is more appropriate to the monitoring of the effectiveness of tactics.

It is to be hoped that neither director is arguing too strongly for one approach to managing H. K is not necessarily asking that the board does not use historical information in order to inform its deliberations and the Production Director does not appear to be arguing for all board meetings to be backward thinking.

(b)   It could be argued that the board ought to provide senior and middle management with a clear strategic direction. Strategies ought to have clear and specific objectives that give management something to work towards. For example, H's board may ask management to develop plans that will increase production capacity by 50% over the next three years.

Once a strategy has been put in place it should be kept under review and changed if necessary. However, changes should be kept to the minimum, otherwise management will become confused and may be demoralised. H's board should aim to motivate management by demonstrating commitment to the strategy rather than actively engaging in making changes to it. Otherwise, strategic management may be driven by day-to-day changes and circumstances and H will have no real direction.

H is a manufacturing company that requires complex and expensive technology. Many changes in strategy will prove expensive to implement. H exists to service demand for components from a wider industry. Many aspects of strategy will be set by H's customers and H will have to be responsive to the industry's demands. It would make considerable sense for H to consider progress towards implementing strategies on a half-yearly basis but it is unlikely that it will be feasible for the company to make meaningful changes of strategic direction twice per year.

On balance, it appears that K's arguments have been influenced by her experience in the service sector, where it is likely to be possible to be far more innovative because the costs of following different strategic directions are likely to be lower.

(c)   The Production Director's arguments raise significant questions about the role of the non-executive director. It would make little sense for K to have a seat on the board if she was not judged capable of making a meaningful contribution to the board's work.

It could be argued that non-executive directors have a significant role to play in providing oversight of the workings of the board as a whole. To an extent, it would be desirable for the non-executives to maintain some distance from the active management of the company, even at the strategic level, because they will then be capable of being a little more impartial in their oversight. K's role could be more concerned with making sure that the executive directors have a clear and consistent direction in mind for the company, rather than in participating in developing a strategy herself.

It may be possible for the non-executive directors to offer some fresh insights that would not have occurred to their colleagues on the executive board, without compromising their independence. K comes from a completely different background and may be able to ask questions that would not be considered by the executive directors. From time to time it is healthy to challenge accepted norms and to ask whether things could be improved. K clearly has an entrepreneurial outlook and that could raise questions about whether H could identify new revenue streams or meet customer needs in a different way.

If the non-executives are to provide effective oversight then they should not be constrained by the executive directors. They should be permitted to raise questions about any aspect of the company's management. The executive directors should recognise that the search and appointment process should ensure that only competent and capable people are appointed to the board and should respect the non-executives accordingly.

Test your understanding 19 – C consultancy (Case study)

Address

Date

Dear Audit Committee,

It was a pleasure meeting with several of your colleagues at C recently. Further to those meetings regarding C's governance arrangements and the management committee, I write to inform you of my findings.

Strengths

The fact that there is no benefit in terms of salary or seniority means that the partners are not likely to be in competition for promotion to the management committee. That has the advantage of ensuring that they focus on winning business and supervising assignments. The management committee will be made up of practising engineers who fully understand the important issues in the running of the firm. The fact that the members will return to normal partnership within three years means that they will not introduce any radical developments that may be beneficial to themselves but harmful to the partnership as a whole.

The partnership will include a number of members who have served on the management committee, which will give them a better understanding of the firm's management.

Weaknesses

Partners may view the need to serve on the committee as an interruption of their professional activities as engineers. Their reduced commitment to assignments during the first two years and withdrawal from assignments in the third year could cost them contact with the architects and contractors on whom they rely for referrals.

Partners may be tempted to take on an excessive workload while serving on the committee and so the firm's leadership will suffer because it is not a top priority. Partners who are eligible for membership of the management committee may feel that it will interrupt their ongoing careers and so may start to lobby for exclusion. That will defeat the objective of every partner taking it in turn and may mean that only those partners who are willing, who may not be the best candidates, will participate.

The annual change of managing partner means that there will be no real continuity in that position, although each new incumbent will have spent the previous two years on the committee.

The fact that there is no room for professional management on the committee means that the administrative aspects of managing this engineering firm may not enjoy the prominence they deserve.

The fact that major strategic decisions are left to the partnership as a whole may mean that the management committee tends not to look beyond the immediate future.

Major strategic changes may be difficult to implement if it is necessary to obtain a majority of the votes from 45 partners.

Should you have any further queries, please do not hesitate to ask.

Yours sincerely

External consultant

Test your understanding 20 – P chemicals (Case study)

(a) **Briefing notes**

To: The Chair

From: A non-executive director

Date: Today

Subject: Suitability of nominees and bonuses

Suitability of nominees

S is employed by a major shareholder, which is regarded as a problem for potential non-executives in terms of the guidance in the Combined Code. There is a risk that S will suffer a conflict of interest in that decisions that are good for P as a whole may not be ideal for C Pensions and vice versa. That problem could be overcome to an extent by recognising S's interest, as and when it becomes an issue, and making sure that there are sufficient independent directors to compensate. S has no skills or experience that would be directly relevant to the strategic management of a manufacturing company. Having said that, it could be that S will bring a fresh perspective to board meetings and so the lack of direct experience could be an advantage. S also has a great deal of experience of managing investment portfolios and that could be valuable in terms of presenting arguments to the board from the perspective of institutional investors. S's experience in that regard could be useful in areas such as financial reporting and so S may be a valuable member of the audit committee.

T is a qualified accountant and will provide skills that will be directly relevant to the financial reporting and control aspects that are generally associated with non-executive directors. T has had a full and varied career and that will give a range of perspectives that may be valuable to P. T's experience includes the manufacturing sector and that may give insights into the management of capital intensive businesses such as P. T has a range of contacts in banking that will undoubtedly be useful when it comes to negotiating with potential lenders. T is about to retire and so should have sufficient time to devote to this position.

U has had very little experience that is directly relevant to the management of P. U's parliamentary career could, however, have provided skills that are of some value, such as assessing the interests of different stakeholders . That could be a major benefit in the management of a company that manufactures chemicals. U's political contacts could also prove valuable, partly in terms of evaluating proposals that could affect P's position and partly in terms of lobbying to ensure that any changes are not too damaging to the company. U's reputation as a former senior politician will give an incentive to act with integrity and that will enhance P's reputation for honest management. The fact that U appears keen to have a number of directorships is a worry because it implies that P will not necessarily have sufficient time and attention. Furthermore, lobbying for companies that have different issues may mean that U will not always be free to put P first when using former political contacts.

(b) **Bonuses**

One concern is that the bonus mechanism may encourage dysfunctional behaviour. The remuneration committee will have to determine bonuses in such a way that directors cannot improve their rewards by making decisions that are harmful to the company, such as cutting expenditure on discretionary areas such as training in order to improve short-term profit at the expense of the long-term.

Assessing the contribution of individual board members will be difficult because it may be difficult to identify the impact that an individual has had on the running of the company. Measuring contribution effectively requires speculation about the performance that would have occurred in the director's absence. That would probably involve discussion with the director, who is hardly objective under these circumstances.

One problem with basing the bonus on the contribution of each individual director is that the executive board members may start to compete with one another for the sake of maximising their bonus. Individual directors may feel that it is in their personal interests to withhold information from the rest of the board and to avoid discussing ideas in case they do not receive full credit for their contribution.

The shareholders may feel that the system is a cynical attempt to extract more pay from the company. The remuneration committee members will have to ensure that they do everything they can to reassure the shareholders that any bonus payments are deserved otherwise the board as a whole may lose the shareholders' confidence.

There is even a danger that the shareholders may start to lose confidence in the ability of the non-executives to act in an independent manner in their contribution to the oversight of the company.

The directors will have to receive a realistic reward for their services; otherwise they may feel disillusioned and demotivated. It probably makes very little difference that they are well paid in relation to P's other managers and employees. They are likely to measure their rewards in relation to the directors of other quoted companies.

Test your understanding 21 – JKL (Case study)

Report

To: Chair

From: A.N. Accountant

Date: Today

Subject: Corporate governance

Introduction

You have asked me to report on the key reforms in corporate governance and risk management that have taken place recently which affect JKL and to recommend (with reasons), which (if any), of those reforms should be adopted by JKL.

This report addresses the following issues: corporate governance, in particular non-executive directors and the audit committee; and risk management, internal control and internal audit. The recommendations are contained at the end of this report.

Corporate governance

Corporate governance in most of the western world is founded on the principle of enhancing shareholder value. Major corporate collapses have been a feature of recent business history in the United Kingdom and elsewhere, and the publicity surrounding these collapses and the actions of institutional investors have raised corporate governance to prominence. The emergence of corporate governance can be seen as a result of regulatory action in response to past failings; changing financial markets including the desire of institutional investors to be more active and the dependence of an ageing population on pensions and savings which have been affected by declining confidence in stock markets.

The main principles of corporate governance are in relation to directors, the remuneration of directors, accountability and audit, relations with shareholders, and in particular with institutional shareholders and disclosure. The 'comply or explain' approach requires listed companies to disclose how they have applied the principles in the Corporate Governance Code and to either comply with the Code or to explain any departure from it. Under the Code, board effectiveness can be summarised as the effective splitting of the roles of chair and chief effective; the role of non-executive directors and the role of remuneration, nomination and audit committees of the board. In JKL, the roles of chair and chief executive are split but JKL does not comply with recommendations in relation to non-executive directors or the audit committee. I shall deal with each of these in turn.

Non-executive directors

The board should include a balance of executive and non-executive directors, and in particular 'independent' non-executives. It is recommended that a smaller company (outside FTSE 350) should have at least two independent non-executive directors. The notion of independence precludes non-executives from having recently been an employee of, or in a material business relationship with the company; receiving performance-related pay or a pension; having family ties or cross directorships; representing a substantial shareholder, or having been a board member for an excessive period of time.

Non-executive directors should be independent in judgement and have an enquiring mind. They need to be accepted by management as able to make a contribution; to be well informed about the company and its environment and be able to have a command of the issues facing the business. Non-executives need to insist that information provided by management is sufficient, accurate, clear and timely.

There should be a formal, rigorous and transparent procedure for the appointment of new directors to the board. Levels of remuneration should be sufficient to attract, retain and motivate directors of the quality required to run the company successfully. All directors should receive induction on joining the board and should regularly update and refresh their skills and knowledge. The board should undertake a formal and rigorous annual evaluation of its own performance and that of its committees and individual directors.

Audit committee

The Code states that the board of smaller companies (below FTSE350) should establish an audit committee of at least two members, who should all be independent non-executive directors. At least one member of the audit committee should have recent and relevant financial experience.

The audit committee has a role to act independently of management to ensure that the interests of shareholders are properly protected in relation to financial reporting and internal control. The main role and responsibilities of the audit committee should include monitoring the integrity of the company's financial statements; reviewing the company's internal control and risk management systems; monitoring and reviewing the effectiveness of the internal audit function; making recommendations to the board for the appointment, re-appointment and removal of the external auditor and approving the terms of engagement and remuneration of the external auditor, including the supply of any non-audit services; reviewing and monitoring the external auditor's independence and objectivity and the effectiveness of the audit process.

There should be no less than three audit committee meetings each year held to coincide with key dates in the financial reporting and audit cycle as well as main board meetings. JKL's audit committees should have, as part of its terms of reference, the responsibility to assess risk management and internal control within JKL. Each of these is considered in turn.

Risk management

Risk management is the process by which organisations systematically identify, evaluate, treat and report risk with the goal of achieving organisational objectives. Risk management increases the probability of success and reduces both the probability of failure and the uncertainty of achieving the organisation's objectives.

A risk management strategy should include the risk profile of the organisation that is the level of risk it finds acceptable; the risk assessment and evaluation processes the organisation practices; the preferred options for risk treatment; the responsibility for risk management and the reporting and monitoring processes that are required. Resources (money, experience and information, etc.) need to be allocated to risk management.

The benefits of effective risk management include being seen as profitable and successful with fewer surprises, predictable results without profit warnings or reporting major exceptional items. Being seen to have a system of risk management is also likely to be reflected in reputation and credit rating.

JKL has no clear risk management system in place and while the board considers risk, it does not do so systematically. Consequently, there may be risks faced by JKL that it has not recognised.

Internal control

The Code incorporates what is known as Risk Guidance, which has developed from the Turnbull Guidance that recommended the adoption by a company's board of a risk-based approach to establishing a sound system of internal control and reviewing its effectiveness.

The board should acknowledge that it is responsible for the company's system of internal control and for reviewing its effectiveness. It should also explain that the system is designed to manage rather than eliminate the risk of failure to achieve business objectives, and can only provide reasonable but not absolute assurance against material misstatement or loss. The board's statement on internal control should disclose that there is an ongoing process for identifying, evaluating and managing the significant risks faced by the company, that it has been in place for the year and up to the date of approval of the annual report and accounts, and that it has been regularly reviewed by the board.

Reviewing the effectiveness of internal control is one of the board's responsibilities, which needs to be carried out on a continuous basis. The Board should regularly review reports on internal control – both financial and non-financial – for the purpose of making its public statement on internal control. When reviewing management reports on internal control, the board should consider the significant risks and assess how they have been identified, evaluated and managed; assess the effectiveness of internal controls in managing the significant risks, having regard to any significant weaknesses in internal control; consider whether necessary actions are being taken promptly to remedy any weaknesses and consider whether the findings indicate a need for more exhaustive monitoring of the system of internal control.

For risk management and for the board's assessment of the adequacy or otherwise of internal control, an internal audit function should be considered.

Internal audit

Internal audit is an independent appraisal function established within an organisation to examine and evaluate its activities and designed to add value and improve an organisation's operations. The main role of internal audit is to provide assurance that the main business risks are being managed and that internal controls are operating effectively.

The need for an internal audit function will depend on the scale, diversity and complexity of business activities and a comparison of costs and benefits of an internal audit function. Companies that do not have an internal audit function should review the need for one on an annual basis. Changes in the external environment, organisational restructuring or adverse trends evident from monitoring internal control systems should be considered as part of this review. An internal audit may be carried out by staff employed by the company or be outsourced to a third party.

In the absence of an internal audit function, management needs to apply other monitoring processes in order to assure itself and the board that the system of internal control is functioning effectively. The board will need to assess whether those processes provide sufficient and objective assurance.

Recommendations

JKL's single non-executive director is not, under the Code, considered to be independent. It is recommended that JKL appoint two independent non-executive directors to the board.

In JKL, the audit committee currently consists of the chair, non-executive director and finance director. It is recommended that the two newly appointed independent non-executives (recommended above) be appointed and that both the chair and the finance director attend, but not be members of, the audit committee.

The audit committee should review JKL's risk management system and put in place an appropriate policy and system that reflects the risks faced.

JKL's internal controls appear to be adequate based on the external auditor's report; however, it is recommended that JKL's board specifically consider the adequacy of the external audit report in reviewing the effectiveness of internal control in JKL.

The audit committee should also consider the outcomes of the recommended risk management system before accepting the adequacy of internal controls.

This report does not recommend the appointment of internal auditors separate to the external audit function. However, once the board has implemented a risk management system and assessed the adequacy of internal controls, the value of internal audit function should be reassessed.

Test your understanding 22 – HFD (Case study)

Briefing notes

To:	The Board
From:	A.N. Accountant
Date:	Today
Subject:	Corporate governance and ethics

(a) Good corporate governance requires that a company be headed by an effective board with a clear division of responsibilities between running the board and running the company/charity with no individual having unfettered decision-making power. There should be a balance of executive and non-executive directors so that no individual or group can dominate the board. There should be a formal and rigorous process for the appointment of directors who should receive induction training. Information should be supplied in a timely manner to board members so that the board can discharge its duties. The board should then evaluate its performance both individually and collectively each year.

These principles do not seem to have been applied at HFD as it is dominated by the chief executive who also acts as chair and appears to dominate the board through his appointment of non-executive directors and his control over the agenda. To meet the principles of good corporate governance, HFD should:

– Separate the roles of chief executive and chair with the chair being a non-executive director.

– Ensure that all directors are independent of influence by the chief executive. Positions should be advertised with interviews being conducted, perhaps initially by an independent person. Appointments should be for a defined period, after which directors should stand for re-election.

– Provide induction training to new board members in the goals and operations of the charity.

– Annually evaluate the performance of each director and the board as a whole.

– Accountability and audit principles of good corporate governance require that a board should be able to present a balanced and understandable assessment of the company's position and prospects, should maintain a sound system of internal control and maintain an appropriate relationship with the company's auditors.

– HFD's Board does not seem to be able to make a balanced and understandable assessment of the company's position and prospects, given the narrow confines of what the CEO/Chair allows it. The CEOs relationship with the external auditors is not appropriate

– To meet the principles of good corporate governance, HFD should:

  – Set an agenda for board meetings that encompasses a wide variety of strategic matters including the charity's strategy, operations, risk management, internal controls and not be limited to financial reports and proposals for funding.

  – Consider meeting more frequently than quarterly.

  – Obtain an independent assessment of the company's internal controls by appointing a firm to act as (outsourced) internal auditor.

  – Affirm the reporting relationship of the external auditors to the board as a whole, and not to the CEO. The external auditors may need to be changed if they are unwilling to accept this changed relationship.

Although it is good practice, it is not necessary to have a separate audit committee, but if not, the functions of the audit committee should be carried out by the full board itself.

The disclosure principle requires that a company's annual report contains a high level statement of how the board operates and the decisions taken by the board and management, details of board members, meetings, performance evaluation, etc. HFD should provide adequate disclosure of board functioning in its annual report to make this aspect of the charity transparent.

(b) CIMA's Code of Ethics for Professional Accountants makes clear that an accountant's responsibility is more than satisfying the needs of a client, he/she must also act in the public interest. It is irrelevant whether or not the CIMA member is paid for his/her services, which are still expected to comply with the ethical principles.

There are 5 fundamental principles in the Code of Ethics: integrity, objectivity, professional competence and due care, confidentiality and professional behaviour.

Of particular relevance to HFD are objectivity, and professional competence and due care. Objectivity may be impeded due to bias because of his/her appointment by the CEO or the influence of the CEO or other persons on the board who may align themselves with the CEO.

The demands of professional competence and due care means that the accountant must look beyond the narrow focus on financial statements set by the CEO to a broader perspective including non-financial risks (mainly in relation to the charities operation) and the adequacy of internal controls (as it is insufficient to rely wholly on the external auditor's annual management letter).

The conceptual framework underlying CIMA's ethical principles requires accountants to risk manage their own position in relation to the work they are performing and in so doing to identify, evaluate and mitigate any risks they face. The main risks faced by an accountant include those relating to self-interested behaviour, self-review, advocacy, familiarity and intimidation.

The major threats faced in relation to HFD are familiarity and intimidation. The accountant has been appointed to the board as a result of some prior business relationship which may affect his/her objectivity. The CEO/Chair of HFD also appears to be a dominating individual and the accountant may be intimidated by this individual, resulting in the accountant's views not being presented accurately and/or forcefully.

The accountant as board member needs to identify and evaluate the risks of familiarity and/or intimidation that s/he faces, and ensure that s/he takes appropriate action (ultimately resignation from the board) to maintain his/her independence and objectivity.

Test your understanding 23

The correct answer is A

Corporate governance is not designed to reduce organisational costs. It may, in fact, have the opposite effect due to the management time and additional staff required by corporate governance codes.

Test your understanding 24 – ADF – (Case Study)

To: Carlos Smith

From: Anne Accountant

Date: 1/5/20XX

Subject: Review of corporate governance arrangements

Dear Mr Smith,

Thank you for your email. I have looked through the information you provided and have identified the following weaknesses:

Lack of diversity of the board of directors

Most of the directors in ADF are older men from country F. There is only one woman on the board.

Having a diverse board can ensure that the company has a wide range of experience to draw on when making decisions.

For example, ADF wants to expand abroad. By having directors from other countries or with experience of these foreign markets, the company would be far better placed to achieve this growth.

Lack of independence of non–executive directors

All the non–executive directors are linked to the Chair. This makes it unlikely that they will act impartially. They are likely to vote along with the Chair.

This could lead them to reject acceptable projects, such as the proposed foreign expansion, merely because the Chair disapproves.

Weak internal audit

The fact that the directors allow ADF to have such an inadequate internal audit function indicates an alarming lack of control. If they are unable to rely fully on the accounts produced, they may find it difficult to implement sensible strategies in the future.

Overall

The ultimate goal of corporate governance is to provide investors with increased confidence in the company and increase the transparency of the board's decisions.

Should investors feel that ADF has poor corporate governance, it can damage ADF's reputation with investors. This may harm its share price and make it harder for the company to raise much needed finance in the future – which is likely to be important if it is planning overseas expansion.

I hope this helps. If you need any further information, please let me know.

Kind regards

Anne

Internal control

Chapter learning objectives

Lead	Component	
A3. Ways of managing risk.	(a)	Discuss roles and responsibilities.
C1. Internal controls systems	(a)	Discuss roles and responsibilities for internal controls
	(b)	Discuss the purpose of internal control
	(c)	Analyse the features of internal control systems
C2. Recommend internal controls for risk management	(a)	Discuss the COSO internal control framework.
	(b)	Assess control weakness
	(c)	Assess compliance failures
	(d)	Recommend internal controls for risk management

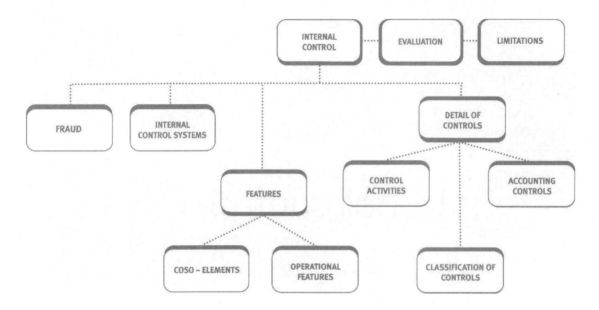

1 Internal control systems

- In order to manage their risks, businesses need to set up internal control systems.

- These internal controls apply across all parts and activities of a business

 Definition

There are a number of different definitions of internal control systems, but all have similar features. One definition is:

> 'The whole system of controls, financial and otherwise, established by the management in order to carry out the business of the enterprise in an orderly and efficient manner, ensure adherence to management policies, safeguard the assets, prevent and detect fraud and error and secure as far as possible the completeness and accuracy of the records.'

An internal control system can be thought of as a system for management to control certain risks and therefore help businesses achieve their objectives.

 Internal controls and risk management

- Internal controls can be considered as part of the risk reduction method of responding to risk.

- The need for a robust system of internal control and risk management is seen as a major element of good corporate governance.

- In the UK for example, the Corporate Governance Code requires the board of directors to review the system of internal control in their organisation, and satisfy themselves that a suitable system is in place.

Objectives of internal control

A definition of an internal control system included:

Definition	Commentary
...the orderly and efficient conduct of its business, including adherence to internal policies'	There will be systems in place from ensuring that all transactions are recorded (so the business is conducted in an orderly manner) to following policies such as provision of good customer service.
...the safeguarding of assets'	Assets, in this case, include buildings, cars, cash etc. (e.g. those things that can be touched), through to other assets including the intellectual property of the company (e.g. those things which cannot be touched but are still an asset of the business).
...the prevention and detection of fraud and error'	This will include fraud and error at the operational level through to the strategic level (e.g. off balance sheet finance or the adoption of incorrect or suspect accounting policies (think of Enron).
...the accuracy and completeness of the accounting records and ...'	Again, ensuring that all transactions are recorded – so liabilities are not 'hidden' and assets are not overstated.
...the timely preparation of financial information.'	Reporting deadlines in many jurisdictions are quite strict (60 days in the US for some reports) hence the need to ensure information is available to produce those reports in a timely fashion.

The main point to note here is that the internal control system encompasses the **whole business,** not simply the financial records.

2 The Turnbull Report

The Turnbull Report was originally published in 1999, and set out best practice regarding internal controls for listed companies in the UK. In October 2005, the Financial Reporting Council issued 'Internal Control – Revised Guidance for Directors on the Combined Code'. The report was an updated version of the Turnbull Report and covered the importance of internal control in companies. In September 2014 the Turnbull Guidance was superseded by the **Guidance on Risk Management, Internal Control and Related Financial and Business Reporting**.

Extracts of the most recent version of the guidance are set out on the following pages:

Applicability and background

(2)   It aims to bring together elements of best practice for risk management; prompt boards to consider how to discharge their responsibilities in relation to the existing and emerging principal risks faced by the company; reflect sound business practice, whereby risk management and internal control are embedded in the business process by which a company pursues its objectives; and highlight related reporting responsibilities.

(3)   While it is hoped that this guidance will be useful to other entities, it is primarily directed to companies subject to the UK Corporate Governance Code (the Code).

(4)   The Code defines the role of the board as being "to provide entrepreneurial leadership of the company within a framework of prudent and effective controls which enables risk to be assessed and managed". Effective development and delivery of a company's strategic objectives, its ability to seize new opportunities and to ensure its longer term survival depend upon its identification, understanding of, and response to, the risks it faces.

(5)   Economic developments and some high profile failures of risk management in recent years have reminded boards of the need to ensure that the company's approach to risk has been properly considered in setting the company's strategy and managing its risks. There may be significant consequences if the company does not do so effectively....

Risk Management and Internal Control

(13) The board has ultimate responsibility for risk management and internal control, including for the determination of the nature and extent of the principal risks it is willing to take to achieve its strategic objectives and for ensuring that an appropriate culture has been embedded throughout the organisation. This guidance provides a high-level overview of some of the factors boards should consider in relation to the design, implementation, monitoring and review of the risk management and internal control systems. Such systems cannot eliminate all risks, but it is the role of the board to ensure that they are robust and effective and take account of such risks.

(14) This guidance asks boards to determine their "principal" risks, rather than "significant" risks as in earlier Code editions. This decision was taken to align the terminology with the new Strategic Report requirements. The term "principal risk" is defined in the FRC's 'Guidance on the Strategic Report'. The FRC considers that in this context the words "principal" and "significant" are interchangeable and that the amendment should not be seen as implying a change in the nature of the risks.

(15) The guidance does not set out in detail the procedure by which a company designs and implements its risk management and internal control systems. Attempting to define a single approach to achieving best practice would be misguided if it led boards to underestimate the crucial importance to high quality risk management of the culture and behaviour they promote.

Board Responsibilities for Risk Management and Internal Control

(24) The board has responsibility for an organisation's overall approach to risk management and internal control. The board's responsibilities are:

- ensuring the design and implementation of appropriate risk management and internal control systems that identify the risks facing the company and enable the board to make a robust assessment of the principal risks;

- determining the nature and extent of the principal risks faced and those risks which the organisation is willing to take in achieving its strategic objectives (determining its "risk appetite");

- ensuring that appropriate culture and reward systems have been embedded throughout the organisation;

- agreeing how the principal risks should be managed or mitigated to reduce the likelihood of their incidence or their impact;

- monitoring and reviewing the risk management and internal control systems, and the management's process of monitoring and reviewing, and satisfying itself that they are functioning effectively and that corrective action is being taken where necessary; and

- ensuring sound internal and external information and communication processes and taking responsibility for external communication on risk management and internal control.

(25) The board's specific responsibility for determining whether to adopt the going concern basis of accounting and related disclosures of material uncertainties in the financial statements is a sub set of these broader responsibilities. A company that is able to adopt the going concern basis of accounting and does not have related material uncertainties to report, for the purposes of the financial statements, is not necessarily free of risks that would threaten the company's business model, future performance, solvency or liquidity were they to materialise. The board is responsible for ensuring this distinction is understood internally and communicated externally.

(26) It is the role of management to implement and take day-to-day responsibility for board policies on risk management and internal control. But the board needs to satisfy itself that management has understood the risks, implemented and monitored appropriate policies and controls, and are providing the board with timely information so that it can discharge its own responsibilities. In turn, management should ensure internal responsibilities and accountabilities are clearly established, understood and embedded at all levels of the organisation. Employees should understand their responsibility for behaving according to the culture.

Establishing the Risk Management and Internal Control Systems

(28) The risk management and internal control systems encompass the policies, culture, organisation, behaviours, processes, systems and other aspects of a company that, taken together:

- facilitate its effective and efficient operation by enabling it to assess current and emerging risks, respond appropriately to risks and significant control failures and to safeguard its assets;

- help to reduce the likelihood and impact of poor judgement in decision-making; risk-taking that exceeds the levels agreed by the board; human error; or control processes being deliberately circumvented;

- help ensure the quality of internal and external reporting; and

- help ensure compliance with applicable laws and regulations, and also with internal policies with respect to the conduct of business.

(29) A company's systems of risk management and internal control will include: risk assessment; management or mitigation of risks, including the use of control processes; information and communication systems; and processes for monitoring and reviewing their continuing effectiveness.

(30) The risk management and internal control systems should be embedded in the operations of the company and be capable of responding quickly to evolving business risks, whether they arise from factors within the company or from changes in the business environment. These systems should not be seen as a periodic compliance exercise, but instead as an integral part of the company's day to day business processes.

Monitoring and Review of the Risk Management and Internal Control Systems

(39) The existence of risk management and internal control systems does not, on its own, signal the effective management of risk. Effective and on-going monitoring and review are essential components of sound systems of risk management and internal control. The process of monitoring and review is intended to allow the board to conclude whether the systems are properly aligned with strategic objectives; and satisfy itself that the systems address the company's risks and are being developed, applied and maintained appropriately.

(40) The board should define the processes to be adopted for its on-going monitoring and review, including specifying the requirements, scope and frequency for reporting and assurance. Regular reports to the board should provide a balanced assessment of the risks and the effectiveness of the systems of risk management and internal control in managing those risks. The board should form its own view on effectiveness, based on the evidence it obtains, exercising the standard of care generally applicable to directors in the exercise of their duties.

(Guidance on Risk Management, Internal Control and Related Financial and Business Reporting' – Financial Reporting Council – September 2014)

3 Features of internal control systems

 COSO model of internal control

COSO (Committee of Sponsoring Organisations) have stated that effective internal control systems consist of five integrated elements.

Control environment

The control environment can be thought of as management's **attitude, actions** and **awareness** of the need for internal controls.

If senior management do not care about internal controls and feel that it is not worthwhile introducing internal controls then the control system will be weak.

Management can try to summarise their commitment to controls in a number of ways:

- Behave with integrity and ethics (corporate governance is covered more thoroughly in Chapter 5).

- Maintain an appropriate culture in the organisation.

- Set up a good structure – for example, an independent internal audit function, and ensure segregation of duties.

- Set proper authorisation limits.

- Employ appropriately qualified staff and conduct staff training.

When auditors assess the control systems of business for the audit, if the environment is poor they will place no reliance on any detailed control procedures.

Risk assessment

Risk assessment (as discussed in chapter 2) feeds directly into the internal control system. A risk assessment must be performed and should identify:

- **Controllable risks** – for these risks, internal control procedures can be established.

- **Uncontrollable risks** – for these risks, the company may be able to minimise the risk in other ways outside the internal control environment. Uncontrollable risks could be risks that are caused by the external environment that the company operates in. For example, the best internal control processes in the world cannot reduce the risk of inflation or the economy going into recession.

Control activities

Once controllable risks have been identified, specific control activities can be undertaken to reduce those risks. There is a huge variety of control activities that companies can adopt at all levels of management and in all parts of the organisation.

Due to the need to adapt and change control systems, most companies use a variety of different control processes to ensure that the business achieves its objectives.

The typical processes that could be used are:

- having a defined **organisation structure**. All staff need to understand how their role fits in with the rest of the organisation to aid their understanding of the job. They need to know who to report to on a daily basis and also points of contact for when they need to deal with other departments or divisions;

- having **contracts of employment** with individuals at all levels. Contracts of employment guide an employee's behaviour. Typically, they include hours of work, job title, salary and pension entitlements, holiday, data protection rules through to codes of dress. A major control within the contract of employment is the section on disciplinary action which outlines what constitutes a disciplinary procedure and the resulting event which will usually include dismissal;

- establishing **policies**, and subsequently procedures to ensure the policies are followed. Organisations typically have policies on health and safety, travel expenses, dignity at work, etc. Procedures might include the setting up of an audit department to ensure that the policies are adhered to;

- setting up a suitable **discipline and reward system.** Discipline has already been mentioned, however, rewards can also control an individual's behaviour. If an employee knows that there is a month-end bonus for meeting a particular sales target then most, if not all, of their actions will be focussed on that outcome. The objective is performance and conformance. However, if rewards are not structured correctly they can lead to 'dysfunctional behaviour' which is covered later in the chapter;

- ensuring a system of **performance appraisal and feedback**. Appraisals are usually at least an annual event (perhaps more often whilst an employee is being trained). During the appraisal the manager and employee should have an opportunity to discuss whether the job is being performed satisfactorily, whether previous objectives have been met, and what any future objectives are. An employee's behaviour is controlled via an appraisal since they know that their manager will be watching their work in order that a discussion can be held. It is an opportunity for the manager and employee to feed back on any issues that concern them or activities which may have been performed well.

Information and communication

In order for managers to operate the internal controls, they need information and therefore a good information system must be set up. The information provided to managers must be:

- Timely.
- Accurate (and therefore reliable).
- Understandable.
- Relevant to the actions being taken.

Computer systems have led to increased quality of information being provided to managers but the systems must be integrated into the business strategies if they are to provide what managers need.

Cyber risks are a specific part of this syllabus because it is so important to the successful running and control of business. This topic is covered in more detail in other chapters.

Monitoring

The company may have produced a very good internal control system but it must be monitored. If the system is not monitored it will be very difficult to assess whether it is out of control and needs amendment. Internal control systems are also dynamic in that they need to evolve over time as the business evolves.

The internal audit function is often the key monitor of the internal control system. Internal auditors will examine the controls and control system, identify where controls have failed so that the failures can be rectified, and also make recommendations to management for new and improved systems. More will be seen in later chapters on internal audit.

Updates to the framework in 2013

In 2013 COSO updated the framework by adding 17 principles. These principles sit within the five components to help explain the fundamentals behind them and to help make the framework more principles-based.

COSO have emphasised that the additional detail is not meant to make it a tick list, but more to make the components clearer and therefore easier to apply.

It is intended to apply to all types of organisation, from profit seeking, to governmental and not for profit. It also, in line with the external changes over the last 20 years, increases focus on non-financial considerations and recognises the increased use of technology.

Components of an internal control system including principles

COSO identify five components of an effective control system.

(1) **Control environment**

This is sometimes referred to as the 'tone at the top' of the organisation. It describes the ethics and culture of the organisation, which provide a framework within which other aspects of internal control operate. The control environment is set by the tone of management, its philosophy and management style, the way in which authority is delegated, the way in which staff are organised and developed, and the commitment of the board of directors.

The control environment has been defined by the Institute of Internal Auditors as: 'The attitude and actions of the board and management regarding the significance of control within the organisation. The control environment provides the discipline and structure for the achievement of the primary objectives of the system of internal control.

The principles that underpin the control environment component are:

- The organisation shows a commitment to ethical values.

- The board has appropriate expertise and oversees the five competencies.

- Management must establish an appropriate organisational structure to help achievement of the objectives

- Human resource policies and practices to help attract, develop and retain suitable talent.

- Accountability of employees for their areas of responsibility.

(2) **Risk assessment**

There is a connection between the objectives of an organisation and the risks to which it is exposed. In order to make an assessment of risks, objectives for the organisation must be established. Having established the objectives, the risks involved in achieving those objectives should be identified and assessed, and this assessment should form the basis for deciding how the risks should be managed.

The risk assessment should be conducted for each business within the organisation, and should consider, for example:

- **internal factors,** such as the complexity of the organisation, organisational changes, staff turnover levels, and the quality of staff

- **external factors,** such as changes in the industry and economic conditions, technological changes, and so on.

The risk assessment process should also distinguish between:

- **risks that are controllable:** management should decide whether to accept the risk, or to take measures to control or reduce the risk

- **risks that are not controllable:** management should decide whether to accept the risk, or whether to withdraw partially or entirely from the business activity, so as to avoid the risk

The principles that underpin the risk assessment component are:

- Clear objectives to allow risk identification and assessment
- That risk identification and analysis does take place across the entity.
- The potential for fraud arising in pursuit of the stated objectives must be considered.
- The internal controls system must be reviewed for changes in the external environment.

(3) **Control activities**

These are policies and procedures that ensure that the decisions and instructions of management are carried out. Control activities occur at all levels within an organisation, and include authorisations, verifications, reconciliations, approvals, segregation of duties, performance reviews and asset security measures. These control activities are commonly referred to as internal controls.

The principles that underpin the control activities component are:

- Select of appropriate controls to mitigate the risks to the achievement of objectives.
- Specifically controls over technology are included.
- Policies and procedures establish how the controls are implemented.

(4) **Information and communication**

An organisation must gather information and communicate it to the right people so that they can carry out their responsibilities. Managers need both internal and external information to make informed business decisions and to report externally. The quality of information systems is a key factor in this aspect of internal control.

The principles that underpin the Information and communication component are:

- Appropriate information is generated and used to assess controls
- The information is communicated appropriately internally to support the internal control process.
- The information is communicated to appropriate external parties.

(5) **Monitoring**

The internal control system must be monitored. This element of an internal control system is associated with internal audit, as well as general supervision. It is important that deficiencies in the internal control system should be identified and reported up to senior management and the board of directors.

The principles that underpin the monitoring component are:

- Appropriate evaluations of the controls are carried out.

- Any issues with controls are communicated to appropriate people (including the board where necessary).

Test your understanding 1

COSO stated that effective internal control systems consist of five integrated elements. These included:

Select ALL that apply

A Risk

B Control activities

C Control environment

D Monitoring

E Information and communication

Test your understanding 2

COSO categorises objective setting into four categories. These do include:

Select ALL that apply

A Strategic

B Management

C Operational

D Reporting

Test your understanding 3

Five elements make up an effective internal control system.

Which of the following is regarded as the most important?

A Risk assessment

B Monitoring

C Information and communication

D Control environment

Operational features of internal control systems

There are considered to be three features of a sound internal control system:

More on sound internal control systems

The Turnbull guidance described three features of a sound internal control system:

- Firstly, the principles of internal control should be **embedded** within the organisation's structures, procedures and culture. Internal control should not be seen as a stand-alone set of activities and by embedding it into the fabric of the organisation's infrastructure, awareness of internal control issues becomes everybody's business and this contributes to effectiveness.

- Secondly, internal control systems should be capable of **responding quickly** to evolving risks to the business arising from factors within the company and to changes in the business environment. The speed of reaction is an important feature of almost all control systems. Any change in the risk profile or environment of the organisation will necessitate a change in the system and a failure or slowness to respond may increase the vulnerability to internal or external trauma.

- Thirdly, sound internal control systems include **procedures for reporting** immediately, to appropriate levels of management, any significant control failings or weaknesses that are identified, together with details of corrective action being undertaken. Information flows to relevant levels of management, capable and empowered to act on the information, are essential in internal control systems. Any failure, frustration, distortion or obfuscation of information flows can compromise the system. For this reason, formal and relatively rigorous information channels are often instituted in organisations seeking to maximise the effectiveness of their internal control systems.

Test your understanding 4

J Company is suffering from working capital problems and the directors wish to make several changes to internal controls over purchases, inventory and sales in order to try and improve cash flow. They feel that currently there is no real commitment or belief in the internal controls system. The sales director keeps high levels of finished goods on site to give customers plenty of choice and the purchasing manager keeps high levels of raw materials as she is afraid of shortages. Each blames the other for J Company's current problems. Suppliers are paid within 25 days despite agreed terms being 30 days because the CEO wishes to maintain good relationships with them. Customers are encouraged to take credit with J Company in order to increase sales. Staff are generally well paid (with sales related bonuses) and staff turnover is low. J Company is seen as a good place to work and management are respected.

Which of the following are likely to be reasons that embedding the principles of internal controls in J's culture will be difficult?

Select ALL that apply.

A   There is a blame culture with the sales and purchasing managers each feeling the other is responsible for cash flow problems.

B   Senior management are not fully committed to solving the working capital problems.

C   Sales related bonuses encourage staff to think of increasing sales rather than whether the debt is recoverable.

D   Staff turnover is low meaning staff will be set in their ways.

E   Staff are well paid and happy in the workplace.

4 The detail of controls

As discussed in the COSO model of internal control, specific control activities will be undertaken to reduce risks. Some examples of organisational controls include:

Segregation of duties

Most accounting transactions can be broken down into three separate duties: authorisation or initiation of the transaction, the handling of the asset that is the subject of the transaction, and the recording of the transaction. This reduces the risk of fraud and the risk of error.

For example, in the purchases system, the same individual should not have responsibility for:

- Making a purchase;
- Making the payment;
- Recording the purchase and payment in the accounts.

If one individual had responsibility for all of these activities they could record fictitious purchases (for personal use) and pay themselves for transactions that had not occurred, which is fraudulent.

Also segregation of duties makes it easier to spot unintentional mistakes.

Physical controls

Physical controls are measures and procedures to protect physical assets against theft or unauthorised access and use. They include:

- using a safe to hold cash and valuable documents;
- using a secure entry system to buildings or areas within;
- dual custody of valuable assets, so that two people are required to obtain access;
- periodic inventory checks;
- hiring security guards and using closed-circuit TV cameras.

Authorisation and approval

Authorisation and approval controls are established to ensure that a transaction must not proceed unless an authorised individual has given his approval, possibly in writing.

For **spending transactions**, an organisation might establish **authorisation limits,** whereby an individual manager is authorised to approve certain types of transaction up to a certain maximum value.

Management control

Controls are exercised by management on the basis of information they receive.

- **Top level reviews.** The board of directors or senior management might call for a performance report on the progress of the organisation towards its goals. For example, senior management might review a report on the progress of the organisation toward achieving its budget targets. Questions should be asked by senior management, prompting responses at lower management levels. In this way, top level reviews are a control activity.
- **Activity controls.** At departmental or divisional level, management should receive reports that review performance or highlight exceptions. Functional reviews should be more frequent than top-level reviews, on a daily, weekly or monthly basis. As with top-level reviews, questions should be asked by management that initiate control activity. An example of control by management is the provision of regular performance reports, such as variance reports, comparing actual results with a target or budget.

Supervision

Supervision is oversight of the work of other individuals, by someone in a position of responsibility. Supervisory controls help to ensure that individuals do the tasks they are required to and perform them properly.

Organisation

Organisation controls refer to the controls provided by the organisation's structure, such as:

- the separation of an organisation's activities and operations into departments or responsibility centres, with a clear division of responsibilities

- delegating authority within the organisation

- establishing reporting lines within the organisation

- co-ordinating the activities of different departments or groups, e.g. by setting up committees or project teams.

Arithmetic and accounting

Controls are provided by:

- recording transactions properly in the accounting system

- being able to trace each individual transaction through the accounting records

- checking arithmetical calculations, such as double-checking the figures in an invoice before sending it to a customer (sales invoice) or approving it for payment (purchase invoice) to make sure that they are correct.

Personnel controls

Controls should be applied to the selection and training of employees, to make sure that: suitable individuals are appointed to positions within the organisation; individuals should have the appropriate personal qualities, experience and qualifications where required; individuals are given **suitable induction and training**, to ensure that they carry out their tasks efficiently and effectively.

Staff should also be given **training** in the purpose of controls and the need to apply them. Specific training about controls should help to increase employee awareness and understanding of the risks of failing to apply them properly.

Remember that any controls recommended in the exam should **cost less than the benefits** they bring. For example, you would not recommend the hiring of a security guard at £35,000 per annum to watch over the petty cash tin which held £100.

Mnemonic

The above controls can be remembered using the mnemonic SOAPSPAM

Supervision, **O**rganisation, **A**rithmetic and accounting, **P**ersonnel, **S**egregation of duties, **P**hysical, **A**uthorisation and approval and **M**anagement.

Test your understanding 5 – Types of control (Integration)

Recommend the types of control that a company could put in place for the following risks:

(1) Shoplifting from a retail business.

(2) Goods being sent to customers but not invoiced.

(3) Poor quality supplies being purchased.

(4) Incorrect prices being charged.

Test your understanding 6

The internal control whereby an accounting transaction is broken into three separate tasks – initiation, handling and reporting, and dealt with by three different staff, is called:

A   Authorisation and approval

B   Supervision

C   Segregation of duties

D   Arithmetic and accounting

Test your understanding 7

The risk that orders could be taken from a customer that is unable to pay or unlikely to pay for a long time could be controlled by:

A   Checking that all goods delivered notes are matched to an invoice

B   All new customers being subject to a credit check

C   Picking goods for despatch by using a copy of the customer's order

D   Customer statements being sent out

Test your understanding 8

X plc has been criticised for its apparent lack of internal control. Staff behaviour is considered to be unprofessional, management don't appear to reprimand staff for this (often because their allocated staff changes frequently) and there is no annual assessment or feedback on staff.

Which of the following controls should help to reduce these problems?

Select ALL that apply

A   Organisation structure

B   Contracts of employment

C   Policies and procedures

D   Discipline and rewards

E   Performance appraisals

Test your understanding 9

The COSO framework consists of 8 interrelated components which include:

Select ALL that apply

A   External environment

B   Risk assessment

C   Control activities

D   Monitoring

Classification of controls

Controls can be understood as falling within three broad categories:

- Financial controls;
- Non-financial quantitative controls;
- Non-financial qualitative controls.

Financial controls

- These controls express financial targets and spending limits.
- Examples include
  - budgetary control
  - controls over sales, purchases, payroll and inventory cycles.

Sales cycle

Objectives of controls

The objectives of controls in the sales cycle are to ensure that:

- sales are made to valid customers
- sales are recorded accurately
- all sales are recorded
- cash is collected within a reasonable period.

Below is a summary of the sales cycle, showing examples of possible risks and the related controls:

Process	Risks	Control procedures
Receive an order.	Orders may be taken from customers that are unable to pay or unlikely to pay for a long time.	All new customers subject to credit check.
Goods are despatched to customer.	Incorrect goods may be sent to customers leading to loss of goodwill.	Pick goods using a copy of the customer's order.
Invoice is raised.	Invoices may be missed, incorrectly raised or sent to the wrong customer.	Checked that all goods delivered notes (GDNs) match an invoice.
Sale is recorded.	Invoiced sales may be inaccurately recorded.	Customer statements sent out (customers let you know if incorrect).
Cash received.	Customer may not pay for goods.	Review aged debt listing and investigate (customer underpaid).
Cash recorded.	Cash received may be stolen.	Regular banking/physical security over cash (i.e. a safe).

A more detailed list of possible risks and control procedures is shown below:

Process	Risks	Control procedures
Receive an order.	Orders may not be recorded accurately.	Confirm order back to customer (or) get all orders in writing.
	Orders may be taken from customers that are unable to pay or unlikely to pay for a long time = financial loss.	All new customers subject to credit check.
		Perform regular credit checks on existing customers.
	Orders cannot be fulfilled and therefore customer goodwill is lost (and possibly the customer).	Credit limit check before order is accepted.
		Check inventory system before issuing order.
		Automatic re-ordering system linked to customer order system.
Goods are despatched to customer.	Goods may not be despatched for orders made.	Use sequentially numbered customer order pads. Send a copy to the warehouse where they are filed numerically and sequence is checked to ensure that all are there (none missing).
	Incorrect goods may be sent to customers leading to loss of goodwill or goods may not be in inventory.	Pick goods using a copy of the customer's order.
		Get the copy signed by the picker as correct.

		When GDN is raised check it matches with the customer order (staple together and file).
		Get the customer to sign a copy of the GDN and return to the company.
		Use sequentially numbered GDNs, file a copy numerically and check that they are all there.
Invoice is raised.	Invoices may be missed, incorrectly raised or sent to the wrong customer.	Copy of sequentially numbered GDN sent to invoicing dept, stapled to copy of the invoice, checked all GDNs are there and having invoice to match.
	Credit notes may be raised incorrectly, missed or to cover cash being misappropriated.	On copy of the invoice sign as agreed to original order and GDN, signed as agreed to customer price list, signed as agreed it adds up properly.
		Credit notes to be allocated to invoice it relates.
		Authorised by manager and sequence check done on a regular basis.
Sale is recorded.	Invoiced sales may be inaccurately recorded, missed or recorded for the wrong customer.	Review receivables ledger for credit balances (paid for goods but no debtor recorded).
		Perform a receivables ledger reconciliation (check info in individual ledger matches that in nominal).
		Computer controls.
	.	Perform receivables ledger control account reconciliation.
		Customer statements sent out (customers let you know if there is an error).

Cash received.	Incorrect amounts may be received.	Agree cash receipt back to the invoice.
	Customer may not pay for goods.	Review receivables ledger for credit balances (customer overpaid).
		Review aged debt listing and investigate (customer underpaid).
		Review aged debt listing regularly, phone when overdue by 30 days, another letter at 45 days final letter threatening legal action at 60 days.
		Refer receivable to solicitor.
Cash recorded.	Cash maybe incorrectly recorded or recorded against the wrong customer account.	Customer statements.
	Cash received may be stolen.	Customer statements.
		Regular banking/physical security over cash (i.e. a safe).
		Reconciliation of banking to cash receipts records.
		Segregation of duties.

The **purchases cycle** is similar to the sales cycle but concentrates upon the risk of staff ordering goods for themselves, more goods being ordered than necessary (leading to obsolescence or theft), payments being made to fictitious suppliers (theft), and goods being overpriced by the supplier.

Controls might include segregation of duties so that one staff member cannot order goods for themselves or payments be made to a fictitious supplier. Recruitment and training procedures in addition to a fraud policy statement might help. Agreeing a supplier invoice to a supplier quote or price list and recomputing the invoice for quantity, price and tax will ensure that the correct amount enters the financial statements.

Bank and cash controls

Bank and cash

Objectives of controls

The objectives of controls over bank and cash are to ensure that:

- cash balances are safeguarded

- cash balances are kept to a minimum

- money can only be extracted from bank accounts for authorised purposes.

Below is a summary showing examples of possible risks to cash and bank accounts and the related controls:

Risks	Control procedures
Cash is stolen from the premises.	Safes/strongroom/locked cashbox with restricted access.
	Tills emptied regularly.
Money is taken from bank accounts for unauthorised purposes (i.e. stolen).	Restricted list of cheque signatories.
	Regular bank reconciliations reviewed by person with suitable level of authority.

A more detailed list of possible risks and control procedures is shown below:

Risks	Control procedures
Cash is stolen from the premises.	• Safes/strongroom/locked cashbox with restricted access.
	• Security locks.
	• Swipe card access.
	• Key access to tills.
	• Night safes.
	• Imprest system.
	• Use of security services for large cash movements.
	• People making bankings vary routes and timings.
	• Tills emptied regularly.
	• Frequent bankings of cash and cheques received.

Money is taken from bank accounts for unauthorised purposes (i.e. stolen).	• Restricted list of cheque signatories. • Dual signatures for large amounts. • Similar controls over bank transfers and on-line banking, e.g. secure passwords and pin numbers. • Cheque books and cheque stationery locked away. • Regular bank reconciliations reviewed by person with suitable level of authority

Controls in other departments

Controls over **human resources** i.e. employees, managers and directors might include:

- Recruitment policies including the completion of an application form and the checking of any relevant qualifications to independent documentation. e.g. certificates;

- References being taken up prior to appointment;

- Continuous training;

- Eligibility to work in the country (visa);

- Contract of employment.

Controls over the **distribution department** might include

- The human resources controls listed above;

- Signed goods received and goods despatched notes;

- Regular inventory counts;

- Monitored CCTV cameras around the distribution depot;

- Security guards at exits;

- Bag searches when staff leave their shift.

Test your understanding 10

B has a chain of service stations across motorways in Country X. These service stations sell fuel, confectionary and newspapers and also have a café offering hot food.

The directors of B are concerned that there have been incidences of fraud in the café's in several service stations and they have linked this to poor recruitment policies. The HR department insists that they carry out rigorous checks before offering positions in the service stations but the directors wish extra controls to be implemented. Since staff turnover in the service stations is so high, it is expected that new controls should make a difference quickly.

Which of the following controls over HR should be implemented to make fraud less likely in the café's at the service stations?

Select ALL that apply.

A   Include induction training for each new member of staff.

B   Only candidates with recent experience of working in a café or restaurant should be recruited.

C   Each new staff member should provide two recent character references before they are offered a job at B.

D   New staff members should be asked to work a six week probationary period before they are given a contract to ensure their suitability for the job.

E   Shift patterns and teams should be varied so that no staff member works alone in the café or with the same team members on a regular basis.

Test your understanding 11

B is a training college offering courses in professional qualifications. Each course has a tutor who lectures from the front of the room and passes around a class register at the start of the day which students sign to confirm attendance. The register is systems generated and any student whose name does not appear on it due to late enrolment is asked to add their name and signature to the bottom so that B can invoice them for the course.

On day one of the course, text books and notes are available at the front of the classroom for students to collect on their way into the room. A separate materials register is left at the front of the room for students to sign to acknowledge they have received materials.

> Recently B's management has received reports of students attending class for the first session and then not returning after morning break. In addition, there have been cases of students being observed simply passing the class register on instead of signing or adding their name to it.
>
> B is concerned that it may be losing revenue if these incidents are occurring on a larger scale.
>
> **Which of the following control procedures could help prevent revenue loss in B?**
>
> Select ALL that apply.
>
> A   Class registers to be taken around the room by and signed under tutor supervision.
>
> B   Class register taken later in the day rather than first thing.
>
> C   Material to be given or sent to students on enrolment rather than left at the front of the room.
>
> D   Tutor to carry out head count to ensure the number of signatures on the register matches the number of people in the room. Discrepancies checked immediately.
>
> E   Only students enrolled and whose names appear on the register should be allowed to attend the course.

Non-financial quantitative controls

- These controls focus on targets against which performance can be measured and monitored.
- Examples include
    - balanced scorecard targets
    - TQM quality measures
- It is important that a feedback loop exists:
    - performance target (standard) set
    - actual result recorded
    - compared with target
    - control action taken (if required).

Non-financial qualitative controls

- These form the day-to-day controls over most employees in organisations.
- Examples include
    - employee training
    - management control methods (such as organisation structure, contracts of employment)
    - physical controls
    - project management.

The Bribery Act

The Bribery Act is a type of non-financial control. It came in to force in the UK on 1st July 2011 and it is designed to bring the UK in line with international norms on anti-corruption legislation. It will make it a criminal offence to give or receive a bribe. It will also introduce a corporate offence of failing to prevent bribery.

The Serious Fraud Office will be able to prosecute both domestic and foreign companies, providing they have some presence in the UK. Bribes committed in the UK and abroad could be prosecuted under the Act.

Some experts have argued the new law could put British companies at a disadvantage as it goes further than similar legislation in other jurisdictions.

Individuals will face up to 10 years in prison and an unlimited fine if found guilty of committing bribery.

For example, a former court worker became the first person to be convicted under the Bribery Act 2010. He was jailed for six years having been convicted of bribery and misconduct in a public office after admitting that he received a bribe in his role as an administrative officer at a Magistrates' Court. The administrative officer pleaded guilty for requesting and receiving a £500 bribe to "get rid" of a speeding charge and to misconduct in public office for other similar offences. He was sentenced to three years for bribery and six years for misconduct in a public office, to be served concurrently.

Test your understanding 12

If found guilty of committing bribery, the UK Bribery Act states that individuals will face:

A   Up to 5 years in prison and an unlimited fine

B   Up to 10 years in prison and an unlimited fine

C   Up to 5 years in prison and a £10,000 fine

D   Up to 10 years in prison and a £10,000 fine

 5   Evaluation of an internal control system

Developing an adequate control system

The first step in designing an adequate control system is to ascertain the objectives of the system in question. For example, the system may be human resources and their objectives are many, but include sourcing, recruiting, training and retaining quality staff.

Secondly, research should be conducted regarding the current systems in place (if any) and communication with employees (questionnaires and interviews for example) would help to collate useful information.

Inputs to the process should be identified to check whether they meet the intended objective (or create the desired output). For example, the objective of retaining quality staff will not be met if, a review process is not carried out when well-trained but unhappy staff repeatedly leave the company.

In order to work out whether the system currently works, the company should have use a comparator, for example, HR may set a target labour turnover figure. If this is met or surpassed then action should be taken since it demonstrates that the current system is not effective at retaining a certain level of staff.

In this example, the control system appears to work – it has identified a problem with labour turnover, however, it has also identified a problem in the HR process. This now needs to be resolved.

New controls can be implemented, such as regular appraisals – giving an employee a forum to discuss their job satisfaction, or setting up a new policy on staff welfare which might include an open-door policy, a whistleblowing policy or even just a suggestion box.

These new processes now also need suitable controls to be put in place and indicators chosen that will be acted on are required. Appraisals need to be done for all staff on, say, a yearly basis. The number of suggestions put in the suggestion box needs to be logged and a record kept of the number which have been actioned.

A responsible individual then needs to ascertain whether these extra controls have led to a reduction in the number of leavers and whether this is now at a satisfactory level. If not, then further corrective action needs to be taken.

Costs v benefits

The internal control system of the business is no different to other business activities – the benefits of maintaining the system must outweigh the costs of operating it. As part of the monitoring process therefore management must consider the costs and benefits.

However, it can be difficult to quantify those costs and benefits as they are often not direct cash costs.

Costs of an internal control system will include:

- time of management involved in the design of the system
- implementation:
  - costs of IT consultants to implement new software
  - training all staff in new procedures
- maintenance of system:
  - software upgrades
  - monitoring and review.

Benefits are to be found in the reduction of the risks and achievement of business objectives.

Limitations of internal control systems

Warnings should be given regarding over-reliance on any system, noting in particular that:

- A good internal control system cannot turn a poor manager into a good one.

- The system can only provide reasonable assurance regarding the achievement of objectives – all internal control systems are at risk from mistakes or errors.

- Internal control systems can be by-passed by collusion and management override.

- Controls are only designed to cope with routine transactions and events.

- There are resource constraints in provision of internal control systems, limiting their effectiveness.

Health and safety at work

To protect employees' health and safety whilst at work, a statement might be issued that all staff are supposed to follow. This statement might include:

The company aims to protect the health, safety and welfare of people at work, and to safeguard others, mainly members of the public, who may be exposed to risks from the way work is carried out...

HSE believes in firm but fair enforcement of health and safety law. This should be informed by the principles of proportionality in applying the law and securing compliance; consistency of approach; targeting of enforcement action; transparency about how the regulator operates and what those regulated may expect; and accountability for the regulator's actions...

Those whom the law protects and those on whom it places duties (dutyholders) expect that action taken by enforcing authorities to achieve compliance or bring dutyholders to account for non-compliance should be proportionate to any risks to health and safety, or to the seriousness of any breach...

...making sure that contacts are targeted primarily on those whose activities give rise to the most serious risks or where the hazards are least well controlled; and that action is focused on the dutyholders who are responsible for the risk and who are best placed to control it – whether employers, manufacturers, suppliers, or others...

Decisions on enforcement action are discretionary, involving judgement by the enforcer. All enforcing authorities should have arrangements in place to promote consistency in the exercise of discretion, including effective arrangements for liaison with other enforcing authorities...

Transparency

Transparency means helping dutyholders to understand what is expected of them and what they should expect from the enforcing authorities...

Investigations are undertaken in order to determine:

- causes;
- whether action has been taken or needs to be taken to prevent a recurrence and to secure compliance with the law;
- lessons to be learnt and to influence the law and guidance;
- what response is appropriate to a breach of the law...

While the primary purpose of the enforcing authorities is to ensure that dutyholders manage and control risks effectively, thus preventing harm, prosecution is an essential part of enforcement...

Prosecution of individuals

Subject to the above, enforcing authorities should identify and prosecute or recommend prosecution of individuals if they consider that a prosecution is warranted. In particular, they should consider the management chain and the role played by individual directors and managers, and should take action against them where the inspection or investigation reveals that the offence was committed with their consent or connivance or to have been attributable to neglect on their part and where it would be appropriate to do so in accordance with this policy. Where appropriate, enforcing authorities should seek disqualification of directors under the Company Directors Disqualification Act 1986.

Publicity

Enforcing authorities should make arrangements for the publication annually of the names of all the companies and individuals who have been convicted in the previous 12 months of breaking health and safety law...

Action by the courts

Health and safety law gives the courts considerable scope to punish offenders and to deter others, including imprisonment for some offences. Unlimited fines may be imposed by higher courts.

Death at work

Where there has been a breach of the law leading to a work-related death, enforcing authorities need to consider whether the circumstances of the case might justify a charge of manslaughter or corporate manslaughter...If in the course of their health and safety investigation, the enforcing authorities find evidence suggesting manslaughter or corporate manslaughter, they should pass it on to the police.

An example of compliance failure could include the death of an employee several years ago.

The employee was clearing a dyke bank of green waste material using a mechanical digger. The employee was trained to be wearing a lifejacket in the event that the digger should slip down the dyke bank into the water, or if the employee fell out of the cab into the dyke water.

The employee found the lifejacket cumbersome to wear and so, despite his training, he chose not to wear it. Unfortunately the digger did slip down the bank into the water, and the employee died from drowning. Several compliance issues were raised during an investigation:

(1)   Had the employee been sufficiently trained to know that the wearing of the lifejacket was compulsory? When was the last time he was trained?

(2)   Was the lifejacket operational? (The canisters blowing up the lifejacket have a finite life.)

(3)   The employee was trapped by the digger, so would the lifejacket have helped?

(4)   Should there have been a second employee assisting the first, so in the event of an accident he could have tried to save the employees life or report the accident to the emergency services?

(5)   Should 'second' employees be advised to assist a drowning colleague?

Many more questions were asked during the investigation, but the employee had ultimately failed to comply with company rules by not wearing the lifejacket. And the company had failed to implement sufficient controls to prevent such an accident.

This compliance failure would be allocated a 'serious' rating due to a 'death at work' and post-investigation many new controls would be implemented to prevent any future occurrence. Employee training would probably feature heavily within any new controls.

6   COSO model applied to fraud prevention

 Fraud

Fraud can be defined as:

'dishonestly obtaining an advantage, avoiding an obligation or causing a loss to another party'

Fraud is a crime, but does not have a precise legal definition. The term 'fraud' refers to an intentional act by one or more individuals among management, those charged with governance, employees or third parties, involving the use of deception to obtain an unjust or illegal advantage. (International Standard of Auditing 240 The Auditor's Responsibility to Consider Fraud in an Audit of Financial Statements).

A distinction is made between:

- **fraud**, which is deliberate falsification, and

- **errors**, which are unintentional mistakes.

Examples of fraud include:

- the theft of cash or other assets

- false accounting: this includes concealing or falsifying accounting records with a view to personal gain or providing false information that is misleading or deceptive

- crimes against consumers or clients, e.g. misrepresenting the quality of goods; pyramid trading schemes; selling counterfeit goods

- employee fraud against employers, e.g. payroll fraud; falsifying expense claims; theft of cash

- crimes against investors, consumers and employees, e.g. financial statement fraud

- crimes against financial institutions, e.g. using lost and stolen credit cards; fraudulent insurance claims

- crimes against government, e.g. social security benefit claims fraud; tax evasion

- crimes by professional criminals, e.g. money laundering; advance fee fraud

- e-crime by people using computers, e.g. spamming; copyright crimes; hacking

Prerequisites for fraud

- A major reason why people commit fraud is because they are allowed to do so.

- The likelihood that fraud will be committed will be decreased if the potential fraudster believes that the rewards will be modest, that they will be detected or that the potential punishment will be unacceptably high.

- Therefore, a comprehensive system of control is needed to reduce the opportunity for fraud and increase the likelihood of detection.

There are three prerequisites for fraud to occur:

- **Dishonesty** on the part of the perpetrator.

- **Opportunity** for fraud to occur.

- **Motive** for fraud.

Fraud risk indicators

Fraud indicators fall into two categories:

Warning signs

Warning signs have been described as organisational indicators of fraud risk. Examples include the following:

- Absence of an anti-fraud policy and culture.

- Lack of management supervision of staff.

- Inadequate recruitment processes and absence of screening.

- Dissatisfied employees who have access to desirable assets.

- Lack of job segregation and independent checking of key transactions.

- Poor physical security of assets.

- Management compensation highly dependent on meeting aggressive performance targets.

- Highly competitive market conditions and decreasing profitability levels within the organisation.

- Rapid changes in information technology.

Fraud alerts

Fraud alerts have been described as specific events or red flags, which may be indicative of fraud. Examples include the following:

- Anonymous emails/letters/telephone calls.

- Emails sent at unusual times, with unnecessary attachments, or to unusual destinations.

- Discrepancy between earnings and lifestyle.

- Unusual, irrational, or inconsistent behaviour. For example members of staff who arrive first in the morning and leave last in the evening, do not take holidays, or who keep an area of the office for their exclusive use and do not share files with others.

- Alteration of documents and records.

- Subsidiary ledgers, which do not reconcile with control accounts.

- Extensive use of 'suspense' accounts.

- Inappropriate or unusual journal entries.

- Confirmation letters not returned.

Fraud risk management strategy

In common with any other type of risk, a risk management strategy needs to be developed for fraud. This strategy should include three key elements:

- Fraud prevention.
- Fraud detection.
- Fraud response.

Together, these should result in a fourth element – risk deterrence.

For example, fraud detection acts as a deterrent by sending a message to likely fraudsters that the organisation is actively fighting fraud and that procedures are in place to identify any illegal activity that has occurred. Similarly, the possibility of being caught will often persuade a potential perpetrator not to commit a fraud.

As well as addressing the legal aspects of fraud, this process operates within the wider context of the organisation's risk management strategy, corporate governance and ethical culture.

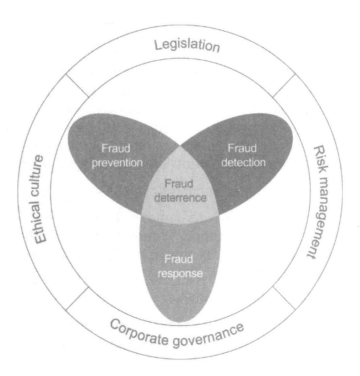

Fraud prevention using the COSO model

The main elements of an internal control system should be in place for dealing with fraud. In general terms, managing the risks of fraud is similar to the management of other types of risk and consists of the following elements:

- **Control environment**. Management should show an active interest in the prevention and detection of fraud. There should also be a fraud policy statement on how to respond to suspicions of fraud, to ensure that timely and effective action is taken in a consistent manner, and that management responsibilities are clear. For example, should initial suspicions be reported to the line manager in whose area of operations the suspected fraud is taking place, or should the matter be reported to senior accounts management for investigation?

- **Risk recognition and assessment**
  - Identify risk areas. Management should identify those areas that are vulnerable to fraud risk.
  - Activities where the risks might be high include cash handling and payments, purchasing and payroll.

- Assess the scale of the risk. The scale of the risk depends on the probability of fraud and the size of potential losses if fraud occurs. It also depends on the measures that are already in place to prevent fraud, and their apparent effectiveness. The scale of the risk to be considered is the 'residual risk' after allowing for the existing control measures.

- **Control activities and procedures**. The responsibility for the management of each risk to specific individuals. Specific controls are suggested below.

- **Information: monitoring and reporting**. Information should be provided regularly to management so that they can monitor performance with respect to efficiency and effectiveness in achieving targets, economy and quality. Effective monitoring can detect certain types of fraudulent activity. A company might use internal auditors to investigate a problem, after line management have established the basic facts. Any risk of continuing fraud should be dealt with if possible, for example by halting further payments or changing operating procedures until the matter is resolved.

- **Monitoring** activities and correcting deficiencies

  - Identify the need for revised controls. The adequacy of existing controls should be evaluated. Where appropriate, the need for specific additional controls should be identified, to reduce or eliminate the risk of fraud.

  - Implement the revised controls.

  - Monitor the implementation of the revised controls, to assess their effectiveness. One way of doing this is to carry out an internal audit investigation.

'The risk management cycle should be treated as an iterative process. If the implementation of revised controls is not sufficient to eliminate the threat of fraud, then the cycle must begin again' (HM Treasury).

Fraud detection

A common misbelief is that external auditors find fraud. This is actually rarely the case – in fact their letters of engagement typically state that it is **not their responsibility** to look for fraud. Most frauds are discovered accidentally, or as a result of information received (whistleblowing).

Some methods of discovering fraud are:

- Performing regular checks, e.g. stocktaking and cash counts.

- Warning signals or fraud risk indicators (see previous section). For example:

  - Failures in internal control procedures

  - Lack of information provided to auditors

  - Unusual behaviour by individual staff members

  - Accounting difficulties.

- Whistleblowers.

Fraud response

- The fraud response plan sets out the arrangements for dealing with suspected cases of fraud, theft or corruption.

- It provides procedures for evidence-gathering that will enable decision-making and that will subsequently be admissible in any legal action.

- The fraud response plan also has a deterrent value and can help to restrict damage and minimise losses to the organisation.

The organisation's response to fraud may include:

- Internal disciplinary action, in accordance with personnel policies.

- Civil litigation for the recovery of loss.

- Criminal prosecution through the police.

 Investigation of fraud

When a fraud comes to light, internal auditors might be asked to investigate it. The purpose of investigating a fraud should be to:

- Establish the facts.

- Establish how the fraud occurred and initially went undetected. Were the internal controls weak or inadequate? Or were the internal controls by-passed or not properly applied?

- Consider whether anyone else might have been involved in the fraud.

- Establish or estimate the size of the loss.

The investigator should look at all relevant documents and files, listen to recorded telephone conversations and read the fraudster's e-mails. Individuals working with the fraudster should be interviewed, such as colleagues, supervisor and manager.

Great care must be taken to ensure that evidence is gathered and maintained in a manner that could be used in any criminal proceedings that the company institutes. The company might also have to defend allegations of unfair dismissal or defamation by an employee who claims they have been wrongly accused.

As a result of an investigation, an auditor should make recommendations about the system. These are likely to be that, if the risk of losses is high, either:

- the existing internal controls are not sufficient to limit the risk; new controls or stronger controls should therefore be introduced, or

- the existing internal controls should be sufficient to limit the risk, but were applied inadequately or were ignored in the past; measures should therefore be taken to ensure that the controls are properly applied in the future.

Test your understanding 13

Theft of the petty cash tin occurred at Y plc. This was the second time it had happened in three years. The tin held £750 in the first instance and £7,500 in the second instance (due to a new van being paid for later in the day). Normally the tin would only hold around £100.

Controls that should be in place to prevent these thefts are:

Select ALL that apply

A   Insurance

B   Maximum limits on the value of cash held

C   Confidentiality

D   Keeping the tin locked when unused

Test your understanding 14

O is a multinational organisation which sells a large number of goods, including books and DVD's online to individual customers. A review of one of the IT systems which processes internet sales has revealed several transactions over the last few months which suggest there has been some 'hacking' or fraudulent access to the customer database. Each transaction resulted in no payment from the customer and transactions being immediately deleted from the customer database so that sales were not recorded.

Which of the following control recommendations may help to prevent a reoccurrence of the issues outlined above?

Select ALL that apply.

A   Only despatch goods where payment has been received in full.

B   Monitor system access from internal sources, using a control log, to identify whether staff in the IT department are placing fraudulent orders.

C   Only sell to those customers who have an account set up with O.

D   Check a number of transactions at regular intervals on a daily basis to make sure they are not deleted.

E   Invest in fraud insurance to cover losses resulting from unauthorised access.

Test your understanding 15

A new member of staff has started working in the receivables department of ABC Ltd. She previously worked in the sales department at ABC's main competitor.

Which controls should be implemented to ensure that the new staff member operates in the correct manner at ABC?

Select ALL that apply

A   Employment contract

B   Confidentiality clause

C   Training

D   Supervision

Test your understanding 16

Examples of non-financial quantitative controls include:

Select ALL that apply

A   An organisation structure

B   Physical controls

C   The number of faulty goods returned

D   The percentage of staff attending training courses each year

Test your understanding 17

The risk that money could be stolen from PQ's bank account could be reduced by:

Select ALL that apply

A   Having a restricted list of dual cheque signatories

B   Locking away cheque books

C   Annual bank reconciliations

D   Having secure passwords and PIN numbers

Test your understanding 18

A sole trader, Yu Yang, owns a new consultancy business employing ten highly-skilled, autonomous staff.

Yu Yang has just attended a new business education lunch, run by a government advisory committee, set up to help new business. The topic of discussion at lunch was internal control systems. Yu Yang has come back to the office enthused by the lunch and looking to start the implementation of new controls.

Advise Yu Yang which THREE of the following are limitations to the effectiveness of internal controls within his consultancy business.

A   An employees could ignore the internal control

B   Internal control systems will only target manufacturing companies

C   Additional controls could negatively affect employee motivation

D   Internal controls can slow down the companies' response time to market

E   There likelihood of a major accident is low given the work of Yu Yang's business, therefore internal controls are not necessary

F   Internal controls are only needed if the company is a limited company

Test your understanding 19

TT is a passenger ferry operator which operates several vessels between busy ports in countries A and B.

One of TT's larger ships was damaged in high winds during a crossing. The damage led to multiple passenger injuries and compensation claims against TT which the company was not adequately insured for. It was acknowledged that TT should not have operated the particular ferry service due to the weather conditions and that control failures were largely responsible for the incident and injuries.

TT has a history of control weakness and the internal audit team have listed the main weaknesses which were in evidence on the day of the incident. The management of TT now wish to establish which control weaknesses contributed to the incident.

Which of the following weaknesses would have made the incident more likely to occur?

Select ALL that apply.

A   Passengers not being provided with suitable safety equipment to use in an emergency.

B   Crew members failing to secure the ship adequately against the weather on departure due to time constraints.

C   TT's internal procedures lacking routine weather checks and instead relying on each ship's captain to decide locally on safety to operate the service.

D   Inadequate checks on the relevance and extent of insurance over incidents involving weather damage.

E   The captain overriding speed controls in order to meet the scheduled arrival time.

Test your understanding 20 – Private hospital (Integration)

A private hospital has a canteen that provides staff and visitors with subsidised meals and refreshments. The canteen's selling prices are supposed to cover running costs, so that there is no net cost to the hospital. Over the past eighteen months the canteen has been reporting losses that have been increasing steadily despite monthly sales remaining constant. The cost of purchases has grown substantially for no apparent reason. The purchasing of supplies and the choice of suppliers is the sole responsibility of the Canteen Manager. The current Canteen Manager has been in post for almost two years.

The hospital's Chief Executive asked the Head of Internal Audit to investigate why the canteen was making losses and a thorough investigation was conducted under the supervision of F, an experienced auditor and qualified accountant. The internal audit team discovered that the losses started shortly after the Canteen Manager changed suppliers. F compared the invoiced prices charged by the new supplier with those charged by the former supplier and discovered that the new supplier was significantly more expensive.

F interviewed the Canteen Manager, who claimed that the change in suppliers was because the new supplier was more reliable and provided higher quality products. F was suspicious and contacted a number of alternative suppliers. None of the potential suppliers whom F contacted would have charged as much as the canteen was paying for basic commodities such as rice and potatoes. Furthermore, the canteen's invoices showed that it was paying far more than the normal market price for branded goods, such as crisps and chocolate bars.

F was in the Canteen Manager's office one lunch time, and saw a laptop computer open at an email to the supplier and investigated further. The Canteen Manager had been using a personal email account to email the owner of the supplier on a daily basis. The emails revealed that:

- the owner had been inflating the selling prices of all goods sold to the hospital by 20%;

- the Canteen Manager passed these inflated invoices for payment; and

- the owner then paid half of the 20% that had been overcharged to the Canteen Manager in cash.

F confiscated the laptop, which was the Canteen Manager's personal property, and submitted it, along with a full report, to the Head of Internal Audit.

Two weeks later, F was asked to meet with the hospital's Chief Executive. The hospital's directors had discussed the report carefully and had interviewed the Canteen Manager and decided that they did not wish to refer the matter to the police. The Canteen Manager had been accompanied by a lawyer, who stated that the Canteen Manager denied all charges of fraud and pointed out that there was very little evidence to support F's accusations. F could have easily falsified the emails on the laptop and the owner of the food supplier had supplied the lawyer with a statement that no payments had been made to the Canteen Manager. The Chief Executive had agreed that the hospital would return the Canteen Manager's laptop and would make him a substantial payment in return for his agreement to resign quietly. The Chief Executive had also promised that the Canteen Manager would receive a positive reference. F was asked to destroy any remaining notes and documents relating to this investigation and to remain silent, not discussing the case with anyone either within the hospital or any third parties.

Required:

Discuss the difficulties associated with proving that the Canteen Manager was fraudulent.

(30 minutes)

Test your understanding 21 – Fraud and mitigation (Integration)

XYS is a company manufacturing and selling a wide range of industrial products to a large number of businesses throughout the country. XYS is a significant local employer, with 2,000 people working out of several locations around the region, all linked by a networked computer system.

XYS purchases numerous components from 500 local and regional suppliers, receiving them into a central warehouse. The company carries about 20,000 different inventory items, placing 15,000 orders with its suppliers each year.

The Accounts Payable Department of XYS has five staff who process all supplier invoices through the company's computer system and make payment to suppliers by cheque or electronic remittance.

Required:

Explain the risk of fraud in Accounts Payable for a company like XYS and how that risk can be mitigated.

(20 minutes)

Test your understanding 22 – College (Case study)

Scenario

A large college has several sites and employs hundreds of teaching staff.

Trigger

The college has recently discovered a serious fraud involving false billings for part-time teaching.

The fraud involved two members of staff. M is a clerk in the payroll office who is responsible for processing payments to part-time teaching staff. P is the head of the Business Studies department at the N campus. Part-time lecturers are required to complete a monthly claim form which lists the classes taught and the total hours claimed. These forms must be signed by their head of department, who sends all signed forms to M. M checks that the class codes on the claim forms are valid, that hours have been budgeted for those classes and inputs the information into the college's payroll package.

The college has a separate personnel department that is responsible for maintaining all personnel files. Additions to the payroll must be made by a supervisor in the personnel office. The payroll package is programmed to reject any claims for payment to employees whose personnel files are not present in the system.

M had gained access to the personnel department supervisor's office by asking the college security officer for the loan of a pass key because she had forgotten the key to her own office. M knew that the office would be unoccupied that day because the supervisor was attending a wedding. M logged onto the supervisor's computer terminal by guessing her password, which turned out to be the registration number of the supervisor's car. M then added a fictitious part-time employee, who was allocated to the N campus Business Studies department.

P then began making claims on behalf of the fictitious staff member and submitting them to M. M signed off the forms and input them as normal. The claims resulted in a steady series of payments to a bank account that had been opened by P. The proceeds of the fraud were shared equally between M and P.

The fraud was only discovered when the college wrote to every member of staff with a formal invitation to the college's centenary celebration. The letter addressed to the fictitious lecturer was returned as undeliverable and the personnel department became suspicious when they tried to contact this person in order to update her contact details. By then M and P had been claiming for non-existent teaching for three years.

The government department responsible for funding the college conducted an investigation and concluded that the college's management had relied excessively on the application controls programmed into administrative software and had paid too little attention to the human resources aspects of the system.

Task

(i)   Write a memorandum to the Board evaluating the difficulties associated with preventing and/or detecting this fraud.

(20 minutes)

(ii)   Write a letter to the Dean of the college which:

(a)   Advises on the weaknesses in the college's systems and procedures; and

(b)   Discusses the suggestion that the human elements of control systems are frequently more important than the software elements in ensuring that records are correct.

(30 minutes)

Test your understanding 23 – G Manufacturing (Case study)

Scenario

G is a manufacturing company that employs 800 production staff and 90 administrative staff. The company operates from a single site.

Trigger

A new Chief Executive was appointed in July. She was recruited from a much larger manufacturing company where she was the Marketing Director. The company is also an indirect competitor of G's.

Since her appointment the Chief Executive has focussed on learning as much as she possibly can about the company's culture. She spent the whole of August meeting representatives from all levels of staff within the company and other stakeholders such as customers and suppliers. She has called a board meeting to discuss her findings.

Her findings are as follows:

- The company manufactures high quality products that are popular with customers. All members of G's staff are proud to be associated with the manufacture of the products.

- G's managers and supervisors take a very relaxed approach when working with subordinates. Staff are empowered to make decisions on their own without consulting their superiors if they are confident that they are acting in the company's best interests.

- The relaxed management style has harmed the control environment immensely. Only a minority of the company's staff take the budgetary control system seriously and hardly any of them pay serious attention to variance reports. In contrast to all other departments, morale in the accounts department is very low because the members of the accounts staff feel that they waste a significant amount of time every month chasing heads of departments for reports and for other important information.

- These attitudes are echoed by external stakeholders. Customers are delighted with the quality of G's products, but often find that G's invoices and monthly statements contain errors. Suppliers claim that invoices submitted to G are settled very promptly 90% of the time, but the remainder have to be chased because G's accounts staff do not always receive accurate and complete records of orders placed and goods received.

The Chief Executive has warned the board that the control environment must be improved as a matter of priority. She proposes to send an email to all staff congratulating them on their achievements on product quality, but stating that the rather lax attitude towards management and record keeping will have to stop. Over time, she plans to impose disciplinary measures on staff who are responsible for bookkeeping errors or delays. She also proposes that G should create an internal audit department to monitor compliance with formal processes and procedures.

The Production Director has argued that the Chief Executive's proposals are counter-productive and that most of the delays and omissions are due to employees giving priority to the creation of an excellent product.

Task:

Write a report to the Board:

(a) Explaining why it is necessary to improve G's control environment; and

(b) Evaluating the Chief Executive's proposal to impose disciplinary measures on staff who are responsible for bookkeeping errors or delays.

(30 minutes)

Test your understanding 24 – U internet (Case study)

Scenario

U is an internet-based company that sells books, DVDs and CDs to consumers. U's customers are required to create an account, to which they register their name, address and credit card details. The customers must also create a password, which they must use whenever they wish to log into their account in order to update their details or place an order. Registered customers can log in and place orders very easily because all of their delivery and payment details are already on file. That feature is one of the main factors behind U's success. The other main factor is that U's software tracks each customer's purchases and uses that information to email recommendations based on past orders. Many customers buy recommended products and the proportion is growing because U's tracking software becomes increasingly accurate as more data is gathered.

Trigger

U has recently suffered a security breach involving 2,000 of its highest spending customers. One of U's analysts had been asked to write a report about those customers' buying habits. The report was required urgently and so the analyst copied the customers' files onto a memory stick, which he took home to analyse on his home PC over the weekend. He copied the final report onto the same memory stick, but lost the stick during the train journey into work.

The analyst had one of his flatmates email him a copy of the report, which was still on the hard drive of his home PC, so the report's deadline was met. The analyst did not report the loss of the memory stick because he did not wish to get into trouble for losing the data. He hoped that anybody who found the stick would simply erase the files.

Over the next two weeks, U started to receive complaints from customers that orders were being placed without the account holders' permission. U's policy in these circumstances is to seek clarification from the account holder and suggest that the order could have been placed by a family member who knew the account password. The volume of complaints was higher than usual and the analyst was asked to investigate them to determine whether there was a security problem. The analyst quickly realised that many of the complaints were from the 2,000 customers whose files were on his memory stick and that the person who had found the stick was abusing that information. He admitted the loss of the memory stick and was suspended.

U's customer services department wrote to all of those customers whose accounts had been compromised and offered to cancel any disputed charges on their accounts. The customers were also advised to contact their credit card providers and to study their card statements carefully in case the thief had used that information to defraud them. Several of these customers complained to a national newspaper and U received many further complaints concerning disputed charges, mainly from customers whose details had not been copied by the analyst.

Task:

Write a report to U's Board which:

(a) Advises on the weaknesses in both the control environment and the internal controls that led to this loss of data;

(b) Recommends, stating reasons, actions that U's board should take:

   (i) to restore the confidence of its existing and potential customers;

   (ii) to prevent similar problems occurring in the future.

(45 minutes)

Test your understanding 25 – V (Case study)

Scenario

V is a quoted company. Its board comprises an equal number of both executive and non-executive directors. The company has a remuneration committee, comprised entirely of non-executives.

Trigger

A major institutional investor in V has written to the chair of the remuneration committee to raise some concerns about the manner in which the performance of V's executive directors is controlled and rewarded.

At present, each of the executive directors receives a fairly substantial fixed annual salary combined with options granted under an executive share option scheme ("ESOS"). The ESOS is designed in order to align the directors' interests with those of the shareholders:

The remuneration committee reviews each director's performance during the financial year and grants a number of share options in accordance with performance.

The options are issued "at the money" (that is, the exercise price is the same as the market price) so that the directors have an incentive to increase the share price.

The options can only be exercised on a specified date that falls three years after their issue.

If a director leaves the company then any outstanding options will lapse without compensation.

The institutional investor has expressed concern about the ESOS arrangement because of the underlying financial implications of the scheme. V first introduced ESOSs in order to motivate the executive directors to act in the shareholders' interests. If the directors work towards maximising V's share price then the options will provide higher returns if they are in the money when they come due for exercise. In addition, V's directors are much less likely to reject positive net present value investment opportunities if they hold options. Normally the directors are more risk averse than the shareholders when it comes to project appraisal, but holding options makes risk-taking more appealing.

The institutional investor is concerned that the options may have encouraged dysfunctional behaviour by the directors, although it is difficult to be certain that that has arisen because of the limited information that is available to the shareholders.

The institutional investor has suggested that the executive directors should be rewarded with a simpler scheme, such as an annual profit-related bonus. At present, it is unclear whether the reward system in place provides the executive directors with meaningful feedback on their performance. As a shareholder, the investor wishes to see a clearer link between the directors' performance and their remuneration.

Task

Write a letter to the institutional investor which:

(i)   Explains why the introduction of ESOSs could motivate V's executive directors to accept positive net present value (NPV) projects;

(ii)   Explains how an ESOS scheme could affect the actions taken by the directors (other than the project appraisal decision).

(30 minutes)

Write a memorandum to the remuneration committee which evaluates the advantages AND disadvantages of rewarding executive directors by paying a bonus based on a simple and transparent measure such as profit.   **(15 minutes)**

Test your understanding 26 – Cliff (Integration)

Day-to-day internal controls are important for all businesses to maximise the efficient use of resources and profitability. Your firm has recently been appointed as auditor to Cliff, a private company that runs a chain of small supermarkets selling fresh and frozen food, and canned and dry food. Cliff has very few controls over inventory because the company trusts local managers to make good decisions regarding the purchase, sale and control of inventory, all of which is controlled locally. Pricing is generally performed on a cost-plus basis.

Each supermarket has a standalone computer system on which monthly accounts are prepared. These accounts are mailed to head office every quarter. There is no integrated inventory control, sale or purchasing system and no regular system for inventory counting. Management accounts are produced twice a year.

Trade at the supermarkets has increased in recent years and the number of supermarkets has increased. However, the quality of staff that has been recruited has fallen. Senior management at Cliff are now prepared to invest in more up-to-date systems.

Task

(i)   Discuss the problems you would expect to find at Cliff as a result of the poor system of internal control.

(ii)   Recommend four improvements to the internal control system at Cliff, explaining the advantages and disadvantages of each.

(35 minutes)

Test your understanding 27 – SPD (Integration)

SPD has been approached by Q, a specialist manufacturer of extremely expensive high performance cars. Q is in the process of developing a new car that will be one of the fastest in the world. The car will be designed to be driven on public roads, but the owners of such cars often take them to private race tracks where they can be driven at very high speeds.

Q has designed an electronics system to enable an average driver to drive the car safely at high speed. The system will monitor the engine, brakes and steering and will compensate for errors that could cause a crash. The system will, for example, sense that the car is about to skid and will compensate for that. The electronics system will be based on a circuit board that Q wishes to have built by SPD.

Building Q's circuit board will pose a number of challenges for SPD. The circuit board will be subject to a great deal of vibration when the car is driven at speed. The cars are expected to last for a very long time and so there could be problems if the circuit boards deteriorate with age. The circuit board will be installed in an inaccessible part of the car where it will be difficult to inspect or maintain.

Many of the components on the board will be manufactured by SPD, but some crucial components will be supplied by a third party that has already been selected by Q.

Required:

Discuss controls that should be in place to reduce the risks faced by SPD if they accept an order from Q.

(15 minutes)

Test your understanding 28 – Rhapsody Company (Integration)

Rhapsody Co supplies a wide range of garden and agricultural products to trade and domestic customers. The company has 11 divisions, with each division specialising in the sale of specific products, for example, seeds, garden furniture, and agricultural fertilizers. The company has an internal audit department which provides audit reports to the audit committee on each division on a rotational basis.

Products in the seed division are offered for sale to domestic customers via an Internet site. Customers review the product list on the Internet and place orders for packets of seeds onto Rhapsody Co's secure server using specific product codes, along with their credit card details. Order quantities are normally between one and three packets for each type of seed. Order details are transferred manually onto the company's internal inventory control and sales system, and a two part packing list is printed in the seed warehouse. Each order and packing list is given in a random alphabetical code based on the name of the employee inputting the order, the date and the products being ordered.

In the seed warehouse, the packets of seeds for each order are taken from specific bins and despatched to the customer with one copy of the packing list. The second copy of the packing list is sent to the accounts department where the inventory and sales computer is updated to show that the order has been despatched. The customer's credit card is then charged by the inventory control and sales computer. Irrecoverable debts in Rhapsody are currently 3% of the total sales.

Finally, the computer system checks that for each charge made to a customer's credit card account, the order details are on file, to confirm that the charge was made correctly. The order file is marked as completed confirming that the order has been despatched and payment obtained.

Required:

In respect of sales in the seeds division of Rhapsody Co

(a)   identify and evaluate weaknesses in the sales system.

(25 minutes)

(b)   provide a recommendation to alleviate each weakness.

(20 minutes)

Test your understanding 29 – Bassoon Ltd (Integration)

Bassoon Ltd runs a chain of shops selling electrical goods all of which are located within the same country.

It has a head office that deals with purchasing, distribution and administration. The payroll for the whole company is administered at head office.

There are 20 staff at head office and 200 staff in the company's 20 shops located in high streets and shopping malls all over the country.

Head office staff (including directors) are all salaried and paid by direct transfer to their bank accounts.

The majority of the staff at the company's shops are also paid through the central salary system, monthly in arrears. However, some students and part time staff are paid cash out of the till.

Recruitment of head office staff is initiated by the department needing the staff who generally conduct interviews and agree the terms and conditions of employment. Bassoon has an HR manager who liaises with recruitment agencies, places job adverts and maintains staff files with contracts of employment, etc.

Shop managers recruit their own staff.

Shop staff receive a basic salary based on the hours worked and commission based on sales made.

The company has a fairly sophisticated EPOS (electronic point of sale) till system at all shops. The EPOS system communicates directly with the head office accounting system.

When making a sale, all staff have to log on with a swipe card which identifies them to the system, and means that the sales for which they are responsible are analysed by the system and commissions calculated.

Store managers have a few 'guest cards' for temporary and part time staff, who generally do not receive commissions.

Store managers and regional supervisors are paid commissions based on the performance of their store or region. Directors and other head office staff usually receive a bonus at Christmas, depending on the company's performance. This is decided on by the board in consultation with departmental managers and put through the system by the payroll manager.

The payroll manager is responsible for adding joiners to the payroll and deleting leavers as well as for implementing changes in pay rates, tax coding and other deductions and for making sure that the list of monthly transfers is communicated to the bank.

The computerised payroll system is a standard proprietary system which is sophisticated enough to incorporate the commission calculations mentioned above which are fed in directly from the EPOS system.

The company employs an IT manager who is responsible for the maintenance of all IT systems and installing new hardware and software.

Required:

Identify the risks inherent in the payroll system at Bassoon Ltd and recommend any changes which you think are appropriate.

(30 minutes)

7   Chapter summary

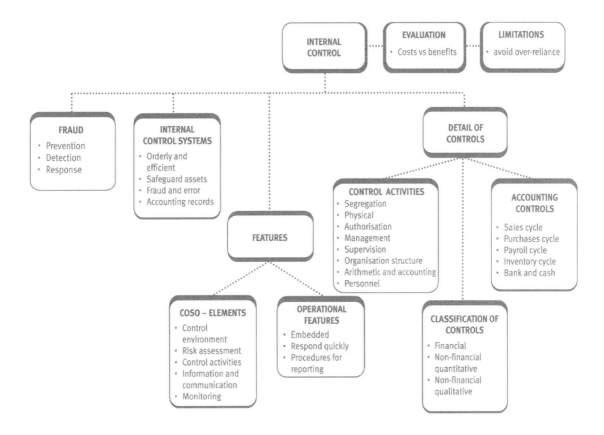

Test your understanding answers

Test your understanding 1

The correct answers are B, C, D and E – The five elements were control environment, risk assessment, control activities, information and communication and monitoring.

Test your understanding 2

The correct answers are A, C and D – The four categories of objective setting are strategic, operational, reporting and compliance.

Test your understanding 3

D

Control environment refers to the attitudes of management and in particular directors towards controls. An organisation may have all of the other five aspects of internal control in place but they cannot be relied upon if management and directors do not regard them as important. Their actions may override or disregard control failures. A poor control environment therefore can undermine an otherwise sound internal control system.

Test your understanding 4

A and B only

- Option A: A blame culture means it is unlikely that staff will integrate controls into their jobs for fear of being blamed if problems are uncovered.

- Option B: The CEO's attitude towards suppliers shows a lack of commitment to solving the problems, as do the views of the sales director and purchasing manager.

- Option C: This may be true but it would not prevent internal controls principles being embedded within J.

- Option D: Similarly, staff who have worked in J Company for a long term may actually be more committed to solving its' problems and happy to incorporate internal controls as part of their jobs.

- Option E: Well-paid happy staff may be complacent but they may also be willing to adapt to change with minimal fuss, especially if they have respect for management.

Test your understanding 5 – Types of control (Integration)

(1) **Shoplifting**

- CCTV cameras in the shop.
- Security tagging of products.
- Stock reconciliations to detect theft.
- Employment of security guards.

(2) **Goods not invoiced**

- Reconcile goods despatch notes to invoices.
- Check sequences of goods despatch notes and invoices.
- Segregation of duties between despatch and invoicing.
- Reconcile stock movement and sales figures.

(3) **Poor quality supplies**

- Inspection of all goods when received.
- Approval of suppliers who can supply high quality.

(4) **Incorrect prices**

- Arithmetic checks on invoices.
- Computer system control to ensure that every invoice is priced on current price levels.
- Authorisation of staff who can change price levels.

Test your understanding 6

The correct answer is C – By definition.

Test your understanding 7

The correct answer is B – By definition. A ensures that all deliveries have been invoiced. C ensures the correct goods are despatched. D will remind the customer to pay but if they are unable to pay it will not help.

Test your understanding 8

The correct answers are A, B, C, D and E – All of the controls should help to some extent.

Test your understanding 9

The correct answers are B, C and D – The COSO framework does not mention the external environment, but does mention the internal environment.

Test your understanding 10

C only

- Option A may help staff learn about B and its operations but not guard against fraud.

- Option B may make the café run more smoothly but not guard against dishonesty.

- Option C may ensure only trustworthy staff are recruited.

- Option D may ensure suitability for the job but any dishonest recruit could just wait six weeks before perpetrating a fraud.

- Option E is not a HR control, rather an operational control.

Test your understanding 11

A, C and D

- Option A: This would ensure every student present signs the register and so is invoiced for the course.

- Option B: This would prevent students turning up, signing in and leaving but it would not pick up those students who do not sign the register at all and so do not get charged.

- Option C: This would prevent theft of material from students not enrolled however may not be practical unless students enrol early.

- Option D: This would ensure that all students signed in and could be invoiced for the course.

- Option E: This may cause a loss in revenue since provided there is room in the class students who turn up on the day should be allowed to attend. They can be invoiced later as long as their details are recorded by B.

Test your understanding 12

The correct answer is B – By definition.

Test your understanding 13

The correct answers are B, C and D – Insurance does not prevent theft. Amounts over £100 should be dealt with by cheque or bank transfer, and not through petty cash. Transactions should be kept confidential – it would appear that someone knew when to steal the tin, while large amounts were held.

Test your understanding 14

A and B only

- Option A: This will prevent deliveries being made without the customer being invoiced or the cash being received.

- Option B: The computer systems appear to have been accessed by third parties with the aim of obtaining goods without paying. It could be that IT staff are actually perpetrating the fraud and this control will detect if this is the case as well as act as a deterrent to staff attempting to place such orders.

- Option C: Since there is a possibility of customer accounts being hacked, this control will not remedy the weakness in the system.

- Option D: This may highlight a reoccurrence of the issue but it will not prevent it from occurring in the first place.

- Option E: This may help minimise financial losses from goods being 'given away' but will not prevent the hacking from occurring.

Test your understanding 15

The correct answers are A, B, C and D – All of the controls should help.

Test your understanding 16

The correct answers are C and D – A and B are non-financial qualitative controls.

Test your understanding 17

The correct answers are A, B and D – Annual bank reconciliations will not be often enough to spot a fraud.

Test your understanding 18

A, C and D

Note:

- B – internal control systems can be applied to service organisations as well
- E – internal controls address more than just major accidents
- F – internal controls are needed for all types of organisation

Test your understanding 19

B, C and E

- Option A may have contributed to more injuries but not made the incident more likely to occur.
- Option D would have caused monetary loss to TT but not made the incident more likely to occur.

Test your understanding 20 – Private hospital (Integration)

There is very little evidence against the manager and the law will almost certainly require the hospital to prove that the Canteen Manager was fraudulent. The material and the information that has been gathered by F is persuasive but most of it could simply be denied by the Canteen Manager.

The hospital can prove that the Canteen Manager's purchases cost more than might have been charged by another supplier, but that is not in itself proof of fraud. The manager could claim to have been careless in permitting the supplier to overcharge the hospital, but could deny any fraudulent intent. The purchases clearly did take place because the food was received and sold through the canteen. The transactions were authorised by the manager, who was empowered to authorise new suppliers and to sign for purchases. All of the documentary evidence proves that the canteen purchases were made from an authorised supplier for the purpose stated in the bookkeeping records.

The only way to prove that the manager had defrauded the hospital would be to seek a formal statement from the supplier that there had been fraudulent collusion. The supplier is owner-managed and the owner is clearly implicated in the fraud. All the owner has to do is to claim that the sales actually occurred at the recorded prices. If the owner admits to participating in the fraud then s/he will be admitting to a criminal offence and will then be open to the threat of criminal charges. The hospital might also be able to reclaim the overstatement of the prices from the owner.

The only correspondence concerning the fraud is in an electronic format. By his own admission, the internal auditor has accessed the email account and so the manager could claim that the files and messages have been tampered with. There is no direct proof that the emails were sent to and from the Canteen Manager and the owner. Anybody could have created that email account and sent and received bogus emails describing a fraud. The manager could simply deny ever having sent or received those messages.

Test your understanding 21 – Fraud and mitigation (Integration)

Computer systems provide a particular opportunity for fraud, although this requires dishonesty by employees, opportunity to commit fraud, and motive. Accounts Payable in particular presents the opportunity for unscrupulous suppliers to claim payment for goods not delivered or services not supplied, or to overcharge. It also provides the opportunity for employees to redirect payments to themselves, or third parties, rather than to the intended supplier, either alone or in concert with third parties.

Some controls are preventative – designed to limit or prevent an event from occurring. This could include physical access controls over the computer system, selection and training of staff, separation of duties between invoice and payment processing or authorisation levels for invoices and payments. Other controls are detective: they identify events that have already occurred, through, for example, the reconciliation of invoices to a supplier statement. Internal audit, based on risk identification and assessment procedures have an important role to play in detective controls. Finally, corrective controls correct events after they have occurred (e.g. recovering overpayments from suppliers, or seeking recompense from employees under a fraud response plan).

It is particularly important that strong controls exist over programme alterations to accounts payable software, physical and logical access controls to accounts payable systems, authorisation levels for invoices and payments and control over forms such as cheques and electronic bank remittances.

The risk of fraud can be reduced through fraud prevention, identification and response policies. Fraud prevention requires an anti-fraud culture and risk awareness which is part of the control environment; sound control systems; and an effective whistle-blowing policy.

Fraud can be identified through regular internal audit checks, warning signals such as late payments, work backlogs, untaken annual leave, and the lifestyle of staff where it is incommensurate with their salary. Fraud response should include disciplinary action under human resource policies, civil litigation for recovery and criminal prosecution.

Test your understanding 22 – College (Case study)

(i)   Memorandum

To: The Board

From: A.N. Accountant

Date: Today

Subject: Fraud mitigation

This fraud would have been extremely difficult to prevent and/or to detect.

The fraud involved collusion between two members of staff. Segregation of duties is one of the most powerful means of preventing fraud, but it can be defeated by fraudulent collusion. It would be virtually impossible to make a system effective without relying on segregation of duties.

The fact that one of the perpetrators was a senior member of staff made it more difficult to prevent. The head of an academic department in a college would be regarded as a trusted member of staff, who would not normally be expected to steal from the college.

Systems are often designed in the expectation that senior members of staff will not betray such trust.

The system was further defeated by the falsification of a record on the personnel department. There was a sound control in place that was only defeated because of a combination of human error and blatant falsification. It would be almost impossible to design any system so that it was foolproof in preventing all mistakes and in preventing fraudulent falsification.

Once the fictitious entry had been made in the personnel files the fraud would be difficult to detect because it would add only a very small amount to the overall payroll. A college would have a large number of lecturers and there would be a substantial turnover in staff.

The only people who could be expected to detect this fraud were implicated in it.

(ii)   Letter

Address

Date

Dear Sir,

I am writing in answer to your request to advise on the weaknesses in the college's systems and procedures. I also cover the suggestion that the human elements of control systems are frequently more important than the software elements in ensuring that records are correct.

Weaknesses

(a) Additions to the payroll should require further authorisation than just the head of the department in which he or she would be teaching. That is not just to prevent fraud and error, but also to ensure that those appointed are competent and well qualified.

Teaching time should be budgeted and allocated to specific classes. That should be part of the normal planning and budgeting process.

Again, that is largely about ensuring that the college obtains value for money from teaching rather than merely trying to prevent fraud and error. This budgeting should be conducted, or at least reviewed in detail, by a dean of faculty or an assistant principal rather than the heads of individual departments.

Pass keys should not be issued to anybody other than designated security and cleaning staff. If a member of staff requires a door to be unlocked then the security guard should open the door personally rather than making a loan of a pass key. Computer passwords should be issued to staff so that they cannot invent their own, easily guessable passwords. The college should have a policy of holding staff responsible for all input made using their electronic identities – regardless of whether they were actually involved – so that they are motivated to take care over logging out of systems and protecting access.

Human controls

(b) It could be argued that the most important aspect of any secure system is authorisation.

Software can compare entries in different files and highlight discrepancies, but it cannot make meaningful decisions about whether a transaction should be processed. For example, a bookkeeping package will process any transaction that is input by a user with access rights, regardless of whether that entry makes sense. The physical security of any system is dependent on the behaviour of the people who operate it. It is, for example, common for security to break down because staff are careless over locking doors or restricting access to authorised personnel. The most important changes that are made, such as amendments to standing data, often require some judgement on the part of the person responsible for authorising the change.

If that person is not careful in agreeing to make the change then the fact that the software is programmed to ensure that the change has been authorised will be almost pointless. Most fraud involving computers tends to be relatively low-tech. For example, the input of fictitious purchase invoices in the hope that this leads to a payment that can be intercepted. Such fraud is more easily detected by a human being than a computer programme.

I hope you have found my advice and suggestions useful. However, if you have any further queries, please do not hesitate to contact me.

Yours faithfully,

A.N. Accountant

Test your understanding 23 – G Manufacturing (Case study)

To: The Board

From: A.N. Accountant

Date: Today

Subject: The control environment at G

Introduction

This report covers an explanation of why it is necessary to improve G's control environment and evaluates the Chief Executive's proposal to impose disciplinary measures on staff who are responsible for bookkeeping errors or delays.

(a) **The control environment**

The control environment is essentially a reflection of the attitudes of senior management towards the operation of the system. If management is seen to condone control weaknesses and compliance failures then the staff at more junior levels will tend to interpret that as an indication that controls do not matter.

It is clear that G's senior management has tolerated a situation in which the staff are concerned only with the technical success of the production process. That has led to problems with the bookkeeping and administrative arrangements, which could prove very costly to the company. The delays and errors in those areas could disrupt cash flows and irritate customers. The fact that the accounts staff are demotivated means that there is a risk that they will leave and so time and energy will have to be invested in appointing replacements.

(b) **Disciplinary measures**

G has been successful because its staff have tended to focus on the quality of the product and the customer satisfaction with the product itself is evidence of that. It may be that the relaxed working relationships mean that staff can focus on product innovation and quality management and that has enhanced the company's reputation. Any changes that are introduced will have to be undertaken with some sensitivity in case they lead to staff becoming demotivated in the process. It may not be constructive to use the threat of disciplinary action in the first instance. The fact that the new Chief Executive is keen to improve the administrative side of the company could be communicated to all staff as a positive step that will make the company more secure and efficient. The company will be unable to function, and to provide employment in the process, if it is unable to pay for materials or to bill customers properly because of accounting errors or lost documentation. It should be possible to communicate a positive attitude and encourage staff to view the accounting aspects of the company's operations as an extension of the whole organisation. The same attitude could be taken towards budgets and variance reports because they can help to ensure the smooth and efficient running of the organisation. The threat of disciplinary action may help to demonstrate that the Chief Executive takes these matters seriously and should send a clear message to staff. The problem is that the workforce is motivated and hardworking and so it may be counter-productive to make that threat unless other approaches have been tried and failed. Quite apart from damaging relations with the workforce, if G threatens to discipline staff and does not carry out that threat, then the impression that errors and delays are acceptable will be reinforced.

The threat of swift and decisive action may motivate and encourage the bookkeeping staff. The fact that the Chief Executive is prepared to take action against employees who make their jobs more difficult could make the bookkeeping staff feel valued and reassured that there will be a change for the better.

Conclusion

In summary, the control environment at G is very important and should be improved. Disciplinary action, where threatened, must be carried out to prevent a future culture of carelessness.

Test your understanding 24 – U internet (Case study)

To: The Board

From: A.N. Accountant

Date: Today

Subject: U's control environment and recommended improvements

Introduction

This report covers the weaknesses in both the control environment and the internal controls that led to this loss of data. It goes on to recommend actions that should be taken to restore the confidence of existing and potential customers, and to prevent similar problems occurring in the future.

The control environment

There appear to be major shortcomings within U's control environment. The analyst's behaviour suggests that staff may be overworked, which will lead to errors and possibly short-cuts such as taking files home. The fact that the analyst was afraid to admit to the loss of the files adds to the sense that the environment is unsupportive and punitive.

Staff should have been trained about the sensitivity of personal details in a company such as U. The information that has been lost may be very personal in nature and could lead to losses because of identity theft and related fraud. Such training should have reduced the risk of a member of staff leaving a file of customer records on an unsecure PC.

Staff should not be permitted to connect personal disk drives to U's computers. There is a danger that these will carry viruses or other malware. Ideally, staff PCs should not have open USB sockets to reduce the risk of this occurring. Any files that need to be shared with colleagues can be transferred over the firm's network.

The files themselves should not be accessible in their entirety. Only accounts staff need details of credit card numbers and so access to those should be restricted to them. Fields within files should be made available to U's staff on a strictly "need to know" basis. The analyst did not need to know customers' names and full postal addresses. It would have been sufficient to have identified customers by a user number and provided the analyst with a buying history for each.

(a) Recommendations

(i)   The first priority is to make a public announcement that all affected customers have been informed about the loss of their records. That will reduce the speculation about the loss and may reduce the number of claims from customers who have not been affected by the loss.

U should close all affected accounts and assist customers to create replacements. That will prevent customers' claims that there are unauthorised charges to their accounts.

U should offer to assist customers who open replacement credit card accounts in order to prevent fraudulent charges. U should reimburse any fees or charges and should also offer a discount or a voucher as a goodwill gesture for the inconvenience.

U should take steps to remedy the control weaknesses and should announce the fact that security has been improved. The fact that sensitive data could be compromised in this way will be a concern to all customers, particularly given that U initially refused to assist affected account holders.

U should quietly change its policy of denying all responsibility for claims of fraudulent charges. Care will have to be taken in case customers attempt to deny liability for genuine purchases in the hope that U will cancel their balance. It is hardly acceptable for U to claim that customers are mistaken about false charges when the company has been responsible for the loss of data.

(ii) The company should make it very clear that the removal of files without authorisation is a serious breach of company rules and that any offenders will be dealt with. The threat should hopefully deter any recurrence and will also ensure that there is no doubt that files cannot be taken home.

If it is ever necessary for files to be taken home there should be a provision made for secure custody of the data. Files could be encrypted and staff could be issued with a company laptop that is password protected and equipped with all relevant antivirus and firewall software.

Conclusion

There appear to be major shortcomings within U's control environment which need to be improved. Several recommendations have been made including a public announcement, closure of all affected accounts, reimbursement of fees and the improvement of future security measures.

Test your understanding 25 – V (Case study)

Address

Date

Dear institutional investor,

I write regarding your recent concerns over director's remuneration at V. This letter should explain why the introduction of ESOSs could motivate V's executive directors to accept positive net present value (NPV) projects, and how an ESOS scheme could affect the actions taken by the directors.

Motivation to accept positive NPV projects

(i) There is a difference between the risk profiles of shareholders and executive directors. Shareholders should hold diversified portfolios, in which case they are subject only to systematic risk. Directors cannot diversify in the same way because each director has only one career and can generally only be an executive director of one company at a time and so the directors are subject to total risk.

A director who is offered an investment that has a positive NPV at the shareholder's required rate of return may implicitly evaluate that investment using a higher rate that reflects total risk and so may reject it.

If the directors hold options then the value of those options is directly related to the total risk of the underlying security and so the directors could be motivated to accept riskier securities in order to increase the value of their options. There is a huge potential gain if the option is in the money when it is time to exercise it, but there is no symmetry because there is no specific loss other than the expiry of the options if it is out of the money. This means that there is effectively only an upside risk to the directors with respect to their options and that may make them less risk averse in project evaluation.

Memorandum

To: The remuneration committee

From: A. N. Accountant

Date: Today

Subject: Executive directors pay

This memorandum evaluates the advantages AND disadvantages of rewarding executive directors by paying a bonus based on a simple and transparent measure such as profit.

Any form of feedback-based control system is designed to ensure that positive impacts are encouraged and reinforced and negative impacts are discouraged and penalised. Feedback measures and controls performance by referring to actual outcomes. From the shareholders' point of view, that suggests that the directors are incentivised to progress towards a specific goal such as increasing profit or share price.

The simplicity of such a scheme makes it easier to understand the directors' motives. A more complicated appraisal and performance scheme may simply create more opportunity for the directors to indulge in dysfunctional behaviour or otherwise play games in order to maximise their rewards at the shareholders' expense.

From the shareholders' point of view, it may be that maximising reported earnings is suboptimal and that a more complicated set of benchmarks would be preferable. On the other hand, a simple benchmark does have the advantage of making the directors accountable for a specific aspect of performance. A simple control and feedback mechanism may be more effective simply because it has the potential to work.

There is a risk that linking pay to reported earnings will simply lead to creative accounting and the overstatement of earnings figures.

Reported earnings is also a relatively short term indicator for most entities. The directors are being encouraged to adopt a planning horizon of twelve months which could mean that longer term cycles, such as the development of new products or the acceptance of longer term projects will be overlooked because a high NPV project may be a short term loss maker. The shareholders will have to ensure that they look out for evidence of such actions rather than simply taking the reported figures at face value.

Internal control

Test your understanding 26 – Cliff (Integration)

(a) Problems expected at Cliff: poor internal control

   (i) I would expect the company to experience some level of over-ordering, leading to reduced profitability as a result of inventory going past its `best before' date.

   (ii) Inventory that is not well-controlled in a supermarket may result in a breach of health and safety regulations which may result in fines or even closure of the supermarkets.

   (iii) I would expect there to be stock-outs leading to the potential loss of business to other supermarkets.

   (iv) I would expect there to be inefficiencies as a result of a lack of central ordering system resulting from quantity discounts not being obtained.

   (v) All of the problems noted above are likely to be exacerbated where local managers or staff are either inexperienced or possibly dishonest – the question states that poorer quality staff have been recruited recently.

   (vi) Supermarket inventory is very easily pilfered either by staff or customers even where it is well-controlled. The lack of regular inventory counts in particular means that pilferage is very easy to hide.

   (vii) I would expect there to be a lack of understanding in the business as a whole as to the availability of new products, products with high margins or other areas in which profitability might be improved.

(b) Four recommendations, explanation of advantages and disadvantages: improvements to internal control

Recommendation 1: that an integrated system be introduced across all supermarkets that links sales, purchases and inventory records.

Advantages

This would provide the company with an overall view of what inventory is held at any particular time, enable it to order centrally and reduce the scope for pilferage. It would result in reduced stock-outs and reduced inventory obsolescence.

Disadvantages

This would require considerable capital investment in hardware, software and training. It would also take control away from local managers which would almost certainly cause resentment.

Recommendation 2: the imposition of regular, or continuous inventory counting procedures together with the prompt update of inventory records for discrepancies found and investigation of the reason for the discrepancies.

Advantages

This would further reduce the possibility of stock-outs and provide evidence of over-ordering, which would enable purchasing patterns to be refined.

Disadvantages

There are costs in terms of staff time and, again, a certain level of resentment among staff who may feel that they are being `spied on', or that they are no longer trusted. Training would also be required and additional administrative work would need to be undertaken by local managers

Recommendation 3: that management accounts are produced on at least a quarterly basis, that figures relating to each supermarket are provided to head office on a monthly basis, and that an analysis is undertaken by head office on the performance of individual supermarkets and inventory lines.

Advantages

This would enable the company to determine which supermarkets are performing better than others. It would also enable the company to identify those inventory lines that sell well and those that are profitable.

Disadvantages

The production of more regular and detailed information will be time consuming. Local managers may feel that they are unable to service the particular needs of their customers if decisions are made on a global basis; customers may feel the same way.

Recommendation 4: that sales price decisions are made by head office.

Advantages

This would enable the company to experiment with the use of `loss leaders', for example, and to impose a degree of consistency across supermarkets to prevent inappropriate pricing decisions being taken by local managers.

Disadvantages

Again, loss of control at a local level is likely to result in resentment and the possible loss of good staff. What sells well in one supermarket may not do so in another. To the extent that head office have less experience of local conditions than local staff, it is possible that inappropriate pricing decisions may be made by head office.

Test your understanding 27 – SPD (Integration)

Reputation risk could be managed by actively warning drivers of the system's limitations. That could involve insisting that Q signs an acknowledgement that the system cannot prevent all crashes. This document should be kept in a safe place at SPD for future reference if need be. The warning could be repeated in the owner's handbook which should be signed for by the driver, and, again, a copy should be kept at SPD.

Any promotional material published by Q should stress that the system is designed to enable drivers to be even safer when driving within their limits but that responsibility for any failure cannot be accepted by SPD.

SPD could insist that the circuit board is designed to "fail safe" conditions. It could have a diagnostic routine programmed into it which will check that it is functioning correctly whenever it is switched on. In the event that this routine fails the circuit board will immobilise the engine. A contract drawn up by their solicitors would be required to absolve SPD of any blame for failure.

SPD should ask Q to accept responsibility for the work done by the third party and get this put in writing. Again a solicitor would need to deal with this. Any lost business due to delays or failures to meet delivery deadlines should be compensated. SPD will also have to insist on its own quality control procedures over this component. That may involve having the right to request details of the technical specification of the part and the subsequent testing of it on a regular basis.

Test your understanding 28 – Rhapsody Company (Integration)

Tutorial note: It is not recommended that you lay out answers to examination questions in a tabular format such as that shown below. Full sentences and paragraphs will ensure that you explain points in enough detail to earn full marks.

Weakness	Evaluation of weakness	Recommendation
Recording of orders Orders placed on the Internet site are transferred manually into the inventory and sales system. Manual transfer of order details may result in information being transferred incompletely or incorrectly, for example, order quantities may be incorrect or the wrong product code recorded.	Customers will be sent incorrect goods resulting in increased customer complaints.	The computer systems are amended so that order details are transferred directly between the two computer systems. This will remove manual transfer of details limiting the possibility of human error.
Control over orders and packing lists Each order/packing list is given a random alphabetical code. While this is useful, using this type of code makes it difficult to check completeness of orders at any stage in the despatch and invoicing process.	Packing lists can be lost resulting either in goods not being despatched to the customer (if the list is lost prior to goods being despatched) or the customer's credit card not being charged (if lost after goods despatched but prior to the list being received in the accounts department).	Orders/packing lists are controlled with a numeric sequence. At the end of each day, gaps in the sequence of packing lists returned to accounts are investigated.
Obtaining payment The customer's credit card is charged after despatch of goods to the customer, meaning that goods are already sent to the customer before payment is authorised.	Rhapsody Co will not be paid for the goods despatched where the credit company rejects the payment request. Given that customers are unlikely to return seeds, Rhapsody Co will automatically incur a bad debt.	Authorisation to charge the customer's credit card is obtained prior to despatch of goods to ensure Rhapsody Co is paid for all goods despatched.

Completeness of orders

The computer system correctly ensures that order details are available for all charges to customer credit cards. However, there is no overall check that all orders recorded on the inventory and sales system have actually been invoiced.	Entire orders may be overlooked and consequently sales and profit understated.	The computer is programmed to review the order file and orders where there is no corresponding invoice for an order, these should be flagged for subsequent investigation.

Test your understanding 29 – Bassoon Ltd (Integration)

Tutorial note: For the case study exam it is not recommended that you lay out answers to examination questions in a tabular format such as that shown below. Full sentences and paragraphs will ensure that you explain points in enough detail to earn full marks.

Risks	Recommendation
Cash paid to part time staff (easier to misappropriate cash).	Apply the payroll system to all employees.
No control over the appointment of head office staff the HR Manager deals with (may recruit unnecessary staff).	Head office staff should be approved by the board.
No control over shop staff, the shop manager recruits own staff.	Should be approved by head office.
Guest cards, could be anybody and they could steal a card to access till at a later date to steal money.	A control system to monitor guest cards so management know who has a specific card.
Lack of segregation of duties, the payroll manager is responsible for all processing.	Split the responsibilities up, maybe get a manager to review the payroll manager's work.
In the question it states the IT manager is responsible for systems, but doesn't state there is restricted access.	Place passwords on the system and change them on a regular basis.

Internal audit

Chapter learning objectives

Lead	Component	
C1. Internal control systems.	(a)	Discuss roles and responsibilities for internal controls
C3. Internal audit in organisations.	(a)	Discuss forms of internal audit
	(b)	Discuss internal audit process
	(c)	Discuss effective internal audit
	(d)	Discuss the internal audit report

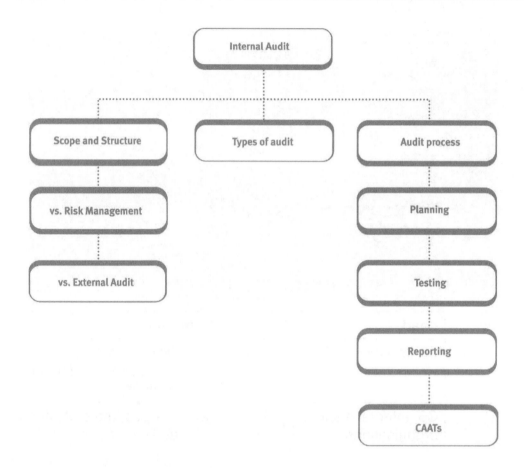

1   Management review of controls

The UK's Turnbull committee says that a review of internal controls should be an integral part of management's role. The board or committees should actively consider reports on control issues. In particular they should consider:

- The identification, evaluation and management of all key risks facing the organisation;

- The effectiveness of internal control – financial, operational, compliance and risk management controls;

- Communication to employees of risk objectives with targets and performance indicators;

- The action taken if any weakness is found.

The report goes on to recommend that the board should consider:

- The nature and extent of the risks which face the organisation;

- The threat of those risks occurring;

- The organisation's ability to reduce the probability and consequences of the risk, and to adapt to any changing risks;

- The costs and benefits of any controls implemented.

An effective internal control system should keep management properly informed about the progress of the organisation (or lack of it) towards the achievement of its objectives. Management and supervisors have a responsibility for monitoring controls in the area of operations for which they are responsible. Internal control might also be monitored by an internal audit function

 What is internal audit ?

Internal auditing is an independent and objective assurance activity designed to add value and improve an organisation's operations. It helps an organisation accomplish its objectives by bringing a systematic approach to evaluating and improving the effectiveness of risk management, control, and governance processes. Internal auditing improves an organisation's effectiveness and efficiency by providing recommendations based on analyses and assessments of data and business processes.

Internal auditing provides value to governing bodies and senior management as an objective source of independent advice.

The scope of internal auditing within an organisation is broad and may involve topics such as the efficacy of operations, the reliability of financial reporting, deterring and investigating fraud, safeguarding assets, and compliance with laws and regulations.

Internal auditing frequently involves measuring compliance with the entity's policies and procedures. However, internal auditors are not responsible for the execution of company activities; they advise management and the Board of Directors (or similar oversight body) regarding how to better execute their responsibilities.

An internal audit function therefore acts as an internal control, to ensure that the internal control system is operating effectively.

 Risk management vs. internal audit

Risk management

- A risk management team would be considered to own the entire risk management process.

- They would be ultimately responsible for all aspects of this process including identification and maintenance of the company's risk register, assessment, prioritisation, treatment of risks and establishment of controls to manage these risks.

- The team would lead the company in developing a risk response strategy and would act in an advisory capacity supporting all areas of the business.

- Provision of training and development by risk staff would facilitate operational managers' ability to identify risks in their area of work and devise controls by which to manage them.

Internal audit

- The role of internal audit is that of monitoring and reviewing the effectiveness of the controls implemented by operational managers.

- In the context of risk management their key activity is in the testing and evaluation of the risk controls (hence ensuring that **those who design controls should not test them**).

- In a wider context the internal audit department can carry out special investigations as directed by management, and can assist the organisation in review of the efficient use of resources.

- Internal audit teams can provide support and assistance to senior management in a range of projects, some of which may fall outside the risk management arena.

- They are often able to contribute to the work of operational teams in identifying risks due to their extensive knowledge of the business, but this is not their primary responsibility.

In summary, risk management identify risks or problems, management devise controls which they think will prevent the risk or problem and the auditors check that the control works. If it doesn't, then it is still a problem and management will implement further or different controls which audit will check again. And so the process goes on until the risk or problem is minimised to the satisfaction of management i.e. it is within the companies attitude to risk.

There are three different parties involved in the process review – risk management, managers and auditors, to ensure independence and the best solution for the company.

 Factors affecting the need for internal audit

There are a number of factors that affect the need for an internal audit department:

Factor	Comment
The scale, diversity and complexity of the company's activities	The larger, the more diverse and the more complex a range of activities is, the more there is to monitor (and the more opportunity there is for certain things to go wrong).
The number of employees	As a proxy for size, the number of employees signifies that larger organisations are more likely to need internal audit to underpin investor confidence than smaller concerns.
Cost/benefit considerations	Management must be certain of the benefits that will result from establishing internal audit and they must obviously be seen to outweigh the costs of the audit.

Changes in the organisational structures, reporting processes or underlying information systems	Any internal (or external) modification is capable of changing the complexity of operations and, accordingly, the risk.
Changes in key risks could be internal or external in nature	The introduction of a new product, entering a new market, a change in any of the PEST/PESTEL factors or changes in the industry might trigger the need for internal audit.
Problems with existing internal control systems.	Any problems with existing systems clearly signify the need for a tightening of systems and increased monitoring.
An increased number of unexplained or unacceptable events.	System failures or similar events are a clear demonstration of internal control weakness.

Where there is no internal audit department, management needs to apply other monitoring processes in order to assure itself and the board that the system of internal control is functioning as intended. In these circumstances, the board will need to assess whether such procedures provide sufficient and objective assurance.

Test your understanding 1

Teddy plc is a small UK-based family run company selling traditional wooden toys from a small chain of shops. The firm has seen rapid sales growth since engaging in e-commerce via a website and selling via large third party online retailers.

The newly appointed Finance Director is the first board member from outside the family and has suggested it would be a good idea for Teddy plc to consider establishing an internal audit department as he has already noticed a large inventory discrepancy.

Which THREE of the following factors are the main reasons for the need for an internal audit at Teddy plc?

A   If a company is listed on the stock exchange it must have an internal audit

B   The growing scale and diversity for Teddy plc suggests there is more to monitor

C   Potential internal control issues are starting to arise at Teddy plc

D   The introduction of e-commerce at Teddy plc

E   The fact the board has majority family members

F   The wish of the shareholders at Teddy plc.

Test your understanding 2

Z is the head of the risk management team at P Co, a large listed manufacturer. P Co also has a well-established internal audit team which is run completely independently of any operational functions within the company in accordance with best practice.

Each year P Co takes on around 20 graduate trainees and in their first month of employment they undergo a detailed induction. As part of this training they listen to presentations on the role of several departments within P Co including internal audit. This year, the board of P Co has decided to ask Z to speak to the graduates about the role of the risk management team and how it differs from that of internal audit.

Z is preparing her presentation. Which of the following should she include and explain as roles of the risk management team?

Select ALL that apply.

A   The maintenance of P Co's risk register

B   The establishment of controls to manage risks

C   The evaluation and testing of risk controls

D   The provision of training and development to operational staff to help them to identify risk

E   Review of the efficient use of resources across the organisation

F   Overall responsibility for risk management within P Co

2   Scope and standard of internal audit work

Scope of internal audit work

The internal audit department will typically have the following scope and objectives as prescribed by the management of the business:

(Do not treat this as a comprehensive list of all the areas that the internal auditor considers, as management may prescribe different functions to meet the needs of their company).

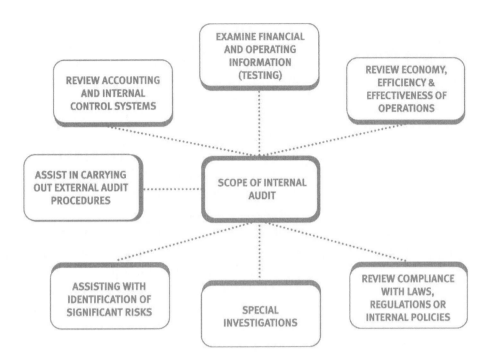

More on scope of internal audit work

Work area	Comment
Reviewing accounting and internal control systems (financial audit)	This is the traditional view of internal audit. The internal auditor checks the financial controls in the company, possibly assisting or sharing work with the external auditor. The internal auditor would comment on whether appropriate controls exist as well as whether they are working correctly. In this work, the internal auditor does not manage risk, but simply reports on controls.
Examining financial and operating information	Internal auditors ensure that reporting of financial information is made on a timely basis and that the information in the reports is factually accurate.
Reviewing the economy, efficiency and effectiveness of operations	This is also called a value for money (VFM) audit (see more later in this chapter). The auditor checks whether a particular activity is cost-effective (economical), uses the minimum inputs for a given output (efficient) and meets its stated objectives (effective).

Reviewing compliance with laws and other external regulations	This objective is particularly relevant under corporate governance codes where the internal auditor will be carrying out detailed work to ensure that internal control systems and financial reports meet stock exchange requirements.
Special investigations	Investigations into other areas of the company's business, e.g. checking the cost estimates for a new factory, or investigating suspected fraud.
Assisting with the identification of significant risks	In this function, the internal auditor does start to work on risks. The auditor may be asked to investigate areas of risk management, with specific reference on how the company identifies, assesses and controls significant risks from both internal and external sources.
Assisting in carrying out external audit procedures	The internal audit team may work closely with the external auditors and provide information that can be utilised in the external audit. There is an obvious benefit to the company from this in the form of a reduction in the audit fee.

Standard of internal audit work

The internal audit function would be expected to carry out their work to a high professional standard. To achieve this the audit function should be well managed and have clear and appropriate procedures for carrying out its work.

It would be expected that:

- There is a formal plan of all audit work that is reviewed by the head of audit and the board/audit committee.

- The audit plans should be reviewed at least annually.

- Each engagement should be conducted appropriately:

  – Planning should be performed.

  – Objectives should be set for the engagement.

  – The work should be documented, reviewed and supervised.

  – The results should be communicated to management.

  – Recommendations for action should be made.

- The progress of the audit should be monitored by the head of internal audit, and if recommendations that the head feels are appropriate are not acted on, the matters should be brought to the attention of the board.

Standards of internal audit work

Internal auditors can follow the same standards as external auditors. However, there are also International Standards for Internal Audit issued by the Internal Auditing Standards Board (IASB) of the Institute of Internal Auditors

- **Attribute standards** deal with the characteristics of organisations and the parties performing internal auditing activities.

- **Performance standards** describe the nature of internal auditing activities and provide quality criteria for evaluating internal auditing services

Attribute standards for internal audit

Objective of standard	Explanation
Independence	The internal audit activity should be independent, and the head of internal audit should report to a level within the organisation that allows the internal audit activity to fulfil its responsibilities. It should be free from interference when deciding on the scope of its assurance work, when carrying out the work and when communicating its opinions
Objectivity	Internal auditors should be objective in carrying out their work. They should have an impartial attitude, and should avoid any conflicts of interest. For example, an internal auditor should not provide assurance services for an operation for which he or she has had management responsibility within the previous year.
Professional care	Internal auditors should exercise due professional care and should have the competence to perform their tasks. They should have some knowledge of the key IT risks and controls, and computer-assisted audit techniques.

Performance standards for internal audit

Area of work	Explanation
Managing internal audit	• The head of internal audit should manage the internal audit activity to ensure that it adds value to the organisation. • The head of internal audit should establish risk- based plans to decide the priorities for internal audit work, consistent with the organisation's objectives. • The internal audit plan should be reviewed at least annually. • The head of internal audit should submit the plan of work to senior management and the board for approval. Independence is maintained by the internal auditor/audit committee being able to decide the scope of internal audit work without being influenced by the board/senior management.
Risk management	• The internal audit department should identify and evaluate significant risk exposures and contribute to the improvement of risk management and control systems. It should evaluate risk exposures relating to governance, operations and information systems, and the reliability and integrity of financial and operating information, the effectiveness and efficiency of operations, safeguarding of assets, compliance with laws, regulations and contracts. Independence is maintained by the internal auditor being given access to information on all these areas and being able to report freely on any errors or omissions found.
Control	• The internal audit department should help to maintain the organisation's control system by evaluating the effectiveness and efficiency of controls, and by promoting continuous improvement. Independence is again maintained by ensuring full provision of information and independent reporting lines (via the audit committee).

Governance	• The internal audit department should assess the corporate governance process and make recommendations where appropriate for improvements in achieving the objectives of corporate governance.
	Independence is maintained by the internal auditor being able to report breaches of corporate governance code without fear of dismissal.
Internal audit work	• Internal auditors should identify, analyse, evaluate and record sufficient information to achieve the objectives of the engagement.
	• The information identified should be reliable, relevant and useful with regard to the objectives of the engagement.
	• The auditors' conclusions should be based on suitable analysis and evaluation.
	• Information to support the conclusions of the auditors should be recorded.
	Independence is maintained by the internal auditor being able to show that normal standards of internal audit work have been followed; that there has been no pressure to 'cut corners' either from senior management or because the internal auditor decided to carry out the work to a lower standard.
Communicating results	• Internal auditors should communicate the results of their engagement, including conclusions, recommendations and action plans.
	• The results should be communicated to the appropriate persons.
	Independence is maintained by the internal auditor being able to communicate to a committee or person separate from the board who also has the power to take appropriate action on the internal auditors' reports.

3 Structure, independence and effectiveness of internal audit

 Structure and independence of internal audit

To ensure that the internal audit function provides an objective assessment of control systems and their weaknesses, there should be measures in place to protect the independence of the internal audit department.

- The internal auditors should be independent of executive management (but have direct access to the highest level of management if required) and should not have any involvement in the activities or systems that they audit (free from operational responsibility).

- The head of internal audit should report directly to a senior director.

- In addition, however, the head of internal audit should have direct access to the chair of the board of directors, and to the audit committee, and should be accountable to the audit committee.

- The audit committee should approve the appointment and termination of appointment of the head of internal audit.

- In large organisations the internal audit function will be a separate department.

- In a small company it might be the responsibility of individuals to perform specific tasks even though there will not be a full-time position.

- Some companies outsource their internal audit function, often to one of the large accountancy firms.

- The internal auditor will review the accounting and control systems, perform testing of transactions and balances, review the 3E's, implementation of corporate policies, carry out special investigations, and assist the external auditors where necessary.

- They should be technically competent and exercise due professional care by planning, supervising and reviewing any work performed. Documentation should be kept, results communicated to management and recommendations made.

Test your understanding 3

The Board of NN, a large drinks manufacturer, decided to set up an internal audit function. The proposal was to appoint an internal auditor at mid-management level who would report directly to the Finance Director.

NN had recently expanded its product range and this had created the need for greater control over internal activities. The need was highlighted by a recent event where internal quality checks were not carried out and thousands of units of production were wasted as a result.

The board discussed whether to promote internally or appoint the new internal auditor from outside the company and they also expressed concerns over the level of authority the internal auditor may expect. Although they recognised the post as important, they believed too much authority might compromise the operational effectiveness of other departments.

Which of the following statements are likely to be correct with respect to the board's deliberations?

Select ALL that apply.

A   Reporting to the Finance Director is a clear threat to the independence of the internal auditor.

B   Recruiting an internal auditor from outside the organisation may help with independence and objectivity.

C   Appointment of an internal auditor will ensure events such as the loss of production due to poor quality control do not re-occur.

D   The internal auditor will not be involved with the work of other departments and so the fears of the board over operational effectiveness are groundless.

E   Internal auditors must operate as a separate department within NN and so a single appointment will not be adequate.

Outsourcing internal audit

In common with other areas of a company's operations, the directors may consider that outsourcing the internal audit function represents better value than an in-house provision. Local government authorities are under particular pressure to ensure that all their services represent 'best value' and this may prompt them to decide to adopt a competitive tender approach.

Advantages of outsourcing internal audit

- Greater focus on cost and efficiency of the internal audit function.
- Staff may be drawn from a broader range of expertise.

- Risk of staff turnover is passed to the outsourcing firm.

- Specialist skills may be more readily available.

- Costs of employing permanent staff are avoided.

- May improve independence.

- Access to new market place technologies, e.g. audit methodology software without associated costs.

- Reduced management time in administering an in-house department.

Disadvantages of outsourcing internal audit

- Possible conflict of interest if provided by the external auditors.

- Pressure on the independence of the outsourced function due to, for example, a threat by management not to renew contract.

- Risk of lack of knowledge and understanding of the organisation's objectives, culture or business.

- The decision may be based on cost with the effectiveness of the function being reduced.

- Flexibility and availability may not be as high as with an in-house function.

- Lack of control over standard of service.

- Risk of blurring of roles between internal and external audit, losing credibility for both.

Minimising these risks

Some general procedures to minimise risks associated with outsourcing the internal audit function will include:

- Controls over acceptance of internal audit contracts to ensure no impact on independence or ethical issues.

- Regular reviews of the quality of audit work performed.

- Separate departments covering internal and external audit.

- Clearly agreed scope, responsibilities and reporting lines.

- Performance measures, management information and risk reporting.

- Procedure manuals for internal audit.

Test your understanding 4

X plc is a financial services company. Shares in X have recently been listed on the UK stock exchange.

You are a Management Accountant of X, and have been talking to your CEO about the need to implement a system of internal controls in order to comply with corporate governance requirements. X already has an Internal Audit function, which reports direct to the CEO. The CEO believes that Internal Audit should be outsourced to one of the many audit firms offering such services, but NOT the company's external auditor.

Advise the CEO which THREE of the following are ADVANTAGES of doing this.

A   Specialist skills may be more readily available

B   Risk of staff turnover is passed to the outsourcing firm

C   Better understanding of the organisation's objectives and culture

D   May improve independence

E   Decisions relating to Internal Audit can be based solely on cost

Ethical threats to independence

Situations could occasionally arise in which an auditor, especially an internal auditor, might be asked to behave (or might be tempted to behave) in a way that conflicts with ethical standards and guidelines.

Conflicts of interest could relate to unimportant matters, but they might also involve fraud or some other illegal activity.

Examples of such ethical conflicts of interest are as follows:

Threat	Example
There could be pressure from an overbearing supervisor, manager or director, adversely affecting the accountant's integrity.	The auditor is asked not to report adverse findings. The threat could be made more personal, e.g. by indicating that the auditor's employment will be terminated if disclosure is made.
An auditor might mislead his employer as to the amount of experience or expertise he has, when in reality the expert advice of someone else should be sought.	The auditor wants to retain his position within the internal audit department or gain respect because of the apparent experience that they have.

An auditor might be asked to act contrary to a technical or professional standard. Divided loyalty between the auditor's superior and the required professional standards of conduct could arise.	An auditor is told to ignore the incorrect application of an accounting standard or the incorrect reporting of directors' remuneration.

Resolution of ethical conflicts of interest

Conflict resolution has been covered earlier.

Effectiveness and efficiency of internal audit

The work of an internal audit department should be monitored to assess

effectiveness in the broader context of the company's risk management systems.

The internal audit process must provide benefits in excess of its cost.

- The **efficiency** of internal audit can be assessed by comparing actual costs and output against a target, such as:
  - the cost per internal audit day
  - the cost per audit report
  - the number of audit reports produced.

- The **effectiveness** of internal audit needs to be measured in a way that indicates the extent to which it provides assurance to management, the audit committee and the board about the effectiveness of the system of internal control.
  - This can be done by identifying evidence of improvements in internal control.

An internal audit report can be prepared for many company activities or systems. E.g. payroll.

If an internal audit was to be performed it might consider the following:

(1) At the front of the report there would usually be an **executive summary**. This would cover the main objectives and scope of the audit, the work performed in brief, the results found and recommendations made.

(2) The **scope of the assignment** would be elaborated on in the next section. This would detail the methodology used e.g. observation, questionnaires, etc, and the areas covered e.g. joiners, leavers, etc.

(3) The next section might be **observations and recommendations** i.e. what the auditor observed during his testing, whether the system was working as it was designed to, and whether any recommendations should be implemented. It should also say who is responsible for any implementations and by when they should be undertaken. The number of recommendations could range from none i.e. the system is working perfectly, to many. This is probably the most practical and most useful part of the report for management.

(4) The recommendations may be **graded by importance**. For example a Level 1 recommendation may need to be implemented immediately since it poses a significant risk to the company, whereas a Level 5 recommendation, say, might be desirable but not necessarily business-critical so can be implemented later.

(5) Finally there will be a **statement of responsibility** from the internal auditor. This will detail any Auditing Standards (standard tests or rules an auditor should follow) used during the course of the work and any limitations in the audit work that was performed. To a cynic, this is the auditors 'get out' clause i.e. some might read it as 'we performed the audit work to the best of our ability, but we can't test everything, so if we missed something, we are sorry but it wasn't our fault'! The auditor will finally **sign** the report.

The internal audit report is often seen as a **'trigger for risk management'** both in the real world and in the CIMA strategic case study exam.

4 Internal and external audit

To a large extent, the work of internal auditors and external auditors is similar, and overlaps. It is therefore important that their efforts should complement each other, rather than duplicate each other.

Comparison of internal to external audit

	External audit	Internal audit
Role required by:	Statute, for limited companies.	Directors and shareholders, usually in larger organisations.
Appointed by:	Shareholders or directors.	Directors, via the Chief Internal Auditor (CIA).
Reports to:	Shareholder (primary duty) and management (professional responsibility).	Directors, via the CIA.
Reports on:	Financial statements.	Internal controls mainly.
Forms opinions on:	True and fair view and proper presentation.	Adequacy of ICS as a contribution to the economic, efficient and effective use of resources.
Scope of assignment:	Unlimited, to fulfil statutory obligation.	Prescribed by directors.

Relationship of internal audit to external audit

The audit plan of the external auditors should be drawn up taking into consideration the work of internal audit, and the extent to which the external auditors can rely on the findings of the internal auditors in reaching their audit opinion.

Factors that the external auditor should consider include:

- the status of internal audit within the organisation

- the scope of the internal audit function

- whether management act on the recommendations of the internal auditor

- the technical competence of the internal auditors

- whether the objectives of the internal audit work are aligned with that of the external auditor

- whether the work of the internal audit function appears to have been planned, supervised, reviewed and documented with due professional care.

Note that there is no particular expectation that the external auditor will be able to rely on the work done by internal audit. The duties of both sets of auditors will differ and hence the work of internal audit may be of very little relevance to the external auditor.

However, in some instances, the external auditors do rely on the internal auditors work if areas of the external auditors audit program have been covered (and the factors mentioned above can be met). Providing the testing performed meets the scope and quality level that the external auditor requires, then the external auditor will place 'some' reliance on the work already performed by internal audit, and consequently reduce the amount of further testing required in order to state an opinion.

However, the external auditors would not place 'total' reliance on the internal auditors work. (They would effectively need to audit the internal auditors work by testing it in part before they could rely on it.)

For example, internal audit might know that during the annual external audit purchase compliance tests are performed to ensure that, say, all purchases are backed up by an order, the order is authorised, etc. The sample normally taken by the external auditor might be, say, 20 transactions. Internal audit could choose to perform this work during the course of the year and present their findings to the external auditor when they arrive to perform the annual audit. The external auditors would then check the internal auditors work by re-performing the compliance tests on a few transactions, say, 3 of the 20. Providing no errors were found, the external auditors would then perform their own, new compliance tests on a reduced number of, say, 5 transactions.

More testing will have been performed since both internal and external audit have been involved, giving a higher assurance level (or lower risk).

Also, this 'sharing' of work can lead to a reduced external audit fee, because some of the testing has been done internally at a reduced cost.

Management letter

In addition to an internal or external audit report, the auditor will usually produce a 'management letter'. This letter usually includes a list of 'issues' that the auditor came across during the course of his audit work.

The letter usually includes a table of:

- issues concerning the auditor (usually a control that could be improved);

- recommendations to implement or improve the controls.

The auditor would usually state a time frame by which the new controls should be implemented and then re-visit the department to ensure that the implementation had taken place.

The management are at liberty to reply to the auditor. They may state that the recommended control has been implemented, or explain why it hasn't been, perhaps because it was too costly, or is on-going.

Test your understanding 5

In a large company which complies with the UK Corporate Governance Code, the head of internal audit should report directly to:

A   A senior director

B   The external auditor

C   The audit committee

D   The risk manager

Test your understanding 6

The primary scope of an internal auditor's work includes:

Select ALL that apply

A   Examining financial and operating information

B   Reviewing compliance with laws and regulations

C   Identifying risk

D   Assisting with external audit procedures

Test your understanding 7

Internal audit can be outsourced. A disadvantage of this might be:

A   Cost

B   Skill

C   Independence

D   Control

Differing perspectives on fraud

The **external auditor** is responsible for identifying material misstatements in the financial statements in order to ensure that they give a true and fair view. By definition then, the external auditor is responsible for detecting any **material** fraud that may have occurred. However, they have no specific responsibility with regard to immaterial frauds. If they identify them, they will be reported to those charged with governance, but there is no duty to identify them.

Internal auditors may be given an assignment:

*   to assess the likelihood of fraud, or if a fraud has been discovered,

*   to assess its consequences and

*   to make recommendations for prevention in the future.

Fraud investigation

Fraud investigation can be carried out by an auditor. It is **not their primary objective** when carrying out an audit, but they are **duty bound to report a fraud if during the course of their work they identify fraudulent activities**.

It is the company directors who are responsible for identifying fraud.

A fraud investigation should cover the following steps:

(1)   Ascertaining the facts of the fraudulent activity.

(2)   Gathering evidence of the crime – documentary, interviews with witnesses, observational, etc.

(3)   Corroborating the evidence.

(4)   Consider whether you have the right of access to the evidence you require. Many cases have been thrown out of court because evidence has been improperly obtained.

(5)   Maintaining confidentiality so that the perpetrator doesn't realise they are being investigated.

(6) Consider the cost of the investigation versus the value of the fraud, although ethically all frauds should be stopped.

(7) Ascertain the value of the fraud.

(8) Consider the loss of reputation if the fraud becomes public.

Test your understanding 8 – SHD (Integration)

SHD is a property development company involved in multiple development projects across the country. In the last year a member of the finance department has established an expenses fraud through the use of a false supplier. Invoices are raised in the name of this supplier on a monthly basis for miscellaneous materials to the various development sites. These invoices are paid directly via the accounts payable system without going to the site project managers.

This fraud has increased the variable costs of construction projects by 15% in the last year, a point which has been identified by the external auditors in their recent audit. The auditors approached the management accountant for further information on the cost increase.

Required:

Discuss the differing views of external auditors and internal auditors to this increase in variable costs.

Test your understanding 9 – Z (Case study)

Scenario

Z is a government agency that is responsible for promoting road safety.

Trigger

Z needs to buy a fleet of 24 buses that have been converted into mobile exhibition spaces so that they can be driven around to educate community groups about the importance of safe road use.

The management board of Z has decided to use a sealed bid system to tender for this fleet of buses. The sealed bid system is as follows:

- Suppliers who wish to bid for the contract to supply and modify 24 buses should submit a sealed bid to Z's chief buyer.

- The bid should be submitted in a plain envelope with a typed label stating "Bus Bid". There should be no other writing on the envelope.

- The bid should identify:
  - (1) The supplier
  - (2) The type of bus to be modified
  - (3) Details of all the modifications to be undertaken
  - (4) The price of supplying 24 modified buses
- On receipt of the sealed envelope the chief buyer of Z will sign across the flap of the envelope and place the bid in the safe.

Z's chief executive contacted the head of internal audit immediately before the end of the bidding process and requested that the internal audit department attend the meeting at which the envelopes would be opened. A senior member of the internal audit department was assigned to the task. In addition, the meeting would be attended by the chief buyer, the head of operations and the departmental manager who would be responsible for managing the exhibitions.

At the meeting the chief buyer announced that four bids had been received. The envelopes were opened in random order by the internal auditor.

The contents were:

Envelope 1: a bid of GBP 2.8 million from supplier L
Envelope 2: a bid of GBP 3.0 million from supplier K and a letter to withdraw a previously submitted bid of GBP 2.0 million
Envelope 3: a bid of GBP 3.2 million from supplier M
Envelope 4: a bid of GBP 2.0 million from supplier K

The details of the bids in envelopes 2 and 4 from supplier K were identical except for the **price.**

Supplier L's bid of GBP 2.8million was rejected immediately because the bidder was planning to use a slightly smaller model of bus than the others and planned to use poor quality materials for the modifications. It was, therefore, agreed that the winning bid would be the revised offer to supply the buses for GBP 3.0 million from supplier K. The head of internal audit was concerned that there could be some irregularities in this bidding process and asked the chief executive to postpone placing an order for the buses until the internal audit department had undertaken an investigation.

Task

(a) Explain THREE factors that could have caused the head of internal audit to be concerned about the bidding process for the buses. **(10 minutes)**

(b) Recommend, with reasons, the work that the internal auditor should undertake if the bidding process for the buses is investigated. **(20 minutes)**

(c) Write a note to the chief executive which recommends TWO advantages and TWO disadvantages of the internal auditor being actively involved in the investigation of suspected fraud.

(15 minutes)

5 Types of audit work

As there are many risks and many controls within a business, there will be many different types of audit that can be performed. All types will essentially ensure the same thing – that the company's processes are being adhered to.

Some different types of audit work are discussed below, but the list is not exhaustive.

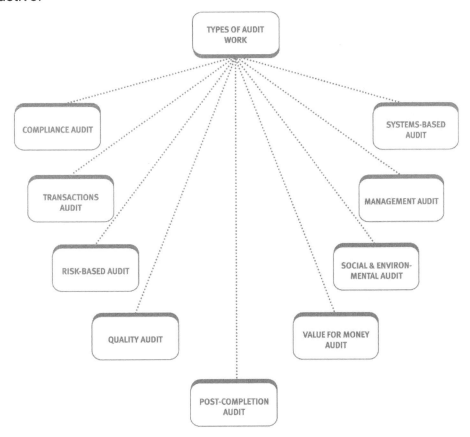

More on audit types

Compliance audit

- Compliance audits check the implementation of written rules, regulations and procedures.

- They were used originally for financial transactions, because the government (tax authorities) needed assurance that the financial figures were correct.

- The concept of compliance has been extended to other areas, such as regulatory inspections and quality audits, where there is a requirement to verify that activities are being performed in strict compliance with approved standards and procedures.

Transactions audit

- A transactions audit involves the checking of a sample of transactions against documentary evidence.

- This method can be used where controls are weak or where transactions are high risk.

Risk-based audit

- A risk-based audit refers to a systems audit in which the auditors use their judgement to decide on the level of risk that exists in different areas of the system, and to plan their audit tests so that more effort is directed towards the most risky areas.

- In this way, less time and effort is spent on elements of the system that are relatively 'safe'.

Quality audit

- A quality audit is a systematic investigation to establish whether quality objectives are being met.

- A quality audit might look into the system for setting quality standards, the relevance of those standards, the system for comparing actual performance against the quality standards and whether the quality controls work effectively.

Post-completion audit (or post-completion review)

- A post-completion audit is an objective and independent appraisal of the measure of success of a project.

- It should cover the project throughout its lifecycle from the planning and implementation stages through to performance after commissioning.

- The review should take place at some time after the project or process has been completed or is being used. Review should not be too soon, where the project or process hasn't been given a chance to 'bed in'. But it should also not be too late where important feedback and learning has not been applied on later projects.

- Its objective is to provide feedback as to the success of a project or otherwise, and acts as a learning tool for future projects.

- Projects are often assessed on three criteria: time, cost and quality. Was the project implemented on time? Did the project come in on budget? Was the project delivered at the expected quality level, or more commonly, did it solve the original issue that prompted the project?

- Post-completion audits are often performed by internal audit, as long as they are not involved in the original design of the project itself. The auditor will source the documentation which stated the original objectives of the project, and then follow the process carried out to ensure that all activities led to the successful completion of these objectives – in an economical, efficient and effective way. If the objectives were not met, why not? And what should be done about it?

The latter four types of audit work will now be considered in more detail.

Value for money audit

An area that internal auditors have been getting increasingly involved in is value for money audits. These have been replaced in terminology more recently by 'best value' audits, but many of the principles remain the same.

In a value for money (VFM) audit the auditor assesses three main areas.

Economy

- The economy of a business is assessed by looking at the inputs to the business (or process), and deciding whether these are the most economical that are available at an acceptable quality level.

Efficiency

- The efficiency of an operation is assessed by considering how well the operation converts inputs to outputs.

Effectiveness

- The effectiveness of an organisation is assessed by examining whether the organisation is achieving its objectives. To assess effectiveness there must be clear objectives for the organisation that can be examined.

More on VFM audit

A VFM audit is 'an investigation into whether proper arrangements have been made for securing economy, efficiency and effectiveness in the use of resources'. It is an audit into the '3 Es' in an item or operation.

- **Economy** means obtaining the required resources at the lowest cost. There would be a lack of economy, for example, if there was overstaffing in a particular department or if an excessive price was paid for materials of the required quality. It is important to remember that economy does not mean achieving the lowest cost possible: it means keeping costs within acceptable limits for obtaining resources of the desired quality.

- **Efficiency** means using the minimum quantity of resources to achieve a given quantity and quality of output. Efficiency can be measured either in terms of:

  - maximising the output for a given quantity of input, such as the maximum quantity of services provided per employee or per £1 spent, or

  - achieving a given quantity of output with the minimum resources possible.

- **Effectiveness** exists when the output from a system achieves its intended aims and objectives.

Managers are responsible for achieving economy, efficiency and effectiveness in the operations for which they are responsible. A VFM audit provides a check to confirm that management is fulfilling this responsibility properly.

VFM audits have commonly been associated with auditing in the public sector, but they are applicable in any type of organisation, in the public or private sectors.

Problems with VFM audits

There are several problems with conducting a VFM audit.

- It might be **difficult to measure outputs**, particularly in government services. For example, the output from an education system can be measured in many different ways, both in terms of the numbers educated and the quality of education. In the health service, outputs might be measured in terms of the numbers of patients treated; on the other hand, successful preventive medicine would be measured in terms of reductions in the numbers of patients treated for particular conditions.

- The **objectives of the activity might be difficult to establish**, particularly in the public sector. For example, what are the objectives of the police service? If an activity has several different objectives, the problem is then how to decide their priorities. For example, the objective of the police force might be to maintain public order, arrest criminals, deter criminals, and so on.

- **The focus must be EITHER on economy and efficiency OR on effectiveness.** It is difficult to report on both issues simultaneously because costs can almost always be reduced by cutting back on the quality of service, while outputs can almost always be improved by spending more.

- **Quality might be ignored when economy and efficiency are measured**. For example, a government might succeed in reducing the costs of secondary education, but only by making schools overcrowded and by lowering the standards of the education provided. VFM tends to focus more on economy and efficiency because those are much easier to measure than effectiveness.

Test your understanding 10 – Seatown (case study)

Scenario

Seatown is located on the coast. The town's main industry is tourism with an emphasis on family holidays and consequently the cleanliness of the town's beaches is a major factor in the town's success.

The town council, which is the local government authority, has a cleaning department that is responsible for keeping the beaches clean and tidy. Early every morning, as soon as the tide has gone out, the beaches are swept using equipment that is towed behind tractors. This equipment skims the top layer of sand and runs it through a filter to remove any litter before returning the cleaned sand to the beach. Most litter takes the form of paper and plastic packaging, but it can include glass bottles and aluminium cans.

To try to prevent litter being left on the beach the town council also places bins on the beaches above the high water mark. Litter bins need to be emptied regularly otherwise holidaymakers pile their rubbish beside the bins and that leads to litter being spread by the wind or by seabirds scavenging for food scraps.

The cost of cleaning the beaches is a major expense for the town council.

Trigger

The management team of the town council has asked the internal audit department to investigate whether the town is getting good "value for money" from this expenditure. The head of internal audit has sought clarification from the town managers on whether the audit should focus on the economy and efficiency of the cleaning operations or their effectiveness. Economy and efficiency audits generally focus on whether cost can be reduced for the same level of service and effectiveness audits ask whether better service can be achieved for the same cost.

Task

Prepare a letter addressed to the town council's internal audit department:

(a)   Recommending, giving reasons, the matters that they should study in order to evaluate the economy and efficiency of the beach cleaning activities.

Your answer should include advice on how to obtain the necessary data and information.   **(20 minutes)**

(b)   Recommending, giving reasons, the matters that they should study in order to evaluate the effectiveness of the beach cleaning activities.

Your answer should include advice on how to obtain the necessary data and information.   **(20 minutes)**

(c)   Explaining why it is easier to investigate the economy and efficiency rather than the effectiveness of the cleaning activities.

(10 minutes)

Social and environmental audit

Environmental audit

An environmental audit is defined as:

'A management tool comprising a systematic, documented, periodic and objective evaluation of how well organisations, management, and equipment are performing, with the aim of contributing to safeguarding the environment by facilitating management control of environmental practices, and assessing compliance with company policies, which would include meeting regulatory requirements and standards applicable.'

It is possible that an 'accounting' trained auditor could be asked to perform one of these audits but it is unlikely that they would be able to perform the task with the proper competence. The auditor is unlikely to have the necessary skills and therefore it would be professionally wrong to accept the assignment.

Social audit

The social audit would look at the company's contribution to society and the community. The contributions made could be through:

- Donations.
- Sponsorship.
- Employment practices.
- Education.
- Health and safety.
- Ethical investments, etc.

A social audit could either confirm statements made by the directors, or make recommendations for social policies that the company should perform.

Environmental reporting

The environmental report that is included in the annual report by many companies is sometimes accompanied by an 'auditors' statement'.

The environmental report produced by companies will normally contain information about:

- Sustainability.
- Targets achieved.
- Compliance with regulations
- Emissions.
- Industrial legacies.
- Obtaining ISO 14001 (environmental management systems).

Many companies conduct an internal audit on these matters, and then have the audit verified by external assessors. It is possible that the external auditor could be asked to be an external assessor, however, it is more likely with environmental matters that the person will be an appropriately qualified environmental assessor.

Management audit

A management audit is sometimes called an **operational audit.**

A management audit is defined by CIMA as 'an objective and independent appraisal of the effectiveness of managers and the corporate structure in the achievement of the entities' objectives and policies'.

- Its aim is to identify existing and potential management weakness and recommend ways to rectify them.'

- This type of audit would require the use of very experienced staff who understand the nature of the business.

More on management audit

The **objectives of a management** audit might be:

- re-focusing resources towards 'mission-critical' objectives

- improving efficiency (improving work flows, eliminating unnecessary activities, eliminating duplicated activities, etc)

- improving the effectiveness of management support tools (such as improvements in controls, automated system support etc)

- assessing the appropriate levels of service for an activity or operation

- identifying cost savings

- identifying opportunities to enhance revenue

- improvements in governance.

The **elements of a management audit** might include:

- a review of policies and procedures

- a general review of workloads, work methods and work flows

- an evaluation of systems and processes

- a review of management practices

- a review of resource utilisation

- a detailed cost analysis.

The **findings of a management audit** might focus not so much on compliance with policies and procedures, but on:

- a lack of technical competence or knowledge of the business amongst managers, and insufficient management training

- an unwillingness to delegate

- regular failure to achieve standards or targets

- inadequate management information systems

- poor communications within or between departments

- poor management/staff relationships

- an absence of clear leadership

- a failure by management to make good decisions.

Systems-based audit

A systems-based audit is an audit of internal controls within an organisation. Although the term refers to any type of system, it is often associated with the audit of accounting systems, such as the sales ledger system, purchase ledger system, receipts and payments, fixed asset records, stock records and so on.

The aim of such an audit is to identify weaknesses in the system (weaknesses in either the controls or in the application of controls, such that there is a risk of material inaccuracy in financial records and statements, or a risk of fraud).

A systems-based audit would take the following steps:

- Identify the objectives of each system
- Identify the procedures
- Identify why the system might not meet its objectives
- Identify ways to manage the above
- Identify if current controls are adequate
- Report on the above.

Test your understanding 11

Checking a sample of transactions against documentary evidence is an example of:

A   A transactions audit

B   A compliance audit

C   A value for money audit

D   A risk based audit

Test your understanding 12

An objective and independent measure of the success of a project is known as:

A   A quality audit

B   A compliance audit

C   A value for money audit

D   A post completion audit

6   The audit process

Introduction

This chapter looks at a typical audit process as it would be carried out by the internal auditor to audit a company's systems or processes. A key point to consider when going through this process is the problems that might be encountered when attempting to audit these different areas.

The audit process

The audit process can be summarised in the following diagram:

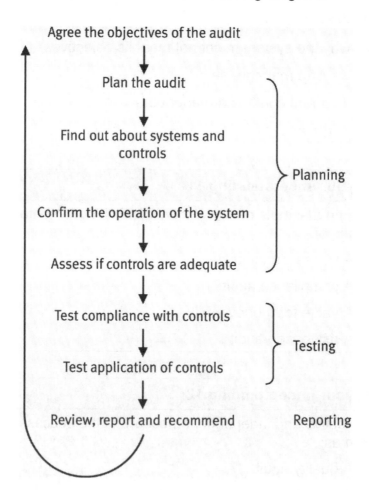

7   Audit planning

Audits should be planned. There should be an audit programme for each financial year, in which the internal auditors set out which activities or operations they will audit, and what the purpose of the audit will be in each case.

- **Objectives of the audit**
  - For example, to check whether the internal controls within a particular operation are adequate and are applied properly.

- **Conduct of the audit**

  - The auditors need to decide what information they need and what investigations they need to carry out.

  - Decisions have to be made about:

    - how to collect and record evidence, and

    - how much evidence to collect

- **Resources and timing**

  - The auditors should assess how much time and effort will be required to carry out the audit, and schedule the work accordingly.

 Risk-based approach

- Most audits are now carried out using a risk-based approach, whereby the auditor assesses whereabouts the key risks are in a system, and then concentrates the audit effort at those key risks.

- The result of this approach is that the audit should be more efficient and effective at achieving its objectives than if another approach were followed.

- Bear in mind from earlier chapters that the internal control system should be built on the back of risk assessments.

- One of the key ways an auditor can try to identify risk is by **benchmarking.**

Types of benchmarking

Benchmarking is the process of comparing one's business processes to best practice from other industries. Management identifies the best firms in their industry, or in another industry where similar processes exist, and compares the results and processes of those studied to one's own results and processes. In this way, they learn how well the targets perform and, more importantly, the business processes that explain why these firms are successful. They often then try to replicate them in their own company.

There are many different types of benchmarking, since it is simply the comparison of one thing to another, but some examples include:

Process benchmarking – the company focuses its observation and investigation on business processes with a goal of identifying and observing the best practices from one or more benchmarked firms. Process analysis is required where the objective is usually to benchmark cost and efficiency. This is increasingly applied to back-office processes where outsourcing may be a consideration.

Product benchmarking – the process of designing new products or upgrades to current ones. This process can sometimes involve reverse engineering which involves taking apart competitor's products to assess their strengths and weaknesses.

Functional benchmarking – a company will focus its benchmarking on a single function e.g. Production, to improve the operation of that function. Complex functions such as Human Resources, Finance and Information Technology are unlikely to be directly comparable in cost and efficiency terms and may need to be disaggregated into processes to make valid comparison.

Competitor benchmarking – involves studying the leading competitor or the company that best carries out a specific function.

Environmental benchmarking – This is the process of collecting, analysing and relating environmental performance data of comparable activities with the purpose of evaluating and comparing performance between or within the entities. Entities can include processes, buildings or companies. Benchmarking may be internal within a single organisation, or – subject to confidentiality restrictions – external between competing entities.

Environmental benchmarking

Environmental and sustainability benchmarking is a tool for comparing the environmental and sustainability performance of different organisations. This form of benchmarking is becoming increasingly important as these issues gain prominence within businesses.

A major retailing company in the UK produces an annual report on their environmentalism and sustainability. It covers many angles, including their targets for:

- recycling and waste management;

- information about their 'green stores' which are built and run using environmental techniques such as using hemp walls, biomass heating systems and rainwater recycling;

- carbon emissions including their investment in their aerodynamic road transport fleet;

- staff shopping where employees and customers are encouraged to donate or swap clothing, etc to manufacture new garments, donate clothing to charities or to reduce waste;

- sustainable supplies including Fairtrade, recycled and organic products;

The company publishes 20 different targets, some with many sub-targets, and gives information on whether they have been achieved, are 'on plan', are 'behind plan' or have been cancelled (and if so, why).

Competitor firms will use this information to generate their own targets, to compare (benchmark) and to learn.

Using the financial statements to benchmark

During the planning stage of any audit, internal or external, the auditor must identify the key risks a company faces. One of the ways an auditor can do this is by using the financial statements or management accounts over several periods or years.

Performing ratio analysis, such as calculating the gross profit margin, net profit margin, and receivable, payable and inventory turnover days will enable the auditor to compare the results with previous years, or their expectations. This may, in turn, help them to identify 'anomalies' or risks that the financial statements are incorrect in certain areas.

For example, imagine a company has had a gross profit margin of 40% and a net profit of 20% for several years. This year the auditor calculates the gross profit margin to be 40% but the net profit margin to have fallen to 15%. This may indicate that certain expenses have inflated or that there may be errors within the expenses (but not sales or cost of sales as this would have affected the gross profit margin also). So the auditor has narrowed down the problem to being somewhere within expenses. They could now calculate each expense as a percentage of sales and compare them to previous years. Let us imagine that the auditor identifies that 'repairs and renewals' has increased dramatically compared to previous years. They would then investigate this account and might identify that several items of expenditure that should have been capitalised (to appear on the statement of financial position) have inadvertently been posted to repairs and renewals. A simple journal correcting this can now be performed. i.e. credit repairs and renewals, debit non-current assets. (Depreciation will need to be recalculated too.)

The auditor would then reperform their ratio analysis, recalculating the net profit margin which should now be in line with the expected 20% of previous years.

On the other hand, there may have been good reason why the net profit margin had fallen. It may be that, say, rent had increased due to their landlord increasing their rental charges. This would not be a financial statement error, but could be ascertained through discussions with the finance department/finance director. In this case, it may be that the financial statements are in fact correct and that in the future the net profit margin is expected to be 15%.

The key point is that the auditor spotted an 'anomaly' or risk, investigated it and resolved to their satisfaction whether there was a risk that the financial statements were incorrect.

Annual audit plan and risk analysis

When preparing an audit plan for the year, the internal auditors should try to focus on those areas of operation where the potential risk to the business is greatest.

One way of assessing risk is to consider, for the operations or procedures subject to audit:

- the inherent risk, and

- the quality of control.

Inherent risk is the risk in the activity or operation, ignoring the controls in the system. For example, a cash based business such as a market stall or a taxi business is inherently risky due to possible theft or mis-declaration of tax payable.

Inherent risk relates both to the severity and the incidence of the risk, i.e.:

- the potential loss if an adverse situation or event arises, and the probability that an adverse situation or event will arise.

The size of the inherent risk will depend on a variety of factors, such as:

- the size of the operations unit, or the size of the expenditure budget

- the nature of the assets used or handled (e.g. systems involving the handling of cash or payments to suppliers have high inherent risk, due to the opportunities for fraud or loss)

- the extent to which procedures are computerised.

The **quality of control** is the perceived quality of the existing controls for the activity. Confidence in the quality of control will be affected by:

- the apparent effectiveness of management and supervision

- pressures on management to achieve targets

- changes in the system activities and procedures

- changes in key personnel

- a high staff turnover

- a rapid expansion in operations and the volume of transactions handled

- the length of time since the last audit of the activity was carried out. Confidence in the quality of controls will diminish over time without fresh reassurance from another audit that the controls are still effective.

The activities which should be given priority for audit are those where the inherent risk is high and the quality of control is low.

Audit risk

This is the risk that the auditors might give an inappropriate opinion on something which they tested i.e. they say that a process is well controlled when in fact it is out of control. Using the example of auditing the financial statements, audit risk has three components elements:

Inherent risk. This is the risk that an amount in the financial statements (for an asset or liability, or a transaction) might be stated as a materially incorrect amount, ignoring the existence of existing internal controls.

Control risk. This is the risk that the existing controls are not sufficient to prevent or detect a material mis-statement of a value in the financial statements.

Detection risk. This is the risk that the auditors' substantive tests will not reveal a materially incorrect amount in the financial statements, if such an error exists.

Materiality

The term 'materiality' is often used in the context of financial reporting. An item in the financial statements is material if its omission or a misstatement of its value would be likely to influence a user of the financial statements. However, materiality cannot be specified mathematically, because it has a qualitative as well as a quantitative aspect.

Materiality should also be considered in relative terms. For example, the risk of valuing an asset incorrectly by $100,000 would be material in the context of a company with assets of $1 million, but far less material in the context of a company with assets of $100 million.

Test your understanding 13

CC is a house builder in Country Y which specialises in developing large sites with many hundreds of houses across all regions of the country. It has an internal audit team who are currently preparing an audit plan for the year ahead focussing on areas of operation where the potential risk to the business is greatest.

Which of the following are inherent risks for CC?

Select ALL that apply.

A   The risk that the economic downturn will encourage management to overstate progress on certain housing developments.

B   The risk that expensive inventory is stolen from sites which are not secured properly overnight.

C   The risk that the internal audit plan omits a particular area of risk which could have significant implications for CC.

D   The risk that government regulations over house building will change and CC will be in breach of new rules.

E   The risk that sites for developments, once work has begun are found to be unsuitable and must be abandoned.

8   Systems investigation and documentation

The auditors should document both the system or operation subject to audit, and their findings or judgements. They will need to ascertain what the system is and also the controls that operate over the system.

Ascertaining systems

The auditor could use the following sources and methods to ascertain how the systems operate:

Flowcharts	These could be examined or created from discussions with staff who use and operate systems.
Interviews/Questionnaires	The staff who operate the system can describe how they use it. This has an advantage over other existing system documentation as it identifies how the staff actually use the system even if this is out of line with the proper procedures.
Systems documentation	The auditor can find the documentation of the system from when it was produced to identify how it operates. Documentation tends to be best for computerised systems as they will have gone through a proper systems development approach and also they tend to be least well understood by users.
Observation	The operation of the system can be observed.

Ascertaining controls

To specifically assess the controls in systems an auditor could use standard control questionnaires. These documents are structured so as to identify all key internal controls and also enable the auditor to assess the quality of the controls.

More on audit tools

Flowcharts

Flowcharts might be used to record:

- the sequence of activities and checks within an operation or procedure
- which individuals carry out each procedure or check.

The advantages of flowcharting the stages in an operation are that:

- a flowchart is more often effective at presenting information in an understandable form than a narrative description
- if there are weaknesses in the controls within an operation, these might be easier to identify by studying a flowchart.

Questionnaires

A questionnaire is a list of questions for which the auditor needs to finds answers in order to gather the information or evidence he needs. The questions should be specific, and should ideally call for a 'Yes' or 'No' answer, although room should be left on the form for additional comments to be added if required.

The answers to the questions help the auditor both to:

- establish the facts, and
- identify potential control weaknesses.

9 Control assessment

Once auditors have ascertained what the controls are, they need to make an assessment of the internal controls and whether they will achieve their objectives.

Example of controls

A company has a small accounting department, in which the same individual is made responsible for accounts payable and also for carrying out the bank reconciliation checks. Ideally, these tasks should be segregated, because there is a risk that the individual might be making payments to their own personal bank account, and the fraud would not be identified by the bank reconciliation process.

To overcome this weakness in the control system, a number of controls might be applied, such as:

- requiring that all payments are reviewed by a senior manager in the company, instead of paid automatically
- a review by the individual's supervisor of all bank reconciliations
- a periodic listing from the company's bank of all the payments out of the company's bank account in the period, for review by a senior manager.

10 Audit testing

Having made an assessment of the existing controls and identified the areas of greatest risk the auditor will move onto the testing.

Auditors need to carry out tests, to ensure that procedures are performed correctly, and that controls to prevent or detect errors are adequate and applied effectively.

Types of testing

 Compliance testing (test of controls):

The test of controls should be carried out to ensure that the controls identified at the planning stage operate as they should.

If the controls are not being complied with then there will be a material weakness in the control system and the result could be serious errors or fraud and the business objectives may not be achieved.

 The results of the compliance testing should indicate whether:

* the controls are effective, or

* the controls are ineffective in practice, even though they appeared adequate 'on paper'.

Substantive testing (test of balances or transactions):

Substantive testing, on the other hand, does not look at the controls in the system – it rather concentrates on the output and ensuring that the output is as expected.

Substantive testing is normally associated with financial systems but can also be used for non-financial systems.

The purpose of the substantive tests is either to:

* confirm that the controls are effective

* where the controls are ineffective, to establish the apparent consequences.

For example, an audit of a quality control system would give the following types of testing:

Substantive test   Monitor the number of quality control failures as a proportion of good output.

Compliance test   Observe the functioning of the quality control staff to ensure they are checking output.

In the exam, students should for look for options with words like **reconcile, analyse, observe, monitor or sample** at the beginning of a sentence that recommends an audit test. Try to avoid options with the word 'check' since that can be construed as vague, unless it explains fully what they would be checking for and why.

Test your understanding 14

Which of the following is a substantive audit test?

A   Observing the functioning of the quality control staff to ensure that they are checking output

B   Matching customer orders to invoices

C   Monitoring the number of quality control failures as a percentage of output

D   Observing staff clocking in and out to ensure that productive time is recorded accurately

Test your understanding 15 – Compliance testing (Integration)

Company X has recently employed John. John went through the company's interview process – after submitting his curriculum vitae and filling in the standard application form, he attended two interviews (one individual and one group). He was then offered the job and asked to start the following Monday.

John has been at X for a month now and his manager is not happy with his work. He is frequently late in to the office, and he frequently makes mistakes in the tasks he is given.

His manager has heard a rumour that the qualification he stated on his application form is false, which could explain his poor work.

Required:

Discuss the problem at X and suggest controls that should be in place to prevent this occurrence.

Detail appropriate compliance tests the internal auditor should perform on the recruitment process to ensure that this does not happen in the future.

> **Test your understanding 16 – Audit testing (Integration)**
>
> Recommend some compliance and substantive tests that could be undertaken by an auditor to check whether errors are occurring in payroll processing. Staff are paid weekly in cash. The objective of the audit is to ensure that:
>
> (i)   payments are only made to genuine employees.
>
> (ii) all deductions from pay are calculated correctly.
>
> (iii) employees are paid only for hours worked.
>
> (iv) deductions are paid over to the appropriate authorities

11   Sampling

With any audit testing it will probably be necessary to undertake some form of sampling.

Sampling is testing a proportion of a population to gain assurance about the population as a whole.

 Audit sampling

The application of audit procedures to less than 100% of the items within an account balance or class of transactions to obtain and evaluate evidence about some characteristic of the items selected in order to form a conclusion on the population.

Risks that occur with sampling

As soon as an auditor decides to sample a population, there are risks that are brought into the audit:

Sampling risk	This is the risk that the auditor's conclusion, based on the results of the sample, may be different from the result that would have been obtained had all items in the population been tested. (This risk can never be removed if sampling is done.)
Non-sampling risk	This is the risk that the auditor may use inappropriate procedures or misinterpret evidence that the test results give. As a result the auditor would fail to recognise an error. (This risk is avoidable if auditors use the appropriate procedures.)

Test your understanding 17

The risk that an amount in the financial statements might be stated as materially incorrect (ignoring the existence of current internal controls) is called:

A   Detection risk

B   Control risk

C   Inherent risk

D   Sampling risk

12   Analytical review

Analytical review is arguably the most important test available to the auditor as they can be used in the audit of most items – both financial and non-financial – and can be used at various points in the audit process.

Definition

Analytical review is the examination of ratios, trends and changes in the business from one period to the next, to obtain a broad understanding of the results of operations, and to identify any items requiring further investigation.

When the results appear abnormal the auditors will investigate more closely to find out the cause(s) by performing further work.

Ratios

During the audit of any part of the financial statements, analytical review often involves the calculation of ratios, such as:

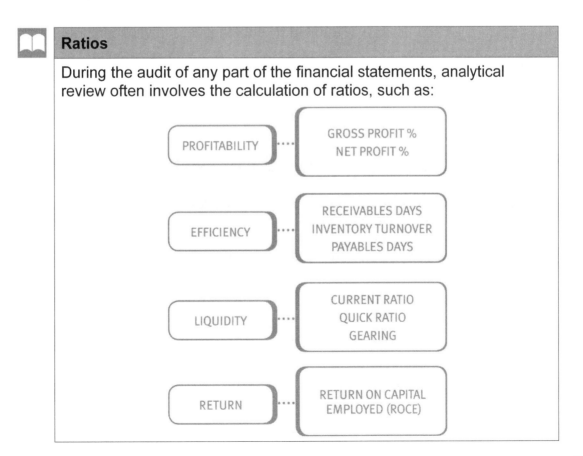

Nature of analytical review

Comparisons of information could be with

Examples

	20X1	20X1	20X0
	Actual	Budget	Actual

- Prior periods/anticipated results

Number of new products launched   9   11   10

- Predictive estimates   Depreciation for year = 15% × y/e cost
- Similar industry info   Staff turnover v industry average

 Uses of analytical review

Analytical review will be used at all stages of the audit.

Planning   They will be used to identify risks, and therefore help in deciding the level of testing, and its nature and timing.

Substantive testing   Analytical review is a very important substantive procedure that can provide sufficient audit evidence in some areas. In practice in the audit of financial information, expenses in the income statement, accruals and prepayments are all audited by substantive analytical procedures.

Overall review   The procedures are used to conclude whether the area being tested is consistent with the auditors' knowledge of the business entity and the expected results.

 Test your understanding 18 – Car dealership (Integration)

You are an internal auditor for a car dealership with a number of branches. You have responsibility for looking at where efficiency gains could be made. From the following information, recommend, with reasons, which region you would look at first.

	North	South	East	West
Number of salesmen	16	12	10	24
Total sales value in the last month (£000)	2,700	2,520	2,320	2,400
Number of sales orders	180	156	160	190
Number of sales discussions	660	364	432	740

More on analytical review

In order to use analytical procedures effectively you need to be able to create an expectation. It will be difficult to create an expectation if operations are significantly different from last year, more so if the changes haven't been planned for. If the changes were planned, we can compare the actual with the forecast. It will also be difficult to use analytical procedures if there have been lots of one-off events in the year as there will be nothing to compare them with.

Test your understanding 19 – D courier company (Case study)

Scenario

F is a member of the internal audit department of D, a courier company. F has recently completed a compliance audit of the extent to which the company's delivery vans are being maintained in accordance with the company's policy.

Each of D's depots has a full-time mechanic. The company's policy is that the depot mechanic is required to check each van's fluid levels and give a road test on a monthly basis. The Depot Manager is responsible for ensuring that every van has been checked in this manner.

Trigger

One of D's delivery drivers was recently involved in a road traffic accident. The police report relating to this accident indicates that the van's brakes had failed because of a leak in the brake pipe. The delivery driver has been charged by the police with an offence because it is illegal to drive a vehicle with defective brakes.

D's Transport Manager has reviewed the van's maintenance log. The log shows that the depot mechanic had not inspected the van during the six weeks before the accident. The Head of Internal Audit has reviewed F's report and has noticed that, although F had visited the depot shortly before the accident occurred, he had reported that policies were being adhered to.

The Head of Internal Audit has asked F to explain why he gave a positive report when records prove that policies had not been adhered to. F explained that the Depot Manager had admitted that the vans had not been inspected as frequently as company policy required because the depot mechanic had been absent for two weeks because of ill health. There were no other qualified mechanics available to carry out these inspections and the depot's repair budget was insufficient to pay for the vans to be inspected by a third party. The Depot Manager had asked F not to note this omission in the audit report because it would lead to disciplinary action, which would harm the Depot Manager's career. F agreed not to report the missed inspections provided that the Depot Manager promised that all of the vans would be inspected as soon as possible when the depot mechanic returned to work.

> The Head of Internal Audit was dissatisfied with F's behaviour alleging F had not acted in an independent manner. F denies that accusation because he has no connection to the Depot Manager or any of the depot's other staff. Additionally, F has pointed out that the Depot Manager could easily have falsified the maintenance records to conceal the fact that the vans had not all been inspected on schedule and a negative internal audit report would simply encourage Depot Managers to falsify their records in future.
>
> **Task**
>
> (a) Evaluate the Head of Internal Audit's assertion that F had not behaved in an independent manner.
>
> (b) Discuss the implications of F's behaviour for the governance of D. The Head of Internal Audit wishes to conduct a thorough investigation into the level and frequency of the inspection of the company's delivery vans.
>
> (c) Prepare a briefing note from the Head of Internal Audit to the internal audit department recommending the tests that could be conducted to ensure that the depot mechanics are inspecting vehicles in accordance with company policy. You should explain the purpose of the tests that you have recommended.
>
> **(45 minutes)**

13 Audit reporting

Audit report

The final stage of an audit is the audit report. In an internal audit assignment the audit report does not have a strict structure, however, it would be expected to feature a number of different parts:

- The objectives of the audit work.

- A summary of the process undertaken by the auditor.

- The results of tests carried out.

- The audit opinion (if an opinion is required).

- Recommendations for action.

When giving recommendations auditors must always ensure that the recommendations are practical and cost-effective.

The auditor will need to consider whether the residual risk will be reduced by the recommendation. If it will not, the recommendation is not worthwhile.

- The internal auditor should have a process of post-implementation review to ensure that recommendations have been actioned by management.

The head of the internal audit team will usually meet with the head of the department being audited and will discuss the points that are being reported. The head of the department being audited can comment on the points raised and the comments are incorporated into the report. This makes the audit process less threatening because the departments being audited know that they will not be reported on to senior management without at least having some advance warning and the opportunity to make their own arguments.

The circulation of the report is also important; typically the internal audit team would discuss the report with the manager of the department being audited. Once this has been done they would submit the report for review within internal audit and then provide the audit committee with a copy. The external auditor would also be able to refer to reports. The content of the report would otherwise remain confidential within the organisation, partly to avoid embarrassing audited managers, whose reputations could be affected by negative reports, particularly if they are taken out of context.

Test your understanding 20

The audit process is made up of the following steps:

A   Plan the audit; document systems and controls; test compliance with controls; report to board

B   Plan the audit; report to the board; document systems and controls; test compliance with controls

C   Document systems and controls; test compliance with controls; report to board; test application of controls

D   Document systems and controls; test application of controls; test compliance with controls; report to board

Test your understanding 21

H is the internal auditor of S Co and has been carrying out work on the purchases cycle to assess the internal controls in place and make recommendations for improvements. He is due to present his findings to the audit committee and has been asked to prepare a report.

Which of the following are sections to be included in the report?

Select ALL that apply

A   Executive Summary

B   Observations and work done

C   A signed opinion

D   Recommendations

E   A statement of compliance with the relevant laws

14 Audit of computer systems

In the case of computer systems, audits are carried out:

- to check whether the system is achieving its intended objectives, and

- in the case of accounting systems, to check that the information produced by the system is reliable.

Problems of auditing computer systems

Auditing computer systems gives some different problems and some new opportunities to auditors to test systems. There are several problems for the auditor of computer systems that do not occur with 'manual' systems, including:

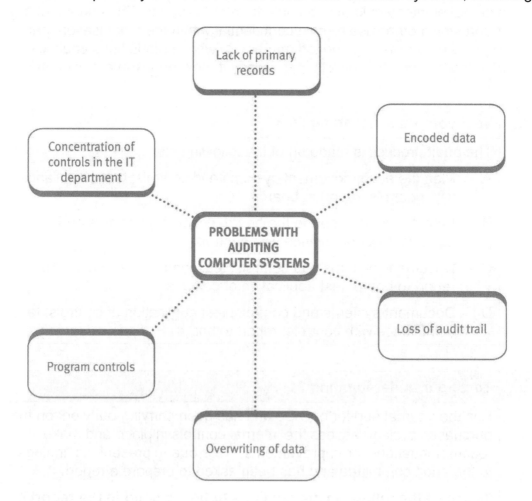

More on problems with auditing computer systems

The auditor may encounter several problems with computer systems that do not occur with 'manual' systems. These include:

- **Concentration of controls** in the IT department. In large computer systems, many of the controls over data are concentrated in the central IT department. This can be a potential weakness in the control system, if users are not aware of an accidental or deliberate corruption of data or programs.

- A **lack of primary records**. In some computer systems, the document originating a transaction might not be created. For example, in an on-line system a customer order received by telephone might be keyed into the system. The system might then generate a despatch document and an invoice, and update the inventory and customer files. The auditor would not be able to trace these documents back to a paper sales order.

- **Encoded data**. When data are entered into a computer system and encoded, there is a risk of error in the input details. Auditors need to consider the effectiveness of program controls, such as data validation checks (including check digit checks) to prevent the acceptance of incorrect data by the system, especially changes to standing data on a master file.

- A **loss of audit trail.** Ideally, in an accounting system, there should be an audit trail providing evidence of the file updates that occur during the processing of a specific transaction. With an audit trail, the auditor can trace a transaction from beginning to end, to confirm that it has been processed correctly. In a manual system, evidence is provided by the existence of hard copy records at each stage of the transaction. Computer systems, however, are generally designed to minimise the amount of paper produced. Control is applied through the output of exception reports, rather than the printout of lists of transactions. The auditor is therefore unable to trace a transaction through the system from originating document to financial statement.

- **Overwriting of data.** When data are stored on a magnetic file, the file will eventually be overwritten with new data. If the auditor needs some of this data to carry out audit tests, it will be necessary to take steps to make the data available. The auditor might therefore need to take copies of data files during the course of the year, and retain them for audit purposes.

- **Program controls.** The auditor has to test the controls in the computer system on which they intend to rely. This means that testing the controls written into the computer programs. To do this, it will be necessary to use computer-assisted audit techniques.

Errors

Additionally, when auditors audit computer systems they need to be aware of the types of errors that occur in the systems. The characteristics of errors are:

- No one-off errors unless deliberate amendment of individual items.
- Systematic errors which repeat across all transactions.
- Higher danger that input errors will not be detected.

Audit approach

The audit approach for computer auditing is often summarised in one of two ways:

- through the computer; or
- round the computer.

Round the computer

Under this approach the auditor does not attempt to understand the operation of the computer system, but rather treats it as a 'black box'. To audit the system, the auditor matches up inputs to predicted outputs to ensure that the outputs are being processed correctly.

The approach is good in that it does not require a high level of expertise of IT in the audit teams, but it is only suitable if the following conditions are met:

- Computer processing is relatively simple
- Audit trail is clearly visible
- A substantial amount of up-to-date documentation exists about how the system works.

Problems with auditing round the computer include:

- Computer files and programs are not tested, hence there is no direct evidence that program is working as documented
- If errors are found it may be impossible to determine why they have happened
- All discrepancies between predicted and actual results must be fully resolved and documented no matter how small (this is because controls are being tested).

Through the computer

This approach actually interrogates the computer files and computer controls and relies much more on the processes that the computer uses.

The auditor follows the audit trail through the internal computer operations and attempts to verify that the processing controls are functioning correctly. The computer controls are directly tested and the accuracy of computer-based processing of input data is verified.

To audit through the computer requires more expertise and a longer set-up time; however, the results can be of very good quality.

This approach utilises different computer-assisted audit techniques (CAATs) such as test data and audit software, discussed below.

 15   Computer-assisted audit techniques (CAATs)

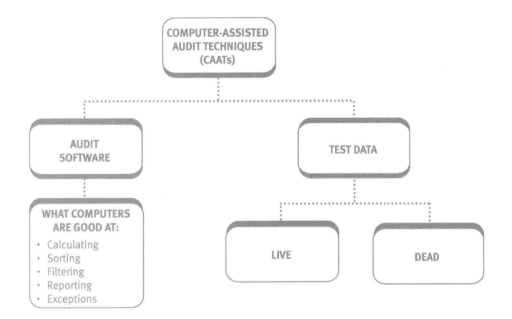

Computer-assisted audit techniques are methods of using a computer to carry out an audit of a computer system. There are two main categories of CAAT:

*   audit software, such as audit interrogation software

*   test data.

Audit interrogation software

Audit software consists of computer programs used by auditors to interrogate the files of a client. Normally the client's data files are input into the audit software program on the auditor's computer, and the auditor can then test those files. Examples of what audit software can do include:

*   Extract a sample according to specified criteria

    –   Random

    –   Over a certain amount

    –   Below a certain amount

    –   At certain dates

*   Calculate ratios and select those outside the criteria

*   Check calculations (for example, additions)

- Prepare reports (budget vs. actual)
- Produce letters to send out to customers suppliers
- Follow items through a computerised system
- Search for underlying relationships and check for fraud.

Packages are generally designed to:

- read computer files
- select information
- perform calculations
- create data files, and
- print reports in a format specified by the auditor.

Audit software enables large volumes of data to be processed very quickly and accurately. The main drawback of audit software is that it can take a long time to set up the systems with the client data, and it will require expertise.

CAATs and fraud detection

Audit software includes a variety of routines for identifying transactions where there could be a suspicion of fraud, such as:

- comparing the home addresses of employees with the addresses of suppliers, to identify employees who are also suppliers
- searching for duplicate cheque numbers
- analysing the sequence of transactions to identify missing invoices or cheques
- identifying suppliers with more than one supplier code or more than one mailing address
- finding several suppliers all with the same address
- listing payments for transactions that fall just within the spending authorisation limit of the individual who has authorised the payment.

Benefits and weaknesses of CAATs

Benefits of CAATs	Examples
CAAT's force the auditor to rely on programmed controls during the audit. Sometimes it may be the only way to test controls within a computer system, therefore enables the auditor to test program controls.	Credit limits within a system can only be changed by the accountant. A computer assisted check will test that this is the case.
Large number of items can be tested quickly and accurately.	Checking the depreciation charged on each asset would be quicker with a computer assisted program than manually.
CAAT's test original documentation instead of print outs, therefore the authenticity of the document is more valid this way.	Actual wages will be tested instead of paper copies.
After initial set-up costs, using CAATs are likely to be cost-effective, as the same audit software can be used each year as long as the system doesn't change.	Examples of use or audit tests (1) Calculation checks (2) Reviewing lists of old or outstanding items and investing those specifically (3) Detecting for unreasonable items (4) Detecting violation of the system rules (5) New analysis (6) Completeness checks (7) Selects samples (8) Identifying exception reporting facilities.
Allow the results from using CAATs to be compared with 'traditional' testing.	If the two sources of evidence agree then this too will increase the overall audit confidence.

Weaknesses of CAATs	Recommendations
CAAT's will be limited depending on how well the computer system is integrated. The more integrated the better the use of CAAT's. For example, the invoices should be computer generated and then processed through the accounts system to feed in to the financial statements.	Ensure understanding of the system to assess whether audit software will be relevant for the company. Need to assess whether there is a need for the audit software.
It takes time to design CAATs tests therefore, may not be cost-effective if the auditor is dealing with a bespoke system, as there may be a lot of set-up costs. The reason for this is it takes time to write specific test data or to program the audit software to the needs of the client.	A cost-benefit analysis from the audit point of view should be carried out prior to deciding to use the audit software.
If the company you are auditing cannot confirm all system documentation is available, then the auditors will be unable to perform the tests effectively due to lack of understanding.	Do not use audit software until these have been identified.
If there is a change in the accounting year, or from the previous year, then the audit software will have to be reset and designed, therefore may be costly.	A cost-benefit analysis from the audit point of view should be carried out prior to deciding to use the audit software.

Test your understanding 22 – Audit software (Integration)

Recommend how audit software could be used in the audit of a mail order company concerned that deliveries are not being invoiced and that stock files are not being updated.

Embedded audit facilities

Embedded audit facilities might be written into a program, particularly in on-line/real-time systems. These facilities can carry out automatic checks or provide information for subsequent audit, such as:

* extracting and storing information for subsequent audit review, with sufficient details to give the auditor a proper audit trail

* identifying and recording items that are of some particular audit interest, as specified by the auditor.

Test data

Test data can be used by inputting the data into the system and checking whether it is processed correctly. The expected results can be calculated in advance, and checked against the actual output from the system. The auditors might include some invalid data in the tests, which the system should reject.

It will only be used if the auditor is intending to do a 'test of controls' audit, and it must be considered cost effective.

Live data = test data are processed during a normal production run.

Dead data = test data are processed outside the normal cycle.

The stages involved in using test data are:

(1) Gain a thorough understanding of how the system being tested is supposed to work and the controls that are included in it.

(2) Devise the test data set. This should be a set of data containing both valid and invalid items. The controls in the system should identify the invalid items.

(3) Run the test data. This can be 'live' (within the normal processing at the client), or 'dead' (outside the normal processing). Live runs give more reliable results but are more risky to operate.

(4) Evaluate the results. It is important that the auditor fully evaluates the results of the test data and does further work if unexpected results occur.

Risks with test data

Risks	Controls
Damage to the system as the system is tested to its limits.	Ensure auditors understand the system and have software support.
Corruption of the systems data if test data are not properly removed.	Ensure process for data removal.
System down time if 'dead' data used.	Establish when system can be used with minimum disruption to the business.

Examples of test data

Tests	Reason for the test
Revenue	
Input an order into the client's system that would cause a customer to exceed their credit limit	The order should not be accepted, or should raise a query whether you are sure you wish to proceed. If this happens then the auditors will have confidence the system is working properly
Input a negative number of items on an order	Ensures only positive quantities are accepted
Input incomplete customer details	The system should not process the order unless all information is completed
Input an excessive amount	There are reasonable checks in the system to identify possible input errors. A warning should appear on the screen confirming the number
Purchases	
Raise an order from a supplier not on the preferred supplier list	A query should be raised as to whether you want to proceed with this transaction
Process an order with an unauthorised staff ID	The system should reject the process altogether or send the request through to an appropriate person for authorisation
Try and make changes to the supplier standing data using the ID of someone who is not authorised to do so	The system should reject the process altogether or send the request through to an appropriate person for authorisation
Payroll	
Try and set up a new employee up on the payroll system using an unauthorised ID	The system should reject the process altogether or send the request through to an appropriate person for authorisation
Try and make employee changes of detail using an unauthorised ID	The system should reject the process altogether or send the request through to an appropriate person for authorisation
Make an excess change, for example increase someone's salary by $1,000,000 by someone authorised	The system should have parameters in place to question this amount, and maybe reject it due to it being outside the normal range

Test your understanding 23

E Company administers payments to home owners to enable them to insulate their homes, or up-grade their heating system. E is in receipt of a central government grant which it must only distribute to home owners whose income is below a certain level or who fall into a 'vulnerable' category, as stipulated by the government guidelines.

E Company must not administer payments twice to the same address, or breach a maximum award amount. E company must also receive proof (in the form of an invoice) that the money awarded has been used for the intended items. E Company maintains computerised records of all payments awarded with inbuilt controls to ensure they do not breach government guidelines.

The internal auditors of E Company are using 'test data' to perform checks on whether the computer controls over awarding payments are working correctly. They are using 'dead data' to test the system.

Which of the following issues is the test data unlikely to detect?

Select ALL that apply.

A   Whether the system will allow a payment which breaches the upper limit to be processed.

B   Whether the system works consistently in the same way

C   Whether the system will allow a payment to be made to the same address twice.

D   Whether the system will allow a payment to be made to an individual not classed as vulnerable or on a low income.

E   Whether an address which has received a grant is valid.

F   Whether 'spot checks' at addresses were carried out correctly.

Test your understanding 24

Factors affecting the need for an audit include:

Select ALL that apply

A   The number of directors

B   Turnover

C   The diversity of the company's activities

D   A change in organisational structure

E   Net assets

Test your understanding 25

The testing and evaluation of controls is usually performed firstly by which one of the following?

A   Risk management

B   External audit

C   Internal audit

D   Management

Test your understanding 26 – G Manufacturing (Case study)

Scenario

G is a manufacturing company that employs 800 production staff and 90 administrative staff. The company operates from a single site.

Trigger

A new Chief Executive was appointed in July 2013. She was recruited from a much larger manufacturing company where she was the Marketing Director. The company is also an indirect competitor of G.

Since her appointment the Chief Executive has focussed on learning as much as she possibly can about the company's culture. She spent the whole of August meeting representatives from all levels of staff from within the company and other stakeholders such as customers and suppliers. She has called a board meeting to discuss her findings. Her findings are as follows:

*   The company manufactures high quality products that are popular with customers. All members of G's staff are proud to be associated with the manufacture of the products.

*   G's managers and supervisors take a very relaxed approach when working with subordinates. Staff are empowered to make decisions on their own without consulting their superiors if they are confident that they are acting in the company's best interests.

*   The relaxed management style has harmed the control environment immensely. Only a minority of the company's staff take the budgetary control system seriously and hardly any of them pay serious attention to variance reports. In contrast to all other departments, morale in the accounts department is very low because the members of the accounts staff feel that they waste a significant amount of time every month chasing heads of departments for reports and for other important information.

- These attitudes are echoed by external stakeholders. Customers are delighted with the quality of G's products, but often find that G's invoices and monthly statements contain errors. Suppliers claim that invoices submitted to G are settled very promptly 90% of the time, but the remainder have to be chased because G's accounts staff do not always receive accurate and complete records of orders placed and goods received.

The Chief Executive has warned the board that the control environment must be improved as a matter of priority. She proposes to send an email to all staff congratulating them on their achievements on product quality, but stating that the rather lax attitude towards management and record keeping will have to stop. Over time, she plans to impose disciplinary measures on staff who are responsible for bookkeeping errors or delays. She also proposes that G should create an internal audit department to monitor compliance with formal processes and procedures.

The Production Director has argued that the Chief Executive's proposals are counter-productive and that most of the delays and omissions are due to employees giving priority to the creation of an excellent product.

Task

Write a briefing note to the Chief Executive recommending, stating reasons, the steps that she should take in order to create an effective internal audit department. **(30 minutes)**

Test your understanding 27 – Multinational car manufacturer

Scenario

M is a multinational car manufacturer. M sells six models of car around the world. Each model has its own assembly factory. Each of the factories is located in a different country and each factory is incorporated as a company. Car assembly is heavily automated, using robots to assemble and weld, and so final assembly is generally in a country that is chosen for its proximity to major markets.

M has many other factories that make components. For example, one factory manufactures all of the music systems for every car sold by M and another manufactures all of the windscreens. These factories can be located in countries that offer low labour costs. For example, the music systems are built using unskilled labour in a developing country.

Each country in which M sells cars has its own M subsidiary that deals with distribution. All sales are to car dealerships and each dealership buys cars directly from its local M subsidiary.

National governments are keen to ensure that intra-group transfers are at arm's length prices and are set so that M will not pay too little tax. Therefore the transfer pricing policy in M is that transfers should be at "market price". Consequently the transfer prices that are used by M do not necessarily reflect the manufacturing costs and so some group members report very small profits. The company's reward system for its senior managers and directors is linked to the profits that are reported by their subsidiary.

M's transfer pricing arrangements take up a great deal of management time. In many cases, arm's length market prices are difficult to identify because there are no direct comparisons available. For example, the subsidiary that manufactures music systems does not sell its products to anyone other than the six assembly companies. Even if similar products can be found that are traded openly by other manufacturers, there are very specific problems with determining an objective market price. For example, there are transport costs and questions over the discounts that are granted for bulk sales. There is an even greater problem with finished cars because M sells its cars at higher prices in more prosperous markets.

Trigger

M's main board is concerned that the company may be investigated by the tax authorities in one or more of the countries where it does business. The Head of Group Internal Audit has been asked to assist the board by conducting an internal investigation in order to establish whether M should change any of its transfer pricing practices.

Task

Write a briefing note to the Board advising on the matters that it should cover when briefing the Head of Group Internal Audit in order to be certain that its requirements are met by the internal audit investigation into M's transfer pricing practices.

Write a note to the Head of Group Internal Audit discussing four factors that they should consider when assessing the possibility that a subsidiary could be investigated by its local tax authority.

(30 minutes)

16   Chapter summary

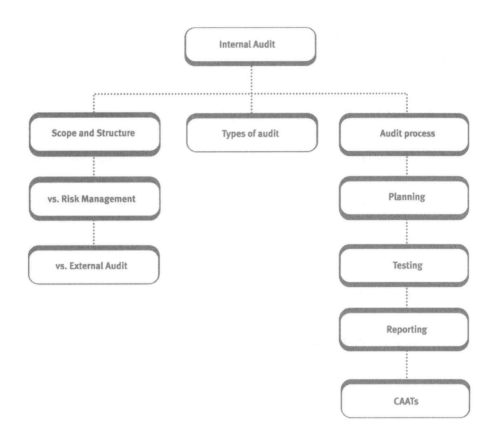

Test your understanding answers

Test your understanding 1

B, C, D

Note:

- A – just because the company is a plc, it does not necessarily follow that it is listed

- E – family run companies do not necessarily have weaker controls or higher risks

- F – while one would hope the shareholders would want an internal audit department, this reason is not as important as the other factors highlighted

Test your understanding 2

A, B and D

- Option C: This is an internal audit role. The risk management team cannot establish controls and then test them objectively.

- Option E: This is a role that internal audit may carry out.

- Option F: This is a responsibility of the board.

Test your understanding 3

A and B only

- Option A: True – The internal auditor cannot report to a director who might be the subject of an internal audit.

- Option B: True – Since objectivity is the key attribute of an internal auditor, an outside appointment, without any personal grievances or conflicts within NN, will be more independent than an internal promotion.

- Option C: False – The internal auditor could review controls over quality control for adequacy but not directly prevent the re-occurrence of any events.

- Option D: False – In carrying out their work, the internal auditors will need to question operational staff and observe them carrying out their roles. This will inevitably take time. However, improvements suggested by internal audit should outweigh any short term loss of efficiency.

- Option E: False – Many organisations have a single internal auditor. Whilst a team and a separate department are ideal, they are not compulsory.

Test your understanding 4

A, B, D

Note:

- C – Internal staff are more likely to have a better understanding of the organisation's objectives and culture

- E – the decision should be based on a range of factors including cost, quality, skills, etc

Test your understanding 5

The correct answer is A – Reporting should be to a senior director. They should also have access to the chair of the board, and be accountable to the audit committee.

Test your understanding 6

The correct answers are A, B and D – Identifying risk is the role of risk management. Internal audit test the controls in place to prevent or detect risk. However, if in the course of internal audit work a risk is identified then it will be reported to risk management (which is a secondary role for audit).

Test your understanding 7

The correct answer is D – By outsourcing the internal audit function control may be lost.

Test your understanding 8 – SHD (Integration)

External audit perspective

External auditors form an opinion on whether the financial statements show a true and fair view. This means they will seek explanations for any unusual items, areas of expenditure, etc so they can form their opinion.

The fact that variable overheads have increased means that they will require evidence (such as approved invoices) to verify these expenses,

They will need to ensure that expenditure is bona fide to the business. If it appears difficult to determine why these expenses have been incurred, then the issue of legitimate business expense is raised.

At the extreme there is the possibility of reporting under the Proceeds of Crime Act of 2002 that the business may have been involved in fraud or money laundering.

Internal audit perspective

The lack of apparent reason for incurring the additional overhead expenses also appears to be a weakness in the internal control systems. Segregation of duties is poor and this has allowed someone to set up a supplier and process invoices for payment to that supplier.

The internal auditors will be concerned by such weaknesses in control and seek to rectify the situation.

They may also notice the increase in expenditure and question the efficient use of resources on the development projects.

Test your understanding 9 – Z (Case study)

(a) The whole point of this type of tendering process is to ensure that each bidder has an incentive to tender at the lowest possible acceptable price. Doing that requires that the bidding parties know as little as possible about one another and that the bids themselves are kept secure.

There are a number of areas of concern in this case: The winning bidder withdrew what would have been the lowest offer and replaced it with a higher bid. There could be an innocent explanation for that, but it is a matter of some concern that the bid was replaced because it could indicate a knowledge of the other bidders' tenders. If that is the case then there could have been some collusion between the bidder and a member of staff in Z's buying department. Alternatively, the bidder could have colluded with the other companies that were most likely to have placed bids for this contract.

The winning bid was not the lowest one submitted. That could signify some favouritism on the part of the selection committee. There may be a perfectly valid justification for rejecting a lower bid, but it seems strange that a bidder for a major contract would submit a tender for a product that is not fit for purpose. The process was not particularly secure. The bids themselves were addressed to a relatively junior manager and were not stored under conditions of great secrecy. The chief buyer could easily have opened incoming bids and put them in replacement blank envelopes without that being obvious to anybody. The internal auditor was not involved until very late in the process and most of those present at the opening were directly involved in the project. The internal audit department could have taken a more active role in the whole process of safeguarding bids and in opening them under secure conditions.

(b) The internal auditor should attempt to establish who had access to the sealed bids after they had been received. It would be an easy matter for anybody who had access to the safe to type a label and put the bid in a new envelope. It would not be particularly difficult to forge a colleague's signature (or for the chief buyer to sign the envelope).

The easiest way for the auditor to determine who had access would be to visit the buying department and to note the location of the safe and the occupants of the office in which it is located. The auditor should use indirect, open-ended questions to determine whether the safe is normally kept locked when the office is occupied and who has access to the key or combination. The opened envelopes, which should have been retained, should be examined and the chief buyer asked to confirm that all of the signatures were genuine. That would effectively mean that the chief buyer was accepting personal responsibility for the bids that were considered. The internal auditor should attempt to establish whether there is any form of relationship between any member of the buying department and the winning bidder. Even those who could not access the safe would possibly know who had tendered from the covering letters, which were kept separately, and that could have permitted the winner to gather information that led to submitting a higher winning bid. The purchase ledger should be checked to determine whether Z had any previous dealings with the winning bidder.

The reasons for the rejection of the cheaper bid should be investigated. The fact that the bus was slightly smaller could be a reason for rejection as could the specification for the modifications, but these might not be material to the selection. If the buses were large enough and within the parameters of the tender document and the materials were of an acceptable specification then the cheapest bid should have been accepted.

(c) **Note**

To: The Chief Executive

From: A.N. Accountant

Date: Today

Subject: The advantages and disadvantages of the internal auditor being actively involved in the investigation of suspected fraud.

Dear Sir,

The advantages include:

The internal auditor should be independent of those who are being investigated. It would be difficult to identify anybody else outside of the buying department with the necessary understanding of the process.

The internal auditor will have the necessary skills to undertake the investigation and also knows and understands the entity's culture and systems. An external auditor could undertake the investigation, but would not have this insight. The entity can be assured of the internal auditor's discretion and so there should be very little risk of the facts leaking out without the board's permission. Internal audit staff are generally professionally qualified and are also trained to be discreet

The disadvantages include:

Using the internal audit department in this way could make it more difficult for the internal auditors to maintain a good working relationship with those under audit. Internal auditors are generally reluctant to investigate potential fraud because it may undermine their relationship with line staff.

The audit could be very time consuming and could be a major distraction from the ongoing schedule of internal audit activities. The internal audit department's time is a valuable resource and it will generally be allocated to specific tasks as part of a plan. The fact that the evidence has been gathered by the company's own staff could undermine its credibility if, say, the company seeks compensation as a result of the investigation or pursues criminal charges. If there has been any staff fraud then the police will require a clear and unambiguous chain of evidence and the fact that colleagues have been involved in the initial investigation may interfere with their ability to build a criminal case. If you have any further queries please do not hesitate to ask.

Best wishes

A.N. Accountant

Test your understanding 10 – Seatown (case study)

Address

Date

Dear Sirs,

Re: The economy, efficiency and effectiveness of beach cleaning activities

(a)   The total cost of all activities should be measured against budget and previous years. That cost should be broken down according to whether it relates to sweeping or emptying bins and by the nature of the expense within that (e.g. labour or vehicle running costs) so that any costs can be identified and managed.

The breakdown of the total should be linked to the cost drivers in order to measure trends or spot anomalies. For example, the cost of running tractors should be divided by the number of tractors or the number of kilometres travelled to determine the cost per vehicle or vehicle-kilometre. Much of this information should be readily available from existing management accounting records maintained by the town.

It may be possible to break costs down to reflect the cost of cleaning specific beaches or stretches of beach. If so, that might indicate whether a particular stretch is costing a disproportionate amount of time and money because of issues over location or problems such as rocks or soft sand. It may be possible to reduce costs by closing such beaches to the public during quieter parts of the holiday season. Analysing costs in this way will almost certainly require staff to maintain logs for a period in order to show how time and resources are being applied.

Any deviations from budget should be investigated, as should any fluctuations in the measures over time.

Comparable statistics should be obtained from other towns in order to determine whether there is scope to benchmark. There is no reason for other towns to withhold that information because the nature of any competition is unlikely to be affected by expenditure on cleaning services.

For the purpose of any comparison the total cost should be related to the number of beaches being cleaned and the length of the beaches in order to adjust for the scale of the operation.

(b) The quantity of refuse collected by each means (sweeping v emptying bins) should be measured in order to reflect the output from the service.

The number of complaints lodged by holidaymakers and residents should be monitored. Those relating to the cleanliness of the beach should be highlighted as an indicator of public perceptions.

The town council should conduct market research to ask beach users what they think about the amenities provided and the questions should include some discussion of the cleanliness of the beach. That should be repeated regularly throughout the holiday season, partly because the problem may change in response to peaks and troughs in the number of users and partly because the use of the beach may change depending on whether families are using it for play during the summer holidays or older couples are simply walking on the beach when the weather is cooler at the beginning and end of the holiday season.

The number of incidents attended by the beach first aiders should be analysed to highlight injuries such as cuts caused by broken glass.

The town council should conduct detailed audits of the beach itself by inspecting areas immediately after the sweeping operation and also during the day. That will require setting a standard for the audit, such as deciding what constitutes a piece of litter (for example, should a small shred of paper that would be difficult to filter out of the sand be counted in the same manner as, say, an empty soft drinks can?)

Compliance with the town council's standards should be monitored. For example, there should be a check to ensure that the bins are actually emptied according to the schedule. Any deviation should be investigated to establish whether that is due to staff failure or because the schedule is impractical.

(c) In general, effectiveness audits are more difficult than economy and efficiency audits.

Economy and efficiency is a matter of cost accounting. The cost of providing the cleaning services is largely a matter of using traditional accounting techniques to analyse data that would be collected for financial reporting and management accounting purposes anyway. There are some subjective decisions that may have an impact, such as identifying relevant costs, but even those problems are largely questions of definition.

Effectiveness involves making some difficult decisions about measuring performance. Surrogates, such as the quantity of litter uplifted, can lead to dysfunctional behaviour because that could encourage more frequent emptying of bins at the expense of sweeping. Sweeping will not necessarily collect a huge quantity of material but it might remove dangerous objects such as broken glass.

It may also be necessary to set targets for the end result of the cleaning activities and that could be difficult. What is an acceptable level of litter? What matters more, perceptions of litter or actual cleanliness? The two could differ because many users may not be aware of litter on the beach.

Should you have any further queries, please do not hesitate to ask.

Yours Faithfully

A.N. Accountant

Test your understanding 11

The correct answer is A – By definition.

Test your understanding 12

The correct answer is D – By definition.

Test your understanding 13

A and D.

- Option A is an inherent risk which exists regardless of internal controls.

- Option B is a control risk.

- Option C is a detection risk.

- Option D is an inherent risk which exists regardless of internal controls.

- Option E is a control risk.

Test your understanding 14

The correct answer is C Substantive tests concentrate on output (the end result) ensuring that it is as expected.

A, B and D are compliance tests (on the process) to test that controls are operating as they were designed to.

Test your understanding 15 – Compliance testing (Integration)

Company X appears to have a recruitment 'process' – application forms and interviews, although this may not have taken the process far enough.

Once a candidate has been selected their application form should be verified, usually by checking their qualifications to actual certificates (not copies) and taking up references (usually two – one work and one personal). There is no mention of this happening at X and may be the reason that John cannot perform the job satisfactorily. The rumour may be true.

John's start date appears to be too soon to enable the aforementioned controls to be implemented. There should be a sufficient period between interview and any start date to enable all claims made on the application form to be verified.

Personnel/human resources should be the department to verify the application form, which they may not have done. Therefore the internal auditor should visit the department, ascertain the recruitment process and test that the process is adhered to.

Compliance tests might include:

- Select a sample of employee files and test to see whether the application form is present.

- From the application forms, trace the references taken up.

- Check that the references were positive i.e. that previous employers found the staff punctual, trustworthy, etc.

- From the application forms, trace the copies of certificates (taken from the originals) which back up any qualifications stated.

- Qualifications could be further tested by contacting the relevant body to ascertain whether they have record of said employee.

The controls at X appear to be ineffective since the process does not cover these vital activities. Alternatively these activities might be part of X's personnel process, and the personnel staff have not followed them. Either way the personnel staff need to be reprimanded and further controls implemented to prevent future occurrences.

Test your understanding 16 – Audit testing (Integration)

Compliance tests

- Look for evidence of the approval of new workers, such as a formal instruction to the payroll department.

- Check that the timesheets are all approved by a supervisor.

- Check that all overtime has been approved.

- Observe the wages payout to ensure:

  - wages are only collected by the person being paid;

  - all staff sign for their wages.

- Ensure that a PAYE/NIC control account is reconciled and reviewed each month by an appropriate manager.

Substantive tests

- Take a sample of timesheets and re-calculate wages and deductions.

- Perform a reconciliation of total hours worked to gross pay and compare month by month.

- Check a sample of payments to the pay rate records to ensure they are being used correctly.

- Re-perform the PAYE/NIC control account for a month to ensure it has been done correctly.

Test your understanding 17

The correct answer is C – Inherent risk.

Detection risk is the risk that the auditor's tests do not reveal a materially incorrect amount.

Control risk is the risk that the existing controls are not sufficient to prevent or detect a material mis-statement.

Sampling risk is the risk that the auditor's conclusion from a sample, may be different from the result that would have been obtained had all items in the population been tested.

Test your understanding 18 – Car dealership (Integration)

A number of performance ratios could be calculated across the different regions to compare performance:

	North	South	East	West
Sales value per salesman (£)	168,750	210,000	232,000	100,000
Sales discussions per salesman	41	30	43	31
Average orders per discussion	0.27	0.43	0.37	0.28
Average value per order (£)	15,000	16,200	14,500	12,600

From the above performance measures it can be seen that the West region is the most inefficient. In all measures this region is at or very near the bottom performance criteria which indicates there should be room for efficiencies. This region should be selected for audit.

Test your understanding 19 – D courier company (Case study)

(a) An independent auditor would report honestly, without any bias or conflict. Independence is an attitude of mind that involves making a truthful report regardless of the consequences. In this case, F appears to have identified with the Depot Manager, despite there being no particular reason for doing so. F has been sympathetic to the Depot Manager's position and that sympathy has resulted in a distorted internal audit report. F's duty was to investigate compliance with a specific rule concerning maintenance and to report the results to senior management. It was not part of F's duty to consider whether a truthful report would harm the Depot Manager's career. The responsibility for deciding whether to take action against the Depot Manager lay with D's board and F should have provided a full report on the circumstances. That report could have included a summary of the Depot Manager's predicament arising because of the absence of the mechanic.

F should not accept responsibility for the impact of a truthful report on the Depot Manager's career. The Depot Manager could have dealt with the fact that there was inadequate cover when the mechanic was absent by reporting the situation to head office. The Depot Manager should not have asked F to deal with this omission retrospectively by lying in the internal audit report.

(b) The internal audit department is a vital element of the control environment in any large entity. The directors rely on internal audit to ensure that formal control processes and procedures are operating as they should. The directors cannot observe the workings of these systems for themselves unless the entity is very small and so the internal audit department provides vital feedback.

If the directors cannot trust the internal audit department to report honestly and accurately then they will have no way of knowing whether their policies and instructions are being carried out. That is a major issue in terms of good corporate governance because the shareholders hold the directors responsible for the governance arrangements and expect them to run the company an effective manner. Cases where problems have arisen because of compliance failures by managers and staff have tended to reflect badly on the board.

F's behaviour is also sending a very clear signal to D's staff. If breaches are not reported and acted upon then staff may decide not to comply. If the internal audit department, whose very existence is to report compliance failures, does not act then the staff could start to become demotivated and lazy. If D's board does not act quickly and decisively then its ability to manage the company effectively will be seriously compromised by this audit failure.

(c) The first thing would be to review the records maintained by the depot. These should indicate that the inspections were carried out and the mechanic should have signed as proof. This test will not actually prove that the tests took place because the mechanic could have signed the documents recklessly, but the signature does at least prove that the staff are willing to accept responsibility for the inspections having been carried out. Internal audit could review the records relating to repairs and breakdowns for each depot. This would be a useful analytical review exercise that could identify any depots that were at a higher risk of not carrying out adequate inspections. Ideally, the cost of repairs should be separated from the cost of routine maintenance.

During branch visits the internal audit staff should be aware of the work being done by the depot mechanics. The depot staff may behave differently during an audit visit, but it would be reassuring to see whether the mechanics were inspecting vehicles. The auditor could supplement these observations by asking the mechanics and the drivers to explain the maintenance procedures in order to establish indirectly whether they volunteered information about the regular fluid checks.

The internal auditor could conduct a spot check on the fluid levels of a sample of vehicles at the depot. These should focus on vans that have recently been checked. If the fluid levels are low then there is a strong likelihood that the checks were not carried out.

Test your understanding 20

The correct answer is A The correct order of events is to: Plan the audit; document systems and controls; test compliance with controls; test application of controls; report to board

Test your understanding 21

A, B and D

- Options A, B and D are typical of an internal audit report on internal controls.

- Options C and E are more in keeping with an **external** audit report.

Test your understanding 22 – Audit software (Integration)

Possible use of audit software:

- Sequence checks on delivery note file and invoice file.

- Computer can check that every delivery results in an amendment to the invoice file and the stock file (with list produced of every exception).

- Exception reports generated of zero value invoices and non-invoiced deliveries.

- Calculation checks on all invoices to ensure in line with price lists. Check on agreement of deliveries against order files.

Test your understanding 23

B, D, E and F

- Option A: The internal auditor can attempt to process payments which both breach and do not breach the upper limit .Those that do breach it should be rejected.

- Option B: Dead data means test data are processed outside the normal cycle. It is not possible to conclude with certainty that the 'live' system would work in the same way.

- Option C: Same address payments should be rejected.

- Option D: The test data will check computer controls, not whether proof of income etc. has actually been seen.

- Option E: As long as an address has not been awarded a payment before it should be accepted by the system. This does not mean it is a valid address, only that it has not been recorded before.

- Option F: The test data will check computer controls, not the work of staff performing spot checks.

Test your understanding 24

The correct answers are B, C, D and E The number of employees (not directors) may affect the need for an audit – the more employees, the higher the risk that supervision may not be an effective control.

Test your understanding 25

The correct answer is C – This is internal audit's key activity, hence ensuring that those who design the controls do not test them.

Test your understanding 26 – G Manufacturing (Case study)

Briefing note

To: Chief Executive

From: A.N. Accountant

Date: Today

Subject: Creating an effective internal audit department

Dear Sir,

Firstly, the board should decide the level of commitment that it is going to make to internal audit. A half-hearted attempt will lead to an under resourced and ineffective department. A realistic staffing level should be decided before anything further is done and the associated costs should be budgeted for.

The terms of reference should be decided. Those will include the powers that will be enjoyed by internal audit and the internal auditor's access to the board. It will be easier to recruit an experienced Head of Internal Audit if it can be shown how the department will be viewed within the organisation as a whole.

The Board should recruit the Head of Internal Audit before interviewing for the other audit staff. That will enable G to offer the Head of Internal Audit the opportunity to have some say in recruitment to ensure that suitable staff are taken on. G should use a recruitment agency to identify suitable candidates because agencies are likely to have access to lists of potential applicants who are interested in moving on to new challenges.

The remainder of the audit team should be recruited, perhaps also using an agency, under the Head of Internal Audit's overall supervision. The team members should have appropriate skills and qualifications, including membership of a professional body, or be working towards a qualification if they are to be employed in a junior role.

The department should be based in a suitable location, with realistic provision for administrative support such as secretarial support. If internal audit is not shown to be adequately resourced then its credibility will suffer in the eyes of the other staff.

The Board should provide internal audit with a statement of the department's powers to request information and documents. Giving internal audit a formal charter within the organisation will help to ensure the department's credibility and its freedom to conduct meaningful investigations.

The initial reports submitted by internal audit will have to be seen to receive the Board's endorsement in order to underpin the directors' support. That could involve requesting a follow-up to deal with any weaknesses or compliance failures. The Board should not take disproportionate action, otherwise the internal audit department will be viewed as a threat, but it should be clear to all staff that the internal audit reports will be read and taken seriously.

Should you have any further queries, please do not hesitate to ask.

Best wishes

A.N. Accountant

Test your understanding 27 – Multinational car manufacturer

(a) **Briefing note**

> **To:** The Board
>
> **From:** A.N. Accountant
>
> **Date:** Today
>
> **Subject:** Investigation into transfer pricing
>
> The board has to provide the Head of Internal Audit with a very clear objective for this audit. This is a very specific task that could prevent the company from being tied up in a number of investigations around the world. The board should identify the problem areas that are likely to prompt a tax investigation in one or more of the subsidiaries and brief the internal auditor accordingly so that the group is aware of the "worst possible case".
>
> The Head of Internal Audit should be briefed on the extent to which evidence should be gathered. This could be a desk-based audit carried out from head office or it could involve local teams visiting subsidiaries. The Head of Internal Audit should be given a detailed budget of the time and resources that are to be invested in this study.

If the audit team is to visit subsidiaries and engage with local management, then the audit staff will have to know how much they are permitted to reveal about the investigation. Transfer pricing is clearly a very controversial matter for M and local managers may be unsettled by any suggestion that pricing policies may be changed.

The timetable should be established. If the board requires the findings quickly then it will either have to accept a less detailed investigation or it will have to reallocate internal audit resources from other areas.

(b) **Note**

To:	Head of Group Internal Audit
From:	A.N. Accountant
Date:	Today
Subject:	Tax investigation

Dear Sir,

I attach some notes regarding factors that should be considered when assessing the possibility that a subsidiary could be investigated by the local tax authority.

National tax rates

The countries that are most likely to investigate transfer prices are those that have the highest tax rates. Ranking tax rates and import tariffs will provide the internal audit team with an indication of the subsidiaries that are at greatest risk of being the subject of an investigation.

Credibility of tax charge

The manipulation of transfer pricing is associated with the underpayment of tax. The internal audit team should calculate the tax paid by each subsidiary as a percentage of accounting profit. A subsidiary with a very low effective rate of tax is more likely to be investigated for the distortion of transfer prices. Alternatively, the authorities may relate the tax charge to other statistics. For example, a company that has a healthy reported revenue and a very small tax liability may be suspected of manipulation

History of tax investigations

The history of individual countries may also be relevant. For example, the UK government was concerned about the potential underpayment of tax by some multinational companies and so any UK subsidiaries may be more at risk of an investigation by the tax authorities

Visible market prices

The nature of the products being supplied may also affect the risk of an investigation. For generic items such as nuts and bolts or spark plugs, there will be a readily observable market that is visible to the tax authorities. If M's transfer prices are close to the observable market prices for such items then there is very little risk that a tax investigation will occur and so there is less point in conducting an audit investigation. If the pricing implications are complicated because there is no meaningful comparison then any tax investigation will be more disruptive and it could be useful to pre-empt that with an audit investigation so that M has its defence ready.

Cyber security threats

Chapter learning objectives

Lead	Component	
D1 Analyse cyber security threats.	(a)	Analyse nature and impact of cyber security risks.
	(b)	Analyse types of cyber security risks
	(c)	Analyse risk of security vulnerabilities
D2 Review cyber security processes	(a)	Review cyber security objectives.

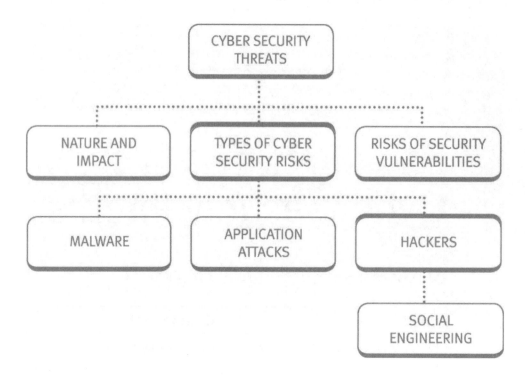

1 Overview of cyber security threats

Organisations deal with a wide variety of sensitive information on a daily basis. It is important to understand what constitutes sensitive information, how it is used, what an organisation's objectives regarding cyber security might be and how different organisations may interact with technology.

1.1 Types of sensitive information

Sensitive information can take many forms. Broadly speaking there are three main types of sensitive information:

- **Personal information**: often referred to a Personally Identifiable Information (PII), this is anything that can be used either on its own or with other information to identify, contact or locate a single person.

- **Business information**: this is anything that may cause a risk to the company if discovered by an external party, for example a competitor. It includes things like research data, marketing plans and new product developments.

- **Classified information**: this usually refers to information that a national government has put special restrictions on where disclosure could harm public safety and security.

Expandable text: Sensitive information

Personally Identifiable Information includes but is not limited to the following:

- Names

- Addresses

- Date of birth

- Credit card numbers

- Bank account numbers

- Personal health information

- Information about sexual activity or orientation

- Information about race or ethnicity

- Information about political opinions

- Information about religious or philosophical beliefs

- Students' registration with an awarding body

- Students' Kaplan ID number!!

The nature of PII such as this means there is an increased risk to an individual if this data is lost, compromised or disclosed without authorisation as it could lead to fraud, financial loss, inconvenience or unfairness. Organisations that do not look after PII could be exposed to significant legal consequences, this is covered in more detail in the risk of security vulnerabilities later in this chapter.

Business information could include, but is not limited to:

- Financial information for internal reporting

- Financial information for external reporting, prior to publication

- Confidential sales information (customer lists, order information)

- Payment card information maintained for ease of customer ordering

- Confidential employee information

1.2 Understanding how technology interacts with the organisation

To enable an organisation to protect itself from any cyber security threats, it must understand how technology interacts with the organisation. This includes the following considerations:

- **Type of technology the company uses:**

    Enterprise Resource Planning (ERP) systems, Data Centres

- **The different ways the organisation is connected with technology:**

  Virtual Private Network (VPN), routers, virtual servers

- **The different service providers the company uses:**

  Cloud provider, software providers, call centres

- **How the company delivers its product or service to the customer:**

  Transmissions to vendors, online retail channel, wholesale customers

All of these factors provide an opportunity for an issue to arise, if they are not properly understood and controlled.

 Expandable text

Type

- **Enterprise Resource Planning (ERP)** systems link a wide range of activities that managers could use to control information flow and employee behaviour. They are often used to automate work traditionally done by the management accountant, such as accounting entries, inventory ordering, monitoring and human resource planning.

- **Data Centres** are large groups of networked computer servers that are usually used by organisations for storage, processing or distributing large amounts of data.

Connection type

- **Virtual Private Network (VPN)** extends a private network across a public network and enables users to send and receive data across shared or public networks as if their computing devices were directly connected to the private network. Often used by organisations whose staff work remotely so they can access shared data drives or intranet.

- **Routers** are networking devices that effectively direct the computing traffic between computers on networks. Data sent using the internet (for example a web page or email) is put in the form of a data packet and the packet is sent from one router to another until it reaches the destination that requested it (web page), or the destination it was told to go to (email).

- **Virtual servers** take advantage of improvements in technology. A modern server is now so powerful that having one server for a single function is very inefficient. Servers can now perform multiple functions and can be located offsite and often controlled by a third party. The resources the server provides are often used by multiple users and each user can administer it as though they have complete control over it.

The Cloud

The cloud is a form of remote data storage. The name 'cloud' is given to it as data storage could be at a great distance from the access point e.g. on another continent remote from the PC rather than held on the PC's local storage. It is not actually stored in a cloud.

Although it uses new technology and concepts, this is similar to very early computing when no-one held data locally and it was all held on a large central computer owned and run by the organisation (at that time known as a mainframe).

Cloud based computing can be outsourced to a third party provider (such as Amazon Web Services (AWS), Google Cloud, Alibaba Cloud) or it can be run in-house.

External cloud operations

There are benefits and risks associated with using outsourced cloud storage.

One of the main benefits is cost:

–   only paying for the storage used

–   in-house staff are not required to maintain and protect the data

The costs relate to the risks involved:

–   remoteness can be a problem, if communications break down you cannot gain access to your data

–   reliance on a third party to protect the integrity of the data

–   sharing storage space with others which may compromise your data

In 2014 there was a high profile breach of a major cloud service provider in which private details, calendars, phone call logs and photographs were stolen. This was possible owing to a control issue that allowed the hackers to make unlimited attempts at guessing the users passwords.

Internal cloud operations

In terms of running internal cloud operations, there are benefits and risks of doing this too.

Benefits

–   Increased control over the storage and back up.

–   No third party is involved reducing the likelihood a third party has access to the information.

Risks

- Increased fixed costs to operate and maintain from physical hardware (remember it is not actually in a cloud it is stored in a physical location somewhere) and infrastructure to staff and training

- If internal systems are breached then it increases the likelihood that all data and back-ups could be compromised

- Lack of access to specialist external knowledge.

An internal cloud solution has the potential to be as good as the organisation is willing to invest in it.

As always, the right solution is subjective and each organisation will select the approach that they feel is the most appropriate for their needs and situation.

Many organisations depend on their digital strategies. The threats to these strategies can be complex and are becoming more so as the reliance on information systems increases. As entities look to exploit greater efficiency from technological advances, new and unforeseen threats are created. Smart technology, and devices being linked together to create networks, increases the vulnerabilities, and a system or a network is only as secure as the weakest device in the network.

Increasing and unexpected threats

In December 2018 over 32 million mobile phone users suffered network outages on the O2 network. The network outages meant that data access was not possible using the mobile network. This is an inconvenience for an individual, but most people have access to Wi-Fi networks at home, at work or in a local coffee shop so can work around it.

However, the issue is that businesses now rely on data connectivity and, as a result of this network outage, some companies like Uber, Deliveroo, Transport for London, and many smaller businesses like market traders who rely on data networks to take credit cards payments, were affected.

As countries' physical defences become stronger, and the use of computers increases, the ability to attack or gather intelligence through physical means diminishes. This has led to an increased focus on cyber warfare, where a nation state seeks to penetrate another nation's computers, online control systems and networks to cause damage, disruption or to try and access confidential information. While a nation may be the intended target, the process can also lead to organisations suffering collateral damage. This collateral damage can result in criminals getting access to confidential PII and this is often sold on the **dark web**.

Expandable text: The Dark web

The **dark web** is part of the internet, but a section that allows further anonymity and the ability to obscure the source or location. This increased privacy allows criminals to prosper, for example selling drugs or stolen payment credentials. Some people call this aspect of the dark web the fraud economy.

People often view the internet as having three parts:

The **surface web** (or clear web) – this is the part of the internet that people use every day, that you can find using a search engine.

The **deep web** – this is also used every day, but you have to log in to access it. For example, details of your online bank account are (or should be) inaccessible from a search engine, but you can access them by logging in.

The **dark web** – you need special technology to be able to access this. The Tor browser or Tor network are the more well-known ways to access the dark web. There is increased use of encryption and use of obfuscation tools to protect privacy. Tor is an acronym for The Onion Router, this is a reference to how it works, that like the vegetable there are many layers to the encryption on the network.

The dark web would be the place that a criminal would sell PII that had been stolen from an organisation. There is a huge market for this kind of information, more so than for intellectual property or an organisation's financial projections.

Expandable text: Legitimate uses of the dark web

Not everything that happens on the dark web is fraudulent or criminal activity. Many companies like Facebook and other social media organisations, and also news services like the BBC have a legitimate service run on Tor software. The BBC state their reason for operating on the Tor network as being to allow audiences who live in countries where BBC News is blocked or restricted access to trusted news, this is part of the BBC World Service mission.

The dark web can be used to protect whistle-blowers and give people access to legitimate services that have been restricted through government censorship like social media or news sites.

It is also used by the military, law enforcement organisations as well as journalists and individuals who wish to keep their browsing activity private.

Use of PII

There's a big market for PII. After a cyber-attack, or more specifically after a cyber-breach at an organisation, it is not just the breached organisation that needs to be concerned.

Customers are not specific to one organisation; they are customers for several and various retailers, institutions and organisations. They are also employees somewhere too, potentially at your organisation. These customers/employees all have passwords, in some cases they may only have one password to make their life easier.

If an employee was involved in a cyber-breach, potentially years ago, they may still be using the same password, or a version of that password, for their login to the work network.

If a criminal gets an email address and a password they are likely to try it on a popular site, for example Amazon, Facebook or a bank. As they try these different sites and sometimes get access, a profile starts to build; home address, a business address, their LinkedIn profile, their role at their organisation. The profile builds and it can be sold on to someone else, who makes more connections. In a legitimate business, this would be referred to as value added.

 Cyber warfare

In June 2017 a global cyberattack called Notpetya primarily targeted the Ukraine on the eve of a national Ukrainian holiday. It is estimated that 80% of infections were in the Ukraine, with several banks, metro systems and the Chernobyl Nuclear power plant going offline.

Germany was also badly hit, with around 9% of the infections reported there, including personal care company Beiersdorf and logistics company DHL. Other collateral damage was reported around the world by firms like the American pharmaceutical company Merck, and Danish transportation, logistics and energy provider Maersk.

1.3   Cyber security and the external environment

It is also important to determine what environmental, technological, organisational and other changes have occurred during the period that could have a significant effect on the entity's cyber security risks and therefore the cyber security risk management program.

Types of changes that could affect cyber security risk management

As an organisation goes about its business, there are a variety of changes that could affect the cyber security risks and therefore the management of those risks. These could include, but are not limited to:

- Expansion – for example adding an additional manufacturing operation. This will require an additional connection to the local area network, which in turn leads to an additional area for protection.

- Acquisition – an acquisition or merger is a very challenging time for an organisation, but part of that challenge often links to integrating different software packages, leading to risks such as data loss during the changeover process and potential breaches through additional access points.

- Restructure – if an organisation were to undertake an internal restructure that would impact cyber security. Reporting lines would change, and IT users would require their access to be updated to match their new roles.

- Hardware update – rolling out any kind of update poses a risk as it means people will need to change the way they do things. Also old hardware must be disposed of securely, as data stored on the hard drive could be accessed if it wasn't correctly wiped and should fall into the wrong hands.

- Regulations – Any changes in legal requirements or regulatory frameworks can have an effect on cyber security risk management. For example the introduction of GDPR in the EU has put pressure organisations that operate in the EU, but has also led other government organisations to consider improvements to their data privacy laws and so could have implications for other companies.

Types of changes that could affect cyber security risk management

In late 2019 and early 2020 a new strain of the coronavirus emerged known as Covid 19. It is hard to know for certain what the longer terms implications of Covid 19 will be, but it is safe to say that it has had significant impact on life on a global scale.

One of the results of the pandemic was a significant increase in homeworking across the globe. According to the Office for National Statistics in the UK, only 5% of the UK labour force worked mainly from home in 2019, but by the end of March 2020 everyone in the country was advised to work from home if at all possible.

This created significant opportunities for cyber criminals both through the volume of people attempting to work remotely, but also through preying on people's anxiety over the pandemic, with emails offering cures and financial support if the individual clicked on a malicious link.

Expandable text: Security implications of homeworking

As well as anxieties about the pandemic there are other issues with increased remote working. It is much harder for IT to monitor computer usage.

- There has been an increase in threat actors pretending to work for an organisations IT team and ask users to reset their log-in passwords by clicking on a link in an email. The link may look legitimate but takes the user to a site where the threat actors record their username and passwords, which the threat actor can either use maliciously or sell on the dark web.

- Threat actors can trick employees into downloading malware from hackers and then they can exploit the user or the organisation, depending on the type of malware (see later section on malware).

- Employees have been sent messages in alternate platforms such as WhatsApp that appear to be from a senior figure requesting money transfers to be made.

- Employees may print sensitive information at home, but then not dispose of it appropriately.

- In the home, staff may connect work devices to other devices, or because of poor encryption of other devices on the home network the work laptop may be compromised by being on the same Wi-Fi network (there is more on the IoT later) as the unencrypted device.

- Employees may be more likely to use their personal laptop or computer rather than work device that has been configured by the organisations IT department. There is more on the issues of bring you own devices (BYOD) in the next chapter.

The next chapter will look at some of the controls that can be applied by organisations

Changeover methods

- **Direct changeover** – This is where the old system is switched off and then the new system is switched on. This is appropriate when the two systems are very different, or it is too expensive to run two systems. Although this method is cheap, it is also risky since if the new system doesn't work properly the company might be unable to revert to their old system quickly. (Also, staff trust in the new system would be lost.)

- **Parallel running** – The old and new systems are run together for a period of time, until it is considered safe to switch the old system off. This method will be costly (inputting data twice and possibly employing more staff to do this), however, it will be less risky than direct changeover.

- **Pilot changeover** – This is where one part of the business changes over first. Once the system operates correctly there, the rest of the business will change over. The pilot department or division could be using direct or parallel changeover. Again, this is a safer method of changeover as only one part of the business will be affected if anything goes wrong. However, when the system is rolled out across the rest of the company there may be different problems in each location and the IT team's resources will be stretched.

- **Phased changeover** – This involves bringing in the new system one part of the business at a time, say, by department or division. It differs from pilot changeover in that all departments or divisions are staggered with respect to receiving the new system. The downside is that this method is time-consuming. However, it is less risky as, should there be a problem in any particular department or division, and the IT staff will be able to deal with the problems one at a time.

TSB software migration

TSB Bank Plc is a retail and commercial bank, based in the UK. They operate around 550 branches across England, Scotland and Wales. They were in the news when they migrated from their old banking systems to a new system geared towards more customer friendly digital banking and provide an example of a **change** that could affect cyber security risk management:

In 2015 the Spanish banking group, Sabadell, acquired TSB from Lloyds Banking Group and wanted to integrate TSB into the same core banking system used by the rest of Sabadell.

The reasons for the change were compelling for Sabadell, providing not just alignment with rest of the group, but also the chance to offer new fintech services that the TSB legacy system couldn't offer, allowing them to compete in new markets for TSB.

Changeover method

TSB chose to move customers across using a pilot approach. They moved some services first, including a new mobile banking app, and planned to move everything else across in the final quarter of 2017. The final stage was delayed, according to TSB to allow for an expected interest rate rise, but as can be the case with a pilot change over, when they did eventually undertake the final stage they had many problems as discussed further below

1.4 Cyber security objectives

The management of the organisation must establish cyber security objectives. As with all good forms of risk management, it is risk based, so the cyber security objectives will link to the cyber security risks that may impact the achievement of the organisations ultimate business objectives.

The Association of International Certified Professional Accountants (AICPA) has identified a reporting framework for cyber security and this outlines some of the key cyber security objectives. They include:

- **Availability**: One of the reasons that the use of websites and applications is so attractive to organisations and individuals is the flexibility of continuous access to, and use of, information and systems. Organisations can make sales 24 hours a day, and customers are not limited to bricks and mortar store opening hours.

- **Confidentiality**: organisations create and obtain a huge amount of information, from proprietary information to personal information, and it must be protected from unauthorised access and disclosure, including complying with privacy requirements.

- **Integrity of data**: organisations must make sure they take steps to prevent unauthorised modification of or destruction of information.

- **Integrity of processing**: Guarding against the improper use, modification, or destruction of systems.

Objectives – online retailer

- **Availability** – an online retail store would need to provide 24 hours a day, 365 days per year access to their website for their customers.

- **Confidentiality** – an online retailer will know many things about each customer, from PII such as name, address, payment details to the things they like, when they shop, how much they spend etc.

- **Integrity of data** – an online retailer must make sure financial information for both internal and external purposes is reliable, and also that customer information is correct and up to date.

- **Integrity of processing** – making sure goods sold are as described on their website and the service matches the description they provide, for example delivery within 2 working days.

TSB software migration – objectives

Continuing the TSB system migration, we can now look at what aspects of their cyber security were affected.

- **Availability** – TSB customers, previously used to 24 hour access to their accounts had been warned of slight disruption but were in fact unable to access their accounts for a five day period.

- **Integrity of data** – as the issue was well publicised, it became an opportunity for unauthorised access. It is reported that fraudulent attacks increased 70 times, with around 1,300 customers defrauded as a result of the failed IT upgrade.

- **Confidentiality** – some customer's personally identifiable information was compromised as many customer reported being able to access other customers' accounts and data.

 RBS – availability issues

In 2012 an outage occurred for RBS, Natwest and Ulster Bank. Customers could not access their funds for a week or more and the banks had to manually update account balances.

RBS received a fine £56m from regulators because of the outage. CA Technologies, who were the software suppliers that caused the outage, paid the bank millions of pounds.

Although the public rarely get to know the true cause of the problems, reports suggest the issue was caused by someone in an RBS operation in India pressing the wrong button.

As well as understanding their cyber security objectives, consideration must be given to how these objectives are established, approved and maintained.

A typical process could be that on a regular basis, the board review overall objectives and approve them as appropriate. These then flow down into the business objectives where the most senior member of the IT team will align the cyber security objectives with them. This would then be approved at board level. This may include stating any industry standards the company complies with – for example PCI DSS (Payment Card Industry Data Security Standards).

 PCI DSS

PCI DSS was brought in to ensure businesses process card payments are secure, protect sensitive cardholder data and help to reduce card fraud. It sets tight controls over the storage, transmission and processing of the cardholder data that businesses handle.

Test your understanding 1

Which of the following are true of cyber risks?

Select ALL that apply.

A   It is a type of operational risk.

B   It could be a deliberate and unauthorised breach of security to gain access to information systems to embarrass, extort or spy on a firm.

C   It could manifest itself through IT issues from poor systems integrity or other factors.

D   It is a strategic risk.

E   The likelihood and impact are reducing all the time.

F   Anti-virus software will stop all cyber risks.

Test your understanding 2

The most risky changeover method is:

A   Phased changeover

B   Pilot changeover

C   Parallel changeover

D   Direct changeover

Test your understanding 3

Ashveer Holloway is a loyal customer of Proud Ltd, a pharmaceutical company. Ashveer was born on 28th January 1990. He buys a specialised medication from Proud, which cannot be sold without prior approval from a doctor because it has an age limit on it due to the strength of the medication. Ashveer needs it to treat a very rare medical condition that he has. He pays for the medication using direct debit and it is delivered to his house on the 1st of each month.

Which of the following pieces of PII do Proud Ltd necessarily hold about Ashveer?

Select ALL that apply.

A   Name.

B   Credit card details.

C   Date of birth.

D   Information about religious beliefs.

E   Personal health information.

F   Proud Ltd customer account number.

G   Address.

Test your understanding 4

An accountancy training company have developed an online system to support their students in their studies. Through this system students can access all of their printed materials, plus additional questions and videos. The company's students all study at different times of the day as they have students all over the world, and the exams they are studying for are have flexible dates, so can be taken all year round.

As the volume of data stored on the system has increased, the training company has noticed that the speed of processing has started to decline. Customer feedback had given them some new ideas about how to set up the online material but this set up idea is not supported by the current system. As a result of these developments, the company has decided to change its systems, to improve both layout and response time. As the online system is so valuable to their customers they have decided to do a phased changeover – to make sure that students can access the system during the changeover process.

Which one of the cyber security objectives are the training provider concerned about by adopting the phased changeover?

A   Integrity of data

B   Integrity of processing

C   Confidentiality

D   Availability

Test your understanding 5

A newspaper article has described a form of technology in the following paragraph:

"This allows the user to extend a company network across a public network, and enables users to send and receive data across shared or public networks as if their computing devices were directly connected to the private network. It is usually secured and requires two step authentication by the user through a password and randomly generated passcodes."

Which one of the characteristics of technology is being described?

A   Type

B   Connection type

C   Service providers

D   Delivery channels

E   Confidentiality

Test your understanding 6

GH are a US based company that specialise in online grocery sales for delivery to customers' homes. They have been very successful and decided to expand geographically. In the last year they have successfully acquired a European grocer who has previously only provided sales from outlets in areas with high population densities in three major European countries. As part of the acquisition, GH are in the process of setting up new systems within the European grocer with a view to launching online sales for delivery in one of the European countries, and increasing this further next year.

Which of the following aspects of the company's environment have experienced changes that could affect the cyber security risk management of GH?

Select ALL that apply.

A   Regulation

B   Expansion

C   Acquisition

D   Culture

E   Hardware update

F   Internal restructure

G   Personally Identifiable Information.

Test your understanding 7

X is a multi-site retail organisation, formed by the recent merger of four independent retailers. You were previously Management Accountant of one of the retail companies, and have recently been appointed Systems Accountant for the merged organisation.

Each of the merged companies currently uses a different information system for the recording and processing of inventory. X is planning to replace these systems with one new system that will be common to every site. You have been talking to the Finance Director about the need to standardise systems, and he has expressed concern regarding the disruption that will be caused by the changeover.

Advise the Finance Director which of the following system changeover methods can be used.

Select ALL that apply

A   Direct

B   Parallel

C   Pilot

D   Phased

2 Types of cyber security risks

2.1 Malware

Malware is the term used for malicious software, regardless of the intended purpose. It can do any number of things, ranging from the stealing of credentials, other information or money to the general wreaking of havoc, or denial of service. There are various way to execute malware, they include:

- **Ransomware** is designed to prevent a business from accessing its data, information or a whole computer system until a specified amount of money is paid.

- **Botnets** are networks of private computers that are infected with a malware and controlled by a "botnet agent" designed to follow the attacker's instructions without the knowledge of the owner of the computer. They are often associated with a DDoS (see 2.2).

- **Trojans** are named after the Trojan horse in an ancient Greek story where a wooden horse was allowed into the city as it was deemed harmless but which concealed soldiers inside ready to attack the city. This type of malware does a very similar thing: it pretends to be a useful piece of software whilst secretly releasing malware into the system, usually with the capability to be controlled by the attacker from a different location, (known as a remote access Trojan or RAT). Once on the system it can then prevent access to the system (ransomware), infect the system damaging and destroying files or act as spyware (see later).

 Banking Trojans

A **banking Trojan** operates in the same way as a Trojan, but was originally targeted specifically at the banking industry. Banks have always been seen as establishments worth attacking throughout history and so have needed to have good security and controls. As online banking came in the same was true, but criminals realised that stealing customer credentials was a more feasible approach to attacking a bank than trying to penetrate their security controls, both virtual and physical.

> As a result of this the first banking Trojans were created. Since then, the scope, technical ability, and focus of the malware authors has changed and evolved to target a range of industries, such as online advertisers, digital analytics firms, social media sites, and communication platforms.

- **Malvertising** is when online advertisements have malware written into their code. It can involve hiding the malicious code in legitimate online advertising networks and web pages. The code may direct the victim to a malicious site where the malware can be installed or it may directly infect the victim's computer when they visit the page that contains the advert, even if the user does not click on anything to do with the online advert. Malvertising is a serious threat that requires little or no user interaction.

- **Viruses** are designed to endlessly replicate themselves and infect programs and files to damage or destroy data. **Worm viruses** spread across networks to infect other devices.

- **Spyware** is designed to spy on the victim's systems without being detected and gather information to send to the hacker. **Keyloggers** are similar – every keystroke typed by the victim is recorded and forwarded to the hacker. This type of malware can result in threat actors recording usernames and passwords which can be used to either gain unauthorised access to a network or sold on the dark web for another threat actor to use illegally.

Advanced malware

There are different types of malware for different types of industries, where the malware will be designed to attack systems or customers of that industry in a particular way, for example the banking Trojans described earlier were originally designed to target the banking industry.

Most malware requires human intervention to infect devices.

The alternative is that there to be an issue in the software being used. The issue may be either unknown to the software developer or it may be that the developer has knowingly left the issue unaddressed. An issue like this is often referred to as a **zero day** exploit.

Polymorphic malware is a type of malware that avoids being identified by systems and networks by constantly changing its identifiable features. It can use any of the above ways to execute malware (spyware, Trojans, viruses) but it's harder for the target to identify. This is becoming more common as attack instigators look to keep malicious software on devices longer to steal more data that will be used in future attacks.

Example: Ransomware

In 2017 ransomware became big news as several outbreaks hit a variety of organisations throughout the year.

- Wannacry shutdown more 80 NHS organisations in England, leading to around 20,000 cancelled appointments, GP surgeries having to return to pen a paper and some hospitals diverting ambulances as they were unable to take anymore emergencies.

- NotPetya later in the year spread through a version of an accounting program that was used in Ukraine. It affected multinational companies such as shipping firm Maersk and pharmaceutical company Merck. NotPetya reportedly cost Merck more than $300 million per quarter in Q3 & Q4 of 2017.

All these attacks stemmed from a weakness in Microsoft's Windows operating system that could run programs on other computers on the same network. It is believed that knowledge of this flaw was originally used by the NSA, who gave it a codename EternalBlue.

Incidents like these have raised the profile of cyber security threats and made more organisations aware of the damage that can be done.

2.2 Application attacks

As with malware, application attacks is the broad term for a variety of different ways of attacking a victim, this time by attacking an application (app). This kind of approach is becoming more common as application development is increasingly based on the web. Whether it is the applications on our smart phones and various connected devices at home or a complex business application, we are using applications more and more and this leads to potential vulnerabilities.

The intention with application attacks is usually the same as with malware attacks – stealing data from database servers, running attack scripts on other users' computers, stealing user credentials, etc.

Below are some of the more common types of application attacks:

- A **denial-of-service (DoS) attack** overwhelms a system's resources so that it cannot respond to service requests. A **Distributed-denial-of-service (DDoS) attack** is also an attack on system's resources, but it is launched from a large number of other host machines that have already been infected by malicious software controlled by the attacker.

Example: Facebook

When a major firm has system downtime (as Facebook did in March 2019 where Facebook, Instagram and Whatsapp were all offline simultaneously for almost 24 hours), the truth about why it happens can take a long time to come out.

The company stated that it had made some changes to server configuration that triggered a series of issues. Many commentators are unconvinced by the explanation and believe that Facebook was flooded with traffic and ultimately overwhelmed by a DDoS attack.

Facebook could be unlikely to admit to an attack of this nature as it would indicate that they are susceptible to such an attack and others may try to exploit this weakness.

- **SQL** (Structured Query Language) **injection** has become a common issue with database-driven websites. It occurs when the attacker uses an unprotected input box on the company's website to execute a SQL query to the database via the input data from the client to server. A successful SQL injection can read sensitive data from the company's database, modify (insert, update or delete) database data, execute administration operations (such as shutdown) on the database, recover the content of a given file, and, in some cases, issue commands to the operating system.

 SQL Query

An SQL query is a request for something to be done on a database.

For example, when logging in to a website you input your username and password. When you press 'enter' the website queries your inputs against the database of usernames and passwords to check for a match. If the query finds a match in the database the user is allowed access, if no match is found then access to that area of the website is not allowed.

- **Cross-site scripting attacks (XSS attacks)** occur when a victim is attacked when they visit another organisation's website. The attacker uses the third-party web resources to run scripts in the victim's web browser or scriptable application. Specifically, the attacker injects malicious code (often associated with JavaScript) into a website's database. When the victim requests a page from the website, the website transmits the page, with the attacker's code as part of the HTML body, to the victim's browser, which executes the malicious script. For example, it might send the victim's cookie to the attacker's server, and the attacker can extract it and use it for session hijacking.

- **Buffer overflow attack** – A buffer overflow occurs when a system cannot store as much information as it has been sent and consequently starts to overwrite existing content. A buffer overflow attack occurs when an attacker sends a malicious programme which deliberately overloads the system and starts to overwrite existing data.

2.3 Hackers

Hacking is the gaining of unauthorised access to a computer system. It might be a deliberate attempt to gain access to an organisation's systems and files to obtain information or to alter data (perhaps fraudulently).

Once hackers have gained access to the system, there are several damaging options available to them. For example, they may:

- gain access to the file that holds all the user ID codes, passwords and authorisations

- discover the method used for generating/authorising passwords

- interfere with the access control system, to provide the hacker with open access to the system

- obtain information which is of potential use to a competitor organisation

- obtain, enter or alter data for a fraudulent purpose

- cause data corruption by the introduction of unauthorised computer programs and processing on to the system (computer viruses)

- alter or delete files

Hackers could be thieves operating from outside the organisation such as business competitors or nation-states. They can also be insiders, such as disgruntled, or otherwise malicious, employees.

Example: Target Corporation

One of the largest department store retailers, Target Corporation, suffered a major security breach in late 2013.

Hackers used credentials they stole from a third party – one of Target's suppliers. The third party supplied heating, ventilation and air conditioning services to Target and, as such, had access to the Target network to monitor energy consumption and temperatures at various stores.

Once into the network, the hacker uploaded malware into the Point of Sale systems. The hackers reportedly used the malware to steal data from around 40 million credit and debit cards in the US in a two to three week period.

This example is explored further later in this chapter and the next chapter.

"Hackers" is a broad term, but there are actually different types of hackers, defined according to their reason for hacking. Regardless of their reason they all require a certain level of skill.

- **Unethical hackers:** these are the stereotypical hackers that hack with malicious intent. They typically break in to secure systems and networks to steal data, destroy it or perhaps just modify it. Critically, it is all done without the company's permission.

- **Ethical hackers** usually hack with the company's permission. They are trying to help the company understand what an unethical hacker may try to do so it can protect the computer network. Some people describe the ethical hacker as a security expert.

There is a third type, that sit in the middle, they are not specifically malicious or well-intentioned, but sell their skills for monetary gain.

Hackers

One of the key elements of a hacker is that they are skilled in some way, whether that is technical skills able to breach security networks, or skilled in **social engineering** (see below) and the ability to deceive people into taking actions that put cyber security at risk.

Another term is often used in cyber security is actor or **threat actor**. A threat actor is a term for an individual or group that, either intentionally or unintentionally, conducts malicious activities against an organisation. Critically, it can include negligence or mistakes by a person or a group of people who do not have malicious intent.

Weaponised documents

A tool often used by a hacker is social engineering, to enable the use of or activation of a **weaponised document**.

A weaponised document is a document that is downloaded from a source (email, website or shared drive) that contains some code, a link or even a video that once activated releases malware onto a system or network.

Social engineering

Social engineering is the manipulation of people to make them perform specific actions or reveal confidential information. The principle relies heavily on the ability to influence people to do something that they wouldn't normally do, or in a lot of cases should not be doing.

Dr Robert Cialdini has studied this area and has identified six principles used to persuade or influence someone. These are:

- **Reciprocity** – this is the idea that people often feel obliged to do something in return for a favour or a gift they have received.

- **Consistency and commitment** – it is human nature to like rhythms or routines – people like to behave as expected, and like people who behave as expected. We may also be influenced to through with our support for something if we had shown an initial interest in it.

- **Consensus** – people like to follow the behavioural norms of others. This is sometimes referred to as social proof.

- **Liking** – people sharing some common traits are more inclined to like each other. People are more likely to do something for someone they like.

- **Authority** – if someone is deemed to be an expert they carry more power.

- **Scarcity** – something that is in short supply is perceived to be more valuable.

In the context of cyber security, social engineering relies on these principles to carry out techniques known as phishing or spear phishing to gain access to a system or network.

- **Phishing** refers to the use of fraudulent messages to try to steal sensitive information such as passwords or credit card numbers, or to install malware onto a user's computer. Phishers often use a combination of communication tools to deceive their victims.

  Examples include: SMS text message – smishing

  Email impersonation

  Telephone calls – voice phishing or vishing

  Fake websites

- **Spear phishing** is when a phishing attempt targets a specific user, rather than a blanket communication sent to many people. Spear phishing usually involves carrying out research into the specific person and their role and interests. This allows the attacker to modify the communication to be more appealing or relevant to the victim, increasing the likelihood of its success.

 Types of phishing attacks

Business Email Compromise (BEC) is a way to phish or spear phish. It is also known as impostor email and CEO fraud. BEC attacks involve impersonating an identity, for example a CEO, CFO or HR director and asking for a particular action to happen or for a piece of information to be sent through.

Domain fraud is sometimes called out bound phishing and is a type of phishing where the threat actors make an email appear to be from a legitimate source, but is actually from a malicious actor. A fraudulent domain name is another example of something that may be purchased on the dark web.

Domain fraud

Domain fraud occurs by using a trusted brand name or service in an email address. For example a widely used service such as PayPal or Amazon may feature in the email address and the branding may be used in the message but it may not actually be from the organisation.

Paypal@service.com or amazonprime@registration.com would look legitimate, but more commonly the organisation (and its domain) would appear after the @ in an email address.

Sometimes it may be customerservice@trustedbrandname*support*.com and by adding an extra word, in this case 'support', to the brand name the threat actor is able to register a new domain that appears to be from a trusted source. In some cases the letter I may be substituted for the number 1 and the attacker relies on the target being lazy or in a rush. Sometimes the urgency is created in the attack by implying a quick response is important to receive the offer, this links to the social engineering principle of scarcity.

Business Email Compromise (BEC)

This is where an email is sent to look like it is from an important individual from within an organisation and asks the receiver to carry out a task like a fraudulent bank transfer, or to supply company data or customer PII.

It is sometimes referred to as imposter email or CEO fraud.

They are difficult for email security to pick up, partly because they are sent in low volumes, but often there is no attachment to scan or URL to check.

They rely on the social engineering principle of authority.

The most common approaches are:

- **Spoofing email fields** – this can be done by changing the reply-to email address to make it look like the email is coming from within the organisation, or adjusting the display name (this is particularly effective on mobile devices that do not display the reply to email address, using domain fraud by making the email appear to be from within the organisation but changing a character, for example a zero could replace the letter 'o'.

- **Using scarcity** – by putting a word like 'urgent' into the subject line, combined with the perceived authority as the email looks like it is from a superior in the organisation can increase the likelihood.

- **Variety** – when the technique first started it was primarily focussed on the CEO and CFO relationship, but now BEC will target more identities.

Individuals working within an organisation are often cited as being one of the biggest cyber security risks. Research has found that employees often feel that they are not part of the information security defence systems. This can lead to individuals taking actions or making choices that compromise the organisation. This is particularly risky when spear phishing is used, as it deliberately focusses on an interest and therefore a weakness in that individual's decision making.

 Example: Social engineering

In 2013 Yahoo were compromised when hackers used social engineering to manipulate an engineer who had special access to the system. The engineer was duped by a spear phishing email and the hackers gained access to every single customer account, more than 3 billion accounts. The data was made available to buy on the dark web.

Yahoo initially said that around 500 million accounts had been compromised; it wasn't until October 2017 that the full extent of the breach was revealed.

Another huge cyber security issue for an organisation to consider too, is reputational damage (as discussed in Chapter 4). Situations like this can cause massive reputational damage as consumers lose trust in the organisation, as well as leading to significant fines.

Social engineering can use many themes to attract attention, the following are some of the more popular themes:

- Food
- Shelter
- Love
- Money

There is understandably some overlap here with the motivation theory and Maslow's hierarchy of needs. By focussing on basic human desires like food and shelter, moving through to social needs like companionship and love the social engineering attack is increasing its chances of success.

 Opportunities for cyber-crime

Earlier in the chapter the new strain of the coronavirus known as Covid 19 was highlighted as a cause of increasing opportunities for cyber-crime. This is because the outbreak has had an impact on where people are in the pyramid of Maslow's hierarchy of needs. The uncertainty over health and wealth means that an email offering a cure or financial support is more appealing now than an equivalent email would have been offering those things before the outbreak occurred.

The governor of New York touched on it in one of his daily addresses during the outbreak, making a statement saying "There is going to be an impact on the economy, not just here in New York but all across the country, and we're going to have to deal with that crisis, but let's deal with one crisis at a time. Let's deal with the crisis at hand and the crisis at hand is a public health crisis."

He is acknowledging that the financial impact of the pandemic is expected to be significant, but the first priority to deal with is to resolve the health crisis.

BEC opportunities

The 2019/2020 Covid 19 pandemic is a prime opportunity for BEC. A scammer could impersonate a superior at an organisation and send an email like this:

"Subject: Urgent

Hi,

We just got placed on lockdown after an outbreak in our area. I don't have access to my desktop so I need you to help me urgently. A payment is overdue to Company Z, please could you wire money to these account details to ensure continuity of supply."

Another common attempt during the pandemic saw threat actors pose as the organisations HR department and then attach a document to the email titled "Work From Home Policy" that had malicious code embedded within it, and the malicious code would be initiated by the recipient clicking on the document.

Social engineering themes

One of the most popular themes in the USA is to include reference to Form W-2 in the subject line. This is the Internal Revenue Service tax form used to report wages paid to employees and the taxes withheld from them.

Social engineering considerations

As well as the social engineering themes and principles mentioned, the instigators of these attacks use other tools to help increase the likelihood of success.

One consideration is the day of the week. Research indicates that there is an increased volume of attacks earlier in the week, with over 50% on a Monday and a Tuesday. The view is that attacks are more likely to be successful when the target is feeling under pressure or in a rush to clear a backlog of work.

Social engineering targets

People are unique, and all operate in subtly different ways, have different habits, different weaknesses and different strengths. This is true in life in general but also in our digital or cyber actions. As such, different people are more or less susceptible to social engineering and provide a different reward for the architect of the social engineering trap.

 Attack targets: people

A CEO may be perceived to be a primary target because of their high profile, importance in decision making and likely access to any data or information they require. As a result a CEO would be considered to yield a potentially significant reward for a social engineering attack.

To counter their appeal, a CEO may have additional security, including training and therefore become less likely to be fooled by an attack, thus making them less attractive to the social engineering instigator.

Employees at this level of an organisation are rarely easily accessible, with relatively few executive email address available on line.

In contrast to this, functions like human resources and customer services are much more easily available online so people can submit job applications (HR) and seek assistance (CS). Because of this increased availability of access and these functions also having access to employ or customer data, they are more attractive targets for attacks.

 Attack targets: further people considerations

The above examples highlight a particular job role and consider the likelihood of attack. The job role is important, but as this chapter has illustrated already, it is not just the role, but the people; the individuals that fill the roles within an organisation that also influence the appeal to attackers.

Here are some considerations for who might be the most susceptible people to attack in an organisation:

- **Use of social media**: not necessarily the amount an individual uses it, but what they reveal on the platform. The more an assailant knows about the victim the more effective their attack can be.

- **Likelihood of clicking**: different personality types are inherently more likely to click on certain things, or just more curious and therefore more likely to click on any link they are sent.

- **Access to customer data**: an individual in a role that has privileged access to customer data would be an attractive target for an attacker. PII is a very valuable commodity on the dark web.

- **Access to confidential business data**: as with customer data, access to confidential information about the organisation or its activities could be a valuable commodity on the dark web.

- **Access to c-suite employees** (c-suite is a term used to describe executive level managers within an organisation): an assistant to an executive director could have access to important information whether it is the executive directors email or calendar, sometimes just a connection is all the threat actor needs.

- **Location**: an individual who often logs in from less secure network connections, like an airport or a café rather than the office or at home, could be more easily attacked.

- **Type of device used**: it is often easier to commit domain fraud or BEC if the target is using a mobile device and cannot see the full email address.

- **Routine**: a routine that is identifiable by a hacker can create an opportunity for attack, either through an offer to make the routine easier or cheaper or by impersonating a person or organisation that is involved in that routine.

 Attack targets: organisations

There is no correlation between the size of organisation and the number of attacks. Larger organisations may appear more appealing because of the perceived extra value and potentially the prestige at being able to breach their security, Facebook for example would give the successful threat actor a lot of credibility, but it would pose a more significant challenge. The defences are likely to be very well prepared and staff very well trained.

A lesser known SME, with a smaller potential payoff, but weaker security in place would therefore provide the opportunity for a threat actor to keep a steady income stream while they work towards a big target.

2.4 Cryptocurrency

The cyber security threats discussed above are made more significant by the development of cryptocurrencies like bitcoin, which make it possible for the perpetrators of ransomware to send and receive money anonymously.

There is more detail on cryptocurrency in chapter 9.

2.5 The internet of things (IoT)

The internet of things is a network of devices, most commonly associated with devices around the home, where machines such as vehicles and home appliances contain software and sensors and communicate with one another either through the Wi-Fi or via Bluetooth.

This allows simple tasks to be controlled and monitored from a remote location, for example; turning the heating on as you are going home.

The internet of things can be applied to various forms of business too: the internet of medical things (IoMT) or the healthcare IoT, the industrial IoT etc. In the business environment remote monitoring and control facilitates greater levels of automation or central control often provides an opportunity for efficiency savings.

IoT for business

The Internet of Things creates vulnerabilities for both individuals and businesses because smart devices are not always sufficiently secure because of poor or no encryption. In these cases threat actors can interrogate the weak link wirelessly to reveal access codes.

A factory's heating system could be controlled by wireless sensors linked to the main server and a threat actor parked outside could pick up the signals. Alternatively, small drones can be used to extend the threat actors reach.

Threat actors might try social engineering to gain access to the network by ringing staff and asking for passwords, or make practical attempts such as trying doors that should be locked, checking desks for passwords that have been written down and left visible etc.

A business must decide whether the convenience that the IoT provides is worth the additional vulnerabilities and therefore security measures that would be required.

Example: Smart breakfast

Fiction has for a long time used the concept of being able to automate repetitive parts of life, for example the semi-automated breakfast in the film "Wallace and Gromit: the wrong trousers". The concept of pressing a button to boil the kettle and start the toaster while you are still in bed is now much more realistic, but the process turns mundane devices into potential security vulnerabilities.

These devices that are interconnected create a network in your home, each device connected to the network create an additional end point of the network and each end point is also an access point for the network.

If the kettle or toaster do not have adequate security features they could allow a threat actor to access the network, to install some malware.

Example: Smart doorbells

The increase in the use of smart doorbells is causing major concern as many of the highest selling versions have very poor security records.

An independent consumer watchdog in the UK called Which has been testing some of the leading devices and found various flaws recurring in many devices such as:

- Weak password policies

- Lack of data encryption

Some of the devices could even be manipulated to steal network passwords and enable a threat actor to hack other smart devices within the residence. One of the smart doorbells tested was even found to send users' home network names and passwords unencrypted to servers in a different country.

This is obviously a concern for home occupiers using these devices, but it also highlights the wider problem that smart device users must be aware of, both personally but also from a business perspective. Saving money by buying a cheaper device can create a weakness on your network and put you or, if this is a business purchase, the organisation at risk.

Whilst many devices are safe because they do encrypt access details, in a business context, many of the risks associated with the IoT can be overcome by running a network cable to replace wireless connections.

At home it may be worth foregoing the convenience of being able to control the lights through your mobile phone and the Wi-Fi network to reduce the risk of a cyber-breach.

Test your understanding 8

The Senior Finance Manager at Hackers Ltd received an email that appeared to be from the Hackers' bank. The email asked for the manager to confirm some security information by clicking on a link and answering several questions. At the end of the week, one of the manager's direct reports flagged some unusual transactions whilst carrying out routine bank reconciliations. There were several large payments to unknown sources.

Which of the following cyber-attacks does it appear that Hackers Ltd were a victim of?

A   Distributed denial of service

B   Botnets

C   Phishing

D   SQL injection

Test your understanding 9

FGY company has been subject to a Ransomware attack.

Which one of the following cyber-threats has FGY become exposed to?

A   Personal and Business Information held on the system has been stolen

B   The company computer system has been shut down until a payment is made to release it

C   The FGY website has been overloaded as a result of multiple simultaneous requests for service being sent from a number of different IP addresses

D   Malware has infected the adverts appearing alongside the company web pages

Test your understanding 10

LPU company has recently been the victim of a cyber-attack.

A member of the company's procurement team logged onto a trusted supplier website using a pre-set user name and password. Unfortunately the cyber-attacker had previously injected the supplier's website with malicious code and was able to access this log-on information as it was entered.

The attacker then used this information to log-on to the supplier site, pretending to be LPU, and was able to gain access to LPU's sensitive business information.

The above cyber-attack is an example of which form of web application attack?

A   Distributed denial of service (DDoS) attack

B   Structured Query Language (SQL) injection attack

C   Cross-site scripting (XSS) attack

D   Buffer overflow attack

Test your understanding 11

One of WRY company's competitors has recently been subjected to a structured query language (SQL) attack.

The board of WRY is keen to ensure their website is not also vulnerable to such an attack.

Which ONE of the following could be employed by the board to help test the robustness of their systems?

A   Internet troll

B   Unethical hacker

C   Ethical hacker

D   Botnet

3   Social media

3.1   What is social media?

Social media is a catch-all term for a range of sites that may provide radically different social interactions.

Illustration 1 – Examples of social media sites

- Twitter is designed to let people share short updates or 'tweets' with others.

- Facebook, in contrast is a complete social networking site that allows for sharing updates, photos, joining events and a variety of other activities.

- LinkedIn is a professional business-related networking site

- Instagram is a free photo-sharing program.

Opportunities offered by social media

Social media offers a number of opportunities. These include:

- **Advertising** – for example, Starbucks is tweeting to customers and you can join their Facebook site to find out about its news and promotions.

- **Brand development** – for example, Volkswagen uses Flickr to develop its brand. Individuals are able to post pictures of their Volkswagen Beetle or their campervan on the site.

- **Big Data analytics** – by monitoring when a brand is mentioned, by who and in what context, marketers are now able to target advertising through social media better than ever before.

- **Method of listening to customers** – sites where customers and potential customers discuss the products of the company, and of its competitors, can be an opportunity to deal with compliments, complaints or support queries openly and honestly, e.g. customer ratings or feedback on Amazon.com or Tripadvisor.co.uk.

- **Real-time information gathering** – in the past it would take days or weeks for businesses to conduct a survey to gather enough responses to generate conclusive data. Now on social media, businesses can gather instant feedback with quick polls.

- **Communication** – for example, Deloitte Australia have held employee performance reviews in World of Warcraft and BDO uses Second Life as an avenue for meetings, presentations and events for staff and for clients.

- **Recruitment and selection** – firms seeking to recruit staff can ensure a wide range of potential candidates see their advert by using social networking sites such as Facebook and Twitter. Organisations can avoid costly recruitment fees and are more likely to find candidates already engaged with their brand.

- **Selection** – many firms are screening candidates by researching their web presence, for example on LinkedIn or Facebook to see what interesting facts, photos and opinions can be found that might be relevant to their future careers.

3.2 Risks of social media to organisations

As always, with opportunity there also risks. Some of the risks presented by social media include:

- **Human error** – a mistake by an employee could range from being hacked after clicking on fraudulent links on their work computer, to making inappropriate comments on social media (either through their personal account, or if they have access to it, via the company account).

- **Productivity** – while there are clearly positives to be gained from social media, if employees can access social media at work it can disrupt their work and reduce the operational efficiency of the company.

- **Data protection** – regulatory requirements are increasing around how companies gather, use and store data about their customers. Firms need to make sure they have secure networks and they comply with all legislation.

- **Hacking** – as with any computer program, a hacker may try to infiltrate social media accounts for malicious reasons, or use social media accounts to harvest data to assist with a social engineering attack, like phishing or a Business Email Compromise attack.

- **Reputation** – any mistakes a company makes on social media, (such as an inappropriate post made by a staff member) could have a negative impact on the brand of the organisation and result in lost customers, sales or even employees.

- **Inactivity** – as maintaining an online presence becomes increasingly important, not using social media or not keeping existing accounts up to date, could be as damaging as using it badly.

- **Costs** – in theory using social media costs nothing, but to use it well, and control the accompanying risks, could cost a significant amount. Also, any fines from non-compliance with regulations could also be significant.

Illustration 2 – Examples of social media problems

- A well-meaning employee at Adidas sent a tweet from the company account congratulating runners for "surviving the Boston Marathon"; unfortunately this brought back images of the 2013 bombing for many social media uses. Adidas very quickly took down the tweet and issued an apology.

- In March 2017, McDonald's posted a surprisingly critical tweet of President Trump: It turned out that the tweeter wasn't McDonald's – in fact someone had hacked into their account to send the tweet. McDonalds quickly removed the offending tweet, but it further illustrates that even multinational organisations are susceptible to hacking in various forms.

- Sometimes the company may do nothing, but a comment from someone else, a celebrity, for example, can lead to issues. A tweet from Kylie Jenner reduced the market value of Snap Inc (the parent company of Snapchat) by $1.3billion, when she posted on a different form of social media that she no longer used the Snapchat application.

3.3 Risks of social media to individuals

The risks of social media are not just to organisations. Poor use of social media can create risks for individuals too:

- **Going viral** – people often make social media posts in a very informal way, without considering who may see it or how it may be perceived. This can lead to a previously little-known person becoming well-known very quickly around the world. The reasons for this fame can be both good (taking a strong stance for a good cause) and bad, for example an ill thought out joke can lead to thousands of abusive responses. People have been known to disable their accounts after receiving such abuse.

- **Internet trolling** – the abusive responses mentioned above are often referred to as trolling. Trolling is where someone uses social media to deliberately upset or incite emotional responses from another individual.

- **Employment** – companies now include social media reviews as part of their recruitment process. People have also lost their jobs as a result of going viral in a negative way.

- **Legal sanction** – law enforcement organisations can view social media posts to help identify where suspects were, or in some cases what they were doing, at a particular time.

- **Physical theft** – posting from a holiday resort overseas, or just posting from a significant distance from home, can signal to thieves that a property is unoccupied and is likely to remain so for several hours or days.

- **Identity fraud** – fraudsters can build up a significant portfolio of information from a social media account with poor privacy settings, such as home address, date of birth, interests etc.

- **Permanence** – once a social media post has been made it is very difficult to remove. Even if you delete it someone else may have already taken a screenshot of your post. This can lead difficulties in the future (going viral, employment issues) even if the person making the post has changed their views or admitted to their mistake.

Test your understanding 12

Squeeks is an app development company based in Donlon, the capital city of a large EU member country. The company first set up in 2007 and due to their innovative approach to application design, customer focus and positive culture, managed to survive a very tough economic environment in the first few years.

They feel that a positive team spirit is vital to their success, and as they have grown, invested heavily in staff entertainment, such as pool tables, massage chairs, games consoles and a free continental breakfast bar. They also feel that it is important for staff to be able to express themselves and so have consciously avoided any kind of social media policy.

What are the consequences that Squeeks faces as a result of its policy on social media?

Select ALL that apply.

A   Employees will raise the profile of Squeeks by putting messages out about their work.

B   Squeeks will be able to monitor the profile of their brand and analyse who is saying what and use this to target advertising

C   An employee may click on a fraudulent link that appears on their social media feed and compromise the Squeeks systems.

D   Theft from a staff member's home because they have been posting about their holiday.

E   An employee making inappropriate comments and damaging Squeaks' reputation.

F   Staff may spend too long on social media and not meet critical deadlines.

G   The company can review the social media activity of potential new recruits to get a better understanding of whether they would fit in with the culture at Squeeks.

4   Risk of security vulnerabilities

Being aware of the vulnerabilities that could create problems for an organisation is one thing, but being aware of the implications of the vulnerabilities is also vital.

Vulnerabilities can be classified as either technical, procedural or physical:

- **Technical deficiencies** include issues like defects in the software being used, or not using appropriate protection (such as encryption) correctly.

- **Procedural deficiencies** are either IT related (for example system configuration mistakes or not keeping software security patches up to date) or user related (for example not complying with company guidelines on changing passwords or using passwords that are too simple).

- **Physical** where a physical event, like a fire or flood, causes damage to the information technology system.

Whatever the reason for the vulnerability, its exploitation can lead to costly problems for the organisation involved.

Procedural deficiencies: the people factor

In surveys by various sources most breaches occur because of human vulnerabilities rather than a technical or physical vulnerabilities. The key procedural deficiency is usually highlighted as phishing related and then other issues such as lost or stolen devices, patches not being installed by the endpoint user, carrying out activity on an unsecure network or location, for example an airport or coffee shop Wi-Fi also featuring as the cause for cyber breaches.

The following are some examples of the implications for an organisation that is compromised in some way:

- **Down time**: where the organisation is unable to carry out normal procedures leading either to loss of production or potentially lost revenue generation opportunities.

Illustration 3 – Lost sales

Even the biggest online retailers suffer downtime, and in July 2018 during Amazon's Prime Day some customers were unable to access the site.

It is believed the site was down for around one hour and based on forecast sales of $3.4 billion across the 36 hour event that equated to almost $100 million of lost sales.

Amazon are not alone – it is estimated that Fortune 1000 companies lose close to $2.5 billion every year because of website downtime.

- **Reputation damage**: where the organisations name and brand value can be negatively affected, leading to lost sales.

Illustration 5 – Domain fraud

Even though the organisation that is subject to the domain fraud is not at fault when a threat actor uses their brand in an attack, this still reduces trust in the organisation that was mimicked in the fraud. It also reduces the effectiveness of legitimate emails that are sent by that organisation.

- **Customer flight**: this is critical with increasing levels of e-commerce. It is often argued the biggest financial consequence is lost business. Especially if the customer is a significant client, thinking about Porter's 5 Forces and power of customers, while an organisation doesn't want to rely on one or two key clients, the reality is this does happen.

Illustration 6 – Facebook

As a result of negative publicity about the way Facebook uses – and allows other companies to use – the data it has collected, and continues to collect, from the active users of its site, it has experienced a decline in user numbers in what the company considers to be its most valuable markets (the US, Canada and Europe).

- **Industry consequences**: in health care and financial services for example, cyber security breaches can be very costly as they are more highly regulated.
- **Termination of employees**: if an employee is responsible for the breach, it could be considered to be misconduct and could lead to lost skills and knowledge to enforce the policies and procedures an organisation has in place.

Illustration 7

A control is only effective if the consequences of breaching that control are enforced on a consistent basis. This could mean an excellent employee has to have their employment ended to ensure that people take the control seriously.

- **Loss of intellectual property or trade secrets**: as well as lost trust in their ability to protect customer details, the threat actor could have compromised the organisation's competitive advantage in the industry.

- **Legal consequences**: fines, lawsuit costs and settlements can be very significant. In 2018 new legislation came in relating to data protection within the EU with significant fines for breaching the legislation.

Legislation surrounding information systems (UK and EU)

General Data Protection Regulation (GDPR)

The GDPR is a regulation in EU law and in the UK replaced the Data Protection Act (DPA), on 25th May 2018.

The GDPR has two main objectives.

- Protection of fundamental rights and freedoms of individual persons with regard to processing personal data.

- Protection of the principle of free movement of personal data within the EU.

The UK Government has published its new Data Protection Bill that repeals the DPA and enshrines the GDPR into UK law post-Brexit.

It is overseen and enforced in the UK by the Information Commissioner's Office (ICO). The aim is to keep personal data secure at all times.

This means:

- Passwords should protect files and digital devices

- Sensitive documents should be locked away whenever they are not in use (and print outs should be picked up promptly.

- Personal data must sent/transmitted securely

- When it is no longer needed, personal data must be securely disposed of (e.g. shredded or securely deleted)

Key principles

The key principles of GDPR are around lawful and responsible use of personal data. It also looks at the appropriate collection of data; just because data can be collected, doesn't mean it should be.

Exemptions to the Act

EU Member States can introduce exemptions from the GDPR's transparency obligations and individual rights, but only where the restriction respects the essence of the individual's fundamental rights and freedoms and is a necessary and proportionate measure in a democratic society to safeguard things like national security and breaches of ethics in regulated professions.

Rights

Data subjects have enhanced rights under the GDPR compared to the DPA. These include, but are not limited to, things like requesting access to the data held about them; in certain situations they can even request their data is deleted. They can also claim compensation for damages caused by infringement of the GDPR from the company controlling or processing their data.

Enforcement

A breach of GDPR could lead to fines as follows:

- An organisation could be fined up to €10,000,000 or 2% of global income for a failure to implement measures to ensure privacy by design and default, or to maintain records or to maintain appropriate security.

- An organisation could be fined up to €20,000,000 or 4% of global income for a failure to comply with the principles of lawfulness, individuals' rights or conditions for consent.

Computer Misuse Act 1990

Computer crime is defined as 'any fraudulent behaviour connected with computerisation by which someone attempts to gain dishonest advantage' (Audit Commission). Computer crime was enshrined within the Computer Misuse Act 1990.

Objectives

The key objective of the Act was to make crimes of 'hacking' and the theft of data.

Unfortunately the Act does not provide a definition of:

- Computer.
- Program.
- Data.

Criminal offences

The Act created three new criminal offences:

- Unauthorised access, e.g. by an employee who exceeds their authority – a minor offence (tried in the Magistrates Court) – penalty six months imprisonment/fine/both.

- Unauthorised access with intent to commit and then facilitate the commission of a further offence, e.g. divert funds – a serious offence – penalty five years imprisonment/fine/both.

- Knowingly causing an unauthorised modification of the contents of any computer with the intention of interfering with the operation of that computer, preventing access to a program or data, or interfering with the operation of the program or the reliability of the data – includes introducing a virus to a system – penalty five years imprisonment/fine/both.

Examples of other legislation

US

In the US there is no single data protection law. Each state has laws protecting the PII of their residents. However it is something that is being reviewed and there are two major acts being considered:

Honest Ads Act

The Honest Ads Act links to perceived foreign interference in US elections. Digital advertising in the 2016 US elections is reported to have reached $1.4billion – around 7 times that spent in the 2012 election. The Act seeks to ensure that companies like Facebook and Google employ reasonable efforts to ensure foreign governments and agents are not purchasing advertising on their platform in order to attempt to influence voters.

The California Privacy Act

Is deemed to be the toughest privacy regulations in America and took effect in 2020. Users are allowed to ask for the data a company has collected about them and who that data has been sold to. It also allows users to request that the company stops selling their data if they do not like how it is being used.

The Act is still not as stringent as the GDPR regulations but allows individuals some similar rights.

Asia-Pacific

Partly because of the implementation of GDPR in Europe, countries like China, Singapore, South Korea, Japan, Australia, Malaysia, and the Philippines have either updated or will be updating their data protection rules and cyber security laws.

China

China has introduced some of the most comprehensive data protection regulations in the Asia-Pacific region. In June 2017 a new Cybersecurity Law was enacted, requiring companies that conduct business in China, even if they do not have a physical presence in the country, to review their data protection policies and ensure compliance.

China is also introducing e-commerce legislation covering areas such as data anonymisation, big data, overseas data transfers, and information security. As with GDPR, any companies that fail to comply with the law could face severe financial sanctions that could include losing their rights to conduct business in China.

Singapore

The country has changed its Personal Data Protection Act to include aspects of the EU GDPR, on areas such as mandatory breach notification and the appointment of a data protection officer.

As a result of this, in early 2018 several insurance and financial organisations based in Singapore received fines for failing adequately secure personal data, or for breaching rules on the use of personal data.

More to come

The California Privacy Act is unlikely to be the last new privacy legislation that organisations will have to deal with. India is considering new legislation, while the United Kingdom is thought to be planning its own legislation once its departure from the European Union is finalised. In the U.S. New York State and Washington State are also considering their own legislation, as is Congress.

Example: Target Corporation

Following on from the Target Corporation example earlier, in March 2015, Target reached a class-action settlement with affected consumers for more than $10 million (once attorney fees were included) and in May 2016, Target settled with affected banks and credit unions for more than $39 million.

Example: GDPR

The first German data protection authority to impose a fine under GDPR fined a social media company 20,000 EUR for failing to ensure data security of processing personal data. The reason for the breach was that a hacker managed to steal and publish 330,000 email addresses and passwords.

Given the levels of fine possible under GDPR, 20,000 EUR may be considered quite a low figure. The reason for such a low fine was that the authority took into consideration the cooperation and willingness of the company to implement its recommendations.

If the data breach at Yahoo (discussed earlier) had happened after GDPR had come into effect, the company would have faced significant fines, in part because of the delay in disclosing the severity of the data breach (GDPR requires companies disclose the breadth of the breach within 72 hours). Given that Yahoo's revenue in 2012 was over $4 billion, depending on a variety of factors, including how cooperative they were, they could have been fined between $80 million and $160 million.

Example: GDPR not just digital

In December 2019, Doorstep Dispensaree, a London pharmacy supplying care homes in the region, was fined £275,000 by the Information Commissioners Office (ICO) for GDPR breach.

The fine related to leaving 500,000 patient records in an unsecured location since before the new regulations were introduced in May 2018.

The documents, that were left in unlocked crates, disposal bags and cardboard boxed in a rear courtyard, contain names, addresses, dates of birth, NHS numbers and medical information.

Test your understanding 13

RPDG is a supermarket chain based in the EU country of Fratugal. They have for many years operated a loyalty scheme that involves customers registering their personal details (such as name, date of birth, address and contact phone number). Once registered the customer swipes their loyalty card at the checkout during the payment process. This allows RPDG to understand more about their customers' shopping habits, including where and when they shopped, what they bought and how much they spent.

RPDG also make sales online 24 hours day, for home delivery. Once customers have set up an account as part of the loyalty scheme, if they log in and order food for delivery, it automatically includes the purchases under the customer's account profile.

From this, RPDG can gain various competitive benefits, for example they have recently improved the layout of their shop to make sure that commonly purchased products are located nearby. Sometimes the results were surprising, such as nappies and alcoholic beverages – the marketing analysts were able to deduce that new parents were less able to go out for an alcoholic drink and so were more likely to consume alcohol at home. They also send offers to customers linked to products they buy regularly (or that are bought regularly by other customers who purchase similar items).

During a recent system upgrade an issue occurred and the upgrade took longer than planned. Some customers were unable to log in to their accounts to make purchases at prime online ordering times. Additionally some customers were unable to log into their own accounts, but were able to login to another customer's account and view and change their customer details. The issue allowing customers to log in to the wrong accounts only lasted for one hour before RPDG were able to restore normal operations. RPDG have made no public, or internal comment about the issue since it occurred over one week ago.

Which of the following would be implications of the systems upgrade issues at RPDG?

Select ALL that apply

A   RPDG could face significant legal fines for the data breach.

B   Staff could be concerned about the personal information held by RPDG about them.

C   RPDG customers may feel reassured by the speed at which the system issue was fixed.

D   RPDG may have lost significant sales revenue during the time that customers were unable to log in.

E   The lack of comment and clarity from RPDG could increase the level of fine they receive.

F   RPDG customers will shop more frequently in store in future to avoid issues where they cannot log in to their accounts.

Test your understanding 14 (integration)

The chapter has taken a detailed look at all the potential considerations for cyber security threats, including types of sensitive information, known modes of attack, the objectives of the organisation and the risks associated with cyber security issues. Using the approaches outlined in this chapter:

(a)   Consider the various cyber security issues facing an organisation like CIMA.

and

(b)   Consider the cyber security issues that face the organisation that you work for.

Test your understanding 15 – Steelcast (Case study)

Scenario

You work as a senior manager for Steelcast a manufacturer of luxury watches. The company have just completed the takeover of another watchmaker, Hantime that makes watches using quartz movement – a technique which Steelcast does not currently use.

Trigger

The finance director stops by your workplace, holding a copy of the local newspaper. You are told the following:

"We have just completed our takeover of Hantime. Our intention has always been to identify and exploit synergies between the two companies, including the development of a range of Steelcast watches that will use the Hantime movements in place of our traditional clockwork mechanisms.

The markets are a little sceptical of the value of our acquisition. I have brought you a copy of an article that appeared in this morning's paper.

The CEO has asked me to draft a briefing before our next meeting and I need your help.

The briefing deals with the need to integrate the two companies' information systems. This is an issue that frequently leads to problems during the period following an acquisition. The manager in charge of Steelcast's IT systems has contacted her counterpart at Hantime and they have arranged to meet as a matter of some urgency to discuss matters.

Newspaper article:

Hiland Business Times

Market analysts sceptical about Steelcast takeover

Steelcast's takeover of Hantime concluded yesterday. Not surprisingly, Steelcast was able to acquire 100% of Hantime's equity. In addition, Steelcast has persuaded the members of Hantime's Board to sign five-year contracts to continue in post.

Steelcast has made no secret of its desire to acquire Hantime's quartz movement technology for its own range of battery-powered luxury watches. Insiders also claim that Steelcast can add some value to Hantime's operations, perhaps by opening up new approaches to marketing and distribution.

Steelcast's share price was a little depressed yesterday, despite the successful completion of the takeover.

Task

I need practical advice on the following matters:

(a) What are the implications if we do not integrate Hantime's information system with that of Steelcast?   **(15 minutes)**

(b) How would you recommend that we should adopt a coherent strategy for integrating the information systems?   **(15 minutes)**

Test your understanding 16 – Flower House (Case study)

Scenario

You work as a senior manager for Flower House Brownies Ltd (FHB) a manufacturer of delicious brownies for sale online and delivered via a logistics provider.

FHB is a fairly small operation with only 2 directors, and a workforce of less than 20 people. They are based on one site in the EU country of Peninsulaland; the currency there is the P$.

Trigger

The finance director asks you into her office.

"We have just decided to expand our online sales opportunities. As you know the managing director has always been very active on social media and has raised awareness of our fantastic brownies through her presence there. She's decided that now is the time to expand our sales operations. We've done very well selling solely through our own website; the profit last year almost doubled from P$44,000 to P$78,000. We will now sell our brownies via an online retailer and, as you know she likes to think big, and so she has chosen the biggest online retailer there is.

I was reading this article and I'm concerned that they are describing FHB perfectly. We use an ERPS system and have a third party cloud storage for our regular customer account details. This would be a really bad time for us to have any issues with this. I know we have used a website security firm but I'm worried we may not have covered all our cyber threats."

Newspaper article:

Peninsula Business Times

Cyber security biggest threat to online retailers

Many online retailers have been caught unawares by the increased legislation around personally identifiable information and cyber security.

The issue seems to stem from organisations not fully appreciating how they interact with technology and therefore the potential access points that any hackers would have.

It's also been very apparent that organisations in Peninsulaland are not aware of the potential issues that cyber vulnerabilities could have and are not clear on what their key objectives are with regard to cyber security.

Task

I need to understand our cyber security issues more clearly. Please could you advise me on the following matters:

(a) Please could you explain the sorts of information we have that needs protecting? Specifically what sort of Personally Identifiable Information we collect and why we need it? Do we hold any other information we need to protect? **(10 minutes)**

(b) Please explain the interactions we have with technology based on our business model? **(10 minutes)**

(c) What should our cyber security objectives be? **(15 minutes)**

(d) What would be the risks to FHB of any cyber security vulnerabilities? **(15 minutes)**

Test your understanding 17

CFD is an SME based in the north of Geeland. They sell and distribute fresh fruit and vegetables to local businesses and private residences. The board have asked ZX, their meticulous IT director, to assess the threats they face from cyber-crime. ZX is aware that while the staff are one of the organisation's greatest assets, they can also be a weakness in the defence against cyber-attacks, ZX therefore provides regular training to onsite staff about good cyber security. ZX is assessing the most likely target for a hacker to target with a social engineering attack.

YX, the CEO of the company, is highly mobile and takes a very hands on approach to customer development. Part of the reason for this is their controlling and risk averse nature. Despite this mobile nature, YX is very thorough with her IT processes and often calls ZX rather than responding over email to any sensitive questions asked.

QY, the delivery driver, is rarely in the office and primarily uses the company smartphone for communication purposes. This also acts as their route planner and a delivery schedule including customer data. QY likes coffee and often stops at an independent coffee shop for a break and to send some personal emails using the company smartphone.

KZ works in the warehouse, and unpacks deliveries from suppliers and packs customer orders. The orders have no customer information included on them, just a list of items and a barcode to scan when complete and stick on the front of the outgoing box. KZ loves social media and often posts videos to various platforms both in and out of work hours.

Which ONE of the following statements is correct?

A   QY is the most likely target for a social engineering attack

B   KZ is the most likely target for a cyber-attack

C   YX should use her emails more often rather than call ZX

D   ZX is the most likely target for a social engineering attack.

E   No threat actor or hacker would attack CFD

5   Summary

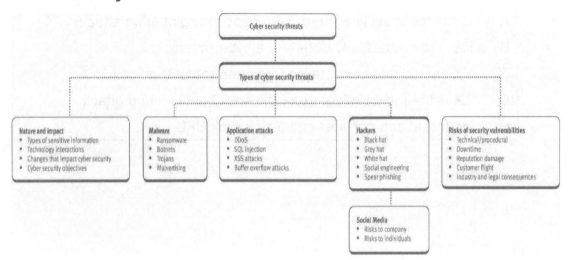

Test your understanding answers

Test your understanding 1

The correct answer is A, B and C

While cyber risks can have very significant consequences for an organisation, they most commonly arise as a result of operational mistakes, so is an operational risk.

Unauthorised breach of information systems is a cyber risk and it could it could manifest itself in the form of poor systems integrity.

As technology is utilised more and more, the likelihood and impact are increasing all the time.

Anti-virus software is a useful part of any defence, but cannot remove cyber risk completely.

Test your understanding 2

The correct answer is D.

This is where the old system is switched off and the new system is switched on at the same time. This is only appropriate where the two systems are very different or it is too expensive to run both. This method is cheap but very risky since if the new system doesn't work then the company may be unable to revert to the old system.

Test your understanding 3

The correct answer is A, C, E, F and G

The name and address are needed for delivery, the personal health information because of the product he buys, the date of birth will have been provided on setting up the customer account, and the account number will have been created then too.

As Ashveer pays by direct debit there is no need for Proud to know his credit card details and there is no reason for them to hold any information about his religious beliefs.

Test your understanding 4

The correct answer is D

As the exams are on demand and can be taken at any point, they want to make sure that the systems remain available to students 24 hours a day, 7 days a week, and 365 days a year.

Test your understanding 5

The correct answer is B

The description is of a virtual private network, which is a connection type.

Test your understanding 6

The correct answer is A, B, C and E

They are expanding through acquisition into a geographical area that has different regulations about data privacy. The target company has not operated online before so may well not have systems and controls in place to comply with the regulations in the way that GH will require. It is likely that the European target will need their computer hardware updated to enable the online sales.

There is unlikely to be an internal restructure – they are more likely to add a new geographical division on to the current structure.

The culture of the target may need to change to fit with GH, but this is unlikely to impact the cyber security risk management of GH.

PII is a type of sensitive information rather than something that will experience change at GH.

Test your understanding 7

The correct answer is A, B and D

Pilot changeover cannot be used, as it assumes that any 'lessons learned' in the first changeover can be transferred to all of the other sites.

We are told that each of the merged companies currently uses a different information system, suggesting that results of one pilot would be of limited usefulness when looking at other locations.

Test your understanding 8

The correct answer is C.

The attackers have used a fraudulent email pretending to be from the company bank to get the information they needed to access the bank accounts themselves.

Test your understanding 9

The correct answer is B.

Ransomware is a type of malicious software designed to block access to a computer system until a sum of money is paid.

Test your understanding 10

The correct answer is C.

The scenario describes an XSS attack.

A DDoS attack occurs where an attacker floods a firm's systems (e.g. its website or servers) with requests from multiple interconnected devices which causes the system to crash.

A SQL injection attack occurs when the attacker is able to inject code into an input box on a company's website (for example an unprotected search box) which then sends a request to the database supporting the website. The attacker could then maliciously download or alter the database.

A buffer overflow occurs when a system cannot store as much information as it has been sent and consequently starts to overwrite existing content. A buffer overflow attack occurs when an attacker sends a malicious programme which deliberately overloads the system and starts to overwrite existing data.

Test your understanding 11

The correct answer is C.

An ethical hacker is someone with the technical knowhow to hack systems who, with the permission of the company, tries to hack the system to identify weaknesses.

An unethical hacker is someone who hacks without permission, often with malicious intent.

An internet troll is someone who posts abusive responses on social media posts.

A botnet is a network of interconnected computers infected with a 'botnet agent' which the attacker can use to control the computers.

Test your understanding 12

The correct answers are C, E, and F.

A, B and G are advantages of social media and Squeeks could benefit from using social media in this way.

D is more of a risk to an individual than to Squeeks.

Test your understanding 13

The correct answers are A, B, D and E.

These are examples of legal consequences (A and E), reputation damage (B) and downtime (D).

Any data breach is likely to concern customers, regardless of how long it took for the company to fix it. In a competitive market like the one in which RPDG operates, issues like this could lead to customers to move to shopping with an online competitor rather than inconveniencing themselves by going to a physical store.

Test your understanding 14 (integration)

(a) CIMA

Types of sensitive information

CIMA have lots of PII about students and members:

Names

Addresses

Date of birth

Credit card details

CIMA contact ID!

From a business perspective they also hold employee details along similar lines plus payment details for staff salaries, and business suppliers.

Technology interactions

They probably use VPNs for remote working for sales staff and potentially for examiners/markers to send questions or candidates' scripts securely. Especially after the global move to home working in 2020.

Software providers (such as Pearson VUE) may be used for exam hosting and CIMA also provide a contact centre for students to email or phone with any queries.

In terms of delivery, they sell CPD courses which can be accessed online, so they require secure channels to transmit them through.

Types of changes

CIMA went through a qualification update – moving from the 2015 syllabus to the current syllabus. This is in part because of the rate of technological advancement and the impact it is having on how finance professionals work.

In terms of systems, in 2015 when CIMA first moved to exams on demand from the previous written exams, they used a direct switch over, so that Nov 2014 was the last sitting for paper based exam, and from 1st Jan all exams were online.

The latest syllabus update seemed to follow a phased changeover with the objective test exams moving in the final part of 2019, while the case studies moved over to the new updated syllabus in early 2020.

Cyber security objectives

- Availability – as a global professional body CIMA will want to have 24/7/365 access to their website so that prospective students, and current students and members can access their accounts and any relevant information as required.

- Confidentiality – As they hold significant PII and operate within the EU they must comply with GDPR and there is a Data Protection Officer listed in their privacy policy.

- Integrity of data – to make any changes to your data you require a CIMA ID and a password to log in.

Cyber security risks

CIMA will be subject to the threats listed from malware, application attacks and hackers. They are probably less likely to be affected by malvertising as there are limited adverts on their websites, although employees may visit sites that host malvertising.

There website may be targeted by a DDoS attack to take it offline, or an SQL injection attack through the log in functions to access students/members personal data.

Social media

CIMA have active social media pages on both Facebook and Twitter which are used to raise awareness of CPD events, syllabus changes and so on.

Risk of security vulnerabilities

Downtime – would lead to lost CPD course sales, and potentially could lose new students.

Reputation damage – given their stature and the current association with best practice cyber reporting, any downtime or hack would have a negative impact on their reputation and credibility.

Customer flight – linked into the downtime, potential new students may be put off by any online issues and choose an alternative professional body.

Legal consequences – with EU operations, any breaches could lead to GDPR sanctions.

These are just a sample of the considerations for an organisation that students and tuition providers may be aware of, there will be other considerations too.

(b)   There is no answer to this, but you can use the headings from a) to help generate ideas of potential issues for your organisation

Test your understanding 15 – Steelcast (Case study)

Integrating IS

It may be that the two companies will operate largely independently of one another and that a lack of integration will cause relatively few problems in terms of operations. There could be difficulties in terms of Hantime scheduling production and making deliveries to meet Steelcast's needs. That problem could be addressed by finding an alternative approach to placing orders and so the impact may not be that serious. Maintaining the group's IS will be complicated if there are two independent systems in operation.

That could mean that maintenance costs and the risks of disruption are doubled. The lack of integration will mean that Steelcast's Board may not be able to request the same level of reporting from Hantime as they take for granted from Steelcast. Requests may be more difficult and more complicated to fulfil. The preparation of consolidated management accounts and financial statements may be complicated by different IS.

Strategy for integration

The first question would be to examine the systems in place in each entity with a view to deciding whether one is superior. It makes sense to change only one system if that would be possible, so that costs and disruption are minimised. The next step would be to work with management teams to determine what they need. Even if we choose to standardise on one or other of the existing systems, it may be worth considering whether that system could be enhanced in a cost-effective manner.

Any local issues need to be taken into account. For example, local regulations might have implications for the accounting system used and so those differences will have to be taken into account. We need to ensure that all specific needs are fully understood by both sides during any ongoing discussions because such differences may not be obvious. There should be a steering committee appointed from the key functional areas in both Hantime and Steelcast. Hantime's representatives should be assured that the intention is not simply to export Steelcast's system to their company.

Test your understanding 16 – Flower House (Case study)

Information that needs protecting

In terms of PII we will have collected this type of information from both employees and customers, particularly our regular customers who have set up an account.

In terms of employees; we will hold details such as name, address, date of birth, bank details etc. We need this for a variety of reasons including paying our staff, complying with law and business continuity planning.

For our customers: we will need name, address and payment details to take payment for their orders, but also to arrange delivery with our logistics provider. For our customers who have set up an account we will hold more information to help identify them: things like dates of birth, and answers to security questions for if they forget their passwords.

We do have other information that needs protecting too: our recipe and mixing /cooking processes give us a competitive advantage, anyone can make a brownie, but they don't all taste as good as the ones we make – which is how we've grown so much over recent times.

Technology interactions

In terms of technological interactions, we obviously have our website that our customers order through. We protect this through a third party security firm and we must regular review this arrangement to ensure they are competitive in terms of their security features and processes. If any of their other clients have had security breaches this could be a concern for us.

Our ever expanding customer base and their details are stored in our third party cloud storage, so again we must ensure that this connection is secure and that our provider follows good security processes.

We also need to make sure our communication channels with our logistics provider are secure as the transmission of PII details to them could lead to potential issues.

Cyber security objectives

There are four core objectives with regard to cyber security: availability, confidentiality, integrity of data and integrity of processing.

Availability – as we are online, we need our website to be available 24 hours a day, 7 days a week 365 days a year, so that our customers can order brownies whenever they need to (whether it is for their own benefit or as a last minute gift for a friend or relative).

Confidentiality – as I have outlined in this email we have both PII and business information that we need to keep secure. We need to make sure that only authorised people have access to all the confidential information we have, whether it is our baking team who make the brownies and are reviewing the recipe/processes or our dispatch team getting the parcels ready to be taken by our logistics provider.

Integrity of data – it is important that the data we retain about our customers remains up to date. Otherwise payments may fail and orders may get delivered to the wrong addresses.

Integrity of processing – we need to ensure that the work we do is consistent with the policies and procedures that we have set up. This is important both to maintain the quality of the brownies we produce and to make sure we comply with hygiene standards in food production and health and safety regulations for our employees. We need to maintain controls over who can amend these policies and procedures, and any legitimate changes must be communicated to our staff appropriately. As we are quite a small operation this should be easy to control at the moment, but we must remain vigilant about these issues as we continue to grow.

Risks of cyber security vulnerabilities

If our website should be unavailable for any reason it could lead to customers being unable to order from us and so we could lose sales. Our website being unavailable would also mean we would lose opportunities to raise awareness about our products and brand.

Potentially even worse, any downtime could lead to customers finding alternative gift ideas or replacements for the brownies we make and sell. We operate in a very competitive environment and any issues with the website being unavailable, of any other cyber related issues, could mean our customers choose a competitor's product over our own.

Another consideration from any issues with cyber security would be reputational damage. Although we our expanding our sales opportunities, it is currently our website that is our core sales point. Going forward we could make sales through other online sources, but any cyber security issues associated with our systems and procedures could mean customers avoid our brownies, regardless of the distribution channel.

Given our location within EU jurisdiction, any cyber security issues are likely to lead to GDPR issues and potential fines. So as well as the lost sales and reputation damage we could be face significant fines, which would put the liquidity of the business at risk and further damage our reputation.

Test your understanding 17

The correct answer is A

QY has access to PII and uses their company mobile phone for both business and personal use, on potentially less secure public networks at the independent coffee shop.

KZ uses social media, but does not appear to have any access to sensitive data, so would be a less attractive prospect for a threat actor.

The CEO and IT director, while they undoubtedly have privileged access to sensitive data, appear to have very good digital hygiene and would be less likely to fall for a social engineering attack. The CEO's approach of not replying to emails or clicking on links is actually an example of good cyber security.

SMEs are often more attractive to threat actors as they may have less advanced cyber security and be easier to attack than a larger organisation.

Cyber security processes

Chapter learning objectives

Lead	Component	
D2 Review cyber security processes	(a)	Cyber security objectives
	(b)	Security controls
	(c)	Centralisation in security

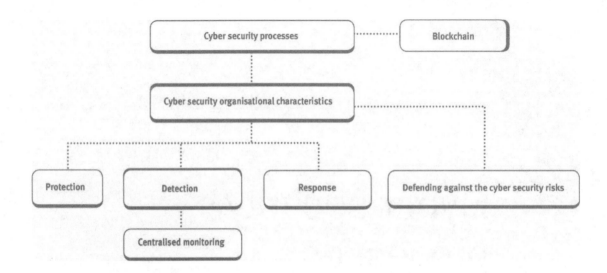

1 Cyber security organisational characteristics

To achieve the security objectives and mitigate the types of risk discussed in the previous chapter, the AICPA cyber security framework recommends a security mechanism based around three principles:

- Protection

- Detection

- Response

These three principles will be applied in different ways across the different levels within the system. Key to their success are factors core to risk management in general: corporate governance, tone from the top and communication of appropriate information for decision making.

1.1 Cyber security risk governance

As part of the reporting framework that the AICPA have devised (see chapter 10 for more detail), management are required to give specific consideration to cyber security risk governance. This would include:

- How the management set the tone from the top.

- Standards for conduct.

- The extent of, and access to, IT expertise at board level.

- Responsibility for overall cyber security within the organisation and across reporting lines.

- The hiring and training of cyber security personnel.

There are various ways for a company to address these governance considerations, they include, but are not limited to:

- A company handbook detailing policies and procedures relating to IT (acceptable use, confidentiality, information security).

- Regular board meetings, potentially quarterly but more or less often as appropriate, where cyber security risk management is discussed.

- In the same way the corporate governance guidelines require recent relevant financial experience on an audit committee, if a director has recent relevant IT experience, it would help with board oversight, although using external IT consultants could also help with this.

- Each organisation has different needs, but consideration should be given to the appointment of a chief information officer (CIO) with overall IT responsibility to the board, a risk committee, a chief risk officer (CRO) with overall responsibility for risk, a chief technology officer (CTO) to look after technology and resources to support internal operations reporting into the CIO and a chief information security officer (CISO) to head up the cyber security program and also report into the CIO.

- As well as appropriate reporting lines and accountability for cyber security, a company needs to make sure it has competent personnel in cyber security roles through the organisation. Hiring appropriately qualified staff is a first step, but making sure they are given time and training to stay up to date in this dynamic area is critical.

 C-suite roles in IT

Responsibility for IT security at organisations varies from the CEO, owner or partner in some smaller organisations through to CISO in organisations with more comprehensive cyber security.

Generally, cyber security experts believe that having a CISO or equivalent person as the head of cyber security is the best practice, with the CISO (or equivalent role) carrying equal authority as the CTO (CIO or Head of IT).

Some organisations combine the roles of CTO and CISO, and this is ok for smaller organisations, but as the organisation grows, best practice suggests that this is too much responsibility for one individual.

1.2 Cyber security information and communication

In chapter 1 we looked at CIMA's risk management cycle and illustrated the importance of information for decision making, with each stage in the cycle providing information to help make appropriate decisions regarding risks and the management of risks. This also applies to cyber security risks, chapter 8 introduced the **cyber security objectives** of an organisation:

- Availability
- Confidentiality
- Integrity of data
- Integrity of processing

It is important that the organisation has appropriate channels and methods for communicating not only its cyber security objectives, expectations and responsibilities, but any key information to both internal and external users.

Internal

For internal communications a company may do any of the following:

- Include cyber security objectives, expectations and responsibilities in a company handbook.

- Have policies available on a shared drive or intranet.

- Initial on boarding training, including signing the handbook to confirm understanding.

- Appropriate reminder training sessions for all staff on an annual basis.

- Annual review of objectives and handbook/training content.

- Designated IT updates for critical/urgent sharing of information

External

For external communications a company may do any of the following:

- Develop an appropriate policy for disclosure of information with external parties.

- Set up communication channels for external parties, including law enforcement, to raise issues

- Use of electronic mail, conference calls, or face to face meetings to disclose any issues.

- Appoint legal and communications teams to be responsible for any media communications.

Cyber security information and communication

Internal

The use of a company hand book and on boarding training is seen as a very good way to set the right tone for all new hires. The employees can be left in no doubt about the importance the organisation places on cyber security when they first start.

Appropriate reviews of this content should be carried out by employees with cyber security responsibilities to make sure it remains relevant, and regular (potentially annual) training for all other staff to help maintain the prominence for all of the workforce.

Employees who have cyber security responsibilities should have additional technical update training to make sure that they remain up to date.

Any employees with access to sensitive data (both employee and customer) will also need additional training to ensure compliance with legislation and appropriate incident management.

External

The policy for external communications should be included in the employee handbook. Any employees who deal with external parties need to receive appropriate training in how to deal with the third parties and what data/information should be made available. In particular legal and confidentiality principles should feature prominently in any policy documents and training.

2 Protection

2.1 Areas to be protected

* **Servers**: a device or program that provides functionality for other programs or devices. A single overall set up is distributed across multiple processes or devices.

  Most personal computers today are capable as acting as a network server, however usually a dedicated piece of hardware carries out the task and has specific capabilities such as a fast processor to facilitate efficient use of the computers on the network.

* **Desktops**: a personal computer designed for regular use at a single location, usually on a desk, due to its size and power requirements. They are normally connected to the server to access shared resources like data storage or hardware like printers.

* **Laptops**: a small, portable version of a desktop, differentiated here because its mobile capabilities increase the risks to the business.

* **Mobile devices**: a computing device small enough to hold and operate in the hand for example smart phones, tablets that now have very similar capabilities to laptops and desktops.

* **Networks**: a method of connecting various devices and allowing them to share resources, applications and other devices. Networks often allow multiple users to share a device, like a printer, or allow easy access to shared files through shared network data storage. Networks can be of differing sizes, from a local area network (LAN) in a particular office, to a company-wide network.

Expandable text – Networks

The internet of things increases the network risks to an organisation. As more devices and end points are linked together, in many cases from different organisations, the more organisations involved, the higher the risk becomes.

Different third parties are at different stages of their life cycle and this can mean that they have different levels of security.

Example: Video conferencing

There was a huge increase in online meetings and video calls in 2020, caused primarily by the move to homeworking but also to enable social interaction between friends and family.

A lot of relatively young organisations therefore saw their applications rise in popularity significantly. As they rose in popularity with the organisations and the general public, they also became more attractive to threat actors as a potential access point to networks. It meant a lot of security updates were needed by the organisations behind these applications.

- **Data storage**: the recording and storing of data and information to be accessed by devices on a network. Often this incorporates the use of cloud based storage, where the data is held on servers in a remote location. Often cloud storage is operated by a third party. The more data an organisation stores, the more attractive they may become to threat actors looking to sell data on the dark web.

- **Business applications**: In modern terminology these are often referred to as apps. They have existed for many years but awareness of apps has been raised by the increased capabilities of technology and in particular mobile devices. Business applications are software tools that allow users to perform certain tasks relating to their work, for example word processing, calculation, graphing and tabulation. Additionally a company may use an accounting application to record its financial data.

2.2 Methods of protection

- **Policies and policy management**: the process of creating, communicating, and maintaining IT policies and procedures within an organisation. These policies can be varied and can range from remote working policies, acceptable use of the internet, protection of personal information, etc. All are designed to protect the company and the employees from harm.

- **Software updates**: Updates contain important changes to improve the performance, stability and security of the applications and operating systems that run on the various types of devices. If the software is not kept up to date then the security features become out of date, which exposes the company to potential hacking attempts.

- **Configurations**: removing or disabling unnecessary functionality from systems can greatly improve the security of systems. Configuration can link to the types of hardware and software that may be used and, in line with policies and procedures, can help protect a company from unauthorised access.

- **Security products**: such as antivirus software can add to system level controls. Failure to use these products can increase the likelihood of a breach either from an attack resulting from visiting an inappropriate site or downloading inappropriate files.

- **Application software controls**: These are controls to ensure that data are correctly input, processed and correctly maintained, and only distributed to authorised personnel.

  Application controls are specific to each application, but can be grouped as follows:

Input controls:

- Checking and authorising source documents manually.
- The use of batch controls.
- Pre-numbered forms.

Processing controls:

- Computer verification and validation checks.
- Error detection controls such as
  - control totals
  - balancing.

Output controls:

- Monitoring of control logs.
- Physical checking of output.

Example: Smart phones

Application controls are not just found in the workplace, most smart phones have application software controls built in to them.

If a new application (app) is downloaded onto a phone it cannot access data on the phone without authorisation. For example a messaging app may ask for permission to access the microphone or photos stored on the phone. Without the user's approval the application is unable access the stored data.

 Example: Purchase ledger

A purchase ledger system might have:

Input controls:

- Some inputs have to be authorised manually – like the addition of a new supplier account.

- Some inputs use batch controls – counting the number of forms to be input, or grouping the inputs in like groups. The system can also notify the input clerk how many forms have been processed. This is can then checked to the physical number to be input and highlights if too few or too many have been input.

Processing controls:

- The software checks that invoiced goods have been ordered and received – linking the details in the purchase ledger and inventory files.

Output controls:

- A supervisor receives a daily exception report, with a nil report in the event of there being no exceptions.

- The supervisor must acknowledge and act upon the exceptions.

IT systems can undermine segregation of duties because they can initiate transactions, move assets and keep records, therefore these systems must be designed very carefully.

2.3 Forms of protection

The first line of defence is to try to protect information assets and systems from attack. Protection can take a variety of forms:

- **Identification**: things like usernames and unique access codes, so that the system has a record of who accessed what and when they did it.

Example: Google documents

Even shared documents on a Google drive have the capability to show who has opened them and, in particular, highlight who has edited them and what changes were made. The identity provided in this case is usually the person's email address.

- **Authentication**: to enable confidence in the identification, each username or unique access code should be verified. This may be by means of a password, or pin number or more recently using biometrics such as a finger print scan or facial recognition software.

Expandable text – Passwords

Password systems can only be effective if users use them conscientiously. There are several inherent problems with a password system:

- Authorised users may divulge their password to a colleague.

- Many passwords may have associations with the user so that a hacker can discover them by experimentation.

- Passwords are often written down close to the computer (e.g. pinned to the notice board inside the office) and so easily discovered.

Passwords have been used for a long time, and quality of passwords is becoming increasingly important; there are a number of precautions that should be adopted:

- Length – it is increasingly common to have to create a password at least 8 characters long.

- Variety – it is often recommended that passwords have a variety of characters for examples upper and lower case letters, numbers, special characters (*&%!)

- Significance – using a date or name that is significant to an individual is advised against. They should be memorable though.

- Change – users should be required to change their passwords regularly

- Unwritten – users should be encouraged never to write down their passwords

- Private – there should be strict controls over passwords – they should never be 'lent' or written down where they can be easily seen.

- Single use – we often hear this term with regard to protecting the environment, but a major issue with passwords is that people re-use passwords for personal and (more critically for organisations network security) for work applications. This can make even badly dated credentials very useful for threat actors on the dark web.

Importance of passwords

Since passwords were first invented by Fernando Corbato in the 1960s they have been an ever increasing part of life and in particular an increasingly critical part of cyber security.

At the time of writing there is an annual World Password Day – on the first Thursday in May – to highlight the importance of a strong password to help protect online data.

There is an increasing feeling that there is too much reliance on the password and the ability of individuals to remember all their passwords safely. The average person has (depending on estimates) over 100 passwords to maintain and remember. This increases cyber risk as people try to resolve these problems by writing down passwords, or using the same password for several things.

Alternative solutions are being introduced like biometric and two factor authentication (this is discussed further in chapter 10).

- **Authorisation**: as well as recording what an individual looks at or enters into the system, it is also possible to limit what any particular user can access within the system. This means that they will only be able to view and enter information appropriate to their skill/employment level.

Example: Password responsibility

As well as guidance about length, variety and significance, it is also important employees are aware of other good practices with passwords.

It is vital that people do not share passwords, and that people do not write them down in obvious places to help them remember them. A common example is sticking a piece of paper with a password on to their laptop or monitor.

To help enforce these behaviours in terms of password quality and password protection, some companies make sure that users know that they are responsible for everything done in the system using their password.

Expandable text – Brute force attacks

Another issue with passwords is that they are susceptible to **brute force attacks**.

A brute force attack is where a computer goes through every possible combination of password (or encryption key) until a match is found. To a human this would take a significant amount of time, but the speed at which a computer can process tasks like this mean it can happen relatively quickly.

To counter this issue most login systems have the ability to block access after a number of unsuccessful password attempts.

Example: Brute force attacks

A typical keyboard has 96 character options.

The reason why an eight character password is recommend is an eight character password has 96^8 combinations (which is over 7.2 quadrillion). Even a very powerful computer would take in the region of 83 days to go through all the possible combinations.

Expandable text – Passwords and quantum computing

While **quantum computing** is currently in its infancy, it will increase the issues associated with passwords.

It will eventually create the ability to harness quantum physics to massively increase processing power. Amongst other things, a quantum computer will be able to break passwords that are associated with encryption with ease.

- **Protecting secrets**: making sure that only authorised people or systems can view the data/information. This is often referred to as **encryption**. The encryption happens both at rest (while the data is stored) and in transit (while the data is being transmitted).

Example: Signal

The messaging service Signal has end to end encryption built into its application so that all messages sent and received are only visible by the intended recipient(s). Not even Signal can view your message. They see this as a vitally important feature because of cases where hackers have illegally accessed private data and photos.

Example: Target Corporation

The attack at Target Corporation (see previous chapter) is said to have resulted partly from the retailer's failure to comply with regulations and properly protect its data by segregating systems handling sensitive payment card data from the rest of its network.

Target initially claimed it was the victim of a sophisticated cyber crime and said it was hard to avoid because of the sophistication.

Target had a valid reason for allowing the HVAC company access to its network, but no individual from the HVAC company should have had authorisation to access anything else in the system other than energy and temperature data.

Payment card Industry Data Security Standard (PCI DSS) specifies that this type of network segmentation should be used to protect sensitive cardholder data.

The malware used to intercept and steal payment card data from Target's POS systems was indeed sophisticated, but the hackers should have been unable to install the malware because of network segmentation practices.

- **Physical security**: is also a key way of protecting hardware, from desktops to smartphones to servers – all should only be accessible by authorised personnel. Attackers may use information they have stolen from online files to break in to a storage facility, or certain access may only be allowed via a specific computer terminal, which is in a secured room. Companies often have policies about how devices should be stored, particularly mobile ones away from the company premises, to reduce likelihood of theft.

  In terms of physically securing premises, there are various basic methods of controlling access to sensitive areas. These include:

  - security guards in buildings
  - working areas to which access is through a locked door or a door with an ID card entry system or entry system requiring the user to enter a personal identification code (PIN number)
  - using safes and lockable filing cabinets
  - closed circuit TV used to monitor what is happening in a particular part of a building – this may be backed up by security video cameras
  - doors automatically locked in the event of a security alarm.

  Additionally, procedural controls to protect files and output include:

  - items containing information like USB drives should not be left lying around on desks and working surfaces
  - computer printout should be shredded or otherwise destroyed before being thrown away.

Location of IT facilities

It is imperative that the location of the system is considered, and hence all equipment is located so as to protect against:

- Fire
- Flood
- Smoke
- Food
- Drinks
- Power failure
- Environment.

- **Email authentication**: is used to help reduce the threat of domain fraud (see chapter 8). Domain Based Message Authentication Reporting and Conformance (DMARC) ensures that legitimate email is authenticated so that people can trust emails from the domains an organisation owns. It also reduces the ability for people to commit fraud from domains that the organisation own.

Expandable text – authentication

Authentication helps reveal who is sending email on your behalf, this reduces the threat of domain fraud and helps protect the reputation of the firm that the perpetrator is trying to mimic in the phishing attempt.

2.4 Personnel controls:

Approaches to attack organisations are constantly evolving, at present the controls to systems, software and networks are seen as quite difficult to breach. The weak link that attackers have identified is the human element, it is estimated that over 90% of current cyber crime is targeted at people through social engineering and often incorporates little or no malicious software whatsoever. This makes personnel controls a key focus of organisations.

The main forms of personnel control are:

- Recruitment controls
- Policies and procedures
- Training
- Supervision and monitoring.

Expandable text – Personnel controls

Recruitment controls – include pre-employment screening of candidates. This can include a review of social media profiles that are publicly available from professional platforms like LinkedIn to more informal platforms like TikTok, Facebook and Twitter. It can also include background checks with previous employers or referees provided by candidates. The aim is to reduce the likelihood of hiring a candidate who increases the cyber risks to the organisation.

Policies and procedures – includes creating guidelines and rules for employees to follow. This could be in the form of confidentiality agreements for employees to sign, an acceptable use policy, information security policy or other such documents. These policies may include incentives for good digital hygiene or an escalation list of potential responses should any individual breach the policies and procedures.

It is important that these are actionable and actioned as appropriate, otherwise if employees feel there will be no consequences the control may be less effective. Examples of policies that may be in place are a limit on the amount of personal web browsing that an individual can do, or to clearly outline the process for an individual to feedback about any emails received that could be a of a suspicious nature.

Training – this is one of the most important controls that an organisation has against the increasing threat posed by social engineering attacks. It must be regular, often to serve as a reminder, so that people don't adopt bad habits. It must also be thorough and reviewed/updated for the changing nature of cyber security and social engineering threats.

Supervision and monitoring – this includes immediate managers supervising employees in their work to ensure they are not using their computers inappropriately, but also centralised monitoring functions reviewing unusual network activity such as an employee logging on to the network at an unusual time or using the network in a way that was inappropriate.

Example: continuous learning

As cyber threats and social engineering attempts are developing and changing all the time, when an employee either reports a new issue or is tricked by a new attack, this is an opportunity, not to name and shame the employee, but to use the story as a learning point for the rest of the organisation.

It is important for the people setting policies and providing the training to understand the profile of the staff in their organisation and adjust the training to help them learn and follow the best practice guidance the organisation produces.

This could be the information security staff learning what is the most convenient or simplest way for an activity to be actioned and making sure that approach is also the safest or most secure way for that activity to be actioned, rather than trying to change the approach to the activity.

Expandable text – contractors and temporary workers

The guidance for personnel controls is often well applied for permanent candidates, but can be more relaxed for temporary workers. Good cyber security processes would see no difference in the recruitment, training, policies and procedures or the supervision and monitoring of temporary workers.

Even though it is for a limited time, if they have access to emails and the organisation network, their compliance with organisation policy is just as important as permanent workers.

Example: Kaplan

At Kaplan employees are required to take annual information security and privacy training, this gives the company opportunity to remind employees of their responsibilities about passwords, social engineering, safeguarding computers, the use of social media, safe remote working, etc.

As well as mandatory completion, the company sometimes initiate tests to check that the training is being complied with. One example was an internally generated phishing email offering free coffee from a well-known coffee outlet- to access the free coffee a link had to be clicked.

The email had several warning signs that it was not a legitimate offer, for example spelling errors. However several employees did click the link, and doing so meant they were assigned additional security training.

Expandable text – limitations of personnel controls

As with any control, personnel controls have their limitations.

Threats constantly changing – threat actors such as hackers are always looking for a new opportunity to exploit, whether it be health insecurities or financial concerns. Most controls and training will be designed to deal with known threats and approaches.

Lapses – humans, by nature, are susceptible to lapses in concentration. If a phishing attack is particularly well designed, an individual or department may be under-resourced and under pressure anyone can make a mistake a click on a link or download a weaponised document.

2.5 Certification

Certificates play a significant part in the protection process and act as a kind of digital handshake. They are particularly important where payments or transmission of sensitive data is concerned.

Certificates can be used to verify the identity of the sender, allow the transmission of encrypted confidential information and also allow the receiver to know whether the information has been tampered with – the equivalent of tamper proof tape in the virtual world. Authentication and protecting secrets are very much part of the certificate's role.

There are different types of certificate. The most common was SSL (secure sockets layer) certificates but these are being replaced by TSL (Transport Layer Security) certificates.

Expandable text – Certificates
There is a public and private part of a certificate. The private part must stay secure and not be transferred between parties.
Within organisations they are often centrally managed to allow users to access the public certificate for a person they want to send encrypted information to.
For external use public certificates are issued by third-party certificate authorities that verify the identification of the parties using them.

Importance of certificates
In the previous chapter one of the examples highlighted the network outages that O2 suffered in December 2018.
The issue was caused by faulty software provided by mobile network equipment group Ericsson. The fault was due to an expired certificate in software versions installed with the customers, meaning the validity and the security of the software could not be verified.
O2 and Ericsson are not the first to suffer issues as a result of expiring certificates, in 2013 Xbox Live and Azure both suffered downtime because of an expired certificate.

2.6 Man in the middle attacks (MitM)

This is a type of attack where the attacker secretly and independently makes connections between two parties and passes messages between them. The aim is to make them think they are communicating directly with each other whilst in reality is the attacker is controlling the conversation. This kind of attack is often used to collect information, to help a further attack, for example discovering specialist knowledge about a target in order to carry out a spear phishing attack.

Certificates are vital in protecting companies and individuals from MitM attacks, allowing both parties to see whether the identity of the person they believe they are communicating with is authentic or not.

Man in the middle attacks

DigiNotar were a Dutch Certificate issuing Authority. A hacker accessed their web server and because of poor enforcement of the rules on the DigiNotar systems, the hackers managed to get through the segmented network protection and access the servers that issued certificates.

From there the hacker started issuing rogue certificates so that the user could start impersonating various domains which enabled them to carry out a large scale MitM attack against gmail users in Iran, intercepting messages to and from an estimated 300,000 gmail users until the hack was discovered. Investigations discovered that over 500 fake certificates were issued and as a result major web browsers revoked trust in certificates issued by DigiNotar.

This event can be linked to reputational risk discussed earlier in the P3 syllabus. For a firm supposedly in the business of helping secure companies and individuals against cyber threats, being hacked in this way was not good for their reputation, and it is unsurprising that shortly after this incident DigiNotar filed for voluntary bankruptcy.

3 Detection

In the modern world it is unrealistic to think that protection strategies will be enough and so, as well as protective and preventative strategies, organisations must also have robust detection strategies in place to identify when (not if) any threats occur.

As with most things, the sooner any issues are detected the easier it (usually) is to fix them. The detection strategies are effectively a computer equivalent to having a security camera set up.

The following are some of the detection strategies that organisations can employ:

- **Event monitoring** – if a log of events is recorded in files then these can be reviewed to look for unusual activity.

- **Intrusion detection and prevention systems** – it is now possible to run applications that can monitor activities on an ongoing basis.

Intrusion detection and prevention systems

Intrusion Detection Systems (IDS): analyse and monitor network traffic for signs of suspicious behaviour that might indicate attackers are using a known cyberthreat to infiltrate the network or steal information. The system works by comparing current network activity to both expected traffic and a threat database to detect problems such as like security policy violations or malware. It is a passive system which will not prevent attacks.

Intrusion Prevention Systems (IPS): behave in the same way as a firewall, creating a filter between the outside world and the internal network. IPS are active applications which will deny suspicious network traffic if it appears to represent a known security threat. However they can only act on security threats that are already identified.

- **Threat monitoring** – studying the way hackers attempt to compromise organisations, including the techniques and the software tools. This can then be used to develop and share intelligence on the types of threats which in turn can help to develop new controls.

- **User reports** – this links into the first point, event monitoring, and the user reports can identify unusual activity.

Example: Threat monitoring and sharing intelligence

Dr Ian Levy, Technical Director at the National Cyber Security Centre NCSC (part of Government Communication Headquarters – GCHQ) was the subject of an attempted hack by a prankster in 2017.

The prankster – who has duped some very high profile individuals – sent Dr Levy an email that looked like it was from a colleague. Dr Levy spotted that something was wrong with the email but he took the unusual step of asking the prankster to help him educate people about the signs to look out for that you have received a phishing or spearphishing email.

A prime example of the security community working together and sharing threat intelligence with each other, but also the wider public.

While there was no malicious intent in this case, the method was very similar to type of emails sent with malicious intent. Dr Levy said that he was very close to clicking on the link that he had been sent and had he been in a rush, or if he had viewed the email after having had an alcoholic drink or two, he probably would have clicked the link.

Together they wrote a blog on the NCSC website, detailing what the prankster had done and how Dr Ian Levy had spotted something was not quite right.

4   Response

As mentioned in the detection section, it is no longer a case of *if* an organisation comes under attack, it is *when*. This means that as well as detection processes and strategies, organisations must also have responses ready. This has led to the creation of Computer Incident Response Teams (CIRTs) or Computer Security Incident Response Teams (CSIRTs).

When an organisation comes under attack, the key role of the CIRT or CSIRT is to keep the business functioning, or some people refer to it as "keeping the patient alive". The primary functions of the CIRT or CSIRT are:

- Minimise any losses

- Restore normal operations as soon as possible

- Assist with any investigations, internally or externally

- Help provide data and information to support decision making and developing a planned response

- Assist with communications during the critical periods, with various stakeholder groups – customers, suppliers, media, etc.

Example: Maersk NotPetya

Maersk chair Jim Hagemann Snabe discussed the 2017 NotPetya malware outbreak at a World Economic Forum event. He described how Maersk had to reinstall their "entire infrastructure" which he then explained was "4,000 new servers, 45,000 new PCs, and 2,500 applications", describing the response "a heroic effort over 10 days" as it should have taken nearer six months.

Whether this was an intentional Disaster Recovery Plan, or accidental is not entirely clear.

In terms of business continuity, Maersk managed to continue operating over that 10 day period, with only a 20% drop in volumes, Jim Hagemann Snabe put it down to "human resilience". This still cost them between $250 and $300 million.

He described the event as a "wakeup call", because Maersk were "average" at cyber security.

He also explained that Maersk were very open about what happened to them in an effort to help others, another example of threat monitoring and sharing intelligence.

Test your understanding 1

The IT director of NBV company is aware that that incidences of malvertising have become increasingly common in the webpages of suppliers to their industry.

Which THREE of the following responses would be MOST suitable to address this threat?

A   Upgrade application firewalls

B   Update antivirus software

C   Encrypt data sent to suppliers

D   Increase the levels of authentication required to log-on to supplier systems

E   Install advert blocking software

Test your understanding 2

YUB company needs to send highly confidential information from its head office to the production system in its overseas manufacturing facility.

Which ONE of the following forms of cyber-security would be MOST likely to ensure that only the intended recipient is able to access the information?

A   Encrypting the data

B   Monitoring access to and use of the system

C   Instituting a network firewall

D   Backing up the data

Test your understanding 3

Bhogal Plc is a software development company that was initially set up by Sachkartar and his friend Justyna. They met at university while studying information technology and remained friends when they started working in IT graduate positions after they left university. They gained several years' experience, but decided they wanted to go into business together.

After several years of growth, they recently floated on their country's stock market. Justyna and Sachkartar are both directors on the board and they have, with the rest of the board, been very focussed on complying with the country's principles-based code of corporate governance.

At a recent meeting with representatives from their risk committee, the discussion moved onto cyber security and how they could improve their cyber security risk governance.

Which of the following would be appropriate actions for Bhogal Plc to take to address cyber security risk governance?

Select ALL that apply.

A   Appoint an external IT consultant to provide the board with some recent relevant IT experience.

B   Create a company handbook detailing policies and procedures on acceptable use of IT, confidentiality and information security.

C   Make sure that they have appropriate cyber security staff, in terms of qualifications and numbers, ensuring that they get regular training to stay up to date.

D   Ensure that at least 50% of the risk committee are non-executive directors

E   Ensure that cyber security risk management is discussed regularly at board meetings.

Test your understanding 4

The cyber security risk management team at PAAH Ltd are working on their internal handbook to advise employees on acceptable use of IT, confidentiality and information security. As part of this document, and for regular training reminders, they intend to include some information on password best practice

Which ONE of the following would be the most secure password to include as an example?

A   P!ssword

B   p8$sw0rD

C   Pa$s3!)

D   Password1234

> **Test your understanding 5**
>
> Howerson Ltd have decided to issue all of their sales team with laptops, and are considering appropriate forms of protection to prevent unauthorised access to company data.
>
> **Which of the following would be appropriate methods of protection to use?**
>
> Select ALL that apply
>
> A   Reviewing configurations of each laptop prior to giving them to their sales team and disabling any unnecessary features.
>
> B   Installing antivirus software on each laptop.
>
> C   Training the sales team on physical security including where to store their laptops when not is use and offsite.
>
> D   Encourage employees to copy any critical information onto a portable USB drive in case they lose their laptop.
>
> E   Download user reports on a regular basis to identify unusual activity.
>
> F   Set up a Computer Incident Response Team for the sales team to contact should they have trouble logging in.

5   Defending against the cyber security risks

The previous chapter covered the types of cyber security risks. As a reminder below are the key security risks:

*   Malware

*   Application attacks

*   Hackers

Being aware of the risk is part of the solution and this section will cover how they can be defended against. The AICPA refer to this as **applied cyber security** and see centralisation as a key aspect of this.

5.1   Desktops

Modern operating systems are now full of security features, from password protected screen savers through to centrally managed software protocols, software updates and security updates "patches" that can be pushed through to the end users' desktop.

The centrally managed software protocols also allows a directory of user profiles which means that users can access their information from multiple locations.

Other defences such as enabling the password protected screensaver when the user leaves their desktop, or logging off the network when the user leaves the desktop unattended are also critical. It can be those within the organisation who are trying to gain unauthorised access to parts of the system. Leaving a computer accessible while leaving it for a short time, for example to go to the toilet or get a drink of water, can often lead to a detailed conversation with another colleague, meaning there is now a potential access point for someone with malicious intentions.

Other centralised controls like an automatic screen lock after a certain number of minutes of computer idle time can also be implemented to protect against this sort of issue.

5.2 Laptops

Laptops have a lot of similarities to desktops, in terms of the security features and the centrally managed security benefits. The key difference, and their main benefit, their mobility, means they have additional risks. Most pertinent being the risk that they could be lost or stolen and this makes whole disk encryption an essential feature to ensure the security of data on laptops.

Also, companies implement policies dictating how laptops and other mobile devices are stored and secured. Often these policies are common sense, like not leaving devices on a car seat or in a car overnight – there is the obvious theft issue, but also devices do not perform well if exposed to extreme temperatures (either hot or cold) and leaving them in a car could increase the risk of this.

In terms of physical security measures, devices can be locked to a desk although this can be fairly easily defeated.

Example: Security cables

Desktops and laptops can sometimes be secured to a desk by a security cable, fairly similar to the type that are used to secure bikes. The idea, as with a bike, is to prevent theft of the device to protect the data stored on it, or to avoid someone attempting to use it to enter the network.

The issue is that, as with bike security cables, with the right tools and enough time, the cable can be broken.

5.3   Mobile devices

Some of the threats associated with mobile devices link to the way the user operates the device. For example, to save time an aircraft engineer may download the company manual on the device so it can be accessed quickly and remotely. While in the short term this may save some time, it may also mean that the version of the manual the engineer is using does not get updated and so procedures are not carried out to exact company specification. Alternatively someone may gain access to the device and alter the manual so that subsequent work is not carried out in accordance with the appropriate safety requirements.

Organisations that allow staff to download key material, must have clear policies in place to ensure staff also download and install any updates. (This would have also been the case for paper documents, that someone must have responsibility for printing out updated policies and procedures to make sure a file or folder stayed up to date.)

Another issue can arise if a device is left logged on for too long. As with humans, our nightly shutdown and sleep help sort and restore our body, regularly shutting down a device allows updates to be installed. Most companies include these types of behaviours in their acceptable use of IT policies.

 Example: Traveller laptops

Some companies whose employees travel to remote or sensitive locations, set up what are referred to as traveller laptops.

These are devices that are specifically for the trip and often have whole disk encryption, with only data necessary for the particular trip set up on the device. When the person returns, files used on the trip are saved and the operating system and files are completely removed and reinstalled for future use. In some cases the computer is destroyed rather than run the risk of compromising proprietary information. The reason for this is that deleted files are often recoverable because they are not immediately overwritten and there is software available that can reinstate deleted files. The only completely secure way to make files inaccessible is to physically destroy the disk, drilling holes in the disk where the data is stored or crushing or burning the hard drive.

This is quite an extreme action and is reserved for particularly sensitive destinations.

5.4   Bring your own device (BYOD)

Some organisations use what is referred to as bring your own device (BYOD) programmes, but then require employees to submit the devices to the same companywide laptop security policies as company owned devices. Users may prefer the convenience of having just one device, however they may have malicious intent to use their device to gain unauthorised access to the organisations network.

As such, some organisations insist on company owned devices only, or if they allow BYOD, they prohibit the download and use of any non-company applications.

As with access to other systems, sometimes companies create different configuration profiles for different types/levels of users.

An issue for BYOD is compatibility of software, as a user may open a file with different software from that mandated by company standards and lose some of the functionality or data.

If a user is allowed to BYOD, but then leaves the organisation, they could easily download information from the network, or already have sensitive information on their own device. As discussed in the traveller laptop example, it can be very difficult to overwrite files completely, opening up issues with regard to sensitive information.

BYOD also creates another endpoint to the network and another attack point for a potential threat actor. This is particularly concerning if the software and security of the device is not up to date.

Another issue with BYOD is that because the users own the device they may choose to use them in a way that is not permissible with company policy. Companies need to be aware of developments in hardware and the possibility that staff could compromise security when they are used. For example, while they are home working they may connect the work device to a smart speaker in the home environment, the smart speaker may not have appropriate encryption and allow easier access to the device being used for work purposes.

5.5 Network configuration management (NCM)

A vital part of the security process, NCM enables companies to set up a network to meet its communication needs. It involves organising and maintaining information about its network such as locations, IP addresses, default settings, even the versions of software that are installed. By doing this the company can enforce policies, segment the network to prevent cross over into different parts of the network, monitor configuration changes and ensure compliance with software updates across a range of devices on the corporate network, from desktops to laptops and mobile devices.

Network level controls like this are very difficult to get round.

Example: University Wi-Fi

The volume of people that may want to access Wi-Fi at an organisation like a university creates potential cyber security issue – that someone may gain unauthorised access.

A possible solution is set up the network configurations so that there are different Wi-Fi networks, for example one for staff (that allows access to potentially sensitive information on the network) and one for students. NCM allows these networks to be set up so that they are completely segregated meaning that there is absolutely no crossover.

Gaining access to the student Wi-Fi would be available with minimal controls, but gaining access to the staff Wi-Fi would require proof that you are on an authorised device.

Example: Network configuration

Network configuration has reduced the effectiveness of ransomware as organisations have the data backed up and accessible so are no longer willing to pay.

The solution for the attackers is to do the exact opposite of locking data away, they are threatening to publish it for everyone to see, an attack known as doxware.

Example: USB drives

As a network expands and more devices are included within a network, so too do the attack points and the vulnerability of a network.

As part of their NCM some companies ban the use of USB drives, as the risk that one containing malware could be inserted to a computer on the network is too great. In terms of assessment of identified risks, and responses using the TARA model, this would be an example of avoiding the risk.

Other approaches include using antivirus software to scan any files that attempt access to the computer – the software should reject any software that is infected. This is an example of a control to reduce the likelihood of (rather than completely prevent) an issue as the antivirus software may be fooled by the malware.

To protect sensitive data held on a USB drive, a company may set up controls requiring the USB drive to be encrypted before any company data can be copied onto it. This protects the company should the device be lost or stolen.

5.6 Firewalls

There are two main types of firewall.

- **Network firewalls** are like perimeter fences around the network and include policies about who can access what areas of the system. They can be used to restrict access to specific websites, or types of websites, for example social media. Access control lists implemented at the network level can be used to provide certain people with access to sites that may not be allowed to other users. Certain mainstream sites are less risky to visit than say a site dedicated to illegal software, and sites that offer something for free, for example music, are more likely to be risky than a site that requires payment for the music. Where content is free, then there has to be some other way for the site to make money, whether through advertising, or installing malicious software onto a computer to mine for data.

  The most common approach, is to block staff access to certain sites or categories of sites, however some more risk averse companies have a list of allowable sites and block access to everything else.

Example: network firewalls

The employees in communications teams like customer service and marketing are often authorised to use social media sites for company purposes, perhaps to assess what is being said on social media about the brand or to start discussions about the brand or raise awareness of product initiatives. However other staff members may not be allowed access as it is often perceived to provide a distraction and reduce productivity.

- **Application firewalls** are additional security to network firewalls and can be used by an organisation to monitor the inputs, outputs and operations of a particular application. It effectively filters damaging content passing through to the application – like viruses or any attempt to exploit a known flaw in the software.

Expandable text – Application Containerisation

In the world of cyber security a container is a method for deploying applications and securing their data on mobile devices. An application is held within a container so it has its own operating environment. Software written specifically for an organisation's environment is put in a container so that employees do not need to use the mobile device's applications for company data. The container is entirely encrypted so company data can be kept safe from mixing with any personal data or malicious applications.

These are popular for basic services such as exchange email or calendar.

5.7 Antivirus and endpoint security

Antivirus software and endpoint security are additional security features that may be used by organisations to augment the security already provided by the centralised management of the operating system.

Endpoint security is vital where organisational systems are accessed by a number of different users, from a variety of locations, with numerous different types of devices. Each device with a remote connection to the network creates a potential access point for anyone wanting to gain unauthorised access to the network.

These sort of security products can help the organisation to comply with internal policies and external standards. They also provide an opportunity to check the integrity of applications and detect viruses on the machine. They have the ability to block accounts and activity if anything of concern is discovered.

Example: Security controls centralised management patches

The Wannacry and NotPetya malware mentioned in the previous chapter, both exploited a flaw in Microsoft's operating system that had been discovered by the NSA and that the NSA used to access information.

The NSA suspected that the information about EternalBlue had been stolen and so they alerted Microsoft. Once Microsoft were aware of the flaw, they issued patches to remove the flaw. Not all users installed the patches and also Microsoft only issued patches to operating systems that were currently supported.

After the Wannacry and NotPetya issues Microsoft took the unusual step of issuing patches to legacy operating systems that they no longer supported.

It is thought that the next wave of ransomware will start once a new vulnerability has been discovered.

Example: high profile attacks and their wider implications

Throughout this section we have used the Wannacry and NotPetya examples, highlighting some high profile companies that the attacks affected. The reality is a lot more companies were also affected by it, but to a less severe extent.

Since these attacks many organisations have increased their focus on cyber security, partly because of the impact it had on companies like Merck & Mearsk, but in many cases because they were also compromised, only in a smaller way.

The attacks brought into sharp focus the problems that can arise of an organisation is not aware of all the devices on its network and the importance of making sure that software is up to date.

5.8 Business continuity and disaster recovery

Most organisations now expect to be subject to a cyber-attack. Therefore part of the cyber risk management process must be to set up business continuity plans and disaster recovery plans (although the use of these plans is not limited to recovery from cyber-attacks).

- **Business continuity planning** – is proactive and designed to allow the business to operate with minimal or no downtime or service outage whilst the recovery is being managed.

- **Disaster recovery planning** – is reactive and limited to taking action to restore the data and applications and acquire new hardware.

Disaster recovery planning takes place in order to recover information systems from business critical events after they have happened. It involves:

- Making a risk assessment

- Developing a contingency plan to address those risks.

Examples of back-ups that organisations use now are:

- **Mirror site** – this is effectively a complete copy of a website, but hosted on a different URL (web address). It can be used to relieve traffic on a server to speed up performance of a website, or it can be used if the main website goes down for any reason. It is a very expensive approach, but if something is business critical it could be cheaper than the costs incurred as a result of not having one if something goes wrong.

- **Hot back up site** – this is a building that physically replicates all of the current data centre/servers, with all systems configured and ready to go with the latest back up.

- **Warm back up site** – this is a building that has all the critical hardware for the servers and systems in place but they will need to be configured and the most recent back up of the data/information installed before the site can take over the organisation's activities.

- **Cold back up site** – this is an area where, should anything go wrong, new hardware could be set up and a recovery operation could begin. None of the hardware needed is actually in place, so it would take a significant amount of time to restore operations. This is the cheapest option.

The location of back-up facilities is also an important issue.

- If the back-up facilities are **too close** then they may be taken offline along with the primary site.

- If the back-up facilities are **too far away**, that could impact on operations.

Finding the right balance for an organisation will require significant consideration.

There are also third party providers who maintain sites, which could be cheaper but could also create problems with ensuing compatibility. Third party providers are likely to have many other commitments to other clients, and this could impact the availability and accessibility of the back-up in a disaster. Particularly as disasters can impact various organisations at the same time.

Shared outages

In 2021 cloud computer provider Fastly had an issue with their global content delivery network. As Fastly underpins a lot of websites, several websites went offline at the same time. The outage impacted websites like Amazon, the New York Times, the UK government website and Reddit to name just a few.

As many organisations and some with significant buying power would all be seeking a resolution at the same time it could mean a slower response time to those the provider deemed less important.

More on disaster recovery plans

An unexpected disaster can put an entire computer system out of action. For large organisations, a disaster might involve damage from a terrorist attack. There could also be threats from fire and flood damage. A disaster might simply be a software or hardware breakdown within a system.

Disaster recovery planning involves assessing what disasters might occur that would pose a serious threat to the organisation, and trying to ensure that alternative arrangements are available in the event that it occurs.

In the case of a computer system for a clearing bank, this would mean having an entire back-up computer system in place that could be brought into operation if a disaster puts the main system out of action.

Not all organisations have extensive disaster recovery plans. Certainly, however, back-up copies of major data files should be kept, so that in the event that the main files are destroyed, the data can be re-created with the back-up files.

System back-ups

All files containing important information should be backed up on a regular basis. Backing up provides protection against the loss or corruption of data due to:

- faults in the hardware (e.g. hard disk)

- the accidental deletion of a file by a computer operator

- damage to a data file by a hacker.

A back-up is simply a copy of the file. If the original file is lost or becomes corrupt, the back-up can be substituted in its place, and the master file can be re-created.

There may still be some loss of data if inputs to the system occurred after the most recent back-up copy of the file was made.

- However, if back-ups are made regularly, the loss of data should be limited. If there are paper records of input transactions made after the most recent back-up copy was made, the file can be brought up to date by re-inputting the data.

- Some systems provide back-up copies of both master files and transaction data files. Copies of these files can be used to re-create an up-to-date master file if the original master file is lost or corrupted.

Back-up copies might be stored on the same physical computer file as the original file, but this is risky, since damage to the physical file will result in the loss of the back-up as well as the main file.

Back-up files can also be created by copying them on to a disk or tape. Where security is important, any such back-up copies should be held in a secure place, such as a safe.

To counter the risk of damage to a file due to a fire or similar disaster at the premises where the IT system is located, a back-up copy might be taken off-site and held somewhere else.

The need for robust disaster recovery plans

In May 2017 British Airways had an issue with the power supply to business critical IT systems which led to BA's check in systems, call centre and website all going off line.

The company was criticised for its failure to have an appropriate disaster recovery plan for systems critical to its core operation. Questions have been raised as to why an uninterruptible power supply was not used, why there was no back-up power supply to start up automatically if the power supply was compromised, and why there was no back-up server running alongside the main system.

The impact of this disaster was still being felt by passengers three days later and is expected to cost the company a significant amount in compensation payments, with some estimates as high as £100 million.

This is an example of a situation where maintaining a hot back up site would have been worth the investment.

Business continuity planning

QuadrigaCX, Canada's leading cryptocurrency exchange company, made international headlines due to their business continuity planning, or rather their lack of it.

The founder Gerald Cotton passed away while travelling to open an orphanage in India due to complication with Crohn's disease. Unfortunately for QuadrigaCX and their clients Mr Cotton had sole responsibility for looking after the funds and coins. This meant he was the only person with the password key to access the money (which was held in what is referred to as cold storage i.e. stored offline to protect the money from hackers).

This meant that money, which some believe may be in the region of $190 million, in both cryptocurrency and normal money, is completely inaccessible. Experts have been brought in to try and break the encryption but so far have been unable to do so.

If the company had been more proactive in their management of the risks, they would have identified that someone with a medical condition being the sole guardian of a business-critical password or key was poor risk management and been able to put controls in place to manage the risk more appropriately.

There is more detail on disaster recovery and business continuity plans in the incident response section of chapter 10.

5.9 ISO27001

ISO27001 is a standard produced by the International Organisation for Standardisation (ISO) and concerns information security management systems. It is a framework that focusses on all aspects of an organisation's information risk management processes. The ISO developed ISO27001 to provide a model for establishing, implementing, operating, monitoring, reviewing, maintaining and improving an information security management system

The key principle behind the standard is, in line with the AICPA approach: to ensure a proactive rather than reactive approach to cyber security risk management.

Expandable text – ISO27001

ISO 27001 uses a top down, risk-based approach and is technology-neutral. The specification defines a six-part planning process:

- Define a security policy.

- Define the scope of the Information Security Management System (ISMS).

- Conduct a risk assessment.

- Manage identified risks.

- Select control objectives and controls to be implemented.

- Prepare a statement of applicability.

The 2005 version of the standard heavily employed the PDCA, Plan-Do-Check-Act model to structure the processes, and reflected the principles set out in the Organisation for Economic Co-operation and Development (OECD) guidelines.

The 27001 standard does not mandate specific information security controls, but it provides a checklist of controls that should be considered in the accompanying code of practice, ISO27002.

The ISO 27002 standard was originally published as a rename of the existing ISO 17799 standard, a code of practice for information security. It basically outlines hundreds of potential controls and control mechanisms, which may be implemented, in theory, subject to the guidance provided within ISO 27001.

In 2013 ISO27001 was updated to place more emphasis on measuring and evaluating how well an organisation's ISMS is performing. A section on outsourcing was also added with this release, and additional attention was paid to the organisational context of information security.

Given the high regard for ISO standards, a lot of larger organisations require B2B partners to be ISO27001 compliant or to be progressing towards compliance before they will do business with them; this a is further risk mitigation.

6 Blockchain technology

6.1 What is Blockchain technology?

A blockchain has been described as a decentralised, distributed and public digital ledger that is used to record transactions across many computers so that the record cannot be altered retroactively without the alteration of all subsequent blocks and the consensus of the network.

Alternatively, it has been defined by the Bank of England as a technology that allows people who do not know each other to trust a shared record of events.

Benefit of a blockchain

The main benefit of blockchain is security. In the digital era, cyber security is a key risk associated with the use of IT systems and the internet. This is because traditional systems have been 'closed', and so modifications to data have been carried out by just one party. If the system is hacked, there is little control to prevent such modifications from happening.

Illustration 1 – A blockchain

A simple illustration is the relationship that individuals have with their banks or credit card companies. If you carry out a transaction with either (for example, you use your credit card to pay for goods or services) only one party records the transaction – your credit card company. How is that company to know that the transaction is valid? If the details appear reasonable, the transactions will be authorised. This allows those who carry out credit card fraud to make their (illegal) gains.

A blockchain provides an effective control mechanism aimed at addressing such cyber security risks. It is a record keeping mechanism that is 'open' or public, as it is a form of distributed ledger; it has been described as a form of collective bookkeeping.

Key features of a blockchain

- In a blockchain system, transactions are recorded by a number of participants using a network which operates via the internet. The same records are maintained by a number of different parties; as a transaction is entered, it is recorded by not just two parties, but instead by all of the parties that make up the overall chain. This can happen because all of the records in the blockchain are publicly available and distributed between everyone that is part of that network.

- When a transaction takes place (for example, between a buyer and a seller) the details of that deal are recorded by everyone – the value, the time, the date and the details of those parties involved. All of the ledgers that make up the blockchain are updated in the same way, and it takes the agreement of all participants in the chain to update their ledgers for the transaction to be accepted.

- The process of verifying the transaction is carried out by computers; it is effectively the computers which make up the network that audit the transaction. If all of the computers review the transaction and verify that the details are correct, the systems of all participants in the blockchain have updated records. The computers work together to ensure that each transaction is valid before it is added to the blockchain. This decentralised network of computers ensures that a single system cannot add new blocks to the chain.

- When a new block is added to a blockchain, it is linked to the previous block using a cryptographic hash generated from the contents of the previous block. This ensures that the chain is never broken and that each block is permanently recorded. It is intentionally difficult to alter past transactions in the blockchain because all of the subsequent blocks must be altered first.

It is this control aspect of blockchain technology which addresses the main concern of cyber security. If anyone should attempt to interfere with a transaction, it will be rejected by those network parties making up the blockchain whose role it is to verify the transaction. If just one party disagrees, the transaction will not be recorded.

Illustration 2 – Cryptocurrency

Bitcoin is a digital currency that was introduced in 2009. Other cryptocurrencies exist, such as Ethereum and Litecoin.

There is no physical version of Bitcoin; all Bitcoin transactions take place over the internet. Unlike traditional currencies, Bitcoin is decentralised, meaning it is not controlled by a single bank or government. Instead, Bitcoin uses a peer-to-peer (P2P) payment network made up of users with Bitcoin accounts.

Bitcoins can be acquired in 2 different ways: 1) exchanging other currencies for bitcoins; and 2) bitcoin mining.

The first method is by far the most common, and can be done using a Bitcoin exchange such as Mt.Gox or CampBX. These exchanges allow users to exchange sterling, dollars etc. for bitcoins.

Bitcoin mining involves setting up a computer system to solve maths problems generated by the Bitcoin network. As a bitcoin miner solves these complex problems, bitcoins are credited to the miner. The network is designed to generate increasingly more complex maths problems which ensures that new bitcoins are generated at a consistent rate.

When a user obtains bitcoins, the balance is stored in a secure 'wallet' that is encrypted using password protection. When a bitcoin transaction takes place, the ownership of the bitcoins is updated in the network on all ledgers, and the balance in the relevant wallets updated accordingly.

There is no need for a central bank to authorise transactions, since they are verified by those computers that make up the system. This therefore has the advantages of speed, reduced cost (transaction fees are small, typically $0.01 per transaction), and increased security.

Additionally, there are no pre-requisites for creating a Bitcoin account, and no transaction limits. Bitcoins can be used around the world, but the currency is only good for purchasing items from vendors that accept Bitcoin.

6.2   The relevance of blockchain technology to accountants

Ultimately, blockchain provides an unalterable, transparent record of all accountancy-related data.

Examples of how blockchain can benefit the accounting profession include:

- Reducing the cost of maintaining and reconciling ledgers.

- Providing absolute certainty over the ownership and history of assets, the existence of obligations and the measurement of amounts owed to a business and owed by a business.

- Freeing up time to allow staff to concentrate on other responsibilities such as planning, valuation, reporting etc., rather than record-keeping.

Blockchain potential

It is believed that blockchain can streamline and speed up organisations business processes, improve defences against cyber risks and reduce or entirely remove the need to use expensive third party security applications.

Some commentators are suggesting that blockchain could do for networks of organisations what enterprise resource planning (ERP) did for an individual business. That is allow an understanding of business operations and common processes across enterprises, improving integration and improving efficiency.

Some benefits of using blockchain include reduced procurement costs, lower inventory levels. The use of crypto currency could even avoid the use of foreign exchange as businesses are using virtual currencies which would result in far lower administrative costs.

6.3   Risks

Despite initial claims that a blockchain was unhackable, like everything it still has risks, and inevitably is not unhackable. As anything increases in use, it becomes more attractive to those wishing to use it for unauthorised purposes, meaning more time gets spent analysing ways to overcome the controls that are in place and to discover how money can be made/stolen.

51% rule

One of the current issues that has arisen is that if a trader controls over 50% of the mining power in a cryptocurrency chain they can overwrite the controls and spend the same money again. As with other aspects, the more mainstream crypto currencies are less likely to be hacked in this way (the cost to do this with Bitcoin would be prohibitive) but it may be possible on some of the smaller exchanges.

7   Centralised monitoring

There has been an increase in the number of organisations whose systems are now accessed by a large variety of devices logging on from all over the world. Users are creating potential points for unauthorised access with every additional device that is used. The need for centralised monitoring of systems activity has also evolved in line with these changes.

There are many components to centralised monitoring, these include:

- **Event logging and aggregation** – modern computer operating systems keep a record of their activity as standard, collecting information such as:

  - Who logged in

  - What programmes they accessed/used

  - What files were used

  - Areas / systems that they tried to access or run, but were unable to

  Most of this information is fairly superficial and generally will not be looked at, but it is essential for administrative and accountability purposes, as well as – if there is an issue – forensic analysis.

  As much of this could be deemed sensitive information, privacy considerations mean that these records should only be viewed by security personnel. Best practice would be to send the records to a central monitoring point either a security operations centre (SOC) or a data centre.

- **Security information and event management (SIEM)** – these systems have been developed to make this monitoring more effective. They work alongside firewalls, antivirus software, IDS/IPS etc and so make event monitoring more effective. SIEMs analyse all of the available data (from the different systems) and look for patterns that suggests unusual activity that could be a security compromise or a possible attack. The ability to piece together all the different sources of information allows the system to identify security risks that the individual systems may miss.

  SIEM systems have allowed organisations to analyse data in a positive and useful way which would previously have been impossible (or at least extremely time consuming and unlikely to yield results).

  When the SIEM system identifies a potential threat, an incident response process can then be initiated.

- **Modern security operations centre (SOC) functions** – SOC have also evolved over time and could have a range of teams or functions:

  - Incident response team

  - Threat intelligence team

  - Hunt team

  - Insider threat team

Expandable text

- Incident response team

  When the SIEM identifies a potential threat, an incident response process is initiated. The focus of this team is business continuity.

- Threat intelligence team

  The mission of the threat intelligence team is to monitor trends and identify threats arising, most commonly in the industry sector that the company operates. These teams then pass on information to the team responsible for monitoring activity via the SIEM.

- Hunt team

  This team operates on the assumption that the organisation has been breached already but no one has yet identified the breach. The hunt team is therefore looking for any sign that there has been an intrusion into the systems.

- Insider threat team

  Research shows that a lot of system breaches come from within the organisation; perhaps from someone who feels they have been unfairly treated (a missed promotion opportunity or a poor performance evaluation) or an employee who is suffering financial challenges. However investigating for internal involvement can have serious considerations (privacy, legal, HR etc).

Example: Threat intelligence and hunt teams

The gap between security breaches and detection is increasing as attackers are often acting in a more discrete manner.

In the Verizon 2018 Data Breach Investigations Report:

- In 87% of breaches it took only minutes or less for attackers to compromise systems.

- Only 3% were discovered quickly, and 68% went undiscovered for months or more.

- The only industry where the threat from insider action is greater than the external threat is in the Healthcare industry. Although human error was found to be a major factor and curiosity was another (for example where a celebrity had recently been a patient).

Test your understanding 6

An oil company uses an IT server for a major system and the management believe that it is essential that the continuity of processing must be assured at all times.

Which of the following risk control measures is the most appropriate for ensuring that this happens?

A   A secure password protection system

B   A standby server

C   Surplus capacity in the memory of the operational server

D   Fire safety measures

Test your understanding 7

GKJ company allows many of its employees to work remotely on mobile devices.

Which ONE of the following actions would it need to implement to ensure its information security management system (ISMS) complied with the ISO27001 standards?

A   Develop a security policy for use of mobile devices

B   Limit use of business applications by mobile devices

C   Forbid employees to leave mobile devices unattended

D   Ban downloading of company policies from central servers

Test your understanding 8

The board of JLK company has been warned by its Threat Intelligence team that a new form of cyber-attack has just been reported by other companies operating in the same industry.

Which TWO of the following responses to the risk identified by the team would be MOST appropriate for inclusion in JLK's cyber-security risk management programme?

A   Review the company security information and event management (SIEM) system for evidence that such an attack has occurred

B   Enter into a blockchain system with other companies in the industry

C   Update network firewalls

D   Conduct an updated assessment of the company's information security risks

E   Require all staff to change the passwords used to access the system

Test your understanding 9

JPI company relies on goods provided by a complex network of interlinked suppliers. It wishes to ensure that all members of the network are able to transact securely with each other.

Which ONE of the following actions would be the MOST appropriate way to achieve this objective?

A   Introduce a blockchain system linking the network members

B   Set up a shared insider threat team

C   Install a network firewall

D   Introduce a network configuration management (NCM) system

Test your understanding 10 (Integration)

Blush is a small makeup business that currently has a little boutique store in the heart of Eastfield. From the success of their new range of jewellery that has been worn and shown on numerous celebrity Instagram pages, Blush have decided to launch their own website. Up to this point, products were only purchased in-store, but the launch of their website will allow their customers to purchase online, either by click and collect at their local Blush boutique store or delivery to their home address.

To use the website customers must register their details by providing their full name, address, phone number and credit card details..

Required:

(a)   **Discuss and explain the increased cyber security risks which Blush will face as a result of the launch of their website.**

                                                      (10 minutes)

(b)   **Recommend appropriate actions which Blush can put in place to mitigate against the increased risks identified in part (a)**

                                                      (15 minutes)

Test your understanding 11 – H training company (Case study)

Scenario

H is a training company that provides executive training in management subjects. H provides short courses that range from a single day to five days. H has five offices and each office has between ten and twenty full-time trainers.

H's courses are very expensive. Delegates are senior managers and company directors. All courses are paid for by employers who are keen to equip their staff with new skills or to update existing knowledge.

Many courses are taught in H's offices to small groups of delegates, each of whom has come from a different company.

These courses are advertised on H's website and some, like "finance for non-financial managers", are taught frequently throughout the year. H will also adapt an existing course or even write a new course from scratch and offer it in-house for a client company. Trainers often have to travel away from home and stay in hotels in order to present in-house courses at clients' offices.

Each course delegate receives a printed copy of the course materials and an electronic copy on a memory stick. Feedback indicates that delegates like to refer to the paper copy during the course and then take the electronic copy for ease of storage and future reference.

Courses are presented using laptops and projectors. Slides are written on an industry-standard presentation software package. H has provided each trainer with a laptop and all of the company's training rooms are equipped with projectors. Client companies also have projectors that are available for presentations.

Each course has a very specific syllabus and the course materials are written to a very high standard. A master copy of the material used on each course, including client-specific "in-house courses" is stored on a PC at H's head office and updated copies are backed up to a server at another office. Courses are reviewed regularly and updated when required. The company-specific courses are held so that they can be adapted if necessary for other companies or to become a general offering.

Trigger

'Image' is very important and H's trainers all take great pride in their personal appearance. They all take care to ensure that they are well dressed. That pride also extends to being seen to have the latest technology. Many of H's trainers have bought themselves tablet computers that they can use instead of their laptops. There are different operating systems for these machines, but all can run the software required to edit and present course materials and all of the trainers have purchased models that can work with standard projectors. The trainers feel that these tablets look more impressive and that they are lighter to pack when they have to work away from home on in-house courses. The tablets have also been used to go online and access H's systems.

H's Head of IT is concerned that there could be problems associated with the trainers using their own tablet computers in this way.

Task

As a senior employee in the IT department write a memorandum to the IT director of H which:

(a)   Discusses the risks associated with H's staff using their own equipment (for example tablets) instead of the laptops provided by H; and

(b)   Recommends, with explanations, the policies and procedures that H should adopt for the use and purchase of laptops and other devices used by the trainers.

(45 minutes)

Test your understanding 12 – Royals (Case study)

Scenario

You are a senior manager in the finance department for Royals, a budget gym operator in the country of Hylandia. Karl Judd, the chief financial officer, has just sat down at your desk. He passes his tablet with the Twitter app open displaying a series of tweets between one of Royals gym staff and several patient recommended by doctors to the Make Hylandia Healthy initiative:

"Take a look at these tweets!

The CEO has just had a call from a senior official at the Ministry of Health, who is furious at the tweets that have been posted in the last 24 hours. This has apparently gone viral. The CEO is demanding that this gym staff member be dismissed immediately.

I've just spoken to one of the regional managers who has already been in contact with Tim Beam, the gym staff member concerned. Tim says he is very sorry for his tweets, but has been under pressure from all the additional work he is having to do. He also stated that he had not had any assistance or information about the Make Hylandia Healthy initiative from head office. The regional manager also pointed out to me that we do not provide any training on social media use to gym staff nor do we operate any policy on staff usage of social media.

What are the ethical issues we need to consider in relation to this incident, both from Royals' perspective as the employer and from the employee's perspective?

Social media is something that is part of daily life, but the CEO will need some convincing that we should not shut down Royals' twitter account completely.

I need some information from you, firstly on the benefits to Royals of using social media as a business communication tool and secondly, how should we control our social media communications to make sure nothing like this happens again?"

Trigger

Alison Tree @alitree454

Just been to my first session at @RoyalsGym. V disappointed. Gym instructor uninterested in me and I won't be going back. So much for helping me get fit #makehylandiahealthy #wasteoftime

Tom Ray @tjray127

@RoyalsGym was a waste of time. No induction help. Had no ideas what to do. Won't be getting fit at this rate #demotivated

Mr Fitness @timebeam123

@alitree454 sorry you were disappointed with my help at Royals today. Perhaps if you spent less time talking to your friends and more time exercising you wouldn't be so unfit #timewaster

Mr Fitness @timebeam123

@tjray127 I've been working at Royals for 3 years – not seen many like you. Clearly you have never set foot in a gym in your life before. Ha. I've got better things to do with my time. #anothertimewaster

Alison Tree @alitree454

@timebeam123 you are meant to encourage us and not be disrespectful to customers. I wonder if your boss @RoyalsGym know how you feel?

Joanne Rouse @JoJoRouse17

@alitree454 I had a dreadful experience too. I attended @RoyalsGym last week on the #makehylandiahealthy programme. As a 60-year old with no previous experience I expected some help. None was given.

Mr Fitness @timebeam123

@JoJoRouse17 let's face it. You're too old to be going to a gym. Put your feet up and have a biscuit! I've had enough of all this chat now. None of you are paying, so you're not real customers anyway. It doesn't matter what you think. #leaveittotheexperts

Task

"Please prepare me briefing notes on the three issues I've just mentioned so that I can advise the CEO on the approaches we should take."

(45 minutes)

8 Chapter summary

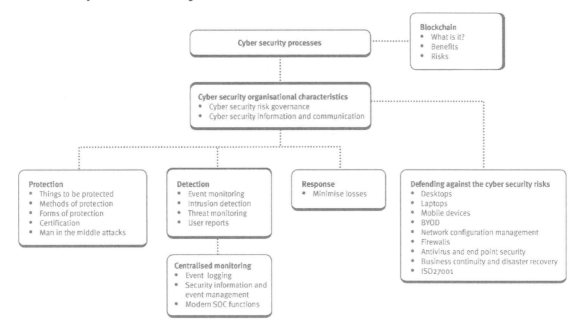

Test your understanding answers

Test your understanding 1

The correct answers are A, B and E

Malvertising occurs where adverts shown on webpages visited by the company system contain malicious code which can infect the computer whether or not the user takes any action (such as clicking on the advert).

Advert blocking software will prevent the adverts from being displayed so that they cannot act.

Application firewalls can prevent viruses passing through to particular applications and antivirus software is designed to prevent viruses but also to detect and remove any that have managed to compromise the system.

Increasing authentication layers and encrypting data would not prevent the adverts from being seen or from infecting NBV's system once they had been displayed.

Test your understanding 2

The correct answer is A

Encryption of data involves scrambling the contents in such a way that only authorised recipients can unscramble and access it.

Monitoring the system may alert the company to attempts by hackers to access the system, a network firewall can prevent company employees from accessing certain sites and backing up data can help the company to reconstruct files in the event that data is lost or corrupted.

Test your understanding 3

The correct answers are B, C and E

These are all ways in which cyber security risk governance can be addressed.

A is a way a company could address cyber security risk governance, but given that both Sachkartar and Justyna have recent relevant IT experience and hold positions on the board they already satisfy this consideration.

There is no requirement for how a risk committee is made up for corporate governance or for cyber security risk governance.

Test your understanding 4

The correct answer is B

It is 8 characters long, with 4 different types of character (3 lower case, 1 uppercase, 2 numbers and a special character.

While A is 8 characters long, it has less variety.

C has good variety but is less than 8 characters.

D is the longest but is very familiar and would be a prime target for a hacker to experiment with.

Test your understanding 5

The correct answers are A, B and C

These are all realistic and appropriate forms of protection to use.

D creates an additional copy of the company data and if lost could compromise company data. A secure back up on a remote server would be more appropriate.

E is a detection technique rather than a form of protection.

A CIRT is a response should a system breach be detected and is not designed to help with routine IT issues.

Test your understanding 6

The correct answer is B

A standby server (in a different location) can ensure continuity of processing, provided that backup files of the system are continually produced (and also stored in a different location).

Test your understanding 7

The correct answer is A

Although the ISO27001 standards require organisations to maintain security policies they do not include any mandatory information security controls. Instead they contain a list of potential controls that may be considered but leave organisations to assess their own specific security risks and develop controls as appropriate.

Test your understanding 8

The correct answers are A and D

JLK's Threat Intelligence team has identified a new form of cyber-attack but at this stage it is not clear how it works to attack the system. Therefore responses to the risk will be high level – assess the risk and seek to identify whether the company has been affected. Specific responses cannot be specified until more is known about how the cyber attack works to threaten the system.

Passwords are a form of authentication that increase an organisation's confidence in the identification of those accessing a system via a legitimate channel.

Blockchain systems will not permit any modification of data within a system unless all the system participants consent.

Network firewalls restrict access to the system by system users.

All these responses might mitigate the risk but only if the new form of cyber-attack exploits the weaknesses they are designed to prevent.

Test your understanding 9

The correct answer is A

Blockchain technology allows for the synchronisation of all data and transactions across a network and each member must verify the transaction before it can be approved. It is increasingly being used to link supply chains.

A network firewall is designed to control access to certain areas inside a computer network.

A NCM system allows for the organisation and maintenance of information about all the different elements in a computer network such as locations, IP address, default settings, versions of software installed etc.

An insider threat team works to identify those within an organisation who may wish use their position to effect a system breach.

Test your understanding 10 (Integration)

(a) **Increased cyber security risks:**

By allowing customers to set up on-line accounts from which to make payments the company will be holding increased amount of Personal Information (such as customer's payment details) which make them more attractive to hackers.

This increases the risk of the following;

Unauthorised access to customer accounts –leading to theft of their confidential Personal Information and / or the making of unauthorised purchases.

SQL injection via unprotected input boxes on the new website (where the attacker is able to inject code into an input box on a company's website which could be used to alter or download the database supporting the website).

Malvertisers maliciously infecting adverts placed on website with malware which can then affect every visitor to that page regardless of whether the visitor actually clicks anything on the page

(b) **Appropriate actions to mitigate against the increased risks:**

Purchase appropriate additional insurance to cover against the increased cyber security risks.

Consider setting up (or appointing an outside company to act as) a security operations centre (SOC) responsible for overseeing cyber-security within the organisation.

Carry out security testing of the system, for example using an ethical hacker, to test the new website to identify any unprotected access points.

Consider whether existing firewalls and malware / virus protection software should be upgraded if needed to protect against additional vulnerabilities.

Introduce a security information and event management system (SIEM) to identify unusual systems activity (such as surges of data traffic across the network) which may suggest there has been a systems breach.

Ensure pop-up blockers take automatic effect whenever any devices on the system access other websites to reduce the exposure to adverts which could contain malware.

Test your understanding 11 – H training company (Case study)

Memorandum

To: IT director

From: Senior IT employee

Date: Today

Subject: The use of tablets – risks, policies and procedures

(a)   **Risks with the use of tablets**

The most immediate risk is that these tablets are being connected to H's servers in order to both download files and upload edited and modified versions. H has no way to ensure that these devices are free of viruses and other malware and so the systems could be corrupted. The laptops are a known quantity and H can specify the security software that must be used and kept up to date

The files that are given to delegates are also potentially open to infection. The delegates could open their organisations up to a threat and H could be held liable.

H's IT staff may not be able to support these devices. If a compatibility issue arises with either hardware or software then the staff will be unable to seek support from H and that could affect the smooth running of a presentation. There are several different platforms for tablet computers and so it would be difficult for H's staff to be familiar with all of them.

Tablets do not always run industry-standard software, but use simplified packages that claim to be able to edit these files.

The creation or modification of a file using a "compatible" software suite may mean the file cannot be opened or that some of the formatting is lost. That could make H's presentations seem far less professional.

Tablets and similar devices may be less robust than a business laptop and so the courses could be disrupted by machines breaking down or failing.

The software running on the tablets may not be licenced and H may be open to accusations of copyright theft if its staff are using unauthorised copies.

In the event that a trainer leaves the company it will not be as easy for H to request the return of its files because they will be on the trainer's personal tablet.

There are very few upside risks, but this arrangement does mean that H's trainers will often appear to be at the forefront of technology. It also gives H the opportunity to experiment with new technology at very little direct cost to the company.

(b) **Policies and procedures over the use of tablets**

The starting point should be to insist that staff use only the hardware and software that have been provided by the company. That will give H control over the platforms that are being used to develop and deliver courses.

H should have a designated evaluation group to evaluate new technology as it becomes available. That group should comprise both IT experts and trainers, so that the new technology can be assessed from both a technical and a practical point of view. H needs to ensure that it makes the best possible use of new technology as and when it becomes available in a reliable and cost-effective product. H should avoid getting carried away by the rush to adopt new technologies that are at the "bleeding edge" because early adopters pay more and bear most of the risks.

New hardware and software should be evaluated against a detailed checklist covering both security and compatibility. H has to be certain that none of its materials will be at risk of infection or corruption and that files will also be capable of being opened, edited, stored and passed onto clients. Security should be evaluated by referring to third-party reviews by security specialists because it is unlikely that H will have sufficient expertise in-house to test the firewall and anti-virus systems on a new computer platform

When new devices require a change in software, such as a switch to a cut-down version of a package that can be run on a tablet, H should insist that the presentations are reviewed slide-by-slide to ensure that they all open and have the required format. H should consider insisting that the materials continue to be updated using industry-standard packages and that the new hardware should be used to present courses using copies of the updated files.

There should be a genuine business reason for making the change to new platforms, otherwise H will be exposed to the risks associated with the new technology simply because trainers want to use the latest "toys". That would not prevent H from agreeing to use new hardware simply for the sake of impressing clients because image is very important in this business.

Test your understanding 12 – Royals (Case study)

Briefing Notes

To: Karl Judd

From: Senior manager

Subject: Social media

Ethical issues

Royals has a duty of care to our employees to train them to carry out their job effectively. I do not believe that we have achieved this in this instance. We must investigate if the claims made by the gym instructor are true, as he could be merely making an excuse for his poor behaviour. But if we find out that gym staff were not fully informed or provided with sufficient guidance regarding this initiative and that gym staff have been over-worked or not given appropriate guidance and support, then this is lack of professional competence on our behalf.

Nevertheless, the gym staff member in question did not act with the correct level of professional behaviour in his responses to the customers using his twitter account. He lacked integrity and objectivity in his responses and in his manner of communicating to customers. There is no excuse for these kind of comments, whatever the pressure he was under. It is certainly not acceptable, particularly if these were carried out via Royal's own twitter account.

We must investigate this situation before we terminate the employment of this gym staff member. It could be considered as gross professional misconduct if proved to be true but we must find out the opinion of other gym staff as to whether his claims about no communication are true. If we do not operate a twitter usage policy and have no training on this as a communication tool, then this is a significant weakness in our training programme and we must immediately instigate a social media usage policy and guidance to all staff immediately.

Benefits of social media as a business communication tool

Social media can help us to generate a huge amount of data about Royals customers in real time. Social media activity could provide us with a wealth of information about our customers, such as who they are, what they like, and how they feel about our brand. Through active engagement and social listening, we can gather relevant customer data and use that information to make improved business decisions.

A presence on social media will also make it easier for our customers to find and connect with us. By connecting with our customers on social media, Royals is more likely to increase customer retention and brand loyalty. Social media ads are also an inexpensive way to promote the business. Social media increases sales and customer retention through regular interaction and timely customer service.

It is now an expectation of customers that businesses have a social media presence. Customers expect fast response times and 24/7 support – just like our service delivery. One of the biggest benefits of social media is using it to increase our website traffic. Not only does social media help direct people to our website, but the more social media shares we receive, the higher our search ranking will be. Also, with social media monitoring we can gain key information about our competitors. This kind of information will allow us to make strategic business decisions to stay ahead of them.

With the help of social media, specifically when it comes to sharing content about the business, all we need to do is share it on our social network accounts. Importantly, social media is a two-way channel where we have the opportunity to enrich relationships with our customers. This kind of social media dialogue between us and our customers is something traditional advertising cannot achieve.

Controlling social media environment

Royals must implement a company-wide staff policy on the usage of social media as soon as possible. Regional Managers should be responsible for initial training and any necessary on-going training and updates on social media usage by staff in their own regions. All new members of staff should be inducted and trained on the appropriate usage of social media when operating as a Royals employee and we must make it clear in staff contracts that violation of our corporate social media usage policies will result in disciplinary action or in extreme cases, dismissal.

Guidance and training should also be given on personal usage to ensure that staff are aware that personal usage violations could have repercussions for Royals. It must be made clear in our social media usage policy that any contact with customers must be carried out in a professional and objective manner and that any correspondence which brings the company name into disrepute will be disciplined. We must make available to staff our disciplinary procedures for any abuse of social media activity.

We should also ensure that a member of the IT team is responsible for monitoring Royals social media activity and that we have some form of process whereby we can actively track any social media activity related to Royals. We must keep up to date on what customers and staff are saying and ensure that it falls within the bounds of what is acceptable to us.

All social media communications from Royals should be provided via one source. We should consider only having one or two members of staff, probably from the marketing team, who respond to any social media comments made by customers, rather than allowing any direct comments from staff to customers. However, we would need to investigate this as we would not want to lose our personal touch with customers.

Cyber security tools, techniques and reporting

Chapter learning objectives

Lead	Component
D3 Discuss cyber security tools and techniques	(a) Discuss forensic analysis
	(b) Discuss malware analysis
	(c) Discuss penetration testing
	(d) Discuss software security
D4 Evaluate cyber risk reporting	(a) Evaluate cyber risk reporting frameworks

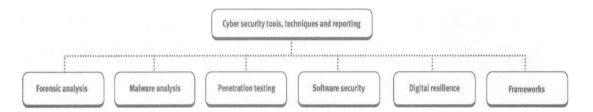

1 Cyber security tools and techniques

Throughout the CIMA syllabus there are examples of companies using techniques to learn from the results of their actions. Whether it is variance analysis or a post completion audit, the common theme of the models is that they look back and learn from events that have occurred.

The obvious aim of cyber security is complete prevention. However this aim is unrealistic and in practice the risk of a cyber-attack is similar to the risk that a project is delayed, or a budgetary target is missed. This chapter explores how companies can look back and learn from any cyber-attacks and so improve their cyber security.

Example: Permanent state of alert
In 2018 it was estimated that small businesses in the UK alone were the target of 65,000 attempted cyber-attacks every day.
Just looking at small businesses, there were sometimes as many as 359,000 attacks in a 24 hour period.
As technology is used more and more this number is only likely to increase.

2 Forensic analysis

As with any crime scene, virtual or physical, something is always left behind. Forensic analysis is the process of examining the things that have been left behind by the attack/attacker to increase understanding about the attack and how the systems were breached to be able to improve defences in the future.

There are three main areas to consider in forensic analysis of cyber-attacks and cyber security. They are:

- **System level analysis**.

- **Storage analysis**

- **Network analysis**.

Each of these will be explored in more detail.

2.1 System level analysis

Once it is known that a system has been compromised, the first stage is to identify what part of the system is affected. This often referred to as looking for 'footprints in the sand' to identify what, if any, changes have been made to the system.

- **System components**: the components of the operating system are often changed after malware has been installed.

- **Configuration changes**: settings of the system and how programmes run can be affected by malware.

- **Services enabled without authorisation**: once the malware is installed the attacker needs to be able to access the system again in the future to enable theft or further intrusion.

- **Fake accounts created**: setting up fake accounts is a common way to re-enter a system.

Example: Social media

Facebook and other social media companies are trying to remove as many fake accounts as possible. Attackers use fake accounts as opposed to hacking into a legitimate user's account – as the user is likely to spot that something is unusual about their account and report it.

In a recent quarterly update, Facebook announced it had disabled almost 1.3 billion fake accounts in a 6 month period.

A significant proportion of the fake accounts were bots (autonomous programs designed to behave like a human) and created with the intention of conducting scams and spreading spam.

Facebook is publishing these sort of statistics for multiple reasons, one is to hold itself accountable, but perhaps a bigger reason is to show to users that it is taking action against this problem.

2.2 Storage analysis

Computers and devices have a huge amount of storage on them which can make locating particular files difficult and conversely make it much easier to hide a file that is not meant to be seen.

The introduction of cloud storage has made this aspect of forensic analysis harder. Since a third party owns the servers that store the data, obtaining access to review any changes can be harder.

Another difficulty with regard to storage analysis is that although files can be deleted, in most cases the deleted files still exist but in an unreferenced way. They continue to take up storage and can even still be accessed (although the recovery process is very time consuming and complex).

Example: Deleted items recovery

In the run up to the 2016 US General Election, the FBI were investigating Hilary Clinton's use of her private computer server for classified information. Reports stated that despite over 30,000 emails having been deleted, the FBI were able to recover some of the emails, both personal and work related.

2.3 Network analysis

Network analysis is focussed on monitoring the amount of data moving across a network at a single point in time, often referred to as network traffic. It is a similar concept to monitoring traffic on the roads, although using quite advanced number plate recognition. The monitoring process doesn't allow the company to see what is in the car (i.e. what data is being transferred), but it does tell you whose car it is that is on the road (i.e. which users are on the network).

As with the traffic flow of cars – usually busy in the morning around 9am and the late afternoon around 5pm – there are patterns in the volume and identity of users on a network at a particular time. If there are unexpected users on the network, or if the level of traffic is unexpectedly high, these could be cause for concern leading to further investigation.

Forensic analysis reviews this network traffic after a cyber attack, to identify patterns in the traffic leading up to the infection. This information can then be used to help detect and mitigate future attacks before they can have an effect. By sharing the data with other organisations, coordinated responses can be developed and IDS / SIEM systems can be improved.

Analysing network traffic using third party cloud storage services can cause privacy issues that would not arise on company-owned hard drives.

Forensic analysis

After the attack on DigiNotar mentioned in the previous chapter, the Dutch government commissioned Fox-IT to carry out forensic analysis on the DigiNotar Network. As always with these incidents, the public never find out the whole story, but some reports say that they were able to find digital "fingerprints" on one of the servers and from this they were able to work out that it was the same attacker who had also compromised another certificate authority called Comodo based in New Jersey in America.

This story suggests that the security preventing unauthorised access to a firm's network appears easier to get round than the security that certificates provide.

A similar situation happened with car security systems. Cars were becoming so hard to break into that criminals were breaking into houses to steal keys to cars, rather than breaking into the cars themselves. The weakest link in any control is often a mistake made by a person, for example leaving the front door unlocked and the car keys near the front door. Relating this example back to cyber security, it could be an employee at a Certificate Authority clicking on phishing email link allowing a hacker access to the network and ultimately being able to issue rogue certificates, rather than the hacker finding a way to impersonate the certificates.

3 Malware analysis

Ideally no malware would get on to an entity's systems, but the reality is it will. Once malware has been identified, analysis of the software should be carried out to understand as much as possible about the malware. The aim of malware analysis is to understand how the malware got on to the computer and its purpose, including whether it was intended specifically for the organisation. Obtaining this information means organisations are better able to improve their defences in the future.

3.1 Reverse engineering

Reverse engineering is a commonly used technique – not just with regard malware. The process is used to deconstruct the subject – to understand how it was designed and how it works. In terms of cyber security and malware, the design and functionality are of interest, but discovering how the malware infiltrated the system provides a key piece of information to help patch flaws and prevent further infiltration.

Developers of malware are aware of the risk that their malware will be discovered and reverse engineered to learn more about it, so they aim to make it as difficult as possible to reverse engineer. A technique known as layering is used to protect the malware code and functionality. Several layers of code are written to protect the malware code and each layer must be uncovered, usually in different ways, before the malware code is revealed. A term used in IT to describe this is obfuscation (making something obscure or unclear). The more bizarre a hacker can make their malware code, the easier it will be for them to protect it.

During reverse engineering, a key aim is to discover whether the attack was targeted or not. Clearly, a targeted attack is more of a concern – it means you have something that someone wants and they have taken the time to write code and hide that code to get at it. Targeted attacks are likely to have better layering as they do not want the target to know where the attack comes from, what they are trying to access and why. Of course, untargeted attacks are still a concern as it means the organisation's security processes have been breached. In the Mearsk example mentioned earlier it probably didn't provide much comfort to know that the NotPetya was targeting the Ukraine – it still caused them significant damage.

Example: targeted attacks

Most targeted attacks are against organisations with a lot of information/data or with significant money. The number one most targeted organisations are Governments, and the second most targeted are financial institutions (for example banks).

3.2 Decompilation and disassembly

Once the layers of code have been removed and the organisation has access to the malware, it is vital that analysis is carried out to understand how it works and why it was put into their system, particularly if it was a targeted attack.

Since the malware will be written in a specific programming language, it is important that appropriate tools are used and people with appropriate skills carry out the task.

As in a fraud investigation, understanding how the opportunity to infect the company's systems occurred and discovering the motive of the attacker will help the company understand what data/information is attractive and how it could be vulnerable.

4 Penetration testing

Penetration testing is another important step in the process of improving cyber security, it is effectively testing how good the cyber security of a company is. This can often involve the use of ethical hackers who are hired to try and penetrate the network or system.

4.1 Network discovery

Network discovery is sometimes called external network or infrastructure penetration test. This part of penetration testing process involves understanding the scope of the network i.e. identifying all of the devices that are on a network and connect with the internet and other external systems. There are obvious devices like desktops, laptops, tablets and smart phones, but as connectivity improves and the "internet of things" develops more and more, other devices are joining the network such as like printers, televisions, alarm systems, thermostats, lights and many more.

Some of the issues that can be discovered through this type of penetration test are:

- Operating systems, applications and server management systems that do not have the most up to date security patches

- Insecure or unused network protocols

- Software, firewalls and operating system that are not configured correctly

> **End points**
>
> The more end points there are on a network, the more access points there are to that network. If any of these access points do not have up to date security features or the latest patches they are a potential vulnerability for that network.

4.2 Vulnerability probing

Once the scope of the network is determined, the next step is to identify the devices on the network that are most vulnerable to intrusion.

Organisations can access online databases of known vulnerabilities or weaknesses that have been identified for common business systems. Software can be used to probe the system and identify, quantify and rank the vulnerabilities in terms of their potential impact.

> **Increased home working**
>
> As organisations move to more flexible working and home working, this presents extra vulnerabilities for the network. It is much easier for IT security to review the devices on their network if they are all on local networks.
>
> If an employee does not have up to date security patches on the device and logs onto the network from home it creates a weakness on that network.
>
> IT will be looking for these types of vulnerabilities and asking the appropriate individuals to take action to update the software on their device.

4.3 Exploiting vulnerabilities

The next step in penetration testing is to attempt to exploit the potential weaknesses by seeing:

(i)   If an ethical hacker can gain access to the system

and

(ii)   What the hacker can exploit using the access that has been gained.

For example setting up a fake administrator profile able to install software (malware) onto the system or send data to an external source without authorisation.

The goal is to understand if access is possible, how long it takes, and what access can be gained. As with most thefts, if the attacker is given long enough they will gain unauthorised access, but if the process is too consuming it can discourage the attacker from persisting.

Example: Printer hackers

In 2018, a YouTube vlogger appealed to his fans to help promote subscriptions to his channel because his position as 'Most subscribed to creator' on YouTube was under threat from another YouTube creator. Some of his followers went to extreme lengths to help.

They exploited security flaws in wireless printers around the world by taking control of them and printing out a message urging the printer's user to unsubscribe from their rival and subscribe to the vlogger instead, then finally urging them to "Fix your printer".

The hackers claim to have accessed over 100,000 printers around the world, but also say that since their hack, people have taken notice and improved security on vulnerable printers. They have also reportedly hacked into other devices such as Google's Chromecast dongle, playing a video asking for subscriptions and again, highlighting the security flaw.

4.4 Internal network penetration testing

An internal network penetration test identifies any vulnerabilities that exist and are accessible to both approved and unapproved users. As an attack can often have internal assistance, this test allows an organisation to test the damage an internal user could do, but also considers if unauthorised access could be possible.

The type of issues identified by this type of test are:

* Inappropriate access by internal users

* Unsecured workstations

* Weak or unchanged passwords

 Example: Kaplan

As part of Kaplan's security processes they have employed someone to try to hack into the system and set up an administrator profile to install malware, or pretty much whatever else they wanted.

This is not a one off event, but something that happens on a regular basis – the hacker comes to a Kaplan office, so is on the internal Kaplan network, and attempts to set up the profile. The first time the person hacked in fairly quickly and was able to do everything they wanted. Kaplan were given a report from the hacker and worked on the various issues identified.

The next time the hacker was asked to attempt to gain access, whilst they did get into the system, they were unable to set up any profiles and failed to access any information or set up any malware.

As ways to hack into systems develop, Kaplan will revisit this security test and continue to work on protecting Kaplan's data.

4.5 Web application penetration testing

This aspect of penetration testing is to identify any security issues from poor design, coding and publishing. In the modern business world, applications are critical to many organisation and are often used to process personal data including payments details; they can even process or store proprietary data.

The type of issues identified by this type of test are:

- Identify potential for injection (lack of validating processes)

- Cross-site scripting opportunities

- the ability for a user to gain access to more of the application or site than they should (often called privilege escalation).

4.6 Wireless network penetration testing

This type of penetration testing is looking for any access points or devices that should not be in an organisations secured environment.

The type of issues identified by this type of test are:

- Open access points or rogue access points

- Badly configured wireless networks

- Accidental duplication of wireless networks

- Insecure wireless encryption

4.7 Simulated phishing testing

Simulated phishing testing is used to assess how susceptible the workforce is to breaking security policies or divulging sensitive information either verbally, in an email or entering it into a website.

 Example: Kaplan

> The example about Kaplan in chapter 9 discussed a situation where an internally generated phishing email offering free coffee from a well-known coffee outlet was sent to all staff, this is an example of simulated phishing testing. The members of staff who clicked on the link were identified as being more susceptible and so received additional training on how to spot suspicious communications and how to react to them.

5 Software security

Software security is the process of writing security into the software. As attacks on software can be complex, the security needs to be considered in different ways, typically there are three levels to consider:

- **Level 1** – This primary level seeks to prevent the attacker from gaining access to the software at all.

- **Level 2** – Unfortunately it is no longer realistic to expect that preventative security will always work, so the second level is concerned with making sure that if a breach occurs an alert notifies the appropriate parties that an attack has breached the level 1 security.

- **Level 3** – While the alert will mean that the appropriate parties can investigate the security breach, time is critical in any attack and in a very short space of time data can be compromised, so the third level takes automatic urgent action, for example locking down accounts and sensitive information.

> **Software security**
>
> These levels of software security, are broadly similar to the overall process outlined in chapter 9 and also in chapter 6 where we looked at internal controls.
>
> Level 1 is prevention – denying the attacker access.
>
> Level 2 is detection – alerting an appropriate cyber security resource about the attempted or successful attack. For example alerting the SIEM.
>
> Level 3 is response – the software has a basic level response built into it to speed up the response time giving the organisation the best chance of minimising the impact of the attack.

5.1 Design review

As with various techniques, if there is a focus on something at the very early stages it is easier to control the costs or make the product/process more efficient. The same is true for software security. An organisation should go right back to the design stage of key processes and systems to make sure that security is part of the design. Some systems and processes may well lack this focus as they were designed long before the realisation of the power and importance that technology would have.

Of particular concern should be accessibility to PII, IP and financial information such as payment details.

> **Design review**
>
> The extent to which our phones, watches and, since the development of the IoT, other devices, have become integral to the way we live and work, was not envisaged when the software for these devices was originally created.
>
> This has led to a need to improve the security features designed into the software.

5.2 Code review

A code review looks at how code is written, with a focus on how someone proves they should be allowed access to a system that contains sensitive information. Often companies have an internal manual detailing best practice and this stage of the review can check that software code is complying with the best practice manual.

In terms of authentication processes, multi factor authentication is being introduced to reduce the risk of hacking and other security breaches and so help to secure an organisation.

 Two step verification compared to two factor authentication

Lots of companies and suppliers are switching to two factor authentication to increase security. Some have previously used two step verification which is still very secure.

Two step verification requires users to input two forms of the same type of information, each from a different source, so for example a password that you remember as a first step, then a password that you are sent via email or SMS as a second step.

Two factor authentication requires the user to prove they should access the system in two different ways, so the first step could be the password that you must remember, but the second step requires something different – like a finger print or proof that you have the trusted device for the account.

5.3 Security testing

Finally in software security, in addition to assessing the strength of the controls in key areas of vulnerability, an internal audit-type review will be required to test whether the controls are actually being carried out (compliance) and are appropriate for the risk area (substantive).

 Software security within organisations

Cyber security and compliance experts say that two of the key software controls in existence in most organisations today are version control and patch management.

Version control – links into network configuration management (NCM) and monitors the various devices on the network to make sure that the software operated is still supported by the software provider. As software gets older, the flaws in that software become better known, and so become more susceptible to hacks. After a given period of time software providers state that a product is at the end of its life and will no longer supported.

> **Patch management** – as discussed earlier this is where the software provider becomes aware of a flaw in their software that could be exploited by an attacker and issues an update to the software to correct the flaw. Again using NCM organisations will push software updates through to devices. Depending on company policy and the severity of the flaw, this can happen at different times. Some companies run updates on a daily basis, others do so less frequently but push through any critical updates ahead of planned updates.
>
> This sort of approach is compliant with ISO 27001 suggested controls.

6 The systems development life cycle (SDLC)

The systems development life cycle is assumed knowledge at this level. However, this can be applied not just to systems, but also software development. There are six stages within the SDLC, with several activities involved:

- Planning – project initiation document, project quality plan, work breakdown structure, budget;

- Analysis – get to the root of the problem via user involvement in the form of interviews and questionnaires, complaints review;

- Design – prototyping;

- Development – build the system which has been agreed on;

- Implementation – staff training, file conversion, documentation, testing;

- Review – post completion audit/review on quality, cost, timescale.

Systems development risks

The development of new computer systems, designed and written for a specific user organisation, is a high-risk venture. It is widely recognised that many new purpose-written systems fail, for several reasons:

- They fail to satisfy the user's real requirements: the system was specified incorrectly.

- They do not provide the data processing or information for which they were designed, or to the quality expected.

- The system was therefore designed and programmed incorrectly.

- They cost much more to develop and run than expected. The system is therefore less efficient than expected.

Controls

Controls should be built into the system development process to reduce these risks. These controls should be implemented at all stages of the systems development life cycle (SDLC).

Examples of systems development controls

Control	Comments
Approval of an outline system specification by the user/IT steering committee.	The proposed system must be specified in terms of what it is expected to provide to the user, in terms of data processing and information quality, and should evaluate the expected costs and benefits. A system should not progress to detailed system design without formal authorisation. By giving formal approval to the system design, the user confirms the objectives of the system.
System designed in detail, using system design standards. The system is fully documented. A detailed system design is produced.	The documentation provides a source for checking in the event of problems with the system. By giving approval to the detailed system design, the user confirms that the programming work should begin.
Programs written using programming standards. All programs fully documented.	The documentation provides a source for checking in the event of problems with the system.
Systems and program testing.	The systems analysts and programmers should carry out their own tests on the programs and the system as a whole, to satisfy themselves that the system objectives have been met.
User testing.	Before the system 'goes live', it should be tested by the user. Before accepting the system for implementation, the user must be satisfied that it meets the planned objectives.
Development timetable and cost control.	The project development should be completed on time and within the budgeted cost. A management/project team should be given the responsibility for monitoring the progress of the project (e.g. using critical path analysis techniques) and its costs.

Control over implementation.	The implementation of the new system should be carefully planned and monitored. There are three methods of implementing a new system:
	• To introduce the system initially in one area or department, as a pilot test. Implement the system universally if the pilot test is successful, and after initial 'teething troubles' have been identified and resolved.
	• To introduce the new system by running it in parallel with the old system, until the new system is operating successfully. Parallel running can be expensive, because it involves running two systems at the same time. However, it should be less risky than an immediate changeover.
	• To make the changeover from old system to new system immediately and in full, without pilot testing or parallel running.
Monitoring the new system: audit of new systems.	A new system should be monitored, with a view to checking that it has been successful and has achieved its objectives. The success of a system should also be assessed in terms of:
	• user satisfaction levels and level of system use
	• actual costs and benefits.

Test your understanding 1

Nimrag Plc are a large national retail chain and recently have suffered a cyber-attack. They identified the breach before any major damage was done, managing to limit the attack to one computer. It was discovered when their network monitoring and logging processes highlighted unusual activity from that desktop even when it was logged off. They were therefore able to detach the computer from the network.

To help them understand what happened and improve their defences in future they are carrying out forensic analysis. The computer affected was an administrator computer which limited access to specific individuals. From reviews of logins to that terminal the company could then review what had been accessed and downloaded.

The breach occurred when one of the senior administrators had accessed their personal webmail account and opened an email that related to their personal areas of interest. It appears that the email had been designed after researching the senior administrator's interests which were openly available on social media.

The file downloaded by the administrator appeared to be legitimate, but hidden inside was unauthorised software that was allowed to run because of poor security awareness by the administrator – the file continuously asked for approval to run until the senior administrator clicked 'ok'.

Which of the following statements are correct?

Select ALL that apply.

A   A policy on social media, preventing access to these sites from work computers, would have prevented this attack.

B   The attack was started by a spear phishing email.

C   User training regarding how personal information can be easily accessed and used would have made the attack less likely to be successful.

D   User access controls to prevent employees visiting personal sites from a sensitive computer would help improve protection at Nimrag.

E   It appears the attack was caused by malvertising on the website the employee visited.

F   User training about how to spot and deal with suspicious emails may have helped reduce the likelihood of this attack.

G   Network monitoring controls should be introduced to help reduce the impact of future attacks.

Test your understanding 2

BHJ bank wishes to improve the cyber security in place over procedures for accessing a customer's financial information within the system. It will now require users to confirm their identities in two different ways before allowing them access to the information.

Which ONE of the following forms of security does this new requirement represent?

A   Two step verification

B   Two factor authentication

C   Two part certification

D   Two layer validation

Test your understanding 3

FTY company is a small family owned business making cakes and biscuits for sale in the local area. The company's systems link its head office, two factories and a temperature-controlled warehouse. The board of FTY is meeting to discuss its cyber security risks.

Which TWO of the following statements made by members of FTY's board members are TRUE?

A   Cyber-attacks are an external threat to the company's systems

B   Keeping anti-malware and anti-virus software up-to-date will ensure the company is protected from cyber-attack

C   Monitoring the amount of data moving across the network at a given time can alert monitors to potential attacks

D   The company will be protected from viruses provided staff never open emails from senders they don't recognise

E   Endpoint protection only works if the scope of the company's network is regularly reassessed

Test your understanding 4

The board of directors at GSD company have been discussing the importance of improving cyber security.

Which THREE of the following statements made by GSD's directors about cyber security are TRUE?

A   The Internet of Things has increased the importance of endpoint security

B   Code reviews to audit application source codes will help establish whether proper system security controls have been built in

C   With the right software security in place the company will be able to prevent the risk of a security breach

D   Unethical hackers can be employed to help the company identify vulnerabilities in the system

E   Business process controls are an important tool in strengthening the company's defences against cyber risk

Test your understanding 5

After a recent cyber attack BTR company has employed a specialist team to perform a forensic analysis to learn more about the attack.

The team has just identified several services that have been enabled so that they can be accessed without authorisation.

Which area of the team's forensic analysis would have been MOST likely to identify this change?

A   System level analysis

B   Vulnerability probing

C   Network analysis

D   Penetration testing

7   Incident response plan

Chapter 9 looked at the process of prevention, detection and response, and in terms of the response, DRP and BCPs were critical aspects of this. Having now covered some more advanced cyber security tools and techniques, it is time to revisit the response aspect, with a look at an incident response plan.

7.1   What is an incident response plan?

A well designed incident response plan will help an organisation to prepare for a potential cyber breach, by creating what might be referred to as blueprint for dealing with the challenges the breach creates. By having guidelines in place, people will be able to respond more quickly, which is critical.

7.2   Creating an incident response plan

The first stage of creating an effective incident response plan is to consider which key functions and departments need to be represented, some suggestions would be representatives from:

- IT

- Security and compliance

- Legal

- Communications/PR

- Senior management

As well as internal members of the organisation, an organisation may also consider including some of the following in this stage:

- Cyber security consultants

- Internet service providers

- Any other outside IT services

As these are key aspects of an organisation's cyber set up, it is better to make sure all the relevant information is available, like for example contact information or contractual agreements.

> **Contractual arrangements**
>
> It is better to understand while the plan is being formulated how timely a response from an external supplier will be, rather than discovering that the contractual arrangements are inappropriate while a cyber-breach unfolds.

Creating a list of roles, responsibilities and contact information means that all employees will know who to contact should they become aware of an issue.

In the CIMA risk management cycle (Chapter 1) the first step was to "Identify the risk areas" and then to "Understand and assess the scale of the risk". The same is true for cyber risks, and at this stage the representatives should be considering what digital assets the organisation has that could be affected by a breach, understand the network set up including interactions with other organisations, as this could be the source of the breach or could lead to a breach at another organisation.

Identifying weaknesses at this stage can help can help resolve these issues before they become a more serious problem.

Weaknesses and potential resolutions

It may be that systems or some parts of the network are incorrectly configured, so the group could implement stricter network segmentation.

There could be some anecdotal evidence of poor credential management by employees, this could lead to a reminder email or a short training session to explain why good password practices are so important.

Risk areas and scale of risk

In this initial review it is important to make sure that it's not only corporate owned assets that are considered; assets that are owned or controlled by third parties should also be included, for example remote workers and any cloud services.

It is also important to appreciate that not all of the working group will be up to date with the latest jargon, so issues should be discussed in terms of the real world impact rather than in depth technical analysis.

The next stage in CIMA's risk management cycle is "Development of risk response strategy". The group should review the current responses that the organisation has in place, and this should include any findings from penetration tests that have been carried out.

Then the cycle moves on to "Prioritisation", and this means going back to "Understanding and assessing the scale of the risk" to consider the weaknesses in cyber security, and the ability to identify potential or actual security compromises. Making sure there is the opportunity for a clear process to investigate any potential issues so that it is possible to quickly identify the extent of a breach and contact the appropriate parties.

Speed of response is often vital in a cyber incident.

Unethical hacker

It's important during these planning stages to think like a malicious hacker; what might an unethical hacker choose to attack? Remember, attackers don't always choose the most valuable asset, selecting several smaller targets that are less well protected helps the attacker build up to a bigger attack.

Once potential targets have been identified, consider what would happen if these targets were compromised. Thinking this through in advance can help the organisation react should this actually happen. It's effectively scenario planning for cyber security.

Maintaining **business continuity** is vital. If key departments, network or systems are compromised, how will the organisation continue to operate?

Clearly planning back up options will enable the organisation to deal more appropriately with any system security issues. This is one of the reasons it is critical to include communications experts from within the organisation, so that templates can be set up and escalation channels can be created.

7.3 Reviewing the incident response plan

The CIMA risk management cycle moves round to "Implement, monitor review and refine", so the incident response plan should too. During the review stage the incident response plan should be considered against the risk appetite of the organisation, and whether it prepares for threats based on an appropriate likelihood/outcome analysis.

All parts of the organisation that need to be involved in the response are aware of the response plan.

Awareness

Once the response plan has been created, talk with stakeholders of the response plan, explain how the response plan works and what they would need to know to carry out their part of the response.

Collaboration helps to make sure that everyone, including departments that are not involved in security understand how to carry out their part of the response.

If the breach relates to email systems being compromised, it would not be appropriate to use email to report the breach.

The incident response should include a triage or workflow to help stakeholders understand where they sit in the process and what events or systems require what response/escalation.

Triage

Triage is a term often used in cyber security. It comes from the medical profession where prioritisation and treatments are decided based on the severity of the patient's condition and their likelihood of recovery with and without any treatment.

In cyber security, the patient would be the technology that has been compromised by a cyber-breach.

The plans should include guidance about how often communication is required, a constant stream of updates can be inefficient, but not enough updates can create anxiety and uncertainty.

During this review stage, it is again critical to try and think like an attacker, and think about how they may breach the system and work from the breach point to gain access to the target.

Internal network penetration testing

Giving an ethical hacker a login similar to a standard remote worker and asking them to try and gain access to confidential information with it would be a useful step to take to help understand the internal manoeuvres that would be required and whether the monitoring systems in place can identify that it is happening. Detecting a breach early in the attack can be very difficult, but can also be vital to reduce the potential damage caused.

The incident plan should be comprehensive enough to cover the most likely and most common issue (remember that it is not always an attack that could compromise the systems it could be a mistake by an employee), but the plans also need to be flexible enough to enable an effective response to the evolving nature of cyber threats.

As part of the review it is worth considering how frequently further reviews will take place. Annually is usually a minimum requirement for such a dynamic area, and more often would be ideal, but it depends on the organisation's cost benefit analysis.

7.4   Testing the incident response plan

Now the plan is formulated and has been reviewed, it's time to practice it with some group training exercises. As with anything, to be really good at something requires practice, and responding to a cyber incident is no different.

A training session should be organised involving people from the incident response plan. The exercise that is created should be a realistic scenario.

Testing

Different training sessions could be organised for different stakeholders in the incident response plan.

For example, for the directors a different executive exercise could be created to determine if they would follow the guidelines appropriately and see if there were any issues, or key deviations from the suggested approach. A key aspect of this type of exercise could be the external communications and cross function collaboration.

For the more technical members of the incident response plan a more detailed exercise could be set up to check that these key players are able to carry out their parts of the plan appropriately.

Penetration testing

In technical scenarios with technical staff, they could carry out an attack on defence training, where one group attempts to be the threat actor and tries to attack the organisations systems without being detected, while the other group attempt to detect where they are in the network, where they've been, how they got there and how to respond to the threat actor.

If the defence team identify the attack line, the exercise should not stop there, it should continue as a real incident would. This may help identify what, where and how an attacker may behave, which could give vital insight into security flaws that were unknown prior to the exercise.

For example, the first response may be to remove compromised machines from the network, but it may be more beneficial to keep the machines running to preserve forensic data.

Documentation of the response and evidence of what has been tampered with should be maintained as it may be required for legal action against a real world attacker. Therefore awareness of this during the test exercise will be important to help prepare for a real life incident.

Once the test has been completed, a review of the scenario and the response is critical to gain maximum benefit from the exercise.

7.5 Implementing the incident response plan

Finally, in the current cyber risks climate, it is not about IF the incident response plan will need to be used, it is WHEN. As discussed in the previous chapter, prevention is an unrealistic expectation.

The key things to do are:

- Keep calm and use the plan
- Understand what is developing
- Track everything
- Involve legal and PR as appropriate
- Use a trusted partner

Implementation – key things

- **Keep calm and use the plan**

  First of all don't panic, use the plan. It's been created, reviewed and tested so it should provide a good basis. Notify the appropriate parties involved in the plan.

- **Understand what is developing**

  Understand the scope and context of the incident; is there a particular asset (server, device, network) that has been compromised? How critical is it for the functioning of the business?

  Does it relate to a specific user? What is the extent of that user's access? Are they aware? Using SIEM data can help answer some of these questions.

  Once the severity of the incident is understand then triage can help prioritise the next steps and enable appropriate escalation.

- **Track everything**

  Collecting and keeping in good condition as much evidence as possible will help the organisation, third party assistance and also potential future legal proceedings.

  Remember, shutting down the systems or devices that are compromised can erase evidence and alert the threat actor.

- **Involve legal and PR as appropriate**

  Once the issue is established it important to include the legal team in proceedings, particular if the incident involves a customer data breach, the response will be scrutinised for regulatory compliance, so gaining legal insight will help keep the response on track.

  In terms of PR the sooner that the organisation are communicating about the issue with external stakeholders the better, if rumours start about a breach, it can do a lot more damage than clear direct communication.

- **Use a trusted third party**

  Not all organisations will have the resources to deal with it themselves, so enlisting the help of an incident response partner can help limit the damage and get the organisation functioning effectively more quickly.

8 Digital resilience

In their book, Beyond Cybersecurity: Protecting Your Digital Business, published in 2015, Tucker Bailey, James Kaplan, Alan Marcus, Derek O'Halloran and Chris Rezek discuss a concept called Digital Resilience. The concept is about doing more than the minimum to protect the company and comply with regulations, but to integrate cyber security into the business operations.

They identify six actions an organisation must consider to achieve their digital resilience, each of the six actions is considered below.

8.1 Identify all the issues

First of all a company must consider what information is at risk, what information an attacker may want and why they may want it. Then they should consider the controls an attacker would need to circumvent to access the data they desire – for example to access a system the user needs a valid username and password, all systems access is logged, data within a system is restricted to a user's needs etc.

The key is then to integrate this knowledge as the defences will be much stronger if they operate together than if they are considered in isolation.

8.2 Aim toward a well-defined target

The logic here, as with all good targets, is to set a cyber security plan that is challenging but attainable – to help motivate people towards achieving it. It is also important to translate it into language that people can understand, so that non IT leaders within the organisation can explain it and make sure that the workforce support the plan.

The well-defined target should include prioritisation of the cyber security risks to the business. Once these have been assessed they can use three types of control to improve the security.

- Business process controls – for example SOAPSPAM (see chapter 6)

- IT controls – for example password protection to login to a system.

- Cyber security controls – for example encryption.

The tendency is often to focus on the final one of these, which can lead to unnecessary expense.

8.3 Work out how best to deliver the new cyber security system

This area links into change management, and looks at how a company takes these challenging targets and turns them into a reality. As with all controls the workforce can often resist what are perceived to be additional controls believing they will inhibit creativity, cause problems with current procedures or increase the time to get things done.

Roles and reporting are important here, and part of the advice is to have a high level manager responsible for all aspects of cyber security, perhaps reporting into the board or potentially dual reporting into the leading risk manager within the company too.

8.4 Establish the risk resource trade offs

Considering the risk resource trade offs takes account of the fact that there is no one solution to managing cyber risk and that different companies have different attitudes towards risk and different risk appetites.

The guidance here is that different options should be created each of which require different levels of resources and reduce risk to different levels. The board can then assess the different options and choose the option that is most appropriate for the organisation.

Example

A company could set up three packages:

Basic – this would be the lowest cost package and lead to the lowest level of security, only covering absolutely essential (legal) requirements.

Standard – this would be a package that included a higher level of security, potentially in line with activities of a business's primary competitors. It would also cost more to implement than the basic package.

Premium – this package would include the top level security, and could potentially differentiate a firm from its rivals. It would also cost a significant amount more than the other packages.

This is just an illustration and four or five different packages maybe created for analysis and selection.

8.5 Develop a plan that aligns business and technology

Meeting regulatory requirements is important for all companies but identifying the key business risk areas and ensuring that cyber security processes are designed to deal with the biggest issues must be a priority.

This should not just be limited to current operations, it is also important for senior people within the organisation to understand internal developments and projects and consider how these will impact cyber security in the future.

Example:

If a company, or some part of the organisation, has just started to use, or is considering using, cloud based software or storage, then it is important that cyber security processes are aligned to this.

8.6 Ensure sustained business engagement

Cyber security is increasingly cited by directors and CEOs as being the biggest risk area for business and so it is one that must be addressed at a strategic level. Financial backing for cyber security is not the only consideration – as with all risks, cyber security risk management requires attention across all aspects of the business from the board level right down to the operational staff.

Example: GDPR and Kaplan

GDPR came into force in May 2018 and to reduce the risk of non-compliance all staff need to be trained. At Kaplan all staff, even those who are not regularly involved with handling private information on computers, have been trained. This includes for example the warehouse staff who prepare the orders for shipment – they are handling personal data and if the wrong delivery note was put into the wrong delivery package this could potentially reveal confidential information to another Kaplan customer.

There are regular updates about GDPR compliance, particularly picking out known issues for people to avoid in future, for example checking emails on a break from teaching, if this displays PII about customers or colleagues on the screen that students can see.

Test your understanding 6

The board of BKM company has been meeting to consider the company's digital resilience as they are planning to launch a digital resilience programme. They plan to integrate cyber security into their business operations using a six step approach.

They have established the cyber risks they are facing and have defined the programme objectives. An organisation structure showing the key roles and responsibilities has been developed and a suitable firm of specialists has been identified to assist BKM develop the programme. A mechanism to track on-going progress and reinforce cyber security has also been agreed.

Based on the information provided which TWO of the following actions from the six-step approach has BKM not yet taken?

A   Establish the risk v resource trade offs

B   Ensure sustained business engagement

C   Develop a detailed plan to align with business and technology

D   Identify all the issues

E   Determine how to deliver the system

9 Frameworks

As cyber security risks and cyber security risk management increase in focus, so too does the need to report on them to stakeholders. At present there is no regulatory requirement to report on cyber security and, because of the complexity and rapidly changing environment in which cyber security sits, it is unlikely any regulatory requirements will come in.

This has left both organisations and stakeholders in a difficult situation. Organisations would like their stakeholders to know that they have robust cyber security procedures in place, but don't know how to convey this to the stakeholder. Equally stakeholders are concerned about whether cyber security is receiving the attention it requires within the organisation but don't know if what they are told has any real meaning.

As a result, frameworks have been created that, although they are not mandatory, give an organisation something credible to show stakeholders to confirm that they do have robust processes and controls in place.

9.1 AICPA

CIMA & AICPA

Since 2011 CIMA and the American Institute of Certified Public Accountants have been working together. In 2012 they launched the Chartered Global Management Accountant (CGMA) designation and in 2016 members of each association approved the creation of a new global association representing management and public accountants on a global level. In 2017 the Association of International Certified Professional Accountants AICPA was formed.

In 2017 the AICPA launched a cybersecurity risk management reporting framework that would:

"Assist organisations as they communicate relevant and useful information about the effectiveness of their cybersecurity risk management programs."

The information included in the reporting framework is designed to:

"Assist senior management, boards of directors, analysts, investors and business partners gain a better understanding of organisations' efforts."

The aim of the framework was to consider the needs of the various stakeholders in any organisation from the board, managers, investors, funding providers, etc by using a common language for risk management reporting – along similar lines to financial reporting principles. Part of the process emphasises that cyber security is no longer just an IT problem (if it ever was just an IT problem), but it is part of the enterprise risk management process.

Cyber security concerns for stakeholders

The board and regulatory authorities are not the only stakeholders concerned with minimising the risk of cyber-attacks and associated losses. Customers and other stakeholders are concerned that their personal information is safe, while investors and business partners are interested in how cyber-attacks would affect the business and therefore their investment.

Some institutional investors have been asking boards about their organisations' cyber security risk management programs as a way to gauge the risk to their investments.

9.2 Cyber security risk management reporting

The framework the AICPA have set up requires management to prepare certain information and then for a qualified accountant at the organisation to review it.

The report has three key components:

- **Management's description**

- **Management's assertion**

- **The practitioner's opinion**

More on the three key sets of information

- **Management's description**

    This is the first section that is completed and provides a description of the firm's cyber security activities, including how the organisation identifies its most sensitive information, how it manages the cyber risks associated with this information, what the key polices and processes it has in place to protect against the risks etc. The descriptions should be in accordance with AICPA description criteria.

    This part of the report provides the context for the next two sections that will be completed.

- **Management's assertion**

    This section gives management the opportunity to state whether, in their opinion, the risks were described in accordance with the criteria and whether appropriate controls were in place and effective.

- **The practitioner's opinion**

    This is the final section completed and is where a qualified CPA accountant gives their opinion on the description of the risks and whether the controls in place are effective.

The AICPA state in its Cybersecurity risk management reporting fact sheet' that the 'use of the reporting framework and related criteria may enhance the confidence that stakeholders place on the entity's cybersecurity communications.'

As such, for a report like this to be effective it should be made available for stakeholders to review. Merely stating that they have carried it out would be unlikely to satisfy all stakeholders about the cyber security of the organisation.

Layout of the report

The final report will actually be laid out in a slightly different order to the order in which it was completed (explained in the expandable text).The Management assertion and the practitioner's opinion are sections 1 and 2 respectively in the report.

These serve as the executive summary where the management and independent accountant highlight the key aspects and overall summary of the report.

In the example on the AICPA website the management's assertion is one page long, and the practitioner opinion (the independent accountants report) is two pages long.

The final section is very detailed and in the example on the AICPA website it is around twenty pages in length.

9.3 Criteria

As with all approaches to analysing risk, identifying key considerations is easier with a model, tool or guide of some description. For example, PESTEL is a classic tool to assist in identifying threats and opportunities for a chosen firm.

To assist with the writing and evaluation of the management description and to improve the comparability of the reports produced the AICPA uses two sets of criteria:

- **Description criteria**

    This is a detailed (33 page) document giving guidance on the areas that should be considered when identifying the cyber security risks the entity faces and the controls it puts in place.

More on the description criteria

The description criteria incorporates the **attributes** of suitable criteria as:

Relevance – to the business operation

Objectivity – free from bias

Measurability – the criteria can be reasonably measured using a consistent approach.

Completeness – that relevant factors (that could affect the decisions of the users of the reports) are not omitted.

There are nine **categories** of description criteria that the management should consider, including the considerations in developing control processes.

- **Nature of business and operations**

  An explanation of what business the entity is involved in and day to day operations.

- **Nature of information at risk**

  Consideration of the types of sensitive information the entity is involved with (creation, collection, transmission, storage) that would be subject to cyber security risk.

- **Cyber security objectives**

  To explain the entity's main cyber security objectives. Consideration should be given to availability, confidentiality, integrity of data and processing, plus the process for establishing, maintaining and approving the objectives.

- **Factors that have a significant effect on inherent cyber security risks**

  These include:

  - technologies, connection types, service providers and delivery channels

  - organisational and user characteristics

  - changes in the period that could affect cyber security risks including environmental, technological, organisational or other aspects

- **Cyber security risk governance structure**

  Consideration of the processes involved in making sure that integrity and ethical values are at the heart of cyber security risk management. It also considers board oversight, accountability, recruitment and development of qualified personnel.

- **Cyber security risk assessment process**
  - consideration to how cyber security risks and other factors that could affect the program have changed in the period.
  - risks related to the achievement of cyber security objectives.
  - considering the risks associated with business partners and vendors.
- **Cyber security communications and quality of cyber security information**

  Disclosure about how objectives, expectation and responsibilities are communicated to appropriate stakeholders, both internally and externally including thresholds for when an event/response requires communication.
- **Monitoring of the cyber security risk management program**

  Disclosure of the process used to assess the effectiveness of key controls in the cyber security risk management program. This should include information about action taken when threats or control weaknesses are discovered.
- **Cyber security control processes**
  - the process for developing a response to, and where necessary mitigating, the assessed risks
  - the characteristics of the entity's IT infrastructure and network
  - the key security processes and policies to address the cyber security risks identified

Illustration of application of description criteria

Below is an example of the disclosures which may be made by a manufacturer, distributor and retailer of consumer products when applying aspects of the description criteria.

- **Nature of business operations**

  What it manufactures, where this takes place, how it makes its sales (online, in store), the main regions it makes sales. Any collaborative ventures used to make sales and distribute goods.
- **Nature of information at risk**

  Financial information for reporting, sales information (customers, pricing, orders), payment card details of customers retained for ease of ordering, customer profiles, product specifications and design ideas, employee information.
- **Cyber security objectives**

  Availability – consideration of the need to provide 24 hours a day, 365 days a year sales opportunities online, the need to supply manufacturing information during shift hours

Confidentiality – keeping employee and customer information confidential and complying with laws around this (including credit card details), corporate data on sales and financial reporting

Integrity of data – preventing the improper modification or destruction of data to support the production of information for internal and external reporting purposes and to assist with business processes.

Integrity of processing – making sure there are controls to prevent improper use, alteration or destruction of systems to support deliveries, processing transactions, manufacturing goods to the correct specifications and protecting employees in hazardous situations in the manufacturing facilities.

Process for establishing, maintaining and approving the objectives – the board establishes and approves overall objectives, this feeds into business objectives and the most senior IT manager aligns cyber security objectives which are then approved at board level. May also include references to relevant standards for example GDPR, ISO 270001 and PCIDSS.

- **Factors that have a significant effect on inherent cyber security risks**

  For a manufacturer, distributor and retailer could include:

  Technologies, connection types, service providers and delivery channels:

  ERP systems

  Cloud provider

  Call centre

  Virtual Private Network (VPN) for a sales team

  Software providers

  Organisational and user characteristics:

  A description of the IT teams organisational structure:

  - Chief Information office (CIO)
  - Teams to support applications, technology and security
  - Chief Technology Officer (CTO) in the technology team
  - Chief Information Security Officer (CISO) in the Security team

  The users of the systems:

  - Customers both consumer & wholesale
  - Any business partner employees with systems access
  - Call centre staff (potentially could be third party)
  - Employees

Changes in the period that could affect cyber security risks it be environmental, technological, organisational or other aspects:

For example an additional manufacturing operations set up, how this was carried out and what IT infrastructure was in place.

Also any security incidents that occurred during the period should be included here:

Any attempted hack e.g. a DDoS on the website, the implications of the attack e.g. any compromised data like PII of consumers or commercial customer info, the work done to fix the issue, potentially including outside contractors helping to review the issue, any changes to security procedures as a result.

- **Cyber security risk governance structure**

  Integrity and ethical values are at the heart of cyber security risk management, may include:

  - Tone from the top

  - Code of ethics

  - Policy and reward structures promoting control and governance

  - Board activities, for examples review meetings

  - Employee policies – code of conduct, employee handbook, IT policy

  Board oversight:

  - Details of the boards IT experience, including NEDs

  - Details of any specific committees for example a risk committee

  Accountability:

  - the work of any risk committees

  - reporting lines for people like the CISO, CTO

  Recruitment and development of qualified personnel in cyber security:

  - Evaluation of applicants education, experience and background checks

  - Signing handbook adhering to policy, confidentiality and non-disclosure agreements.

  - Regular training as required

  - Policy on contractors

  - Organisational charts

  - Annual appraisals

  - Policies on performance improvements for underperforming staff

- **Cyber security risk assessment process**

  The process used to identify cyber security risks and other changes that could affect the risk management program and to assess risks related to the achievement of cyber security objectives.

  - Annual risk assessments

  - Internal audit cyber security reviews

  - Vulnerability assessments and penetration tests

  Considering the risks associated with business partners and vendors:

  - Vendors assessed against cyber threat criteria

  - Tiering system based on the goods/services provided and the importance to the company

  - Vendors must detail hardware, software and information requirements of the work done

  - PII or confidential information only disclosed as appropriate

  - Annual risk assessments, including regulatory requirements, changing vendors, economic changes

- **Cyber security communications and quality of cyber security information**

  Disclosure about how objectives, expectation and responsibilities are communicated to appropriate stakeholders, both internally and externally.

  - Internal policies, available as required (intranet)

  - Handbook, signed upon hiring

  - Training course

  - Cyber security specialists to undertake additional training

  - Communication policy to report security events (e.g. phishing attacks)

  Including thresholds for when an event/response requires communication.

  - Disclosure policy

  - Events assessed by appropriate committees

  - Legal and communications experts used as required

- **Monitoring of the cyber security risk management program**

  Effectiveness of controls in the cyber security risk management program.

  - Any frameworks involved (ISI 270001), NIST cybersecurity framework.

  - Internal audit tests

  - Regular vulnerability assessments and penetration tests

  - Reports from external suppliers (cloud services)

  - Risk based assessments (internal and external)

  Information about action taken when threats or control weaknesses are discovered.

  - The work of any risk committees

  - Vulnerability tracking including any mitigation required

  - Use of KPIs to assess responses to threats or weaknesses

- **Cyber security control processes**

  The process for developing a response to the assessed risks.

  - Development of any committees

  - Work of committees

  - Insurance (business disruption)

  The characteristics of the entities IT infrastructure and network

  - Description of internal networks

  - Cloud based applications and management

  - Segmentation to limit exposure of any breach

  - Controls over any third party access, for example call centre work

  - Authentication processes used for any employees using a VPN connection

  The key security processes and policies to mitigate the cyber security risks identified

  - Policies and procedures about use of information

  - Preventative measures such user specific access, data back up, antivirus software, patch management

  - Detective measures like a security team monitoring activity for unusual events and a response plan

  - Reviews of process capacity to assess adequateness and alert levels established and set

> - DRP and BCP processes, back up sites with sprinkler systems to put out fires, secured physical access to site
> - Policies for retention and destruction of data in accordance with legal requirements

- **Control criteria**

  This is even more detailed (over 300 pages) document giving guidance on the types of risks and controls that may have been identified in the description criteria and examples of other controls that could be used, that managers and qualified accountants can use in their assertions and reports. There are significant references to the COSO Internal Control Framework, which should not be surprising given that cyber security risk management is concerned with considering the effectiveness of the controls in the organisation's program.

 Example of information in the control criteria guidance:

The document is a wide ranging document, but this gives an insight into the contents.

Consideration:

The organisation has a structure, reporting lines and responsibilities to aid the development, operation and monitoring of systems to manage security risks.

Example risk:

The structure does not provide necessary resources or enable appropriate flow of information to manage security risks.

Possible control:

The organisation reviews organisational structure, reporting lines and responsibilities as part of its ongoing risk assessment and revises these as appropriate to meet system and security needs.

Consideration:

Physical access to the facility/facilities where the data centres (or other critical equipment) are located is limited to authorised personnel only.

Example risk 1:

Unauthorised access could be gained to the location leading to damage, fraudulent processing or information being compromised.

Possible control 1:

The organisation issues ID cards to all authorised personnel and the facility has an access control system at all entry and exit points.

Example risk 2:

A person who has had access revoked either through termination of employment or change in employment role continues to access the facility.

Possible control 2:

The personnel responsible for access to the facilities review access to the restricted facility on a regular basis and requests for changes are made promptly.

Consideration:

Processing capacity is sufficient to meet usage requirements including at peak demand requirements

Example risk:

Processing capacity is insufficient to meet system requirements and peak demand requirements.

Possible control:

Processing capacity is monitored on an ongoing basis and assessed against KPIs.

Consideration:

Disaster recovery plans (DRP) to support system recovery are tested to make sure they meet the organisation's commitments and system requirements.

Example risk:

DRPs are not designed appropriately and backups are not enough to allow recovery of the system to meet the organisation's commitments and system requirements.

Possible control:

Business continuity plans (BCPs) and DRPs including restoring backups are tested at least annually. Test results are reviewed and plans are adjusted accordingly.

Consideration:

Mitigating controls exists to prevent or detect and correct errors in processing to meet processing integrity and system requirements.

Example risk:

Processing error, fraudulent action or another external event leads to data loss.

Possible control:

Daily incremental backups are automatically performed and full weekly backups are also carried out.

Consideration:

Confidential information is protected during system design, development, testing and implementation to meet organisational confidentiality and system requirements.

Example risk:

Data used in test systems is not appropriately protected from unauthorised access and loss.

Possible control:

The organisation uses masking software to create test data that removes and replaces any confidential data with dummy data prior to the creation of the test database.

Consideration:

The organisation's privacy commitments are communicated to internal and external users appropriately, and internal users are able to carry out their roles as required while adhering to those commitments.

Example risk:

Internal and external users are not aware of the privacy commitments and how PII is collected and used.

Possible control:

The organisation makes its privacy commitments and practices available to all data subjects both internal and external upon first collection of data, and any updates to policy are communicated as appropriate and through agreed preferences to the data subject.

This gives a flavour of the content, but it is impossible to reproduce it all in this chapter. There are huge amounts of information available to help an organisation implement the AICPA cyber security risk management framework. Further research is possible just type it into a search engine, but be careful to only click on secure and trusted sites.

9.4 NIST cybersecurity framework

 NIST

The NIST is the National Institute of Standards and Technology. It is a non-regulatory agency of the US department of Commerce. As with many governments around the world they seek to give advice about cyber security. In the UK GCHQ has a section called the National Cyber Security Centre that gives advice to UK organisations and individuals about staying safe online.

The NIST cybersecurity framework is voluntary guidance to help organisations mitigate cyber security risk. As with the AICPA framework, part of the framework covers communications with internal and external stakeholders.

The Cybersecurity Framework consists of three main components:

Implementation Tiers

Implementation Tiers provide context – helping organisations to choose the appropriate level of rigor for their cybersecurity programmes and often used as a communication tool to discuss risk appetite, mission priority, and budget.

Core

The core provides a set of desired cybersecurity activities and outcomes using simple easy to understand language. The core is based on five principles:

- **Identify** threats to an organisations systems and data

- **Protect** against threats.

- **Detect** when a system has been breached.

- **Respond** effectively to systems breaches

- **Recover** any compromised data and the systems affected.

Profiles

Profiles help the organisation map its own requirements and objectives, risk appetite, and resources against the desired outcomes included in the core.

9.5 AIC Triad

Another commonly used approach to cyber security is the AIC Triad (sometimes also referred to as CIA Triad (although it has no connection to the Central Intelligence Agency) and also the Security Triad). The model is aimed at helping organisations understand information security and set up policies to help protect the organisation.

It is known as the AIC (or CIA) Triad because of the three elements that underpin it, seen by many as the most important aspects of cyber security.

- **Availability** – put simply systems must be online and available, otherwise organisations cannot do business.

- **Integrity** – making sure that people who modify data are authorised to do so means the data is more likely to be accurate and trustworthy.

- **Confidentiality** – when data is being stored and when it is in use or in transit there need to be rules in place to limit access to those who are authorised to use it.

Hopefully you will recognise these as being fundamental concepts that are part of the AICPA approach, but this provides a more accessible approach, and therefore is more likely to be the start point for smaller businesses.

AIC Triad in more detail

- **Availability**

  As online is increasingly becoming the main way that organisations do business, keeping the system online becomes more and more important. Organisations can use a variety of methods to help protect against downtime:

  - Keeping up to date with software patches
  - Understanding networks requirements and busy times
  - Disaster recovery planning
  - Business continuity planning

- **Integrity**

  Integrity relates to how trustworthy the data is, so it is important to ensure that is cannot be altered during processing and only authorised users have access to make changes. Some of the considerations to protect integrity are:

  - User access controls
  - Checks on data to ensure it is the same before and after transmission
  - Version controls, so if data is accidentally deleted back up can be restored.

- **Confidentiality**

  Confidentiality and privacy are often used interchangeably in the way the AIC triad works. It is focused on putting controls in place to ensure that private information is only viewed by those authorised to see it. Often companies will categorise data relating to different levels of risk should it fall into the wrong hands, with more stringent controls in place around the most sensitive data.

  Considerations to ensure confidentiality include:

  - Training on risk factors and protecting against them including:
  - Social engineering approaches
  - Password best practices
  - Data encryption

Technological advances mean that all frameworks including the AIC triad must evolve. Some developments that pose particular challenges include:

Big data – extra challenges arise because of the huge volume of information that needs to be protected, the variety of sources and types of information and the speed with which it is updated. Making use of it can be challenging, but also making sure that it is accessible, trustworthy and private can become very costly.

Internet of things – as with any network, the more you increase the size, the more access points are created and so the bigger the threat becomes. The issue for the AIC triad is both privacy and security.

Privacy – it may only be fragments of data that are accessible from each of the various endpoints, but when they are collated they can constitute personally identifiable information.

Security – while computers get regular software patches and invariably have good security configurations, many of the devices in the IoT that connect to them don't have the ability to receive software updates or do not require passwords.

9.6 Framework limitations

While the use of these frameworks is widely encouraged to give structure to organisations as they develop controls for the increasingly important threats from digital technology, warnings should be given regarding over-reliance on any particular framework, noting in particular that:

- Even the best cyber security defences can be defeated if the threat actor is determined enough, and has the time and the resources to do it.

- A framework can only provide reasonable assurance regarding the achievement of an organisations objectives – remember a cyber-security framework is effectively an aspect of internal control and all internal control systems are at risk from mistakes or errors.

- The frameworks can be expensive to implement, and a cost benefit analysis should be carried out to check that the cost to implement the framework and controls being considered does not outweigh the benefits.

- Cyber security such as patches and anti-virus software are only designed to cope with known threats or weaknesses.

Test your understanding 7

BPR company has included the following paragraph in its Assertion of Management section at the start of its cyber security risk management report.

We assert that the description throughout the period January 1, 20X1, to December 31, 20X1, is presented in accordance with the description criteria. Our cyber security team, which has unparalleled cyber security expertise, has performed an extensive evaluation of the effectiveness of the controls included within the cyber security risk management program throughout the period, using the required criteria for security, availability, and confidentiality. Based on this evaluation, we assert that the controls were effective throughout the period January 1, 20X1, to December 31, 20X1, to achieve the entity's cyber security objectives based on the control criteria.

Which one of the following attributes, required by the AICPA 2017 cyber security risk management reporting framework, has been breached by this paragraph?

A   Relevance

B   Objectivity

C   Measurability

D   Completeness

Test your understanding 8

KQT company was advised that it could purchase cyber security insurance to mitigate some of the risks associated with a cyber security attack and after an investigation to determine whether it would be worthwhile, purchased appropriate cover with a reputable insurance company.

The board is aware that this decision may impact the disclosures included its report 'Description of KQT company's cyber security risk management program' which is produced in accordance with the AICPA 2017 cyber security risk management reporting framework.

Which of the following matters should be disclosed in the report?

Select ALL that apply

A   The insurance company used

B   The insurance policies chosen

C   The process for identifying which risks could be mitigated by the purchase of insurance

D   The amount spent on cyber security insurance

E   The role of insurance in the company's risk control processes

Test your understanding 9

FHG company designs and manufactures technologically advanced products which it sells to business customers via an on-line ordering and payment system. The market is highly competitive, and employees are required to sign confidentiality agreements before they are appointed, after which they are entered into the payroll system by an outsourced payroll service. FHG company is financed by a mixture of equity and long-term bank loans.

The board of FHG is aware of the requirement to consider the needs of stakeholders when reporting on its cyber security risk management programme.

Which of the following stakeholders should FHG take into account when producing their report?

Select ALL that apply

A   Competitors

B   Shareholders

C   Customers

D   Payroll service providers

E   Lenders

Test your understanding 10

The management of WRT company are confident that the controls they have set up to protect the company against the risk of a cyber security attack are effective. They intend to communicate this to stakeholders in the company's cyber security risk management report, which is being produced in accordance with the AICPA 2017 cyber security risk management reporting framework.

Which section of the report should management use to communicate their belief in the effectiveness of the control environment?

A   Description of the cyber security risk management program

B   Practitioner's opinion

C   Management's assertion

D   Chief information security officer (CISO)'s report

Test your understanding 11

In order to improve the cyber security risk management, the board of YTD company have insisted that all employees must read and then sign a copy of the cyber security risk policy handbook.

The company cyber risk security team is now considering the content to be included in its report 'Description of YTD company's cyber security risk management program' which is to be produced in accordance with the AICPA 2017 cyber security risk management reporting framework.

Which TWO of the following heads within the report would be MOST likely to contain a reference to this policy?

A   Cyber security objectives

B   Factors affecting inherent cyber security risks

C   Cyber security risk assessment process

D   Cyber security communications

E   Cyber security risk governance structure

Test your understanding 12 – Nouveau Cakes (Case study)

Scenario

Nouveau Cakes Ltd is an online cake making and delivery company based within close proximity to the capital city and with good transport links to the rest of the country. They offer to make delicious cakes for any special occasion, with a wide variety of designs and deliver them to the customer's door within 24 hours of ordering on their website.

They have been in operation for 5 years and originally started when founder and current executive chair Larissa Shazam became disillusioned with her office job and decided to follow her passion for cake baking. She originally auditioned for a television bakery contest to try and raise her profile but failed to get through the auditions. Undeterred she started doing local cake making and delivery within her home town and surrounding village.

She quickly built up a good reputation, and started to use social media to raise her profile. Requests for cakes started to come in from further afield due to her presence on social media and, keen to capitalise on this interest, she collaborated with a local distribution company and applied to the bank for financing to increase the size of her operation.

The company now has its own website which is the primary source of its orders and regular customers are able to set up an account for ease of ordering and payment. The company has had to collaborate with a national logistics company for their next day delivery services as the demand for its cakes is increasing throughout the country.

Trigger

The finance director asks you in her office, she's holding a copy of the local newspaper, and is looking concerned.

"Thank you for the work you did for me last week, it was really useful. I need your help again, I've just been reading about a local company that has suffered a major setback due to a hacker gaining access to their customer database. I'm concerned that as we expand, we may become a target for such activities. We have hundreds of regular customers who have set up an account and have stored payment details.

A friend of mine works in IT and is obsessed by cyber security and was telling me all about the various frameworks and how they can be reported now. I didn't really understand it all, but I understand there are loads of different approaches and that there is currently no standard approach. I wondered if we should be doing something on cyber security now. I know Larissa is considering listing the company if our success continues, she's even talking about overseas expansion!

Task

Please can you prepare the following for me for a meeting I have with Larissa and the rest of the board tomorrow morning. I need it within the hour so I can have a good look over it and ask you any questions:

(a)   Outline the issues that we should be considering with regard to cyber security.   **(15 minutes)**

(b)   An evaluation of the benefits and risks of adopting a cyber security framework.   **(15 minutes)**

(c)   A brief evaluation of the cyber security frameworks available and a recommendation for which one we should use.   **(15 minutes)**

Test your understanding 13 – Couchweb (Case study)

Scenario

You work as a senior manager for Couchweb, a media streaming company which offers access to media content over the internet at any time and from anywhere. Subscribers pay a small monthly fee, in return for which they can log into Couchweb's website and view content online. Subscribers can connect to the service using almost any device that can access the internet, including smart televisions, laptops, tablets and smartphones.

The content is exclusively entertainment, primarily TV programmes and movies. Subscribers log in using their own devices and can search Couchweb's catalogue until they find something they wish to watch. The chosen content is then streamed to their device. They can watch their choice of programmes while they are connected to the site, but until now, they have not been able to download the material to watch offline.

Trigger

The finance director asks you in her office, she's holding a copy of the local newspaper, and is looking concerned. She passes a copy to you.

Newspaper article:

Mayland Daily News

Couchweb launches new app

Couchweb has launched a new app that permits subscribers to download up to five programmes or movies to a portable device such as a laptop, tablet or smartphone. This was created in response to feedback from subscribers, who would like to watch their favourite TV programme while commuting but cannot always access the internet while doing so.

Once a subscriber reaches the limit of five items, the website prevents the download of further content until one or more of the previous downloads have been deleted. The content is encrypted to prevent it from being copied and used for some other purpose.

Couchweb reported an enthusiastic uptake of the new service. More than 11 million subscribers had downloaded the new app within 24 hours of its launch.

"As you can see from this newspaper article, we launched the new download app yesterday. However we have already had to suspend the download service. Ronsteel Productions, one of the studios that license most of our content to us, has already discovered some of its programmes on internet pirate sites. The electronic signatures on those files indicate that they originated from Couchweb.

In preparation for the launch of the app, we encrypted copies of the files. These should have been impossible to play other than through the subscriber's app, linked to the subscriber's Couchweb account. The encryption has been extensively tested, but we now know that it is possible to defeat it.

We have been able to identify the subscribers who were responsible for the pirated copies and have cancelled their subscriptions.

Task

The CEO has asked me to brief him later today and I need your help in preparing for the briefing. I need practical advice on the following matter:

(a)   How would Enterprise Risk Management (ERM) provide an effective approach to the prevention of this type of incident at Couchweb in the future?   **(30 minutes)**

Test your understanding 14

The system development lifecycle has six stages. The correct order of four of the stages is:

A   Analysis; Development; Design; Review

B   Analysis; Design; Development; Implementation

C   Planning; Analysis; Development; Design

D   Planning; Design; Analysis; Review

Test your understanding 15

CP Ltd are implementing a new, bespoke computer system to replace an existing system. The stages they have gone through so far include the purchase and installation of the hardware, software development, system testing, staff training and the production of system documentation. This will be followed by:

A   File conversion, database creation and changeover

B   File conversion, database creation and review

C   Changeover and review

D   Changeover and maintenance

10 Chapter summary

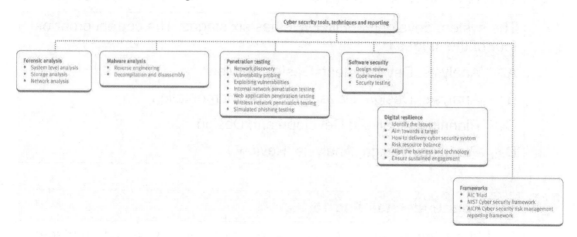

Test your understanding answers

Test your understanding 1

The correct answers are B, C, D and F.

The attack did start from a spear phishing email, a spear phishing email is one that is specifically targeted at a particular user.

User training to help people understand what information is available about them online, how it can be used, and how to spot suspicious emails may have prevented the attack happening.

User access controls preventing employees visiting sites of personal interest on work computers would have prevented this attack.

A policy on social media preventing access to these sites from work computers would not have stopped this attack, the infection didn't come from a social media site and preventing employees from using social media entirely is unlikely to be enforceable.

The attack seems to describe a Trojan malware, as it is disguised in what seems to be a legitimate file. There is no mention of advertising on the websites visited which is how malvertising works.

Nimrag already have network monitoring controls and they appear to be working well having limited the damage caused in this case.

Test your understanding 2

The correct answer is B

Two factor authentication is a method of confirming the identity of a user in two different ways (e.g. password plus finger print).

Two step verification is another method of confirming a user's identify by using one type of information (for example passwords) but using the information from two different sources (e.g. user-remembered plus texted code).

Certification is a method of protecting data sent between two parties which is locked using a public code but can only be unlocked using a private code.

Test your understanding 3

The correct answers are C and E

Networks are often more extensive than businesses realise and endpoint protection must be extended to cover any new entry points. Levels of data traffic across a network can often be predicted and unusual levels can be signs of suspicious activity.

Cyber attacks can come from disgruntled employees inside the organisation.

Malware and virus protection software are vital but are not sufficient to guarantee an organisation is safe from cyber-attack (in practice all organisations are always at risk).

Emails containing viruses can come from known senders (or purport to).

Test your understanding 4

The correct answers are A, B and E

The Internet of Things (Connecting everyday objects via the Internet) has expanded the size of corporate networks, increasing the number of access points and thus increasing the importance of endpoint security.

Basic business process controls are as important as IT and cyber security controls in protecting businesses from cyber risk.

Code reviews are designed to audit source code and verify the existence and correct working of security controls.

Unethical hackers are malicious hackers working without the company's permission – ethical hackers work with the company to help identify system weaknesses.

No level of software security can fully eliminate the risk of a security breach.

Test your understanding 5

The correct answers is A

System level analysis is designed to identify what parts of the system have been affected. Network analysis focuses on monitoring levels of traffic across a network. Penetration testing is the process of determining how robust the company's cyber security defences are and vulnerability probing is part of that process – finding the devices on the network that are most vulnerable to intrusion.

Test your understanding 6

The correct answers are A and C

Establishing the risks satisfies step one – identifying the issues. Defining the programme objectives satisfies step two – setting well defined targets.

The planned organisation structure and appointment of a specialist firm satisfies step three – determining how to deliver the system.

However step four – the risk v resource trade-off is outstanding – management have not yet been offered a range of options to decide what level of protection they need and are prepared to resource.

Step five – a detailed plan which aligns with their business and technology requirements has also not been developed.

Step six – ensuring sustained business engagement is satisfied by the work done to track progress and reinforce the controls adopted.

Test your understanding 7

The correct answer is B

Objectivity requires that the report is free from bias. Statements such as 'unparalleled expertise' should therefore be avoided.

Test your understanding 8

The correct answers are C and E

The disclosures included in the description do not need to cover the specifics of the insurance cover selected – but should instead focus on how the decision regarding the use of insurance are taken and the role that insurance plays in helping to mitigate risks that cannot effectively mitigated otherwise.

Test your understanding 9

The correct answers are B, C, D and E

The AICPA lists senior management, board members, analysts and investors and business partners as the key stakeholders interested in the management of an entity's cyber security risk.

A cyber security attack could impact FHG's stakeholders in many ways. Lenders may be concerned that liquidity (and therefore FHG's ability to pay its debts) could be impacted by an attack on the on-line purchase and payments system.

An attack on this system could also compromise the Business Information the company holds on its customers.

Shareholders may be concerned that confidential product design information could become compromised affecting profitability and Payroll service providers may have an interconnected system which would be affected by any attack on FHG.

FHG's competitors may be interested in their cyber security risk but would not be considered key stakeholders for the purposes of the report.

Test your understanding 10

The correct answer is C

The AICPA recommends a three part report into an entity's cyber security risk management program.

Management describe the program in an often lengthy description section.

They then provide a separate assertion section in which they confirm that the description provided meets the AICPA description criteria and that their controls are effective.

An independent practitioner (a certified public accountant) then carries out an assurance engagement on the same areas and expresses their opinion.

A CISO may assist the board and the independent practitioner but they do not produce a separate section of the report.

Test your understanding 11

The correct answers are D and E

A cyber security risk policy for employees forms part an enterprise's overall governance structure. The use of the handbook is a way of communicating relevant cyber security information internally.

Test your understanding 12 – Nouveau Cakes (Case study)

Issues to consider on cyber security

One of the first things we must consider on cyber security is what information we have that needs protecting, this could be customer, staff or business information. Any PII we hold on employees or customers (such as names, addresses, payment details) must be protected. As this is a legal consideration in most countries, we should be doing it already. In terms of business information, our recipes are the standards that our staff follow and should any of these be altered it would adversely affect our business.

We also need to consider the types of technology we use, for example servers for hosting our website, the database we store customer details on, the communication channels we have with our 3rd party providers such as the delivery company etc.

We have also undergone fairly recent changes in terms of the growth that we have experienced. Often a change to business operations leads to a change in the way we use technology, and this will usually add to the cyber security considerations. For example, moving to online ordering is a significant change and involves collecting PII from a website and storing it on our database.

Social media is an important consideration as we used this to grow our business. Now we have our own website it is important that if we keep our social media pages they remain up to date – if not it could tarnish our reputation. Also someone could potentially gain unauthorised access to our accounts and post inappropriate comments.

Other risks would include malware infecting our systems, in an attempt to steal information, phishing attacks from hackers, or application attacks to either take our website offline or gain access to our customer PII.

Benefits and risks of adopting a cyber security framework

Benefits

The benefits of adopting a recognised approach to cyber security are plentiful. First and foremost as with any risks, being aware of the risks that we face, the potential impact and likelihood of them, being able to prioritise the key issues and put appropriate controls in place, is vital.

As technology is critical to our business operations, following recognised guidelines will help us make sure that we have considered as many of the issues as possible and will help us to respond when an issue occurs. It is a question of when rather than if; we may not be specifically targeted by an attack, but we could still be compromised by an attack that targets a software flaw.

Most cyber security frameworks don't just focus on how to prevent an attack, they also include responses to an attack - this would help us to get our operations back in order as quickly as possible. With our primary source of orders coming from our website, reducing the downtime we have is vital. If a customer cannot access our website they will most likely find another cake company that they can order from and we may not just lose one sale but future sales too.

Risks

There is a risk that we apply a framework and then assume this means we are now completely protected against cyber security risk. This is not the case; as with any control, cyber security controls can be circumvented by collusion and error, indeed the human element in any control systems creates a weakness – we can all make mistakes. Using a framework to assist our risk management of cyber security is good practice but it cannot completely eliminate the cyber threats that can impact our business.

Technological advancements are rapid and varied, and so too are the risks that we face – from any source but particularly with regard to cyber threats. This means that regular review, reinforcement and refinement of policies is vital. For example, a key control would be to train all our employees, even those involved with making the cakes or decorating the cakes, about basic controls like password security and avoiding social engineering. However we should make sure that we give them regular reminders to make sure they do not slip into bad habits and we can update them to any changes.

Evaluation of the cyber security frameworks

AIC Triad

The AIC triad is a nice simple approach to help an organisation understand the information security risks it faces and the potential responses it could take. AIC stands for availability, integrity and confidentiality.

In the same way that I started this piece of work, it starts with understanding what information we have that could be of interest to others and therefore we need to protect, like our customer data and our recipes. The integrity aspect considers how we make sure the data we have is trustworthy, i.e. only changeable by authorised users. For example our customers updating their delivery addresses or payment information, or authorised staff updating the recipes we use for the cakes. It also requires that we consider how we keep our systems online in the event of a breach or attack, i.e. that we have a disaster recovery plan.

NIST cyber security framework

The NIST framework provides voluntary guidance. As with the AIC triad, it is aimed at helping organisations understand the issues it must consider to mitigate cyber risk. This one has five principles, so is more detailed than the AIC triad and therefore it could be argued would help protect our organisation more robustly.

ISO27001

This is from the International Organisation for Standardisation and so carries with it additional credibility. This kind of standard would give additional credibility to NC if we were to move into business-to-business sales. It follows very similar risk management processes including setting up a security policy, using risk assessment and managing the risks identified, and preparing a statement on the risks and controls in place. It does not mandate specific controls, but does provide a checklist of controls to consider.

AICPA cyber security risk management reporting

This is probably the most comprehensive and detailed of the frameworks that exist at present, as such it would probably be the most expensive for NC to undertake, but the result would be that our consideration and controls would be perceived to be of the highest order. Again, it cannot guarantee that NC would be immune from cyber security threats, but would show our stakeholders that we take cyber security very seriously. Given that Larissa has talked to you about listing, this level of reporting would certainly give investors more confidence in our cyber security risk management.

Summary

Given our current size, I think that we should start by using either the AIC triad or the NIST framework. This will give us a good basis for control and if we continue to expand we could look to adopt ISO27001 and the AICPA cyber security risk management reporting.

Test your understanding 13 – Couchweb (Case study)

Enterprise Risk Management (ERM)

It could be argued that it is disappointing that Couchweb has not implemented ERM already because ERM is essentially a process that ensures that risk management is considered in the context of business strategy. ERM would ensure that Couchweb had a proportionate and realistic approach to the identification and management of risks, avoiding risks that exceeded the company's risk appetite. Risks would be addressed in a top down manner, with staff at all levels being aware of the risks associated with their areas of responsibility. There would be systems and procedures in place to manage those risks and staff would be motivated to adhere to them.

ERM would have given Couchweb's risk management a formal direction, which should have both reduced the likelihood of a problem and offered a defence in the event that a problem arose in the future. For example, Couchweb is heavily dependent upon IT for both the delivery of its service and for the processing of subscribers' payments. An ERM system would ensure that the Board took an active interest in IT security and continuity of service and made sure that the necessary resources were available to staff to deal with risks. Staff would be aware of the systems and procedures and there would be regular compliance tests to ensure that these functioned properly.

It could, however, be argued that Couchweb's exposure to risk would not have been reduced by the adoption of ERM. Taking the piracy case as an example, the company was well aware of the threat and had put an encryption system in place to address that. ERM would not necessarily have affected the safeguards put in place by Couchweb because the risk had been formally evaluated in this case and had been addressed by what appeared to have been a realistic response. As with any risk management process, Couchweb was left with a residual risk that it chose to accept and so it was unfortunate that the piracy occurred. The only way to prevent it from occurring would have been to have continued to restrict access to streaming only.

There may be a risk that ERM could create a false sense of comfort if it is approached in a mechanical, box-ticking way. Couchweb clearly understood the risks associated with this new venture and had taken the necessary steps to prevent them. The introduction of ERM may formalise risk management, which is potentially beneficial, but it could also prove a distraction from the ongoing business of identifying and managing the risks themselves. Couchweb's business model requires the company to focus a great deal of attention on specific risks such as those relating to IT systems and that focus may be weakened slightly by a wider process.

Test your understanding 14

The correct answer is B – the six stages in the correct order are Planning, Analysis, Design, Development, Implementation and Review.

Test your understanding 15

The correct answer is A – New files will need to be created for the new system. This will be followed by implementation, by whichever changeover method is deemed appropriate. Review and maintenance are stages after implementation.